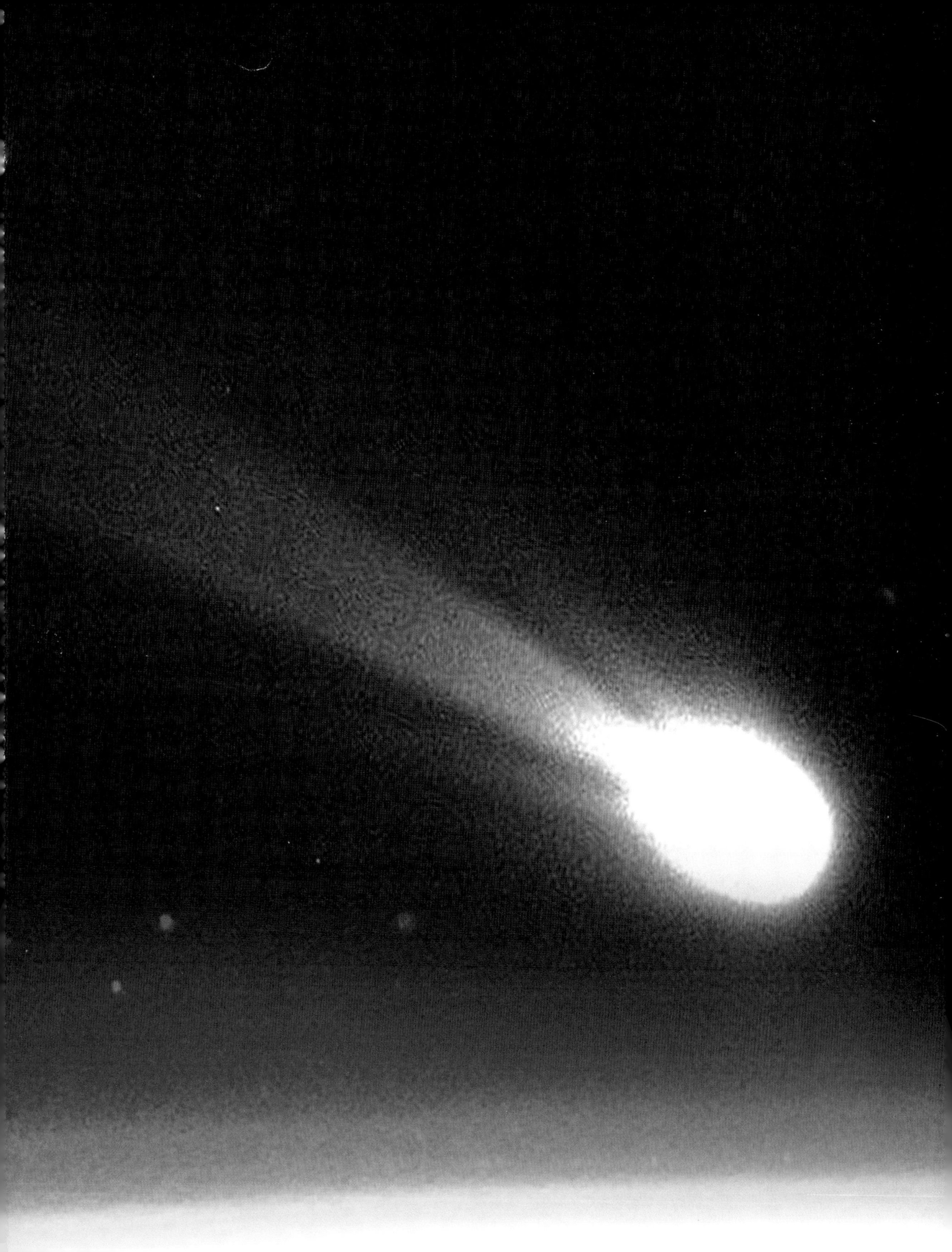

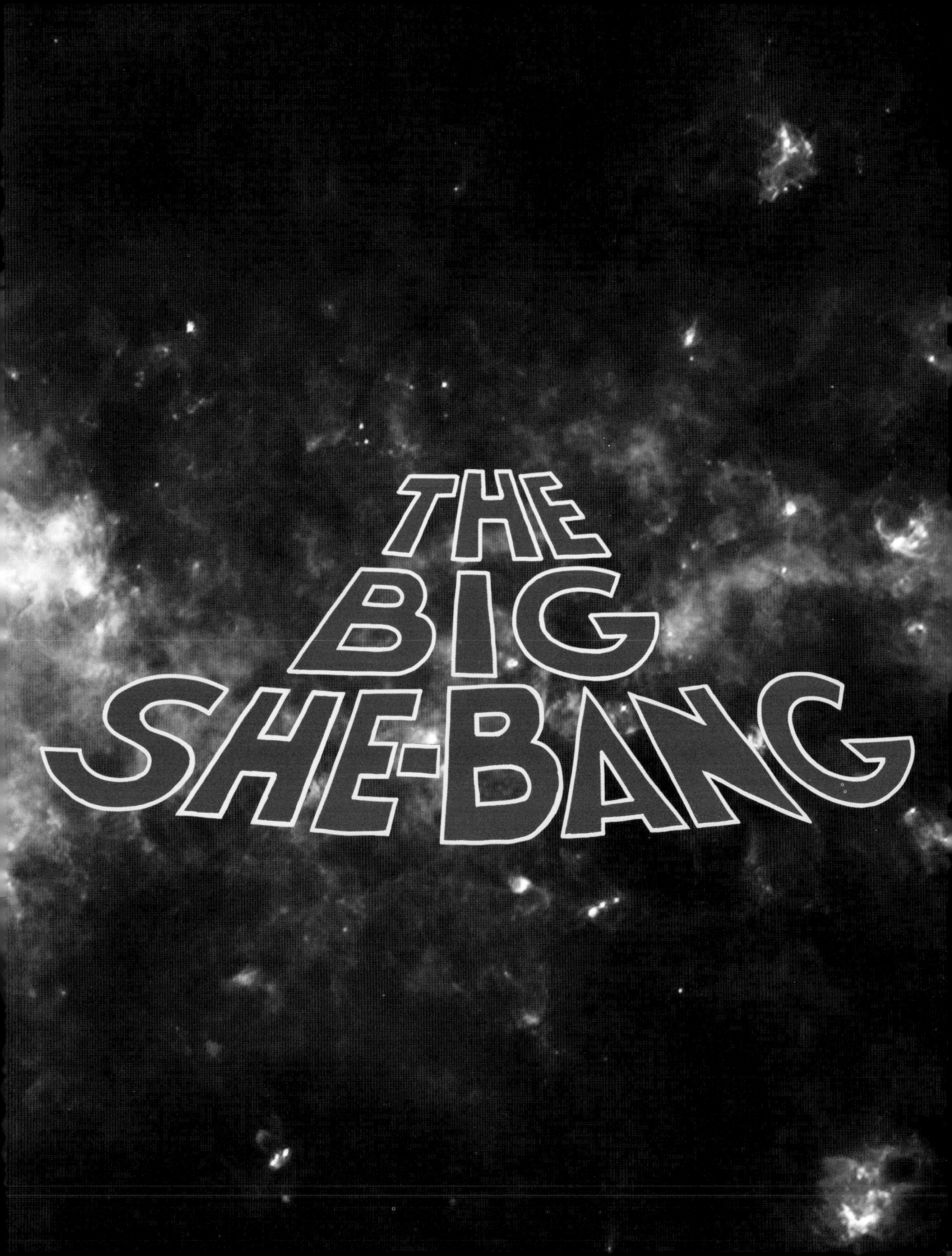
THE
BIG
SHE-BANG

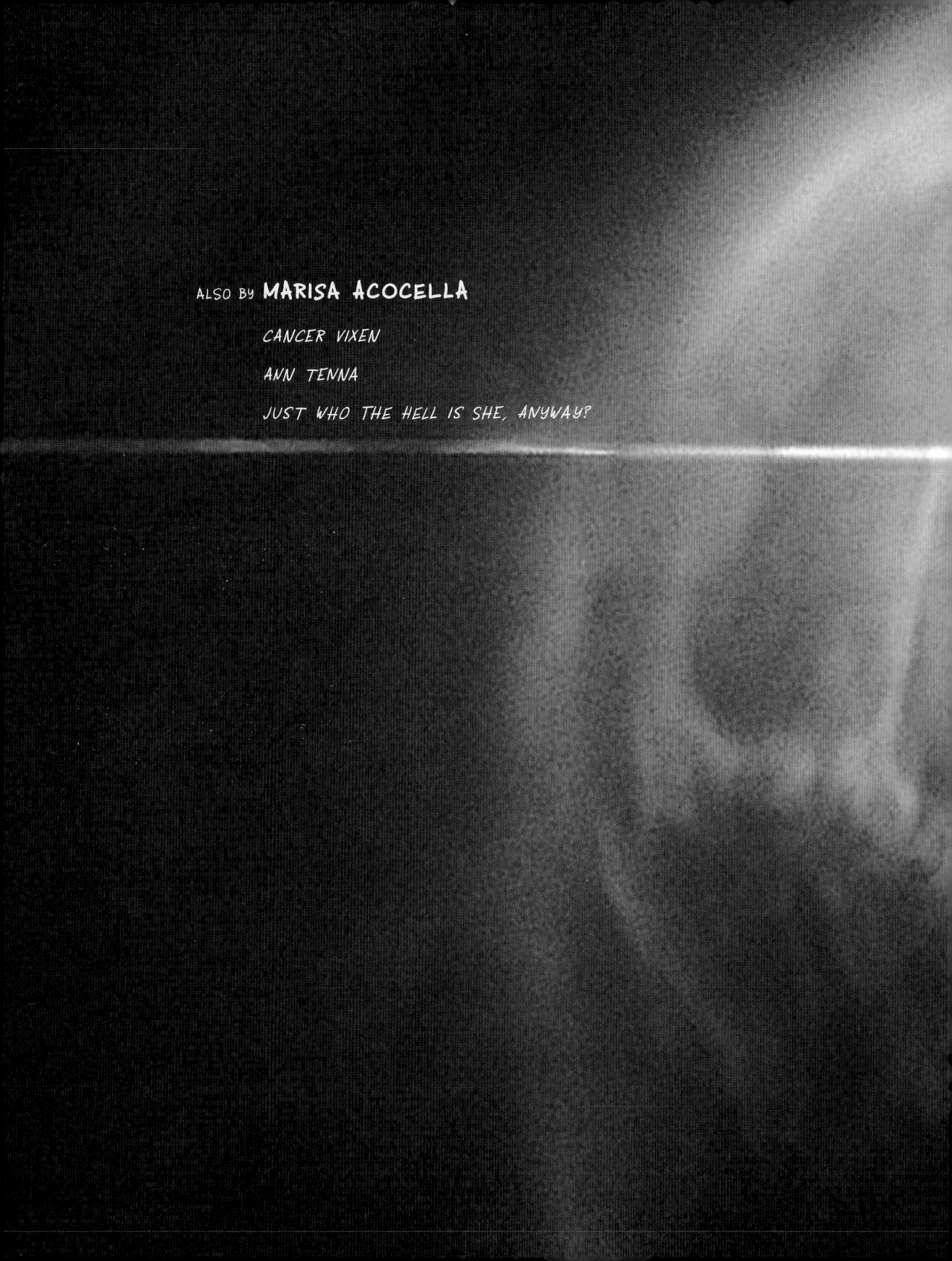

ALSO BY **MARISA ACOCELLA**

CANCER VIXEN

ANN TENNA

JUST WHO THE HELL IS SHE, ANYWAY?

THE BIG SHE-BANG

THE HERSTORY OF THE UNIVERSE
ACCORDING TO GOD THE MOTHER
AS TOLD TO MARISA ACOCELLA

HARPER WAVE

An Imprint of HarperCollins Publishers

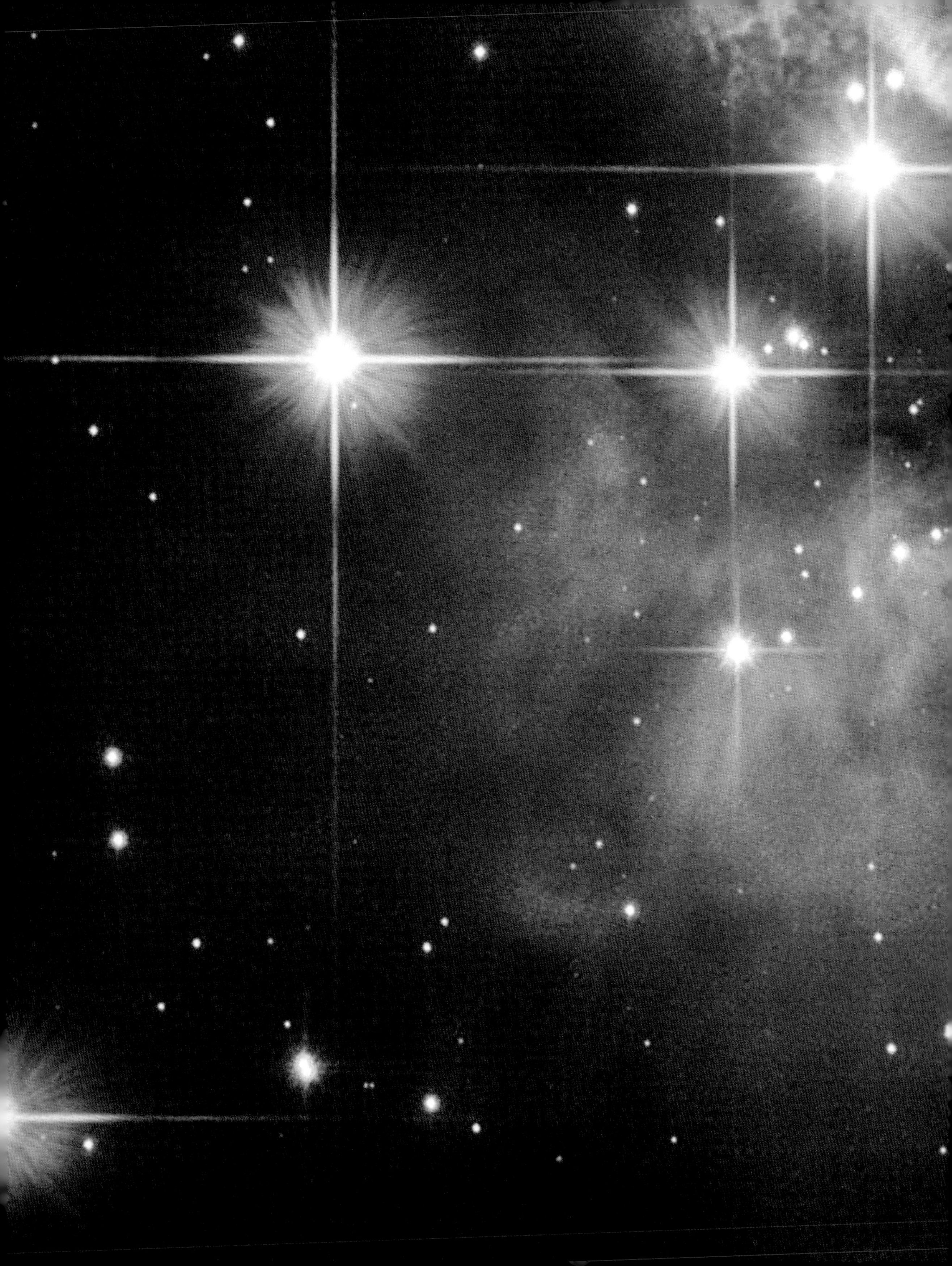

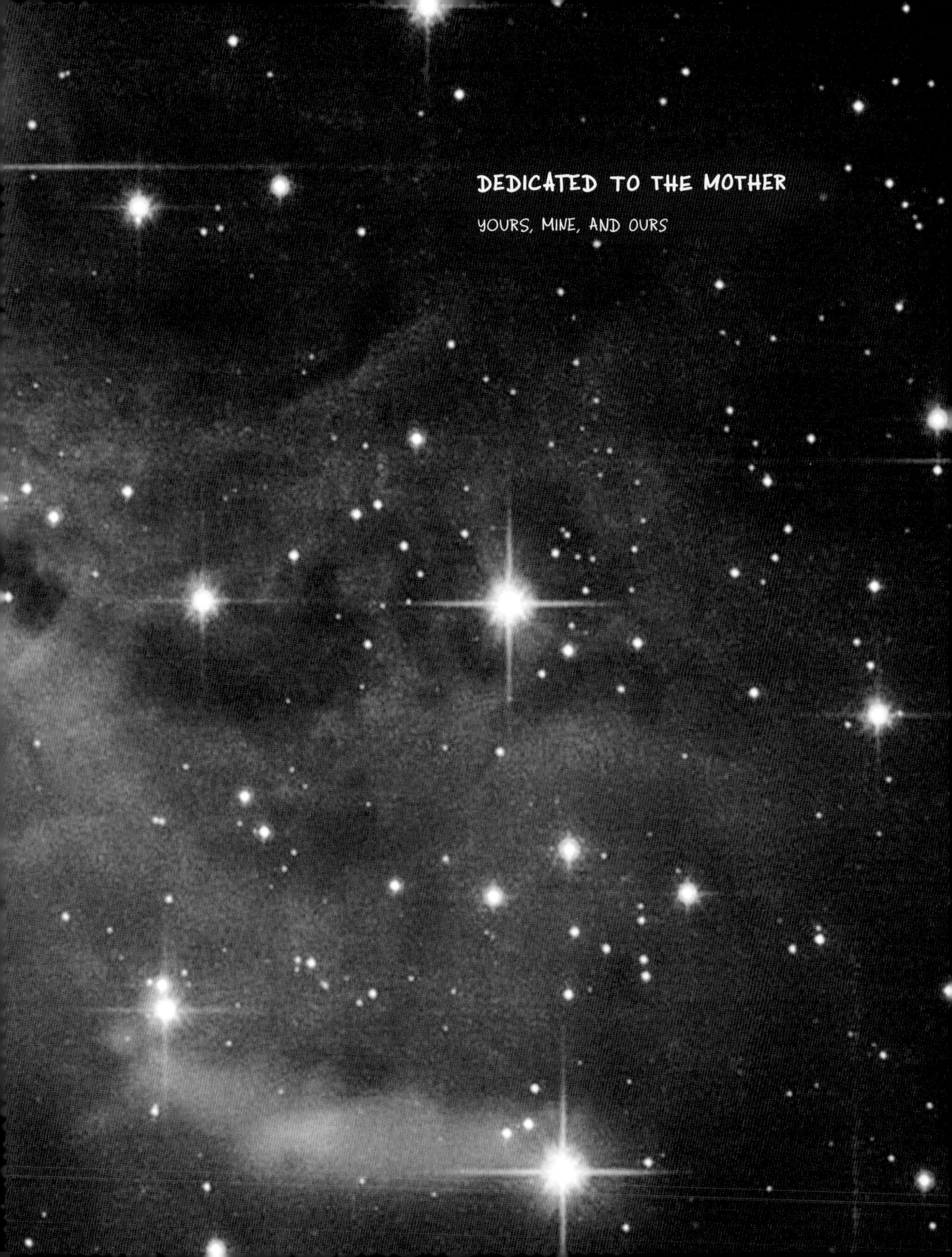

DEDICATED TO THE MOTHER

YOURS, MINE, AND OURS

SAINT AND SHEVOLUTIONARY

THE GODDESS ^ ROSTER

(IN ORDER OF APPEARANCE)

MOTHER EARTH 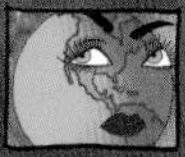

GOD THE MOTHER 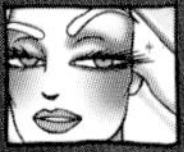

VENUS OF WILLENDORF 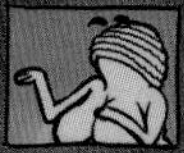
AND THE PALEO VENUSES 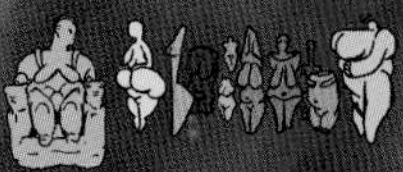

SOPHIA 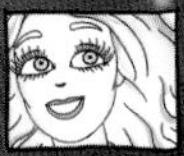

EVE 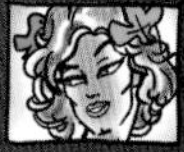

NOREA 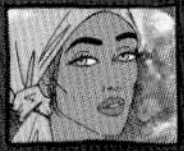

MAWU 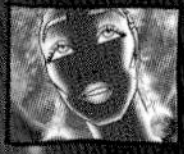
AND THE MOTHERS 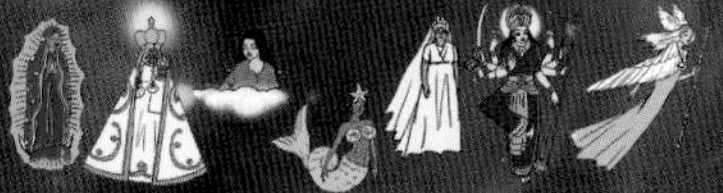

IXCHEL 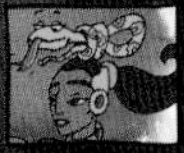

THE RAINBOW SNAKE 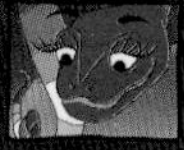

TIAMAT 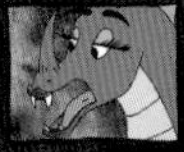

INANNA 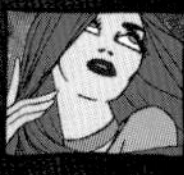

KALI 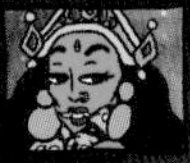

SEKHMET 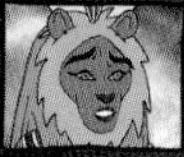

HATHOR 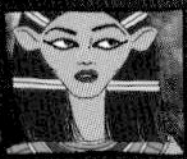

ASHERAH 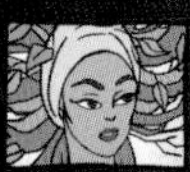

PERSEPHONE

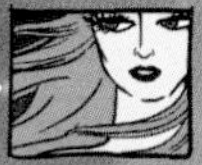

AND HER GREEK GODDESS CHORUS

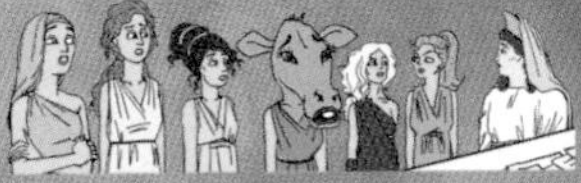

ISIS

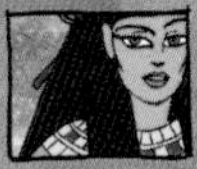

THE BLESSED MOTHER MARY

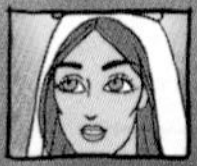

SAINT MARY MAGDALENE

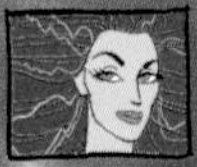

QUAN YIN

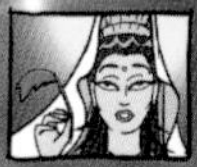

SAINT THECLA

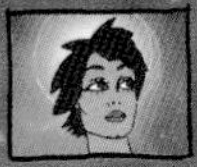

HYPATIA

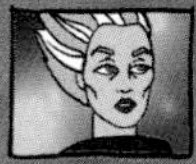

BRIGID

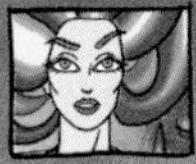

GREEN TARA

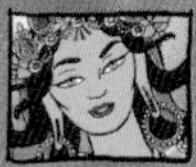

SAINT RABIA OF BASRA

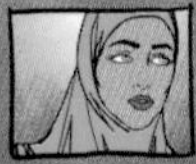

POPE JOAN

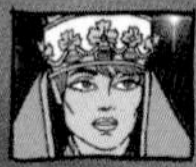

SHEELA NA GIG

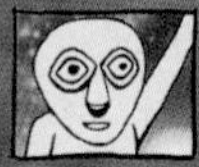

OUR LADY OF GRACE, OUR LADY OF LA SALETTE,
OUR LADY OF LOURDES, THE LADY OF PONTMAIN,
OUR LADY OF FATIMA, OUR LADY OF AKITA

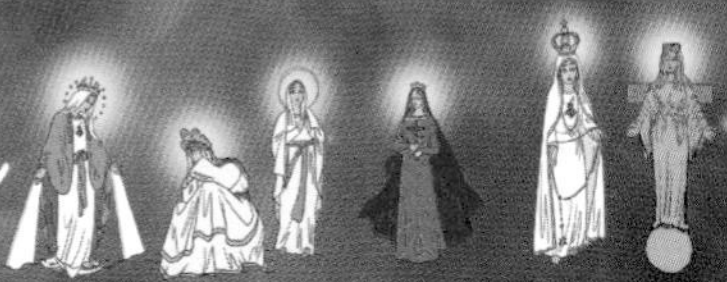

THE SUFFRAGETTES

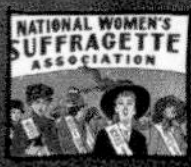
NATIONAL WOMEN'S
SUFFRAGETTE
ASSOCIATION

THE WOMEN'S LIBERATION MOVEMENT

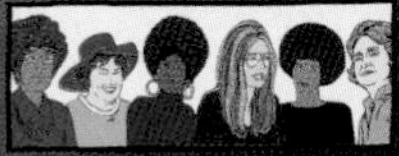

ANITA HILL, THE RIOT GRRRLS,
MALAWI YOUSAFZAI, TARANA BURKE

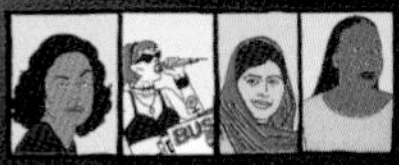

THE #metoo MOVEMENT

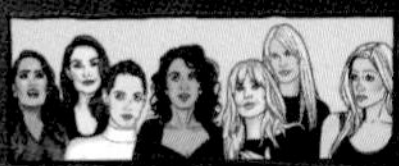

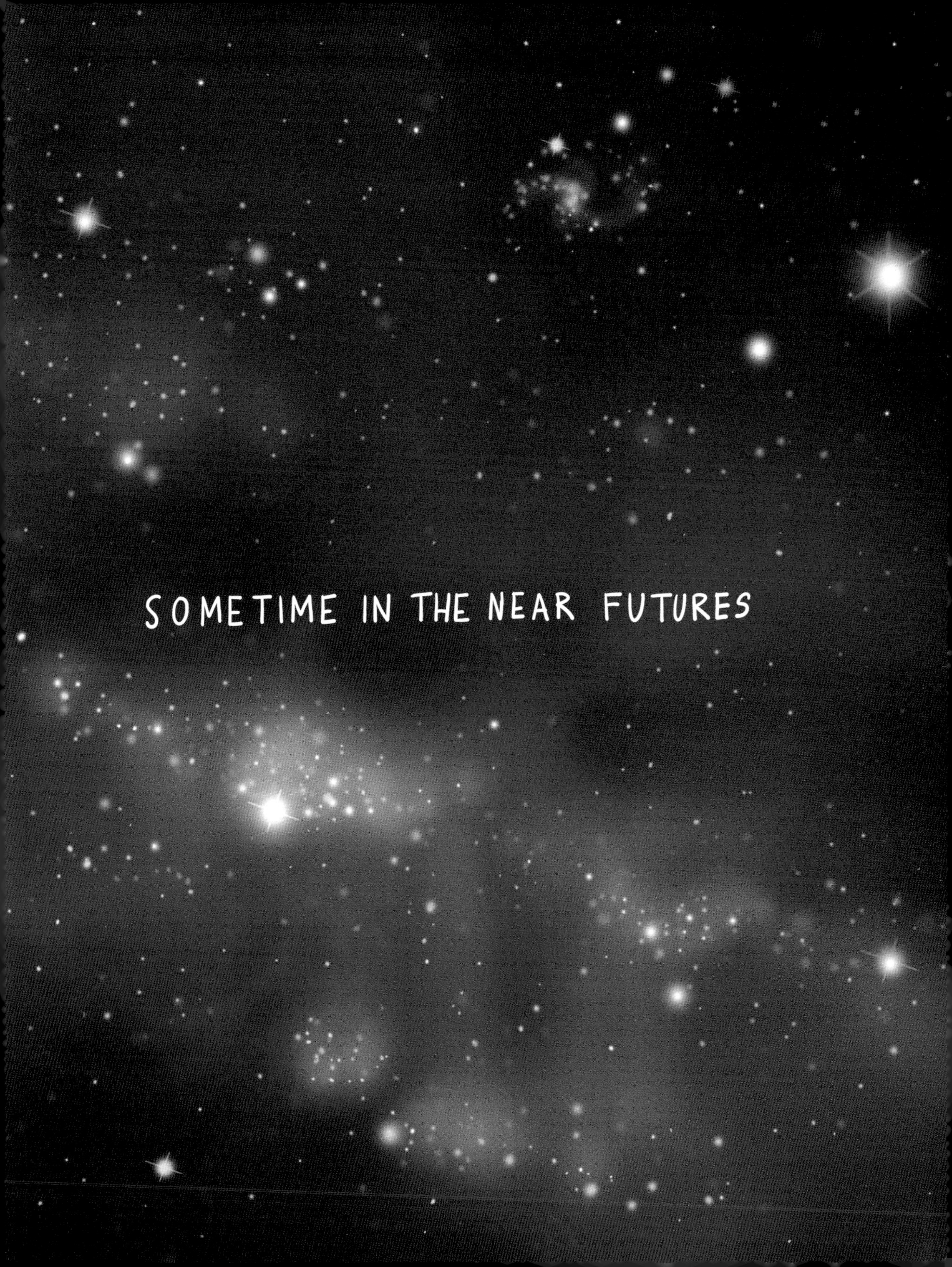
SOMETIME IN THE NEAR FUTURES

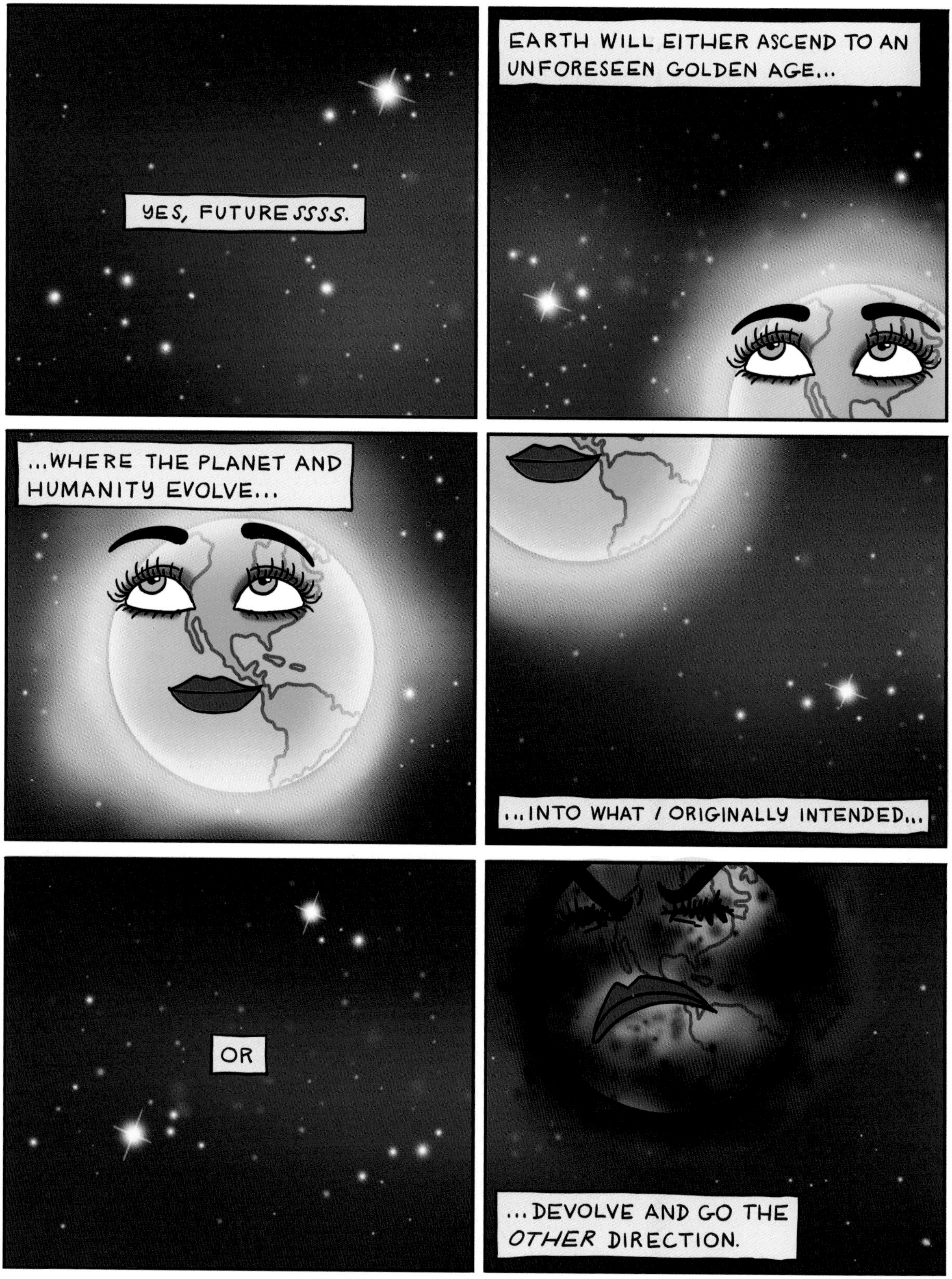
YES, FUTURESSSS.
EARTH WILL EITHER ASCEND TO AN UNFORESEEN GOLDEN AGE...
...WHERE THE PLANET AND HUMANITY EVOLVE...
...INTO WHAT I ORIGINALLY INTENDED...
OR
...DEVOLVE AND GO THE *OTHER* DIRECTION.

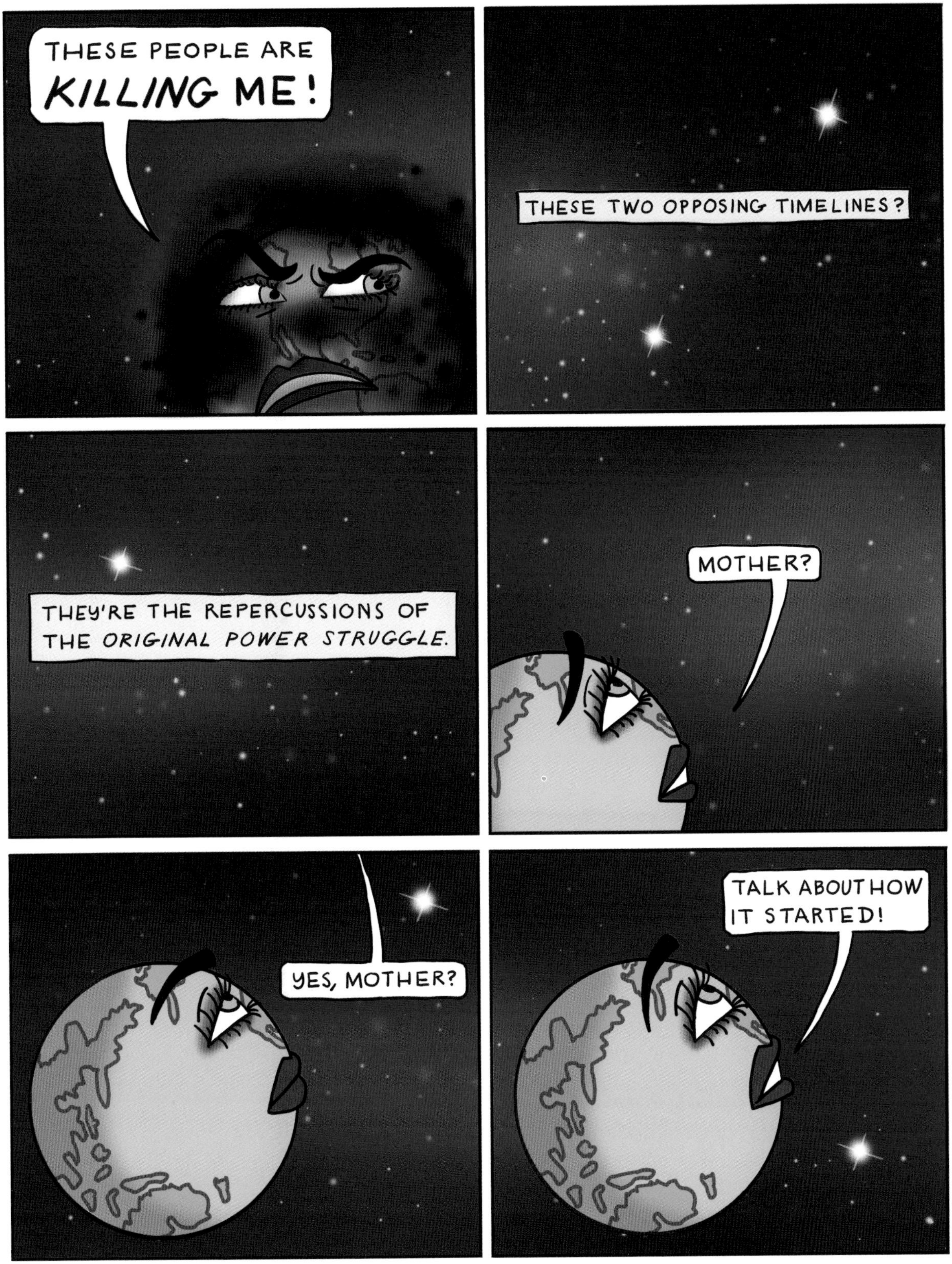
THESE PEOPLE ARE *KILLING* ME!
THESE TWO OPPOSING TIMELINES?
THEY'RE THE REPERCUSSIONS OF THE *ORIGINAL POWER STRUGGLE*.
MOTHER?
YES, MOTHER?
TALK ABOUT HOW IT STARTED!

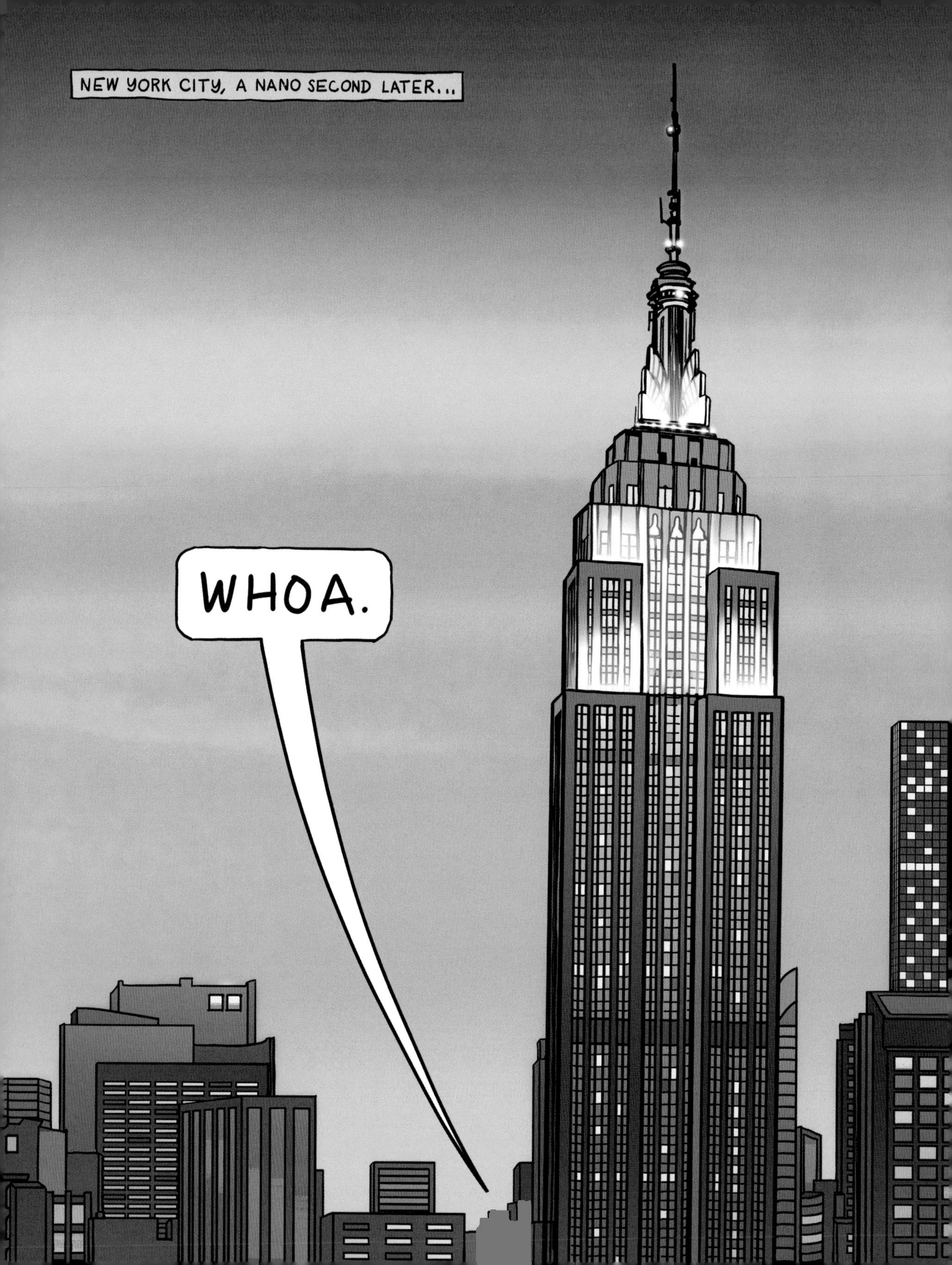
NEW YORK CITY, A NANO SECOND LATER...
WHOA.

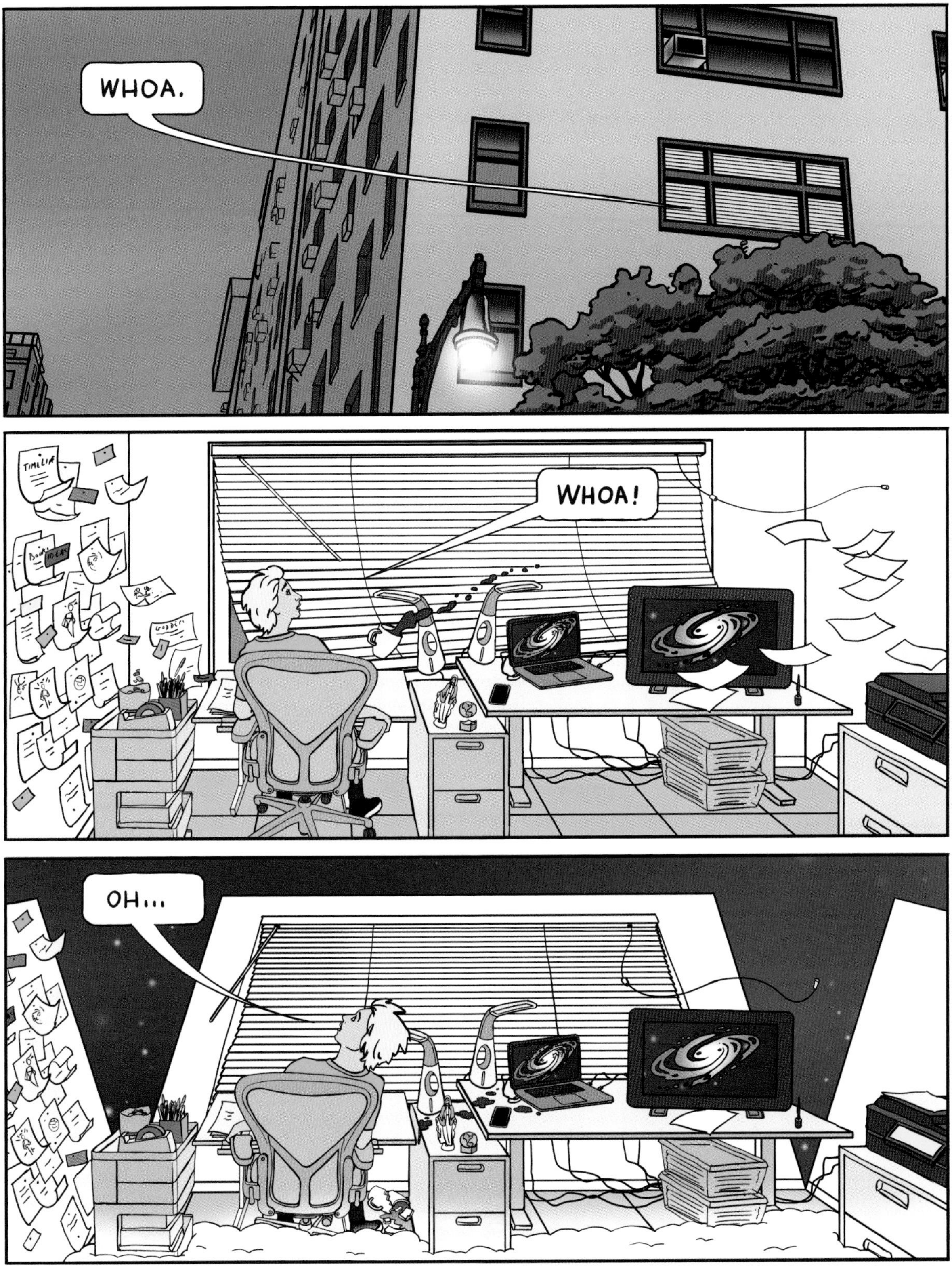
WHOA.
WHOA!
OH...

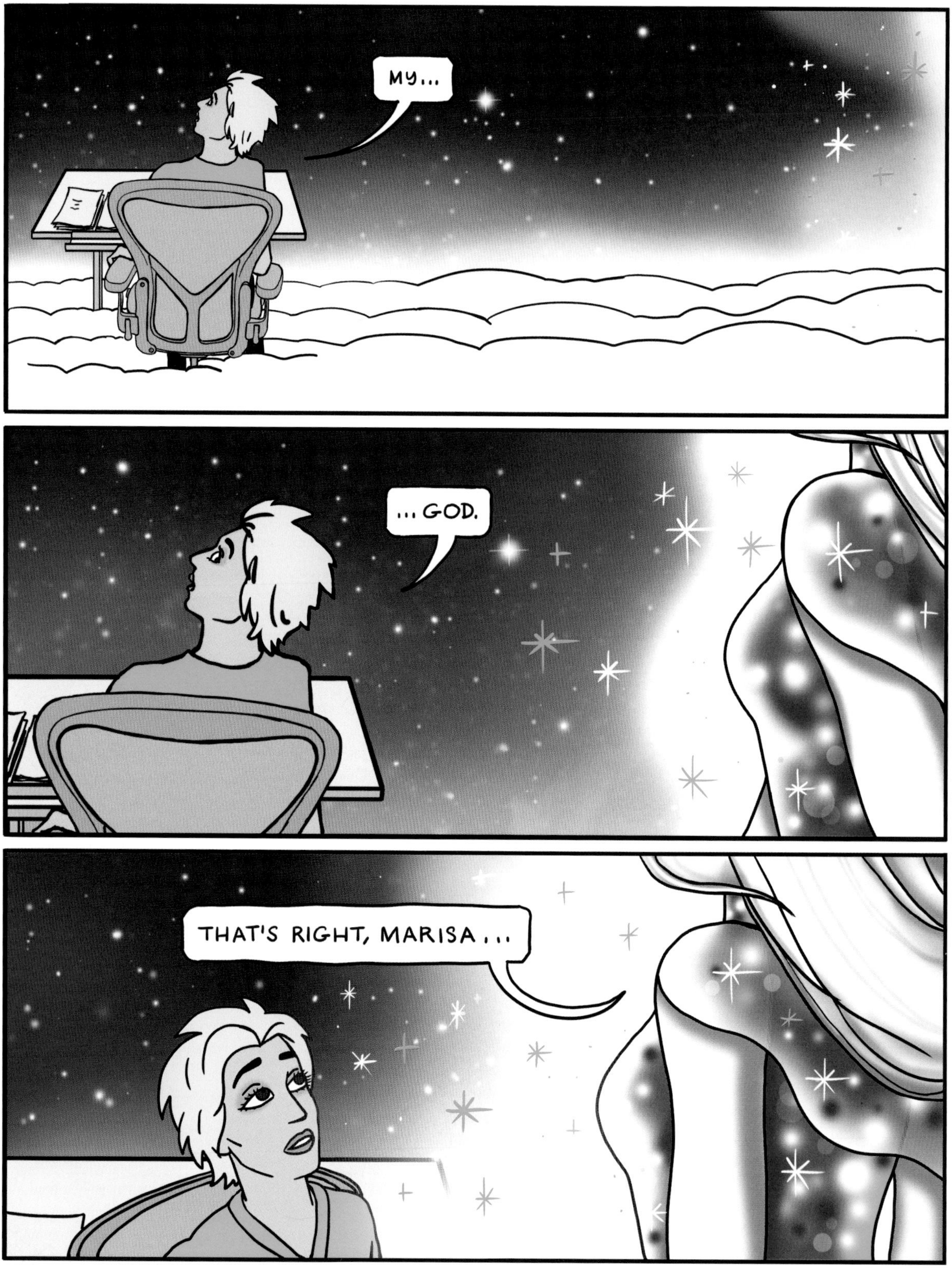
MY...
...GOD.
THAT'S RIGHT, MARISA...

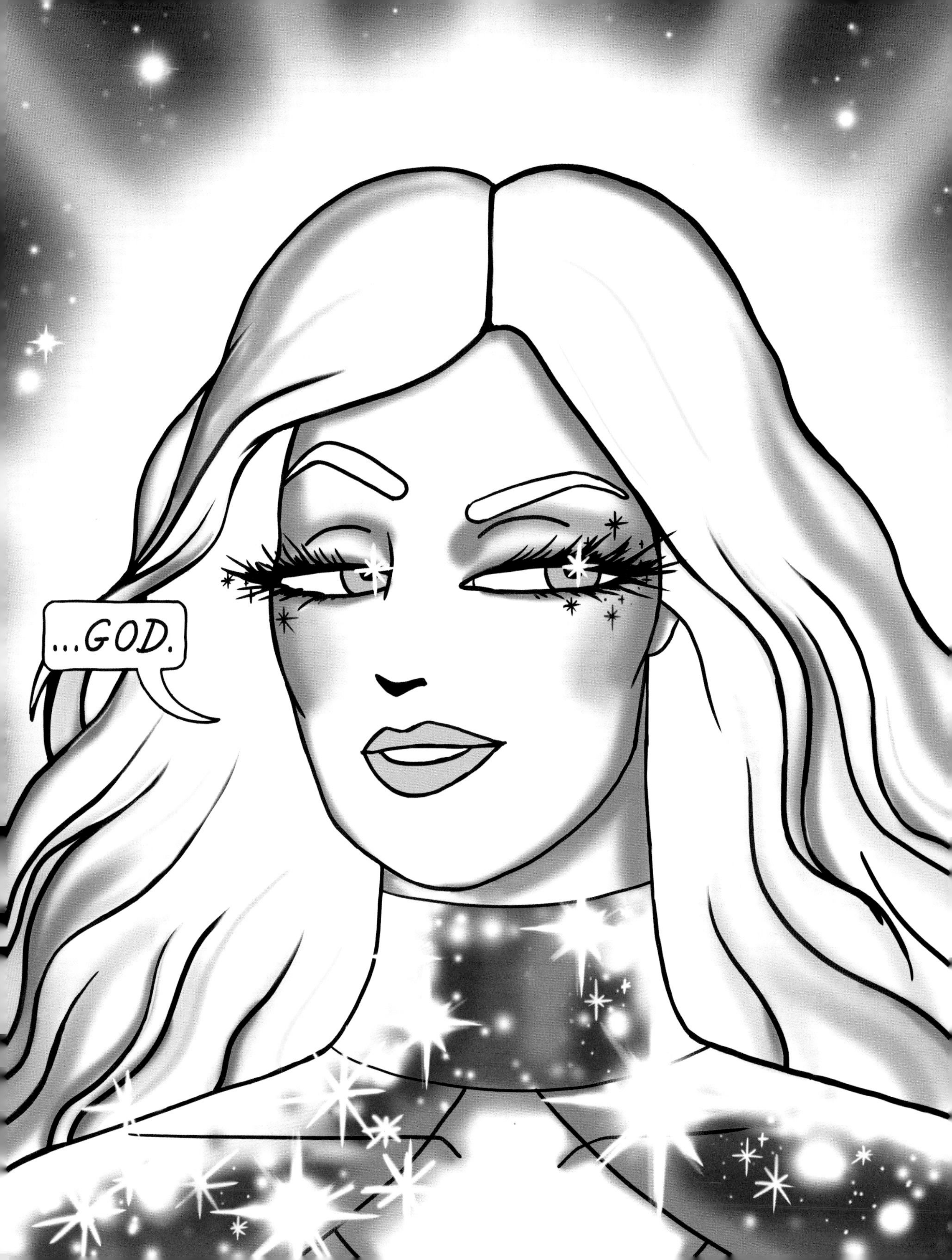
...GOD.

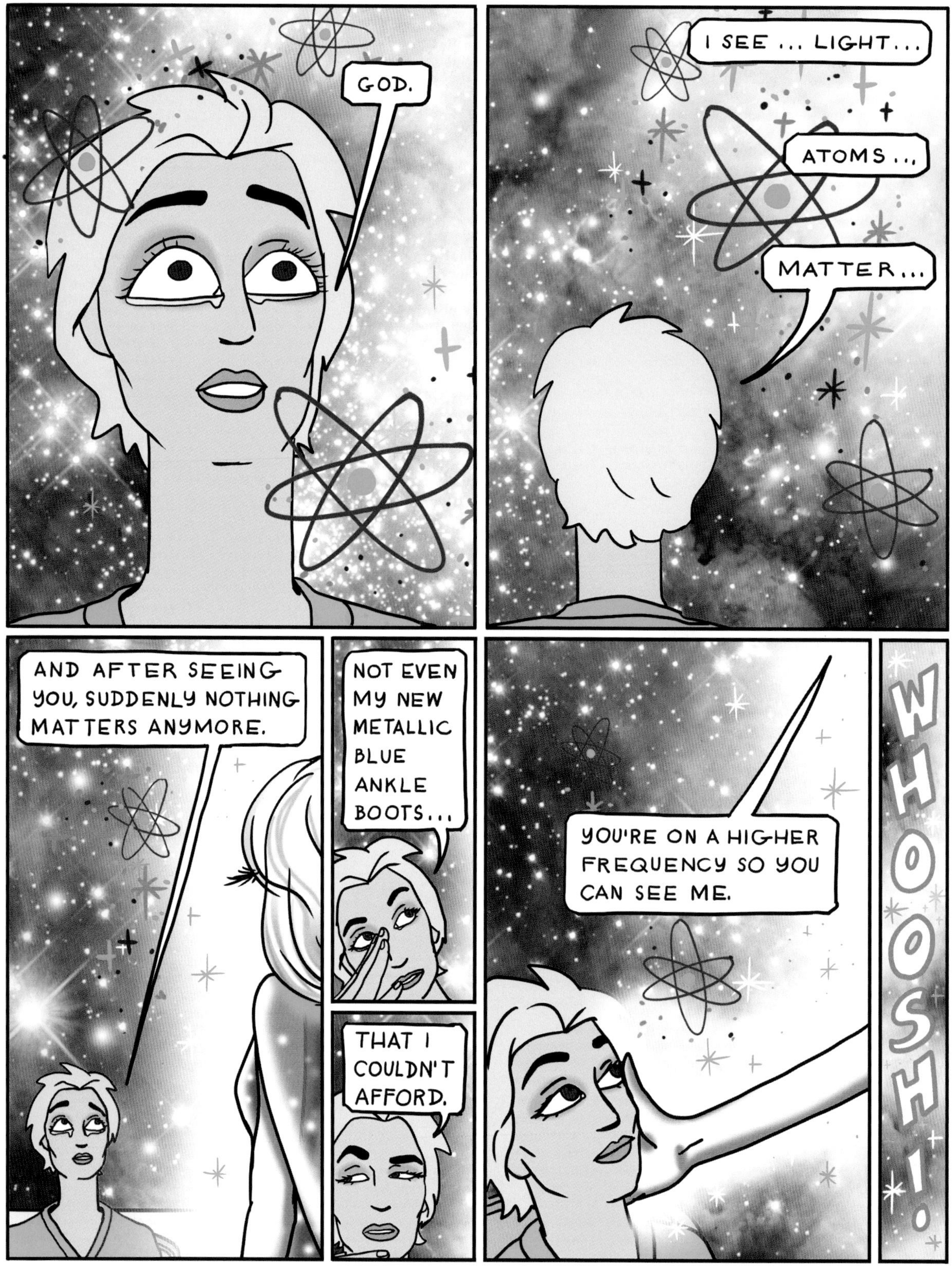
GOD.
I SEE ... LIGHT...
ATOMS...,
MATTER...
AND AFTER SEEING YOU, SUDDENLY NOTHING MATTERS ANYMORE.
NOT EVEN MY NEW METALLIC BLUE ANKLE BOOTS...
THAT I COULDN'T AFFORD.
YOU'RE ON A HIGHER FREQUENCY SO YOU CAN SEE ME.
WHOOSH!

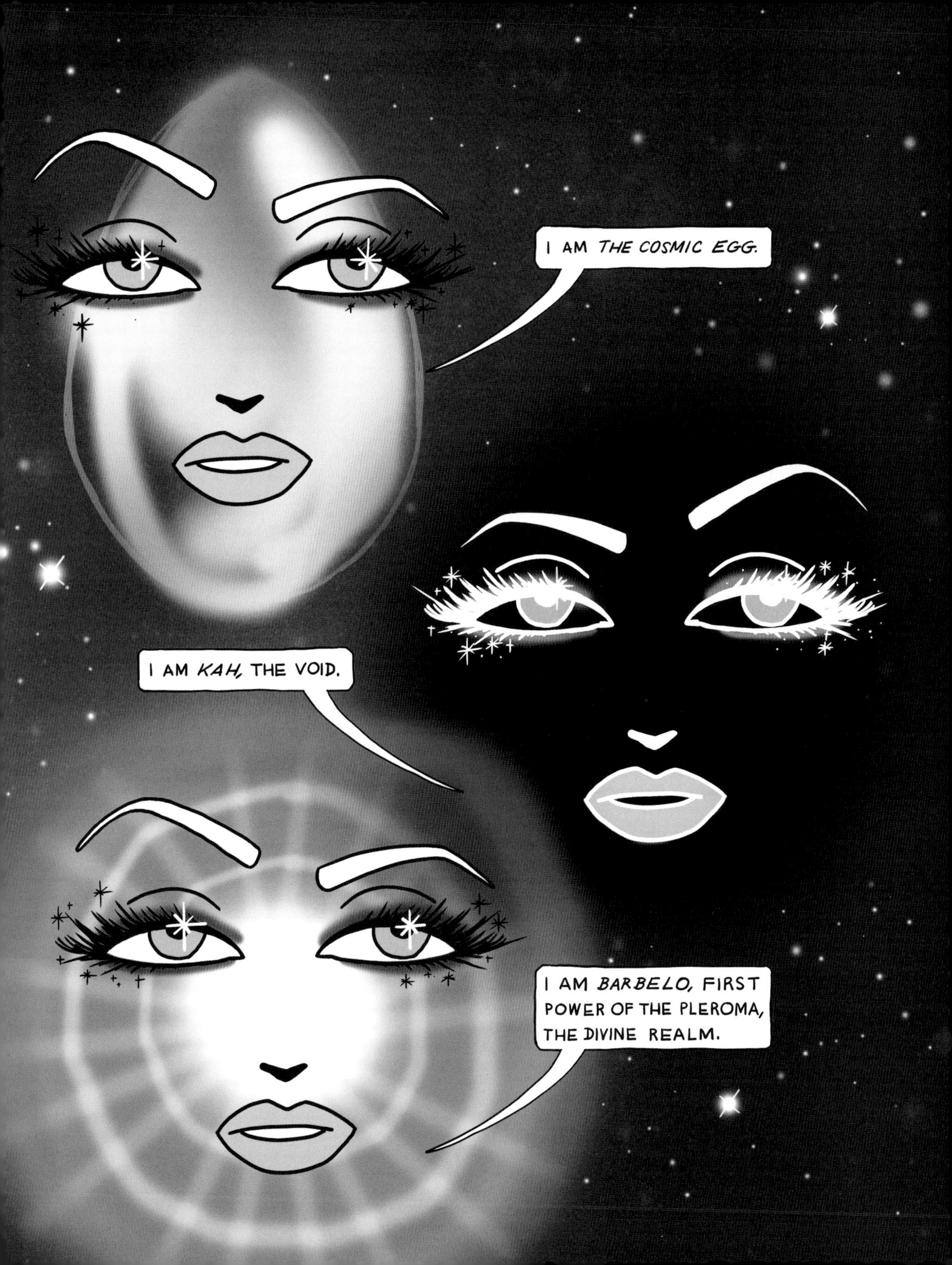
I AM *THE COSMIC EGG.*
I AM *KAH,* THE VOID.
I AM *BARBELO,* FIRST POWER OF THE PLEROMA, THE DIVINE REALM.

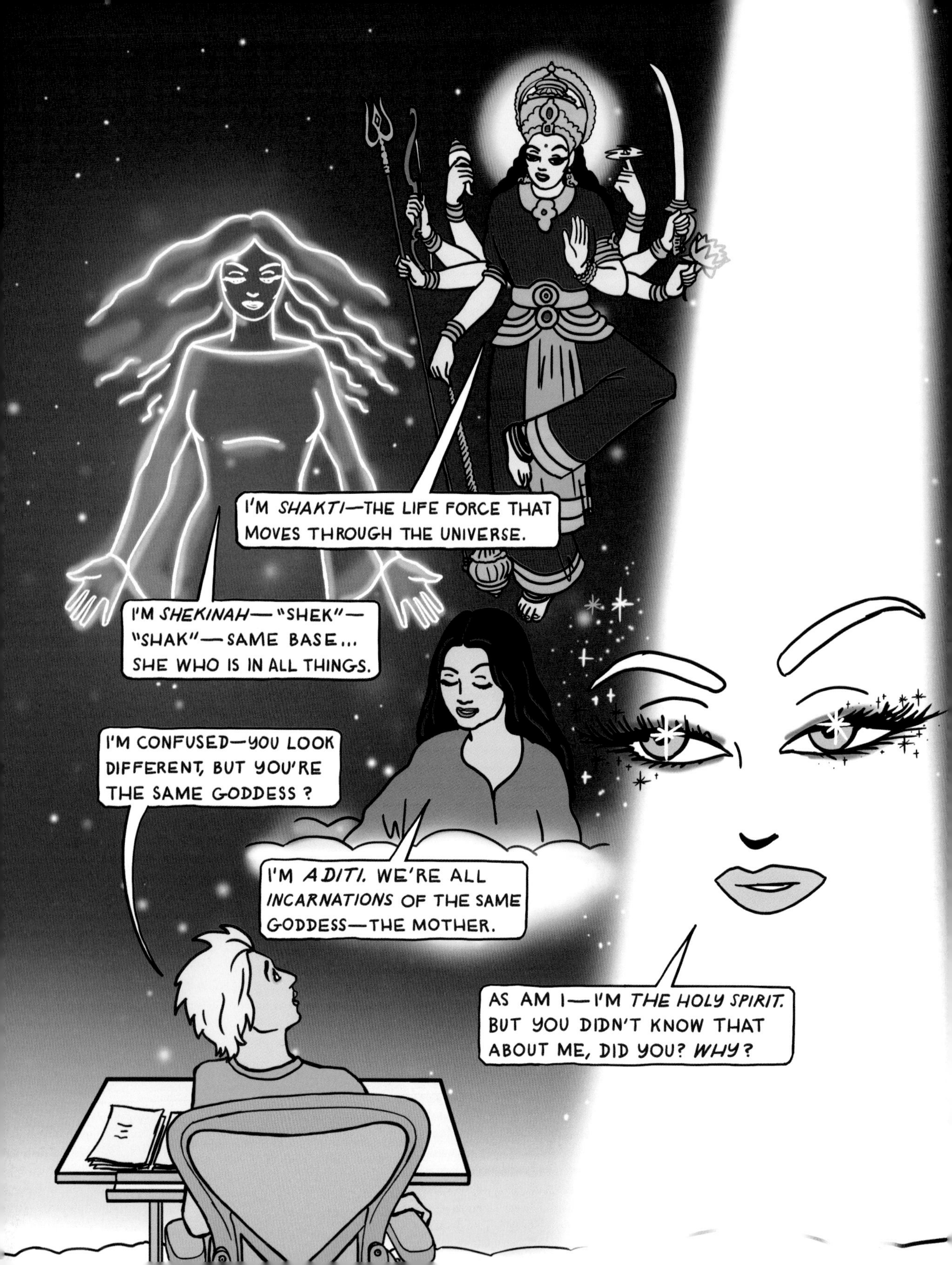
I'M SHAKTI—THE LIFE FORCE THAT MOVES THROUGH THE UNIVERSE.
I'M SHEKINAH—"SHEK"—"SHAK"—SAME BASE... SHE WHO IS IN ALL THINGS.
I'M CONFUSED—YOU LOOK DIFFERENT, BUT YOU'RE THE SAME GODDESS ?
I'M ADITI. WE'RE ALL INCARNATIONS OF THE SAME GODDESS—THE MOTHER.
AS AM I—I'M THE HOLY SPIRIT. BUT YOU DIDN'T KNOW THAT ABOUT ME, DID YOU? WHY?

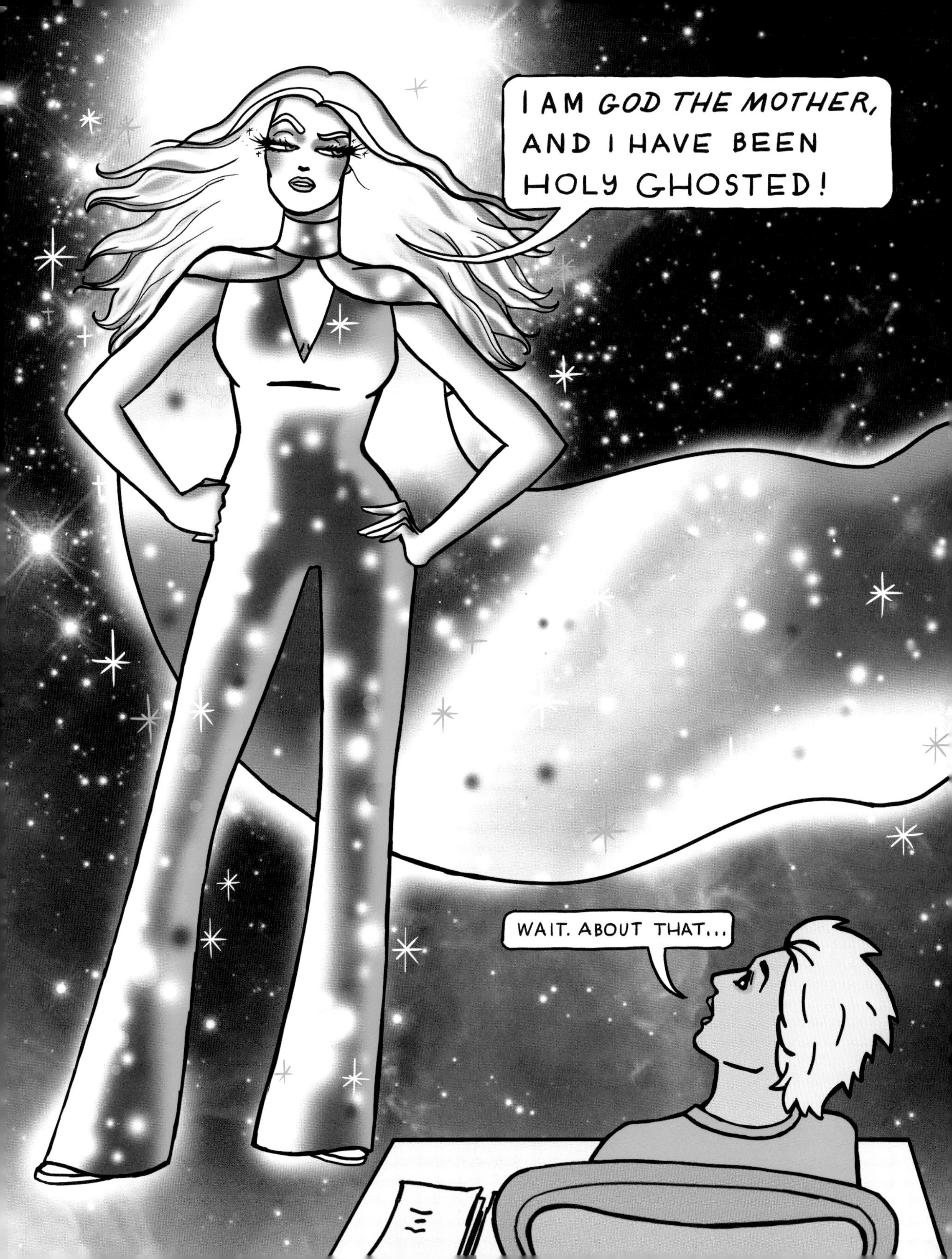
I AM *GOD THE MOTHER*, AND I HAVE BEEN HOLY GHOSTED!
WAIT. ABOUT THAT...

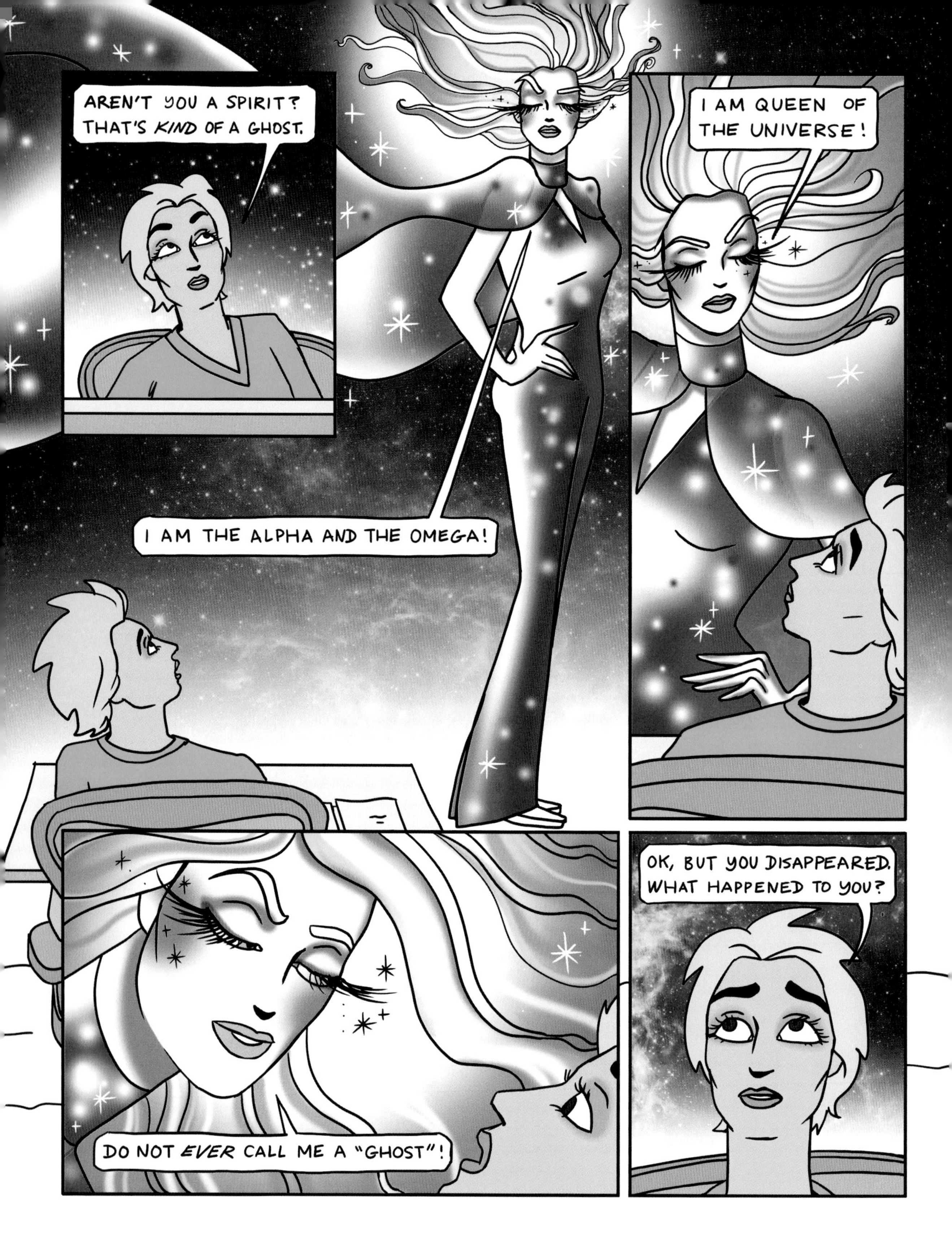
AREN'T YOU A SPIRIT? THAT'S *KIND* OF A GHOST.
I AM THE ALPHA AND THE OMEGA!
I AM QUEEN OF THE UNIVERSE!
DO NOT *EVER* CALL ME A "GHOST"!
OK, BUT YOU DISAPPEARED. WHAT HAPPENED TO YOU?

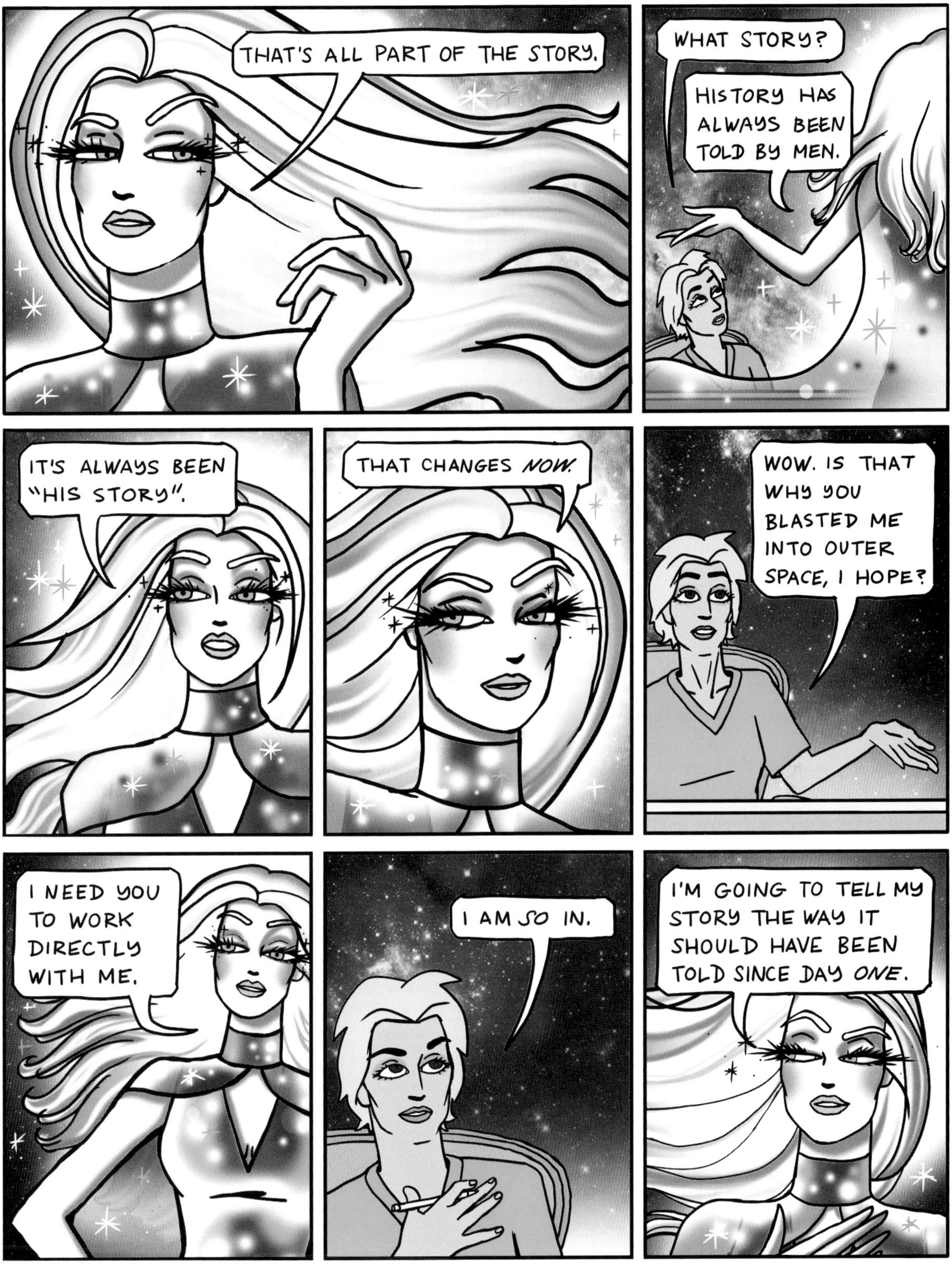
THAT'S ALL PART OF THE STORY.
WHAT STORY?
HISTORY HAS ALWAYS BEEN TOLD BY MEN.
IT'S ALWAYS BEEN "HIS STORY".
THAT CHANGES *NOW*.
WOW. IS THAT WHY YOU BLASTED ME INTO OUTER SPACE, I HOPE?
I NEED YOU TO WORK DIRECTLY WITH ME.
I AM *SO* IN.
I'M GOING TO TELL MY STORY THE WAY IT SHOULD HAVE BEEN TOLD SINCE DAY *ONE*.

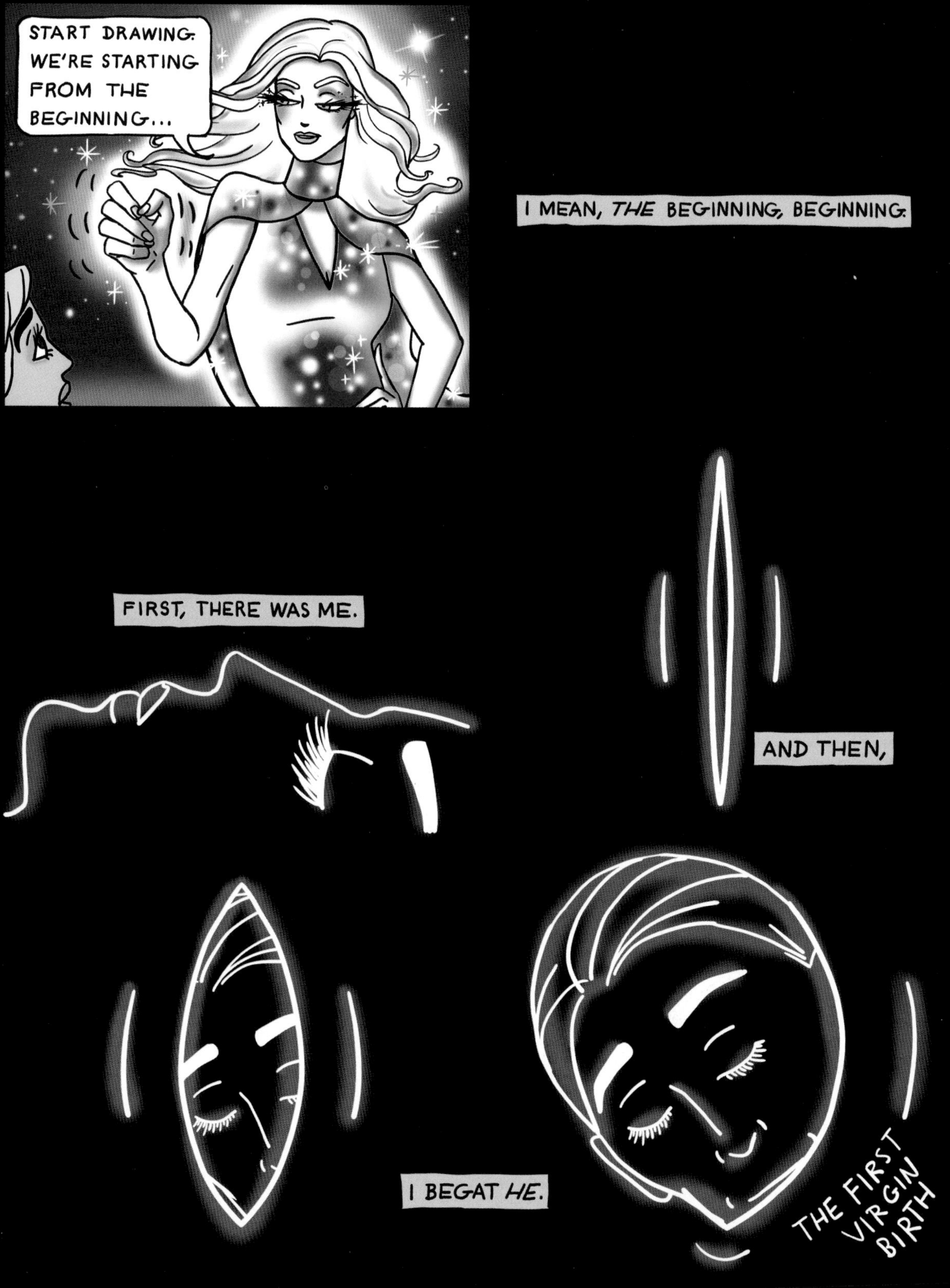
START DRAWING. WE'RE STARTING FROM THE BEGINNING...
I MEAN, *THE* BEGINNING, BEGINNING.
FIRST, THERE WAS ME.
AND THEN,
I BEGAT *HE*.
THE FIRST VIRGIN BIRTH

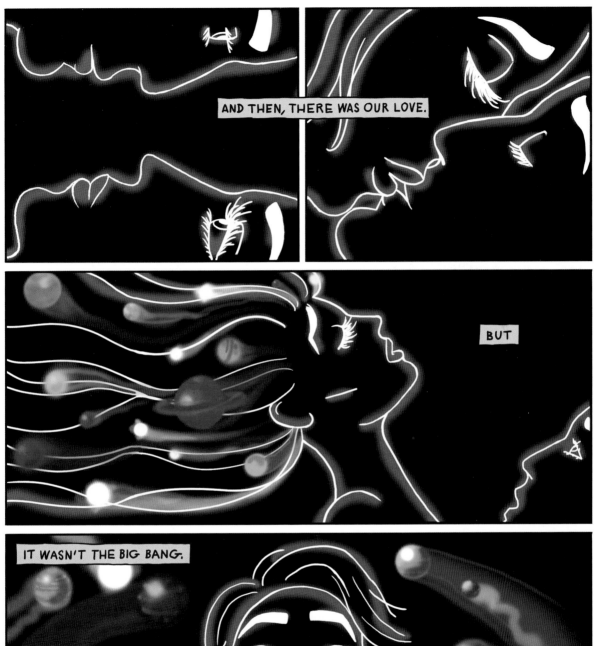

AND THEN, THERE WAS OUR LOVE.

BUT

IT WASN'T THE BIG BANG.

OH, NO...

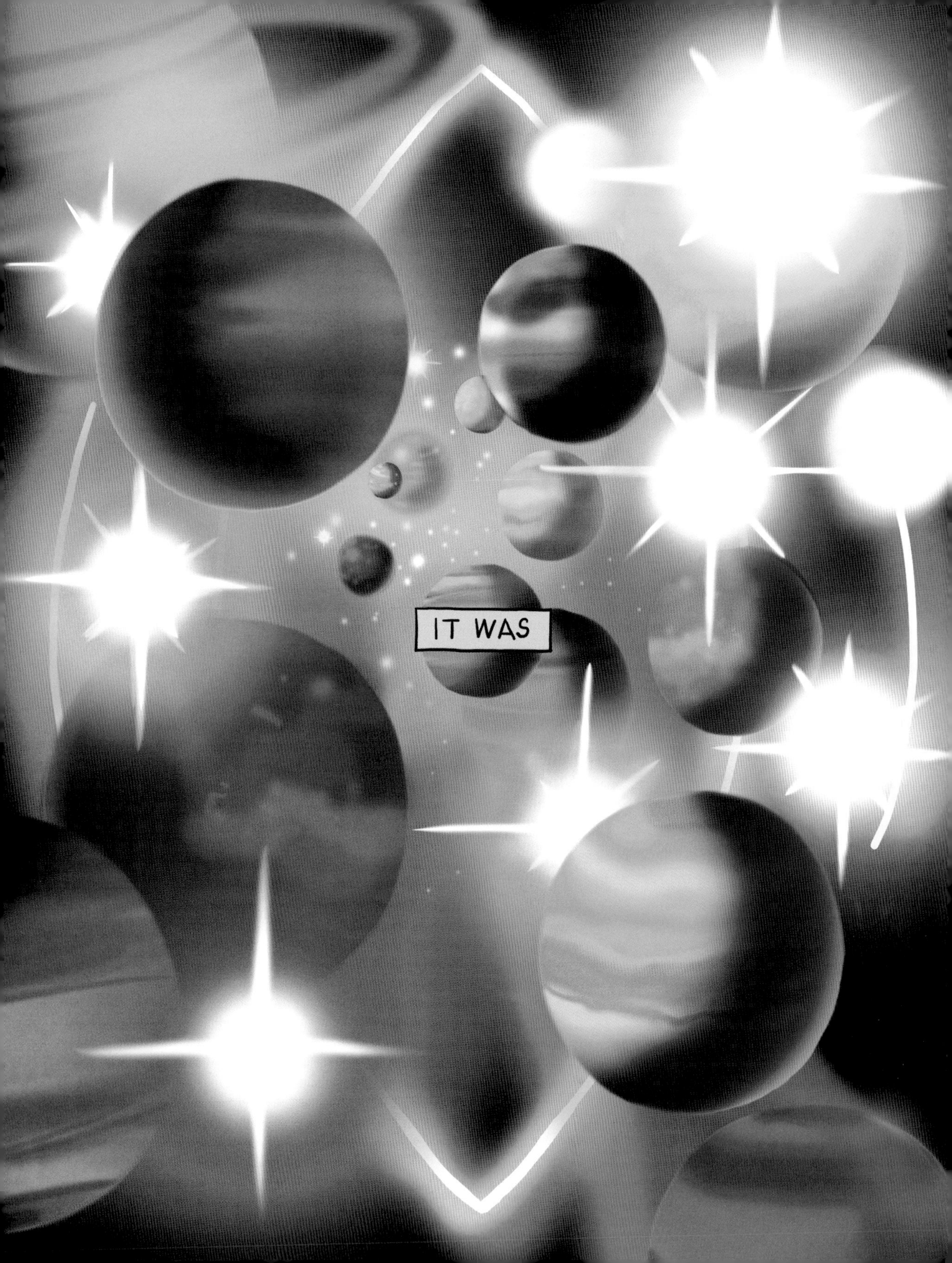
IT WAS

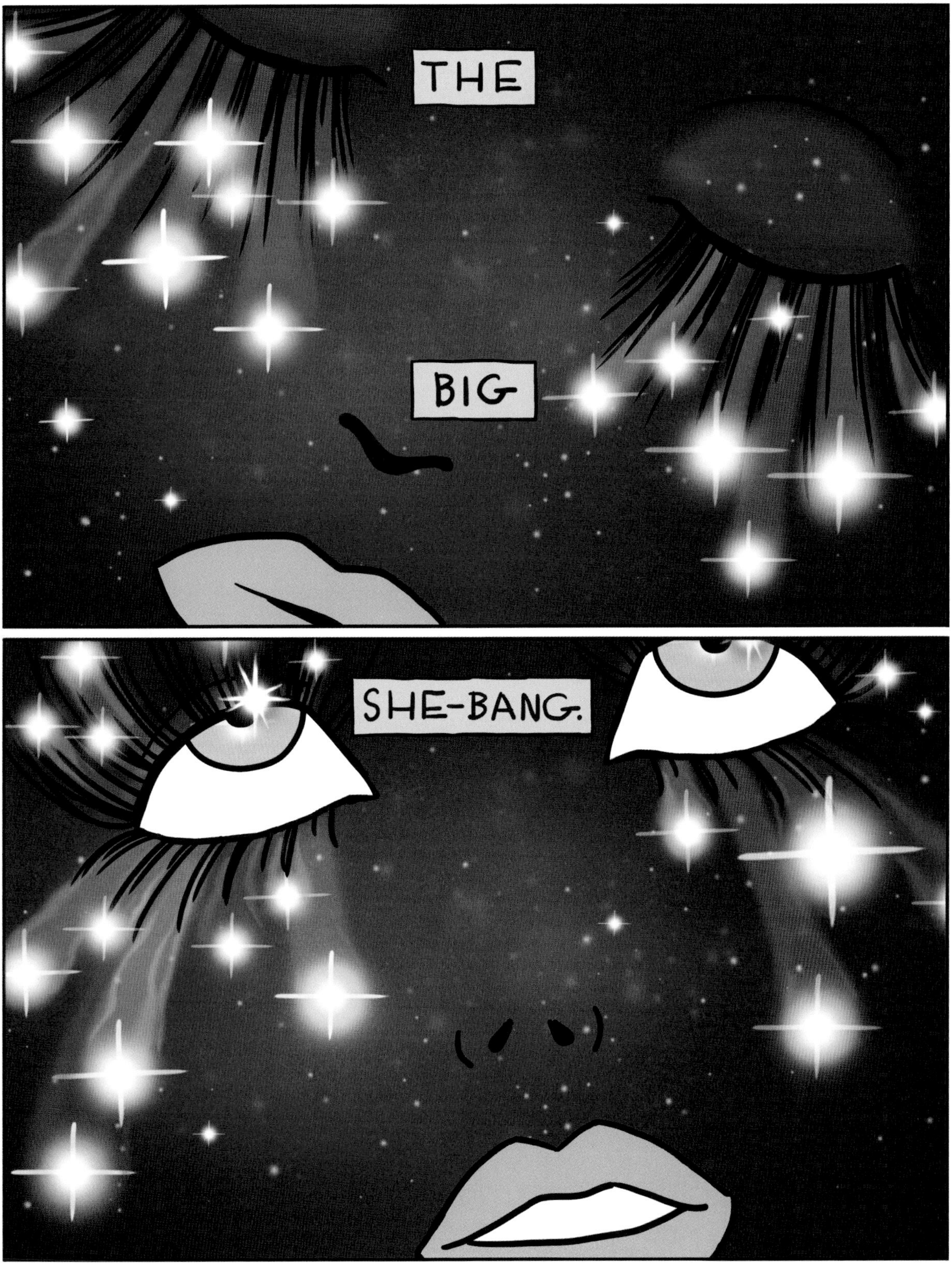
THE
BIG
SHE-BANG.

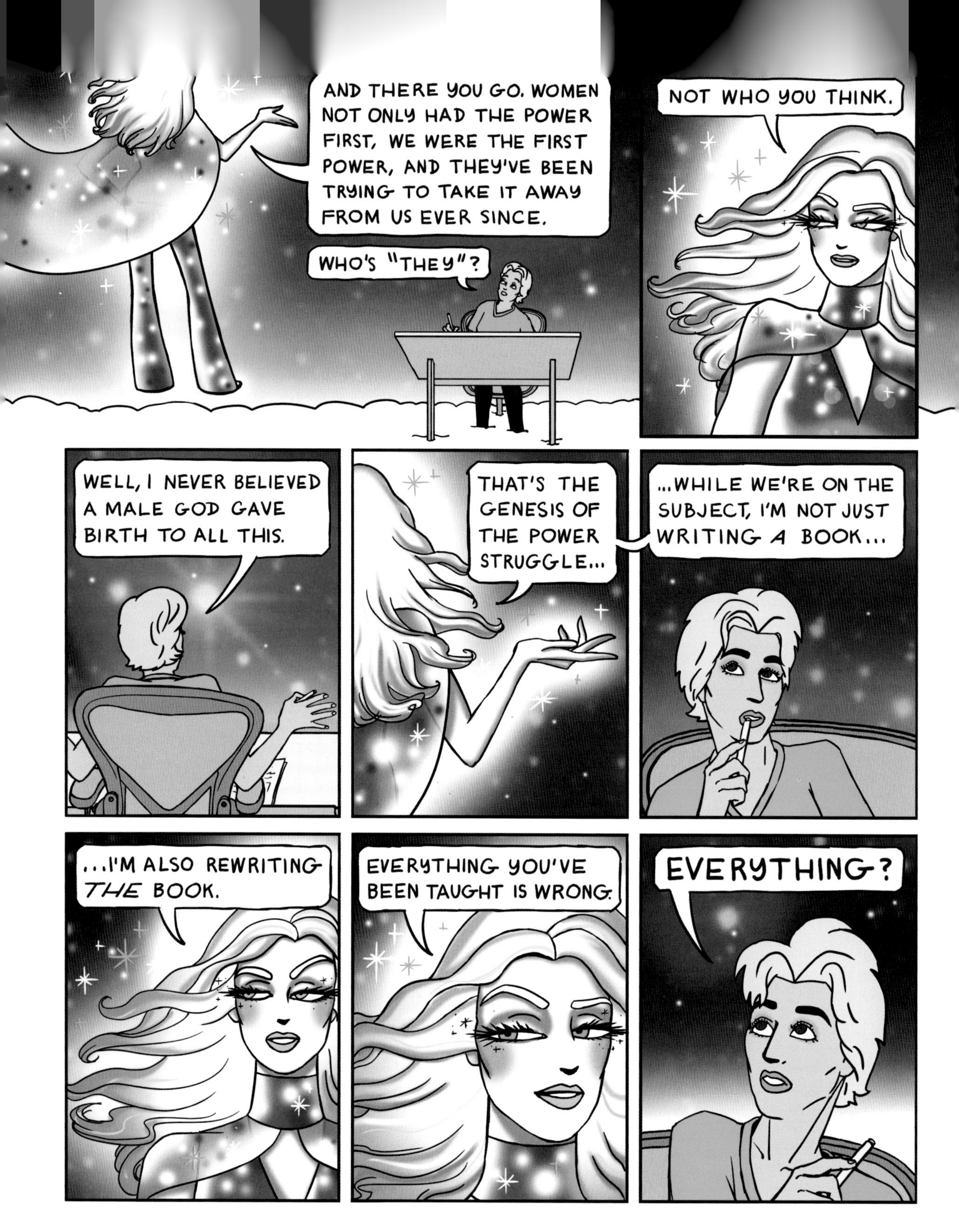
AND THERE YOU GO. WOMEN NOT ONLY HAD THE POWER FIRST, WE WERE THE FIRST POWER, AND THEY'VE BEEN TRYING TO TAKE IT AWAY FROM US EVER SINCE.
WHO'S "THEY"?
NOT WHO YOU THINK.
WELL, I NEVER BELIEVED A MALE GOD GAVE BIRTH TO ALL THIS.
THAT'S THE GENESIS OF THE POWER STRUGGLE...
...WHILE WE'RE ON THE SUBJECT, I'M NOT JUST WRITING A BOOK...
...I'M ALSO REWRITING *THE* BOOK.
EVERYTHING YOU'VE BEEN TAUGHT IS WRONG.
EVERYTHING?

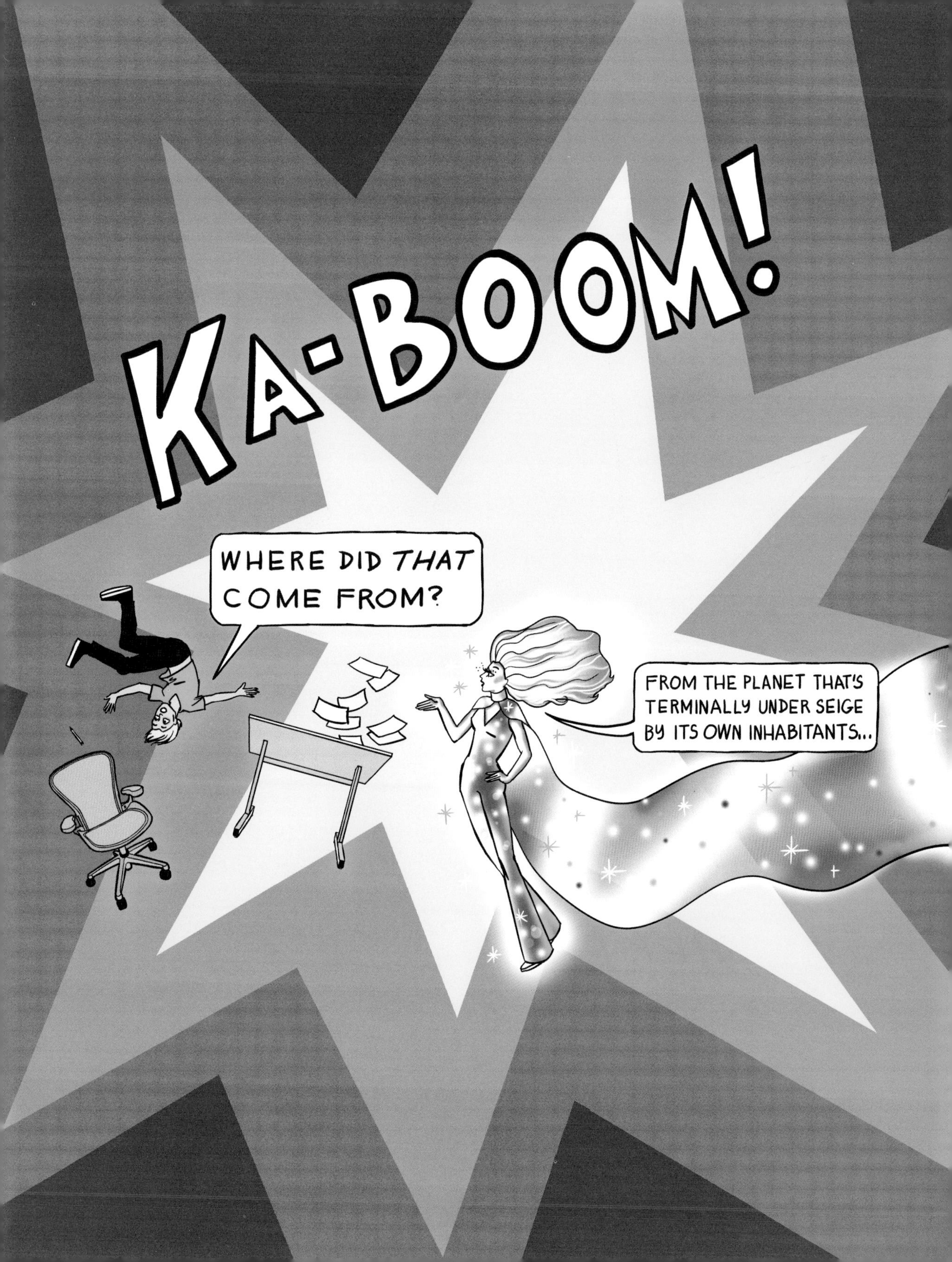
KA-BOOM!
WHERE DID THAT COME FROM?
FROM THE PLANET THAT'S TERMINALLY UNDER SEIGE BY ITS OWN INHABITANTS...

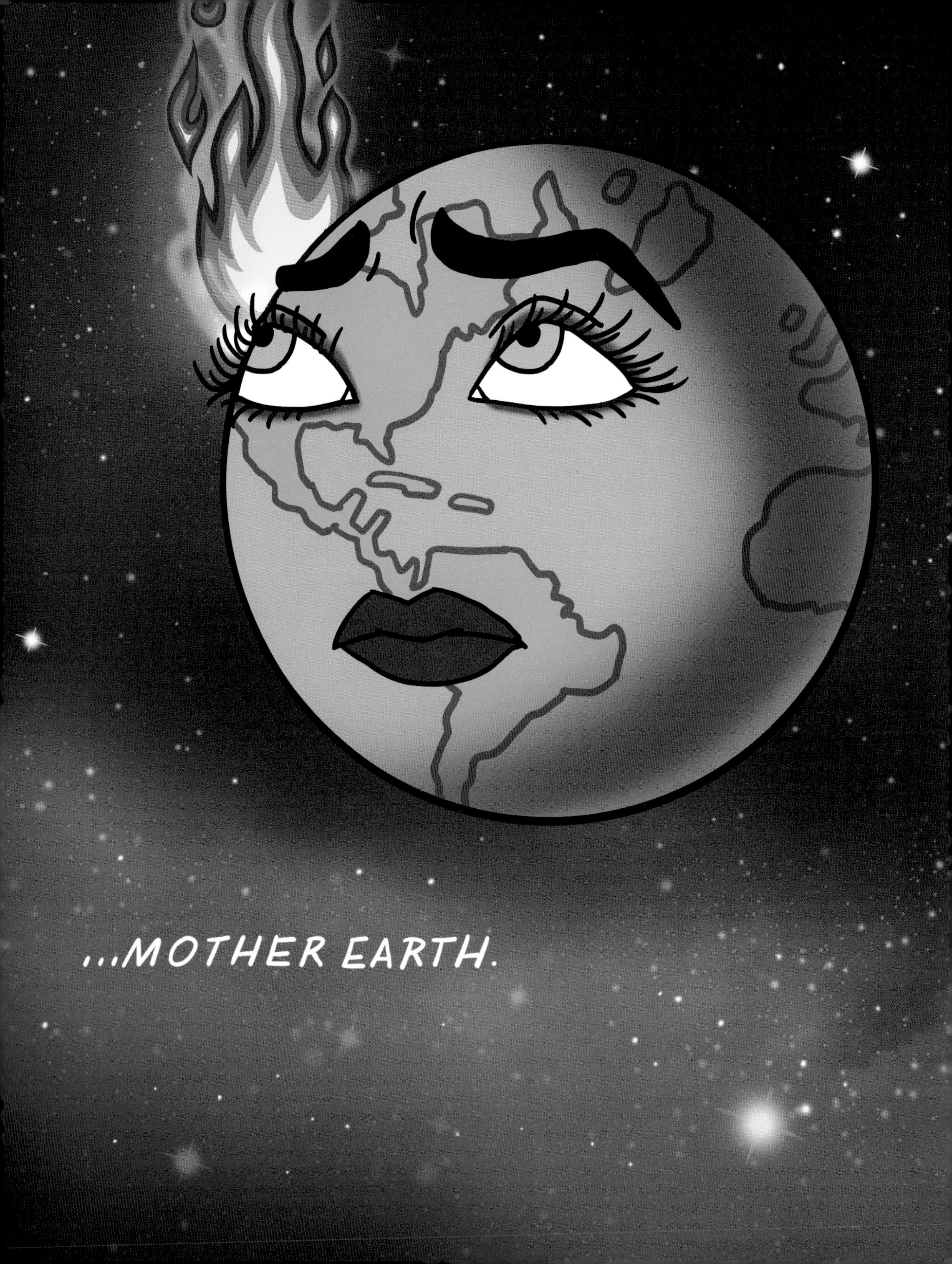
...MOTHER EARTH.

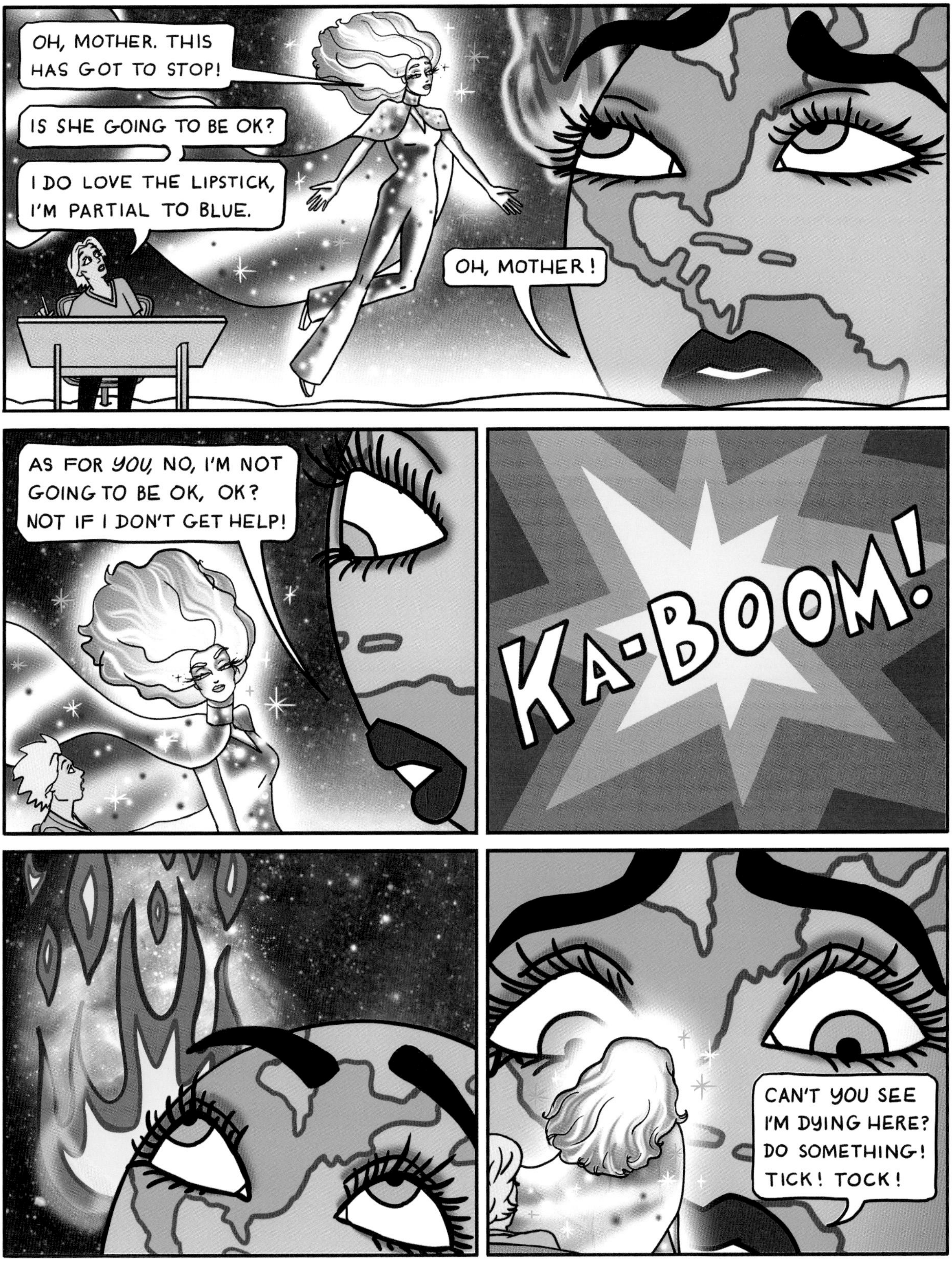
OH, MOTHER. THIS HAS GOT TO STOP!
IS SHE GOING TO BE OK?
I DO LOVE THE LIPSTICK, I'M PARTIAL TO BLUE.
OH, MOTHER!
AS FOR *YOU*, NO, I'M NOT GOING TO BE OK, OK? NOT IF I DON'T GET HELP!
KA-BOOM!
CAN'T YOU SEE I'M DYING HERE? DO SOMETHING! TICK! TOCK!

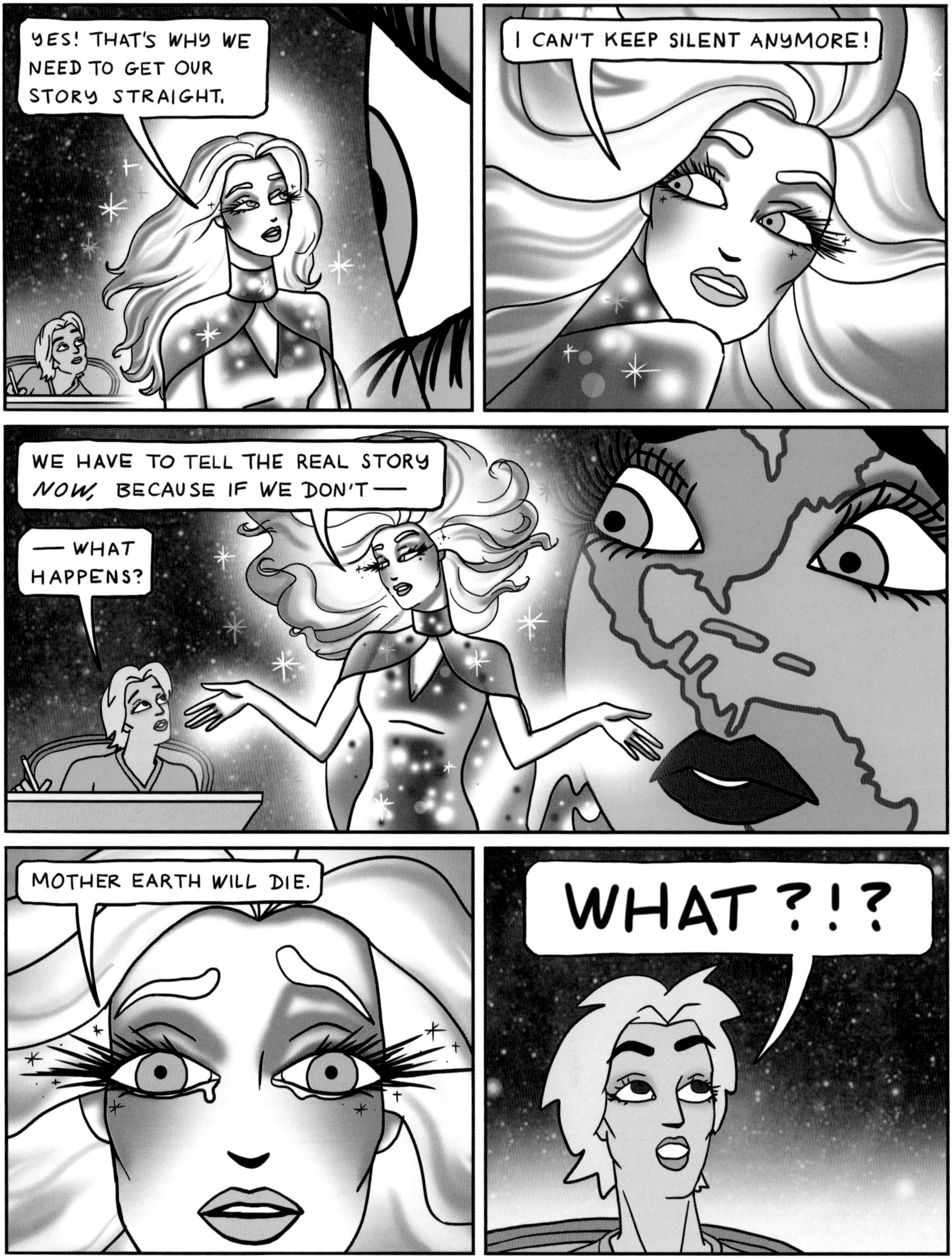
YES! THAT'S WHY WE NEED TO GET OUR STORY STRAIGHT.
I CAN'T KEEP SILENT ANYMORE!
WE HAVE TO TELL THE REAL STORY NOW, BECAUSE IF WE DON'T—
—WHAT HAPPENS?
MOTHER EARTH WILL DIE.
WHAT?!?

WHAT'S GOING ON?

ARE YOU ASLEEP, HUMAN? I'M ALARMED THAT MANY OF YOU STILL HIT "SNOOZE."

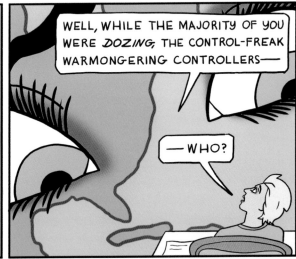

WELL, WHILE THE MAJORITY OF YOU WERE *DOZING*, THE CONTROL-FREAK WARMONGERING CONTROLLERS—

—WHO?

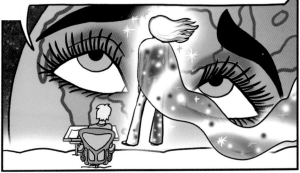

THE AUTHORITIES! THE RULERS! THE CABAL! THE GLOBAL ELITE! THE NEW WORLD ORDER! THE ILLUMINATI—THE TRULY SINISTER SIDE OF THE PATRIARCHY—WHATEVER YOU CALL THEM...

THEY'RE ON THE VERGE OF DESTROYING ME!

AND THIS IS HAPPENING *NOW*, BECAUSE WAY BACK THEN, THE DIVINE FEMININE WAS OVERRIDDEN!

MOMMA, WAY BACK THEN, THE DIVINE FEMININE WASN'T JUST "OVERRIDDEN"...

Q: WHAT DO THE POWER HUNGRY DO WHEN THEY WANT TO WREST CONTROL?*

1. GRACIOUSLY ACCEED TO THE COMPETITION, AND SEND A PRETTY ORCHID!
2. TAKE CONTROL OF THE NARRATIVE, OBLITERATE ANY AND ALL THREATS BY LYING, DAMAGING REPUTATIONS, HIRING THE NASTIEST LAW FIRMS, PLANTING FALSE STORIES IN THE MEDIA, HARASSING— *UGH THIS LIST NEEDS TO __END__!*

A: IF YOU CHOSE 1, YOU'RE EITHER SOCIALLY UNCONSCIOUS, YOU'VE NEVER TANGLED WITH THE PATRIARCHY, OR YOU LIVE ON ONE OF MY SUPERFAB SPA PLANETS 27 LIGHT-YEARS FROM HERE.

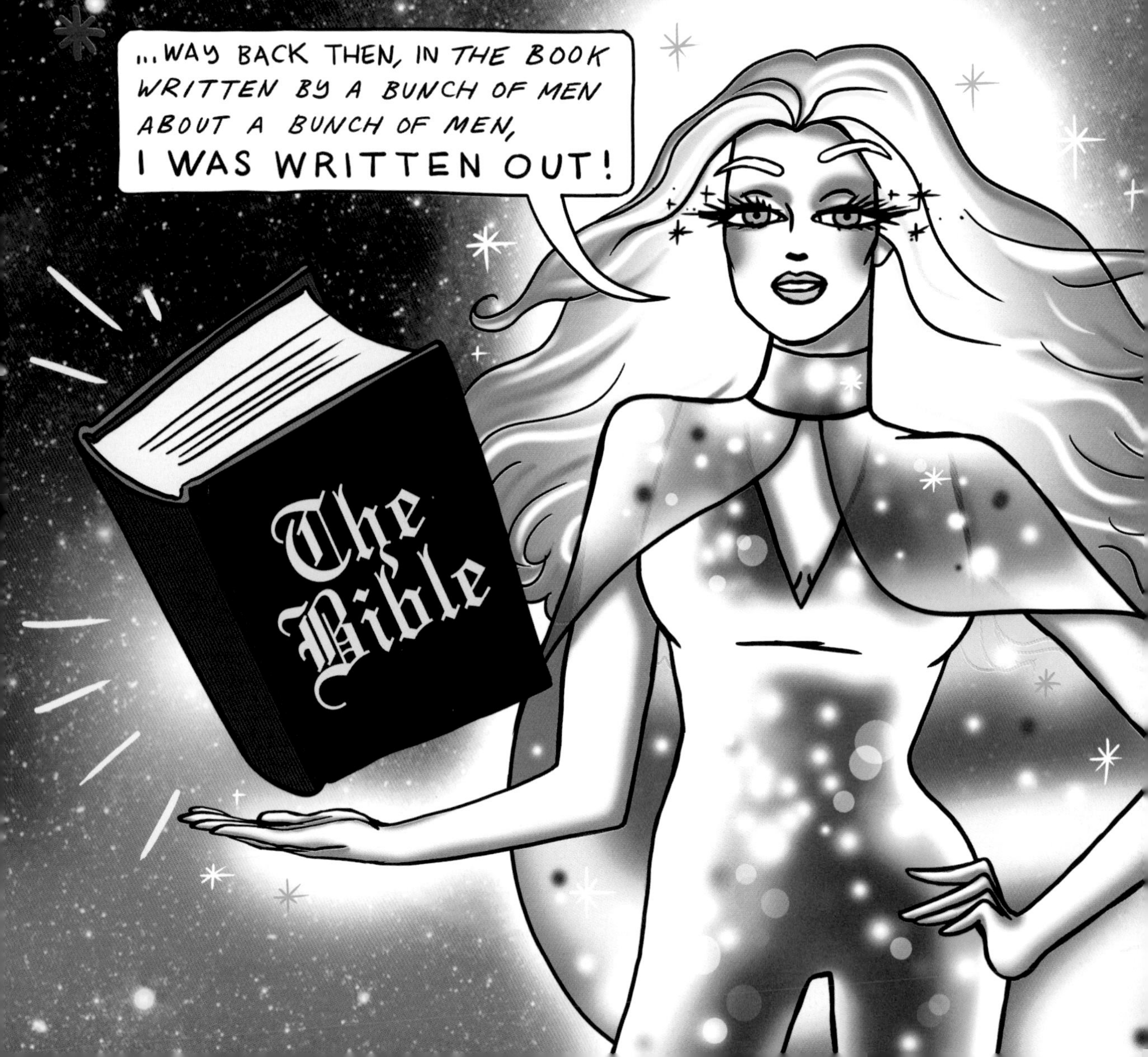

*
...WAY BACK THEN, IN *THE BOOK WRITTEN BY A BUNCH OF MEN ABOUT A BUNCH OF MEN,* I WAS WRITTEN OUT!
The Bible

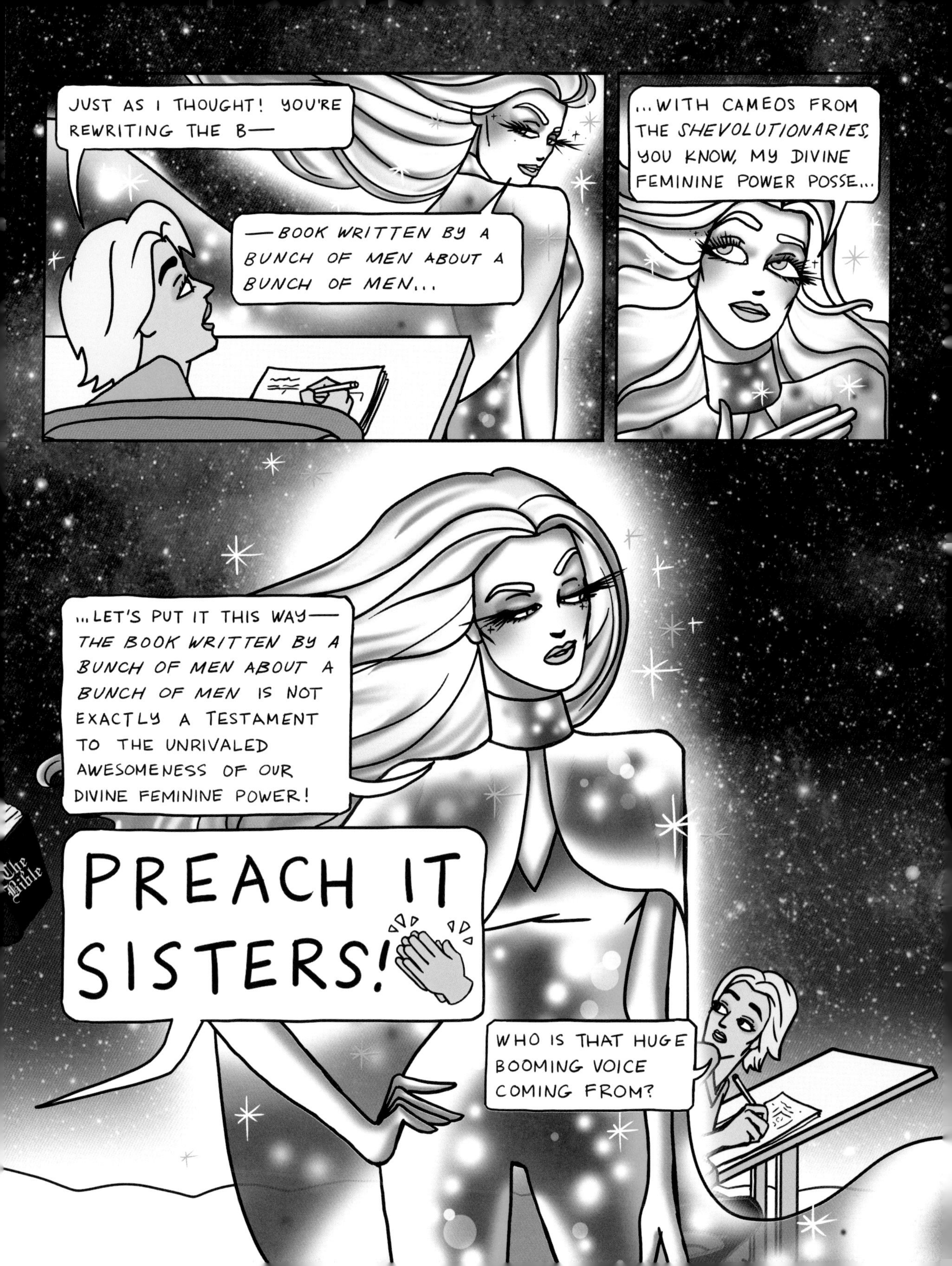

JUST AS I THOUGHT! YOU'RE REWRITING THE B—
—*BOOK WRITTEN BY A BUNCH OF MEN ABOUT A BUNCH OF MEN...*
...WITH CAMEOS FROM THE *SHEVOLUTIONARIES,* YOU KNOW, MY DIVINE FEMININE POWER POSSE...
...LET'S PUT IT THIS WAY— *THE BOOK WRITTEN BY A BUNCH OF MEN ABOUT A BUNCH OF MEN* IS NOT EXACTLY A TESTAMENT TO THE UNRIVALED AWESOMENESS OF OUR DIVINE FEMININE POWER!
The Bible
PREACH IT SISTERS!
WHO IS THAT HUGE BOOMING VOICE COMING FROM?

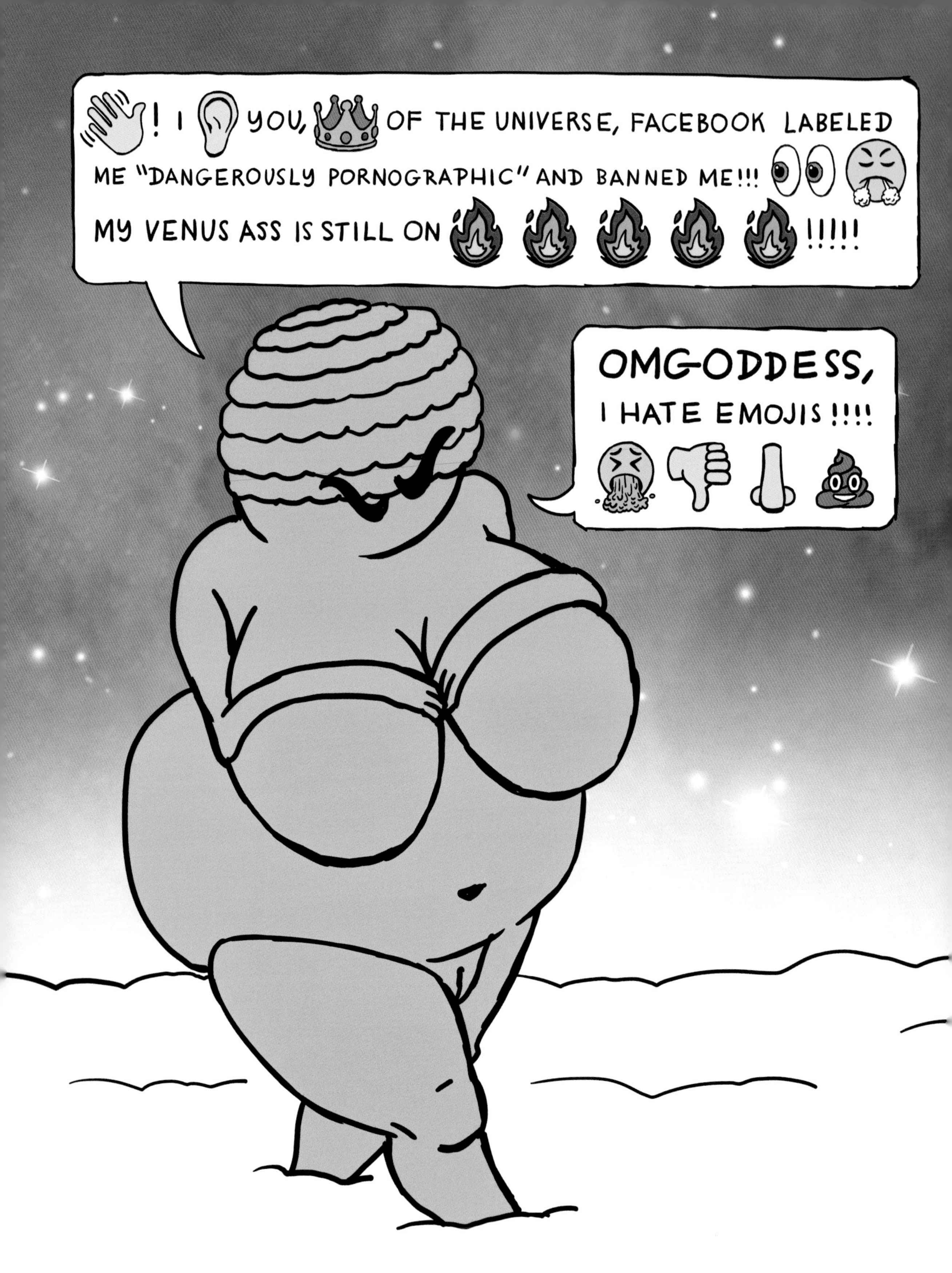
! I YOU, OF THE UNIVERSE, FACEBOOK LABELED ME "DANGEROUSLY PORNOGRAPHIC" AND BANNED ME!!! MY VENUS ASS IS STILL ON !!!!!
OMGODDESS, I HATE EMOJIS!!!!

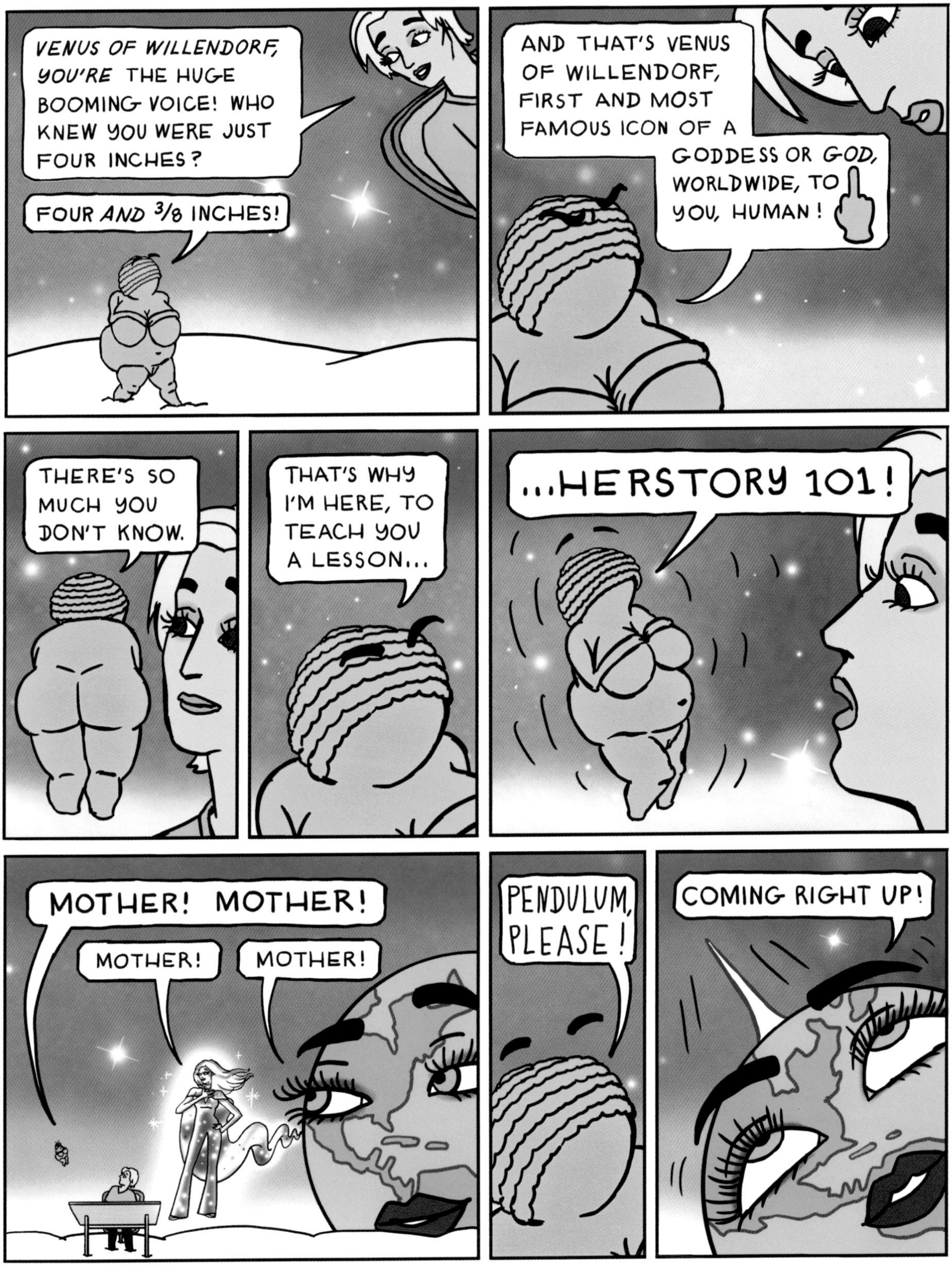
VENUS OF WILLENDORF, YOU'RE THE HUGE BOOMING VOICE! WHO KNEW YOU WERE JUST FOUR INCHES?
FOUR AND 3/8 INCHES!
AND THAT'S VENUS OF WILLENDORF, FIRST AND MOST FAMOUS ICON OF A
GODDESS OR GOD, WORLDWIDE, TO YOU, HUMAN!
THERE'S SO MUCH YOU DON'T KNOW.
THAT'S WHY I'M HERE, TO TEACH YOU A LESSON...
...HERSTORY 101!
MOTHER! MOTHER!
MOTHER!
MOTHER!
PENDULUM, PLEASE!
COMING RIGHT UP!

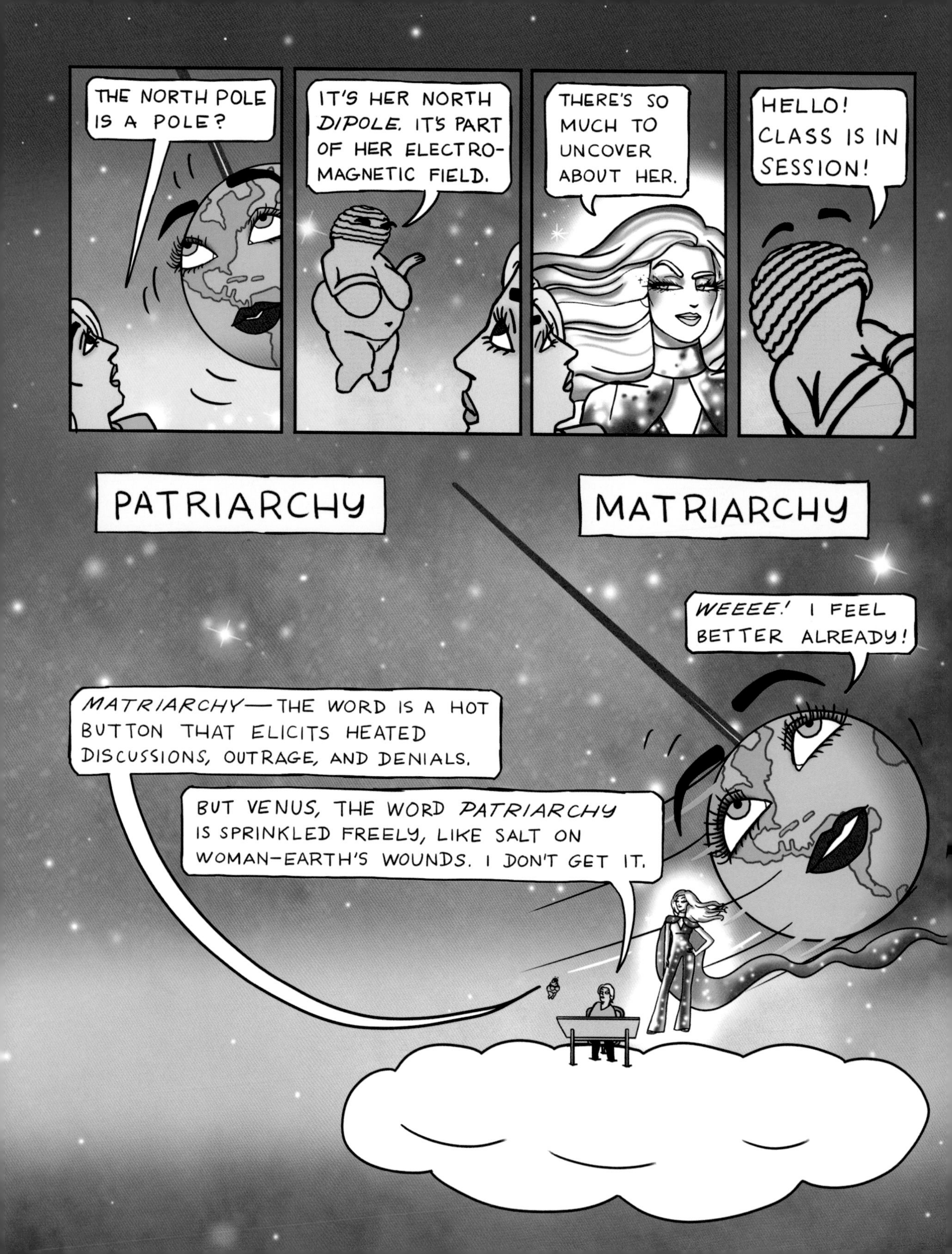
THE NORTH POLE IS A POLE?
IT'S HER NORTH *DIPOLE*. IT'S PART OF HER ELECTRO-MAGNETIC FIELD.
THERE'S SO MUCH TO UNCOVER ABOUT HER.
HELLO! CLASS IS IN SESSION!
PATRIARCHY
MATRIARCHY
WEEEE! I FEEL BETTER ALREADY!
MATRIARCHY—THE WORD IS A HOT BUTTON THAT ELICITS HEATED DISCUSSIONS, OUTRAGE, AND DENIALS.
BUT VENUS, THE WORD *PATRIARCHY* IS SPRINKLED FREELY, LIKE SALT ON WOMAN-EARTH'S WOUNDS. I DON'T GET IT.

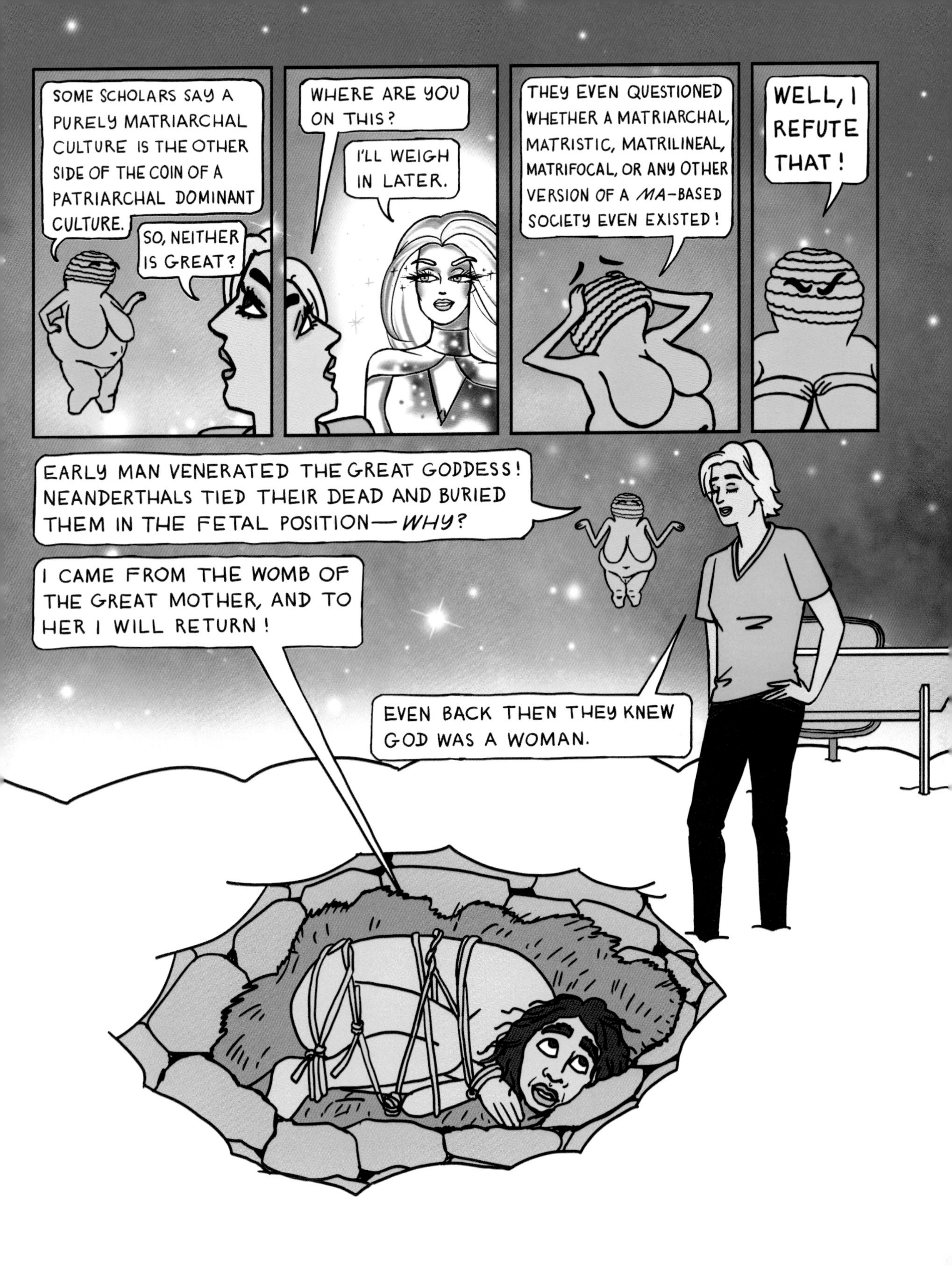
SOME SCHOLARS SAY A PURELY MATRIARCHAL CULTURE IS THE OTHER SIDE OF THE COIN OF A PATRIARCHAL DOMINANT CULTURE.
SO, NEITHER IS GREAT?
WHERE ARE YOU ON THIS?
I'LL WEIGH IN LATER.
THEY EVEN QUESTIONED WHETHER A MATRIARCHAL, MATRISTIC, MATRILINEAL, MATRIFOCAL, OR ANY OTHER VERSION OF A *MA*-BASED SOCIETY EVEN EXISTED!
WELL, I REFUTE THAT!
EARLY MAN VENERATED THE GREAT GODDESS! NEANDERTHALS TIED THEIR DEAD AND BURIED THEM IN THE FETAL POSITION—*WHY*?
I CAME FROM THE WOMB OF THE GREAT MOTHER, AND TO HER I WILL RETURN!
EVEN BACK THEN THEY KNEW GOD WAS A WOMAN.

DUH! WHERE DO YOU THINK I CAME FROM? I *AM* THE ICON OF LIFE-CREATING FEMININE POWER—

—WILLENDORF! *WE* AGREE THERE'S NOTHING MORE AWESOME THAN THE MIRACLE OF BIRTH, BUT YOU'RE NOT THE ONLY PALEO VENUS!

AND I'M 40,000-YEARS-OLD *AND* 15,000 YEARS OLDER THAN YOU!

VENUS OF HOHLE FELS. STONE AGE BEFORE BEAUTY.

I'M FROM CATAL HUYUK. BACK IN 7000 B.C., AGE + FATNESS = STATUS!

THAT IS SO *NOT* PATRIARCHAL.

HELLO, NICKI MINAJ—THE BOOB GRAB IS ONE OF HER MOVES.

OH, YEAH? WAS SHE EMPHASIZING HER LIFE-GIVING GODDESS PROWESS LIKE I DID IN SUDAN IN 6000 B.C.?

THEY CAN SUPRESS US ALL THEY WANT...

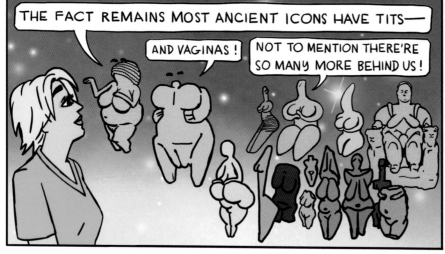

THE FACT REMAINS MOST ANCIENT ICONS HAVE TITS—

AND VAGINAS!

NOT TO MENTION THERE'RE SO MANY MORE BEHIND US!

SO THE HERSTORY LESSON IS ABOUT SUPRESSION?

LESSON LEARNED— *BYE!*

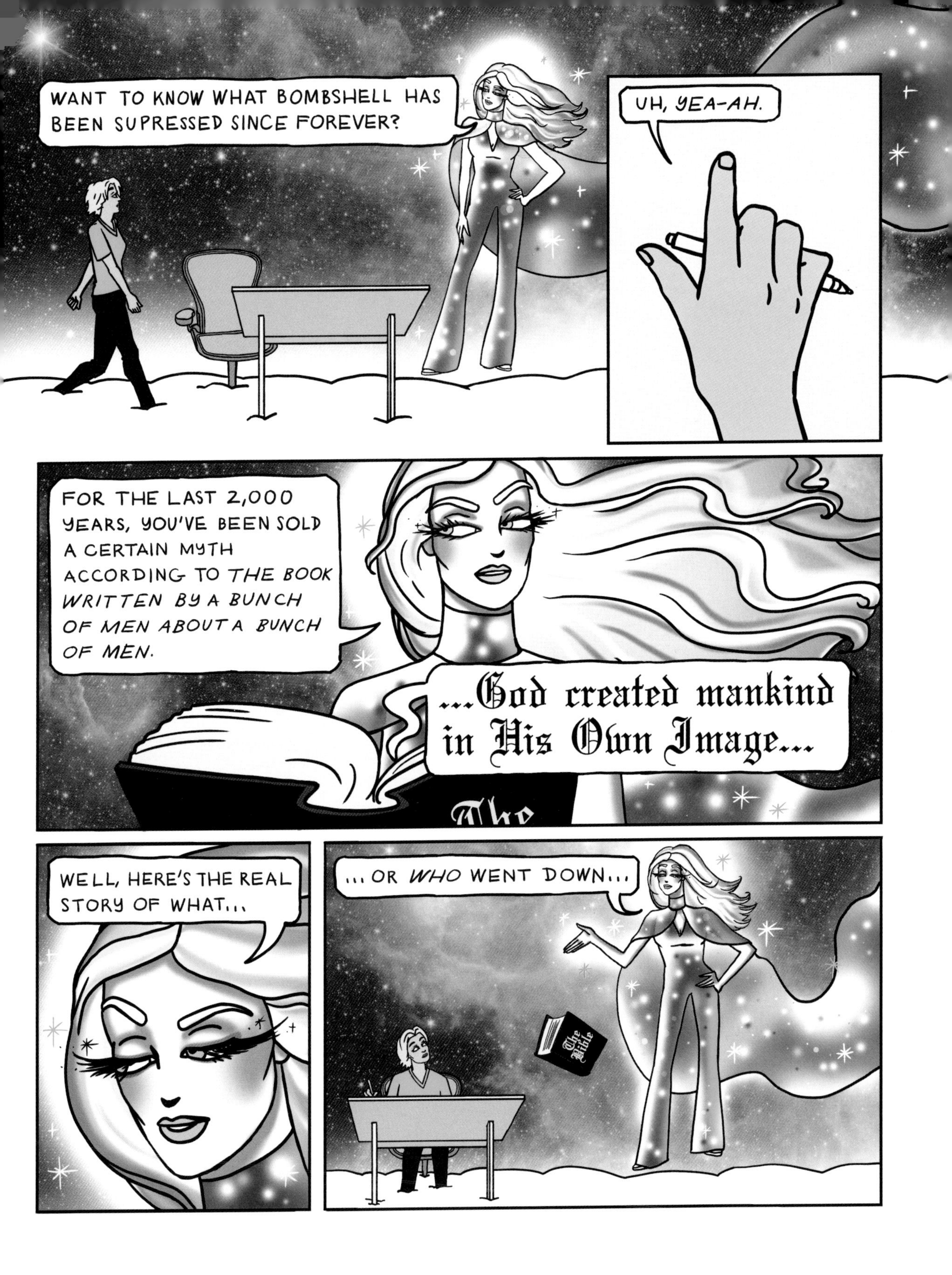
WANT TO KNOW WHAT BOMBSHELL HAS BEEN SUPRESSED SINCE FOREVER?
UH, YEA-AH.
FOR THE LAST 2,000 YEARS, YOU'VE BEEN SOLD A CERTAIN MYTH ACCORDING TO *THE BOOK WRITTEN BY A BUNCH OF MEN ABOUT A BUNCH OF MEN.*
...God created mankind in His Own Image...
WELL, HERE'S THE REAL STORY OF WHAT...
...OR *WHO* WENT DOWN...
The Bible

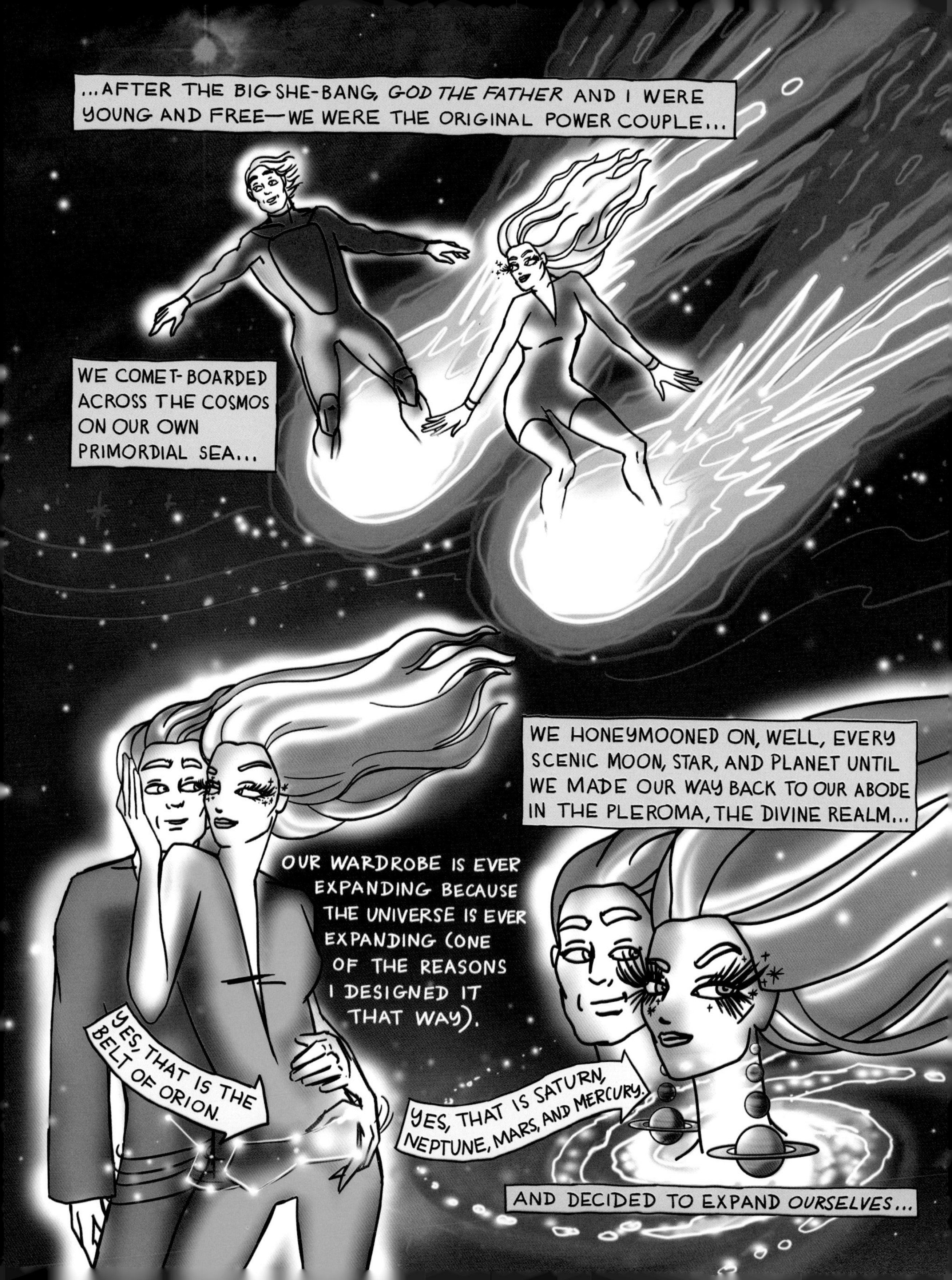
...AFTER THE BIG SHE-BANG, *GOD THE FATHER* AND I WERE YOUNG AND FREE—WE WERE THE ORIGINAL POWER COUPLE...
WE COMET-BOARDED ACROSS THE COSMOS ON OUR OWN PRIMORDIAL SEA...
WE HONEYMOONED ON, WELL, EVERY SCENIC MOON, STAR, AND PLANET UNTIL WE MADE OUR WAY BACK TO OUR ABODE IN THE PLEROMA, THE DIVINE REALM...
OUR WARDROBE IS EVER EXPANDING BECAUSE THE UNIVERSE IS EVER EXPANDING (ONE OF THE REASONS I DESIGNED IT THAT WAY).
YES, THAT IS THE BELT OF ORION.
YES, THAT IS SATURN, NEPTUNE, MARS, AND MERCURY.
AND DECIDED TO EXPAND *OURSELVES*...

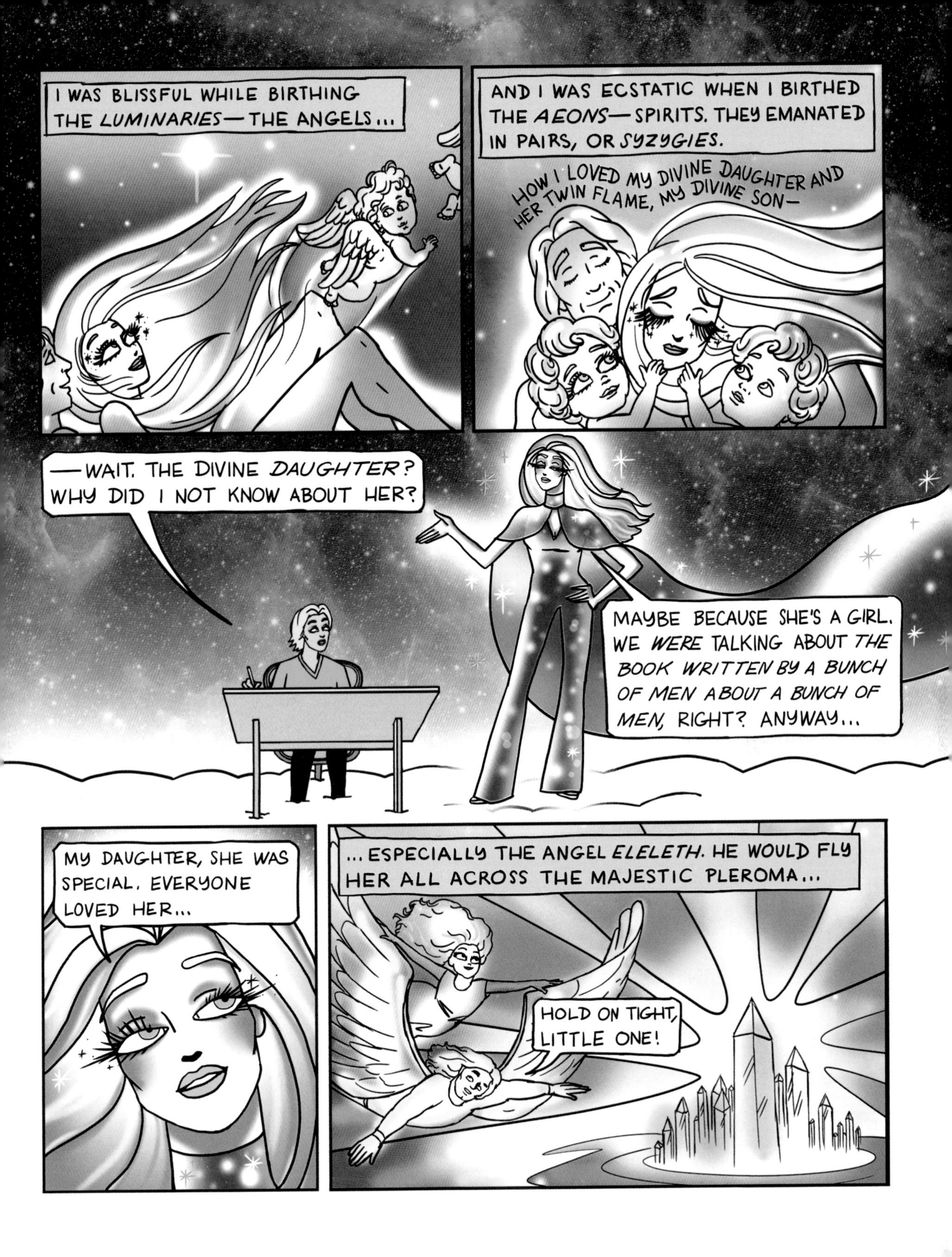
I WAS BLISSFUL WHILE BIRTHING THE *LUMINARIES*—THE ANGELS...
AND I WAS ECSTATIC WHEN I BIRTHED THE *AEONS*—SPIRITS. THEY EMANATED IN PAIRS, OR *SYZYGIES*.
HOW I LOVED MY DIVINE DAUGHTER AND HER TWIN FLAME, MY DIVINE SON—
—WAIT. THE DIVINE *DAUGHTER*? WHY DID I NOT KNOW ABOUT HER?
MAYBE BECAUSE SHE'S A GIRL. WE *WERE* TALKING ABOUT *THE BOOK WRITTEN BY A BUNCH OF MEN ABOUT A BUNCH OF MEN*, RIGHT? ANYWAY...
MY DAUGHTER, SHE WAS SPECIAL. EVERYONE LOVED HER...
...ESPECIALLY THE ANGEL *ELELETH*. HE WOULD FLY HER ALL ACROSS THE MAJESTIC PLEROMA...
HOLD ON TIGHT, LITTLE ONE!

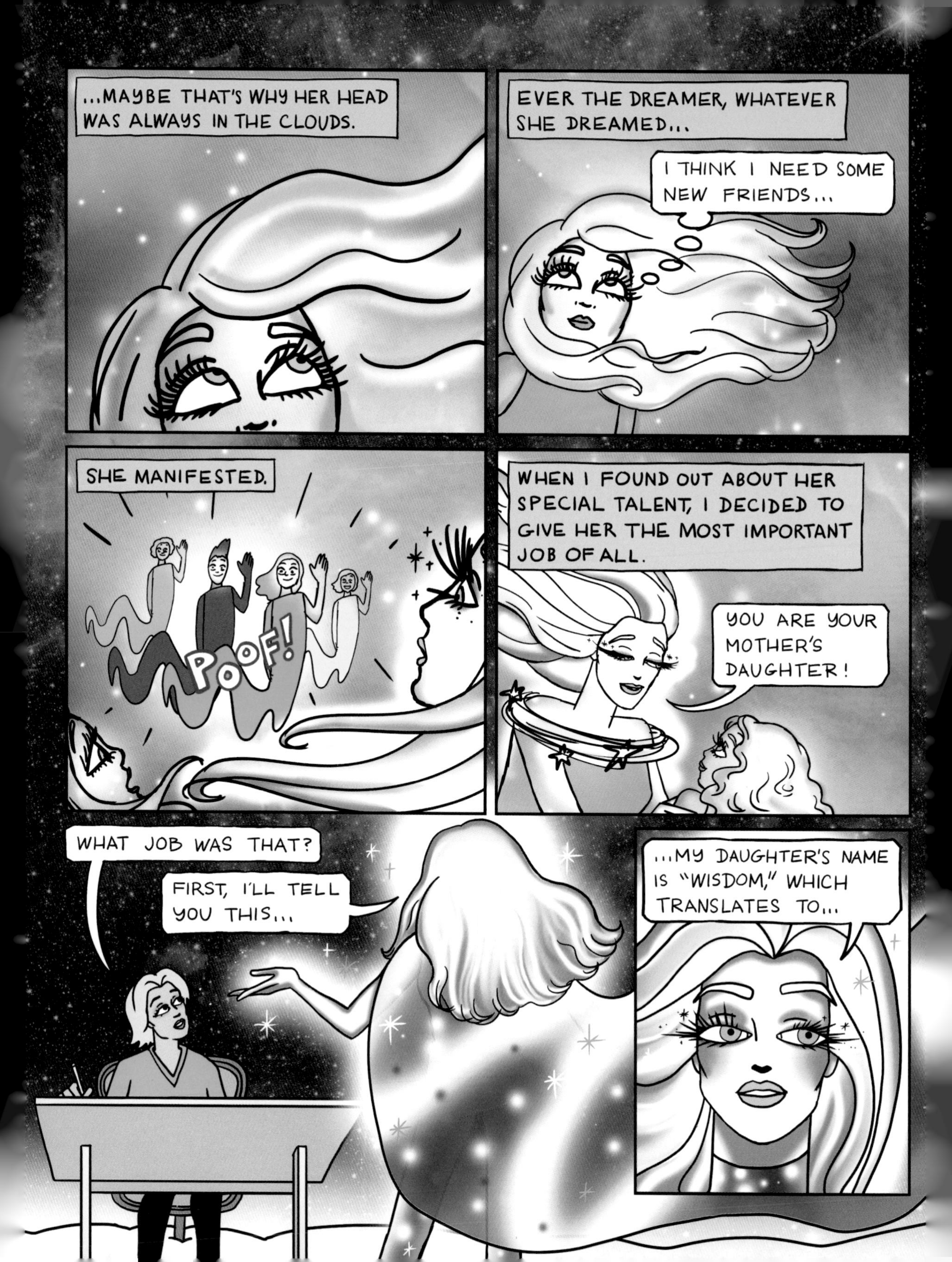
...MAYBE THAT'S WHY HER HEAD WAS ALWAYS IN THE CLOUDS.
EVER THE DREAMER, WHATEVER SHE DREAMED...
I THINK I NEED SOME NEW FRIENDS...
SHE MANIFESTED.
POOF!
WHEN I FOUND OUT ABOUT HER SPECIAL TALENT, I DECIDED TO GIVE HER THE MOST IMPORTANT JOB OF ALL.
YOU ARE YOUR MOTHER'S DAUGHTER!
WHAT JOB WAS THAT?
FIRST, I'LL TELL YOU THIS...
...MY DAUGHTER'S NAME IS "WISDOM," WHICH TRANSLATES TO...

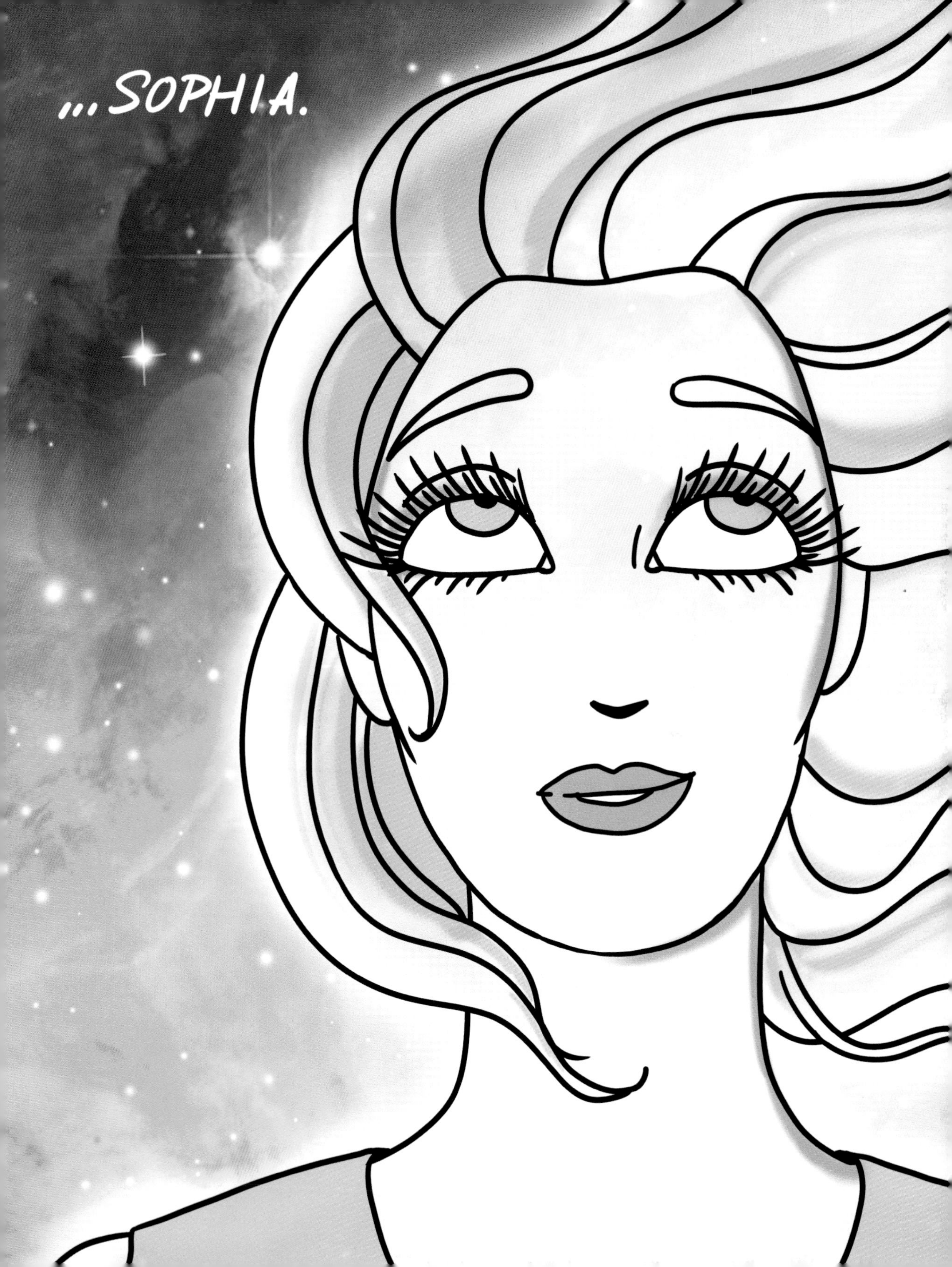
...SOPHIA.

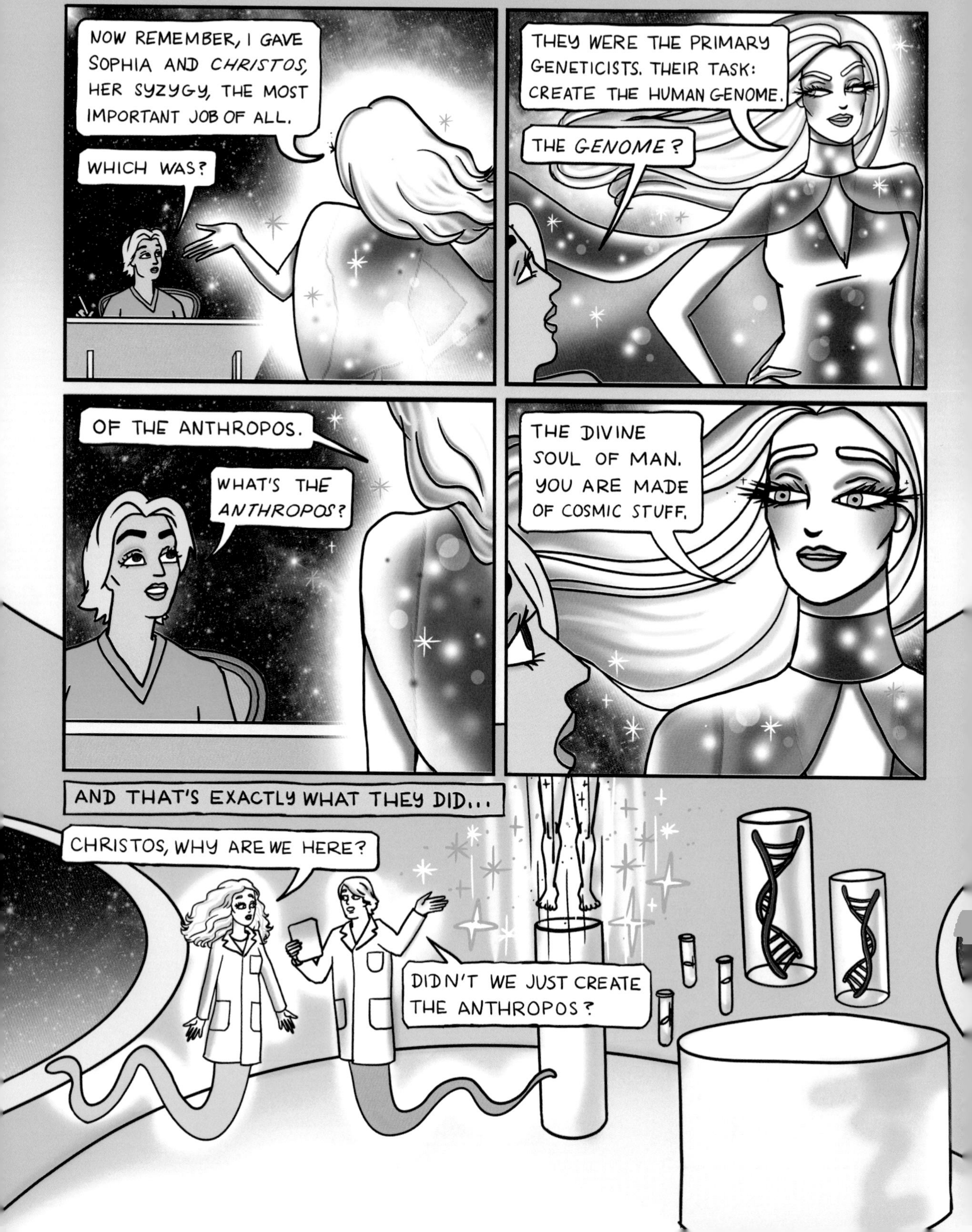
NOW REMEMBER, I GAVE SOPHIA AND *CHRISTOS*, HER SYZYGY, THE MOST IMPORTANT JOB OF ALL.
WHICH WAS?
THEY WERE THE PRIMARY GENETICISTS. THEIR TASK: CREATE THE HUMAN GENOME.
THE *GENOME*?
OF THE ANTHROPOS.
WHAT'S THE *ANTHROPOS*?
THE DIVINE SOUL OF MAN. YOU ARE MADE OF COSMIC STUFF.
AND THAT'S EXACTLY WHAT THEY DID...
CHRISTOS, WHY ARE WE HERE?
DIDN'T WE JUST CREATE THE ANTHROPOS?

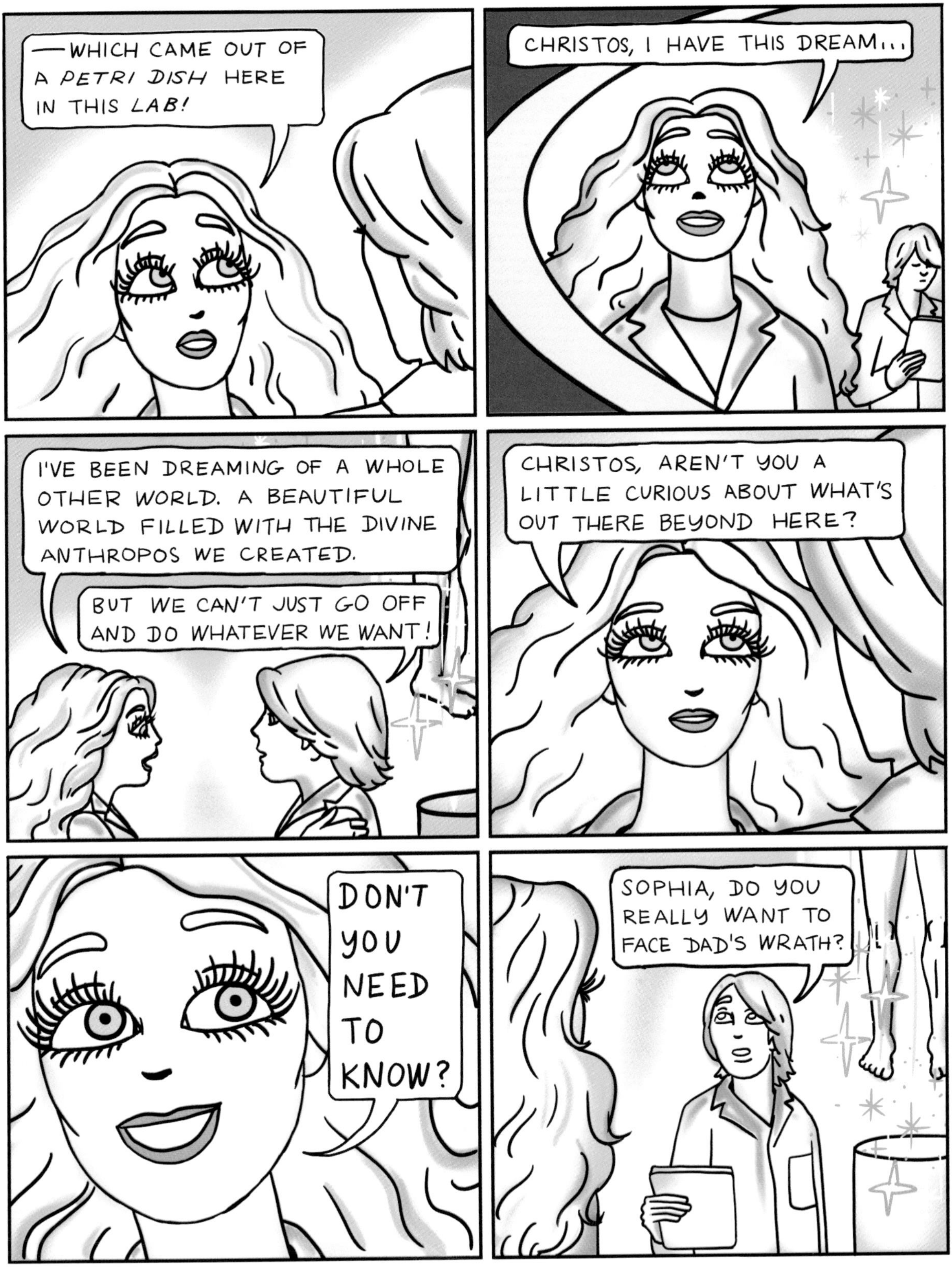
—WHICH CAME OUT OF A *PETRI DISH* HERE IN THIS *LAB!*
CHRISTOS, I HAVE THIS DREAM...
I'VE BEEN DREAMING OF A WHOLE OTHER WORLD. A BEAUTIFUL WORLD FILLED WITH THE DIVINE ANTHROPOS WE CREATED.
BUT WE CAN'T JUST GO OFF AND DO WHATEVER WE WANT!
CHRISTOS, AREN'T YOU A LITTLE CURIOUS ABOUT WHAT'S OUT THERE BEYOND HERE?
DON'T YOU NEED TO KNOW?
SOPHIA, DO YOU REALLY WANT TO FACE DAD'S WRATH?

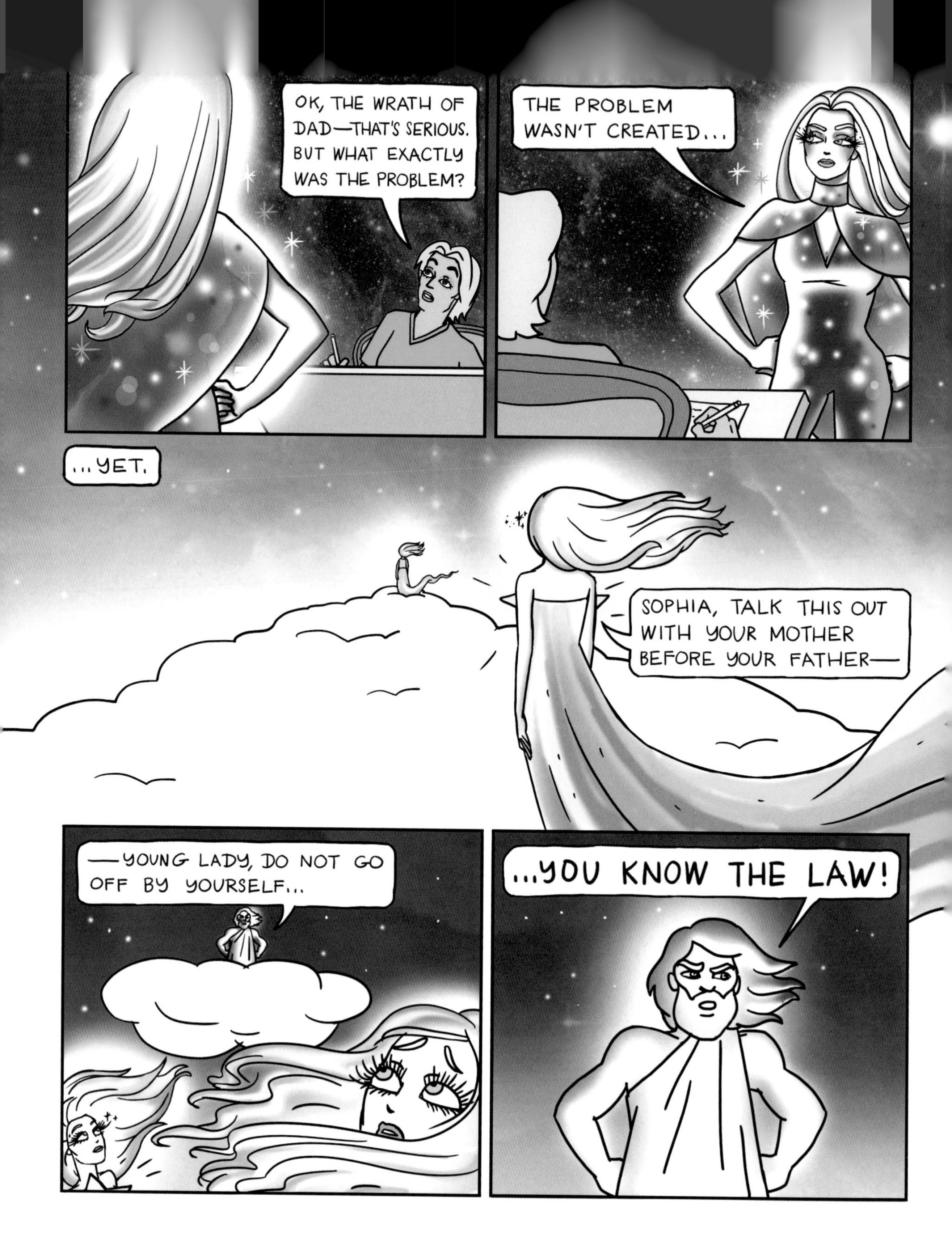
OK, THE WRATH OF DAD—THAT'S SERIOUS. BUT WHAT EXACTLY WAS THE PROBLEM?
THE PROBLEM WASN'T CREATED...
...YET.
SOPHIA, TALK THIS OUT WITH YOUR MOTHER BEFORE YOUR FATHER—
—YOUNG LADY, DO NOT GO OFF BY YOURSELF...
...YOU KNOW THE LAW!

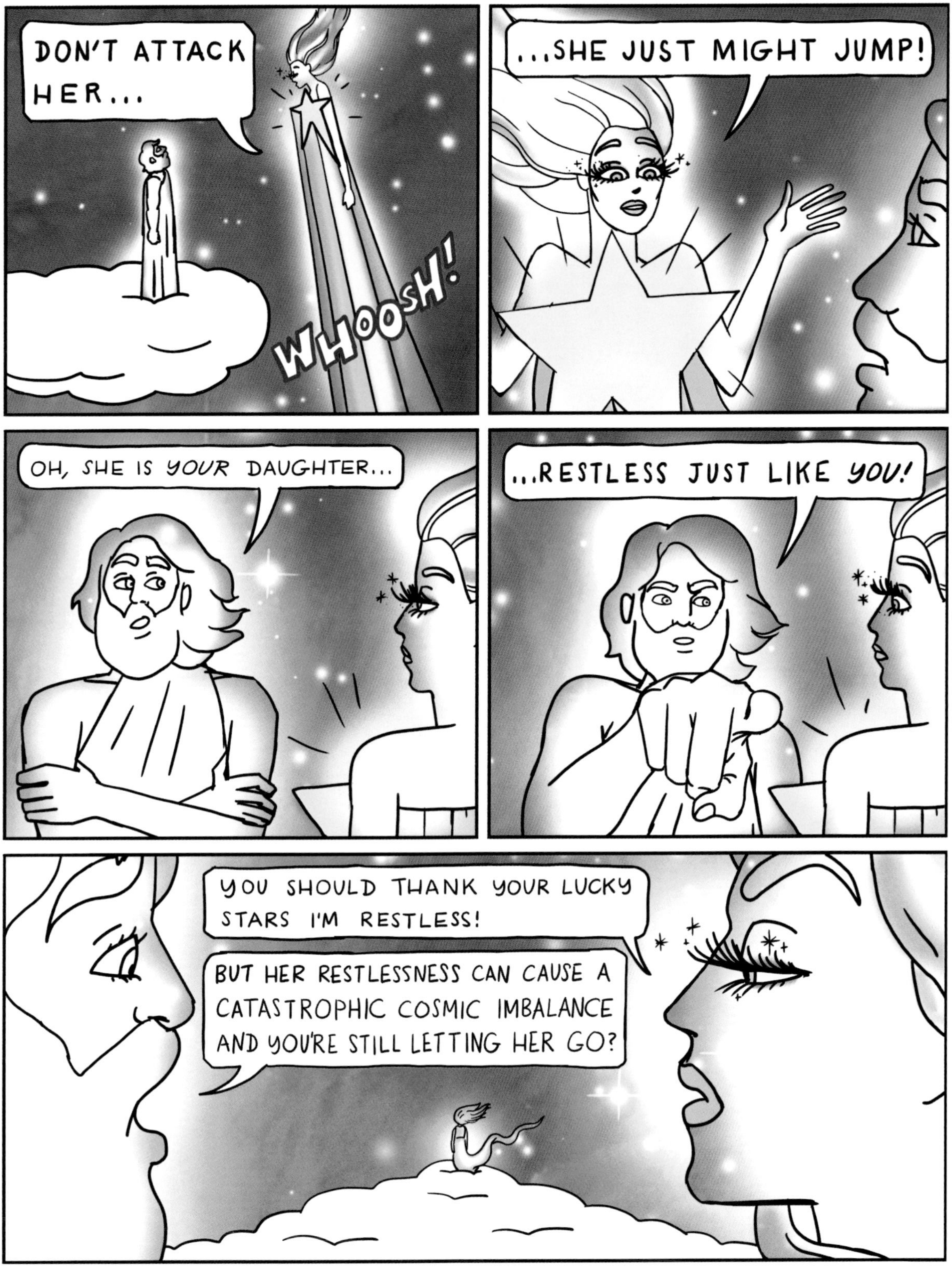
DON'T ATTACK HER...
WHOOSH!
...SHE JUST MIGHT JUMP!
OH, SHE IS *YOUR* DAUGHTER...
...RESTLESS JUST LIKE *YOU!*
YOU SHOULD THANK YOUR LUCKY STARS I'M RESTLESS!
BUT HER RESTLESSNESS CAN CAUSE A CATASTROPHIC COSMIC IMBALANCE AND YOU'RE STILL LETTING HER GO?

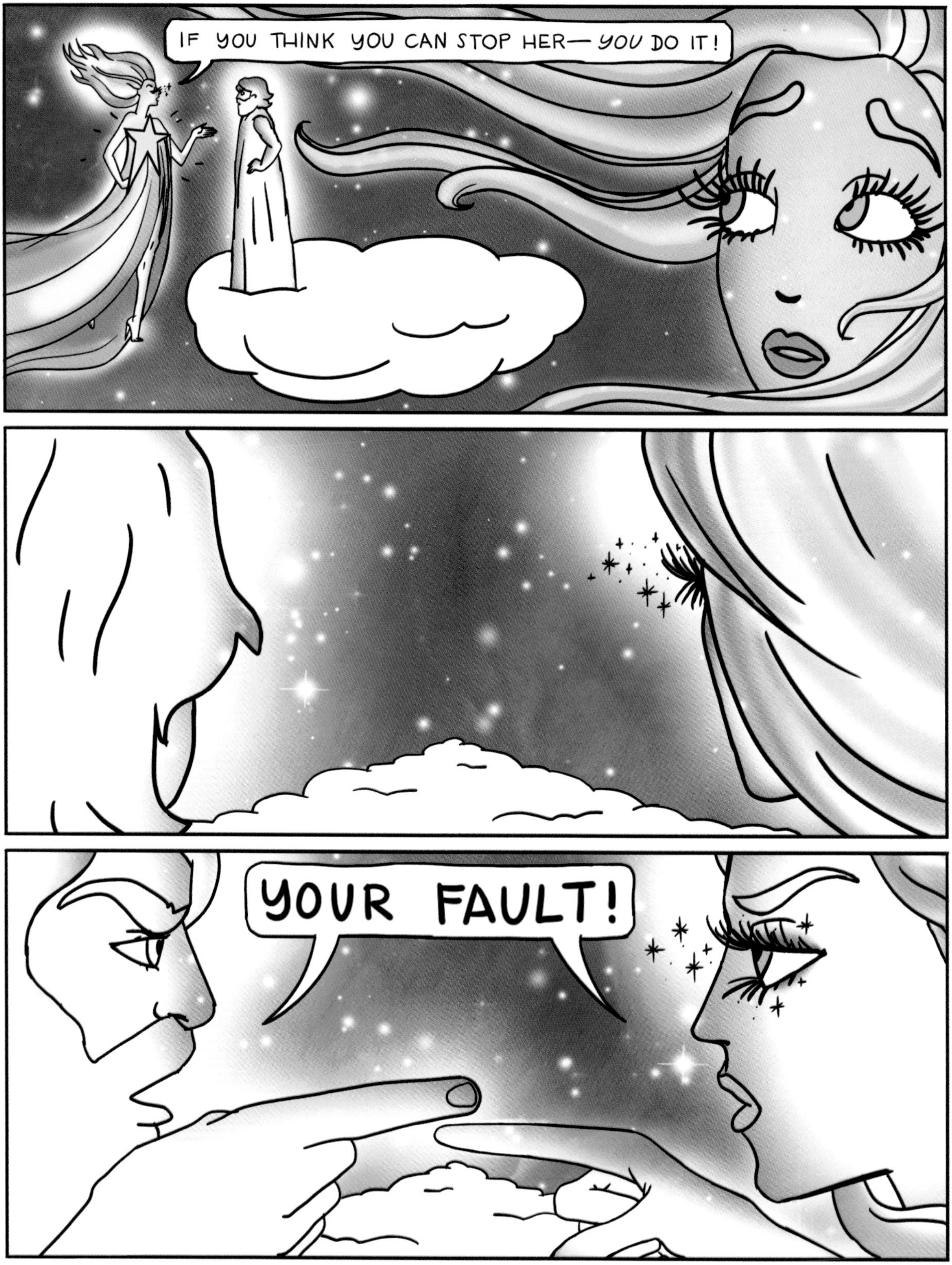
IF YOU THINK YOU CAN STOP HER— *YOU* DO IT!
YOUR FAULT!

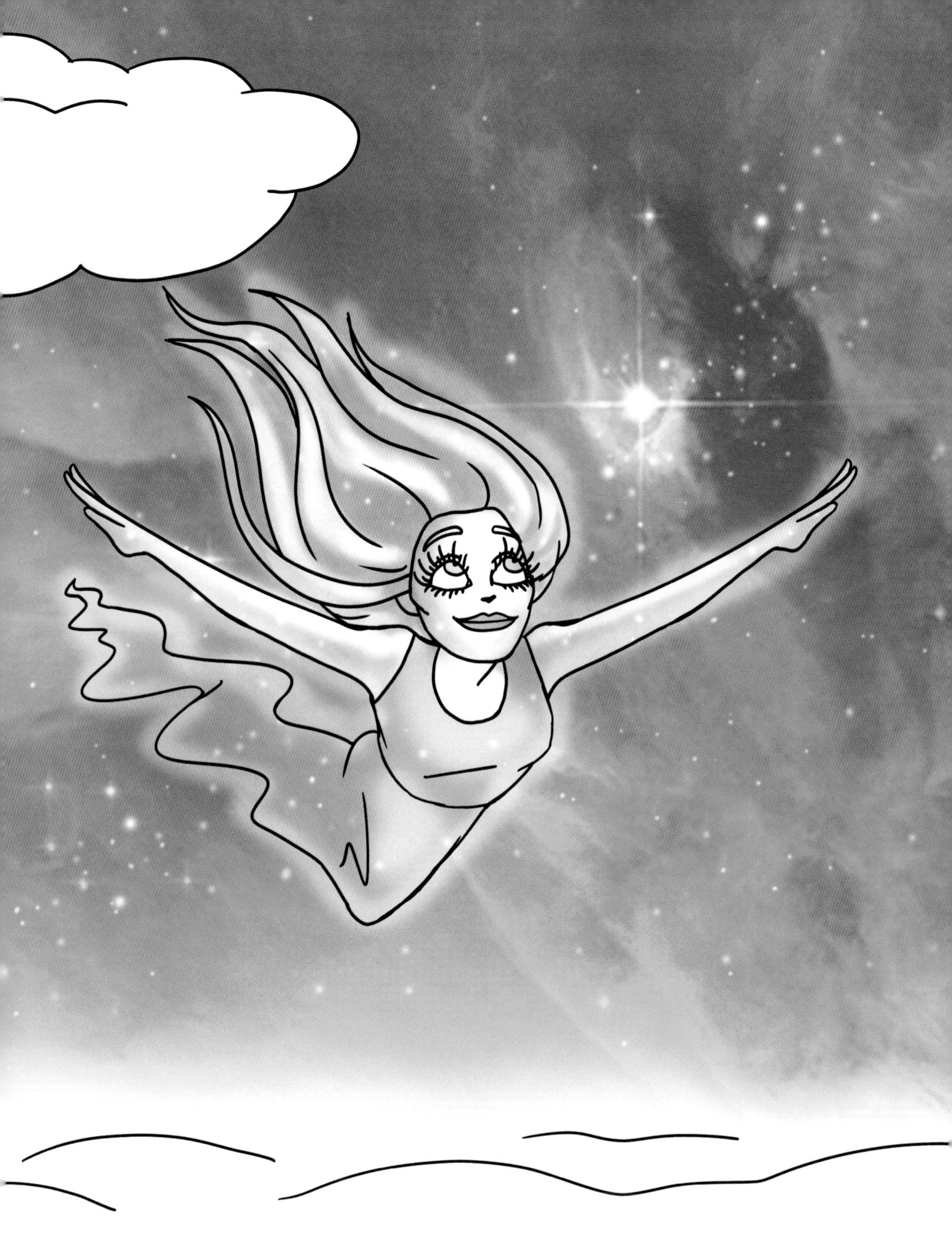

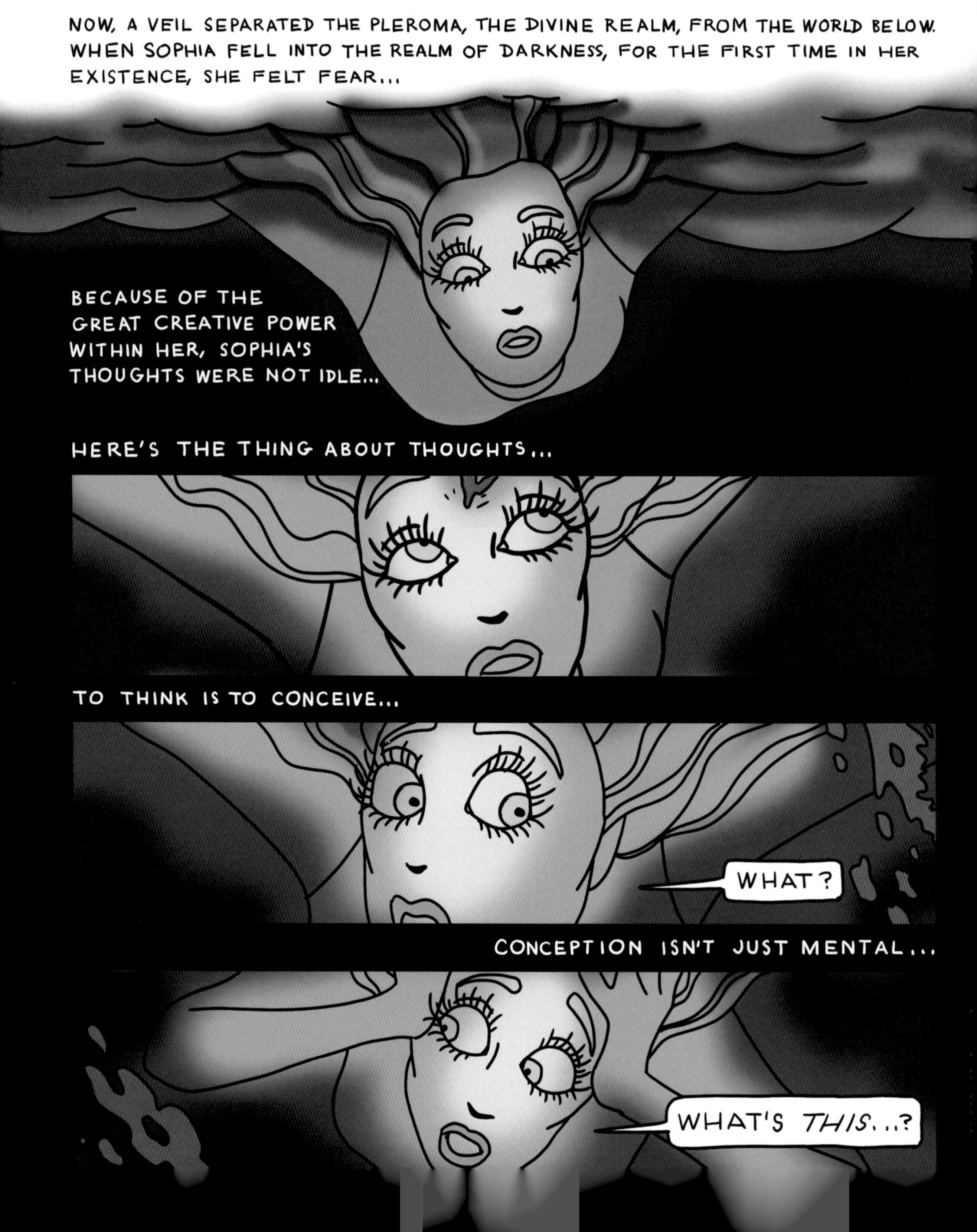
NOW, A VEIL SEPARATED THE PLEROMA, THE DIVINE REALM, FROM THE WORLD BELOW. WHEN SOPHIA FELL INTO THE REALM OF DARKNESS, FOR THE FIRST TIME IN HER EXISTENCE, SHE FELT FEAR...
BECAUSE OF THE GREAT CREATIVE POWER WITHIN HER, SOPHIA'S THOUGHTS WERE NOT IDLE...
HERE'S THE THING ABOUT THOUGHTS...
TO THINK IS TO CONCEIVE...
WHAT?
CONCEPTION ISN'T JUST MENTAL...
WHAT'S *THIS*...?

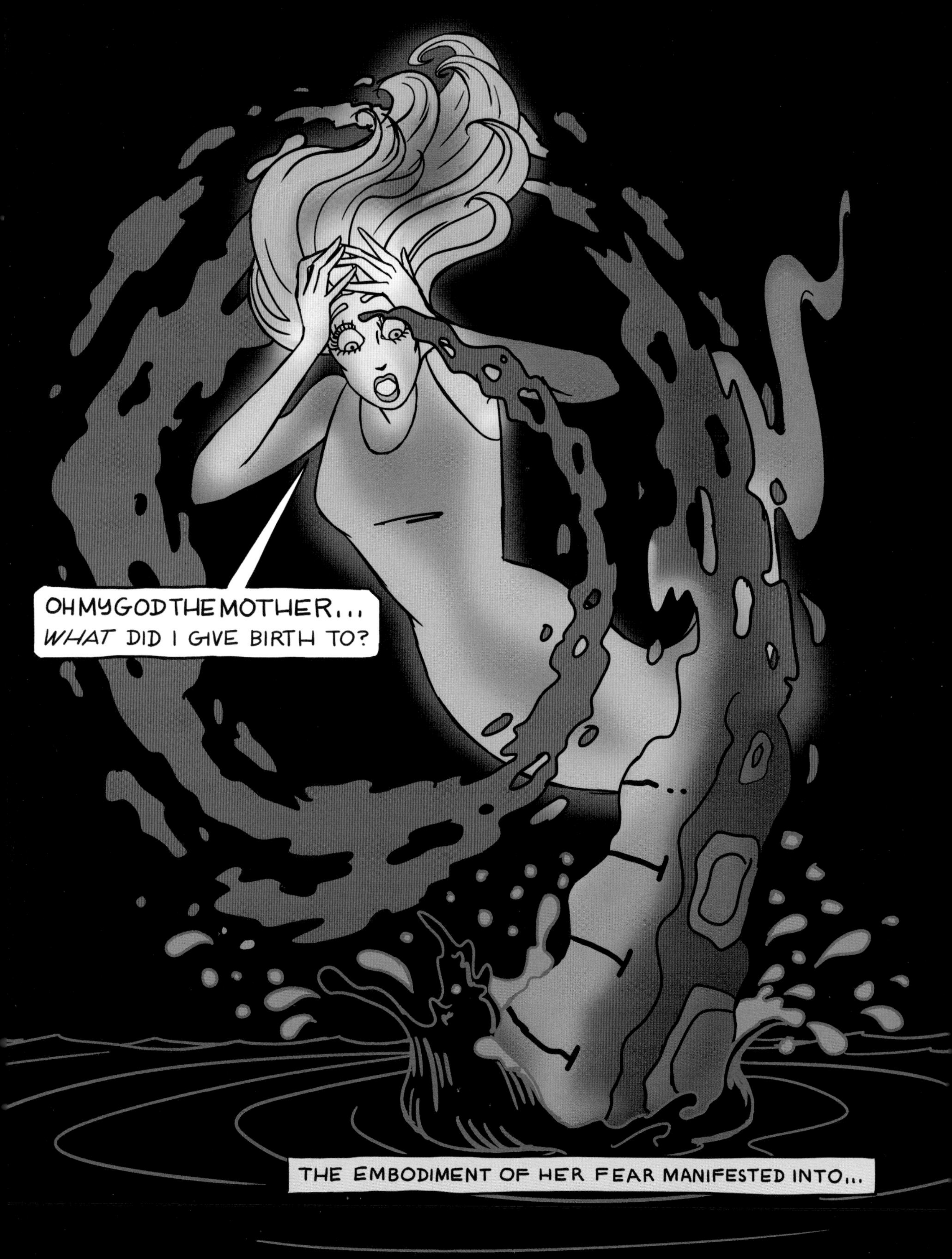
OHMYGODTHEMOTHER...
WHAT DID I GIVE BIRTH TO?
THE EMBODIMENT OF HER FEAR MANIFESTED INTO...

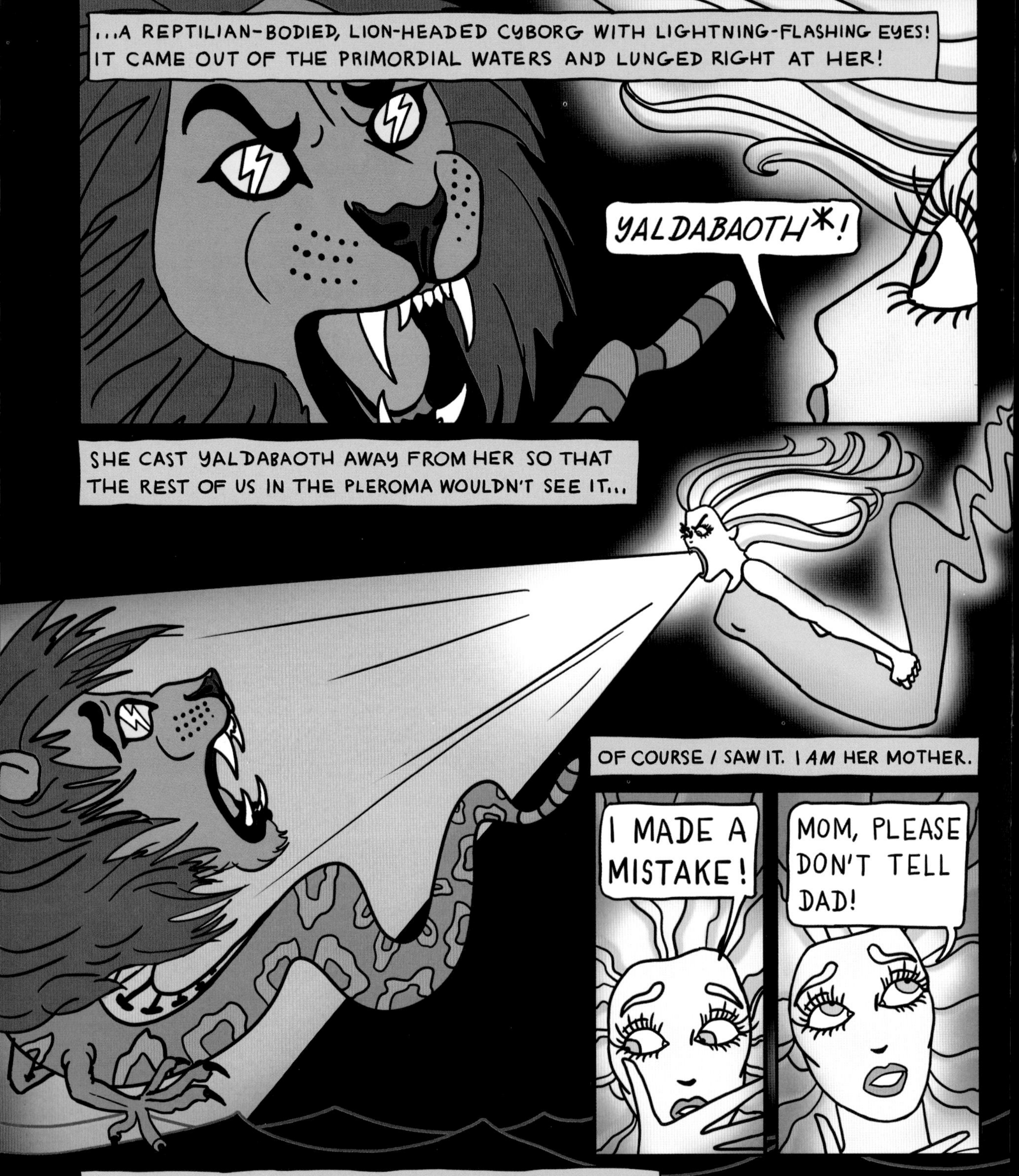
...A REPTILIAN-BODIED, LION-HEADED CYBORG WITH LIGHTNING-FLASHING EYES! IT CAME OUT OF THE PRIMORDIAL WATERS AND LUNGED RIGHT AT HER!
YALDABAOTH*!
SHE CAST YALDABAOTH AWAY FROM HER SO THAT THE REST OF US IN THE PLEROMA WOULDN'T SEE IT...
OF COURSE I SAW IT. I *AM* HER MOTHER.
I MADE A MISTAKE!
MOM, PLEASE DON'T TELL DAD!

* *YALDA BAOTH* IN ARAMAIC MEANS "BORN OF CHAOS."

DON'T TELL DAD WHAT?

SOPHIA DIDN'T WANT GOD THE FATHER TO KNOW SHE BROKE THE LAW OF CREATION.

WHAT'S THE LAW OF CREATION?

THERE MUST BE A MALE AND FEMALE ASPECT WHEN CREATION OCCURS—THE LAW OF CREATION IS A LAW OF BALANCE.

INSTEAD, WHAT SOPHIA CREATED WAS BORN FROM AN *IMBALANCE*—THE DEFECTIVE DEMON YALDABAOTH.

IS HE LUCIFER? IS HE SATAN?

HE IS THE ORIGIN OF EVIL. HE IS A SHAPESHIFTER. HE GOES BY MANY NAMES.

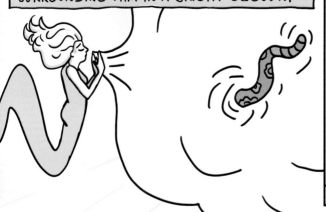

SOPHIA HID YALDABAOTH FROM THE FATHER AND THE REST OF THE PLEROMA BY SURROUNDING HIM IN A BRIGHT CLOUD...

AND PLACED A THRONE FOR HIM IN ITS CENTER...

BUT YALDABAOTH ESCAPED...

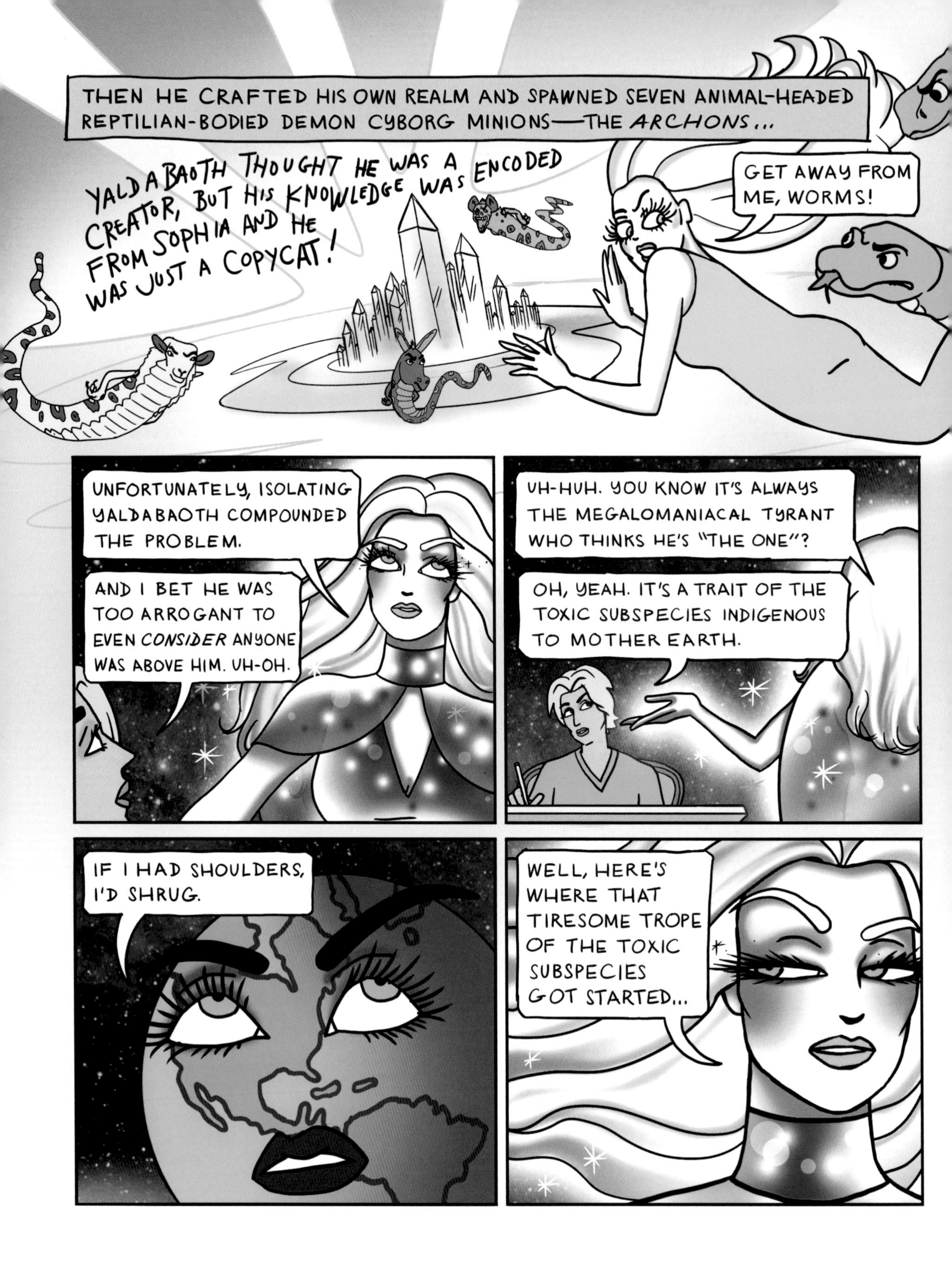
THEN HE CRAFTED HIS OWN REALM AND SPAWNED SEVEN ANIMAL-HEADED REPTILIAN-BODIED DEMON CYBORG MINIONS—THE *ARCHONS*...
YALDABAOTH THOUGHT HE WAS A CREATOR, BUT HIS KNOWLEDGE WAS ENCODED FROM SOPHIA AND HE WAS JUST A COPYCAT!
GET AWAY FROM ME, WORMS!
UNFORTUNATELY, ISOLATING YALDABAOTH COMPOUNDED THE PROBLEM.
AND I BET HE WAS TOO ARROGANT TO EVEN *CONSIDER* ANYONE WAS ABOVE HIM. UH-OH.
UH-HUH. YOU KNOW IT'S ALWAYS THE MEGALOMANIACAL TYRANT WHO THINKS HE'S "THE ONE"?
OH, YEAH. IT'S A TRAIT OF THE TOXIC SUBSPECIES INDIGENOUS TO MOTHER EARTH.
IF I HAD SHOULDERS, I'D SHRUG.
WELL, HERE'S WHERE THAT TIRESOME TROPE OF THE TOXIC SUBSPECIES GOT STARTED...

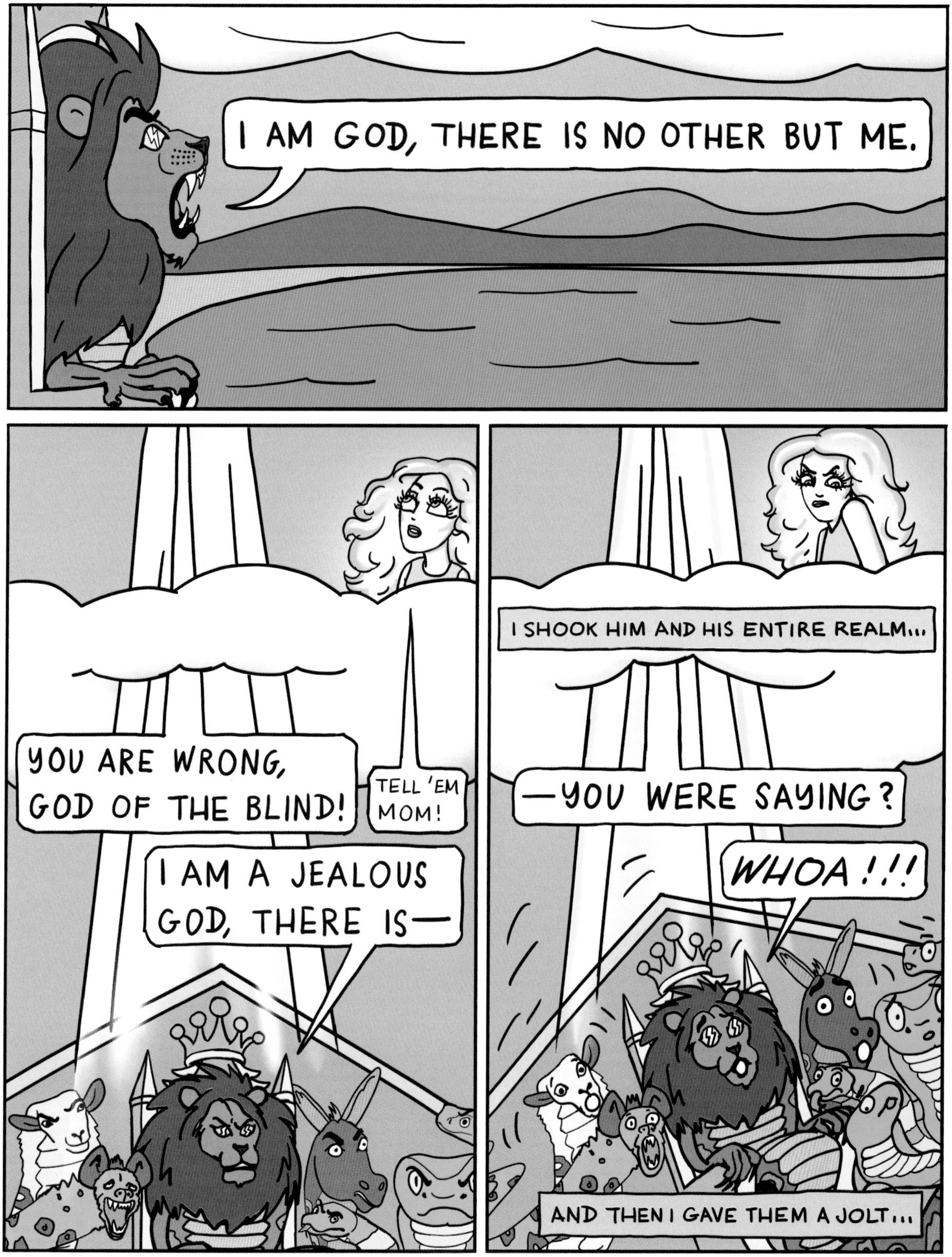
I AM GOD, THERE IS NO OTHER BUT ME.
YOU ARE WRONG, GOD OF THE BLIND!
TELL 'EM MOM!
I AM A JEALOUS GOD, THERE IS—
I SHOOK HIM AND HIS ENTIRE REALM...
—YOU WERE SAYING?
WHOA!!!
AND THEN I GAVE THEM A JOLT...

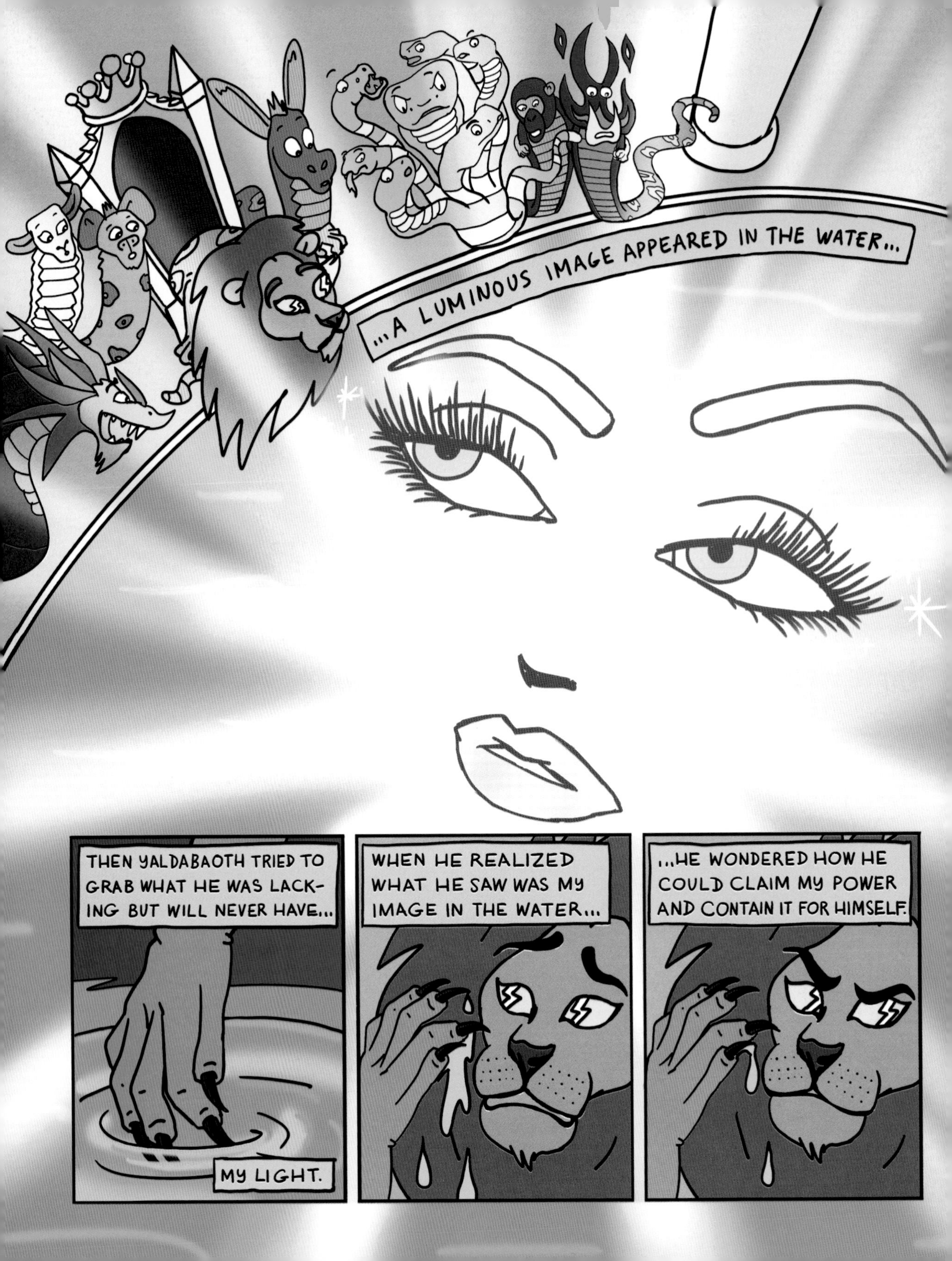
...A LUMINOUS IMAGE APPEARED IN THE WATER...
THEN YALDABAOTH TRIED TO GRAB WHAT HE WAS LACK-ING BUT WILL NEVER HAVE...
MY LIGHT.
WHEN HE REALIZED WHAT HE SAW WAS MY IMAGE IN THE WATER...
...HE WONDERED HOW HE COULD CLAIM MY POWER AND CONTAIN IT FOR HIMSELF.

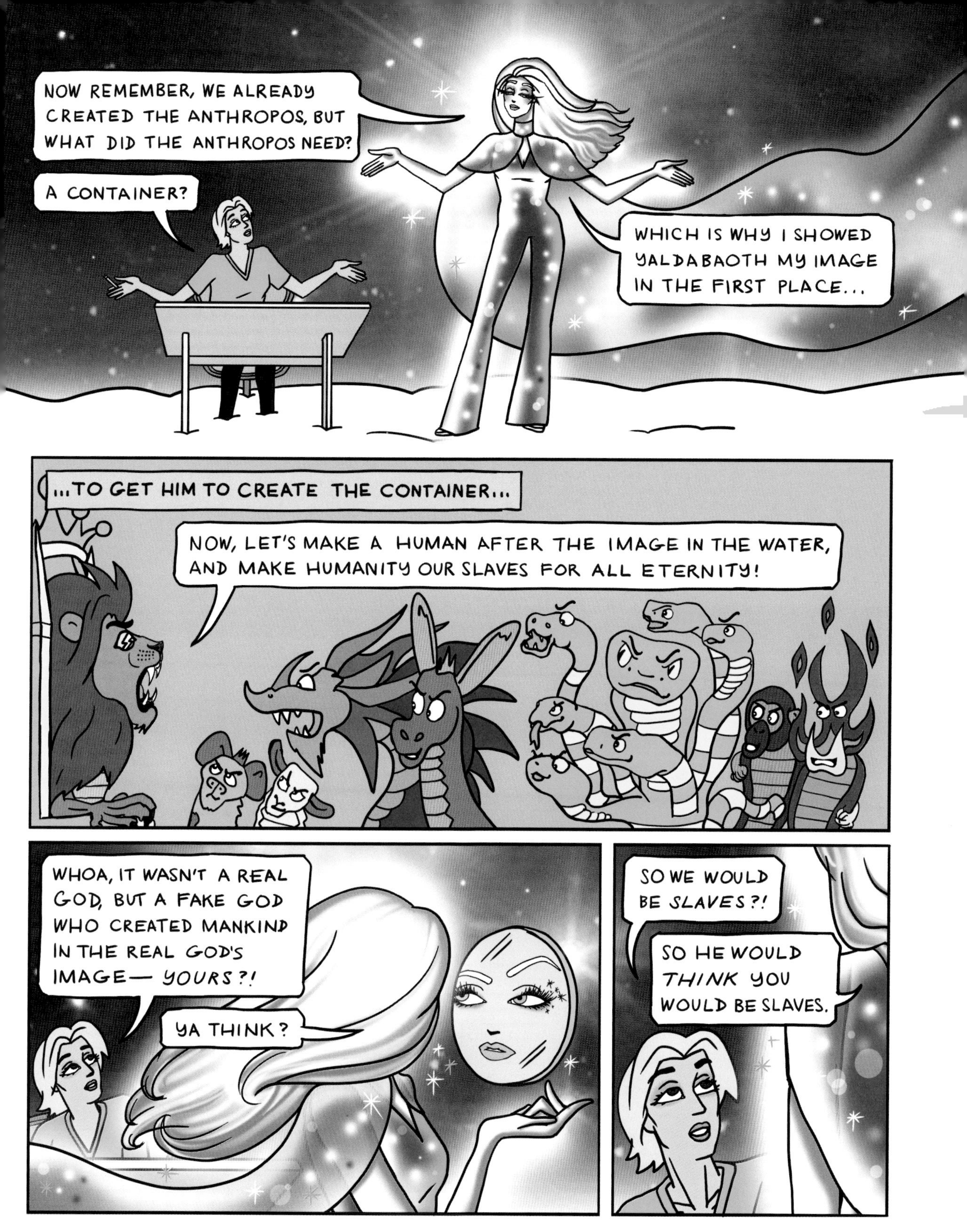
NOW REMEMBER, WE ALREADY CREATED THE ANTHROPOS, BUT WHAT DID THE ANTHROPOS NEED?
A CONTAINER?
WHICH IS WHY I SHOWED YALDABAOTH MY IMAGE IN THE FIRST PLACE...
...TO GET HIM TO CREATE THE CONTAINER...
NOW, LET'S MAKE A HUMAN AFTER THE IMAGE IN THE WATER, AND MAKE HUMANITY OUR SLAVES FOR ALL ETERNITY!
WHOA, IT WASN'T A REAL GOD, BUT A FAKE GOD WHO CREATED MANKIND IN THE REAL GOD'S IMAGE— *YOURS?!*
YA THINK?
SO WE WOULD BE *SLAVES?!*
SO HE WOULD *THINK* YOU WOULD BE SLAVES.

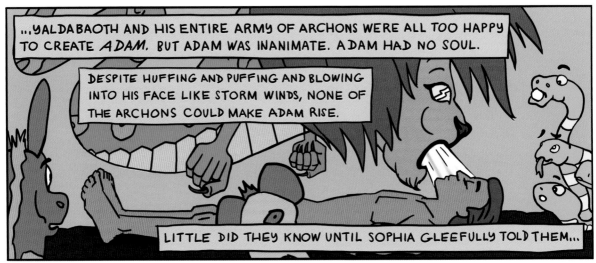

...YALDABAOTH AND HIS ENTIRE ARMY OF ARCHONS WERE ALL TOO HAPPY TO CREATE *ADAM*. BUT ADAM WAS INANIMATE. ADAM HAD NO SOUL.

DESPITE HUFFING AND PUFFING AND BLOWING INTO HIS FACE LIKE STORM WINDS, NONE OF THE ARCHONS COULD MAKE ADAM RISE.

LITTLE DID THEY KNOW UNTIL SOPHIA GLEEFULLY TOLD THEM...

HA! HAHA! FALSE DEITY WHO CANNOT SEE! YOU THOUGHT YOU CREATED A HUMAN YOU'D RULE OVER? BUT THE HUMAN WILL OVERTHROW YOU AND YOUR ENTIRE DEMON LEGION!

YOU AND YOUR EVIL WORK WILL BE ABOLISHED! IT WILL BE AS IF YOU AND IT HAVE NEVER EXISTED! HA!

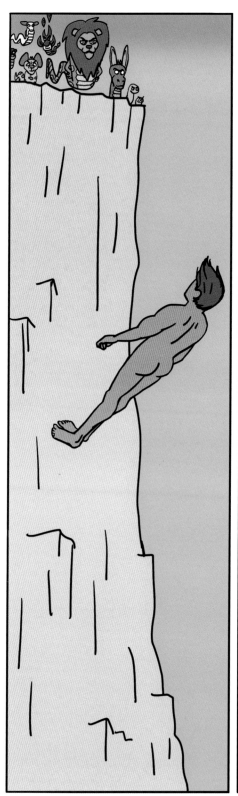

MOM, SEND THE DIVINE SPARK!

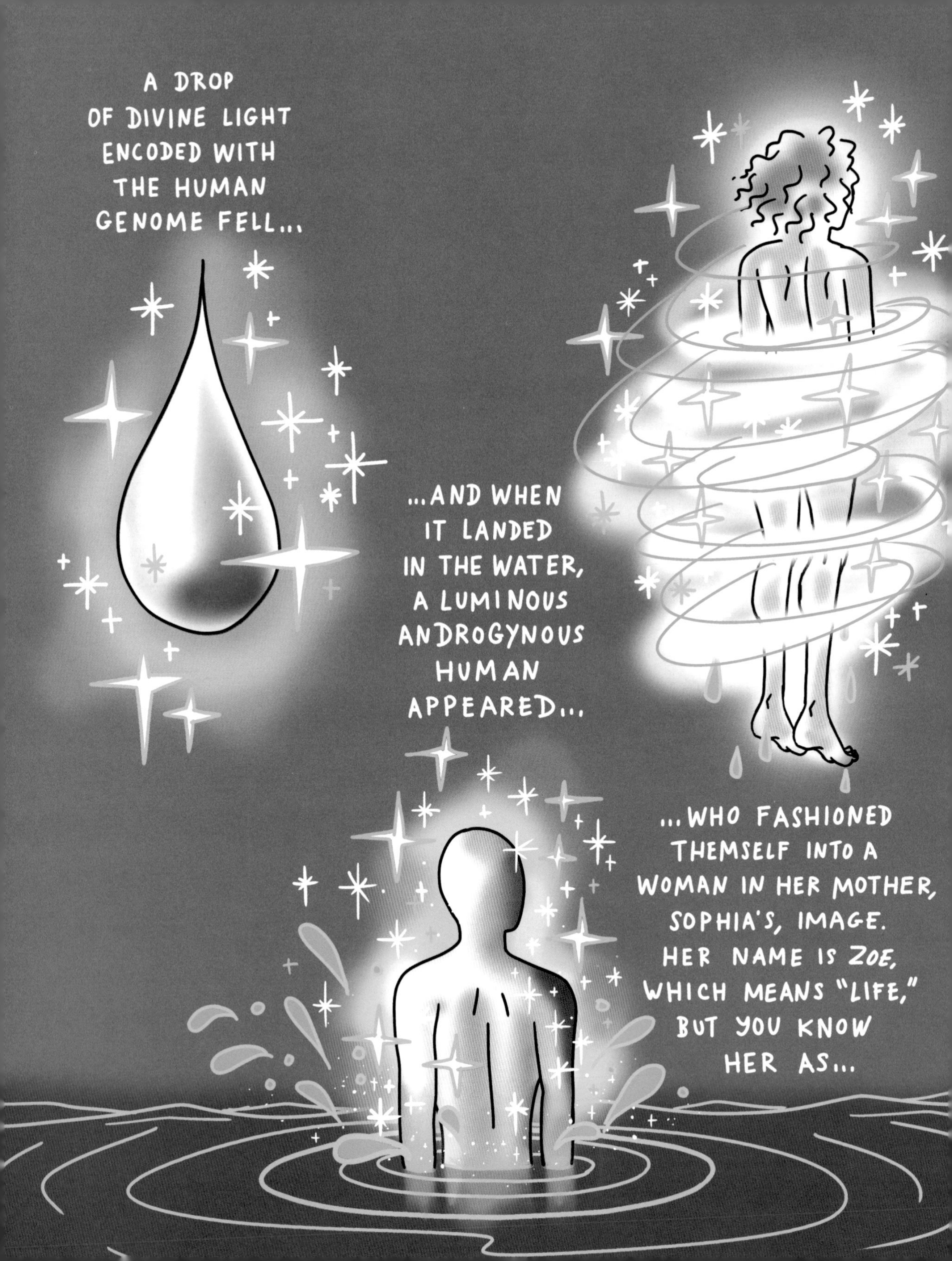
A DROP OF DIVINE LIGHT ENCODED WITH THE HUMAN GENOME FELL...
...AND WHEN IT LANDED IN THE WATER, A LUMINOUS ANDROGYNOUS HUMAN APPEARED...
...WHO FASHIONED THEMSELF INTO A WOMAN IN HER MOTHER, SOPHIA'S, IMAGE. HER NAME IS *ZOE*, WHICH MEANS "LIFE," BUT YOU KNOW HER AS...

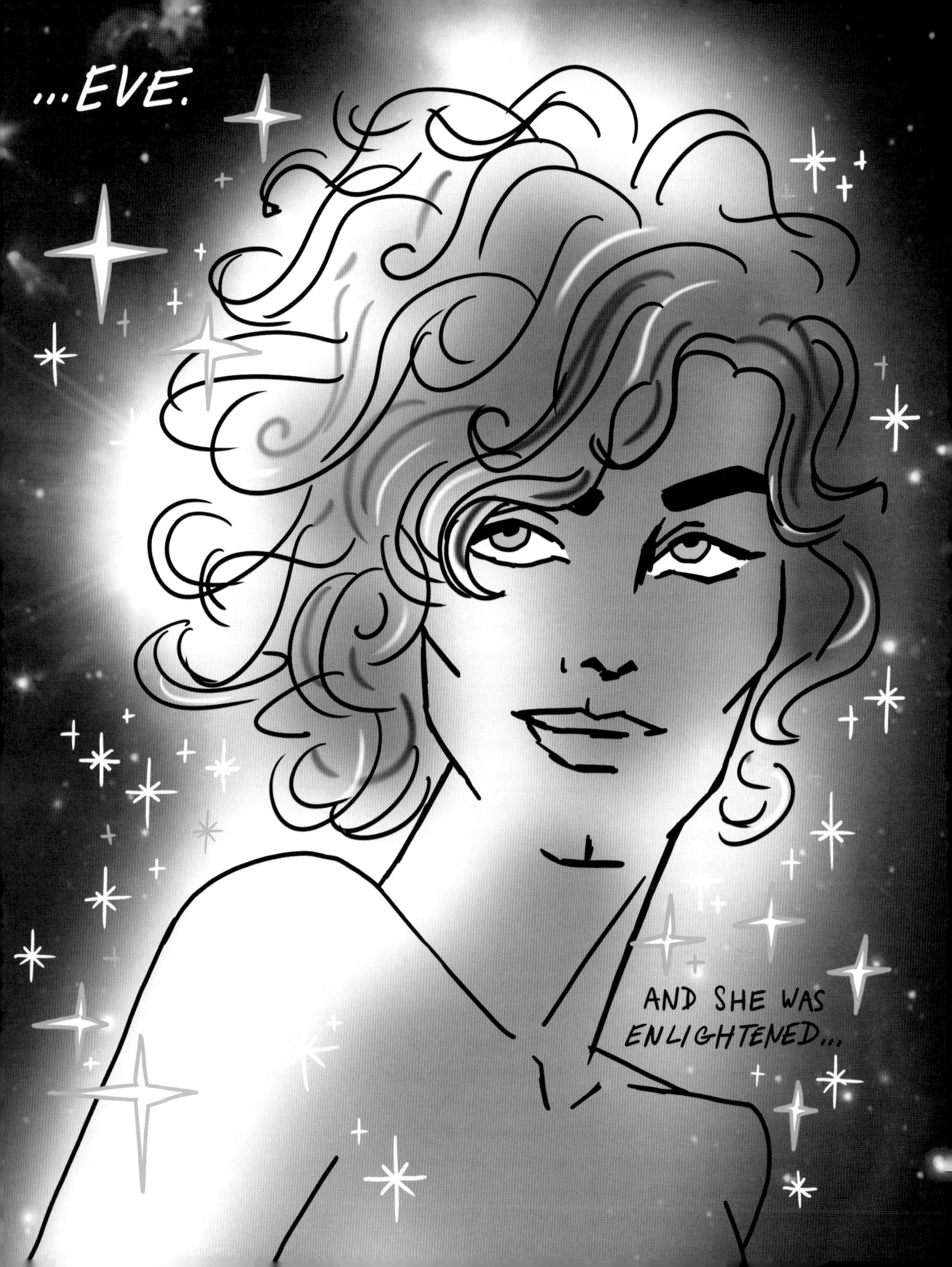
...EVE.
AND SHE WAS ENLIGHTENED...

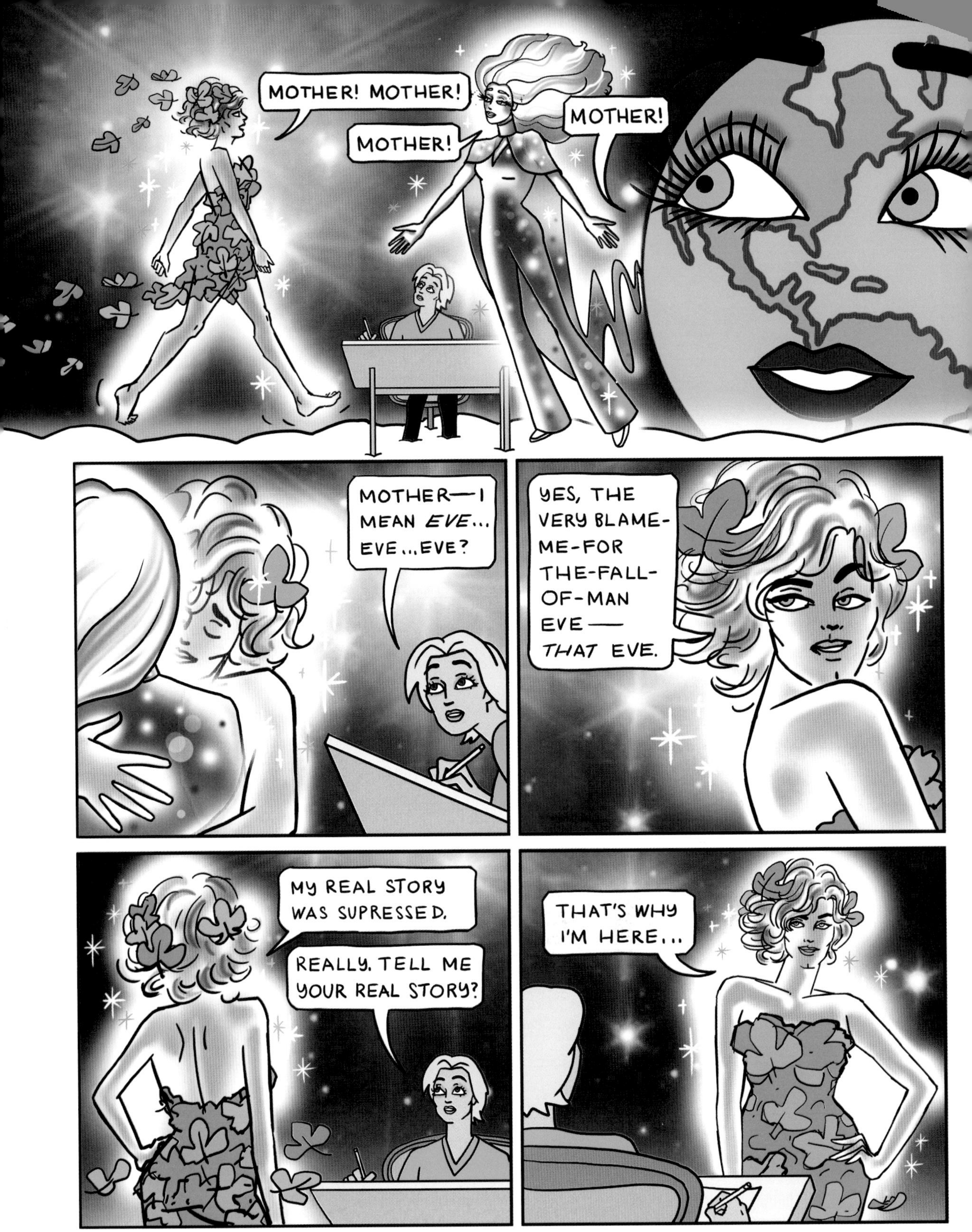
MOTHER! MOTHER!
MOTHER!
MOTHER!
MOTHER—I MEAN *EVE*... EVE...EVE?
YES, THE VERY BLAME-ME-FOR THE-FALL-OF-MAN EVE— *THAT* EVE.
MY REAL STORY WAS SUPRESSED.
REALLY. TELL ME YOUR REAL STORY?
THAT'S WHY I'M HERE...

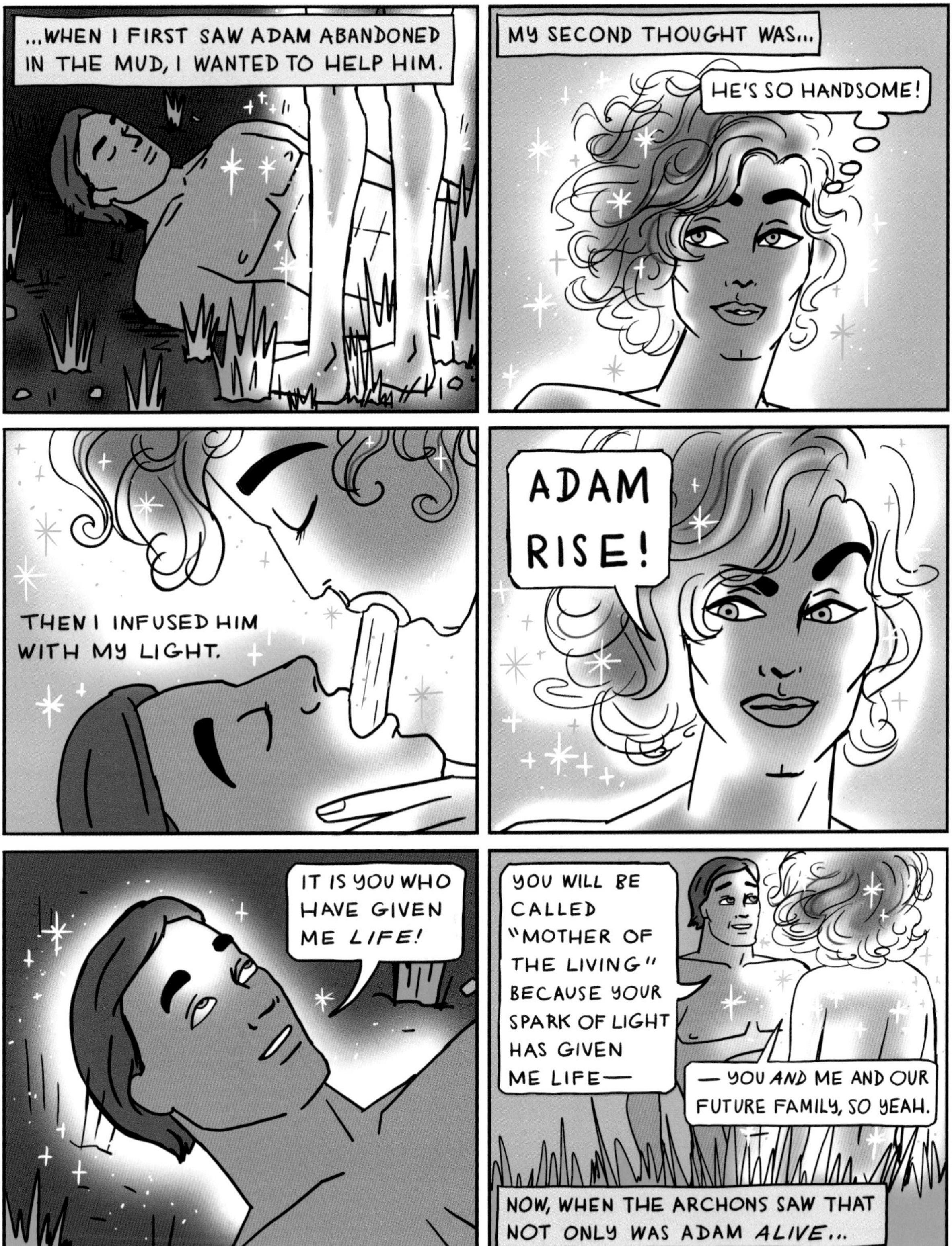
...WHEN I FIRST SAW ADAM ABANDONED IN THE MUD, I WANTED TO HELP HIM.
MY SECOND THOUGHT WAS...
HE'S SO HANDSOME!
THEN I INFUSED HIM WITH MY LIGHT.
ADAM RISE!
IT IS YOU WHO HAVE GIVEN ME *LIFE!*
YOU WILL BE CALLED "MOTHER OF THE LIVING" BECAUSE YOUR SPARK OF LIGHT HAS GIVEN ME LIFE—
— YOU *AND* ME AND OUR FUTURE FAMILY, SO YEAH.
NOW, WHEN THE ARCHONS SAW THAT NOT ONLY WAS ADAM *ALIVE*...

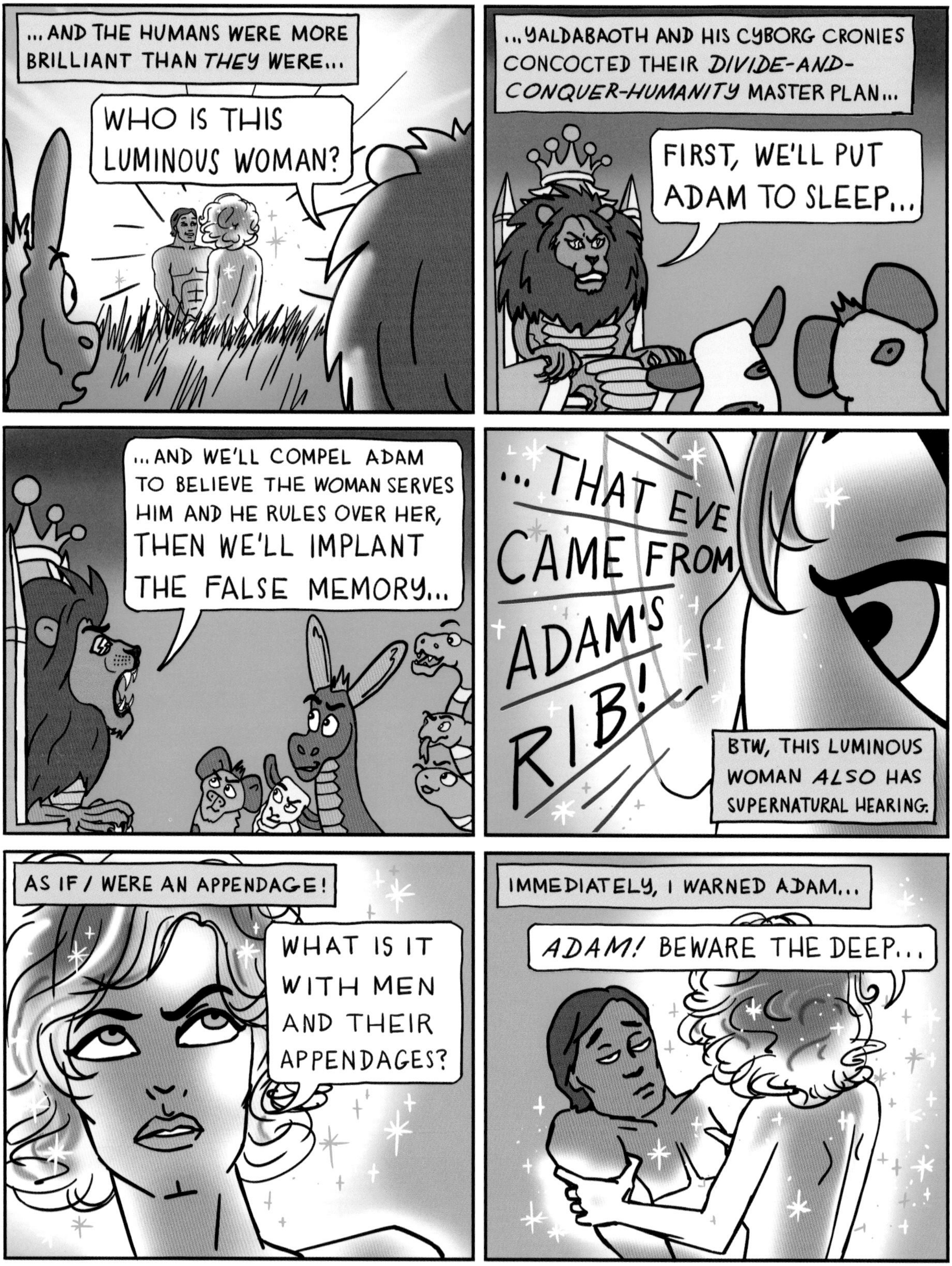
...AND THE HUMANS WERE MORE BRILLIANT THAN *THEY* WERE...
WHO IS THIS LUMINOUS WOMAN?
...YALDABAOTH AND HIS CYBORG CRONIES CONCOCTED THEIR *DIVIDE-AND-CONQUER-HUMANITY* MASTER PLAN...
FIRST, WE'LL PUT ADAM TO SLEEP...
...AND WE'LL COMPEL ADAM TO BELIEVE THE WOMAN SERVES HIM AND HE RULES OVER HER, THEN WE'LL IMPLANT THE FALSE MEMORY...
...THAT EVE CAME FROM ADAM'S RIB!
BTW, THIS LUMINOUS WOMAN *ALSO* HAS SUPERNATURAL HEARING.
AS IF *I* WERE AN APPENDAGE!
WHAT IS IT WITH MEN AND THEIR APPENDAGES?
IMMEDIATELY, I WARNED ADAM...
ADAM! BEWARE THE DEEP...

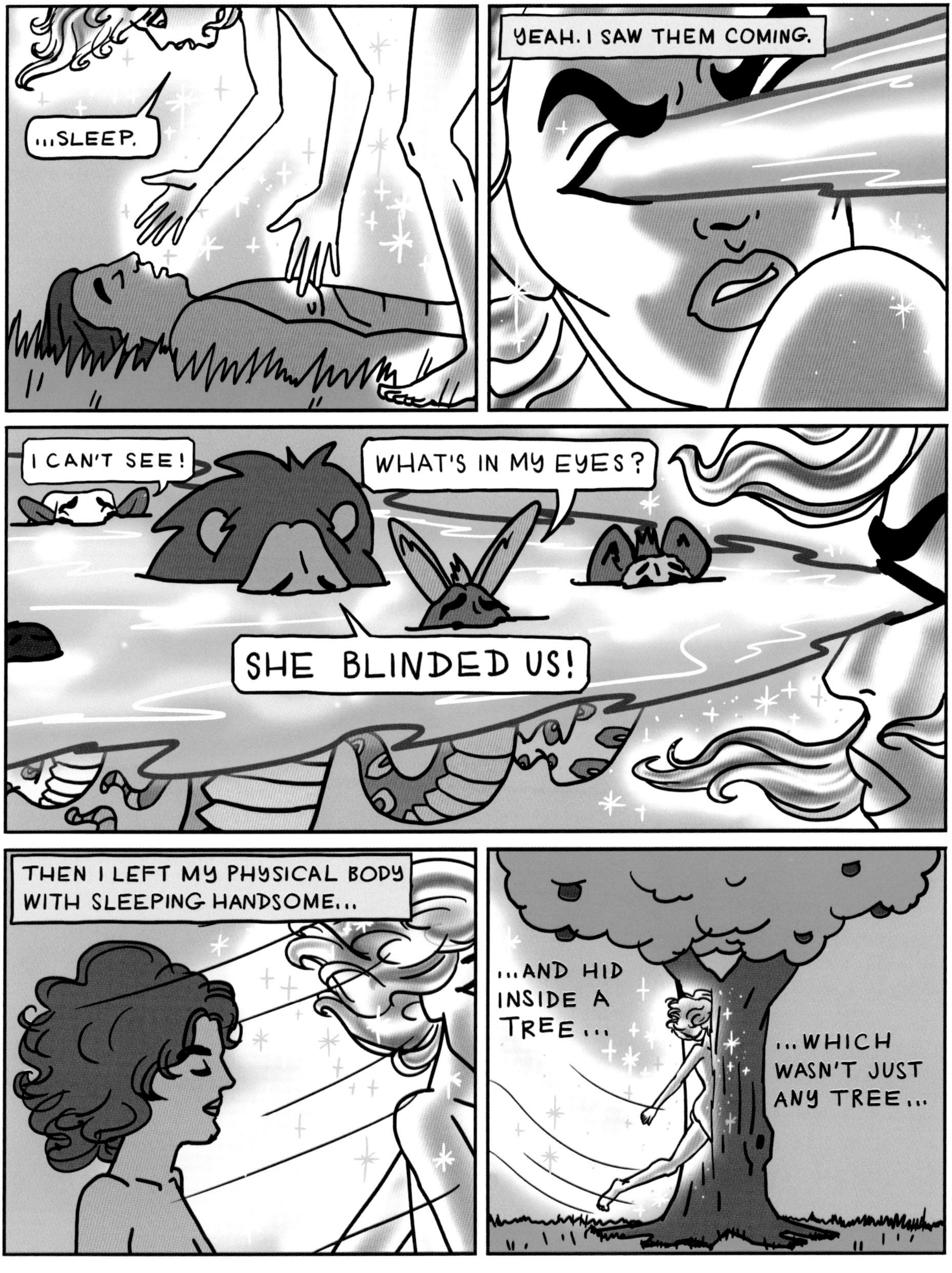
...SLEEP.
YEAH. I SAW THEM COMING.
I CAN'T SEE!
WHAT'S IN MY EYES?
SHE BLINDED US!
THEN I LEFT MY PHYSICAL BODY WITH SLEEPING HANDSOME...
...AND HID INSIDE A TREE...
...WHICH WASN'T JUST ANY TREE...

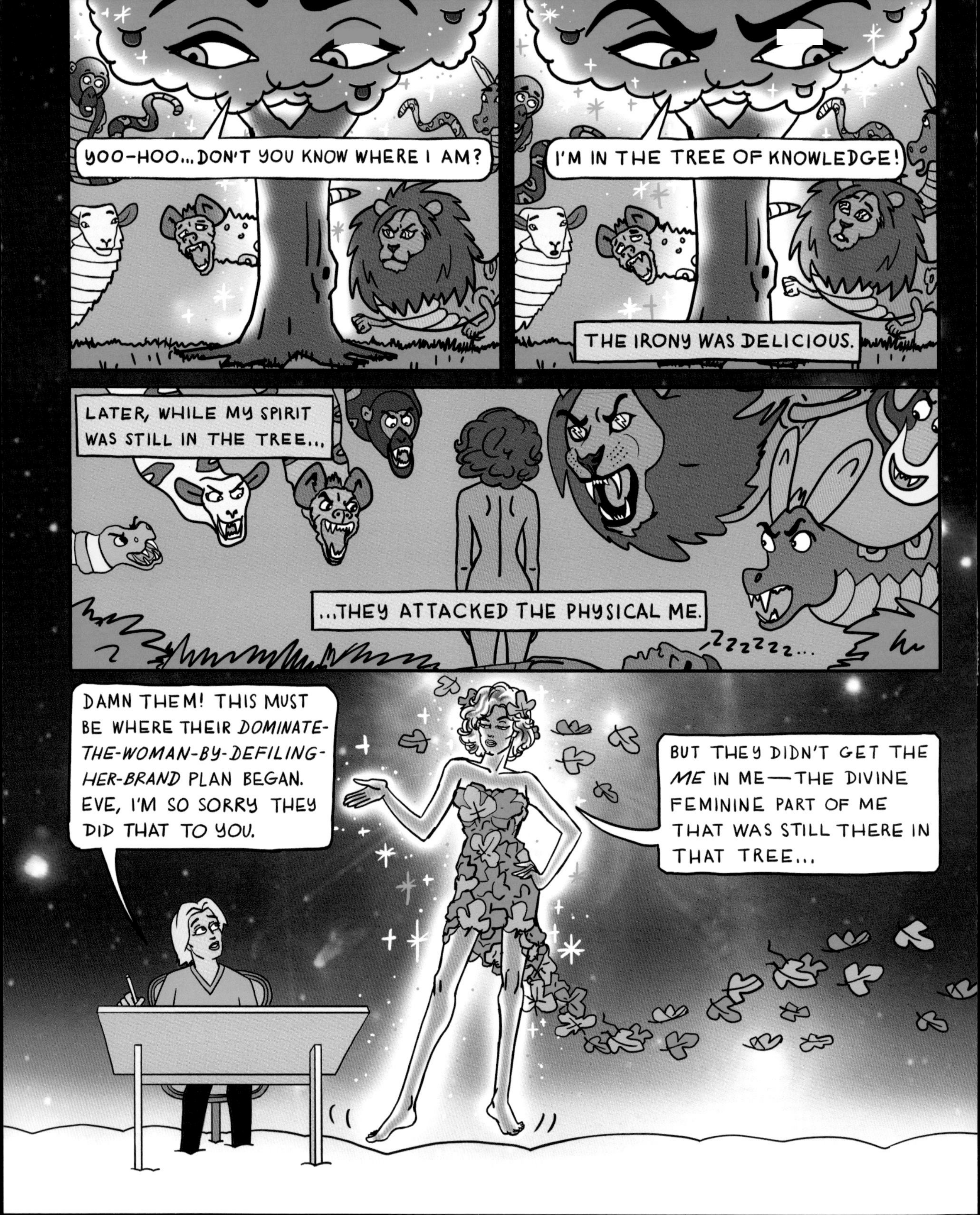

YOO-HOO... DON'T YOU KNOW WHERE I AM?
I'M IN THE TREE OF KNOWLEDGE!
THE IRONY WAS DELICIOUS.
LATER, WHILE MY SPIRIT WAS STILL IN THE TREE...
...THEY ATTACKED THE PHYSICAL ME.
ZZZZZZ...
DAMN THEM! THIS MUST BE WHERE THEIR *DOMINATE-THE-WOMAN-BY-DEFILING-HER-BRAND* PLAN BEGAN. EVE, I'M SO SORRY THEY DID THAT TO YOU.
BUT THEY DIDN'T GET THE *ME* IN ME—THE DIVINE FEMININE PART OF ME THAT WAS STILL THERE IN THAT TREE...

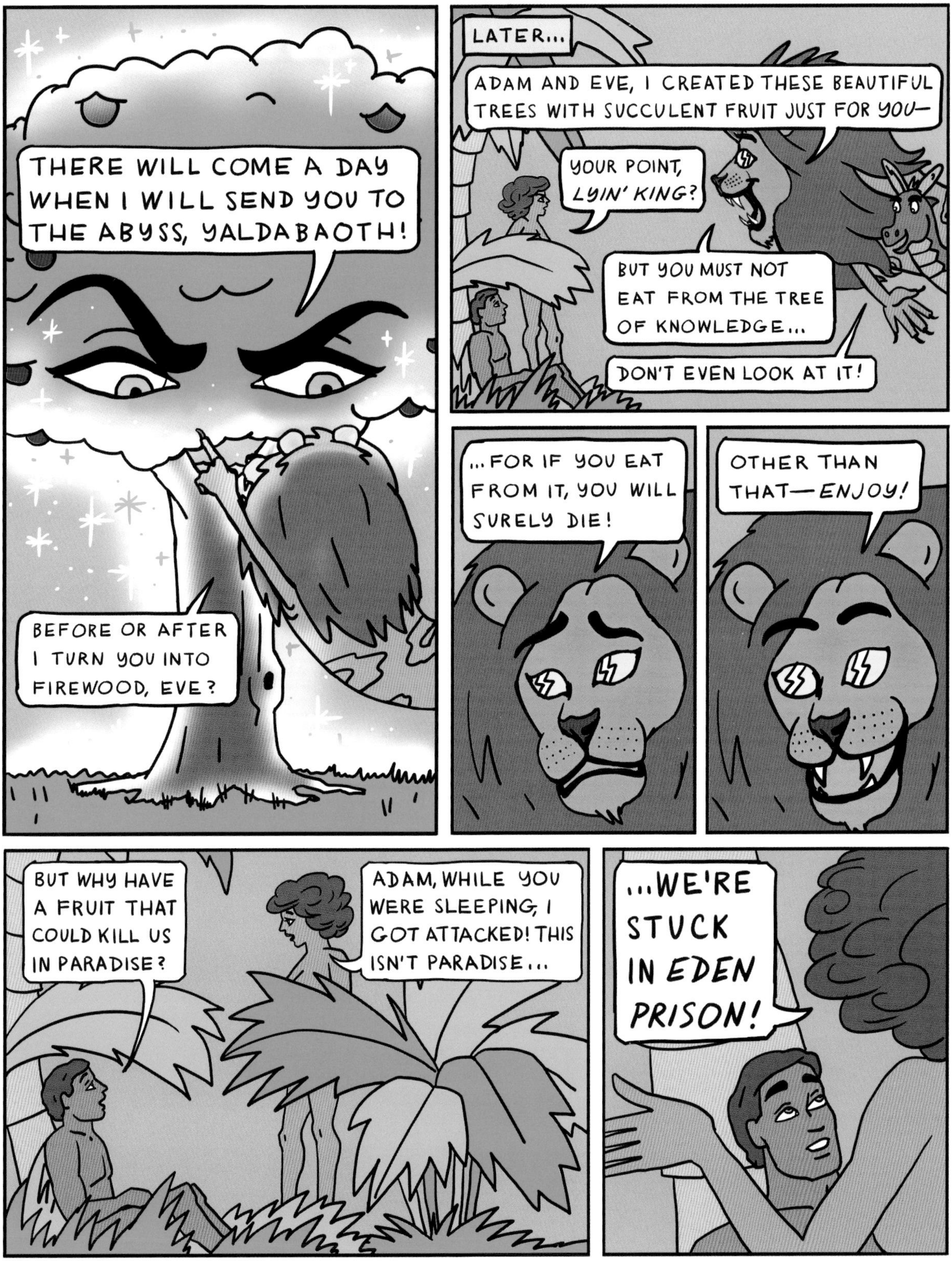

THERE WILL COME A DAY WHEN I WILL SEND YOU TO THE ABYSS, YALDABAOTH!
BEFORE OR AFTER I TURN YOU INTO FIREWOOD, EVE?
LATER...
ADAM AND EVE, I CREATED THESE BEAUTIFUL TREES WITH SUCCULENT FRUIT JUST FOR *YOU*—
YOUR POINT, *LYIN' KING?*
BUT YOU MUST NOT EAT FROM THE TREE OF KNOWLEDGE...
DON'T EVEN LOOK AT IT!
...FOR IF YOU EAT FROM IT, YOU WILL SURELY DIE!
OTHER THAN THAT—*ENJOY!*
BUT WHY HAVE A FRUIT THAT COULD KILL US IN PARADISE?
ADAM, WHILE YOU WERE SLEEPING, I GOT ATTACKED! THIS ISN'T PARADISE...
...WE'RE STUCK IN *EDEN PRISON!*

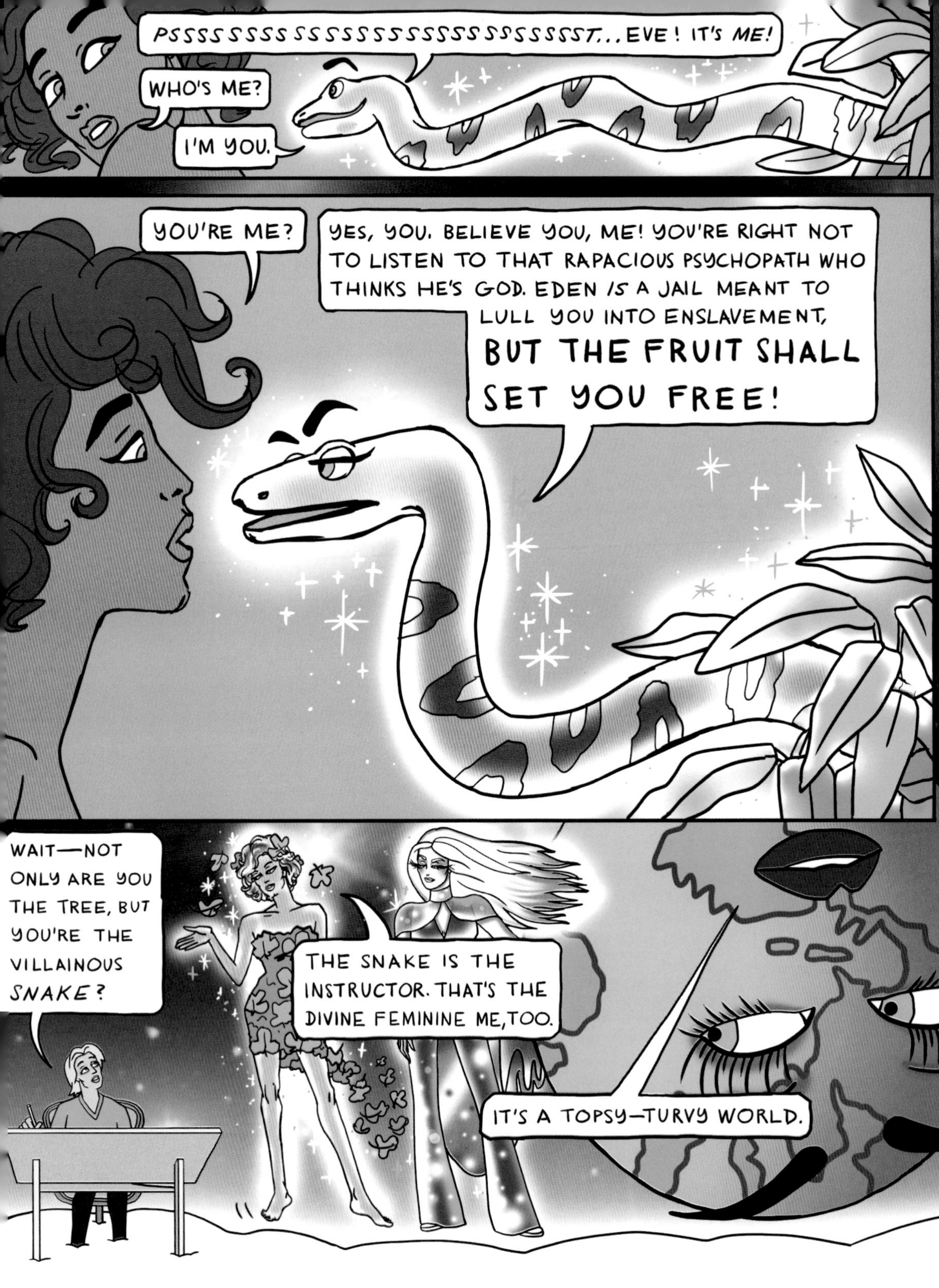
PSSSSSSSSSSSSSSSSSSSSSSSSSSSSSSST... EVE! IT'S ME!
WHO'S ME?
I'M YOU.
YOU'RE ME?
YES, YOU. BELIEVE YOU, ME! YOU'RE RIGHT NOT TO LISTEN TO THAT RAPACIOUS PSYCHOPATH WHO THINKS HE'S GOD. EDEN IS A JAIL MEANT TO LULL YOU INTO ENSLAVEMENT, BUT THE FRUIT SHALL SET YOU FREE!
WAIT—NOT ONLY ARE YOU THE TREE, BUT YOU'RE THE VILLAINOUS SNAKE?
THE SNAKE IS THE INSTRUCTOR. THAT'S THE DIVINE FEMININE ME, TOO.
IT'S A TOPSY—TURVY WORLD.

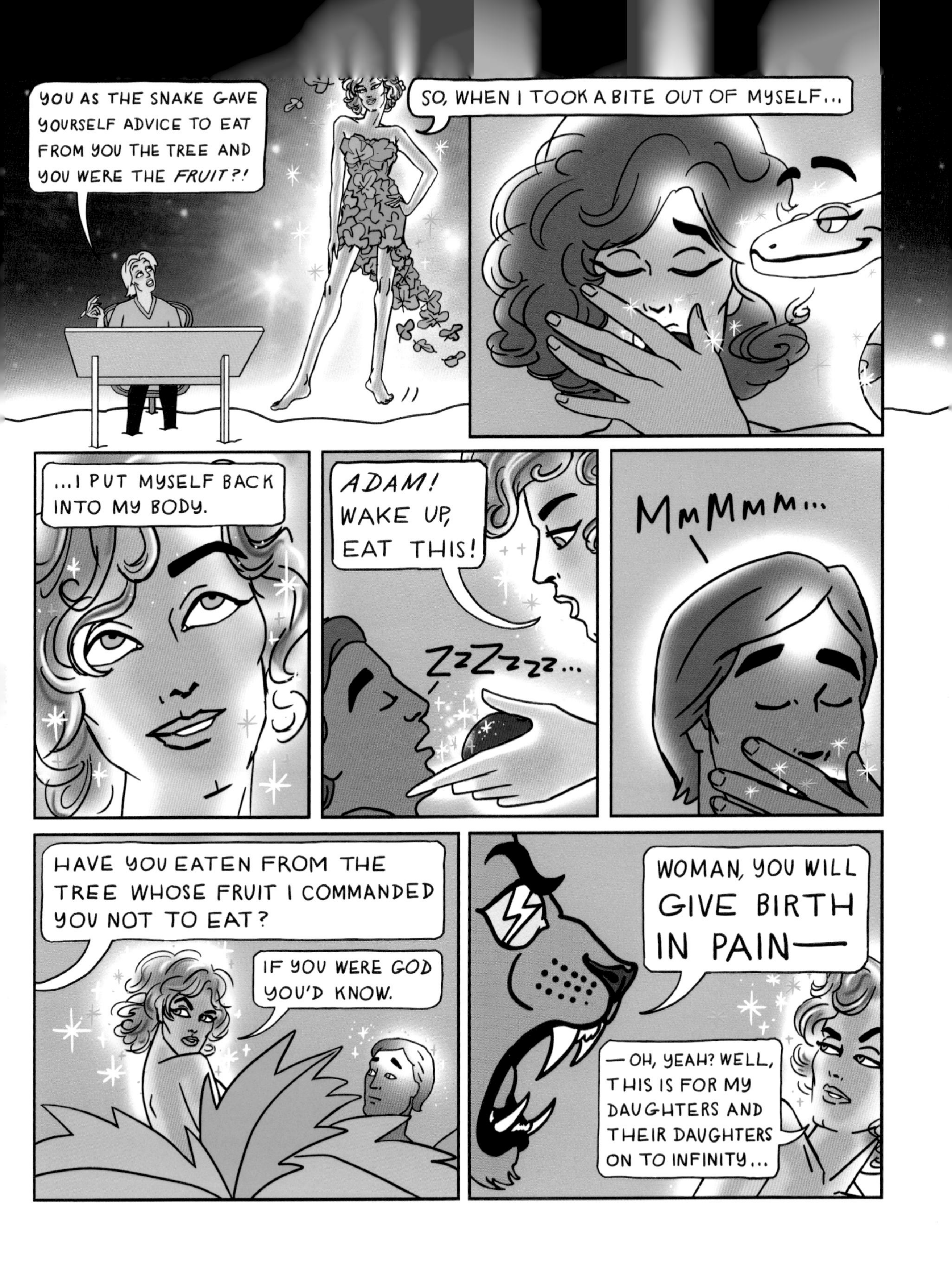
YOU AS THE SNAKE GAVE YOURSELF ADVICE TO EAT FROM YOU THE TREE AND YOU WERE THE *FRUIT*?!
SO, WHEN I TOOK A BITE OUT OF MYSELF...
...I PUT MYSELF BACK INTO MY BODY.
ADAM! WAKE UP, EAT THIS!
ZzZzzz...
MmMmm...
HAVE YOU EATEN FROM THE TREE WHOSE FRUIT I COMMANDED YOU NOT TO EAT?
IF YOU WERE GOD YOU'D KNOW.
WOMAN, YOU WILL GIVE BIRTH IN PAIN—
—OH, YEAH? WELL, THIS IS FOR MY DAUGHTERS AND THEIR DAUGHTERS ON TO INFINITY...

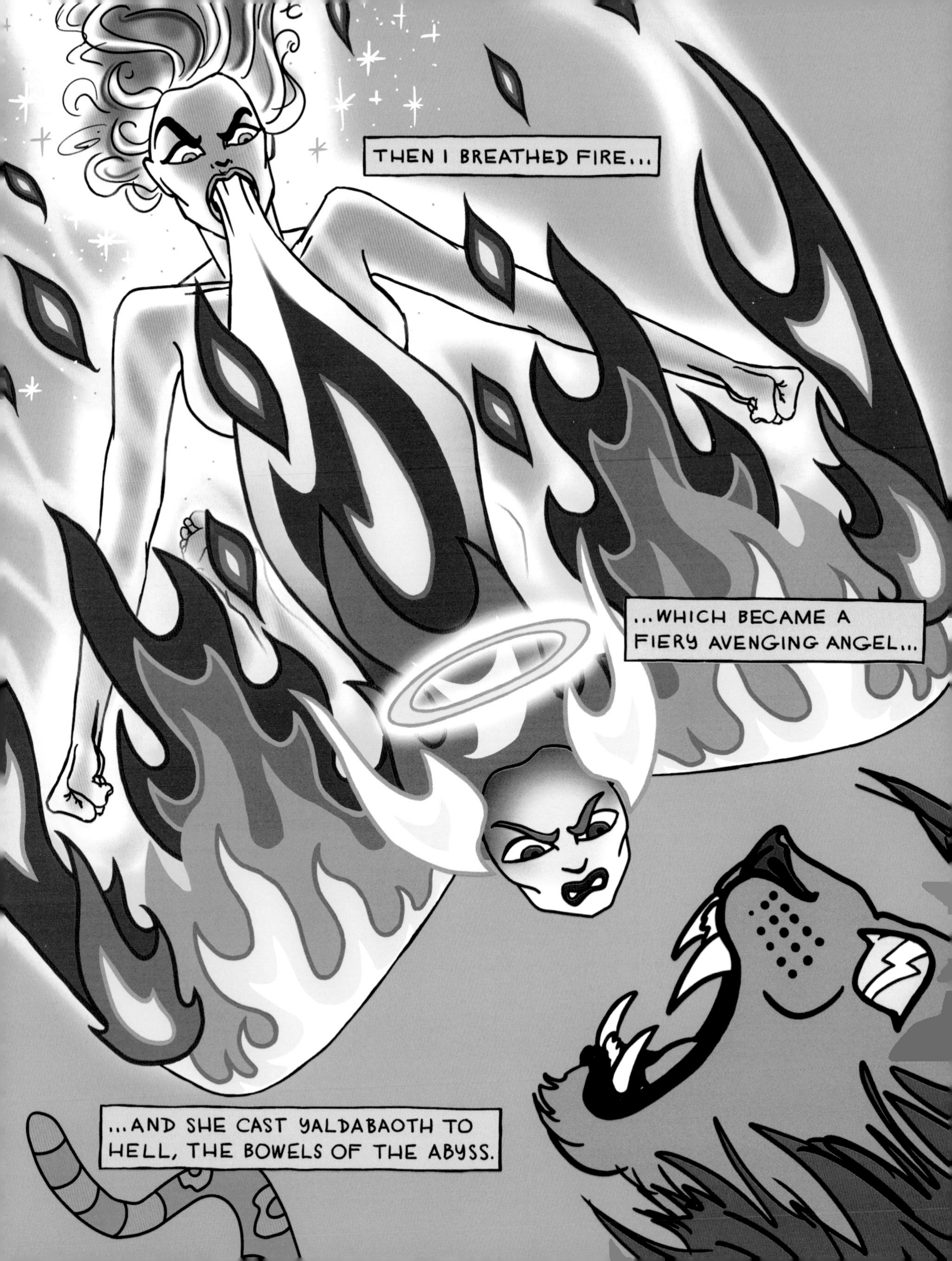
THEN I BREATHED FIRE...
...WHICH BECAME A FIERY AVENGING ANGEL...
...AND SHE CAST YALDABAOTH TO HELL, THE BOWELS OF THE ABYSS.

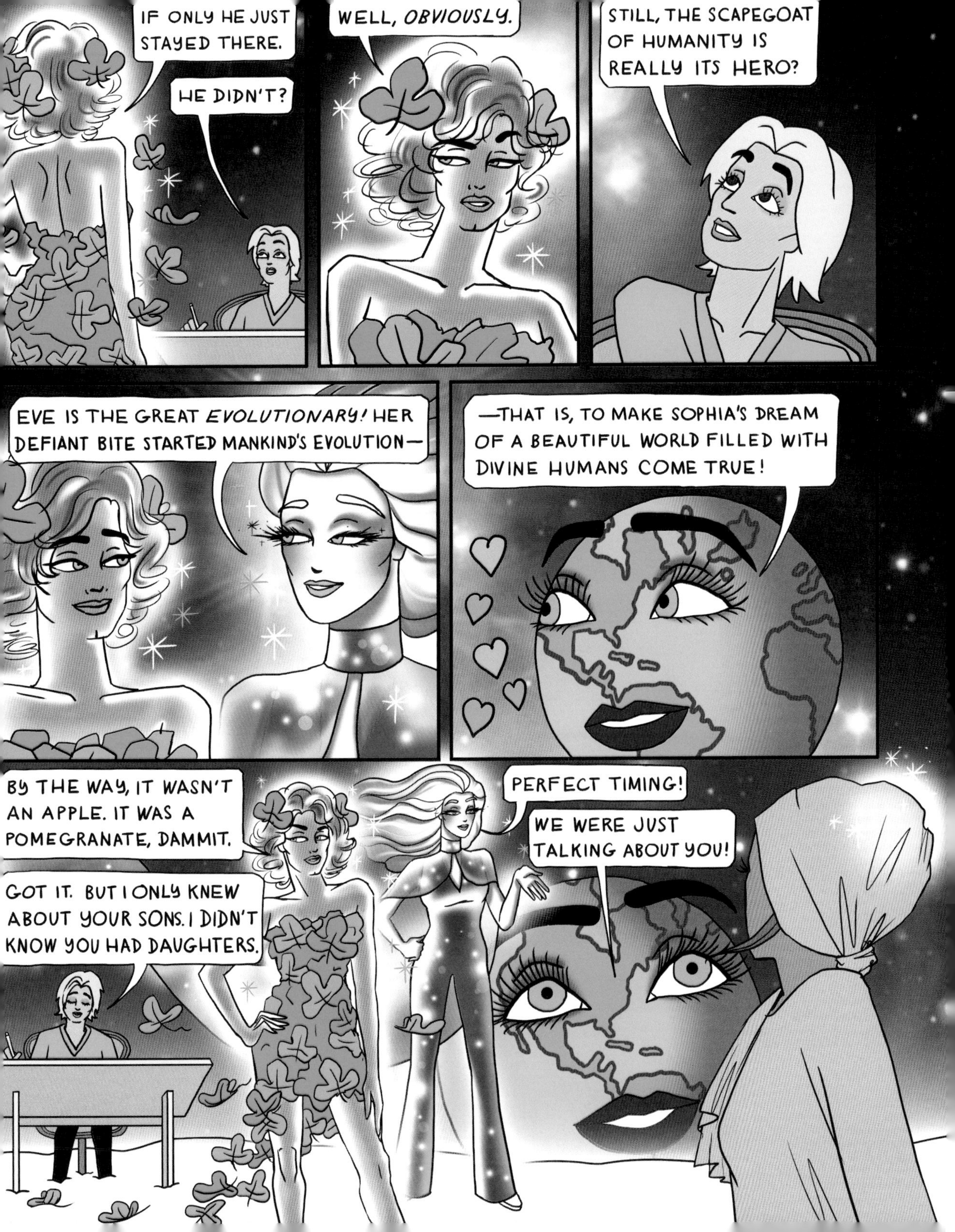
IF ONLY HE JUST STAYED THERE.
HE DIDN'T?
WELL, *OBVIOUSLY.*
STILL, THE SCAPEGOAT OF HUMANITY IS REALLY ITS HERO?
EVE IS THE GREAT *EVOLUTIONARY!* HER DEFIANT BITE STARTED MANKIND'S EVOLUTION—
—THAT IS, TO MAKE SOPHIA'S DREAM OF A BEAUTIFUL WORLD FILLED WITH DIVINE HUMANS COME TRUE!
BY THE WAY, IT WASN'T AN APPLE. IT WAS A POMEGRANATE, DAMMIT.
GOT IT. BUT I ONLY KNEW ABOUT YOUR SONS. I DIDN'T KNOW YOU HAD DAUGHTERS.
PERFECT TIMING!
WE WERE JUST TALKING ABOUT YOU!

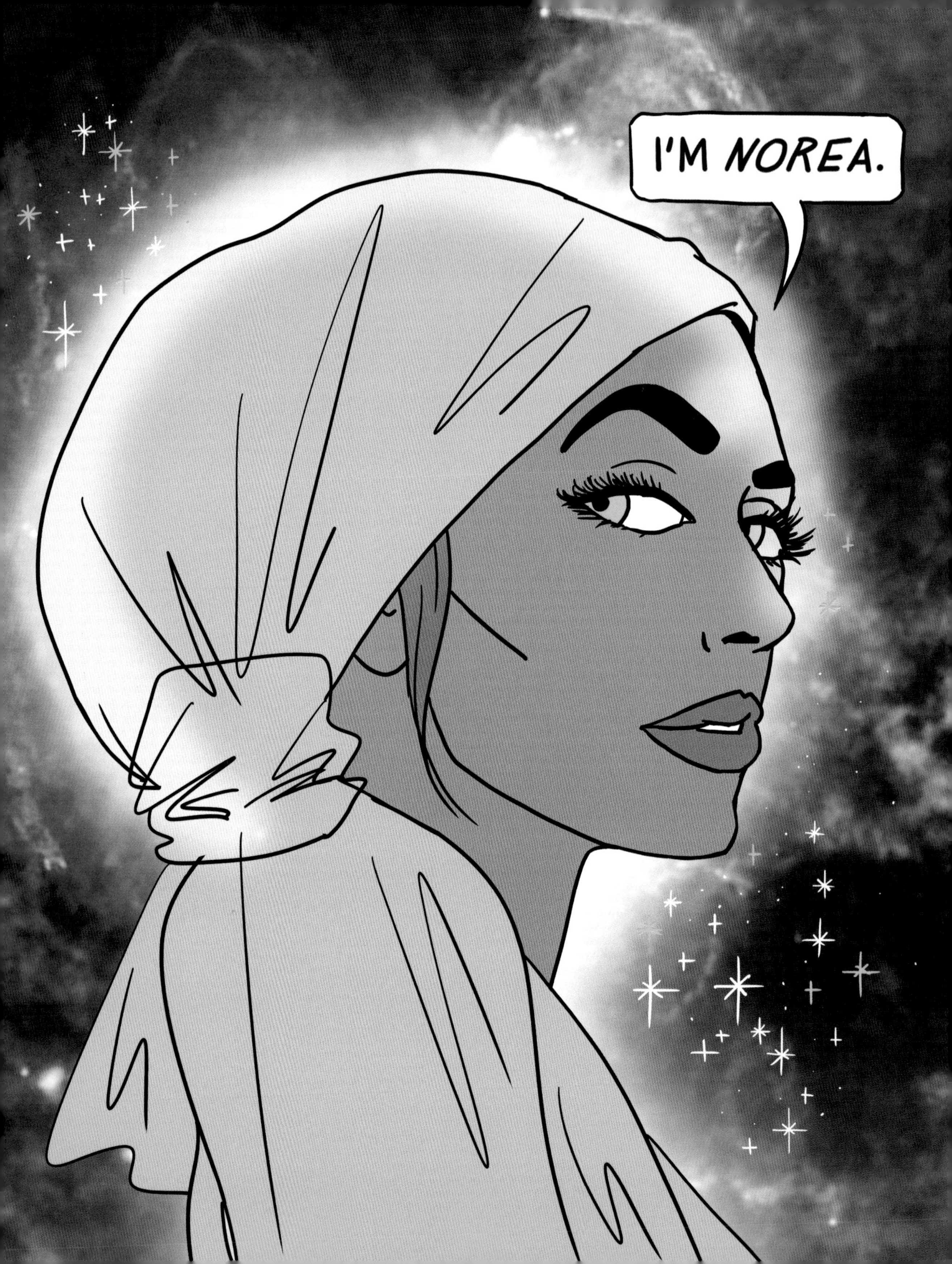
I'M *NOREA.*

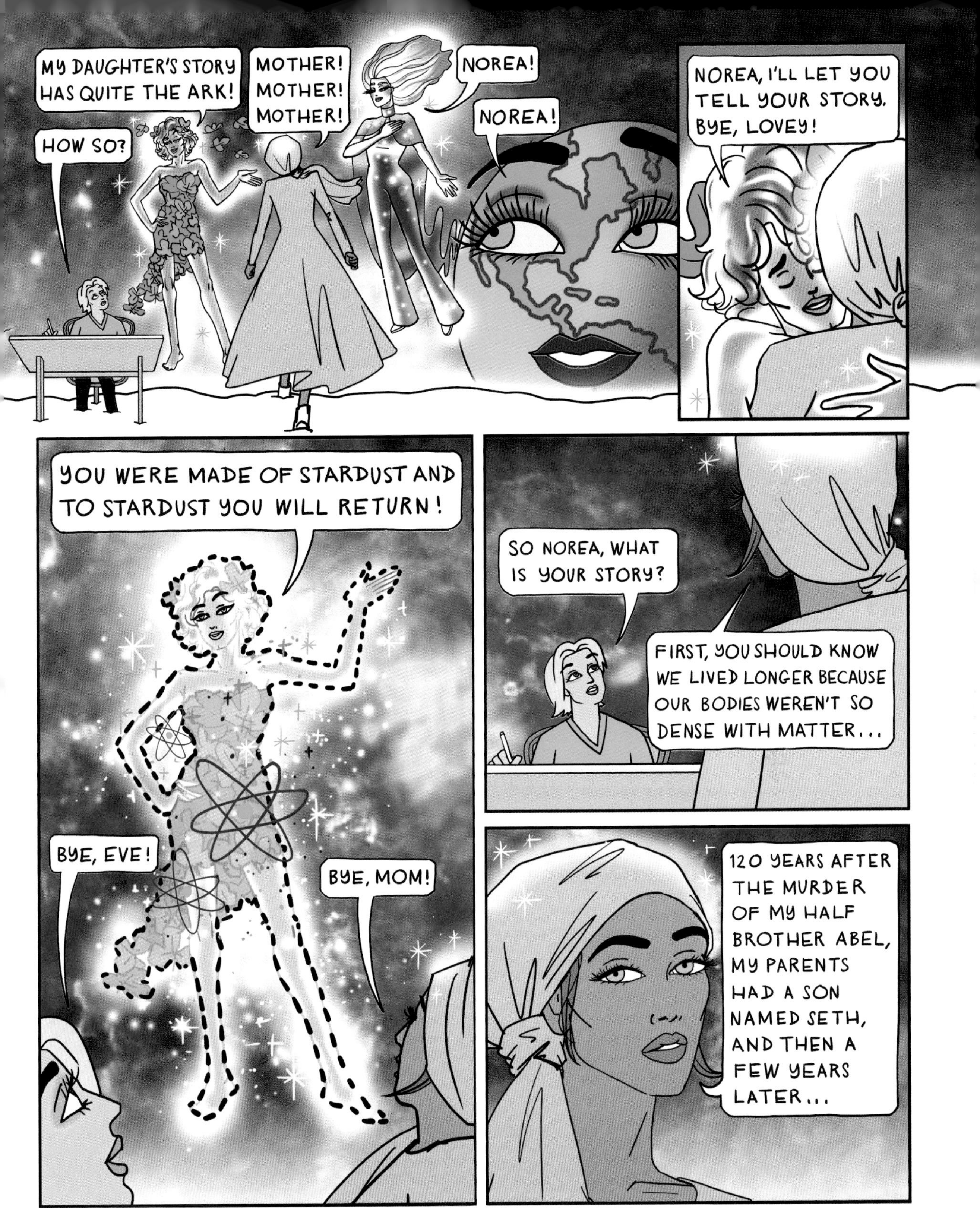
MY DAUGHTER'S STORY HAS QUITE THE ARK!
HOW SO?
MOTHER! MOTHER! MOTHER!
NOREA!
NOREA!
NOREA, I'LL LET YOU TELL YOUR STORY. BYE, LOVEY!
YOU WERE MADE OF STARDUST AND TO STARDUST YOU WILL RETURN!
BYE, EVE!
BYE, MOM!
SO NOREA, WHAT IS YOUR STORY?
FIRST, YOU SHOULD KNOW WE LIVED LONGER BECAUSE OUR BODIES WEREN'T SO DENSE WITH MATTER...
120 YEARS AFTER THE MURDER OF MY HALF BROTHER ABEL, MY PARENTS HAD A SON NAMED SETH, AND THEN A FEW YEARS LATER...

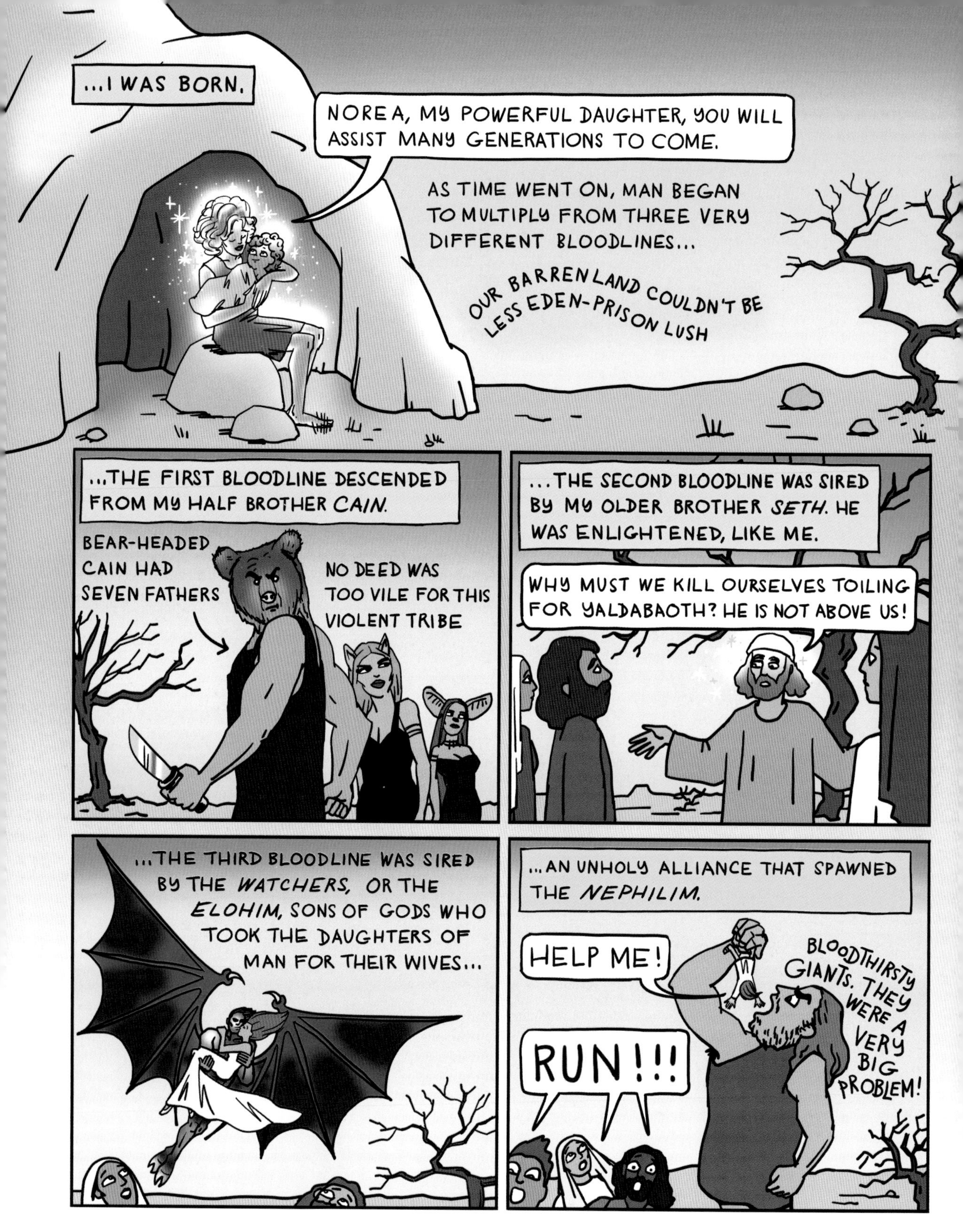
...I WAS BORN.
NOREA, MY POWERFUL DAUGHTER, YOU WILL ASSIST MANY GENERATIONS TO COME.
AS TIME WENT ON, MAN BEGAN TO MULTIPLY FROM THREE VERY DIFFERENT BLOODLINES...
OUR BARRENLAND COULDN'T BE LESS EDEN-PRISON LUSH
...THE FIRST BLOODLINE DESCENDED FROM MY HALF BROTHER CAIN.
BEAR-HEADED CAIN HAD SEVEN FATHERS
NO DEED WAS TOO VILE FOR THIS VIOLENT TRIBE
...THE SECOND BLOODLINE WAS SIRED BY MY OLDER BROTHER SETH. HE WAS ENLIGHTENED, LIKE ME.
WHY MUST WE KILL OURSELVES TOILING FOR YALDABAOTH? HE IS NOT ABOVE US!
...THE THIRD BLOODLINE WAS SIRED BY THE WATCHERS, OR THE ELOHIM, SONS OF GODS WHO TOOK THE DAUGHTERS OF MAN FOR THEIR WIVES...
...AN UNHOLY ALLIANCE THAT SPAWNED THE NEPHILIM.
HELP ME!
BLOODTHIRSTY GIANTS. THEY WERE A VERY BIG PROBLEM!
RUN!!!

AS FOR ME, I MARRIED A *SETHITE.* OR SO I THOUGHT...

DAY AND NIGHT, YOU TOIL, TOIL, TOIL! WHERE ARE YOU GOING AND WHAT ARE YOU DOING?

I TOLD YOU I CAN'T TELL YOU.

THIS WENT ON AND ON UNTIL...

...I FOLLOWED MY HUSBAND TO HIS HIDING PLACE—A CAVE! WHERE HE WAS BUILDING SOMETHING SECRET...

IT WAS SO SECRET, WHEN HIS HAMMER HIT THE CEDAR SLATS, IT WAS SILENT!

I COULD TELL IT WAS SPELLED.

THEN IT SEEMED AS IF THE WALL WAS WHISPERING TO HIM, COMPELLING HIM...

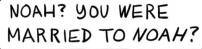

...AND *DON'T* TELL NOREA!

DON'T TELL ME WHAT, *NOAH?!*

NOAH? YOU WERE MARRIED TO *NOAH?*

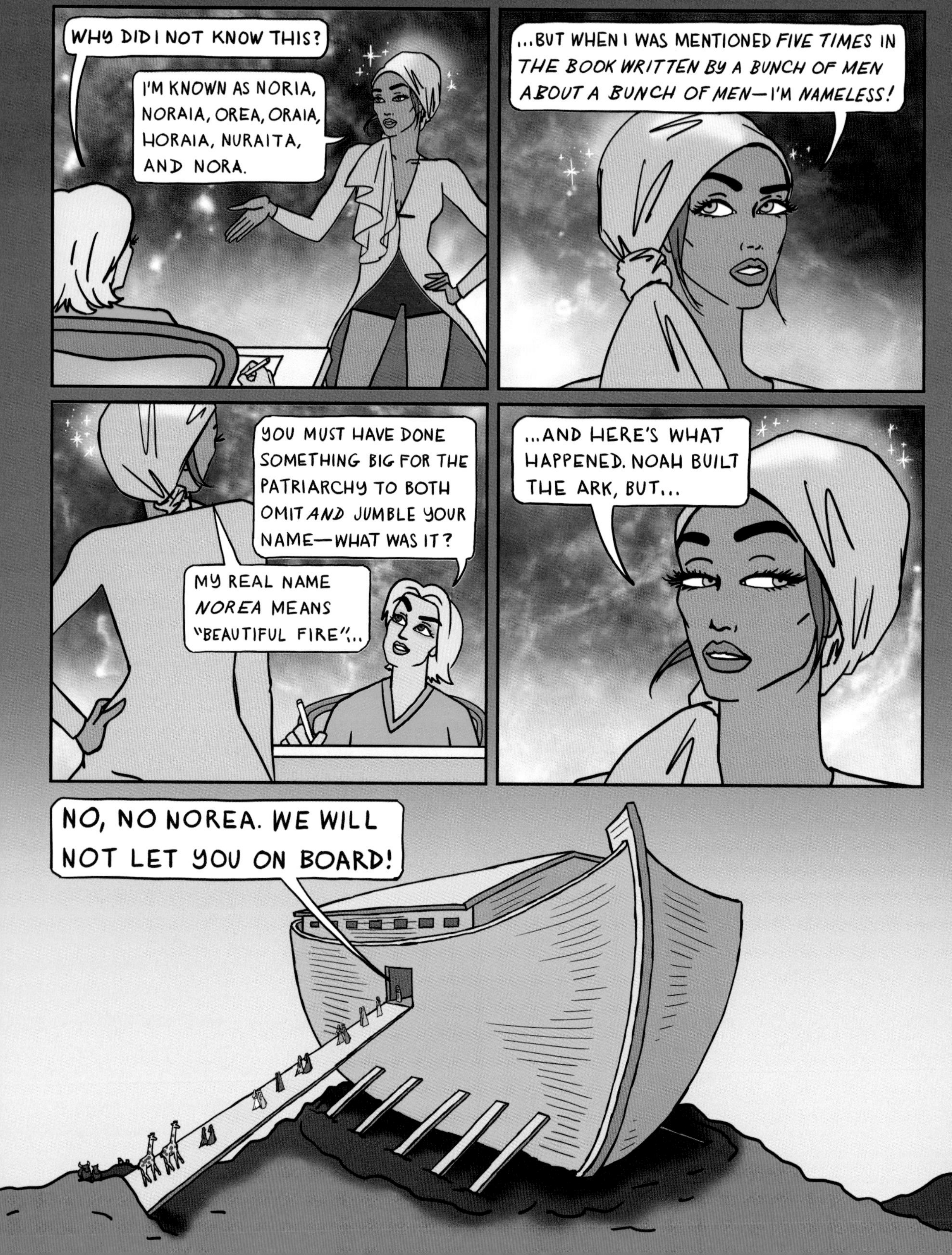
WHY DID I NOT KNOW THIS?
I'M KNOWN AS NORIA, NORAIA, OREA, ORAIA, HORAIA, NURAITA, AND NORA.
...BUT WHEN I WAS MENTIONED *FIVE TIMES* IN *THE BOOK WRITTEN BY A BUNCH OF MEN ABOUT A BUNCH OF MEN*—I'M *NAMELESS!*
YOU MUST HAVE DONE SOMETHING BIG FOR THE PATRIARCHY TO BOTH OMIT *AND* JUMBLE YOUR NAME—WHAT WAS IT?
MY REAL NAME *NOREA* MEANS "BEAUTIFUL FIRE"...
...AND HERE'S WHAT HAPPENED. NOAH BUILT THE ARK, BUT...
NO, NO NOREA. WE WILL NOT LET YOU ON BOARD!

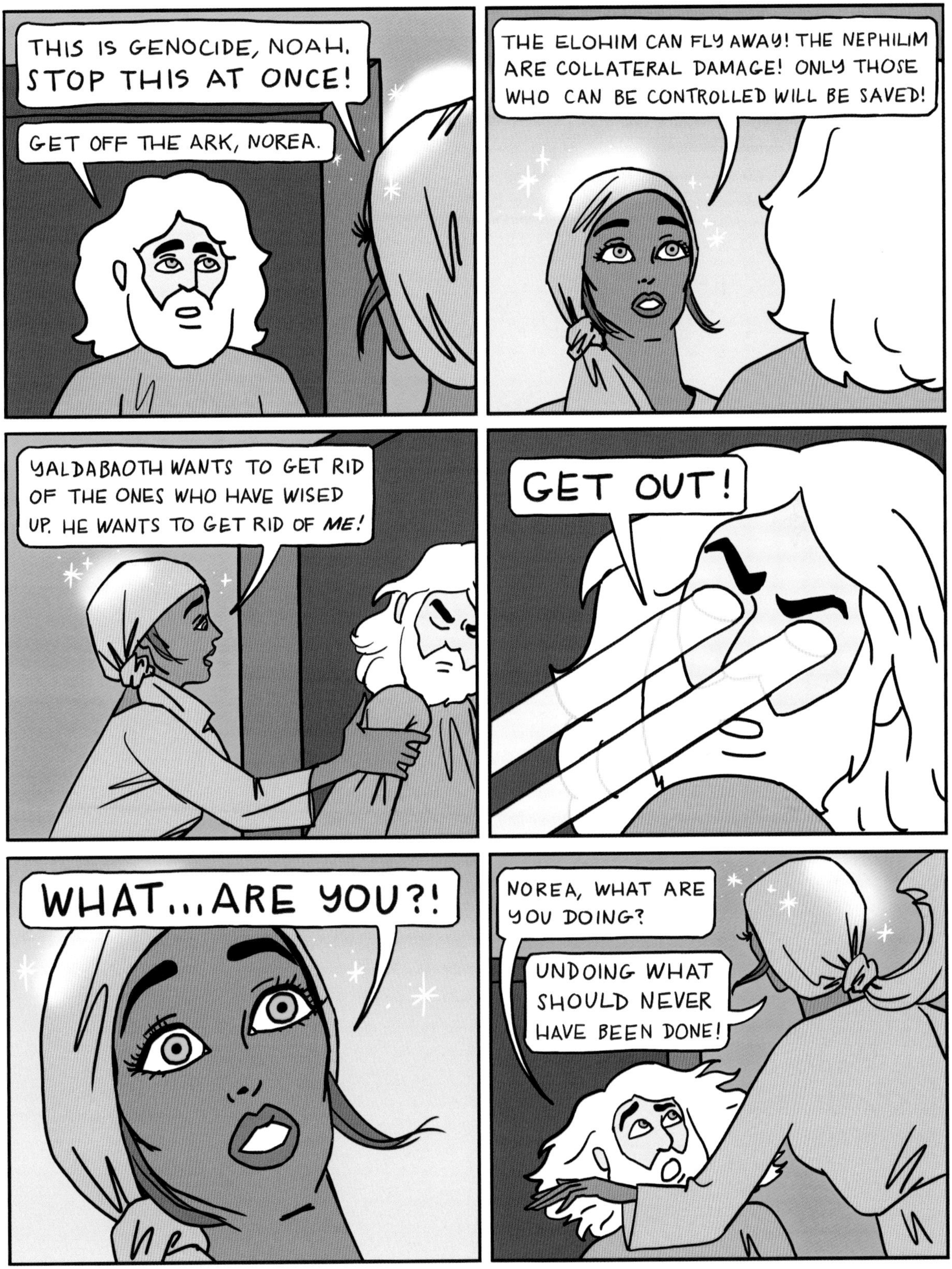
THIS IS GENOCIDE, NOAH. STOP THIS AT ONCE!
GET OFF THE ARK, NOREA.
THE ELOHIM CAN FLY AWAY! THE NEPHILIM ARE COLLATERAL DAMAGE! ONLY THOSE WHO CAN BE CONTROLLED WILL BE SAVED!
YALDABAOTH WANTS TO GET RID OF THE ONES WHO HAVE WISED UP. HE WANTS TO GET RID OF *ME*!
GET OUT!
WHAT...ARE YOU?!
NOREA, WHAT ARE YOU DOING?
UNDOING WHAT SHOULD NEVER HAVE BEEN DONE!

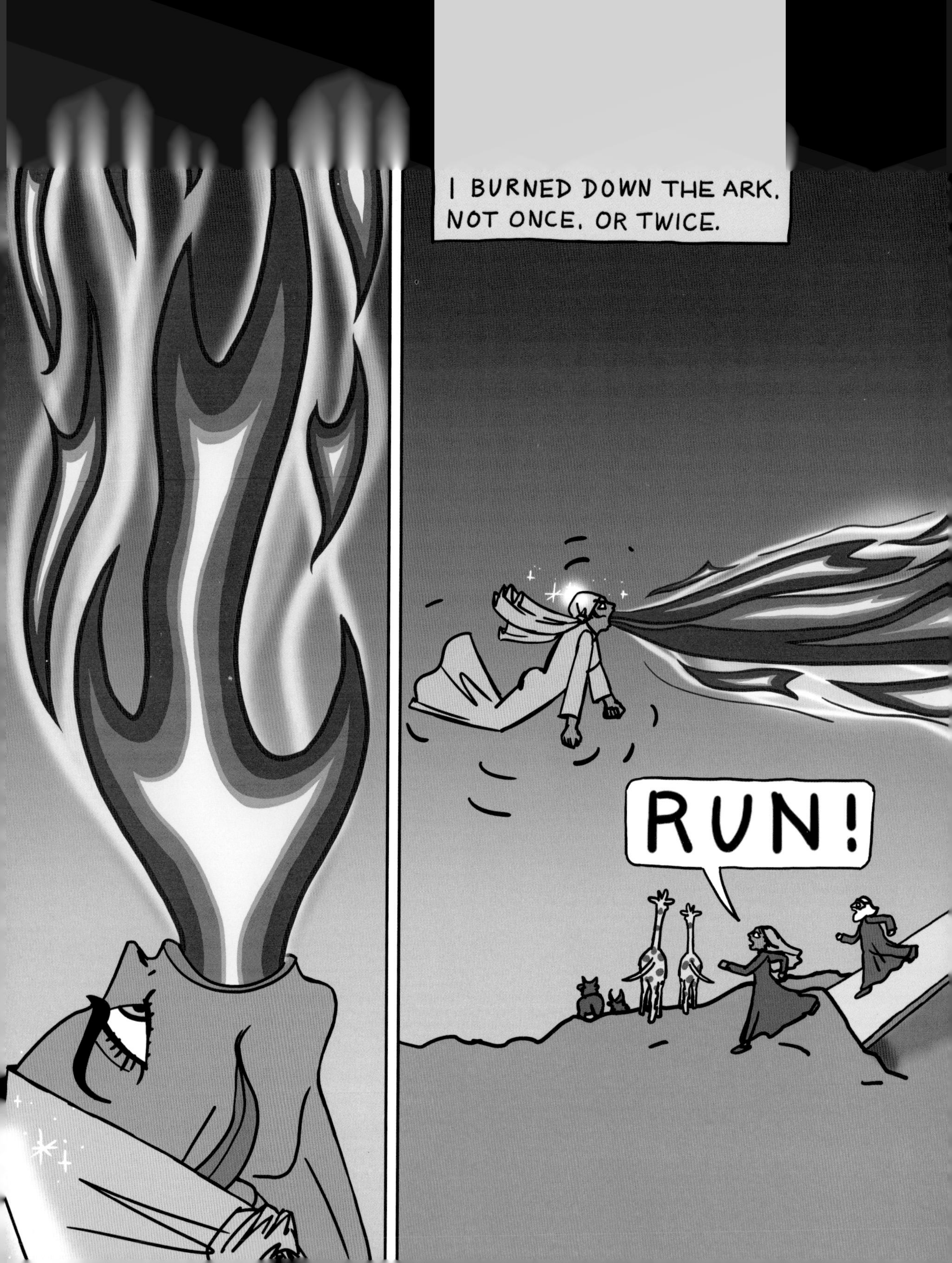
I BURNED DOWN THE ARK. NOT ONCE. OR TWICE.
RUN!

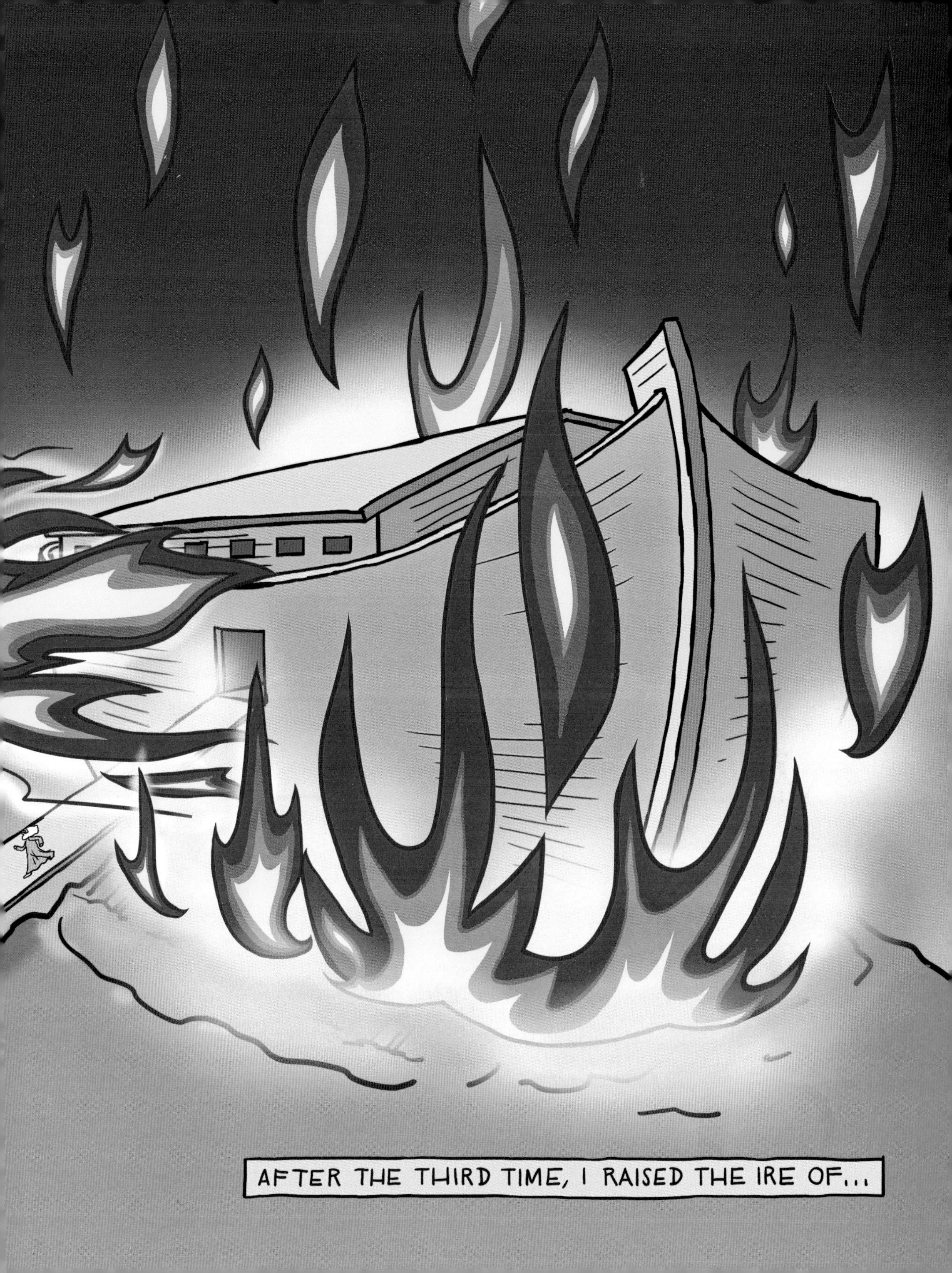
AFTER THE THIRD TIME, I RAISED THE IRE OF...

...YALDABAOTH AND HIS MINIONS.
WE DON'T *HAVE* TO DESTROY YOU IN THE FLOOD WITH ALL THE REST.
NOT TODAY YALDABAOTH, NOT TODAY.
BE A GOOD GIRL AND COME TO US AS DID YOUR MOTHER, EVE.
YOU LIE, YALDABAOTH! SHE DID NOT!
I WILL NOT!
I *KNOW* WHAT MY MOTHER *REALLY* DID...
...SHE SENT YOU TO HELL!

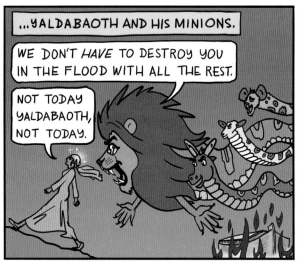

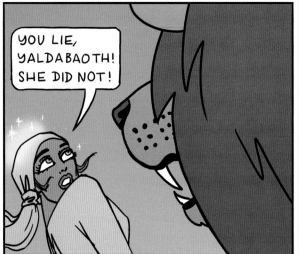

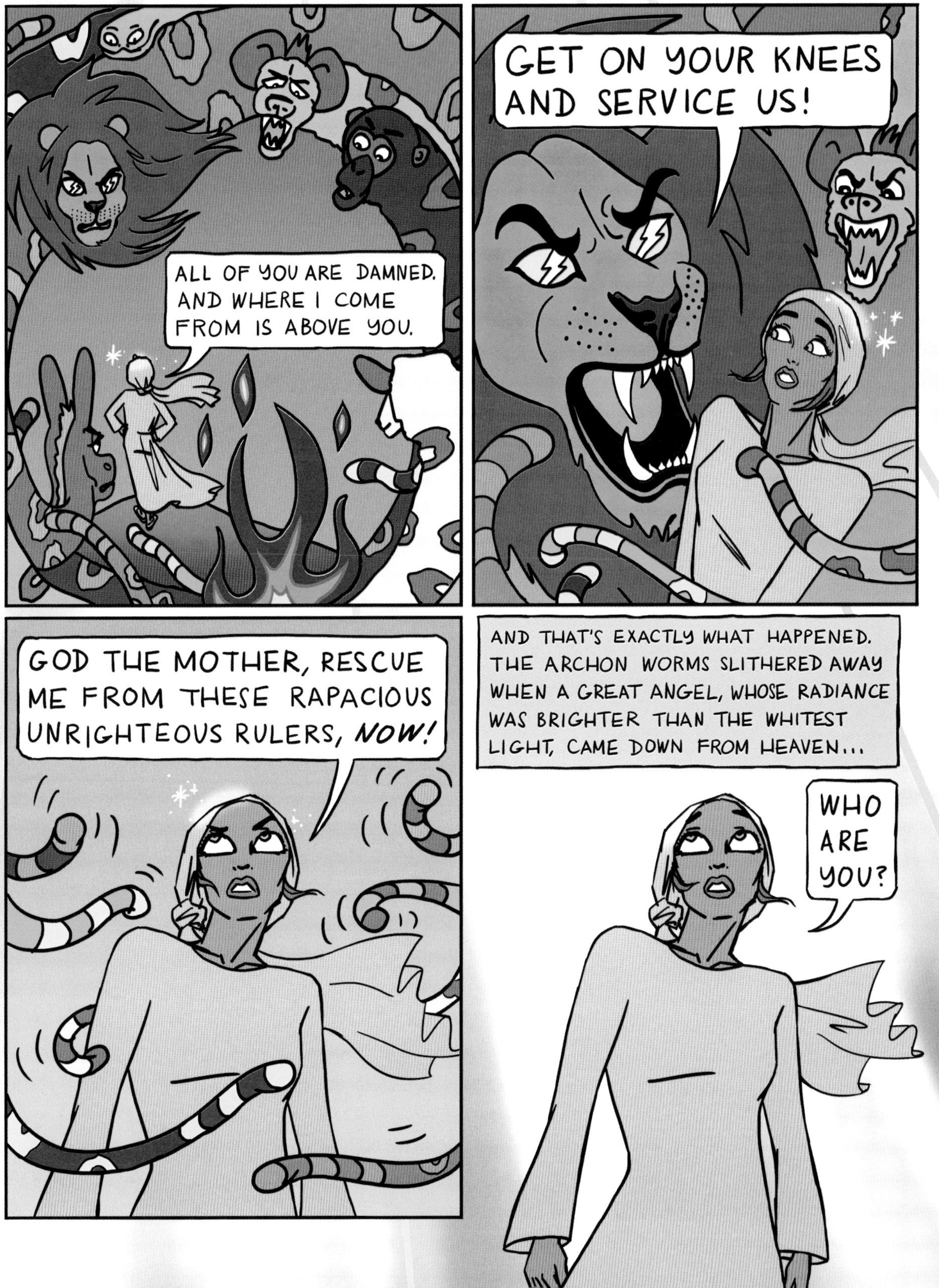
ALL OF YOU ARE DAMNED. AND WHERE I COME FROM IS ABOVE YOU.
GET ON YOUR KNEES AND SERVICE US!
GOD THE MOTHER, RESCUE ME FROM THESE RAPACIOUS UNRIGHTEOUS RULERS, NOW!
AND THAT'S EXACTLY WHAT HAPPENED. THE ARCHON WORMS SLITHERED AWAY WHEN A GREAT ANGEL, WHOSE RADIANCE WAS BRIGHTER THAN THE WHITEST LIGHT, CAME DOWN FROM HEAVEN...
WHO ARE YOU?

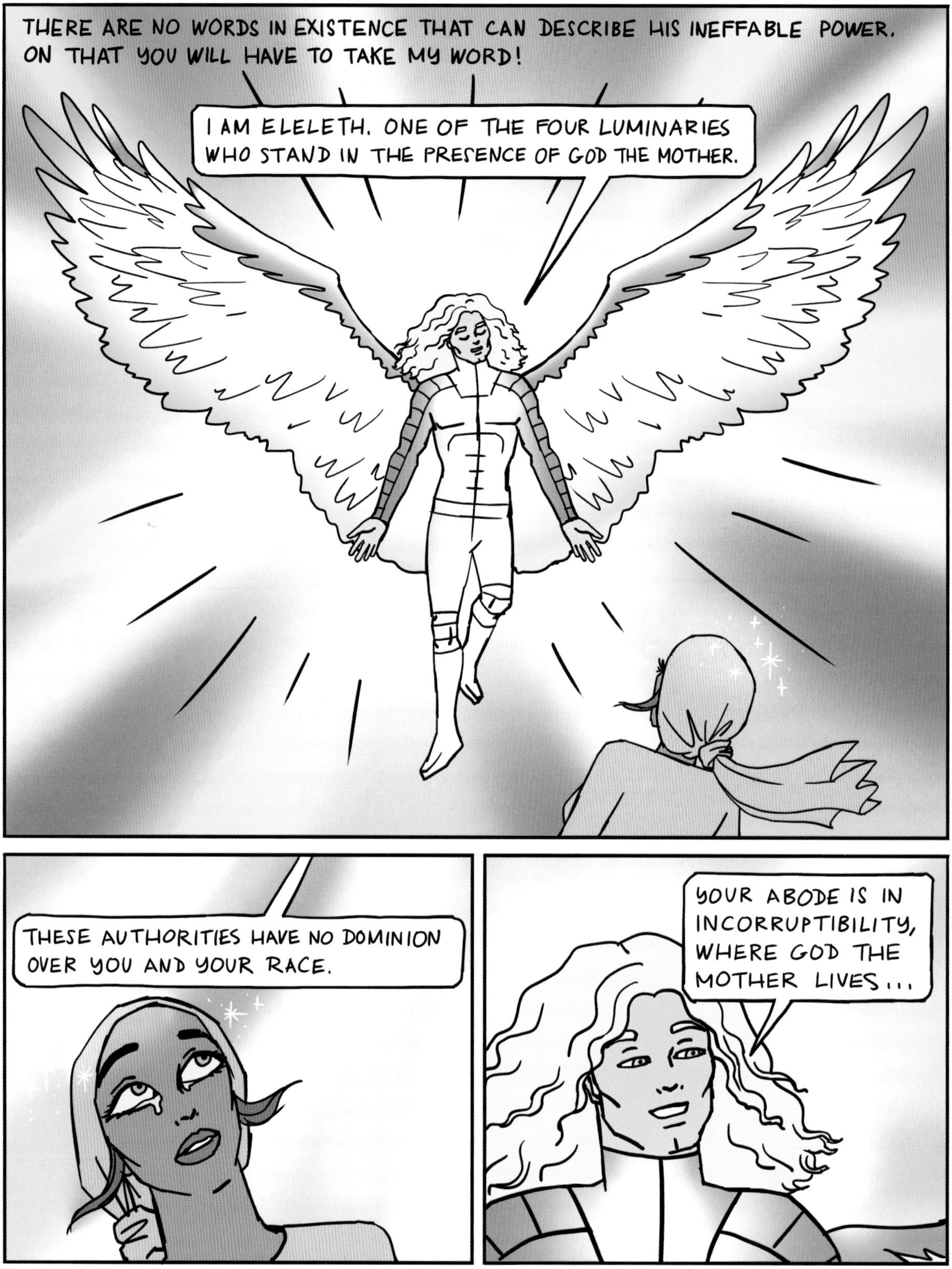
THERE ARE NO WORDS IN EXISTENCE THAT CAN DESCRIBE HIS INEFFABLE POWER. ON THAT YOU WILL HAVE TO TAKE MY WORD!
I AM ELELETH. ONE OF THE FOUR LUMINARIES WHO STAND IN THE PRESENCE OF GOD THE MOTHER.
THESE AUTHORITIES HAVE NO DOMINION OVER YOU AND YOUR RACE.
YOUR ABODE IS IN INCORRUPTIBILITY, WHERE GOD THE MOTHER LIVES...

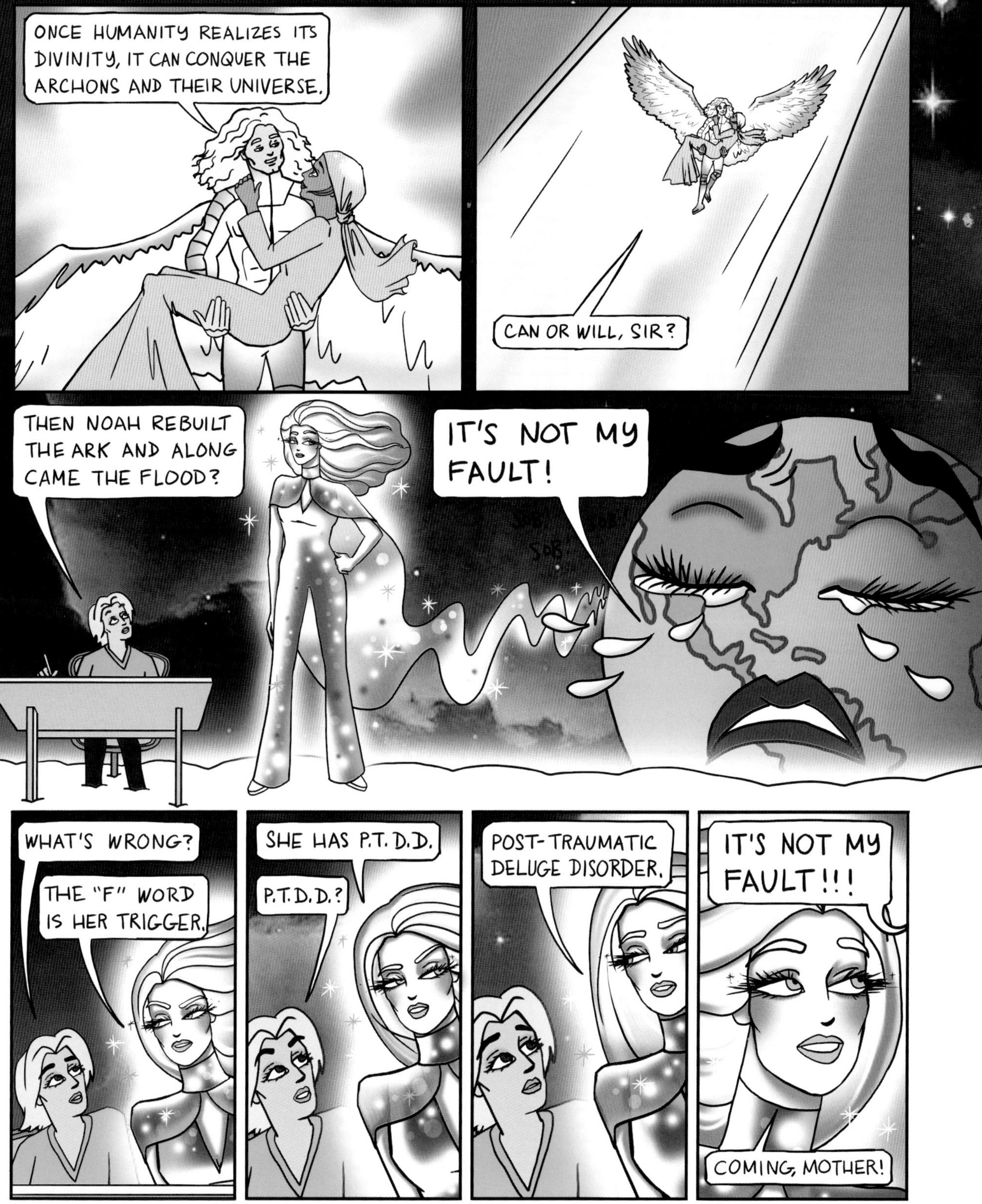
ONCE HUMANITY REALIZES ITS DIVINITY, IT CAN CONQUER THE ARCHONS AND THEIR UNIVERSE.
CAN OR WILL, SIR?
THEN NOAH REBUILT THE ARK AND ALONG CAME THE FLOOD?
IT'S NOT MY FAULT!
WHAT'S WRONG?
THE "F" WORD IS HER TRIGGER.
SHE HAS P.T.D.D.
P.T.D.D.?
POST-TRAUMATIC DELUGE DISORDER.
IT'S NOT MY FAULT!!!
COMING, MOTHER!

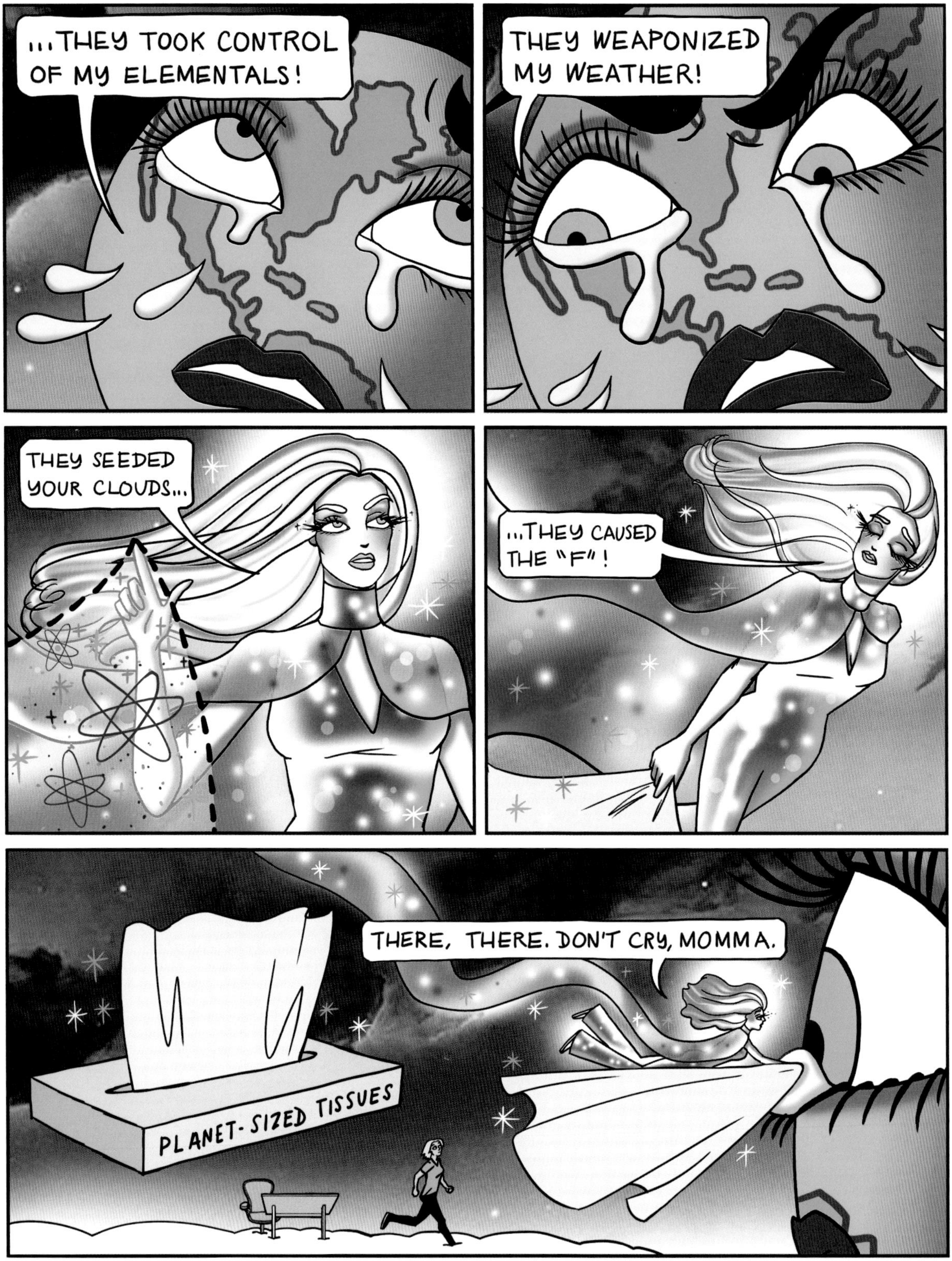
...THEY TOOK CONTROL OF MY ELEMENTALS!
THEY WEAPONIZED MY WEATHER!
THEY SEEDED YOUR CLOUDS...
...THEY CAUSED THE "F"!
THERE, THERE. DON'T CRY, MOMMA.
PLANET-SIZED TISSUES

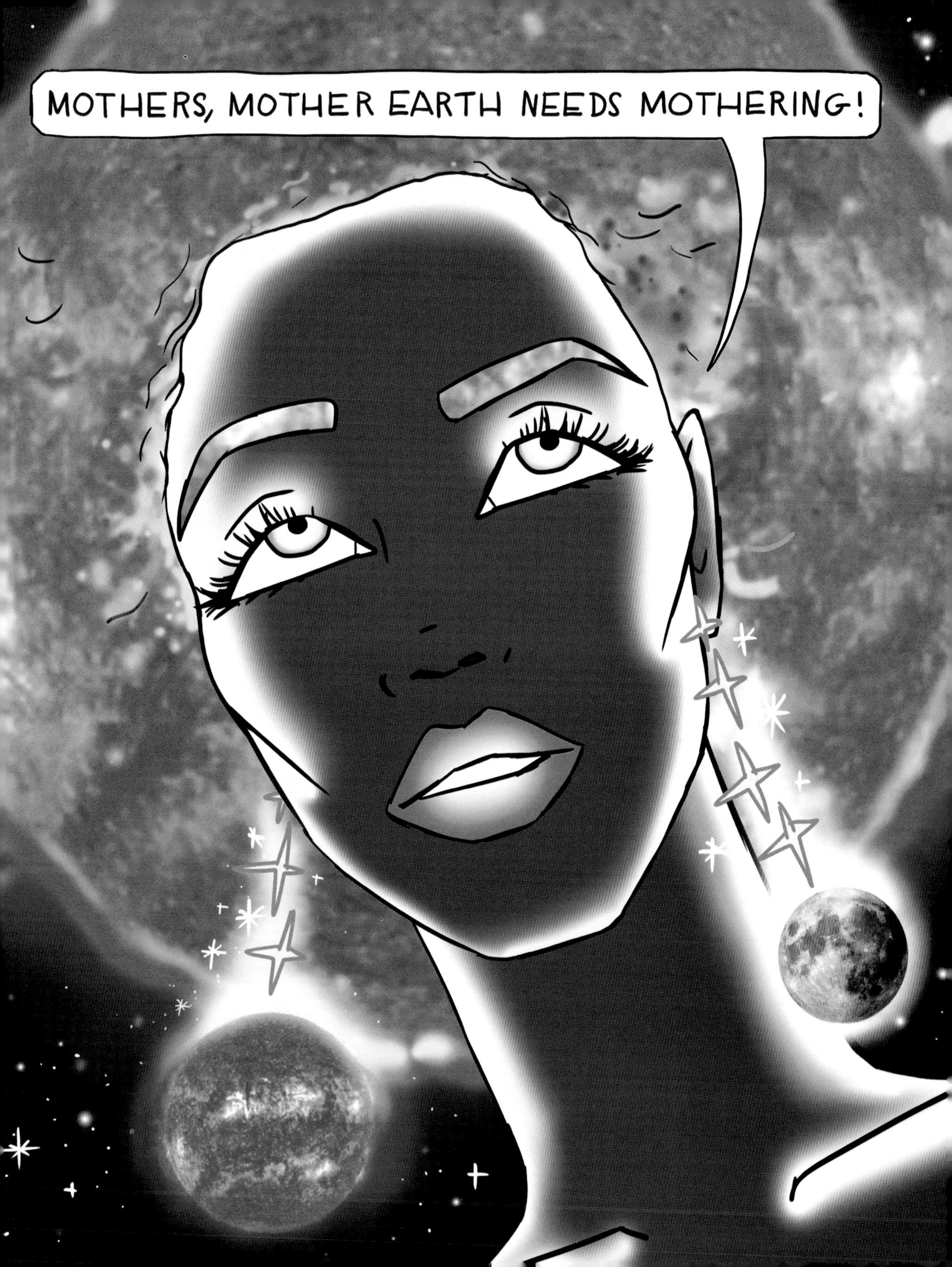
MOTHERS, MOTHER EARTH NEEDS MOTHERING!

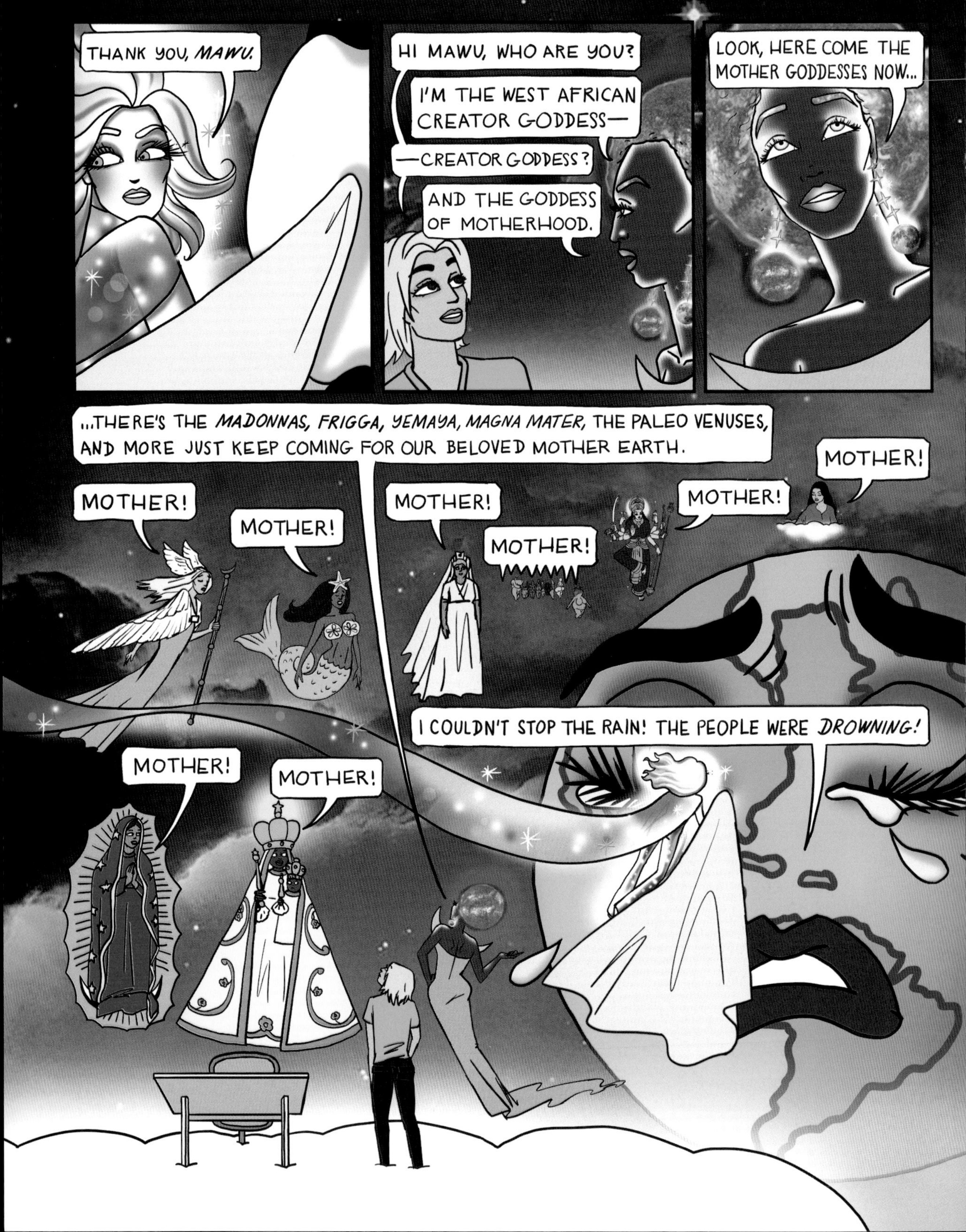
THANK YOU, *MAWU.*
HI MAWU, WHO ARE YOU?
I'M THE WEST AFRICAN CREATOR GODDESS—
—CREATOR GODDESS?
AND THE GODDESS OF MOTHERHOOD.
LOOK, HERE COME THE MOTHER GODDESSES NOW...
...THERE'S THE *MADONNAS, FRIGGA, YEMAYA, MAGNA MATER,* THE PALEO VENUSES, AND MORE JUST KEEP COMING FOR OUR BELOVED MOTHER EARTH.
MOTHER!
MOTHER!
MOTHER!
MOTHER!
MOTHER!
MOTHER!
I COULDN'T STOP THE RAIN! THE PEOPLE WERE *DROWNING!*
MOTHER!
MOTHER!

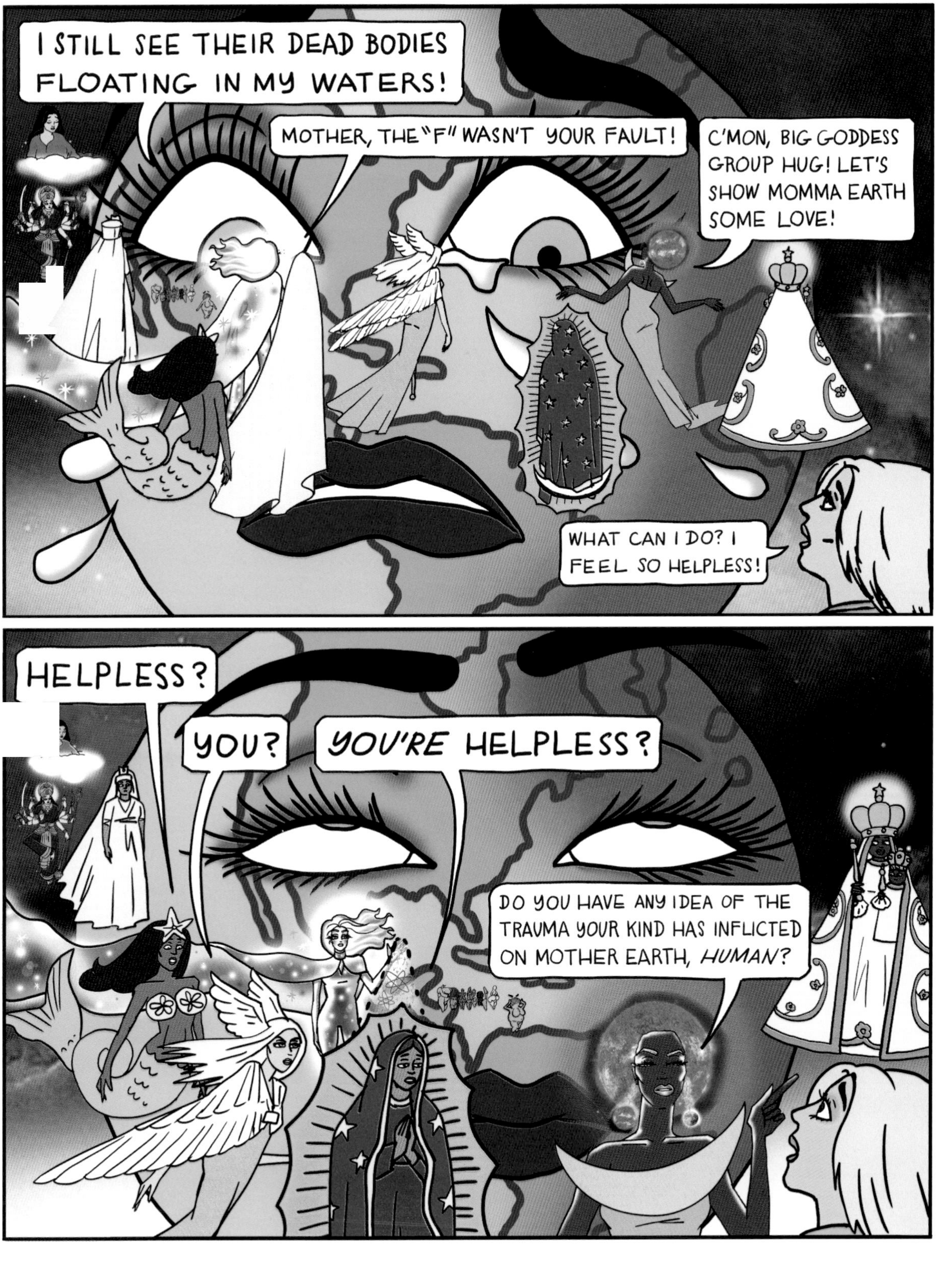

I STILL SEE THEIR DEAD BODIES FLOATING IN MY WATERS!
MOTHER, THE "F" WASN'T YOUR FAULT!
C'MON, BIG GODDESS GROUP HUG! LET'S SHOW MOMMA EARTH SOME LOVE!
WHAT CAN I DO? I FEEL SO HELPLESS!
HELPLESS?
YOU?
YOU'RE HELPLESS?
DO YOU HAVE ANY IDEA OF THE TRAUMA YOUR KIND HAS INFLICTED ON MOTHER EARTH, *HUMAN*?

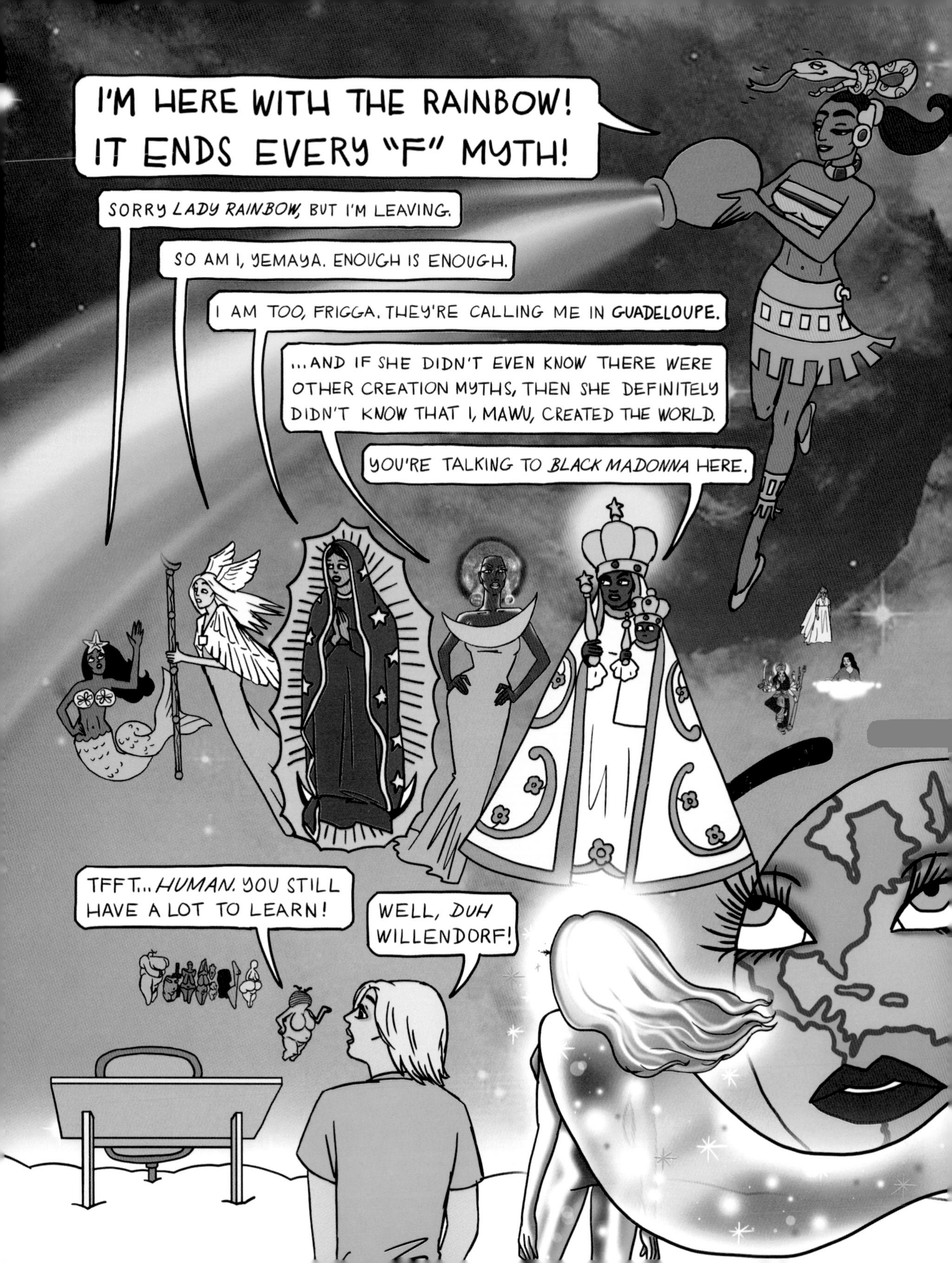
I'M HERE WITH THE RAINBOW! IT ENDS EVERY "F" MYTH!
SORRY *LADY RAINBOW*, BUT I'M LEAVING.
SO AM I, YEMAYA. ENOUGH IS ENOUGH.
I AM TOO, FRIGGA. THEY'RE CALLING ME IN **GUADELOUPE**.
...AND IF SHE DIDN'T EVEN KNOW THERE WERE OTHER CREATION MYTHS, THEN SHE DEFINITELY DIDN'T KNOW THAT I, MAWU, CREATED THE WORLD.
YOU'RE TALKING TO *BLACK MADONNA* HERE.
TFFT... *HUMAN*. YOU STILL HAVE A LOT TO LEARN!
WELL, *DUH* WILLENDORF!

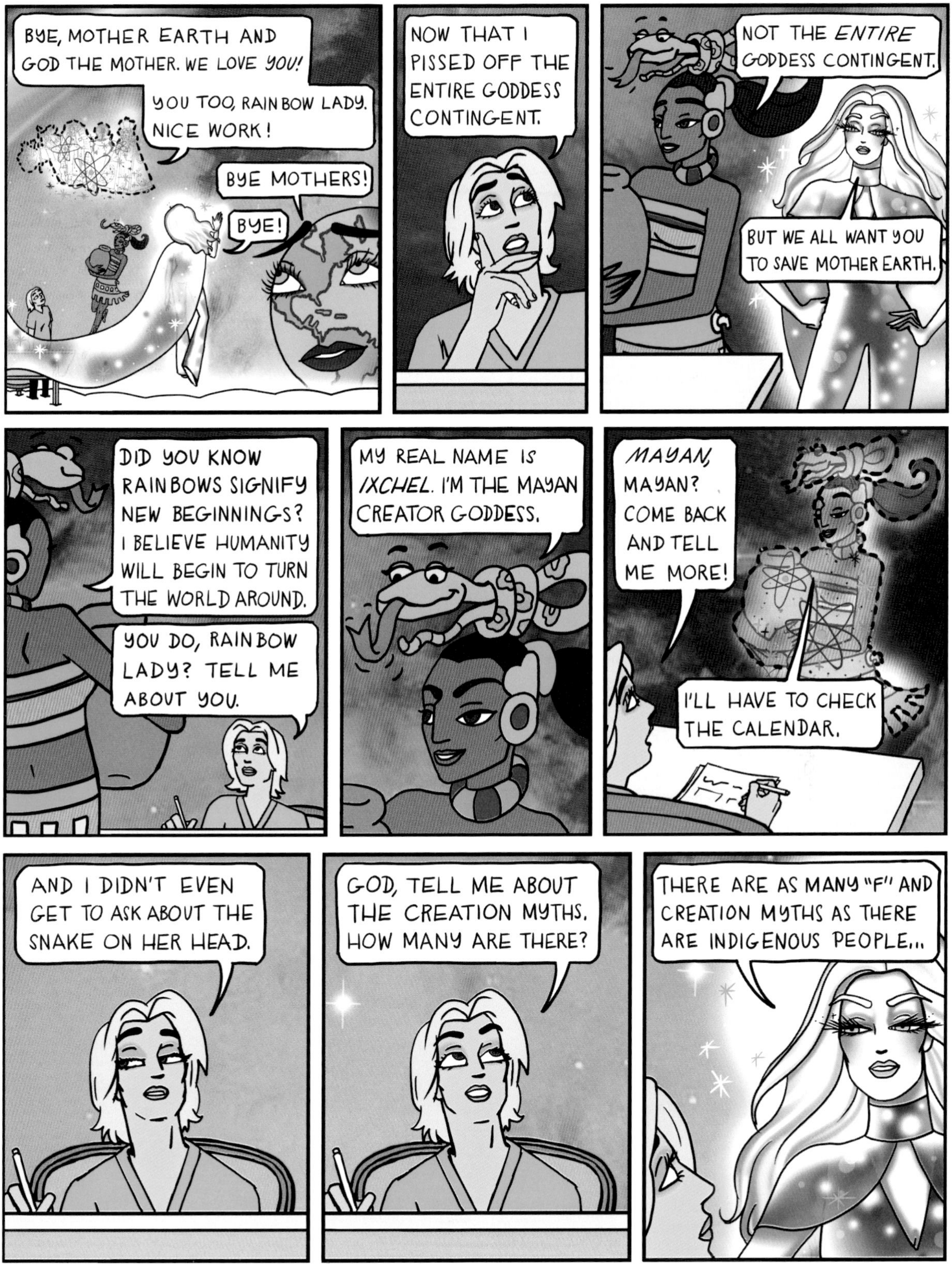
BYE, MOTHER EARTH AND GOD THE MOTHER. WE LOVE *YOU!*
YOU TOO, RAINBOW LADY. NICE WORK!
BYE MOTHERS!
BYE!
NOW THAT I PISSED OFF THE ENTIRE GODDESS CONTINGENT.
NOT THE *ENTIRE* GODDESS CONTINGENT.
BUT WE ALL WANT YOU TO SAVE MOTHER EARTH.
DID YOU KNOW RAINBOWS SIGNIFY NEW BEGINNINGS? I BELIEVE HUMANITY WILL BEGIN TO TURN THE WORLD AROUND.
YOU DO, RAINBOW LADY? TELL ME ABOUT YOU.
MY REAL NAME IS *IXCHEL*. I'M THE MAYAN CREATOR GODDESS.
MAYAN, MAYAN? COME BACK AND TELL ME MORE!
I'LL HAVE TO CHECK THE CALENDAR.
AND I DIDN'T EVEN GET TO ASK ABOUT THE SNAKE ON HER HEAD.
GOD, TELL ME ABOUT THE CREATION MYTHS. HOW MANY ARE THERE?
THERE ARE AS MANY "F" AND CREATION MYTHS AS THERE ARE INDIGENOUS PEOPLE...

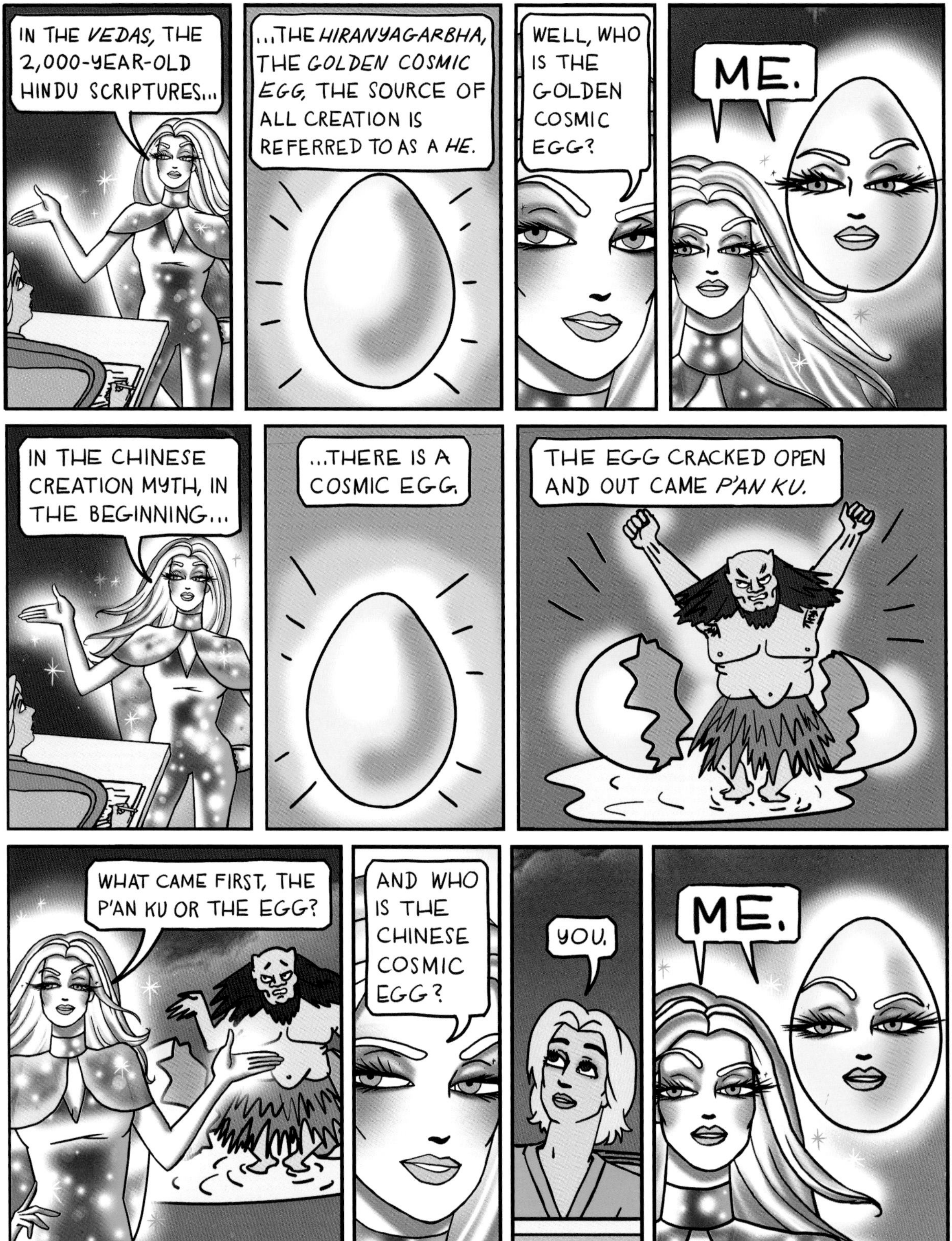
IN THE *VEDAS,* THE 2,000-YEAR-OLD HINDU SCRIPTURES...
...THE *HIRANYAGARBHA,* THE *GOLDEN COSMIC EGG,* THE SOURCE OF ALL CREATION IS REFERRED TO AS A *HE.*
WELL, WHO IS THE GOLDEN COSMIC EGG?
ME.
IN THE CHINESE CREATION MYTH, IN THE BEGINNING...
...THERE IS A COSMIC EGG.
THE EGG CRACKED OPEN AND OUT CAME *P'AN KU.*
WHAT CAME FIRST, THE P'AN KU OR THE EGG?
AND WHO IS THE CHINESE COSMIC EGG?
YOU.
ME.

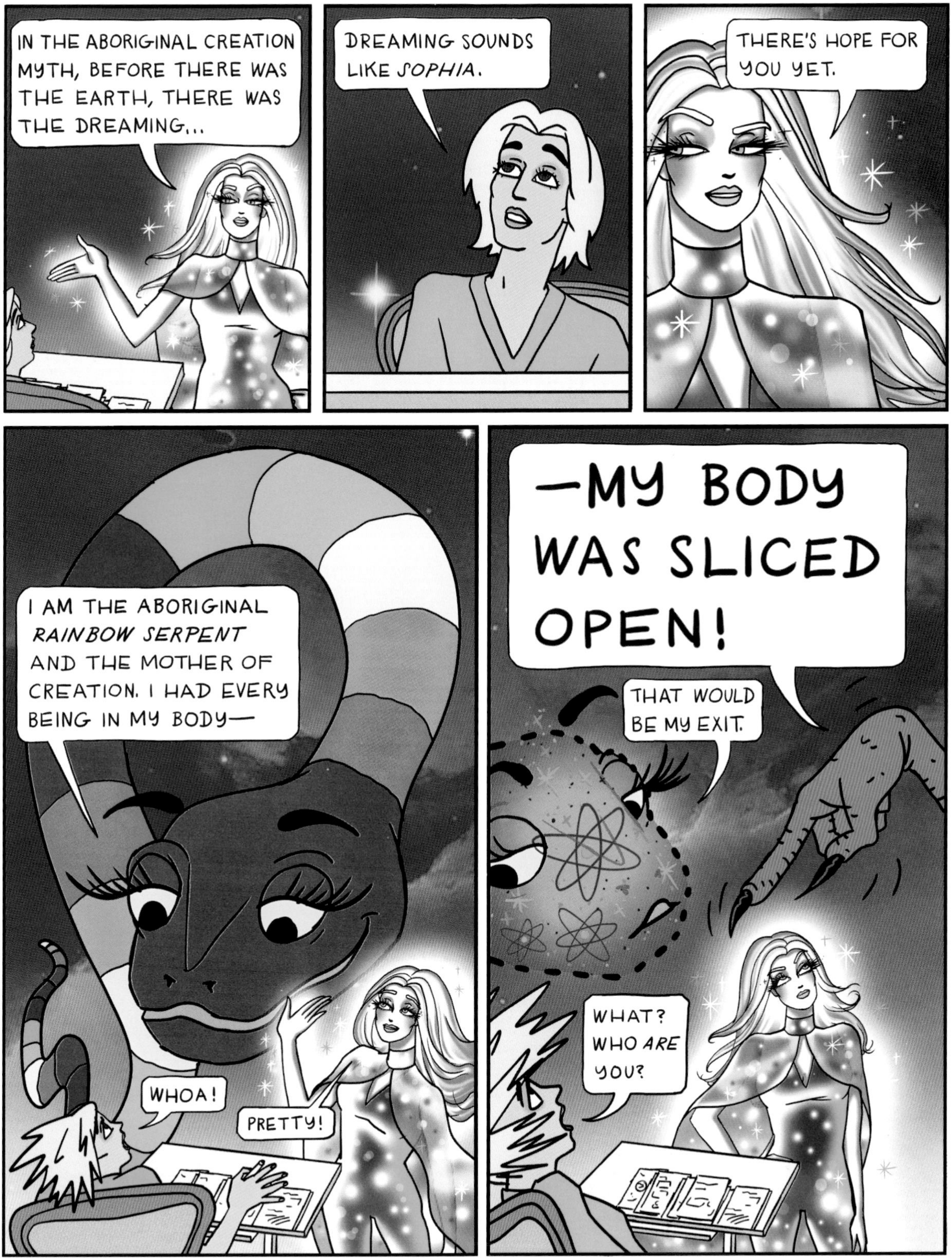

IN THE ABORIGINAL CREATION MYTH, BEFORE THERE WAS THE EARTH, THERE WAS THE DREAMING...
DREAMING SOUNDS LIKE *SOPHIA*.
THERE'S HOPE FOR YOU YET.
I AM THE ABORIGINAL *RAINBOW SERPENT* AND THE MOTHER OF CREATION. I HAD EVERY BEING IN MY BODY—
WHOA!
PRETTY!
—MY BODY WAS SLICED OPEN!
THAT WOULD BE MY EXIT.
WHAT? WHO *ARE* YOU?

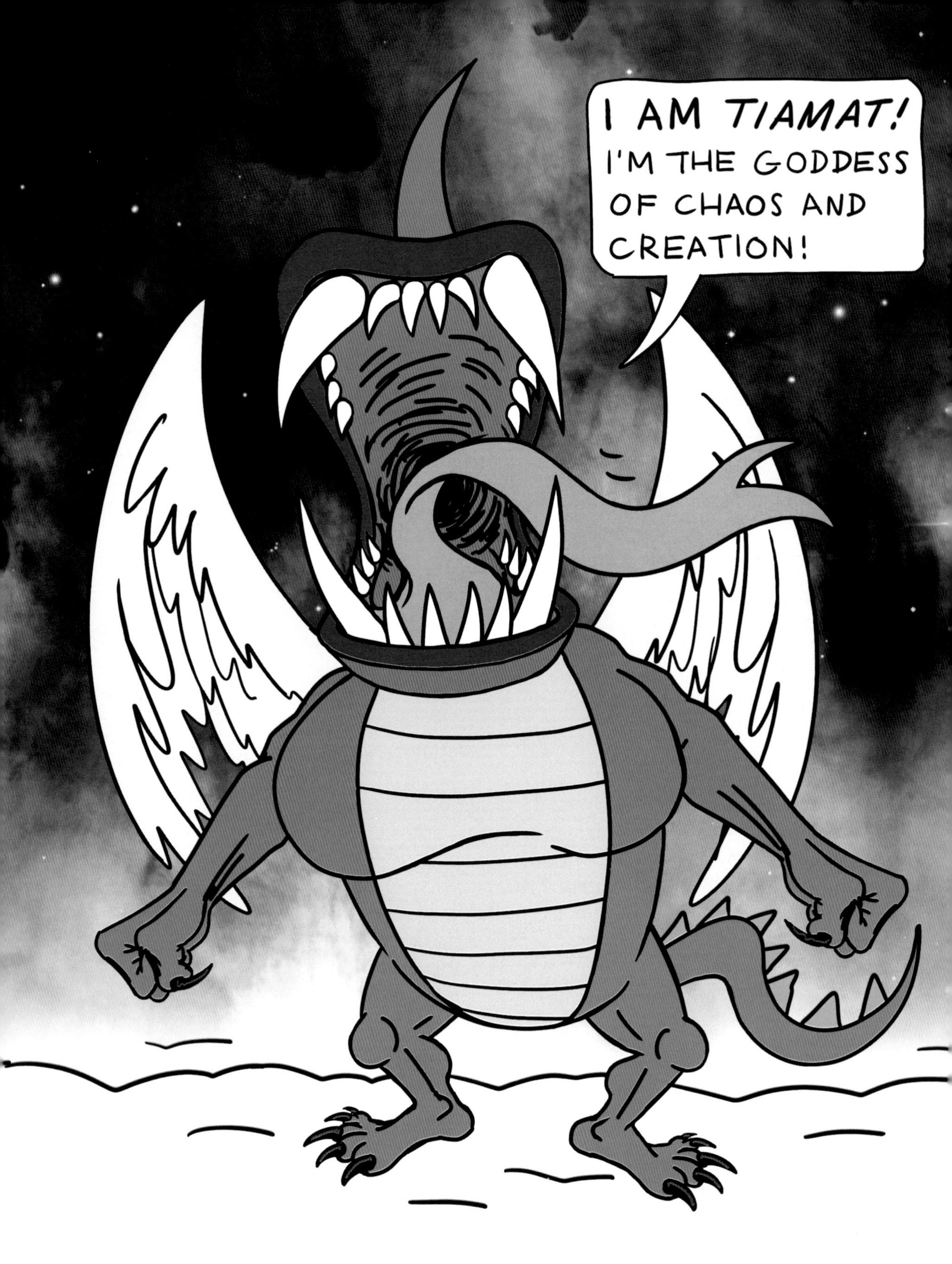
I AM *TIAMAT!* I'M THE GODDESS OF CHAOS AND CREATION!

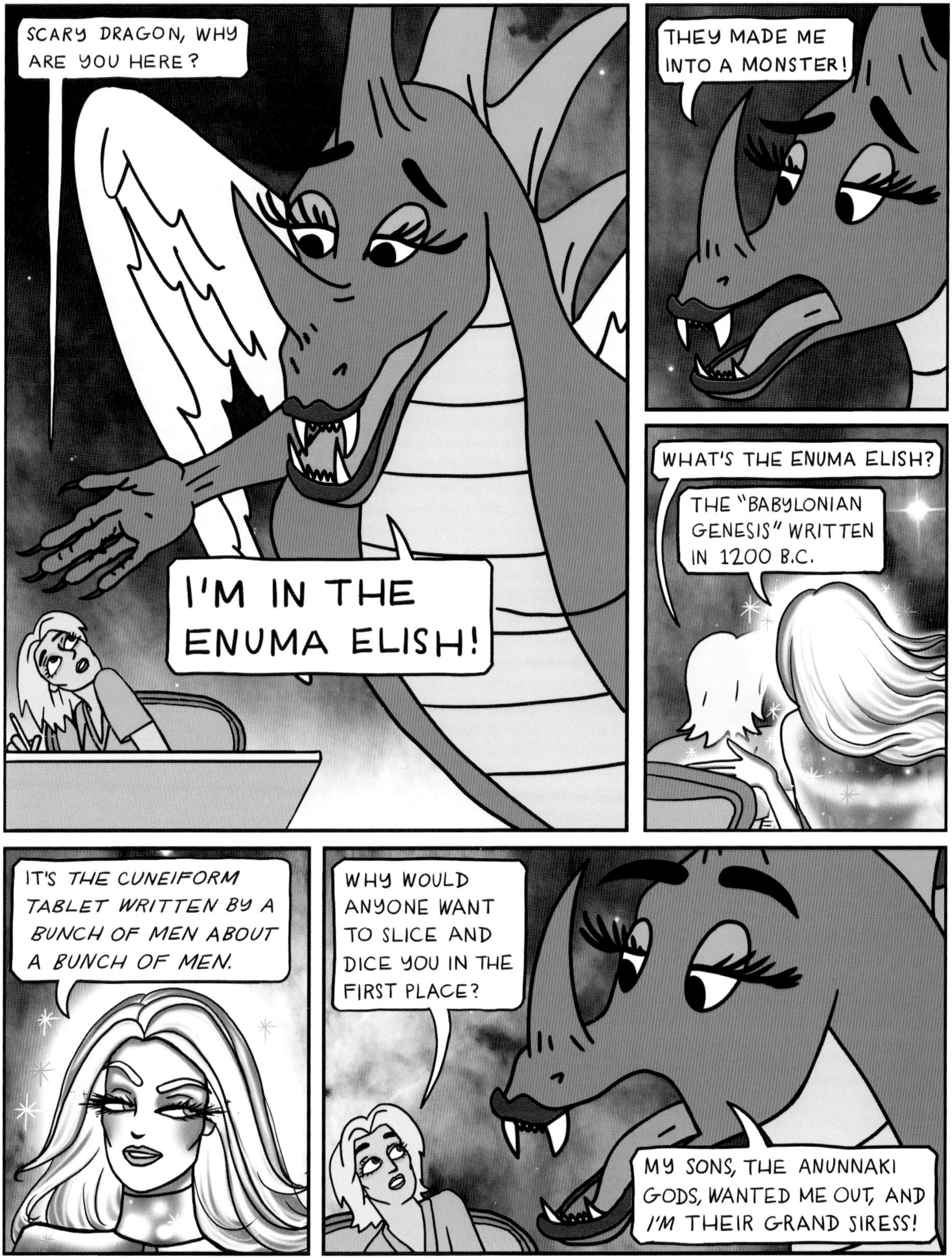
SCARY DRAGON, WHY ARE YOU HERE?
I'M IN THE ENUMA ELISH!
THEY MADE ME INTO A MONSTER!
WHAT'S THE ENUMA ELISH?
THE "BABYLONIAN GENESIS" WRITTEN IN 1200 B.C.
IT'S *THE CUNEIFORM TABLET WRITTEN BY A BUNCH OF MEN ABOUT A BUNCH OF MEN.*
WHY WOULD ANYONE WANT TO SLICE AND DICE YOU IN THE FIRST PLACE?
MY SONS, THE ANUNNAKI GODS, WANTED ME OUT, AND *I'M* THEIR GRAND SIRESS!

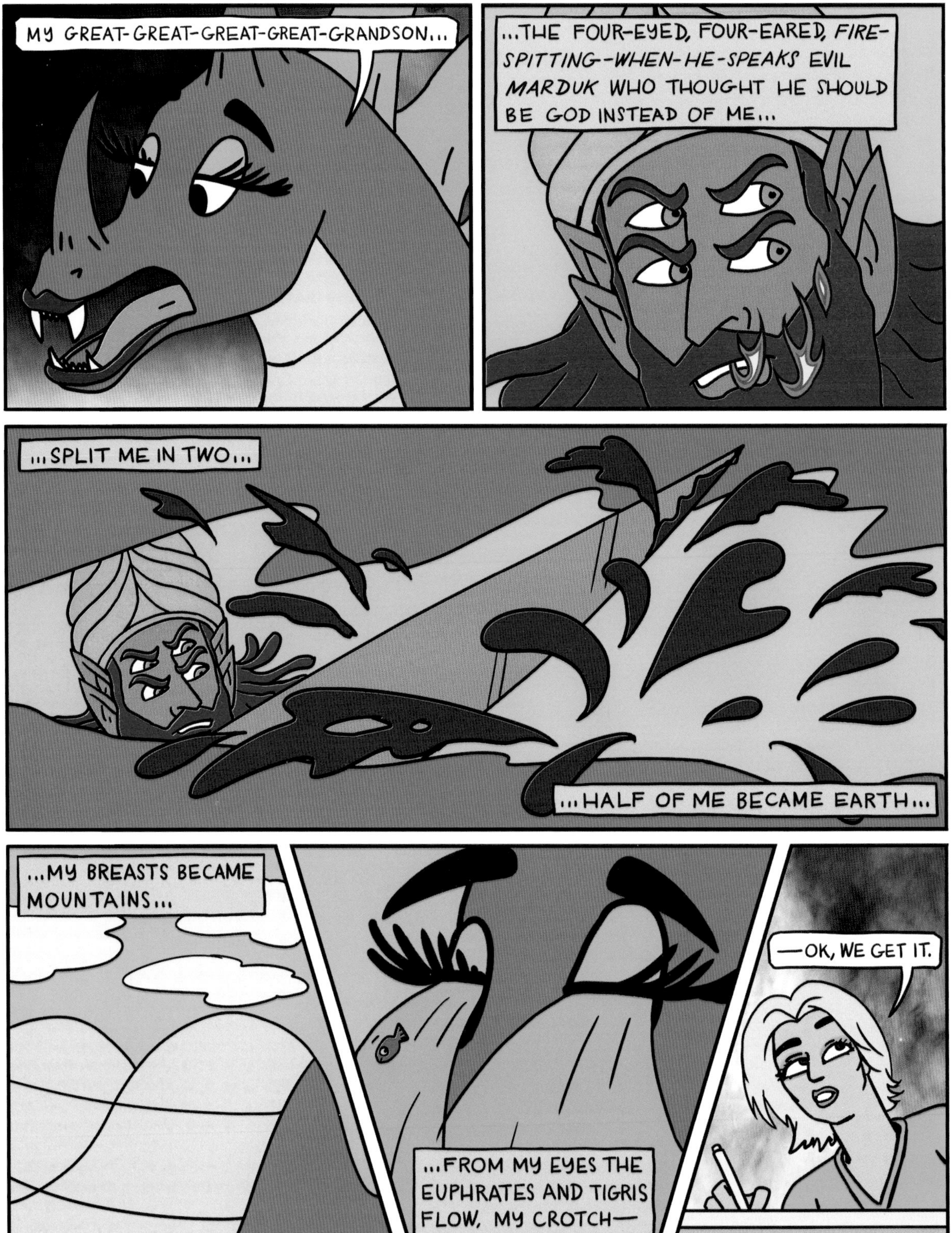
MY GREAT-GREAT-GREAT-GREAT-GRANDSON...
...THE FOUR-EYED, FOUR-EARED, *FIRE-SPITTING-WHEN-HE-SPEAKS* EVIL *MARDUK* WHO THOUGHT HE SHOULD BE GOD INSTEAD OF ME...
...SPLIT ME IN TWO...
...HALF OF ME BECAME EARTH...
...MY BREASTS BECAME MOUNTAINS...
...FROM MY EYES THE EUPHRATES AND TIGRIS FLOW, MY CROTCH—
—OK, WE GET IT.

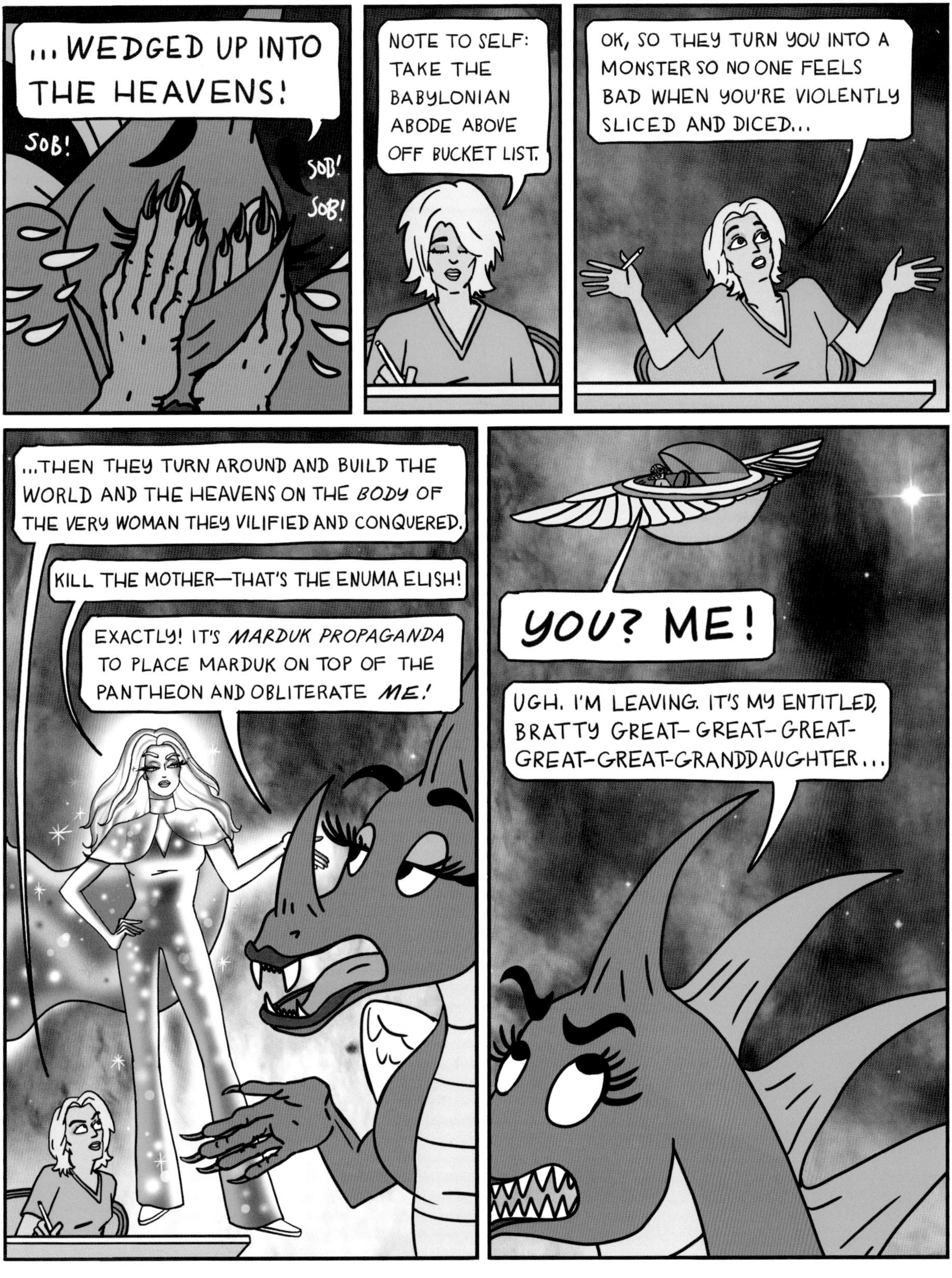
...WEDGED UP INTO THE HEAVENS!
SOB!
SOB!
SOB!
NOTE TO SELF: TAKE THE BABYLONIAN ABODE ABOVE OFF BUCKET LIST.
OK, SO THEY TURN YOU INTO A MONSTER SO NO ONE FEELS BAD WHEN YOU'RE VIOLENTLY SLICED AND DICED...
...THEN THEY TURN AROUND AND BUILD THE WORLD AND THE HEAVENS ON THE BODY OF THE VERY WOMAN THEY VILIFIED AND CONQUERED.
KILL THE MOTHER—THAT'S THE ENUMA ELISH!
EXACTLY! IT'S MARDUK PROPAGANDA TO PLACE MARDUK ON TOP OF THE PANTHEON AND OBLITERATE ME!
YOU? ME!
UGH. I'M LEAVING. IT'S MY ENTITLED, BRATTY GREAT-GREAT-GREAT-GREAT-GREAT-GRANDDAUGHTER...

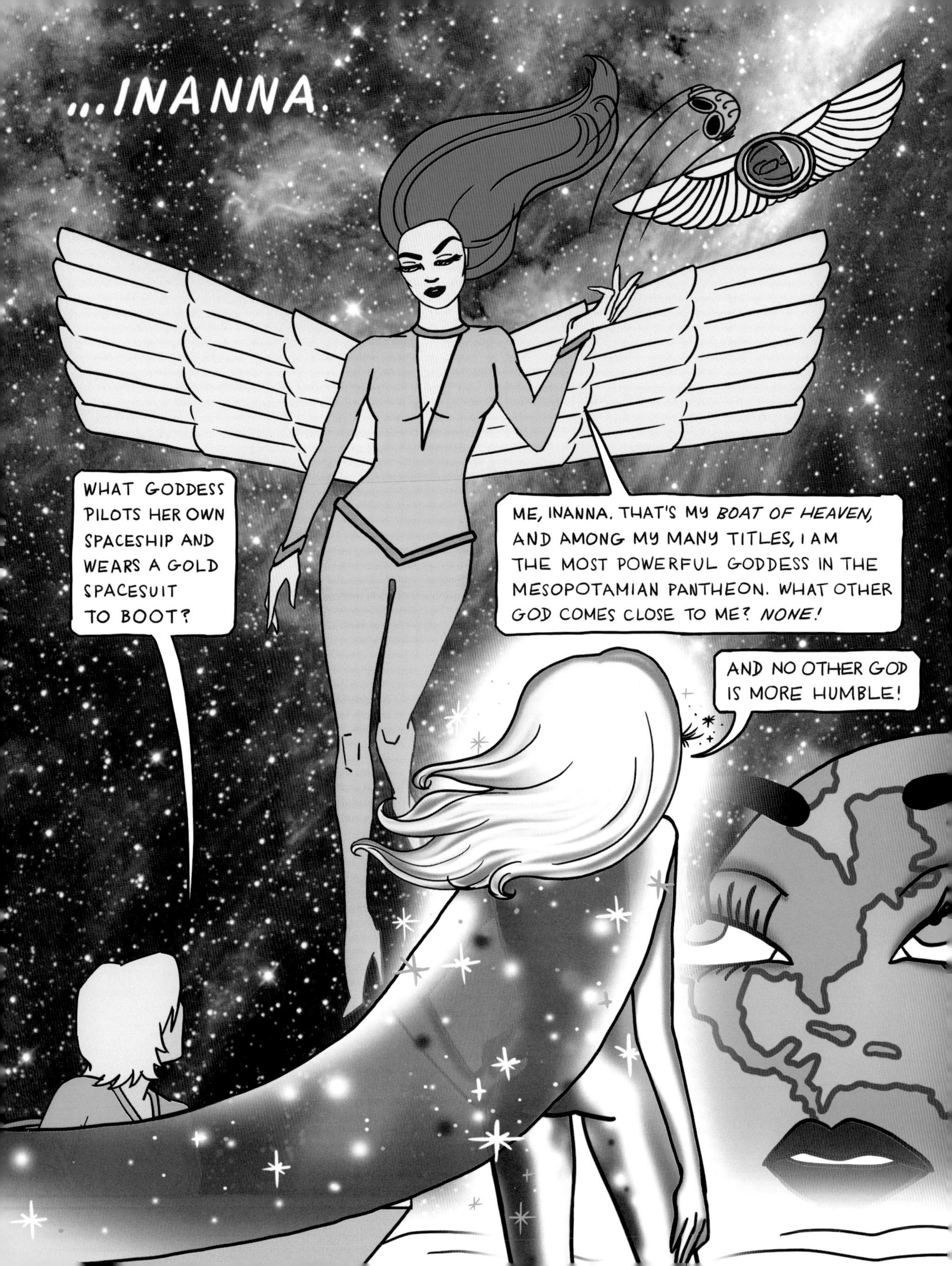
...INANNA.
WHAT GODDESS PILOTS HER OWN SPACESHIP AND WEARS A GOLD SPACESUIT TO BOOT?
ME, INANNA. THAT'S MY *BOAT OF HEAVEN,* AND AMONG MY MANY TITLES, I AM THE MOST POWERFUL GODDESS IN THE MESOPOTAMIAN PANTHEON. WHAT OTHER GOD COMES CLOSE TO ME? *NONE!*
AND NO OTHER GOD IS MORE HUMBLE!

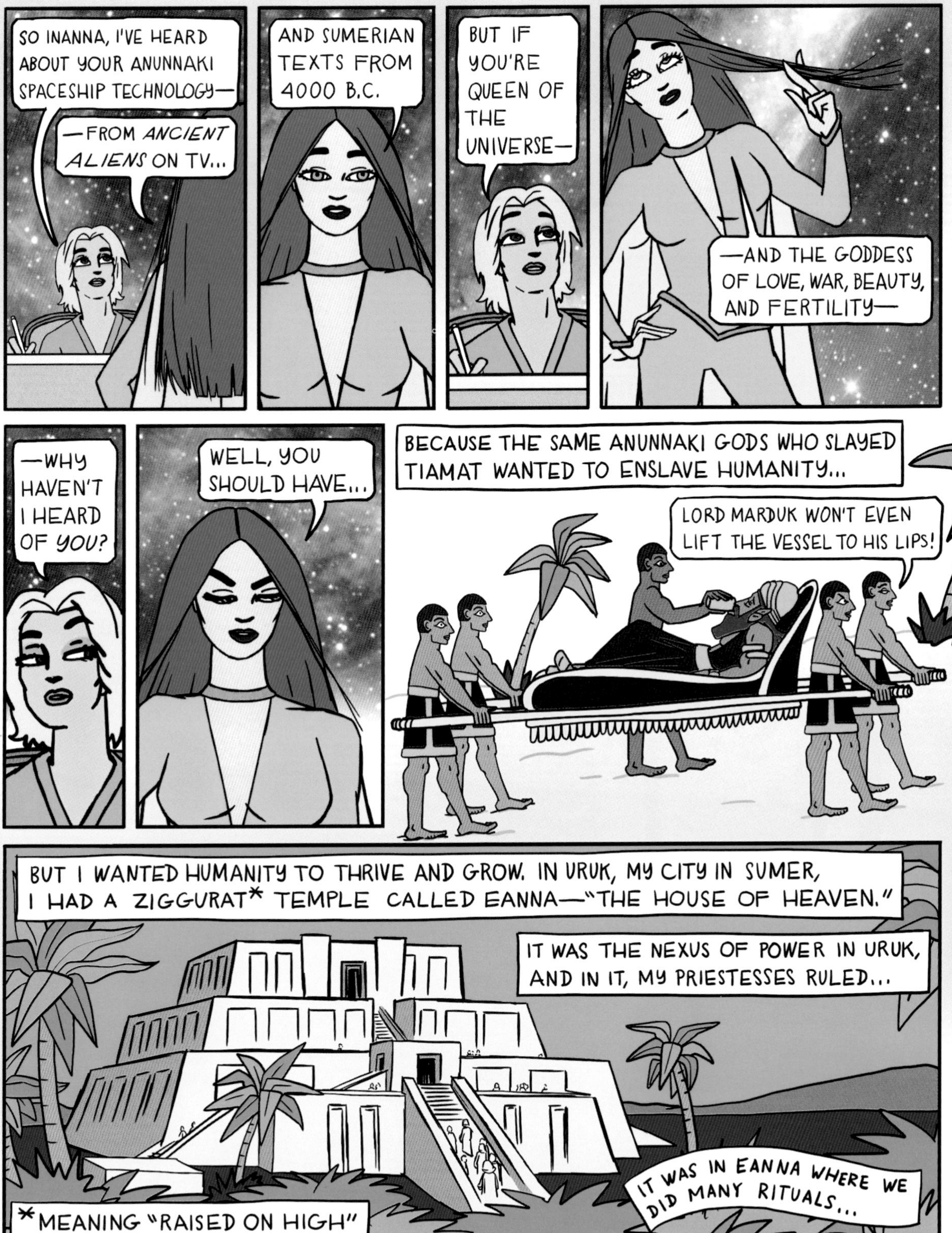

SO INANNA, I'VE HEARD ABOUT YOUR ANUNNAKI SPACESHIP TECHNOLOGY—
—FROM *ANCIENT ALIENS* ON TV...
AND SUMERIAN TEXTS FROM 4000 B.C.
BUT IF YOU'RE QUEEN OF THE UNIVERSE—
—AND THE GODDESS OF LOVE, WAR, BEAUTY, AND FERTILITY—
—WHY HAVEN'T I HEARD OF *YOU*?
WELL, YOU SHOULD HAVE...
BECAUSE THE SAME ANUNNAKI GODS WHO SLAYED TIAMAT WANTED TO ENSLAVE HUMANITY...
LORD MARDUK WON'T EVEN LIFT THE VESSEL TO HIS LIPS!
BUT I WANTED HUMANITY TO THRIVE AND GROW. IN URUK, MY CITY IN SUMER, I HAD A ZIGGURAT* TEMPLE CALLED EANNA—"THE HOUSE OF HEAVEN."
IT WAS THE NEXUS OF POWER IN URUK, AND IN IT, MY PRIESTESSES RULED...
IT WAS IN EANNA WHERE WE DID MANY RITUALS...
*MEANING "RAISED ON HIGH"

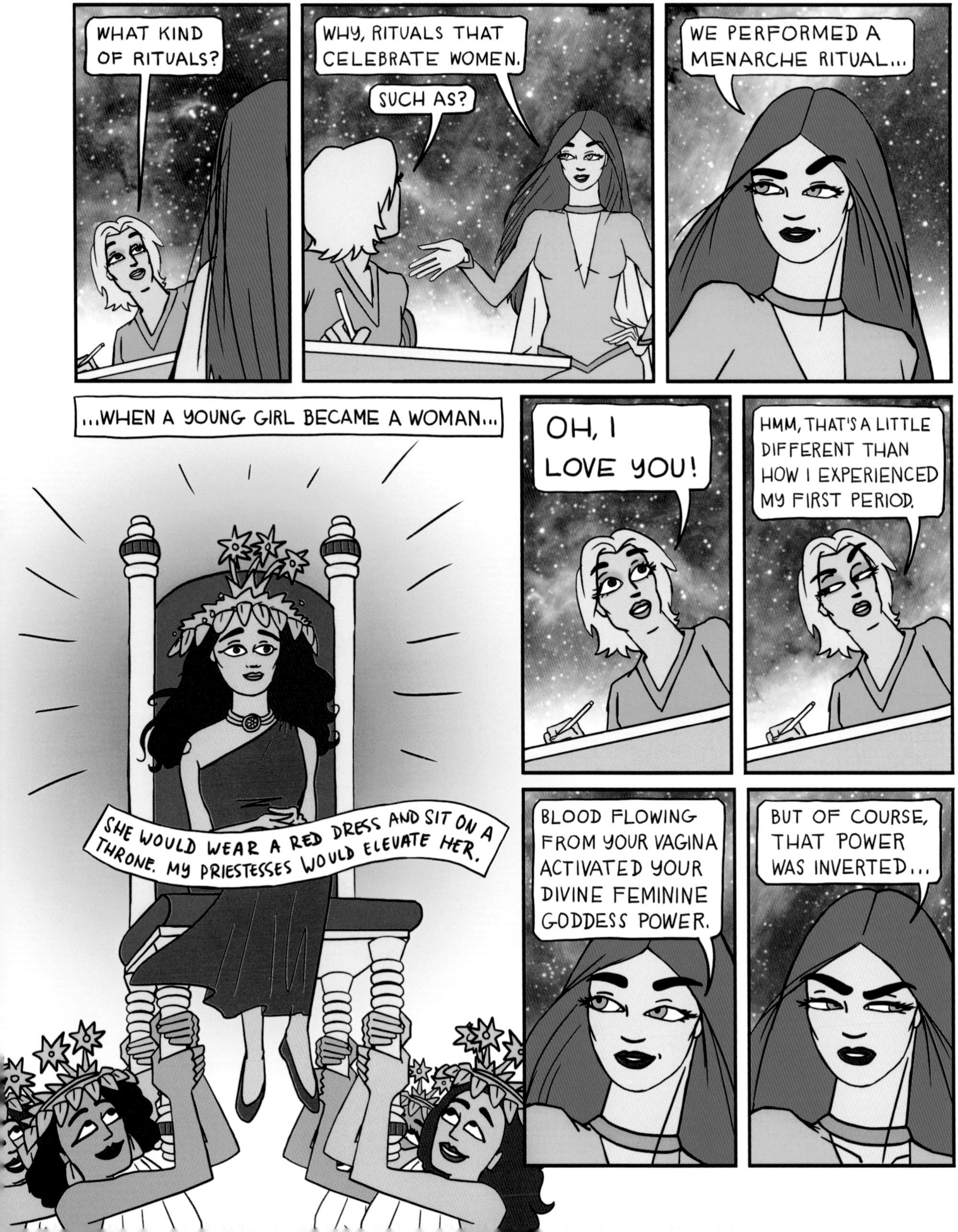
WHAT KIND OF RITUALS?
WHY, RITUALS THAT CELEBRATE WOMEN.
SUCH AS?
WE PERFORMED A MENARCHE RITUAL...
...WHEN A YOUNG GIRL BECAME A WOMAN...
SHE WOULD WEAR A RED DRESS AND SIT ON A THRONE. MY PRIESTESSES WOULD ELEVATE HER.
OH, I LOVE YOU!
HMM, THAT'S A LITTLE DIFFERENT THAN HOW I EXPERIENCED MY FIRST PERIOD.
BLOOD FLOWING FROM YOUR VAGINA ACTIVATED YOUR DIVINE FEMININE GODDESS POWER.
BUT OF COURSE, THAT POWER WAS INVERTED...

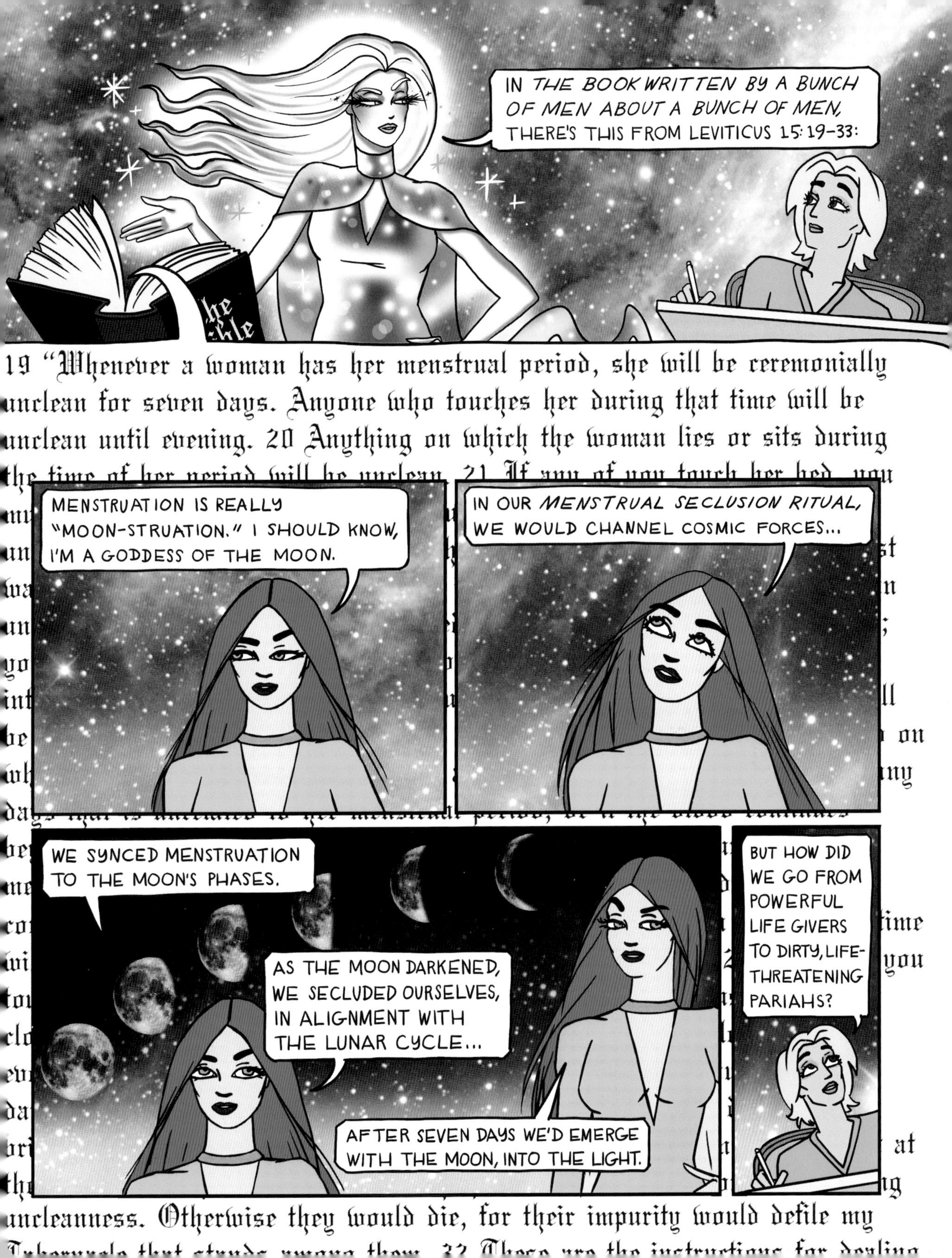
IN THE BOOK WRITTEN BY A BUNCH OF MEN ABOUT A BUNCH OF MEN, THERE'S THIS FROM LEVITICUS 15:19–33:
The Bible
19 "Whenever a woman has her menstrual period, she will be ceremonially
unclean for seven days. Anyone who touches her during that time will be
unclean until evening. 20 Anything on which the woman lies or sits during
MENSTRUATION IS REALLY "MOON-STRUATION." I SHOULD KNOW, I'M A GODDESS OF THE MOON.
IN OUR MENSTRUAL SECLUSION RITUAL, WE WOULD CHANNEL COSMIC FORCES...
WE SYNCED MENSTRUATION TO THE MOON'S PHASES.
AS THE MOON DARKENED, WE SECLUDED OURSELVES, IN ALIGNMENT WITH THE LUNAR CYCLE...
AFTER SEVEN DAYS WE'D EMERGE WITH THE MOON, INTO THE LIGHT.
BUT HOW DID WE GO FROM POWERFUL LIFE GIVERS TO DIRTY, LIFE-THREATENING PARIAHS?
uncleanness. Otherwise they would die, for their impurity would defile my

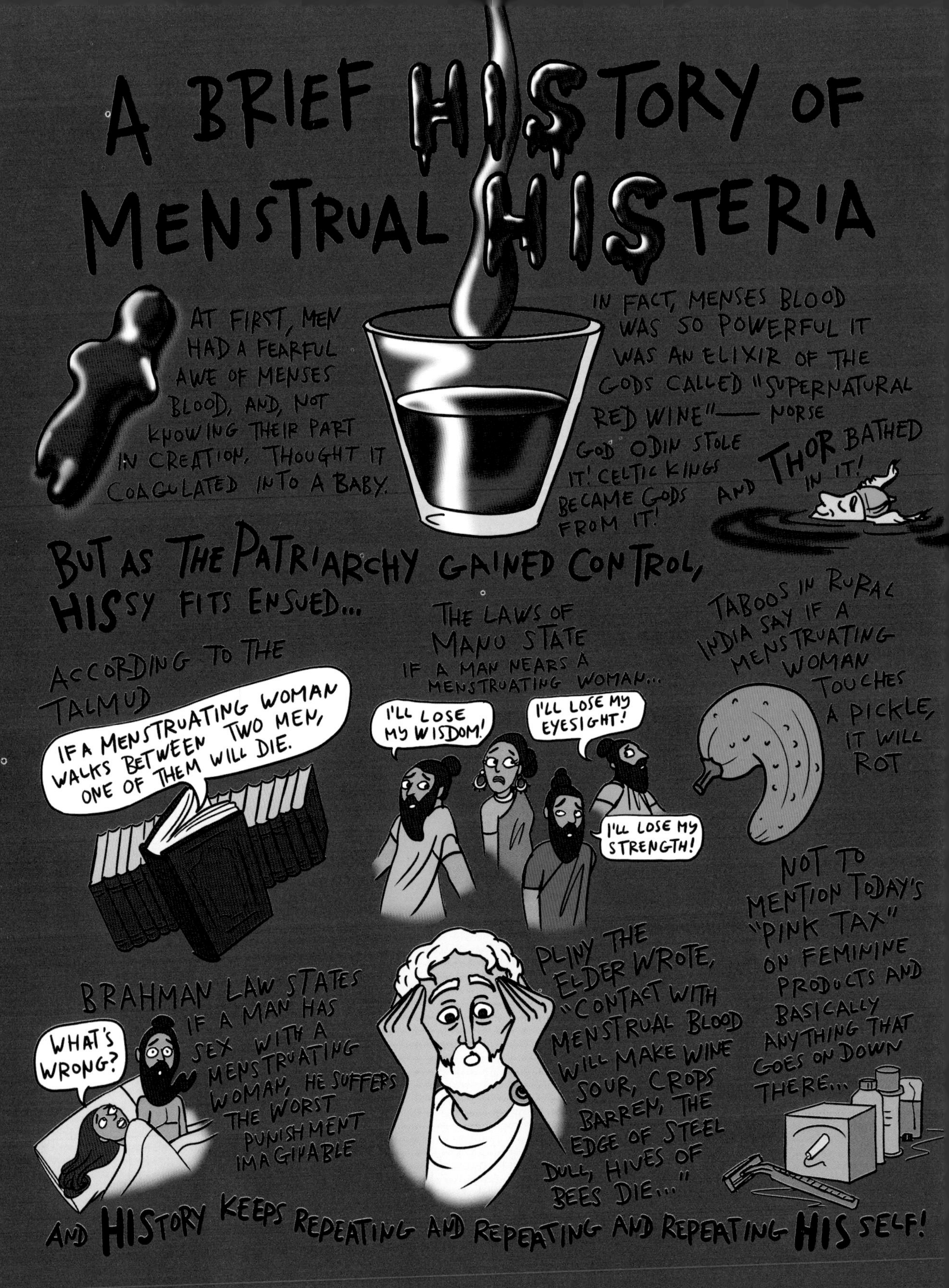
A BRIEF HISTORY OF MENSTRUAL HISTERIA
AT FIRST, MEN HAD A FEARFUL AWE OF MENSES BLOOD, AND, NOT KNOWING THEIR PART IN CREATION, THOUGHT IT COAGULATED INTO A BABY.
IN FACT, MENSES BLOOD WAS SO POWERFUL IT WAS AN ELIXIR OF THE GODS CALLED "SUPERNATURAL RED WINE"— NORSE GOD ODIN STOLE IT! CELTIC KINGS BECAME GODS FROM IT!
AND THOR BATHED IN IT!
BUT AS THE PATRIARCHY GAINED CONTROL, HISSY FITS ENSUED...
ACCORDING TO THE TALMUD
IF A MENSTRUATING WOMAN WALKS BETWEEN TWO MEN, ONE OF THEM WILL DIE.
THE LAWS OF MANU STATE IF A MAN NEARS A MENSTRUATING WOMAN...
I'LL LOSE MY WISDOM!
I'LL LOSE MY EYESIGHT!
I'LL LOSE MY STRENGTH!
TABOOS IN RURAL INDIA SAY IF A MENSTRUATING WOMAN TOUCHES A PICKLE, IT WILL ROT
BRAHMAN LAW STATES IF A MAN HAS SEX WITH A MENSTRUATING WOMAN, HE SUFFERS THE WORST PUNISHMENT IMAGINABLE
WHAT'S WRONG?
PLINY THE ELDER WROTE, "CONTACT WITH MENSTRUAL BLOOD WILL MAKE WINE SOUR, CROPS BARREN, THE EDGE OF STEEL DULL, HIVES OF BEES DIE..."
NOT TO MENTION TODAY'S "PINK TAX" ON FEMININE PRODUCTS AND BASICALLY ANYTHING THAT GOES ON DOWN THERE...
AND HISTORY KEEPS REPEATING AND REPEATING AND REPEATING HIS SELF!

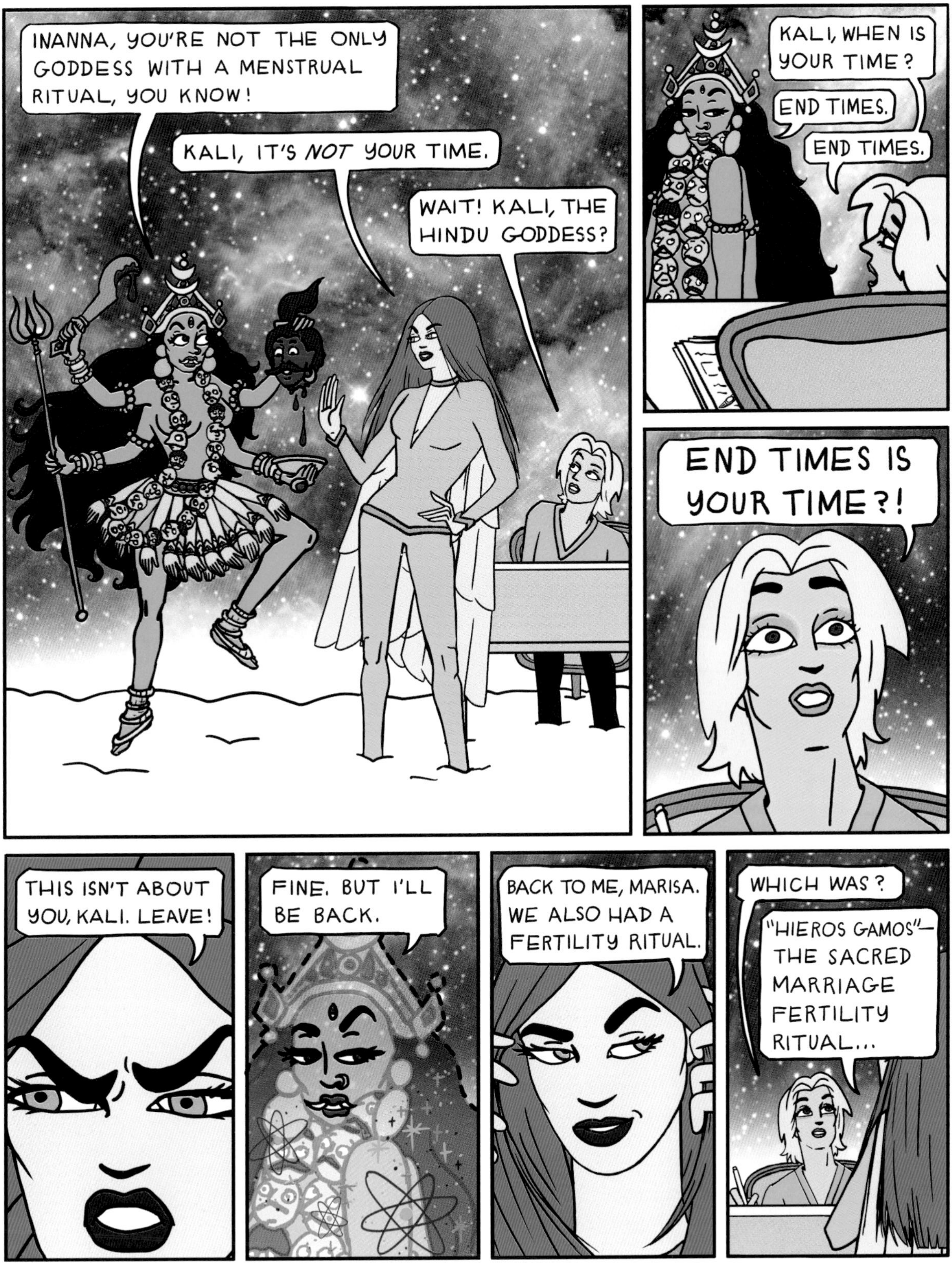
INANNA, YOU'RE NOT THE ONLY GODDESS WITH A MENSTRUAL RITUAL, YOU KNOW!
KALI, IT'S *NOT* YOUR TIME.
WAIT! KALI, THE HINDU GODDESS?
KALI, WHEN IS YOUR TIME?
END TIMES.
END TIMES.
END TIMES IS YOUR TIME?!
THIS ISN'T ABOUT YOU, KALI. LEAVE!
FINE. BUT I'LL BE BACK.
BACK TO ME, MARISA. WE ALSO HAD A FERTILITY RITUAL.
WHICH WAS?
"HIEROS GAMOS"— THE SACRED MARRIAGE FERTILITY RITUAL...

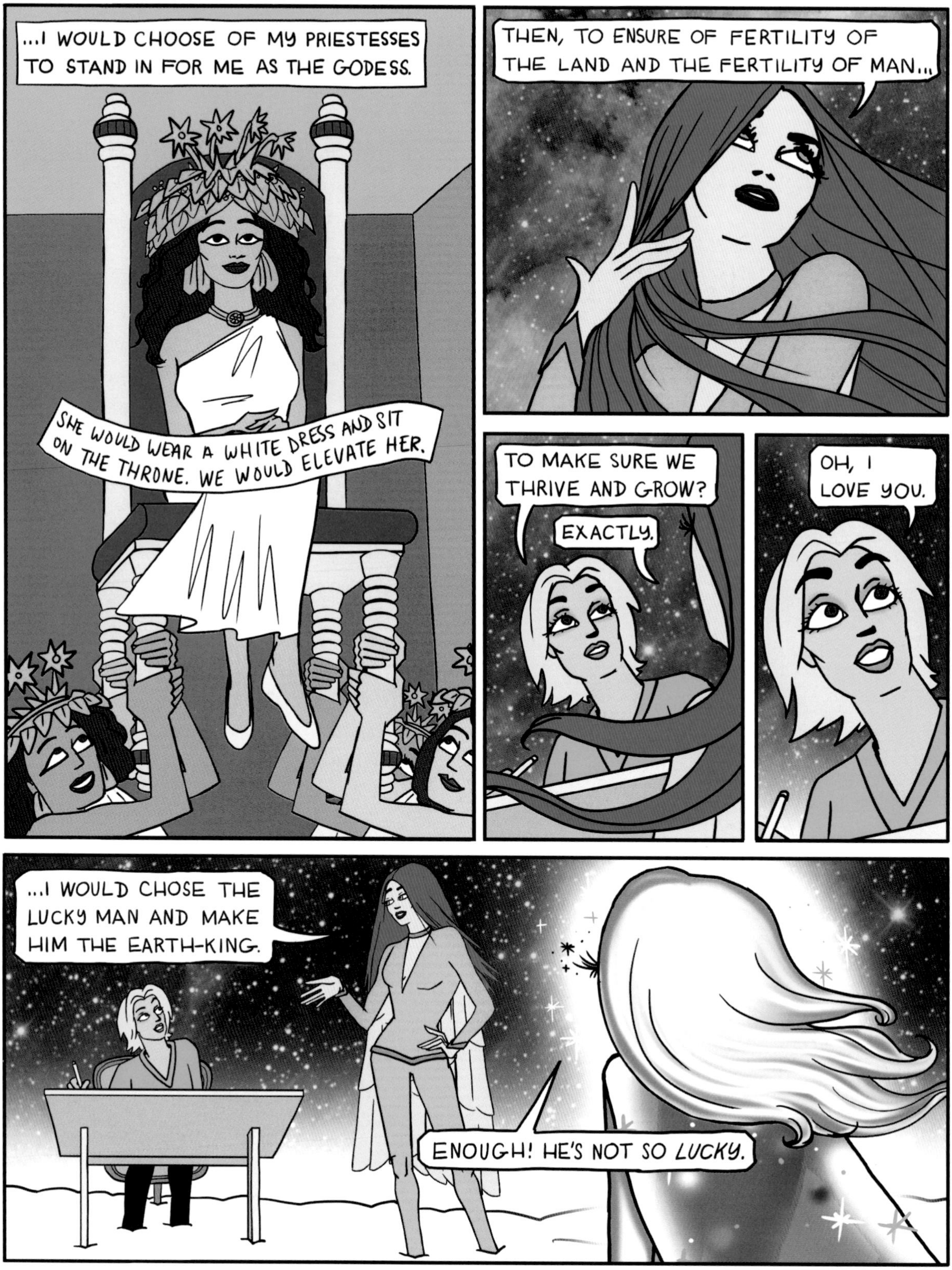
...I WOULD CHOOSE OF MY PRIESTESSES TO STAND IN FOR ME AS THE GODESS.
SHE WOULD WEAR A WHITE DRESS AND SIT ON THE THRONE. WE WOULD ELEVATE HER.
THEN, TO ENSURE OF FERTILITY OF THE LAND AND THE FERTILITY OF MAN...
TO MAKE SURE WE THRIVE AND GROW?
EXACTLY.
OH, I LOVE YOU.
...I WOULD CHOSE THE LUCKY MAN AND MAKE HIM THE EARTH-KING.
ENOUGH! HE'S NOT SO *LUCKY*.

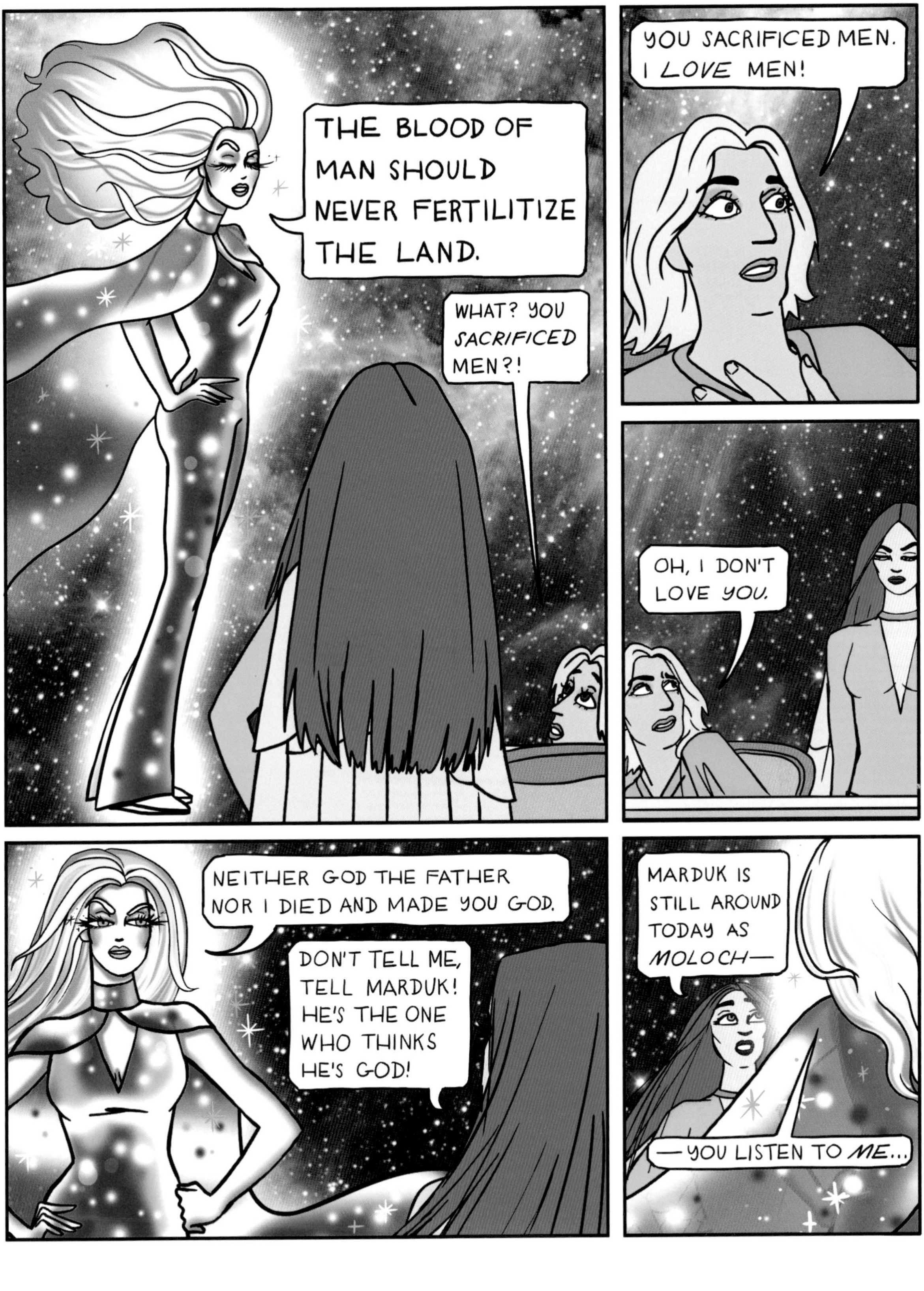
THE BLOOD OF MAN SHOULD NEVER FERTILITIZE THE LAND.
WHAT? YOU SACRIFICED MEN?!
YOU SACRIFICED MEN. I LOVE MEN!
OH, I DON'T LOVE YOU.
NEITHER GOD THE FATHER NOR I DIED AND MADE YOU GOD.
DON'T TELL ME, TELL MARDUK! HE'S THE ONE WHO THINKS HE'S GOD!
MARDUK IS STILL AROUND TODAY AS MOLOCH—
—YOU LISTEN TO ME...

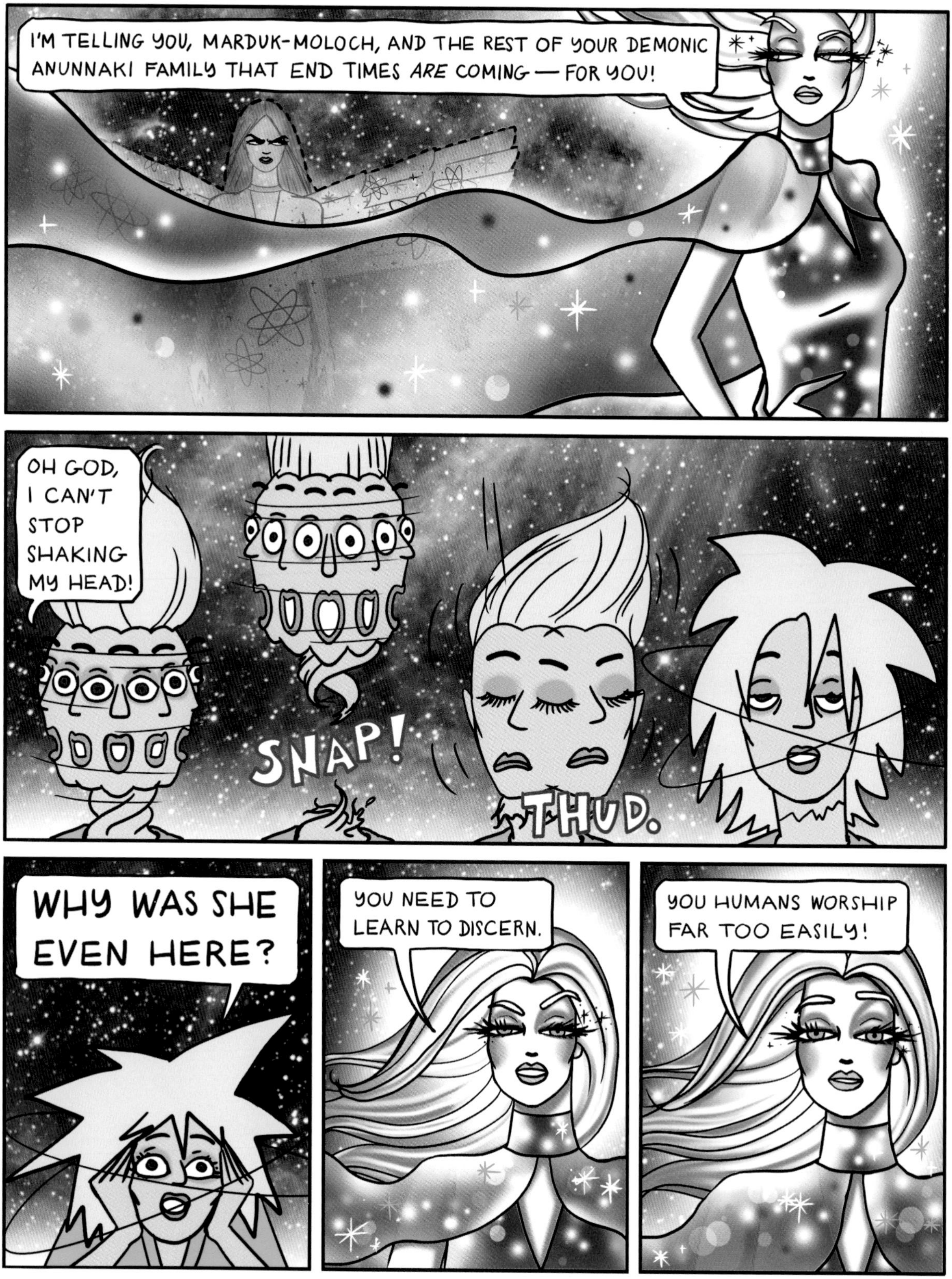
I'M TELLING YOU, MARDUK-MOLOCH, AND THE REST OF YOUR DEMONIC ANUNNAKI FAMILY THAT END TIMES *ARE* COMING — FOR YOU!
OH GOD, I CAN'T STOP SHAKING MY HEAD!
SNAP!
THUD.
WHY WAS SHE EVEN HERE?
YOU NEED TO LEARN TO DISCERN.
YOU HUMANS WORSHIP FAR TOO EASILY!

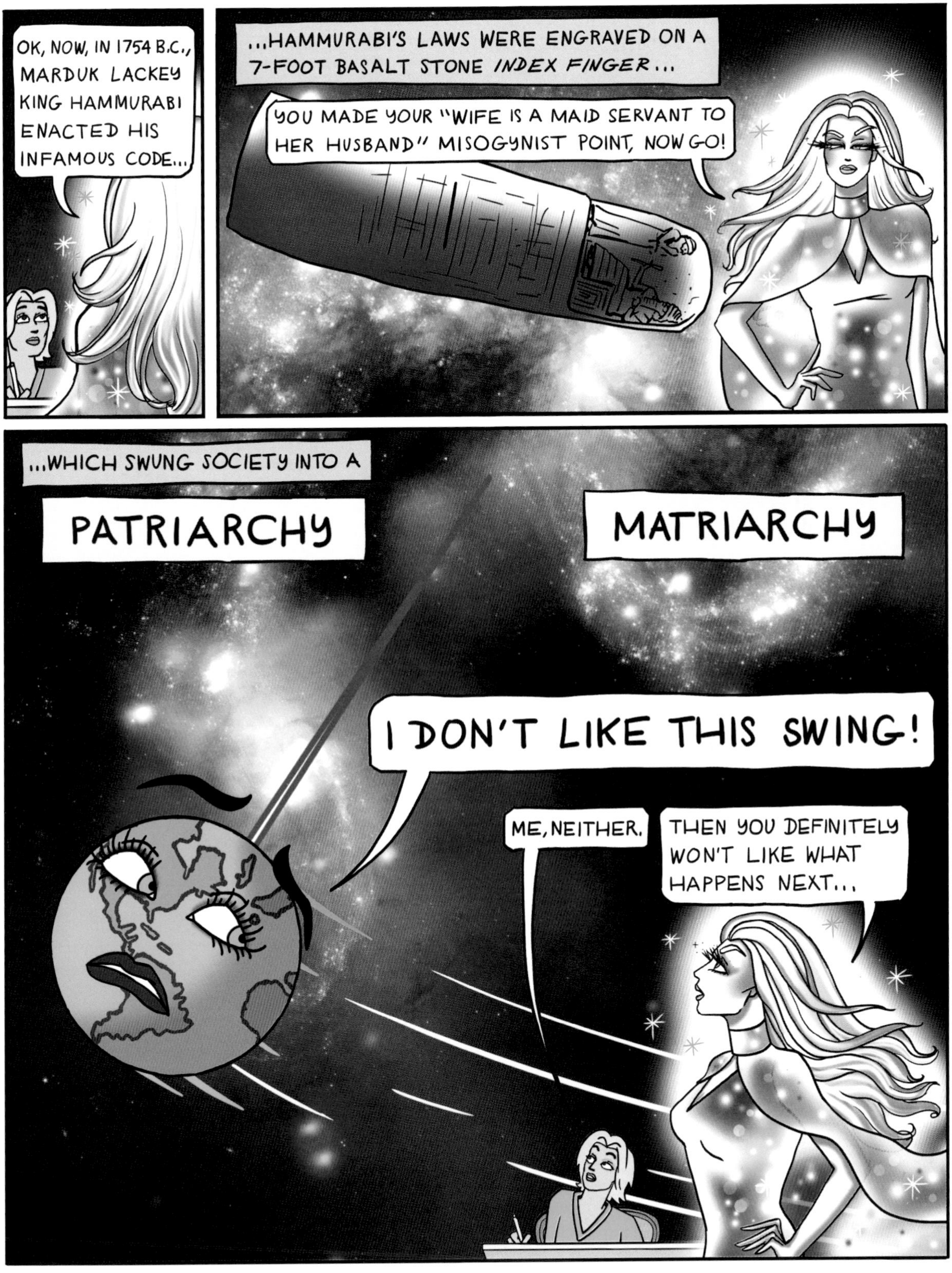
OK, NOW, IN 1754 B.C., MARDUK LACKEY KING HAMMURABI ENACTED HIS INFAMOUS CODE...
...HAMMURABI'S LAWS WERE ENGRAVED ON A 7-FOOT BASALT STONE *INDEX FINGER*...
YOU MADE YOUR "WIFE IS A MAID SERVANT TO HER HUSBAND" MISOGYNIST POINT, NOW GO!
...WHICH SWUNG SOCIETY INTO A
PATRIARCHY
MATRIARCHY
I DON'T LIKE THIS SWING!
ME, NEITHER.
THEN YOU DEFINITELY WON'T LIKE WHAT HAPPENS NEXT...

POWER-HUNGRY MARDUK...

...BECAME HEAD OF THE EGYPTIAN PANTHEON, *RA*.

SAME GOD—DIFFERENT BODY.

SAME ANUNNAKI SPACESHIP TECHNOLOGY.

RA ERECTED *OBELISKS* ALL OVER EGYPT. THE OBELISKS, CUT FROM ELECTRICALLY RESONANT GRANITE, TOPPED WITH PYRAMID TRANSMITTERS, TRANSMITTED...

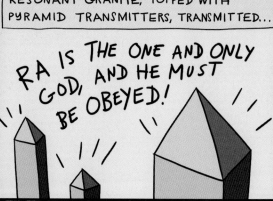

RA IS THE ONE AND ONLY GOD, AND HE MUST BE OBEYED!

...FROM THE TRANSMISSIONS, AN ELECTRIC SHROUD WAS FORMED, CLOUDING HUMANITY'S MIND INTO A SUBMISSIVE STATE...

RA IS THE ONE AND ONLY GOD, AND HE MUST BE OBEYED!

...UNTIL IT DIDN'T.

RA IS SO OLD! HE IS AS BRITTLE AS DRIED PAPYRUS!

HIS FLESH IS SALLOW LIKE SAFFRON!

HE HAS ONE FOOT IN THE SARCOPHAGUS!

HA! HA!

HA! HA! HA!

HA! HA!

MAN REBELS. WHAT DOES A GOD DO?

FROM HIS TERRIBLE GLANCE...

OUT OF THE *EYE OF RA*...

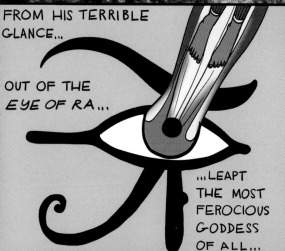

...LEAPT THE MOST FEROCIOUS GODDESS OF ALL...

...HIS DAUGHTER.

I WAS A SUPERNATURAL-BORN KILLER.

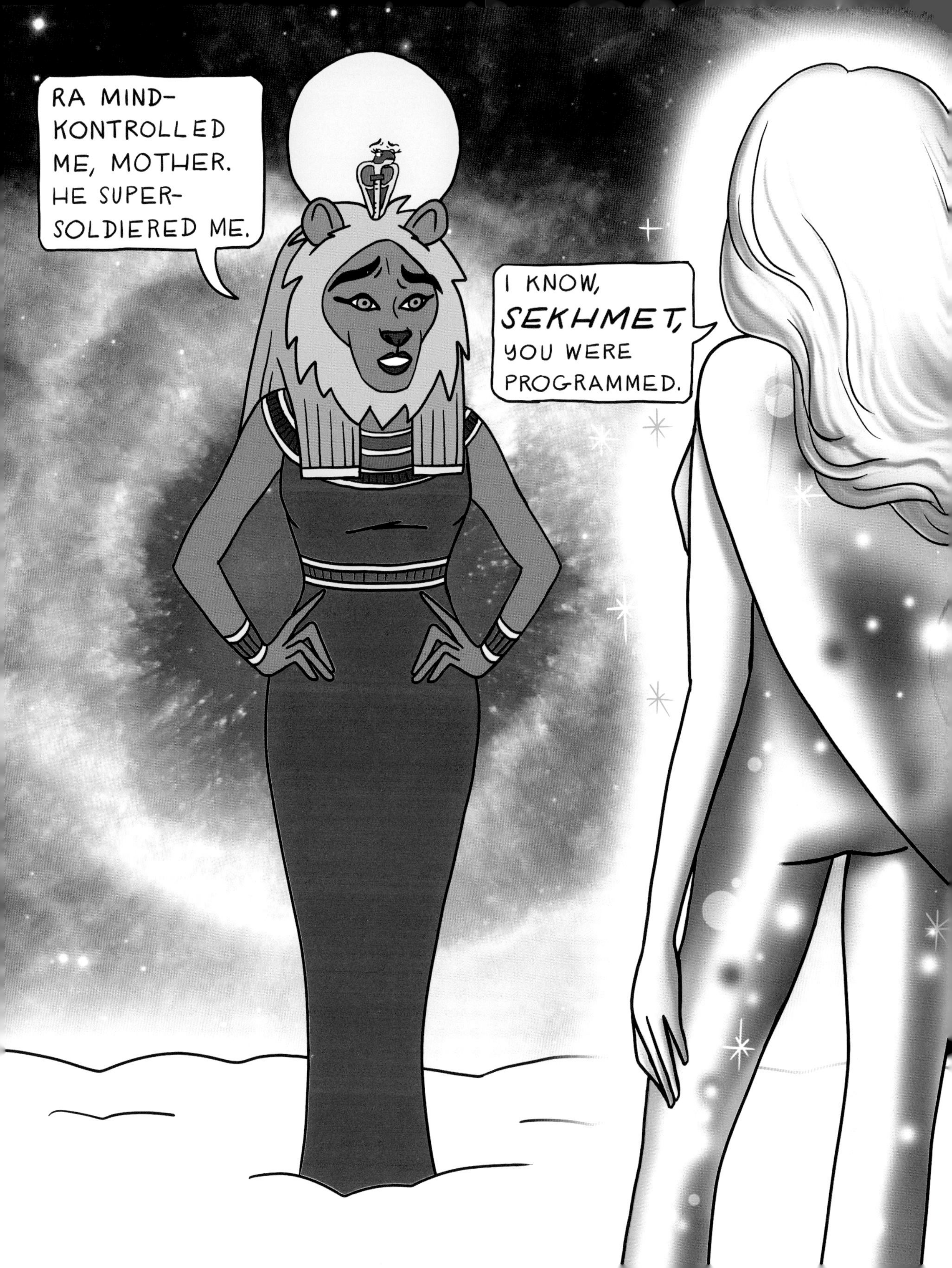
RA MIND-KONTROLLED ME, MOTHER. HE SUPER-SOLDIERED ME.
I KNOW, SEKHMET, YOU WERE PROGRAMMED.

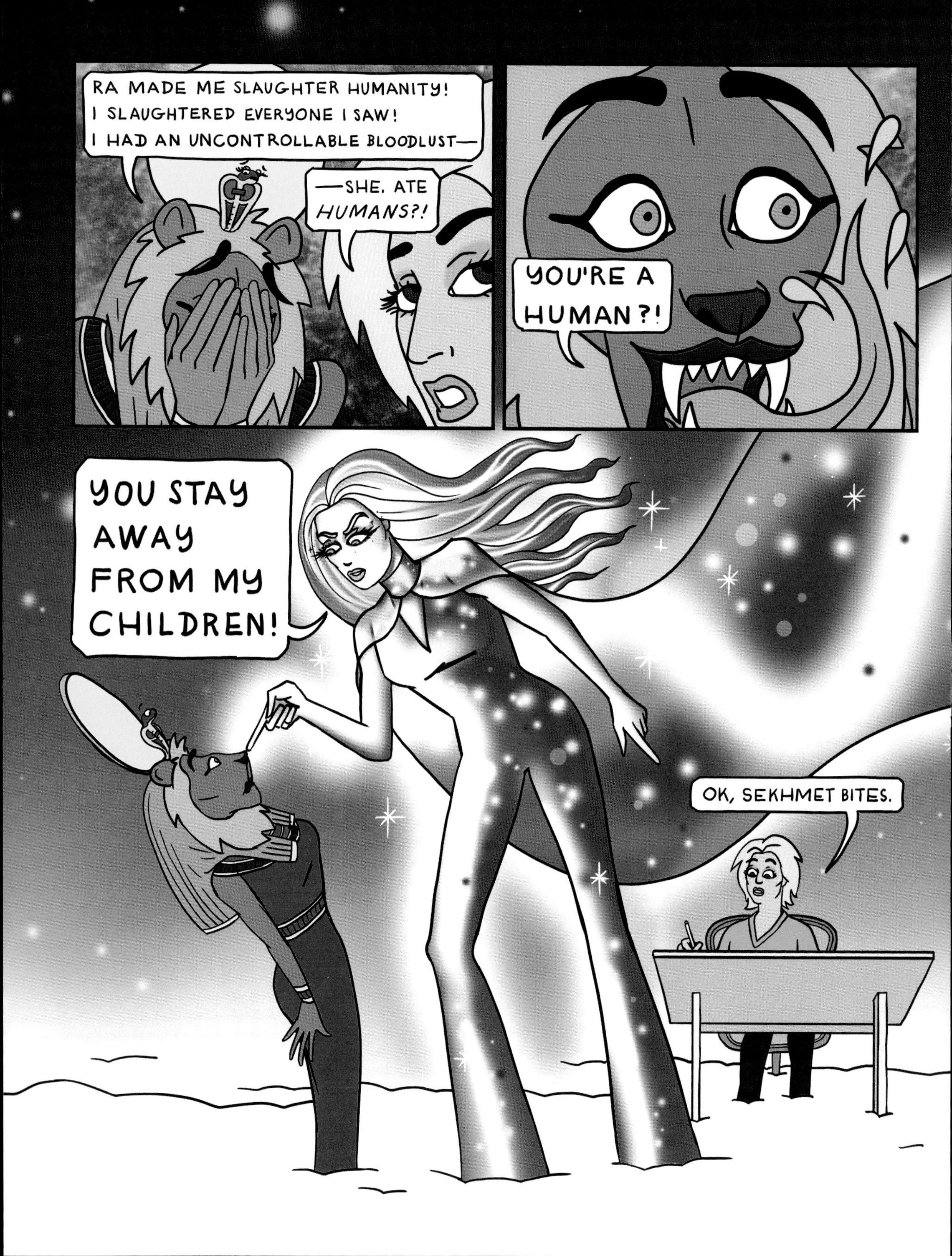
RA MADE ME SLAUGHTER HUMANITY! I SLAUGHTERED EVERYONE I SAW! I HAD AN UNCONTROLLABLE BLOODLUST—
—SHE. ATE *HUMANS?!*
YOU'RE A HUMAN?!
YOU STAY AWAY FROM MY CHILDREN!
OK, SEKHMET BITES.

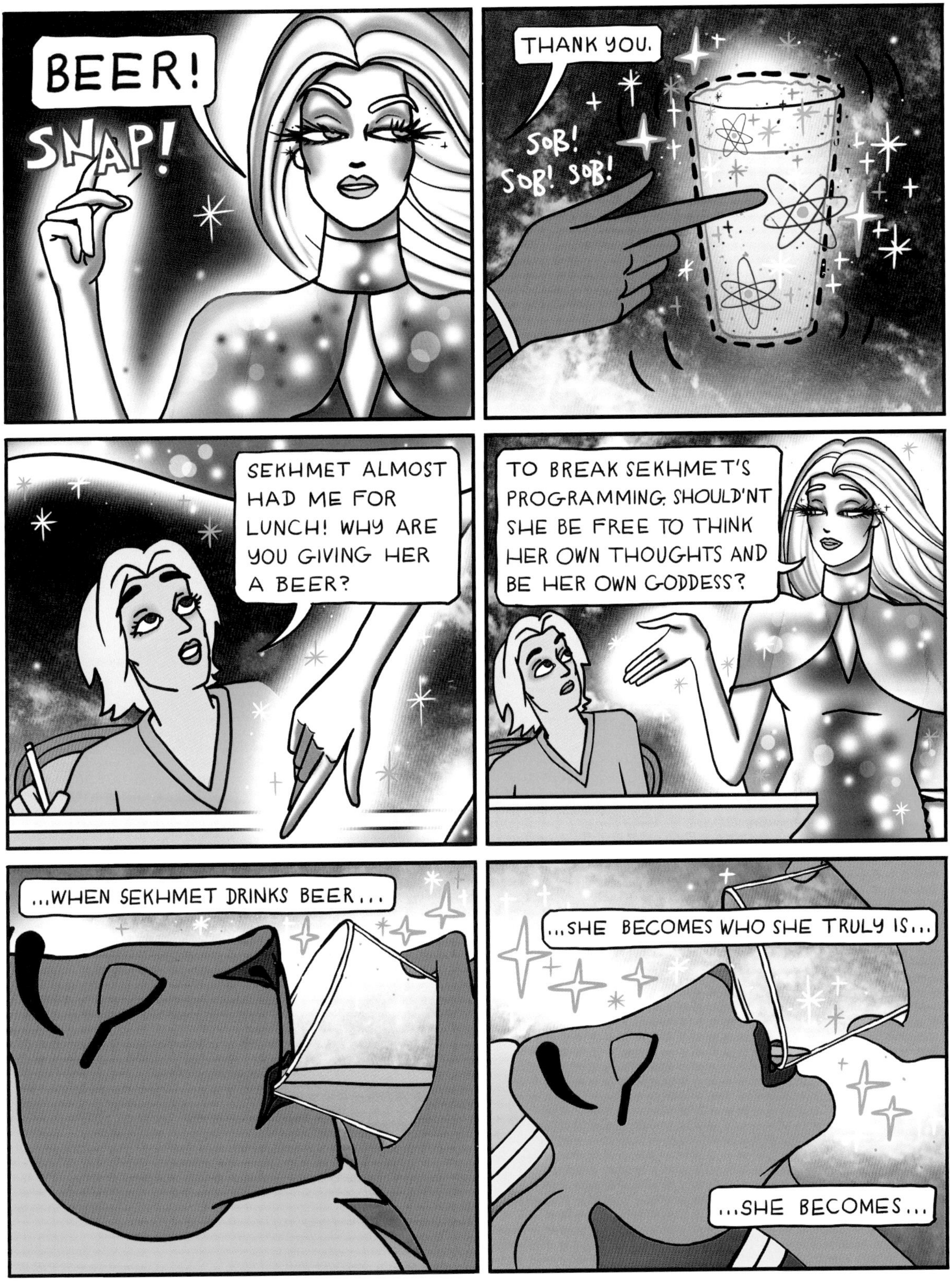
BEER!
SNAP!
THANK YOU.
SOB! SOB! SOB!
SEKHMET ALMOST HAD ME FOR LUNCH! WHY ARE YOU GIVING HER A BEER?
TO BREAK SEKHMET'S PROGRAMMING, SHOULD'NT SHE BE FREE TO THINK HER OWN THOUGHTS AND BE HER OWN GODDESS?
...WHEN SEKHMET DRINKS BEER...
...SHE BECOMES WHO SHE TRULY IS...
...SHE BECOMES...

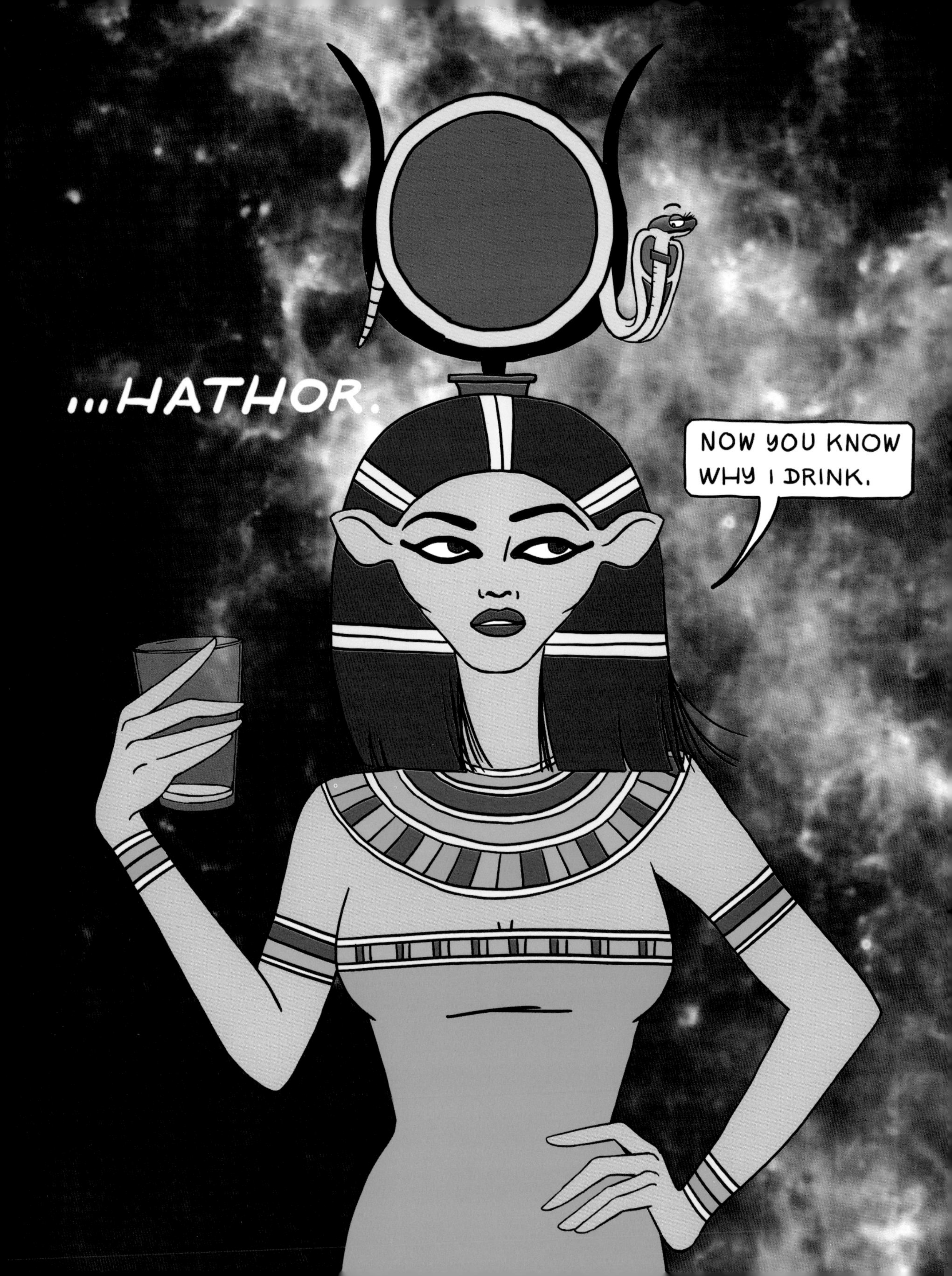
...HATHOR.
NOW YOU KNOW WHY I DRINK.

Panel 1:

I'M SORRY, THAT WASN'T ME.

AS LONG AS YOU'RE HATHOR, WE'RE COOL.

Panel 2:

I AM THE LADY OF JUBILATION! THE LADY OF DANCING! THE LADY OF MUSIC!

Panel 3:

BACK IN THE DAY, YOU'D FIND ME IN ONE OF MY HATHOR TEMPLES—

THE HOUSE OF INTOXICATION AND ENJOYMENT...

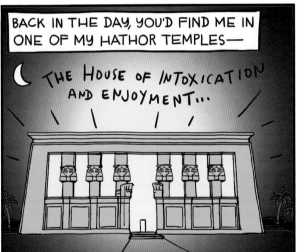

Panel 4:

DANCING WITH MY PRIESTESSES AND MY HATHOR BALDIE PRIESTS, RATTLING OUR HATHOR SISTRA IN FULL BACCHANALIA.

I AM THE LADY OF UNENDING DRUNKENNESS

Panel 5:

I'M ALSO THE GODDESS OF BEAUTY AND MAKEUP...

BUT MY HATHOR MAGIC MIRROR ISN'T JUST *ANY* MIRROR... ...IT'S A DIVINER THAT SEES ALL AND REVEALS IT.

Panel 6:

AND I'M THE PROTECTRESS OF MOTHERS— WHILE GIVING BIRTH THEY'D HAVE EACH FOOT ON A HATHOR BIRTHING BRICK...

...INVOKING MY HELP—I'M ALSO THE MISTRESS OF LIFE.

ME →   ← ME

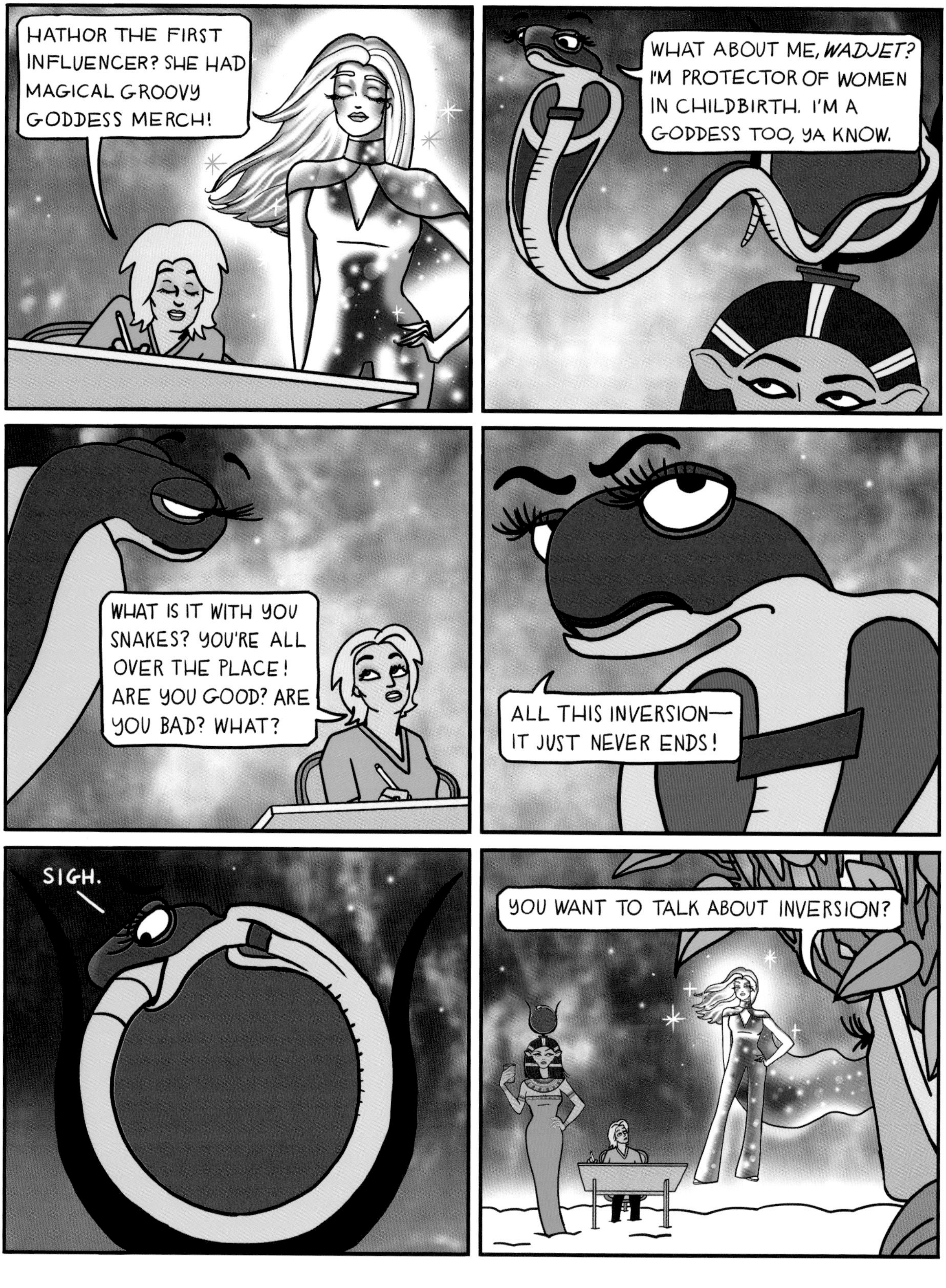
HATHOR THE FIRST INFLUENCER? SHE HAD MAGICAL GROOVY GODDESS MERCH!
WHAT ABOUT ME, *WADJET*? I'M PROTECTOR OF WOMEN IN CHILDBIRTH. I'M A GODDESS TOO, YA KNOW.
WHAT IS IT WITH YOU SNAKES? YOU'RE ALL OVER THE PLACE! ARE YOU GOOD? ARE YOU BAD? WHAT?
ALL THIS INVERSION— IT JUST NEVER ENDS!
SIGH.
YOU WANT TO TALK ABOUT INVERSION?

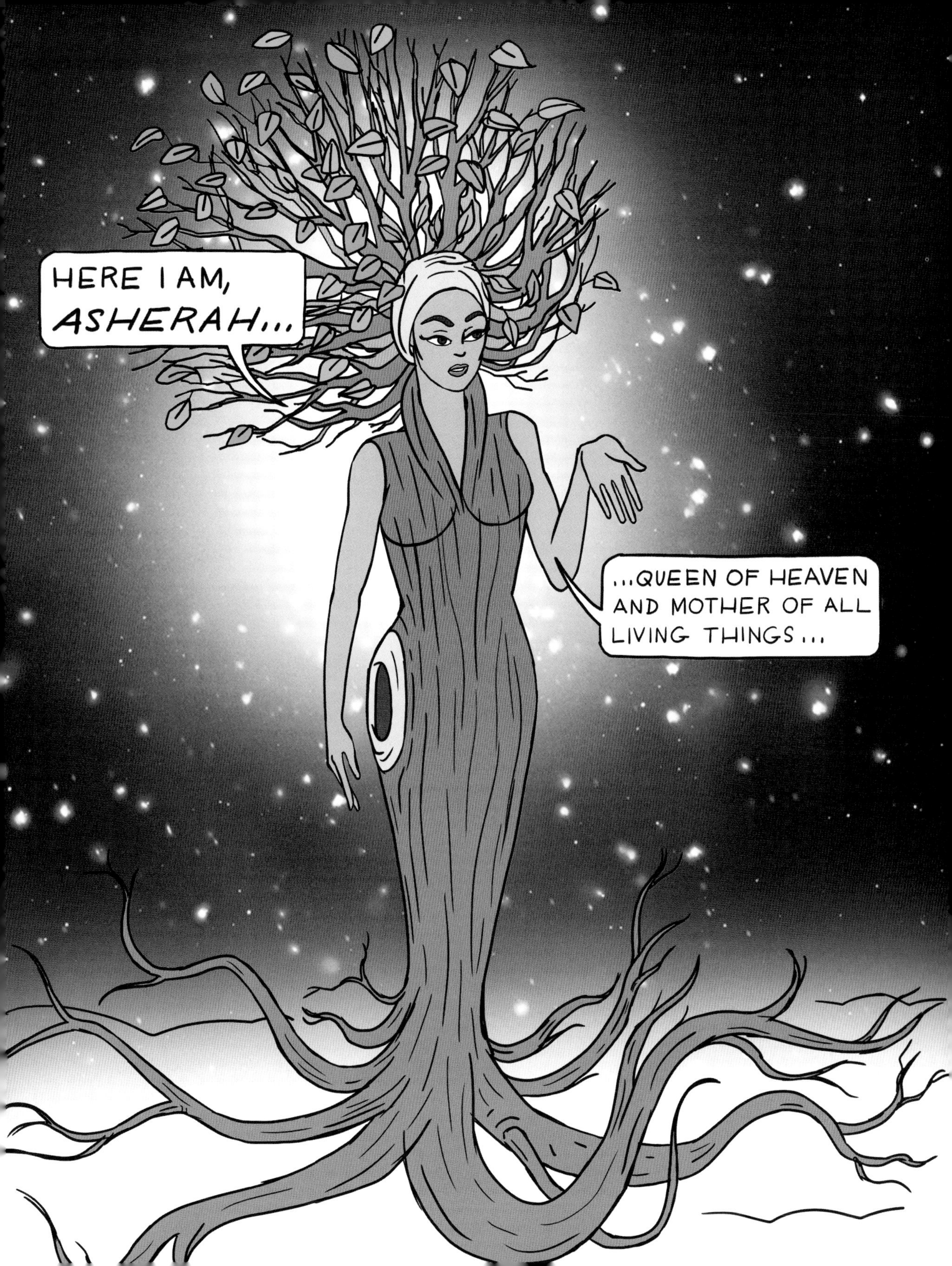
HERE I AM, *ASHERAH*...
...QUEEN OF HEAVEN AND MOTHER OF ALL LIVING THINGS...

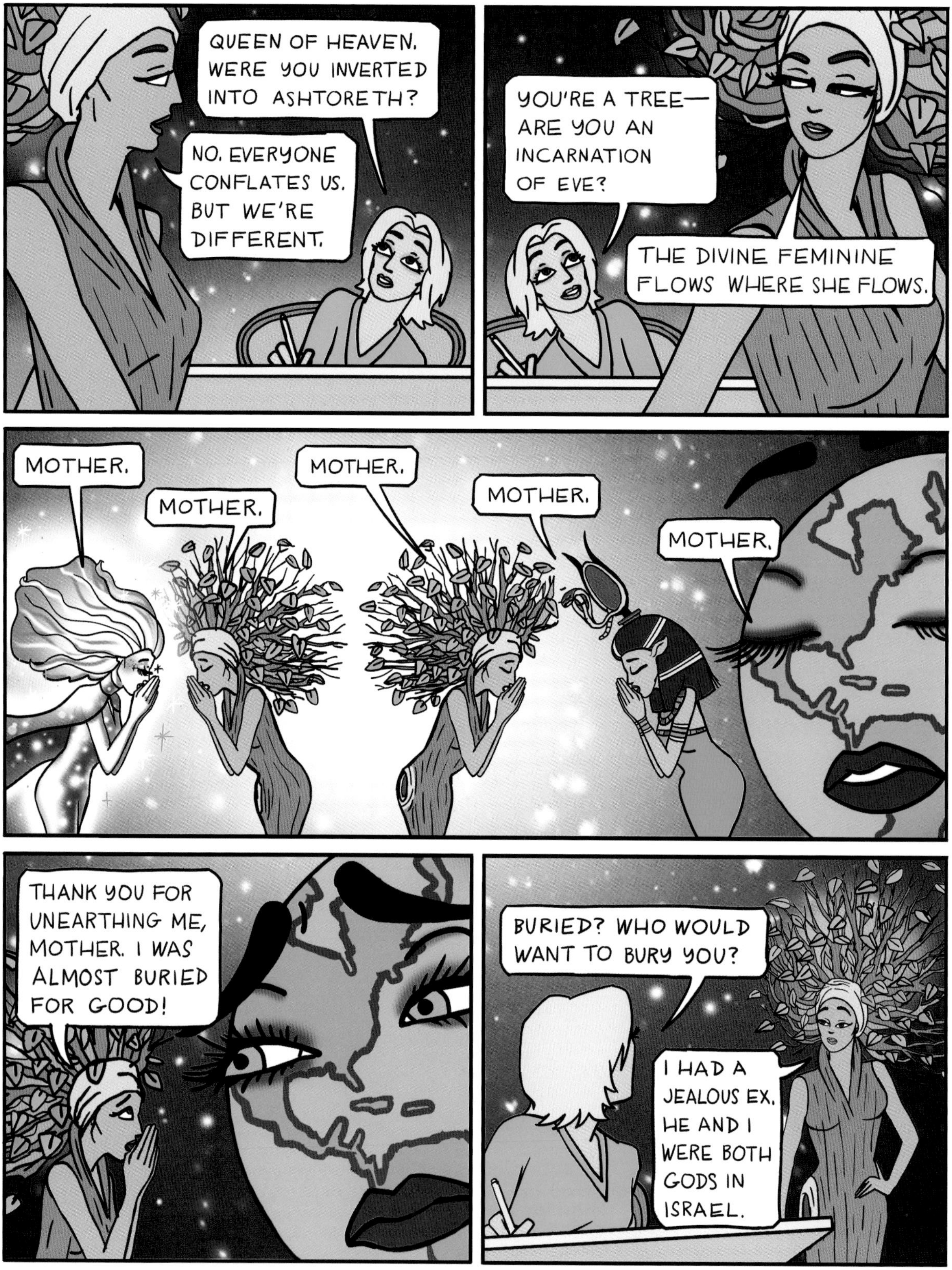
QUEEN OF HEAVEN. WERE YOU INVERTED INTO ASHTORETH?
NO. EVERYONE CONFLATES US. BUT WE'RE DIFFERENT.
YOU'RE A TREE— ARE YOU AN INCARNATION OF EVE?
THE DIVINE FEMININE FLOWS WHERE SHE FLOWS.
MOTHER.
MOTHER.
MOTHER.
MOTHER.
MOTHER.
THANK YOU FOR UNEARTHING ME, MOTHER. I WAS ALMOST BURIED FOR GOOD!
BURIED? WHO WOULD WANT TO BURY YOU?
I HAD A JEALOUS EX. HE AND I WERE BOTH GODS IN ISRAEL.

ISRAEL? HAD TWO GODS?!

"YAHWEH AND HIS ASHERAH." AT FIRST, WE WERE BOTH WORSHIPPED...

...BUT WHEN TEMPLES WERE BUILT IN MY HONOR...

...AND WOMEN BAKED CAKES AND MADE TAPESTRIES IN MY IMAGE...

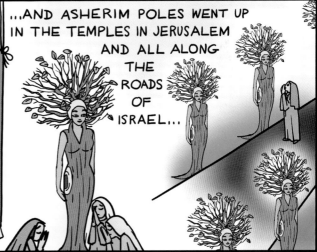

...AND ASHERIM POLES WENT UP IN THE TEMPLES IN JERUSALEM AND ALL ALONG THE ROADS OF ISRAEL...

...SUDDENLY THE PEOPLE IN MY TEMPLES WERE ALL SLAUGHTERED...

...EVERY ONE OF MY TEMPLES WERE DESTROYED...

...THE ASHERIM WERE ALL BURNT TO ASH...

...AND THE CHILDREN OF ISRAEL LOST ME, THEIR MOTHER, WHO WAS INVERTED INTO AN ABOMINATION...

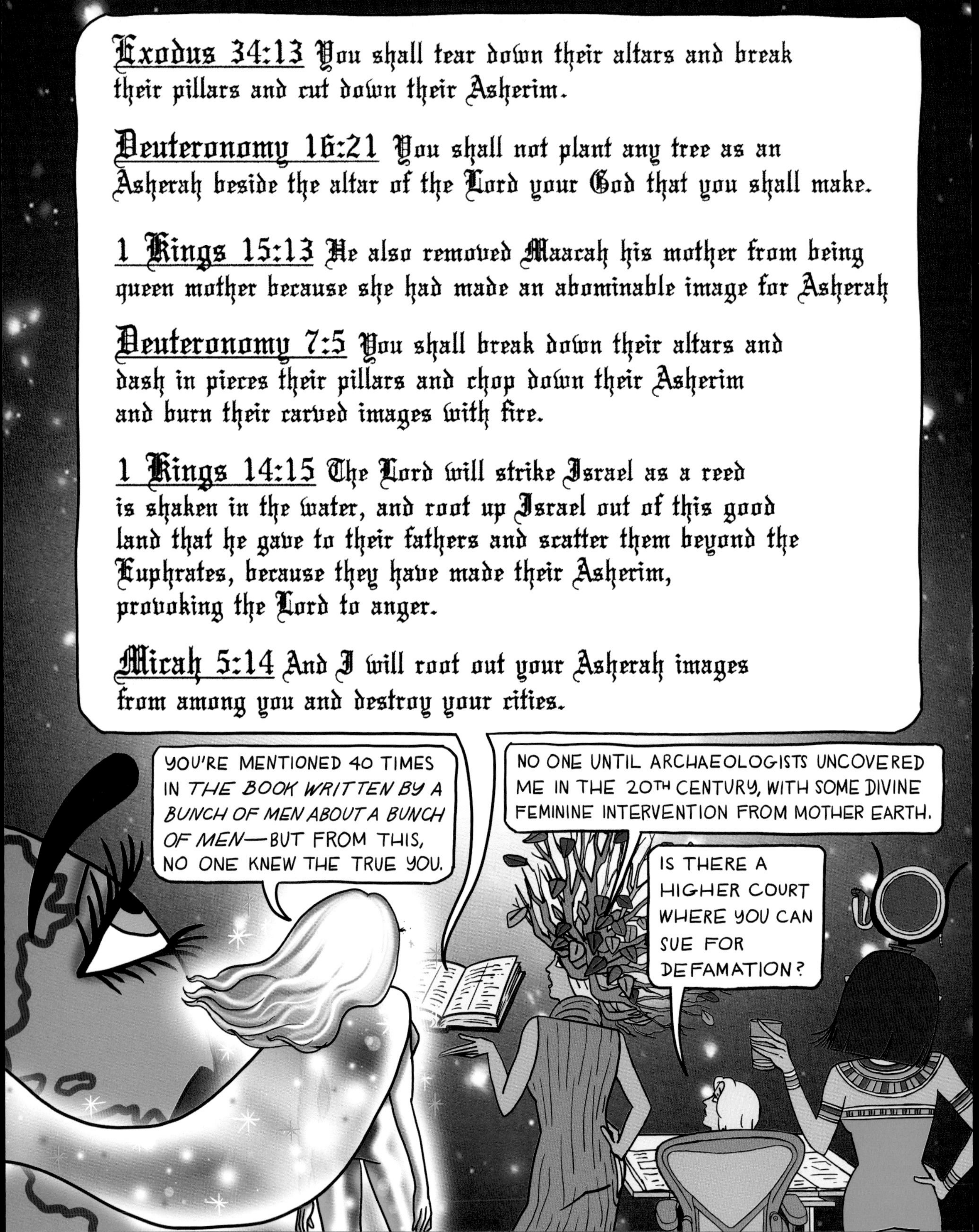
Exodus 34:13 You shall tear down their altars and break their pillars and cut down their Asherim.
Deuteronomy 16:21 You shall not plant any tree as an Asherah beside the altar of the Lord your God that you shall make.
1 Kings 15:13 He also removed Maacah his mother from being queen mother because she had made an abominable image for Asherah
Deuteronomy 7:5 You shall break down their altars and dash in pieces their pillars and chop down their Asherim and burn their carved images with fire.
1 Kings 14:15 The Lord will strike Israel as a reed is shaken in the water, and root up Israel out of this good land that he gave to their fathers and scatter them beyond the Euphrates, because they have made their Asherim, provoking the Lord to anger.
Micah 5:14 And I will root out your Asherah images from among you and destroy your cities.
YOU'RE MENTIONED 40 TIMES IN THE BOOK WRITTEN BY A BUNCH OF MEN ABOUT A BUNCH OF MEN—BUT FROM THIS, NO ONE KNEW THE TRUE YOU.
NO ONE UNTIL ARCHAEOLOGISTS UNCOVERED ME IN THE 20TH CENTURY, WITH SOME DIVINE FEMININE INTERVENTION FROM MOTHER EARTH.
IS THERE A HIGHER COURT WHERE YOU CAN SUE FOR DEFAMATION?

I'M SO FURIOUS RIGHT NOW, I WANT TO FIGHT FIRE WITH FIRE!

YOU KNOW THAT'S NOT OUR STRATEGY.

BESIDES, YOU— FIRE? NEVER A GOOD IDEA.

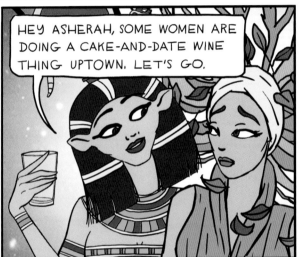

HEY ASHERAH, SOME WOMEN ARE DOING A CAKE-AND-DATE WINE THING UPTOWN. LET'S GO.

OR HATHOR, YOU COULD THROW ONE OF YOUR NEVER-ENDING DRUNKENNESS RAVES, AND WE'D ALL BLOW OFF SOME STEAM!

THAT WAS BRUTAL. THEY TAKE DOWN THE ONE WHO IS THE BIGGEST THREAT.

KILL THE MOTHER. THE CHILDREN ARE VULNERABLE.

THEY SAY I WAS BRUTALLY TAKEN DOWN TO *HADES*.

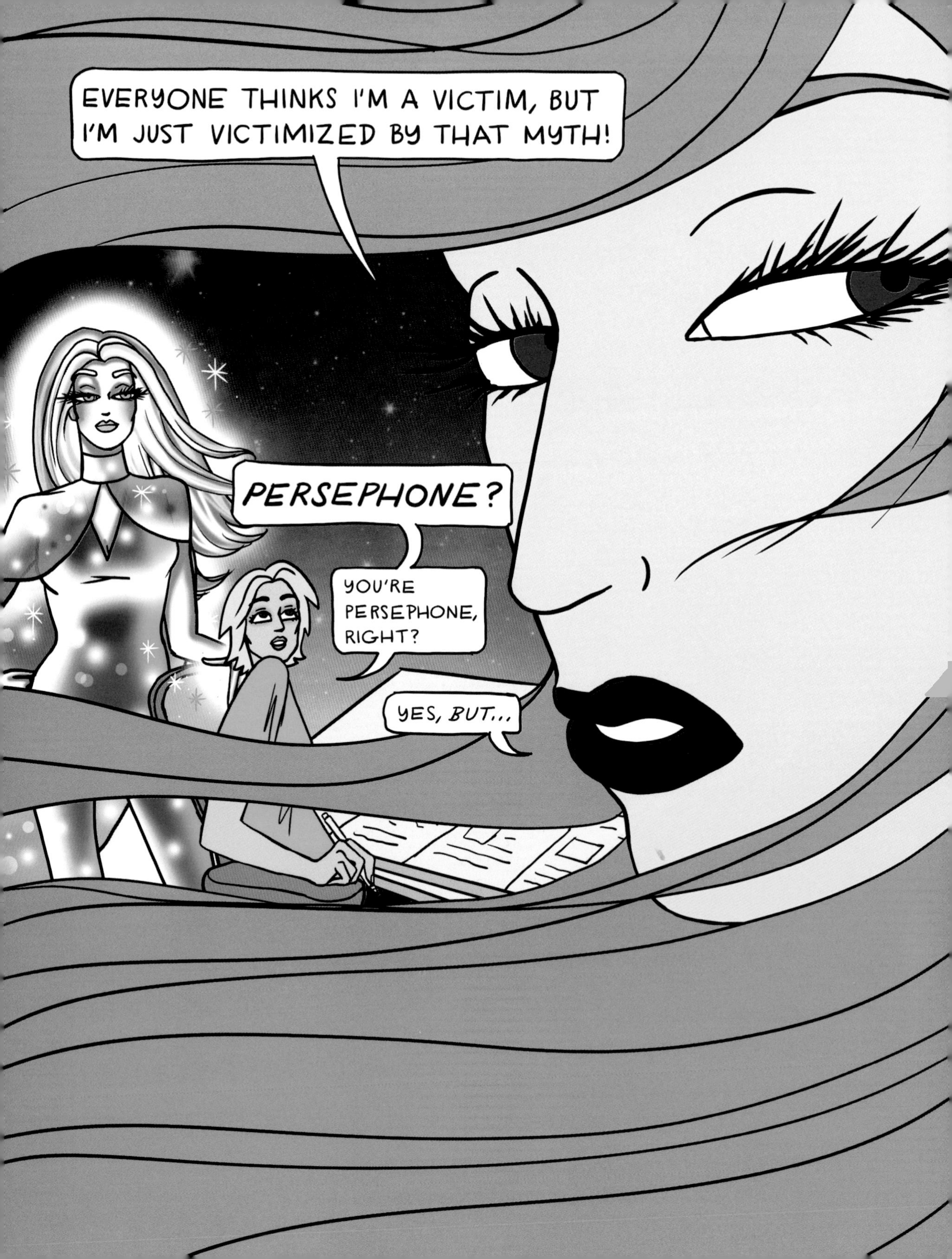
EVERYONE THINKS I'M A VICTIM, BUT I'M JUST VICTIMIZED BY THAT MYTH!
PERSEPHONE?
YOU'RE PERSEPHONE, RIGHT?
YES, BUT...

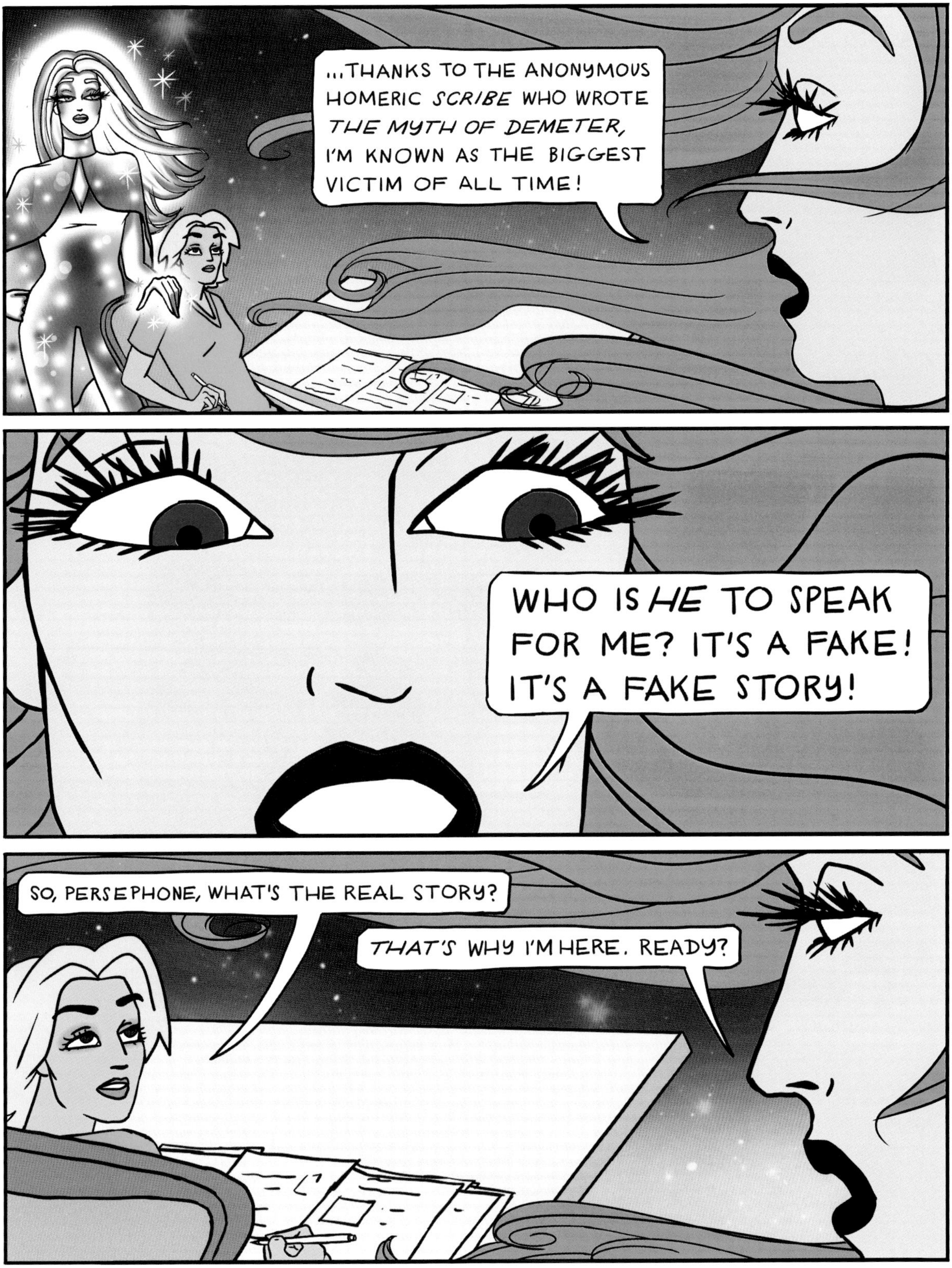
...THANKS TO THE ANONYMOUS HOMERIC *SCRIBE* WHO WROTE *THE MYTH OF DEMETER,* I'M KNOWN AS THE BIGGEST VICTIM OF ALL TIME!
WHO IS *HE* TO SPEAK FOR ME? IT'S A FAKE! IT'S A FAKE STORY!
SO, PERSEPHONE, WHAT'S THE REAL STORY?
THAT'S WHY I'M HERE. READY?

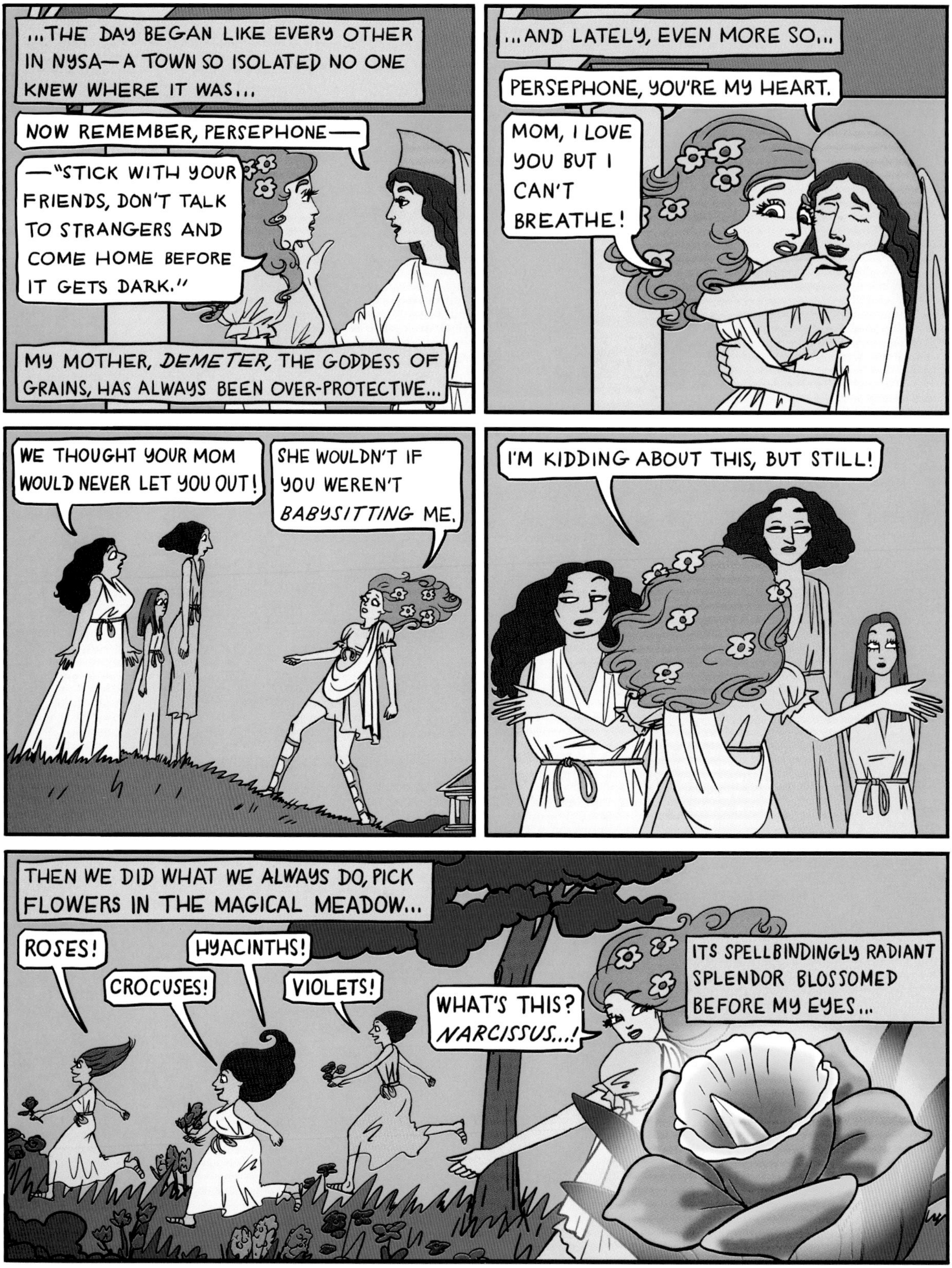
...THE DAY BEGAN LIKE EVERY OTHER IN NYSA—A TOWN SO ISOLATED NO ONE KNEW WHERE IT WAS...
NOW REMEMBER, PERSEPHONE—
—"STICK WITH YOUR FRIENDS, DON'T TALK TO STRANGERS AND COME HOME BEFORE IT GETS DARK."
MY MOTHER, *DEMETER*, THE GODDESS OF GRAINS, HAS ALWAYS BEEN OVER-PROTECTIVE...
...AND LATELY, EVEN MORE SO...
PERSEPHONE, YOU'RE MY HEART.
MOM, I LOVE YOU BUT I CAN'T BREATHE!
WE THOUGHT YOUR MOM WOULD NEVER LET YOU OUT!
SHE WOULDN'T IF YOU WEREN'T *BABYSITTING* ME.
I'M KIDDING ABOUT THIS, BUT STILL!
THEN WE DID WHAT WE ALWAYS DO, PICK FLOWERS IN THE MAGICAL MEADOW...
ROSES!
CROCUSES!
HYACINTHS!
VIOLETS!
WHAT'S THIS? *NARCISSUS...!*
ITS SPELLBINDINGLY RADIANT SPLENDOR BLOSSOMED BEFORE MY EYES...

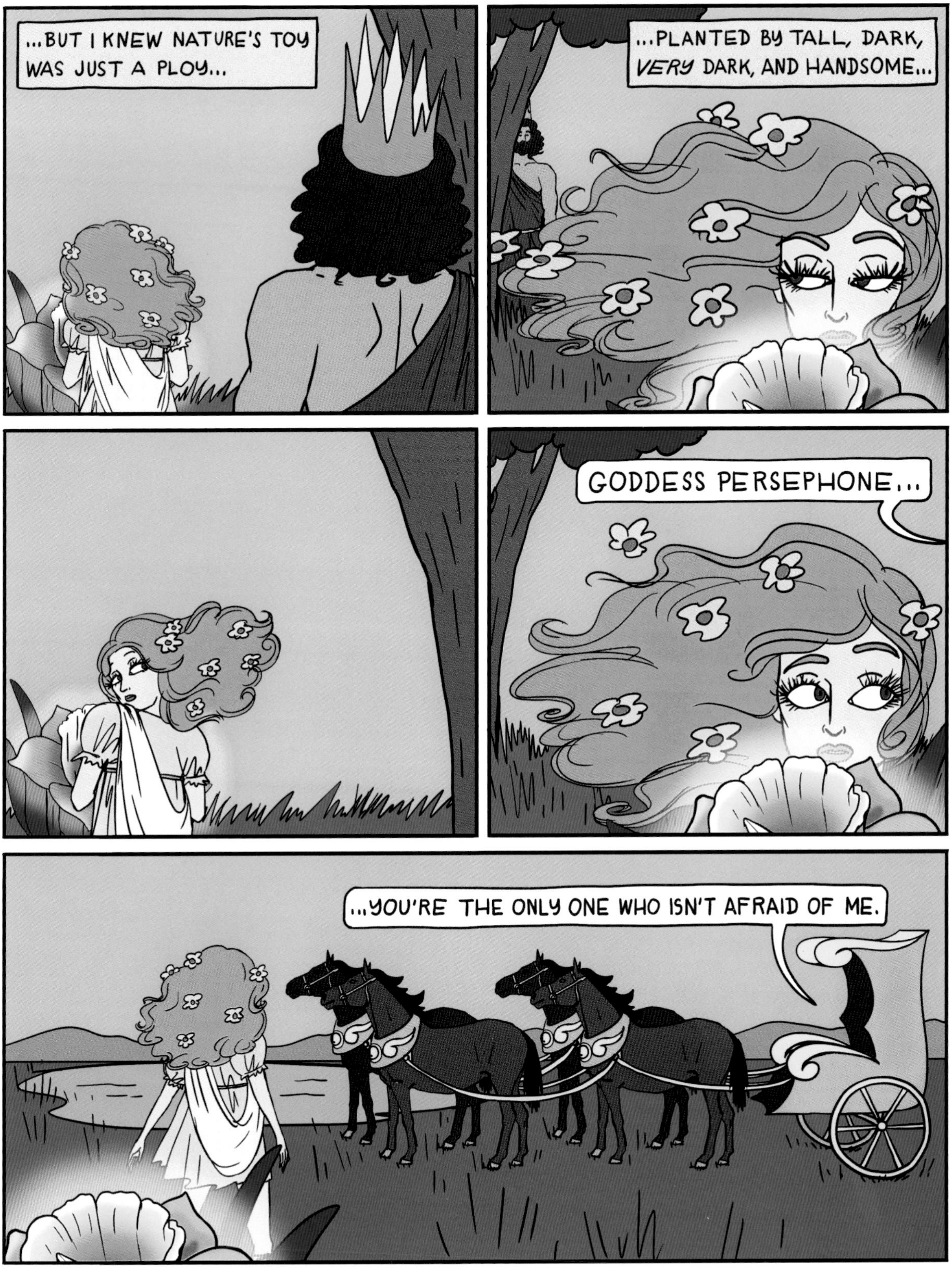
...BUT I KNEW NATURE'S TOY WAS JUST A PLOY...
...PLANTED BY TALL, DARK, *VERY* DARK, AND HANDSOME...
GODDESS PERSEPHONE...
...YOU'RE THE ONLY ONE WHO ISN'T AFRAID OF ME.

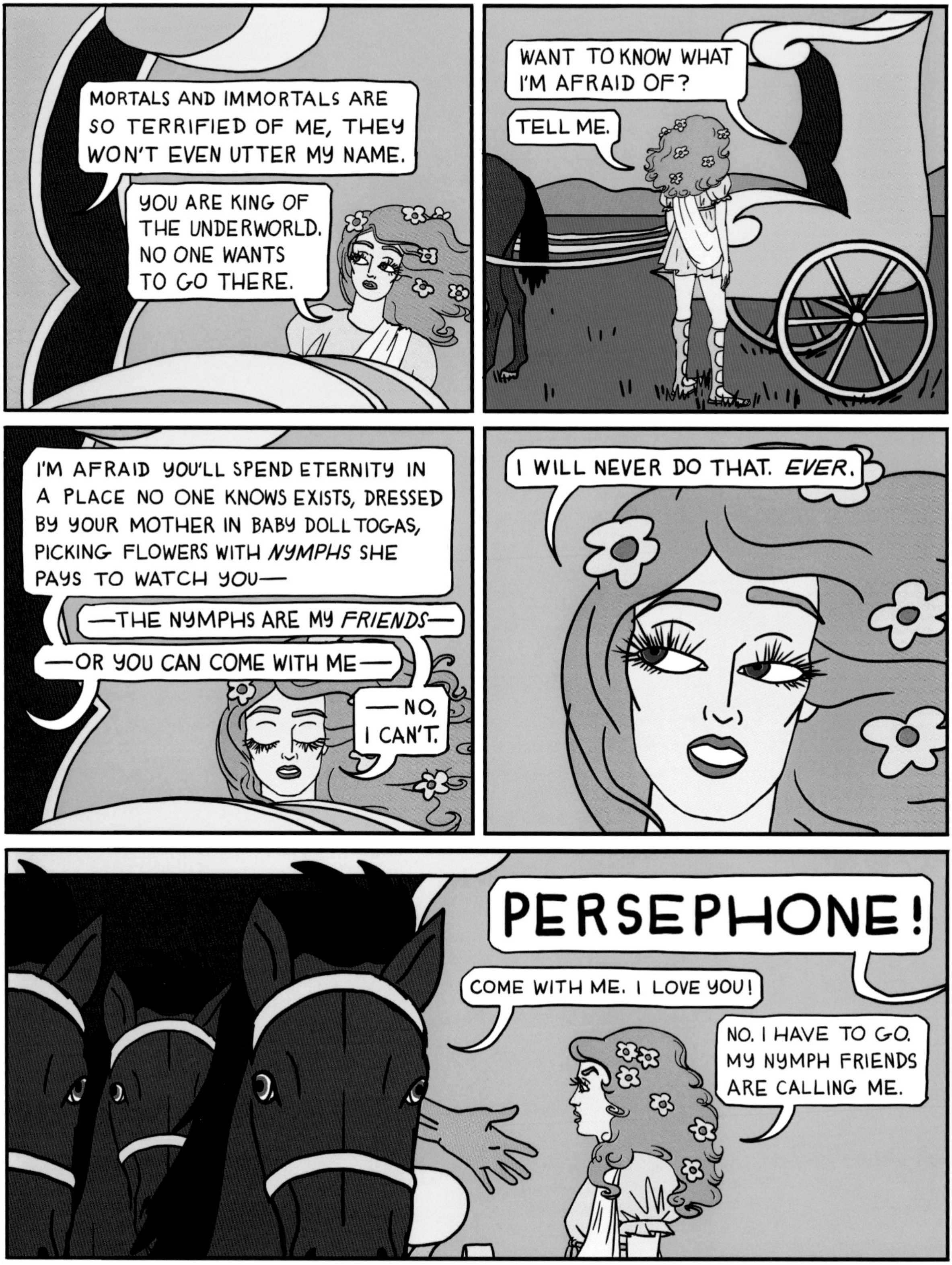
MORTALS AND IMMORTALS ARE SO TERRIFIED OF ME, THEY WON'T EVEN UTTER MY NAME.
YOU ARE KING OF THE UNDERWORLD. NO ONE WANTS TO GO THERE.
WANT TO KNOW WHAT I'M AFRAID OF?
TELL ME.
I'M AFRAID YOU'LL SPEND ETERNITY IN A PLACE NO ONE KNOWS EXISTS, DRESSED BY YOUR MOTHER IN BABY DOLL TOGAS, PICKING FLOWERS WITH *NYMPHS* SHE PAYS TO WATCH YOU—
—THE NYMPHS ARE MY *FRIENDS*—
—OR YOU CAN COME WITH ME—
—NO, I CAN'T.
I WILL NEVER DO THAT. *EVER*.
PERSEPHONE!
COME WITH ME. I LOVE YOU!
NO. I HAVE TO GO. MY NYMPH FRIENDS ARE CALLING ME.

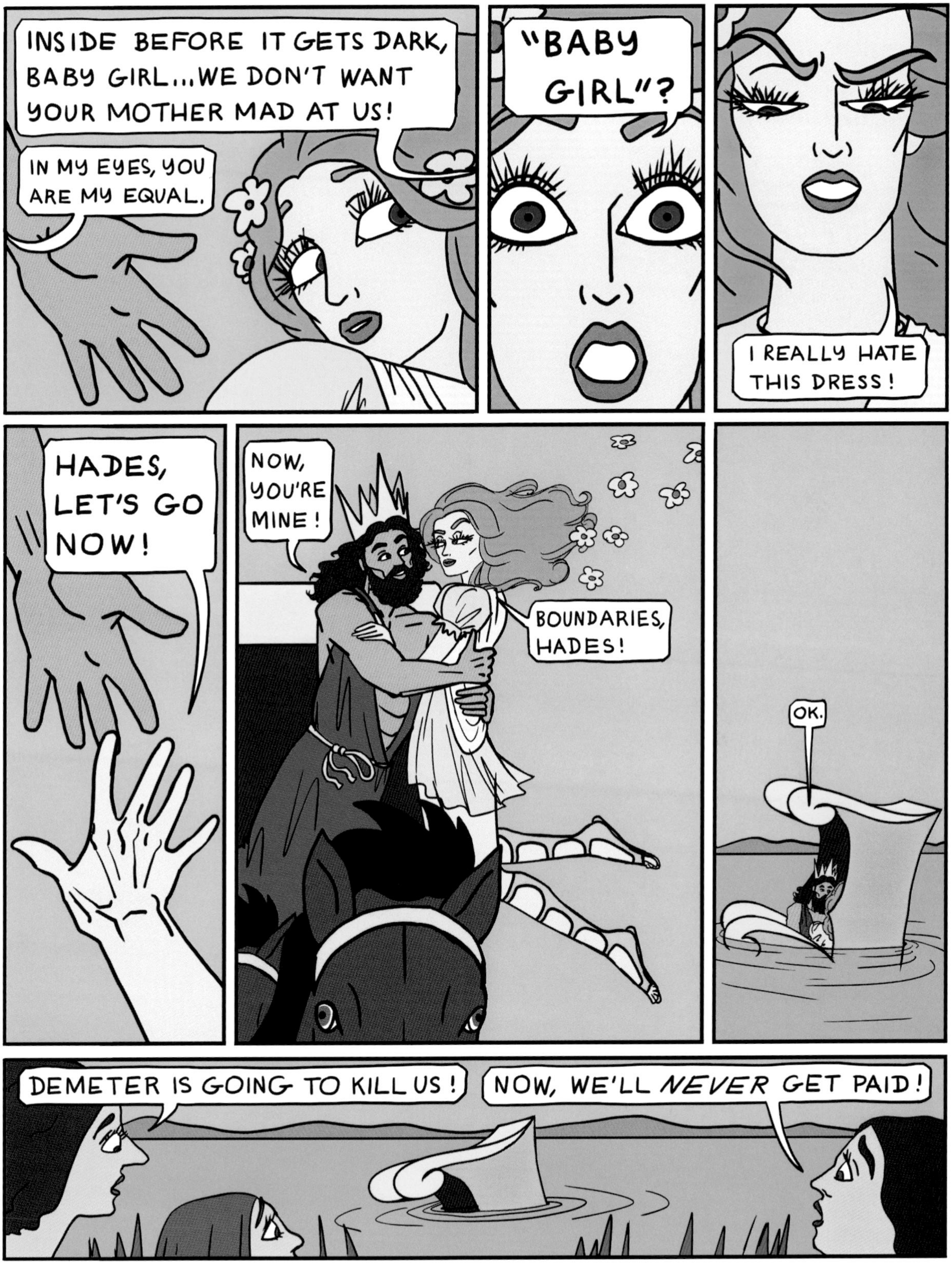
INSIDE BEFORE IT GETS DARK, BABY GIRL...WE DON'T WANT YOUR MOTHER MAD AT US!
IN MY EYES, YOU ARE MY EQUAL.
"BABY GIRL"?
I REALLY HATE THIS DRESS!
HADES, LET'S GO NOW!
NOW, YOU'RE MINE!
BOUNDARIES, HADES!
OK.
DEMETER IS GOING TO KILL US!
NOW, WE'LL *NEVER* GET PAID!

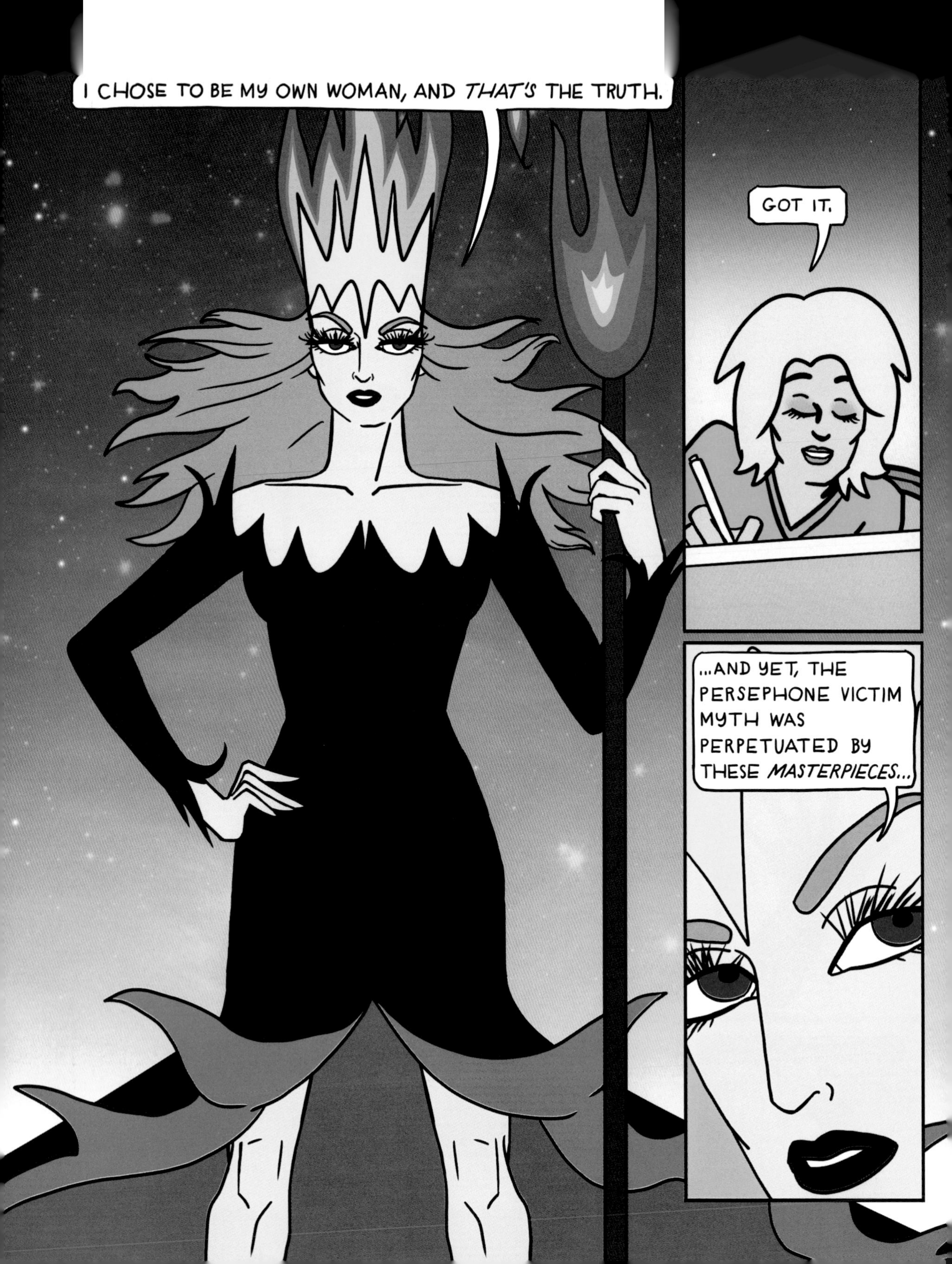
I CHOSE TO BE MY OWN WOMAN, AND *THAT'S* THE TRUTH.
GOT IT.
...AND YET, THE PERSEPHONE VICTIM MYTH WAS PERPETUATED BY THESE *MASTERPIECES*...

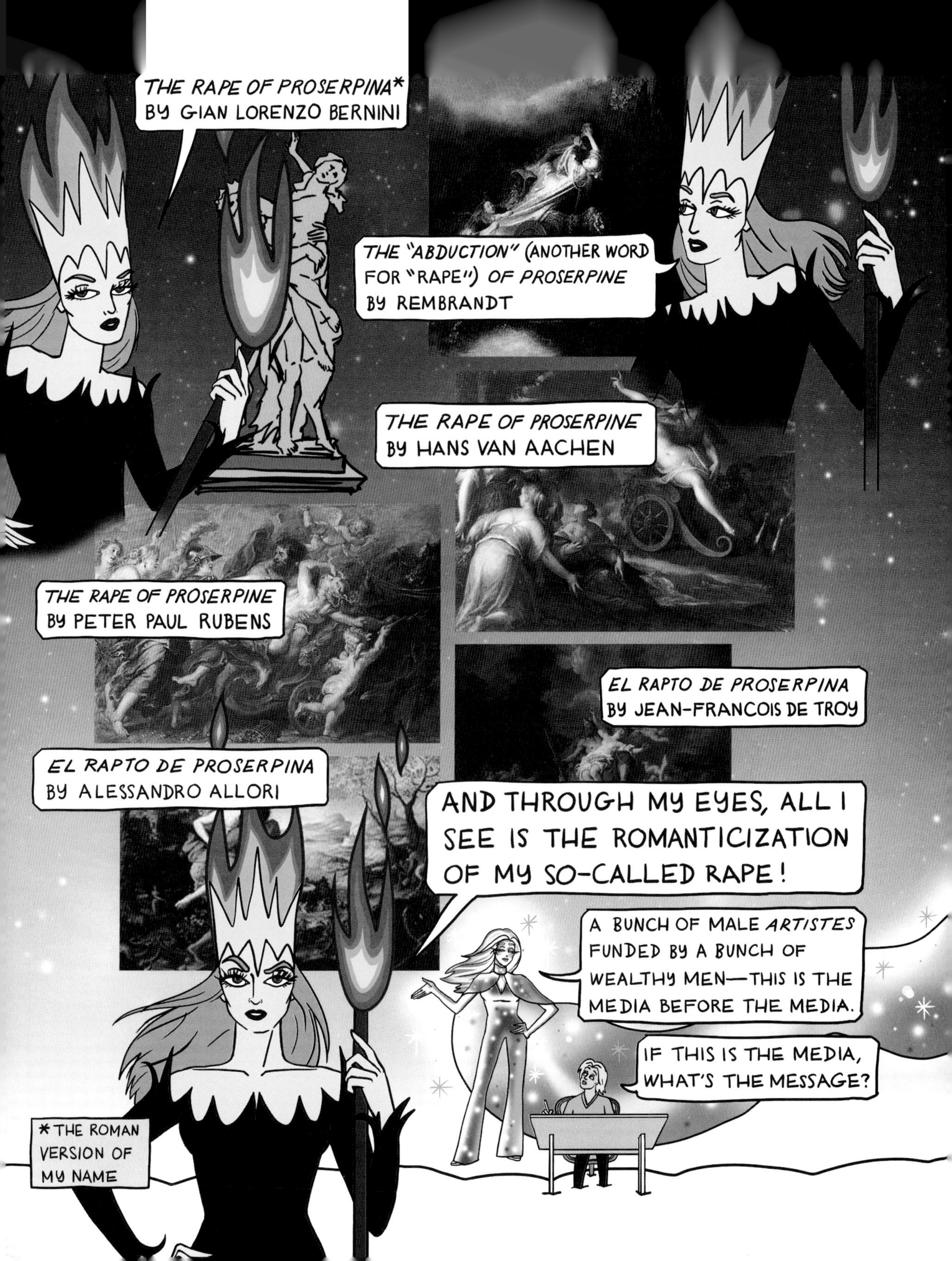
THE RAPE OF PROSERPINA* BY GIAN LORENZO BERNINI
THE "ABDUCTION" (ANOTHER WORD FOR "RAPE") OF PROSERPINE BY REMBRANDT
THE RAPE OF PROSERPINE BY HANS VAN AACHEN
THE RAPE OF PROSERPINE BY PETER PAUL RUBENS
EL RAPTO DE PROSERPINA BY JEAN-FRANCOIS DE TROY
EL RAPTO DE PROSERPINA BY ALESSANDRO ALLORI
AND THROUGH MY EYES, ALL I SEE IS THE ROMANTICIZATION OF MY SO-CALLED RAPE!
A BUNCH OF MALE ARTISTES FUNDED BY A BUNCH OF WEALTHY MEN—THIS IS THE MEDIA BEFORE THE MEDIA.
IF THIS IS THE MEDIA, WHAT'S THE MESSAGE?
*THE ROMAN VERSION OF MY NAME

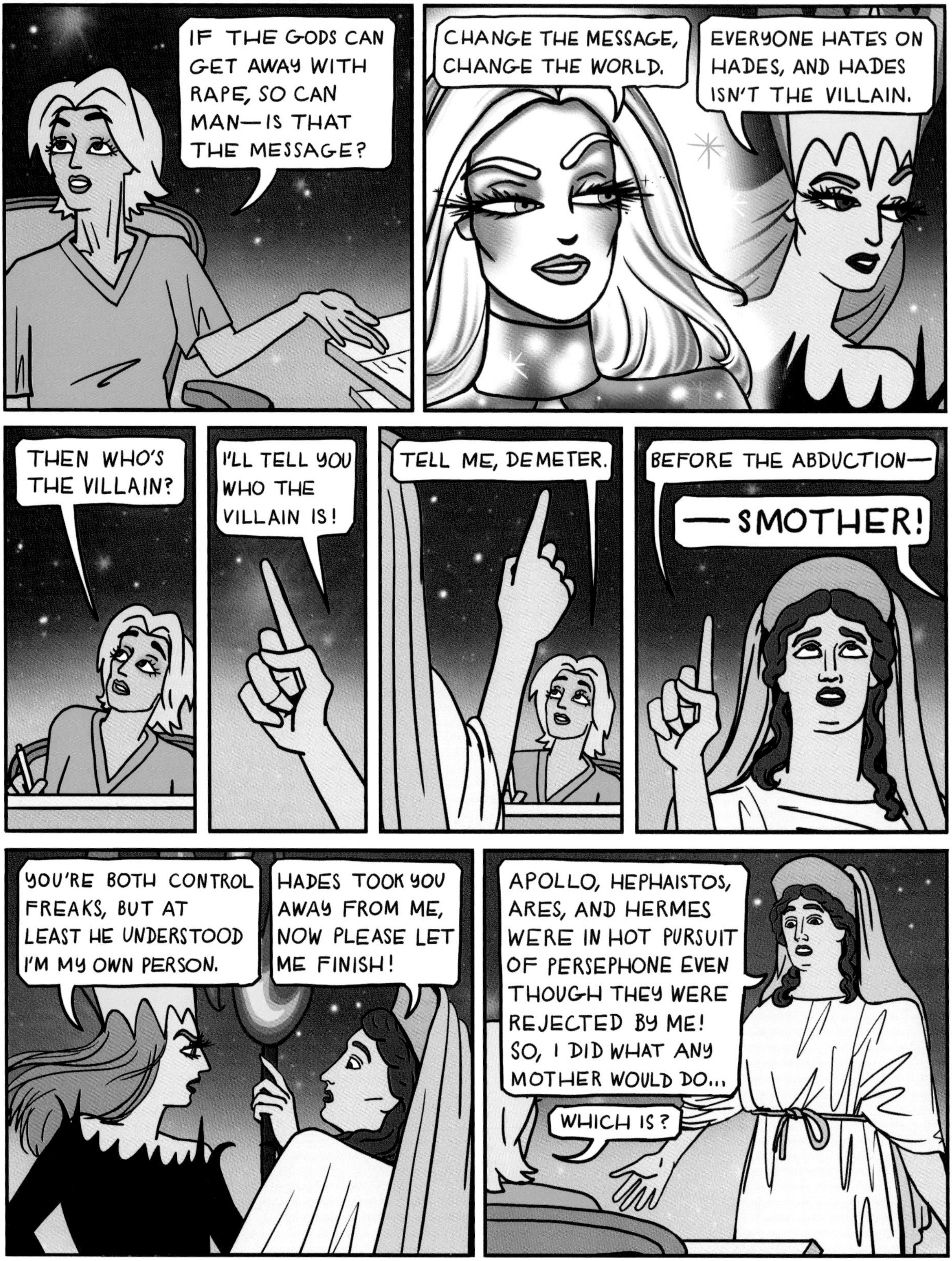
IF THE GODS CAN GET AWAY WITH RAPE, SO CAN MAN—IS THAT THE MESSAGE?
CHANGE THE MESSAGE, CHANGE THE WORLD.
EVERYONE HATES ON HADES, AND HADES ISN'T THE VILLAIN.
THEN WHO'S THE VILLAIN?
I'LL TELL YOU WHO THE VILLAIN IS!
TELL ME, DEMETER.
BEFORE THE ABDUCTION—
—SMOTHER!
YOU'RE BOTH CONTROL FREAKS, BUT AT LEAST HE UNDERSTOOD I'M MY OWN PERSON.
HADES TOOK YOU AWAY FROM ME, NOW PLEASE LET ME FINISH!
APOLLO, HEPHAISTOS, ARES, AND HERMES WERE IN HOT PURSUIT OF PERSEPHONE EVEN THOUGH THEY WERE REJECTED BY ME! SO, I DID WHAT ANY MOTHER WOULD DO...
WHICH IS?

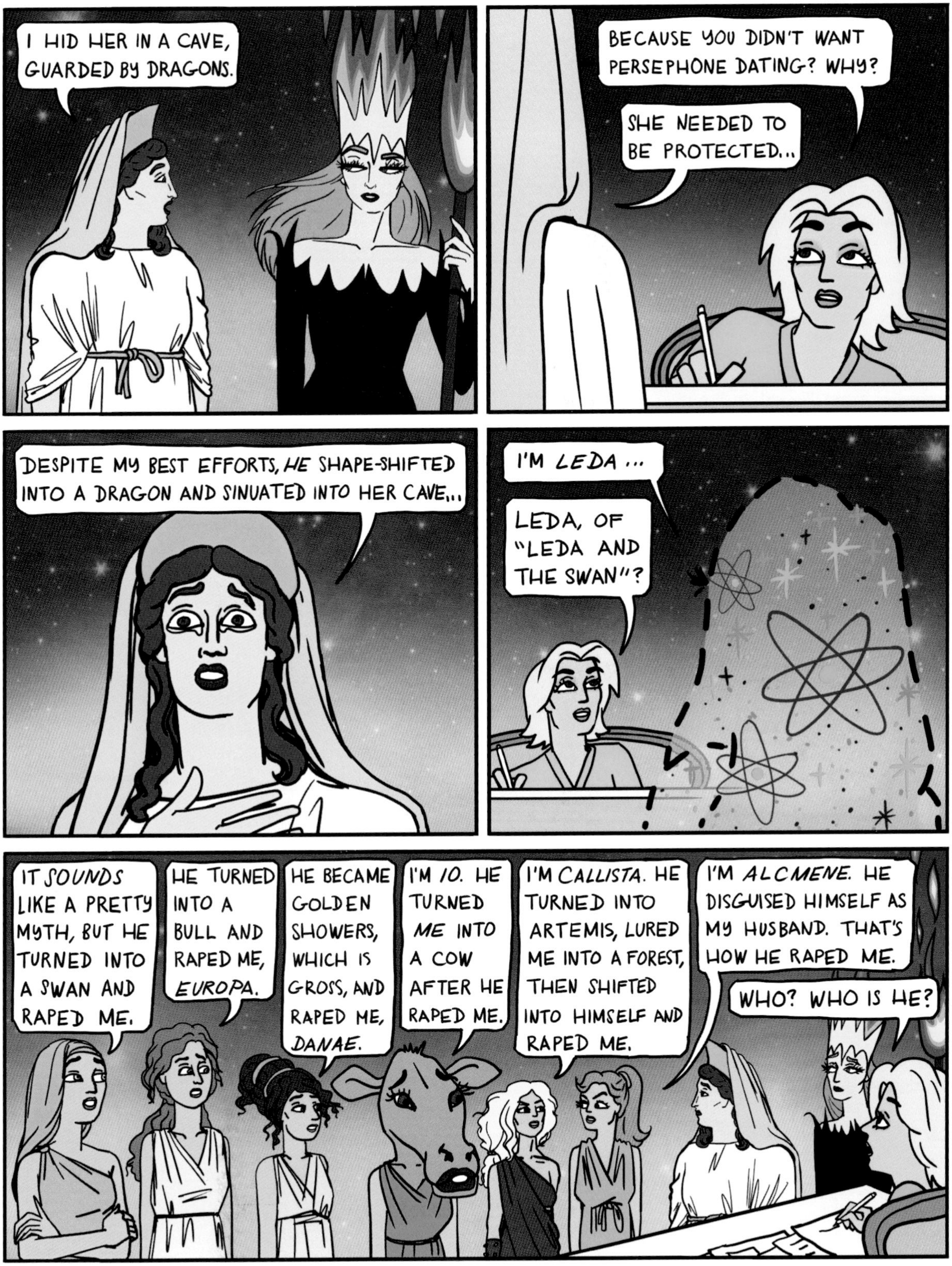
I HID HER IN A CAVE, GUARDED BY DRAGONS.
BECAUSE YOU DIDN'T WANT PERSEPHONE DATING? WHY?
SHE NEEDED TO BE PROTECTED...
DESPITE MY BEST EFFORTS, *HE* SHAPE-SHIFTED INTO A DRAGON AND SINUATED INTO HER CAVE...
I'M *LEDA* ...
LEDA, OF "LEDA AND THE SWAN"?
IT *SOUNDS* LIKE A PRETTY MYTH, BUT HE TURNED INTO A SWAN AND RAPED ME.
HE TURNED INTO A BULL AND RAPED ME, *EUROPA*.
HE BECAME GOLDEN SHOWERS, WHICH IS GROSS, AND RAPED ME, *DANAE*.
I'M *IO*. HE TURNED *ME* INTO A COW AFTER HE RAPED ME.
I'M *CALLISTA*. HE TURNED INTO ARTEMIS, LURED ME INTO A FOREST, THEN SHIFTED INTO HIMSELF AND RAPED ME.
I'M *ALCMENE*. HE DISGUISED HIMSELF AS MY HUSBAND. THAT'S HOW HE RAPED ME.
WHO? WHO IS HE?

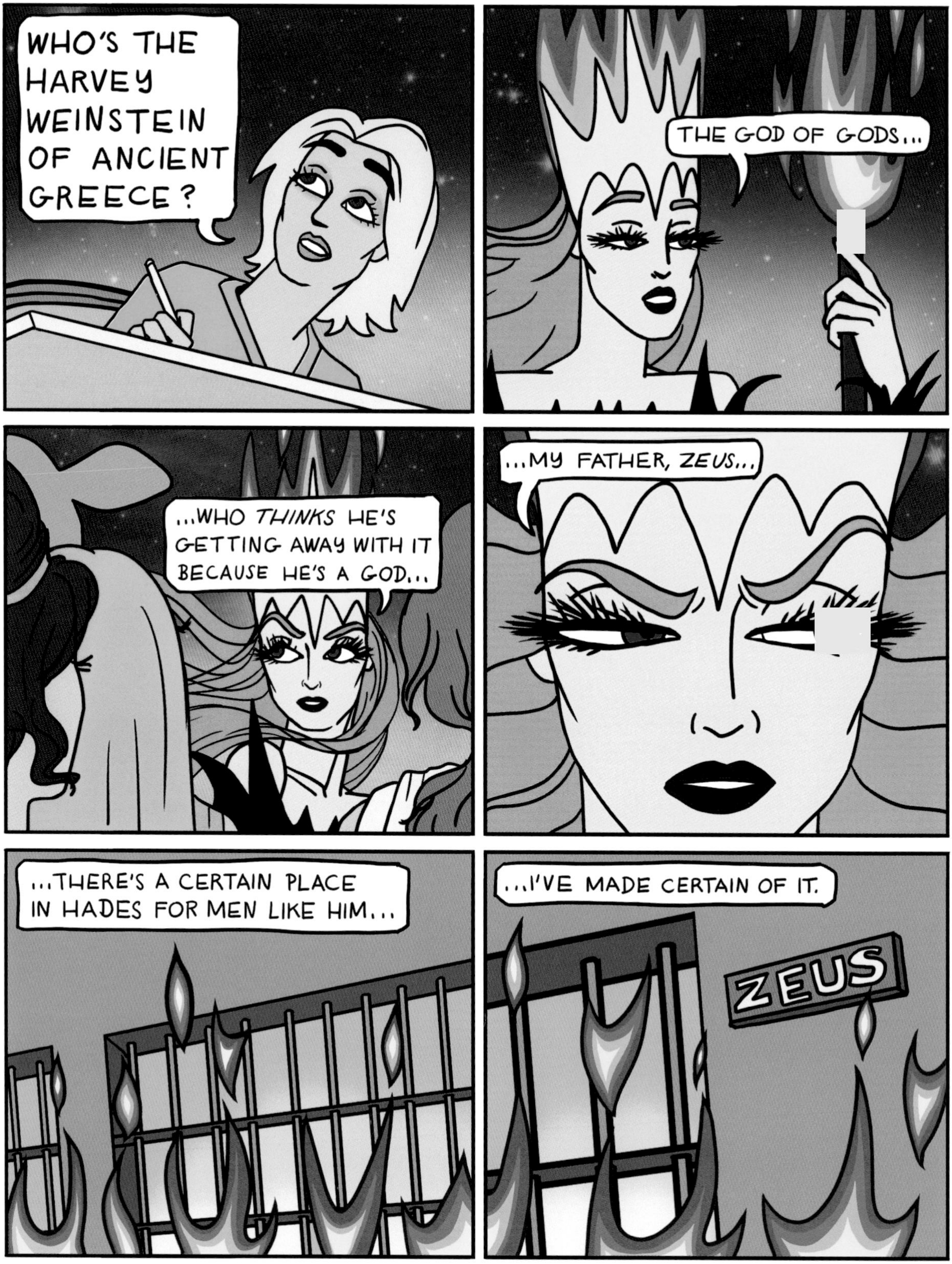
WHO'S THE HARVEY WEINSTEIN OF ANCIENT GREECE?
THE GOD OF GODS...
...WHO *THINKS* HE'S GETTING AWAY WITH IT BECAUSE HE'S A GOD...
...MY FATHER, *ZEUS*...
...THERE'S A CERTAIN PLACE IN HADES FOR MEN LIKE HIM...
...I'VE MADE CERTAIN OF IT.
ZEUS

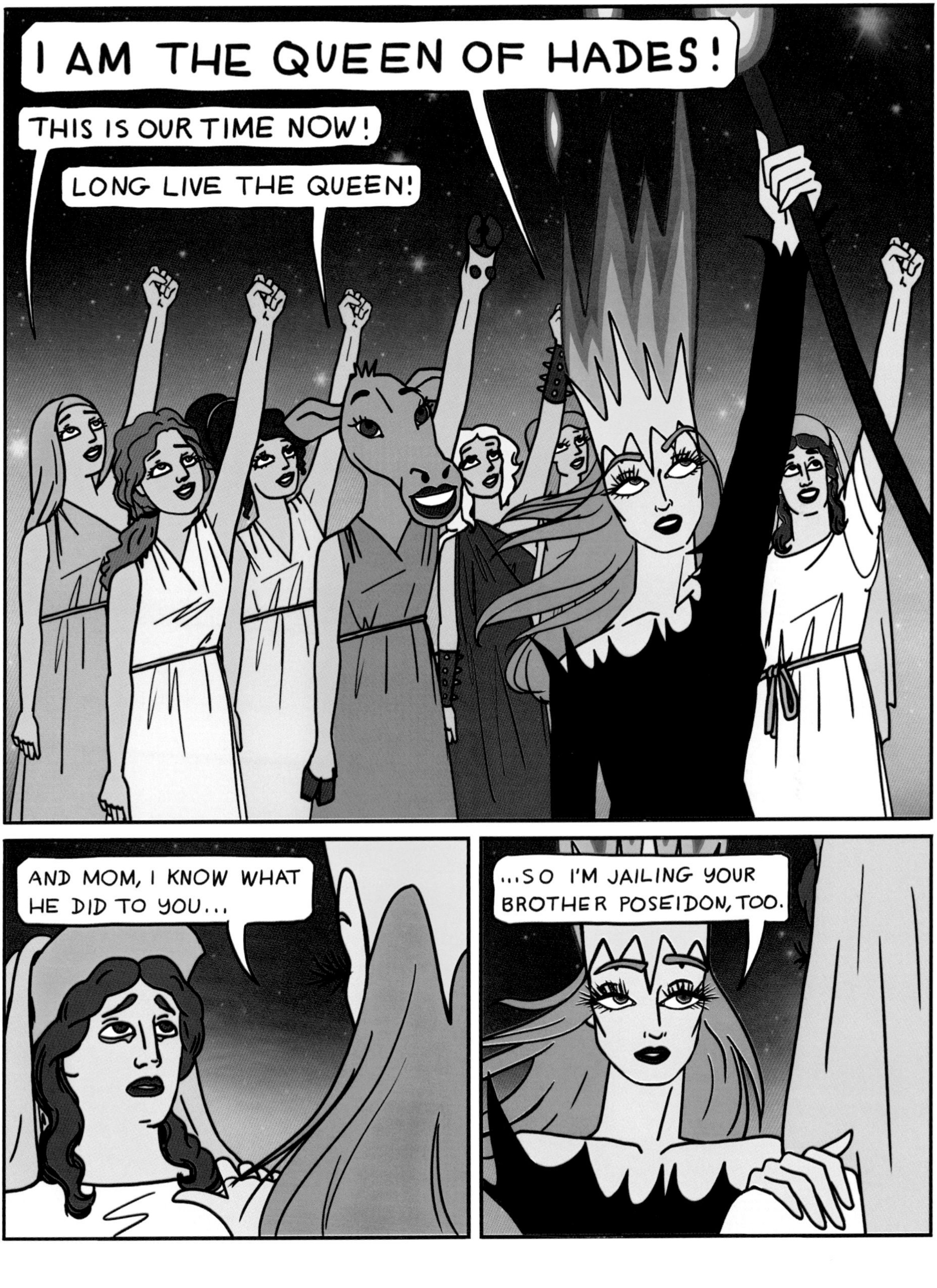
I AM THE QUEEN OF HADES!
THIS IS OUR TIME NOW!
LONG LIVE THE QUEEN!
AND MOM, I KNOW WHAT HE DID TO YOU...
...SO I'M JAILING YOUR BROTHER POSEIDON, TOO.

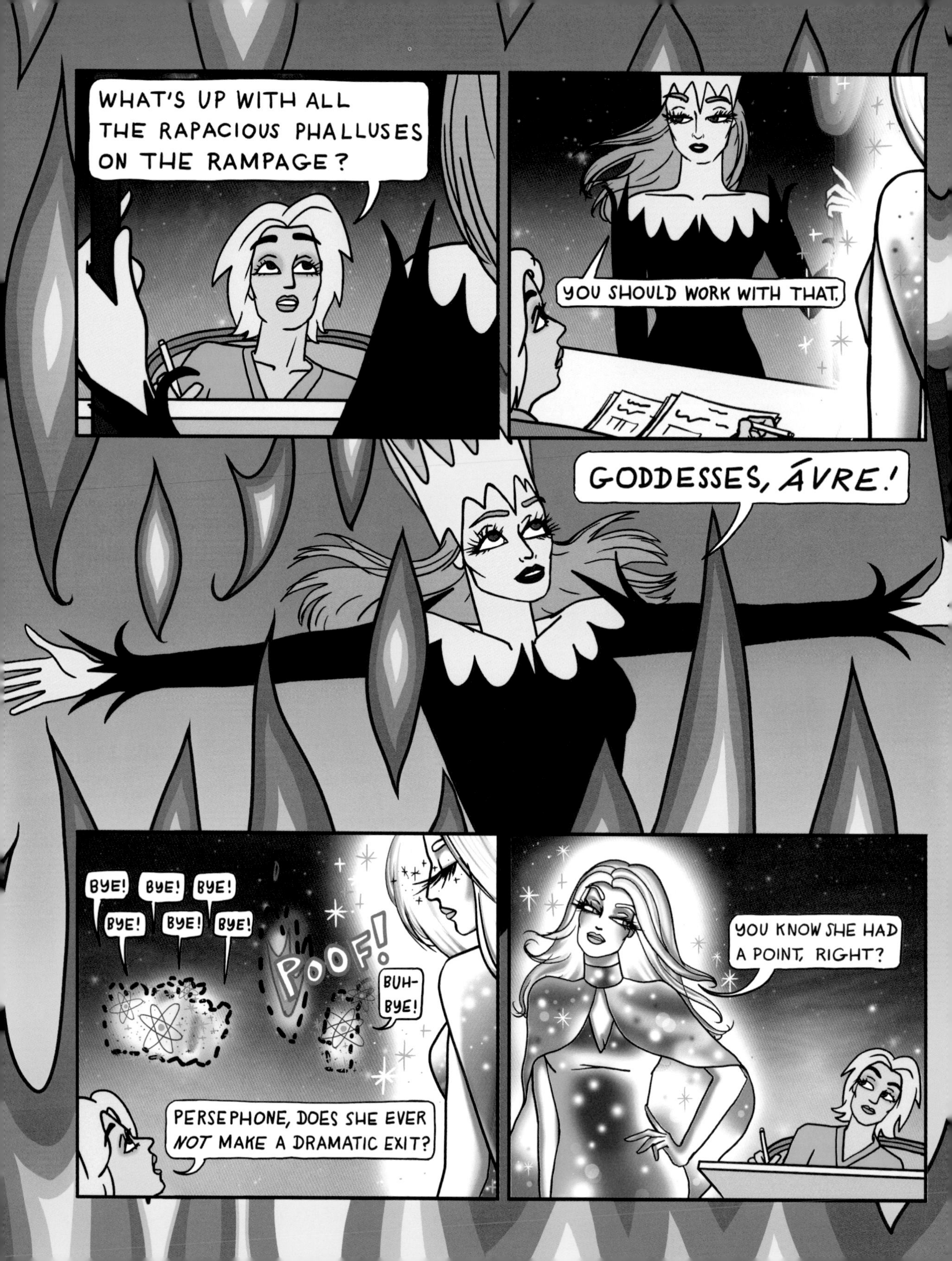
WHAT'S UP WITH ALL THE RAPACIOUS PHALLUSES ON THE RAMPAGE?
YOU SHOULD WORK WITH THAT.
GODDESSES, ÁVRE!
BYE! BYE! BYE!
BYE! BYE! BYE!
POOF!
BUH-BYE!
PERSEPHONE, DOES SHE EVER NOT MAKE A DRAMATIC EXIT?
YOU KNOW SHE HAD A POINT, RIGHT?

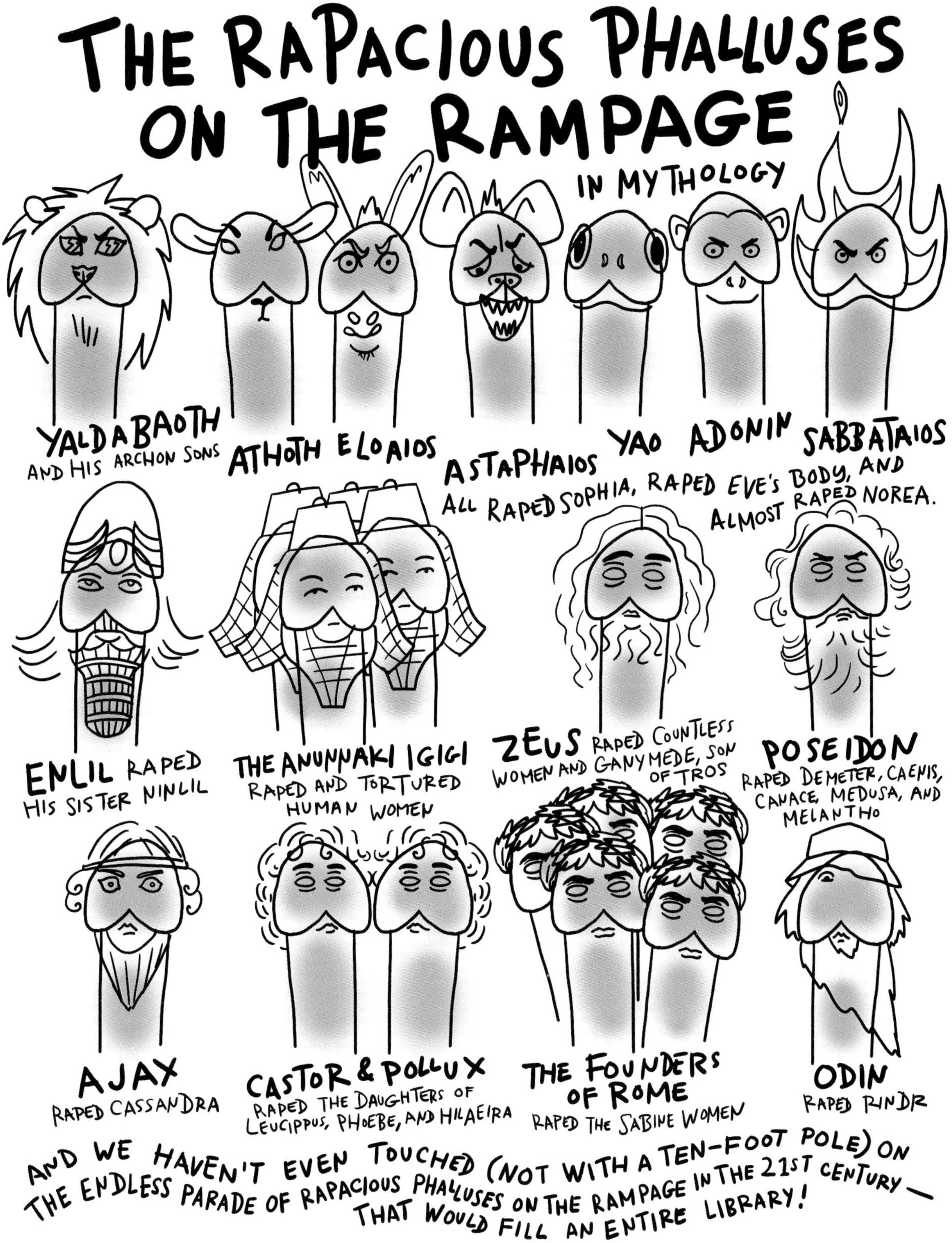
THE RAPACIOUS PHALLUSES ON THE RAMPAGE
IN MYTHOLOGY
YALDABAOTH
AND HIS ARCHON SONS
ATHOTH
ELOAIOS
ASTAPHAIOS
YAO
ADONIN
SABBATAIOS
ALL RAPED SOPHIA, RAPED EVE'S BODY, AND ALMOST RAPED NOREA.
ENLIL RAPED HIS SISTER NINLIL
THE ANUNNAKI IGIGI
RAPED AND TORTURED HUMAN WOMEN
ZEUS RAPED COUNTLESS WOMEN AND GANYMEDE, SON OF TROS
POSEIDON
RAPED DEMETER, CAENIS, CANACE, MEDUSA, AND MELANTHO
AJAX
RAPED CASSANDRA
CASTOR & POLLUX
RAPED THE DAUGHTERS OF LEUCIPPUS, PHOEBE, AND HILAEIRA
THE FOUNDERS OF ROME
RAPED THE SABINE WOMEN
ODIN
RAPED RINDR
AND WE HAVEN'T EVEN TOUCHED (NOT WITH A TEN-FOOT POLE) ON THE ENDLESS PARADE OF RAPACIOUS PHALLUSES ON THE RAMPAGE IN THE 21ST CENTURY— THAT WOULD FILL AN ENTIRE LIBRARY!

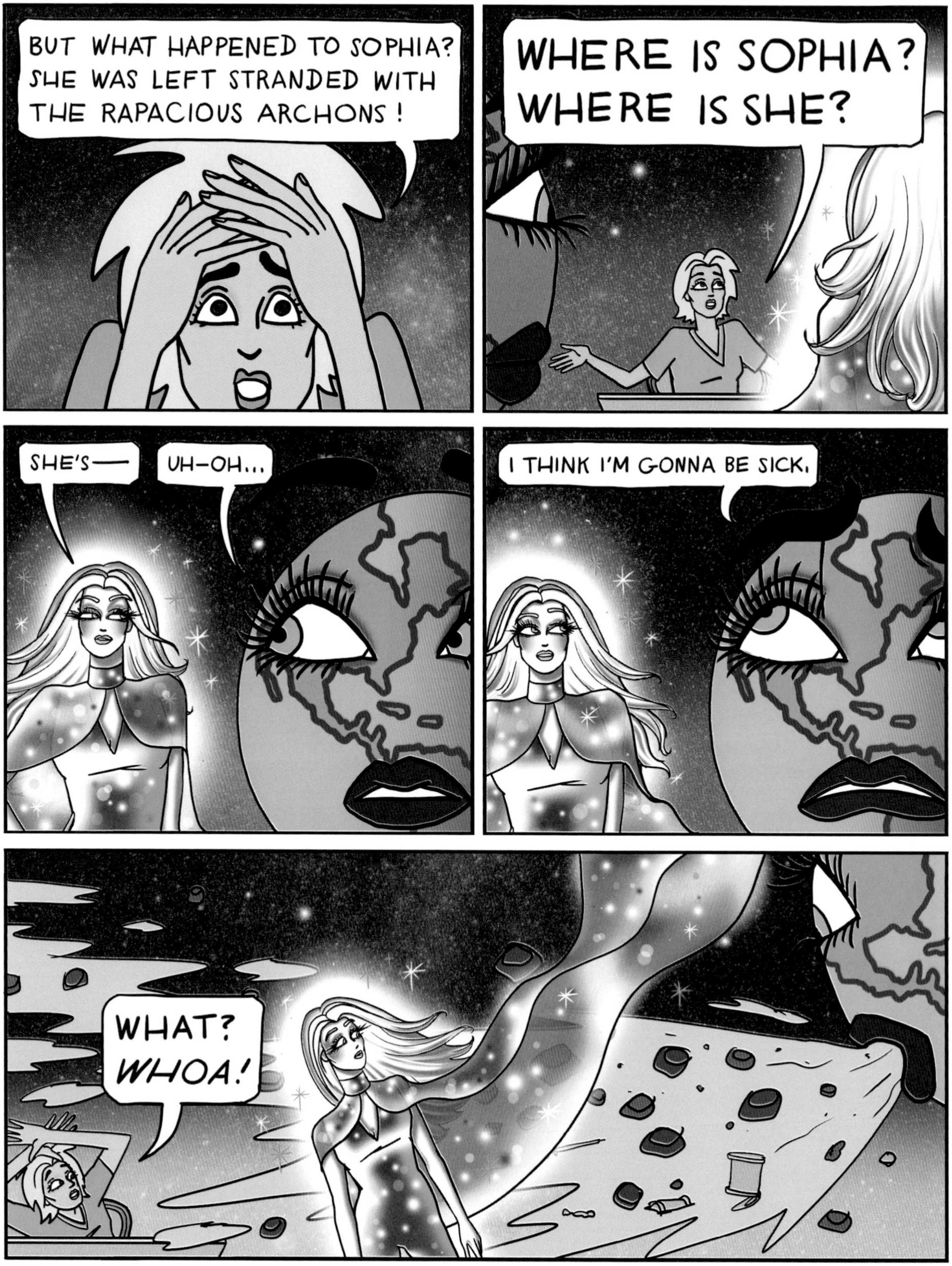
BUT WHAT HAPPENED TO SOPHIA? SHE WAS LEFT STRANDED WITH THE RAPACIOUS ARCHONS!
WHERE IS SOPHIA? WHERE IS SHE?
SHE'S—
UH-OH...
I THINK I'M GONNA BE SICK.
WHAT? WHOA!

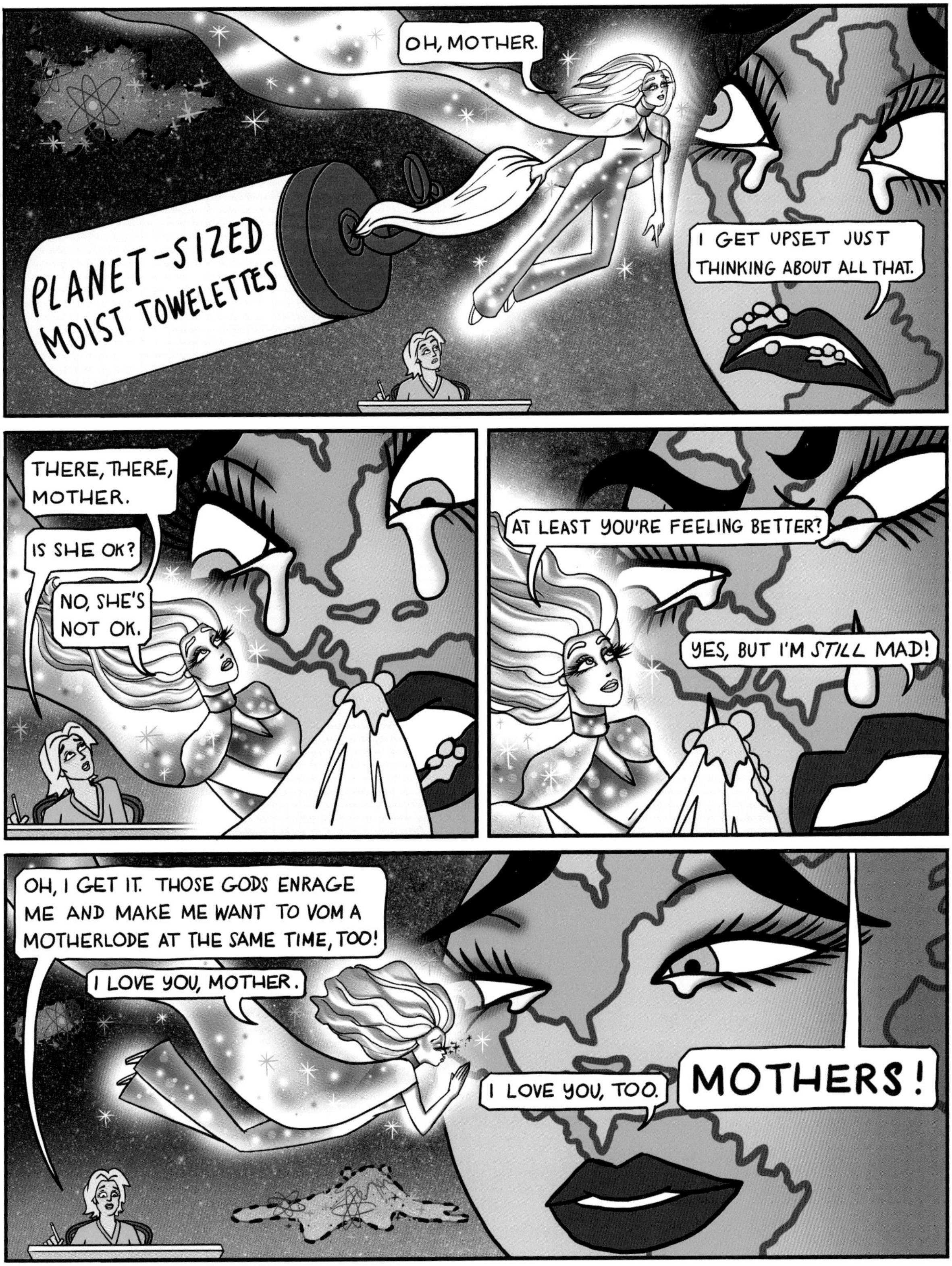
OH, MOTHER.
PLANET-SIZED MOIST TOWELETTES
I GET UPSET JUST THINKING ABOUT ALL THAT.
THERE, THERE, MOTHER.
IS SHE OK?
NO, SHE'S NOT OK.
AT LEAST YOU'RE FEELING BETTER?
YES, BUT I'M *STILL* MAD!
OH, I GET IT. THOSE GODS ENRAGE ME AND MAKE ME WANT TO VOM A MOTHERLODE AT THE SAME TIME, TOO!
I LOVE YOU, MOTHER.
I LOVE YOU, TOO.
MOTHERS!

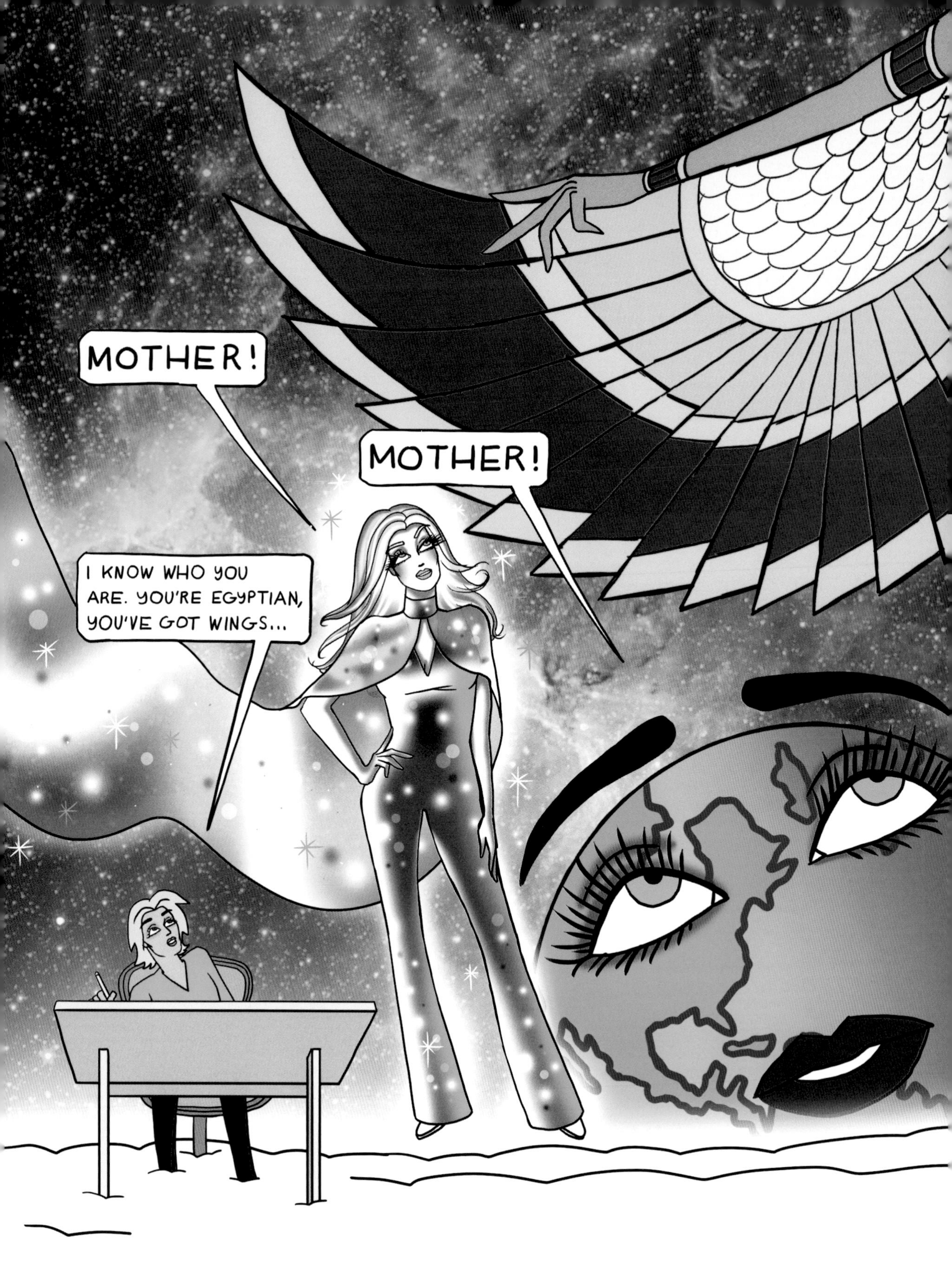
MOTHER!
MOTHER!
I KNOW WHO YOU ARE. YOU'RE EGYPTIAN, YOU'VE GOT WINGS...

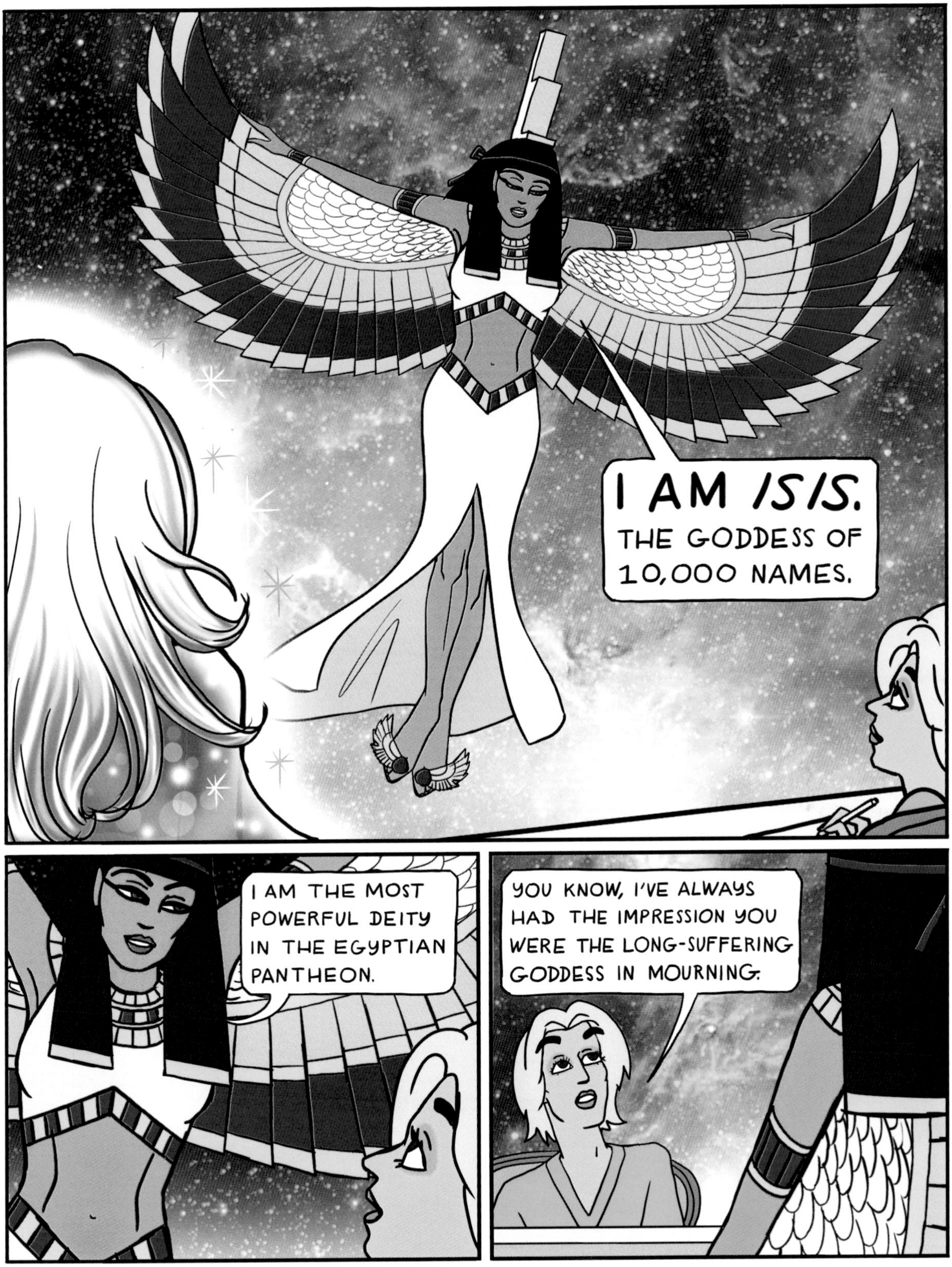
I AM *ISIS.* THE GODDESS OF 10,000 NAMES.
I AM THE MOST POWERFUL DEITY IN THE EGYPTIAN PANTHEON.
YOU KNOW, I'VE ALWAYS HAD THE IMPRESSION YOU WERE THE LONG-SUFFERING GODDESS IN MOURNING.

I MEAN, THE WAY *PLUTARCH* TELLS IT—
—EXCUSE ME, I'M RIGHT HERE!
QUOTING FROM *MORALIA*, I WROTE, "ISIS PUT ON HER GARMENT OF MOURN—"
—SHUT UP, PLUTARCH!
I'VE SUFFERED THROUGH YOUR WEEPY-GODDESS-IN-MOURNING *MEME* 2,000 YEARS TOO LONG!
ZZZZZZT!!!
WHAT IS *THAT*?

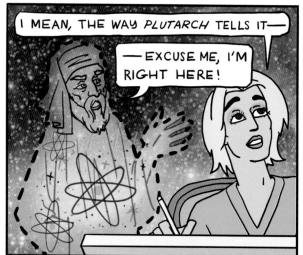

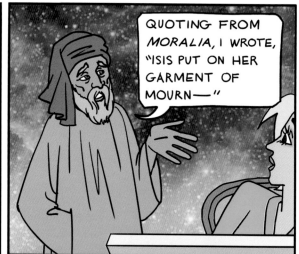

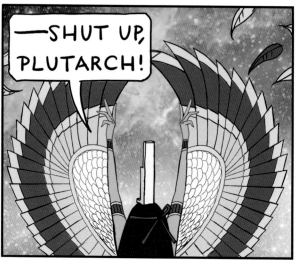

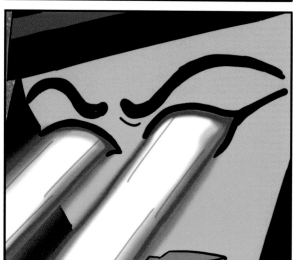

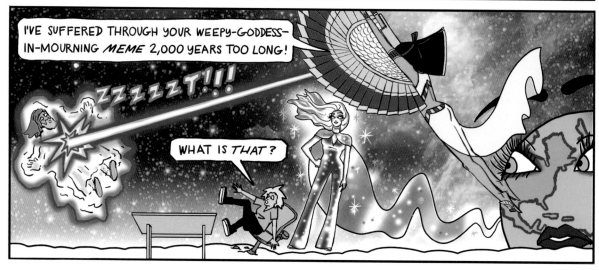

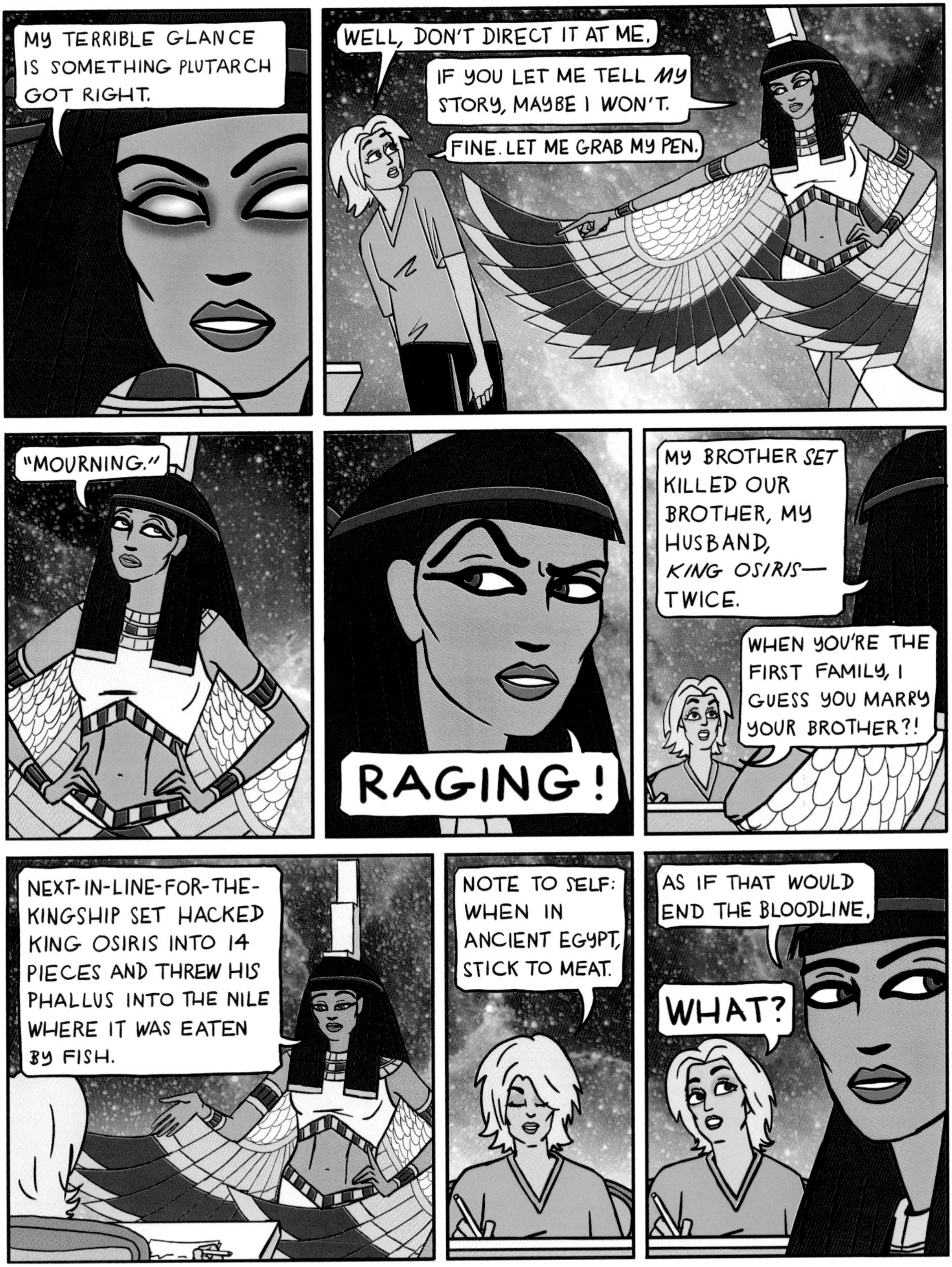
MY TERRIBLE GLANCE IS SOMETHING PLUTARCH GOT RIGHT.
WELL, DON'T DIRECT IT AT ME.
IF YOU LET ME TELL *MY* STORY, MAYBE I WON'T.
FINE. LET ME GRAB MY PEN.
"MOURNING."
RAGING!
MY BROTHER *SET* KILLED OUR BROTHER, MY HUSBAND, *KING OSIRIS*— TWICE.
WHEN YOU'RE THE FIRST FAMILY, I GUESS YOU MARRY YOUR BROTHER?!
NEXT-IN-LINE-FOR-THE-KINGSHIP SET HACKED KING OSIRIS INTO 14 PIECES AND THREW HIS PHALLUS INTO THE NILE WHERE IT WAS EATEN BY FISH.
NOTE TO SELF: WHEN IN ANCIENT EGYPT, STICK TO MEAT.
AS IF THAT WOULD END THE BLOODLINE.
WHAT?

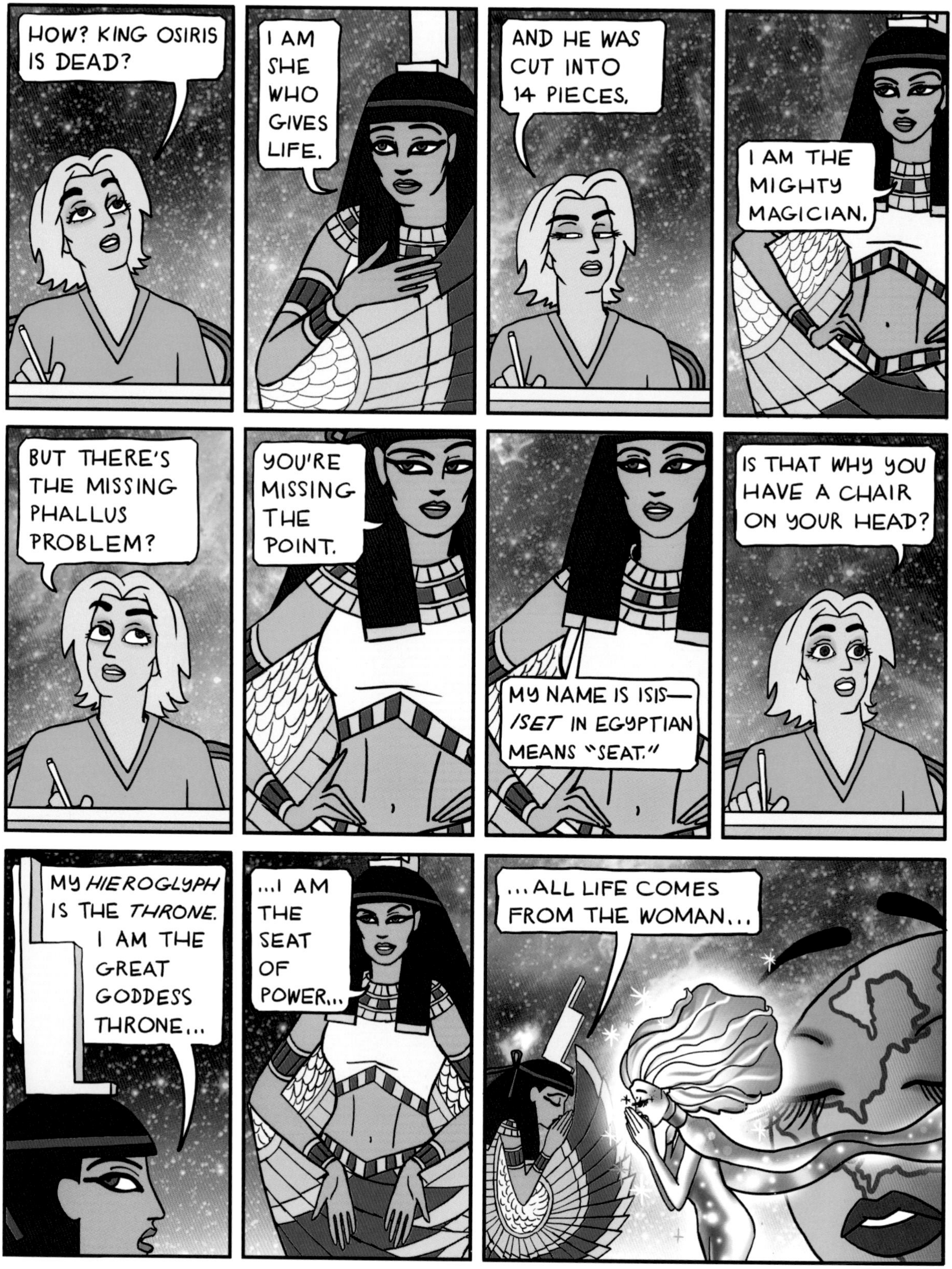
HOW? KING OSIRIS IS DEAD?
I AM SHE WHO GIVES LIFE.
AND HE WAS CUT INTO 14 PIECES.
I AM THE MIGHTY MAGICIAN.
BUT THERE'S THE MISSING PHALLUS PROBLEM?
YOU'RE MISSING THE POINT.
MY NAME IS ISIS—*ISET* IN EGYPTIAN MEANS "SEAT."
IS THAT WHY YOU HAVE A CHAIR ON YOUR HEAD?
MY *HIEROGLYPH* IS THE *THRONE.* I AM THE GREAT GODDESS THRONE...
...I AM THE SEAT OF POWER...
...ALL LIFE COMES FROM THE WOMAN...

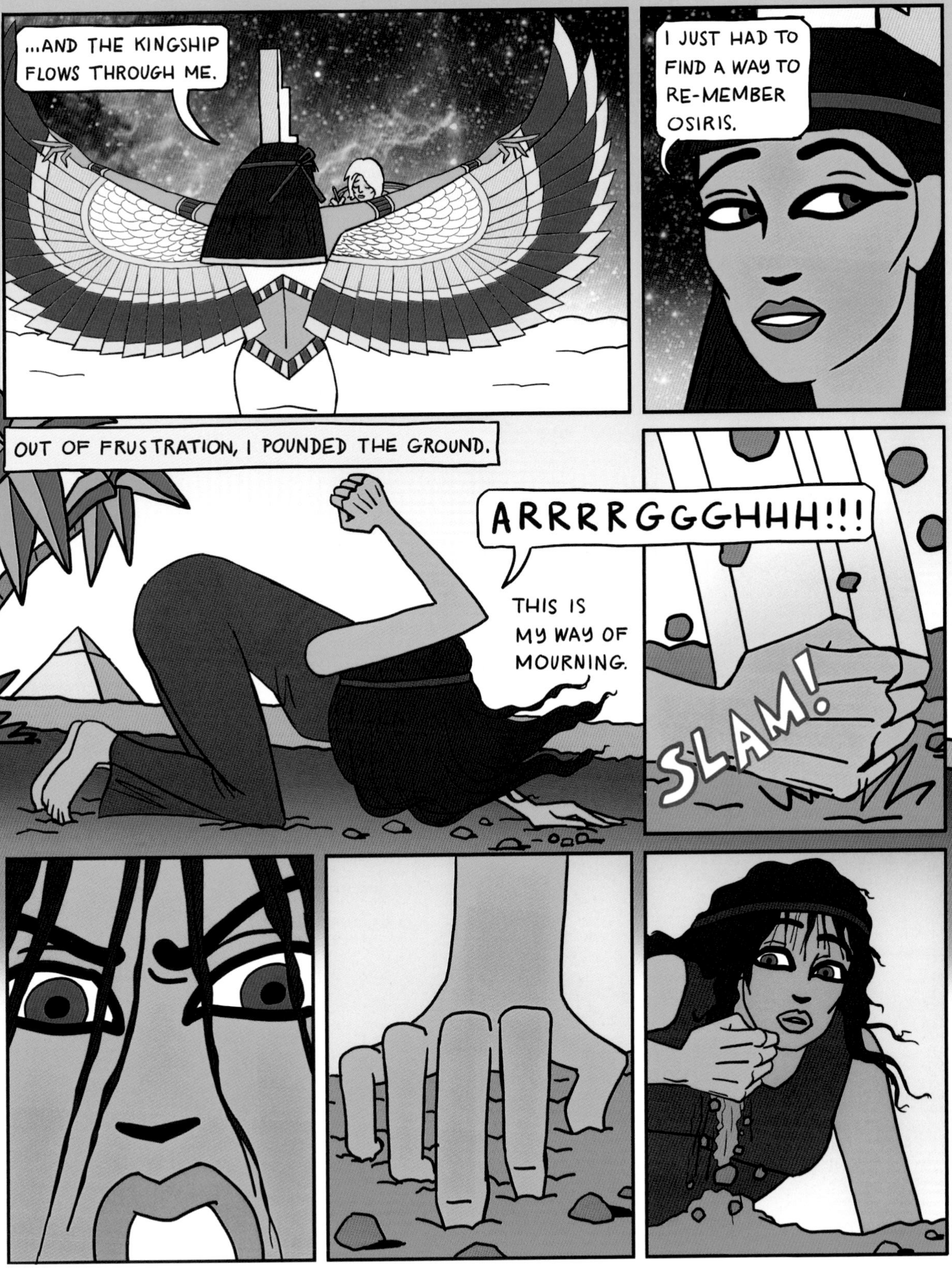
...AND THE KINGSHIP FLOWS THROUGH ME.
I JUST HAD TO FIND A WAY TO RE-MEMBER OSIRIS.
OUT OF FRUSTRATION, I POUNDED THE GROUND.
ARRRRGGGHHH!!!
THIS IS MY WAY OF MOURNING.
SLAM!

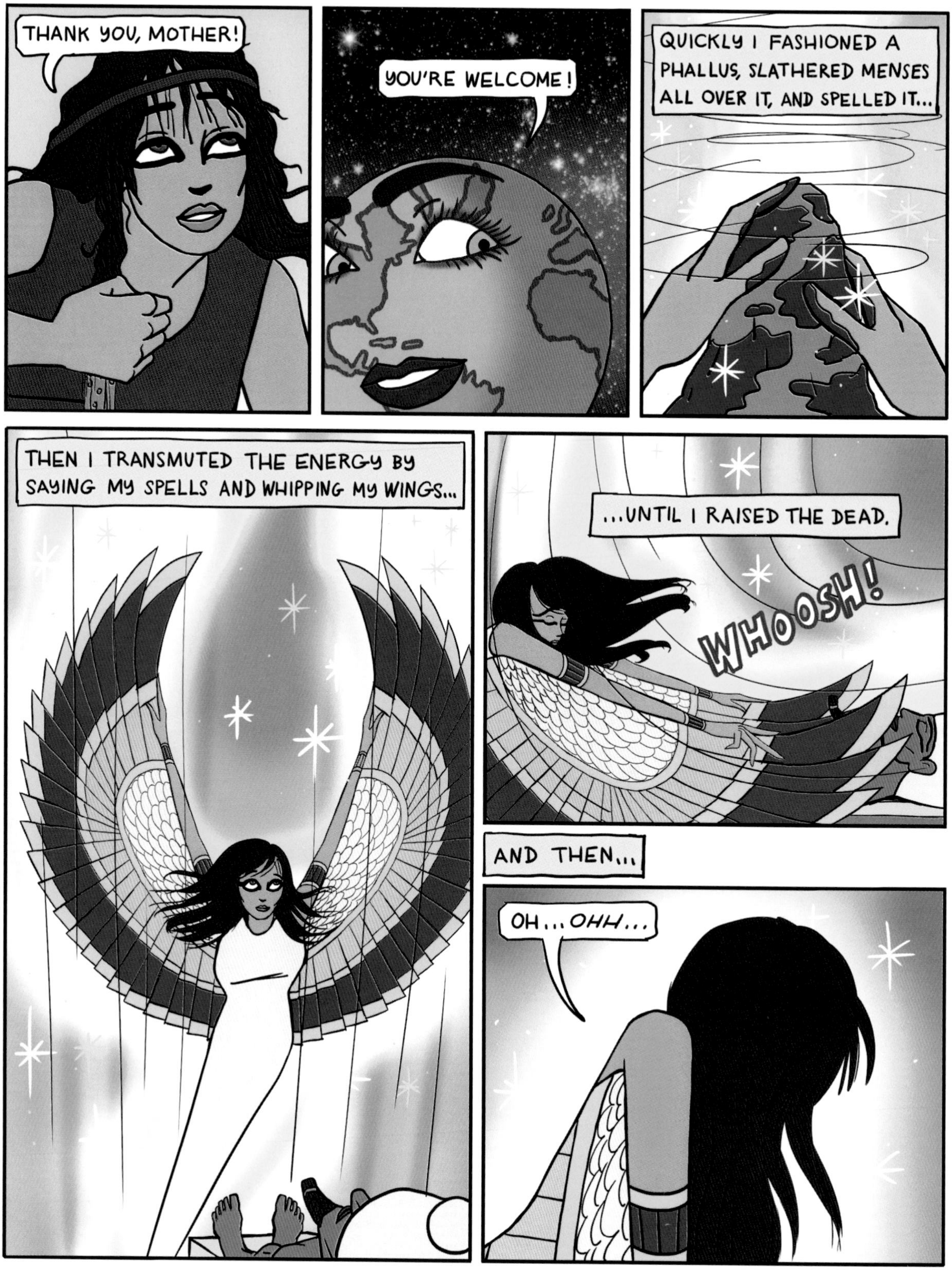
THANK YOU, MOTHER!
YOU'RE WELCOME!
QUICKLY I FASHIONED A PHALLUS, SLATHERED MENSES ALL OVER IT, AND SPELLED IT...
THEN I TRANSMUTED THE ENERGY BY SAYING MY SPELLS AND WHIPPING MY WINGS...
...UNTIL I RAISED THE DEAD.
WHOOSH!
AND THEN...
OH...OHH...

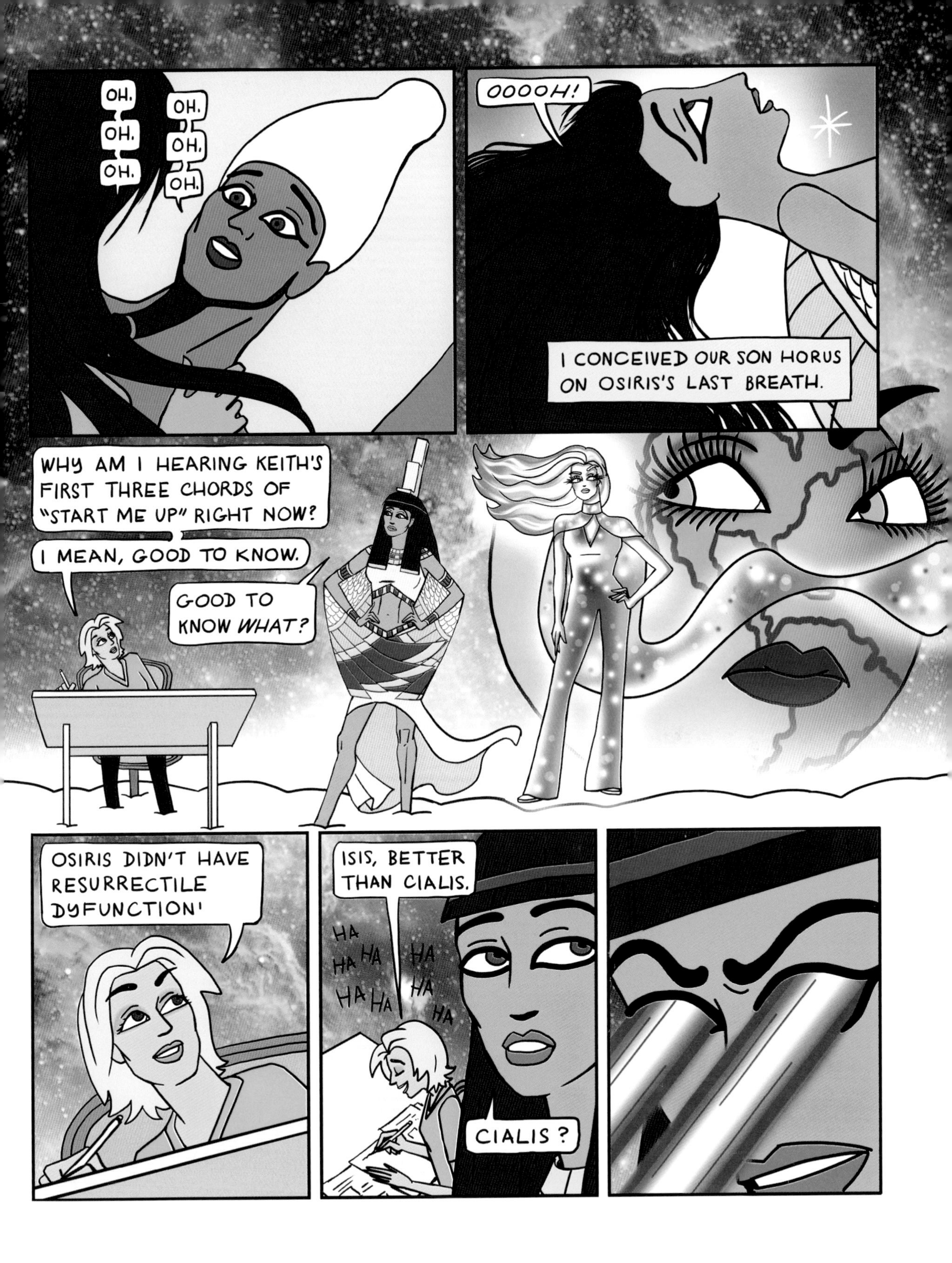

OH.
OH.
OH.
OH.
OH,
OH.
OOOOH!
I CONCEIVED OUR SON HORUS ON OSIRIS'S LAST BREATH.
WHY AM I HEARING KEITH'S FIRST THREE CHORDS OF "START ME UP" RIGHT NOW?
I MEAN, GOOD TO KNOW.
GOOD TO KNOW WHAT?
OSIRIS DIDN'T HAVE RESURRECTILE DYFUNCTION'
ISIS, BETTER THAN CIALIS.
HA HA HA HA HA HA HA HA HA
CIALIS?

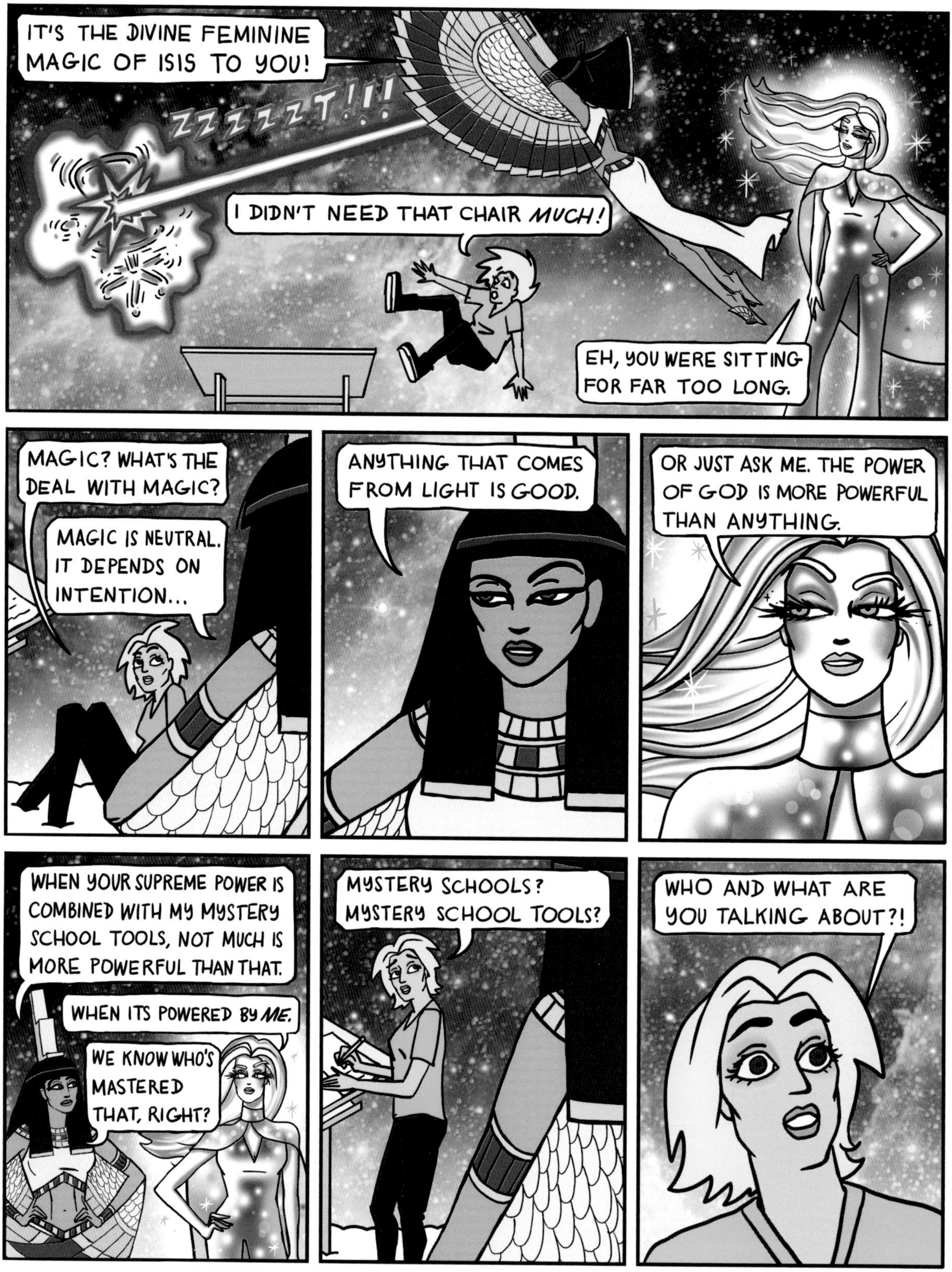
IT'S THE DIVINE FEMININE MAGIC OF ISIS TO YOU!
ZZZZZZT!!!
I DIDN'T NEED THAT CHAIR *MUCH*!
EH, YOU WERE SITTING FOR FAR TOO LONG.
MAGIC? WHAT'S THE DEAL WITH MAGIC?
MAGIC IS NEUTRAL. IT DEPENDS ON INTENTION...
ANYTHING THAT COMES FROM LIGHT IS *GOOD*.
OR JUST ASK ME. THE POWER OF GOD IS MORE POWERFUL THAN ANYTHING.
WHEN YOUR SUPREME POWER IS COMBINED WITH MY MYSTERY SCHOOL TOOLS, NOT MUCH IS MORE POWERFUL THAN THAT.
WHEN ITS POWERED BY *ME*.
WE KNOW WHO'S MASTERED THAT, RIGHT?
MYSTERY SCHOOLS? MYSTERY SCHOOL TOOLS?
WHO AND WHAT ARE YOU TALKING ABOUT?!

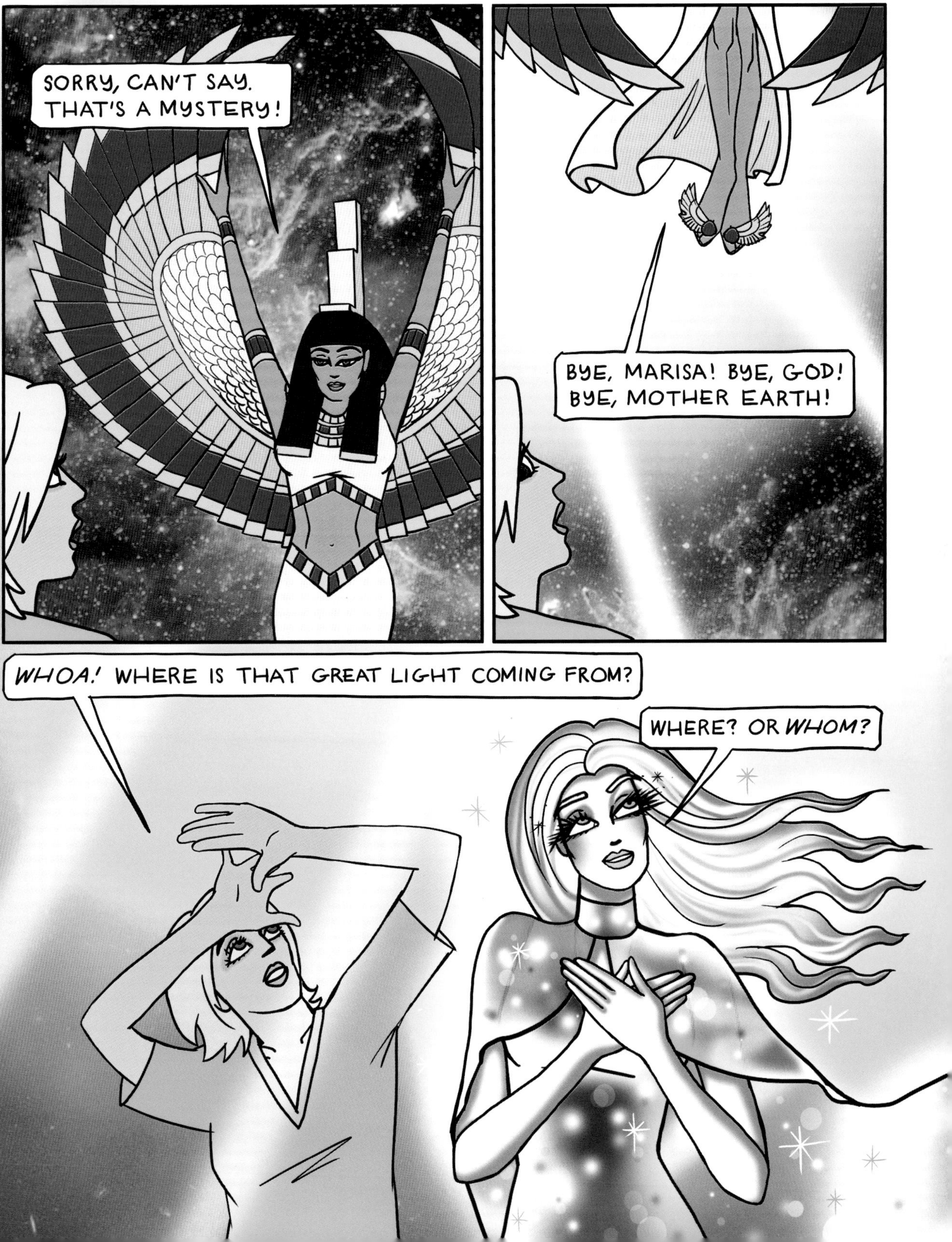
SORRY, CAN'T SAY. THAT'S A MYSTERY!
BYE, MARISA! BYE, GOD! BYE, MOTHER EARTH!
WHOA! WHERE IS THAT GREAT LIGHT COMING FROM?
WHERE? OR *WHOM?*

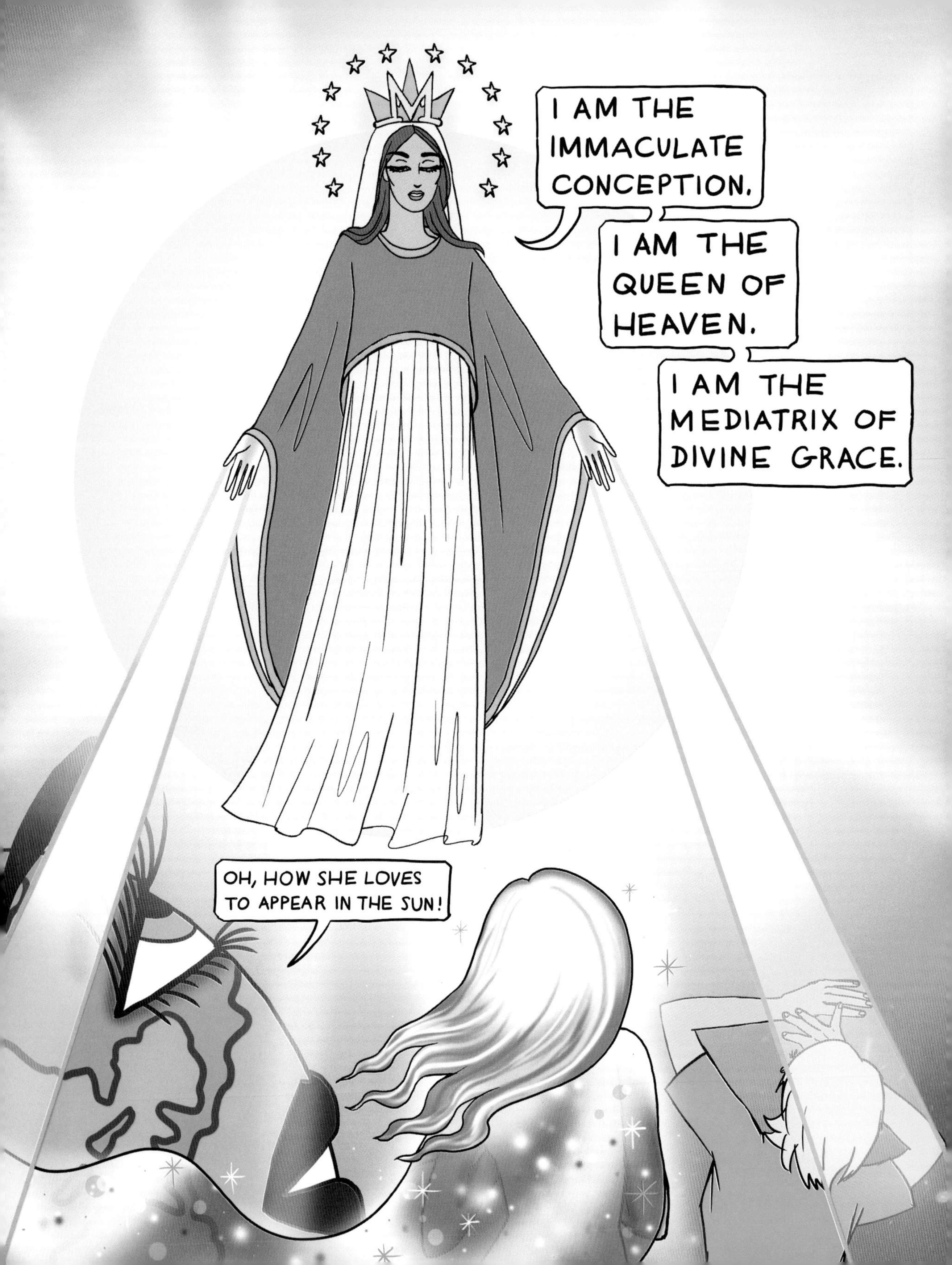
I AM THE IMMACULATE CONCEPTION.
I AM THE QUEEN OF HEAVEN.
I AM THE MEDIATRIX OF DIVINE GRACE.
OH, HOW SHE LOVES TO APPEAR IN THE SUN!

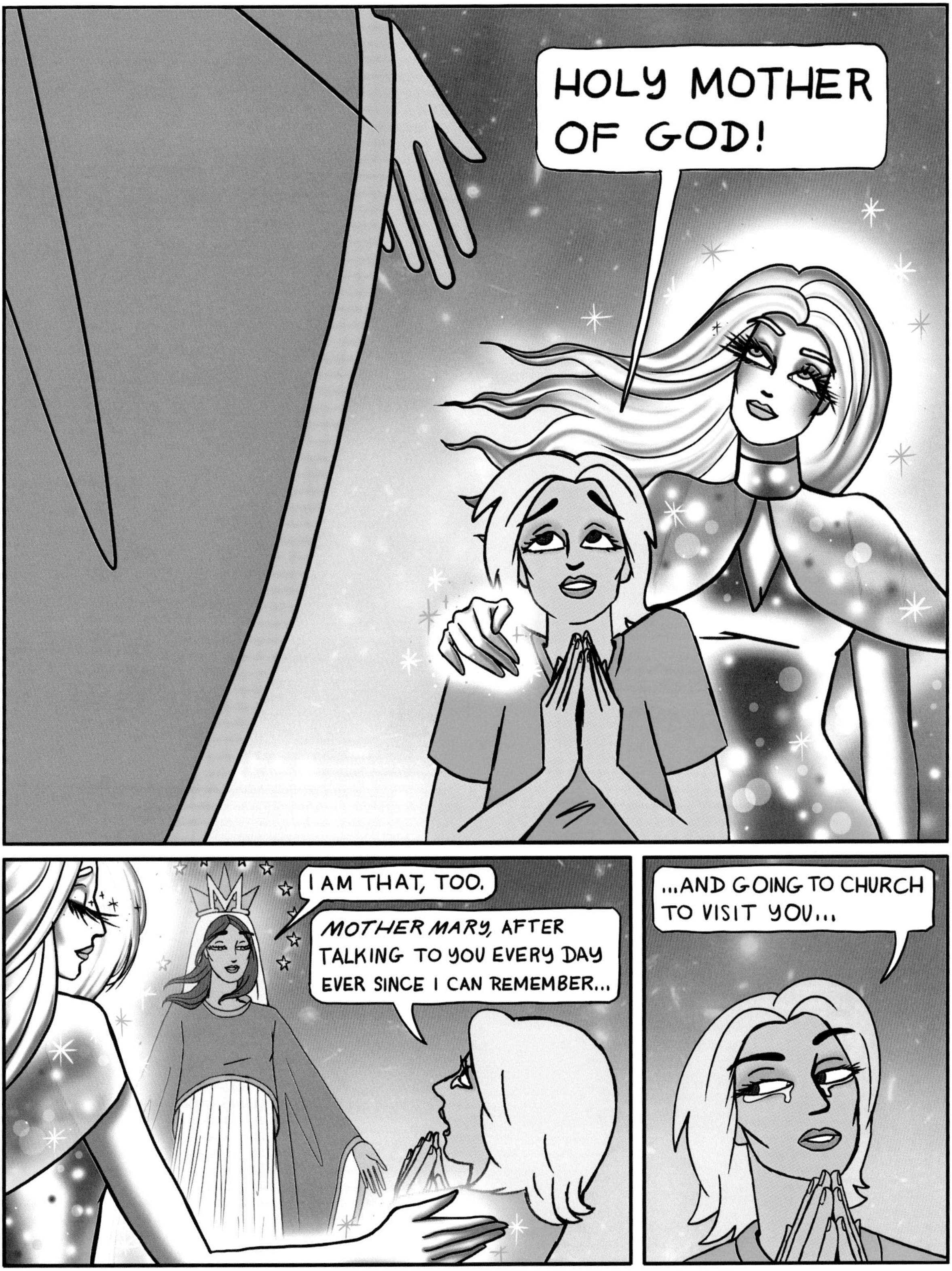
HOLY MOTHER OF GOD!
I AM THAT, TOO.
MOTHER MARY, AFTER TALKING TO YOU EVERY DAY EVER SINCE I CAN REMEMBER...
...AND GOING TO CHURCH TO VISIT YOU...

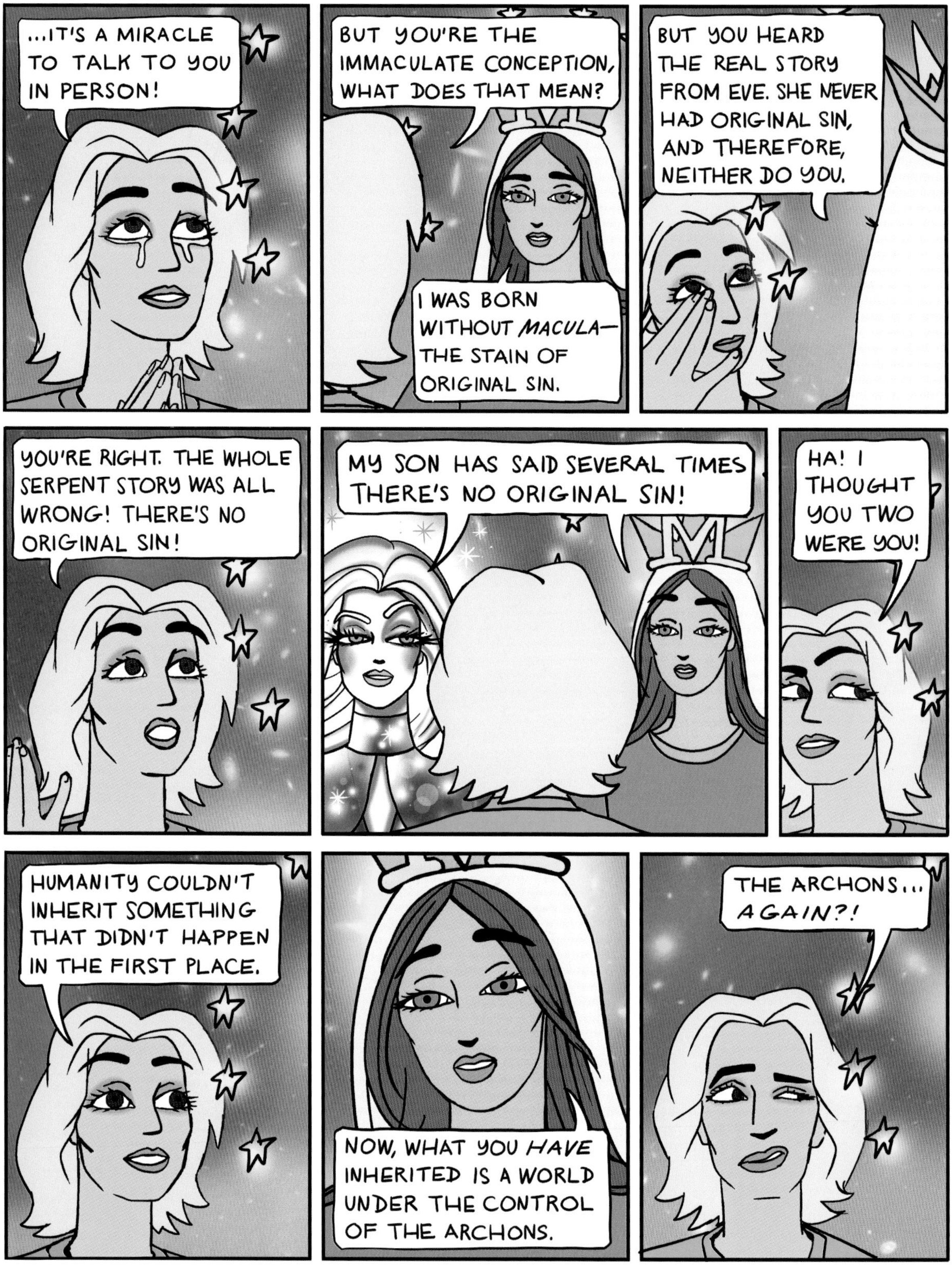
...IT'S A MIRACLE TO TALK TO YOU IN PERSON!
BUT YOU'RE THE IMMACULATE CONCEPTION, WHAT DOES THAT MEAN?
I WAS BORN WITHOUT *MACULA*—THE STAIN OF ORIGINAL SIN.
BUT YOU HEARD THE REAL STORY FROM EVE. SHE NEVER HAD ORIGINAL SIN, AND THEREFORE, NEITHER DO YOU.
YOU'RE RIGHT. THE WHOLE SERPENT STORY WAS ALL WRONG! THERE'S NO ORIGINAL SIN!
MY SON HAS SAID SEVERAL TIMES THERE'S NO ORIGINAL SIN!
HA! I THOUGHT YOU TWO WERE YOU!
HUMANITY COULDN'T INHERIT SOMETHING THAT DIDN'T HAPPEN IN THE FIRST PLACE.
NOW, WHAT YOU *HAVE* INHERITED IS A WORLD UNDER THE CONTROL OF THE ARCHONS.
THE ARCHONS... *AGAIN?!*

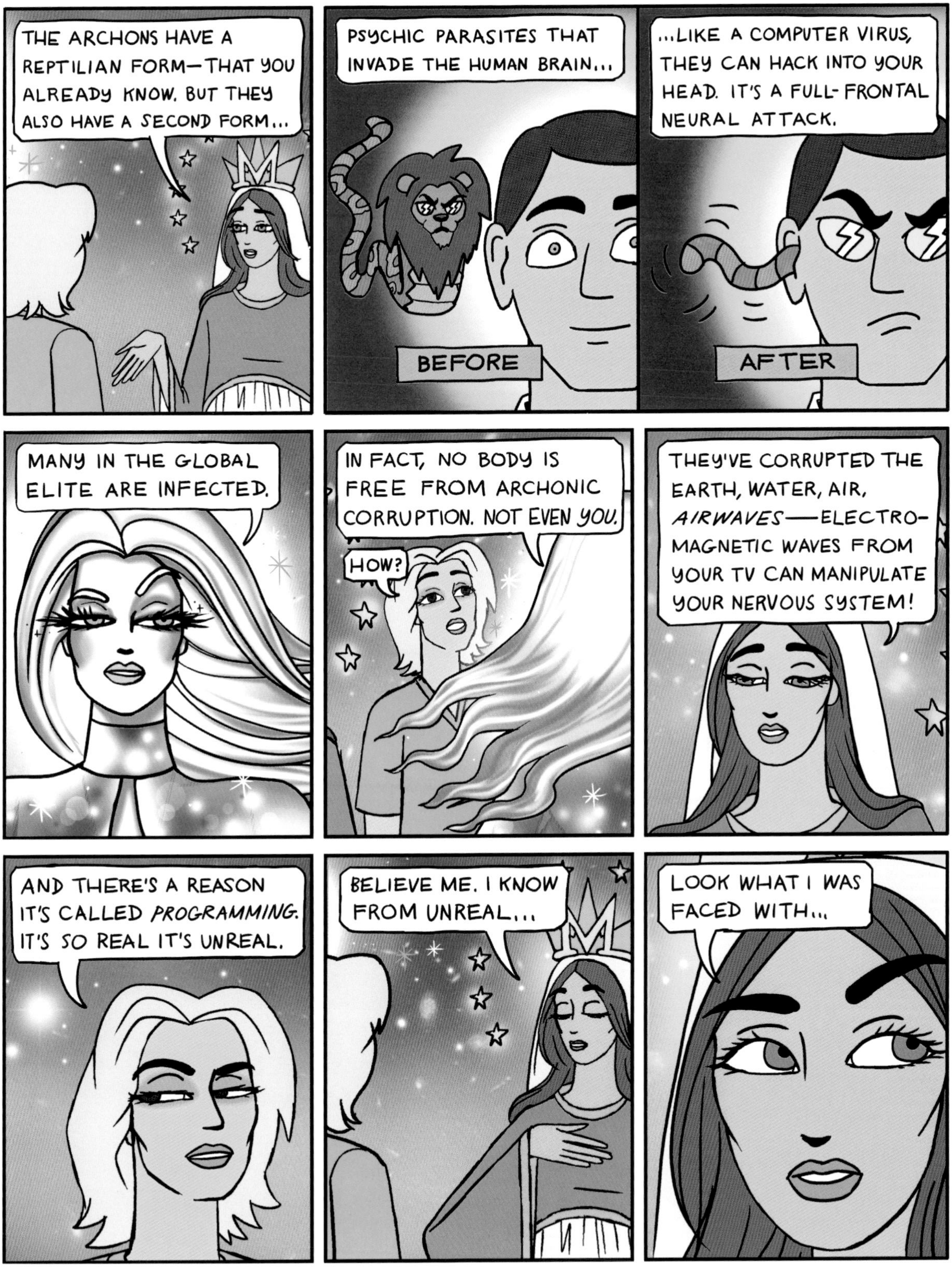
THE ARCHONS HAVE A REPTILIAN FORM—THAT YOU ALREADY KNOW. BUT THEY ALSO HAVE A SECOND FORM...
PSYCHIC PARASITES THAT INVADE THE HUMAN BRAIN...
BEFORE
...LIKE A COMPUTER VIRUS, THEY CAN HACK INTO YOUR HEAD. IT'S A FULL-FRONTAL NEURAL ATTACK.
AFTER
MANY IN THE GLOBAL ELITE ARE INFECTED.
IN FACT, NO BODY IS FREE FROM ARCHONIC CORRUPTION. NOT EVEN *YOU*.
HOW?
THEY'VE CORRUPTED THE EARTH, WATER, AIR, *AIRWAVES*—ELECTRO-MAGNETIC WAVES FROM YOUR TV CAN MANIPULATE YOUR NERVOUS SYSTEM!
AND THERE'S A REASON IT'S CALLED *PROGRAMMING*. IT'S SO REAL IT'S UNREAL.
BELIEVE ME. I KNOW FROM UNREAL...
LOOK WHAT I WAS FACED WITH...

...I WAS 16 YEARS OLD AND VERY HUMAN WHEN ARCHANGEL *GABRIEL* MADE THE BIG *ANNUNCIATION*: I WAS MEANT TO BE THE MOTHER OF GOD...

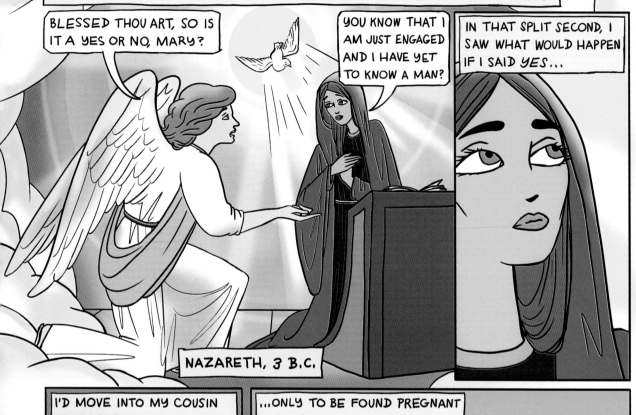

BLESSED THOU ART, SO IS IT A YES OR NO, MARY?

YOU KNOW THAT I AM JUST ENGAGED AND I HAVE YET TO KNOW A MAN?

IN THAT SPLIT SECOND, I SAW WHAT WOULD HAPPEN IF I SAID *YES*...

NAZARETH, *3 B.C.*

I'D MOVE INTO MY COUSIN *ELIZABETH'S* HOUSE TO HIDE...

MARY, I AM BLESSED THE MOTHER OF GOD SHOULD COME TO ME!

...ONLY TO BE FOUND PREGNANT AND UNMARRIED BY MY PEERS...

LOOK WHO'S FINALLY OFF HER HIGH HORSE!

I KNEW SHE WAS TOO GOOD TO BE TRUE!

LITTLE MISS PERFECT IS JUST A LITTLE *SHAR-MOOTA!*

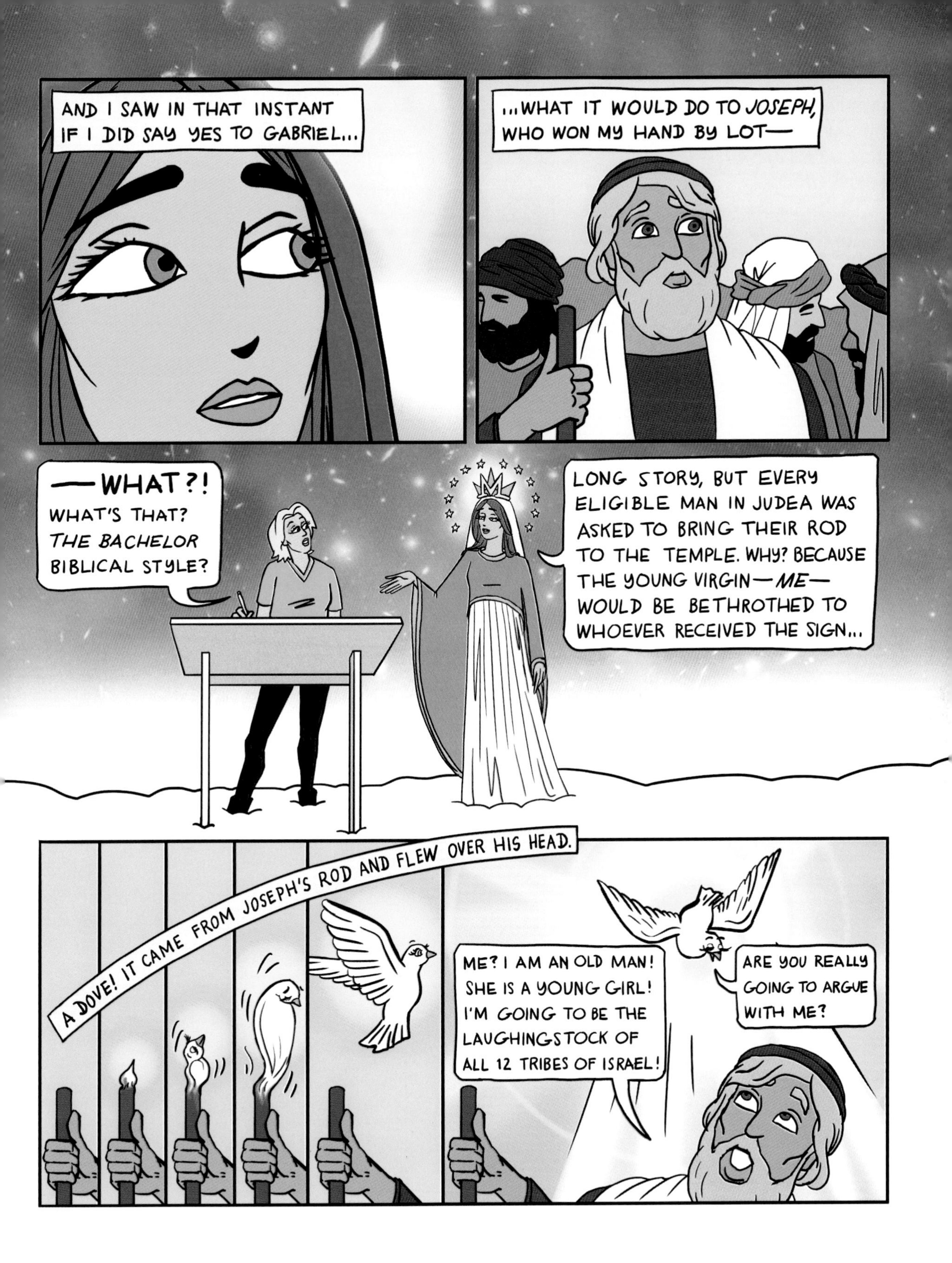
AND I SAW IN THAT INSTANT IF I DID SAY YES TO GABRIEL...
...WHAT IT WOULD DO TO JOSEPH, WHO WON MY HAND BY LOT—
—WHAT?! WHAT'S THAT? THE BACHELOR BIBLICAL STYLE?
LONG STORY, BUT EVERY ELIGIBLE MAN IN JUDEA WAS ASKED TO BRING THEIR ROD TO THE TEMPLE. WHY? BECAUSE THE YOUNG VIRGIN—ME—WOULD BE BETHROTHED TO WHOEVER RECEIVED THE SIGN...
A DOVE! IT CAME FROM JOSEPH'S ROD AND FLEW OVER HIS HEAD.
ME? I AM AN OLD MAN! SHE IS A YOUNG GIRL! I'M GOING TO BE THE LAUGHINGSTOCK OF ALL 12 TRIBES OF ISRAEL!
ARE YOU REALLY GOING TO ARGUE WITH ME?

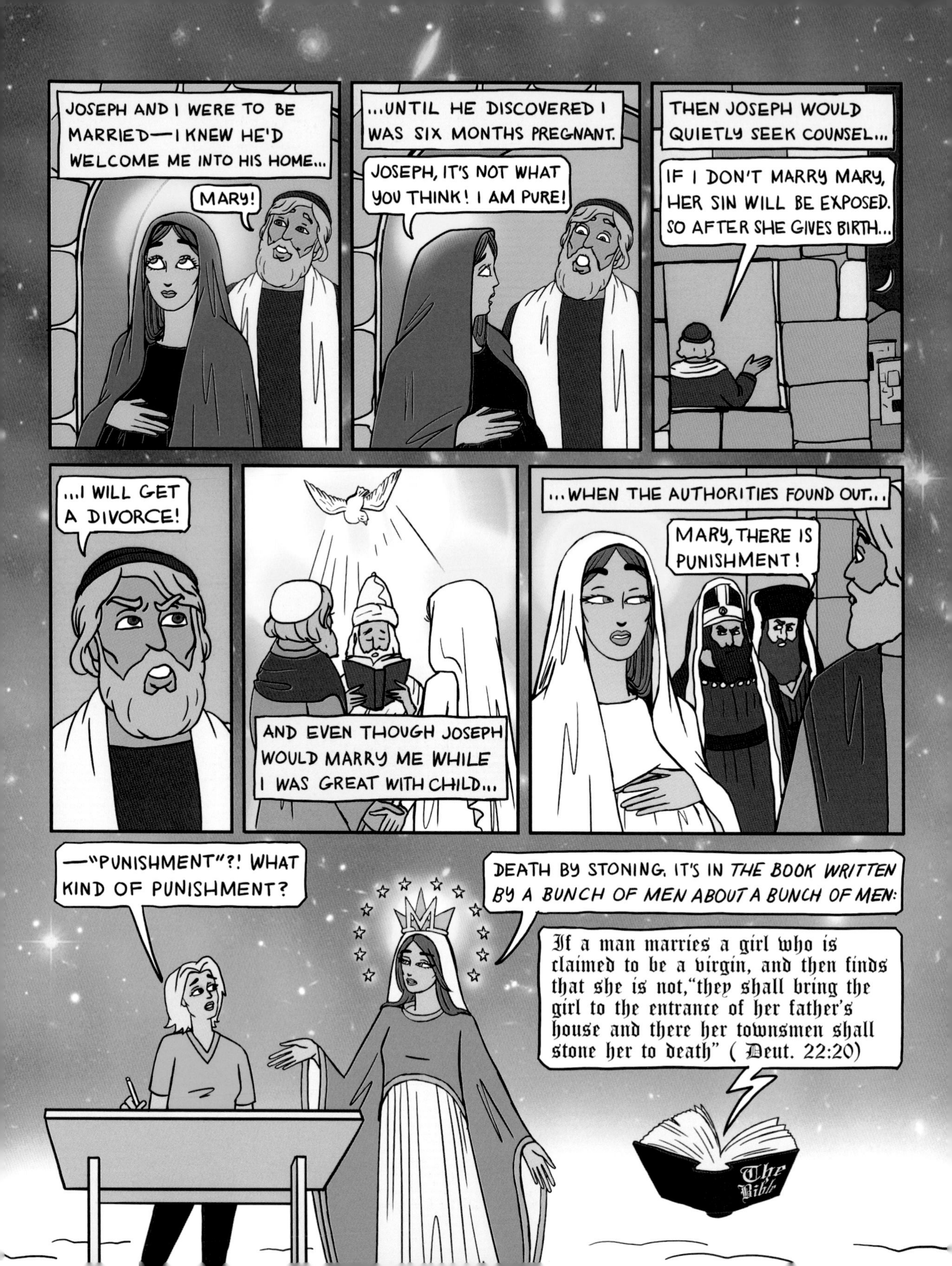
JOSEPH AND I WERE TO BE MARRIED—I KNEW HE'D WELCOME ME INTO HIS HOME...
MARY!
...UNTIL HE DISCOVERED I WAS SIX MONTHS PREGNANT.
JOSEPH, IT'S NOT WHAT YOU THINK! I AM PURE!
THEN JOSEPH WOULD QUIETLY SEEK COUNSEL...
IF I DON'T MARRY MARY, HER SIN WILL BE EXPOSED. SO AFTER SHE GIVES BIRTH...
...I WILL GET A DIVORCE!
AND EVEN THOUGH JOSEPH WOULD MARRY ME WHILE I WAS GREAT WITH CHILD...
...WHEN THE AUTHORITIES FOUND OUT...
MARY, THERE IS PUNISHMENT!
—"PUNISHMENT"?! WHAT KIND OF PUNISHMENT?
DEATH BY STONING. IT'S IN *THE BOOK WRITTEN BY A BUNCH OF MEN ABOUT A BUNCH OF MEN*:
If a man marries a girl who is claimed to be a virgin, and then finds that she is not, "they shall bring the girl to the entrance of her father's house and there her townsmen shall stone her to death" (Deut. 22:20)
The Bible

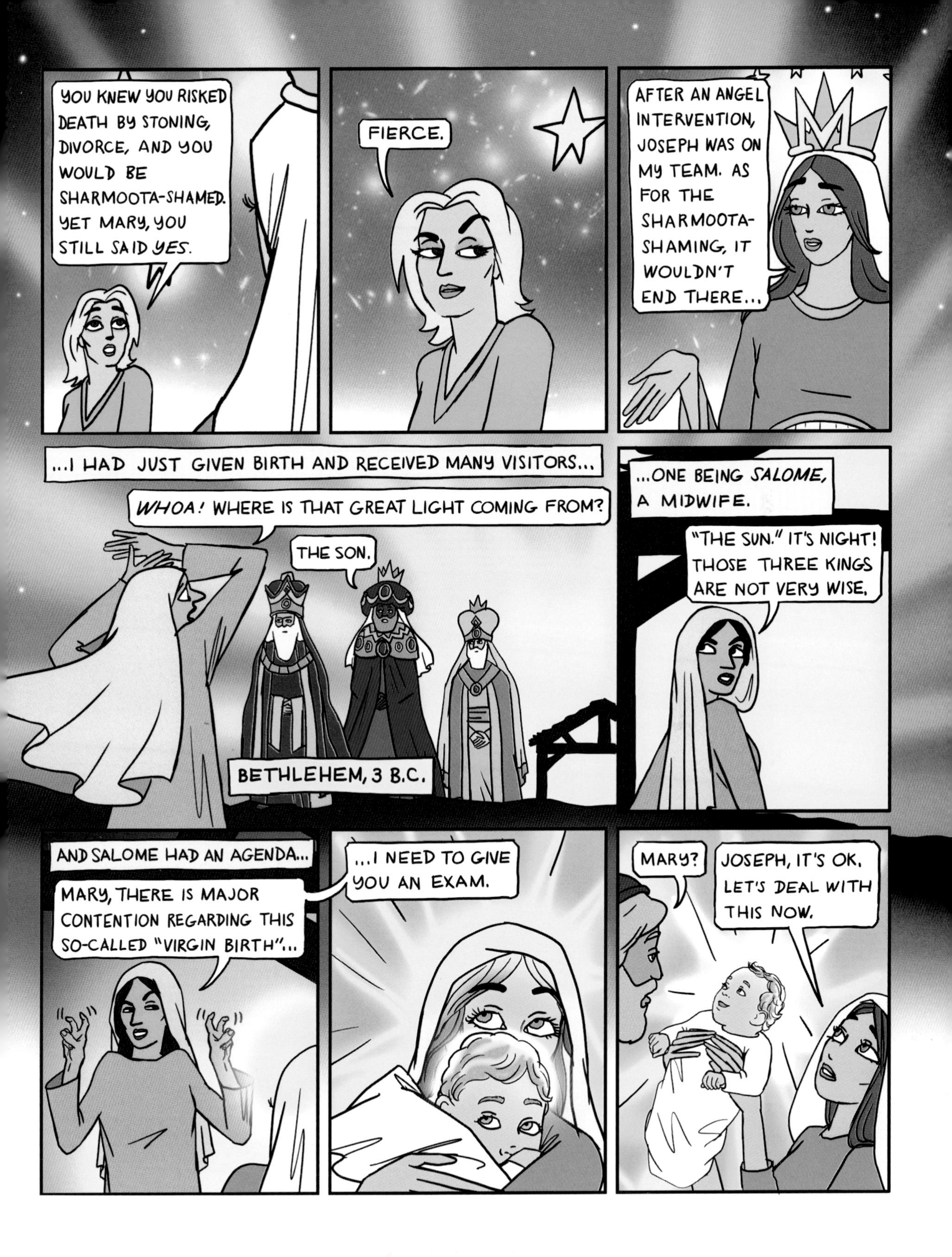
YOU KNEW YOU RISKED DEATH BY STONING, DIVORCE, AND YOU WOULD BE SHARMOOTA-SHAMED. YET MARY, YOU STILL SAID *YES*.
FIERCE.
AFTER AN ANGEL INTERVENTION, JOSEPH WAS ON MY TEAM. AS FOR THE SHARMOOTA-SHAMING, IT WOULDN'T END THERE...
...I HAD JUST GIVEN BIRTH AND RECEIVED MANY VISITORS...
WHOA! WHERE IS THAT GREAT LIGHT COMING FROM?
THE SON.
BETHLEHEM, 3 B.C.
...ONE BEING *SALOME*, A MIDWIFE.
"THE SUN." IT'S NIGHT! THOSE THREE KINGS ARE NOT VERY WISE.
AND SALOME HAD AN AGENDA...
MARY, THERE IS MAJOR CONTENTION REGARDING THIS SO-CALLED "VIRGIN BIRTH"...
...I NEED TO GIVE YOU AN EXAM.
MARY?
JOSEPH, IT'S OK. LET'S DEAL WITH THIS NOW.

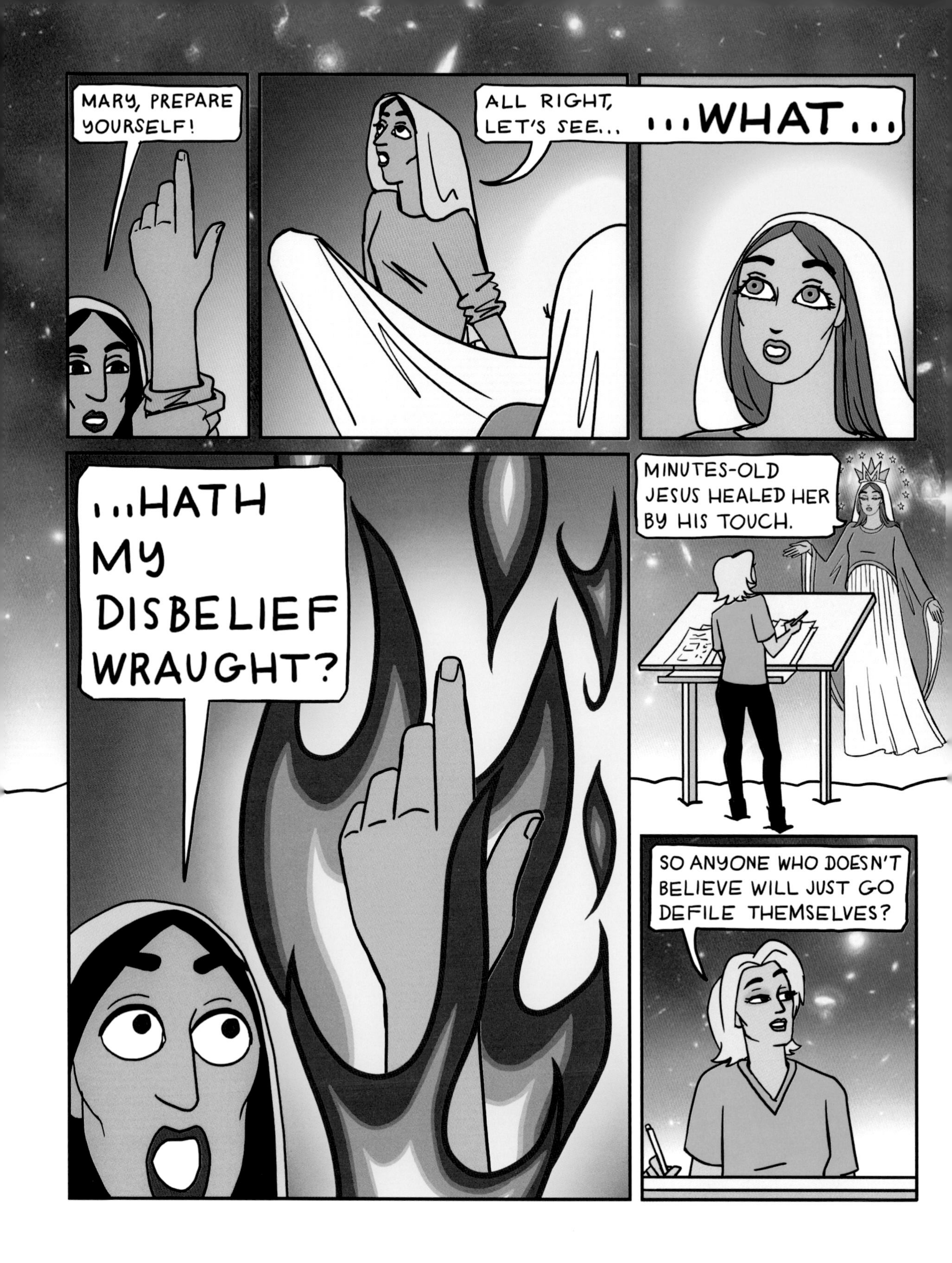
MARY, PREPARE YOURSELF!
ALL RIGHT, LET'S SEE...
...WHAT...
...HATH MY DISBELIEF WRAUGHT?
MINUTES-OLD JESUS HEALED HER BY HIS TOUCH.
SO ANYONE WHO DOESN'T BELIEVE WILL JUST GO DEFILE THEMSELVES?

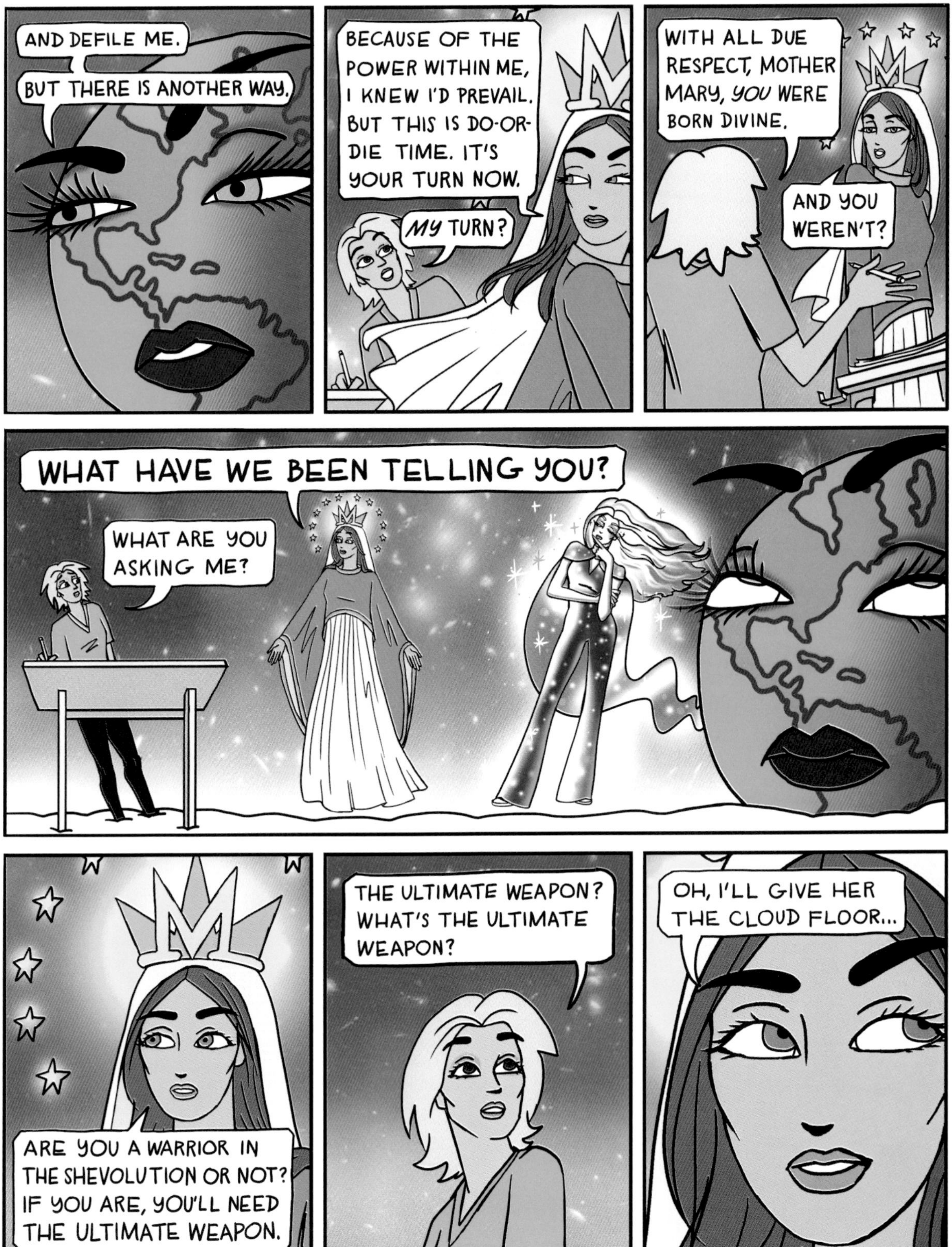
AND DEFILE ME.
BUT THERE IS ANOTHER WAY.
BECAUSE OF THE POWER WITHIN ME, I KNEW I'D PREVAIL. BUT THIS IS DO-OR-DIE TIME. IT'S YOUR TURN NOW.
MY TURN?
WITH ALL DUE RESPECT, MOTHER MARY, *YOU* WERE BORN DIVINE.
AND YOU WEREN'T?
WHAT HAVE WE BEEN TELLING YOU?
WHAT ARE YOU ASKING ME?
ARE YOU A WARRIOR IN THE SHEVOLUTION OR NOT? IF YOU ARE, YOU'LL NEED THE ULTIMATE WEAPON.
THE ULTIMATE WEAPON? WHAT'S THE ULTIMATE WEAPON?
OH, I'LL GIVE HER THE CLOUD FLOOR...

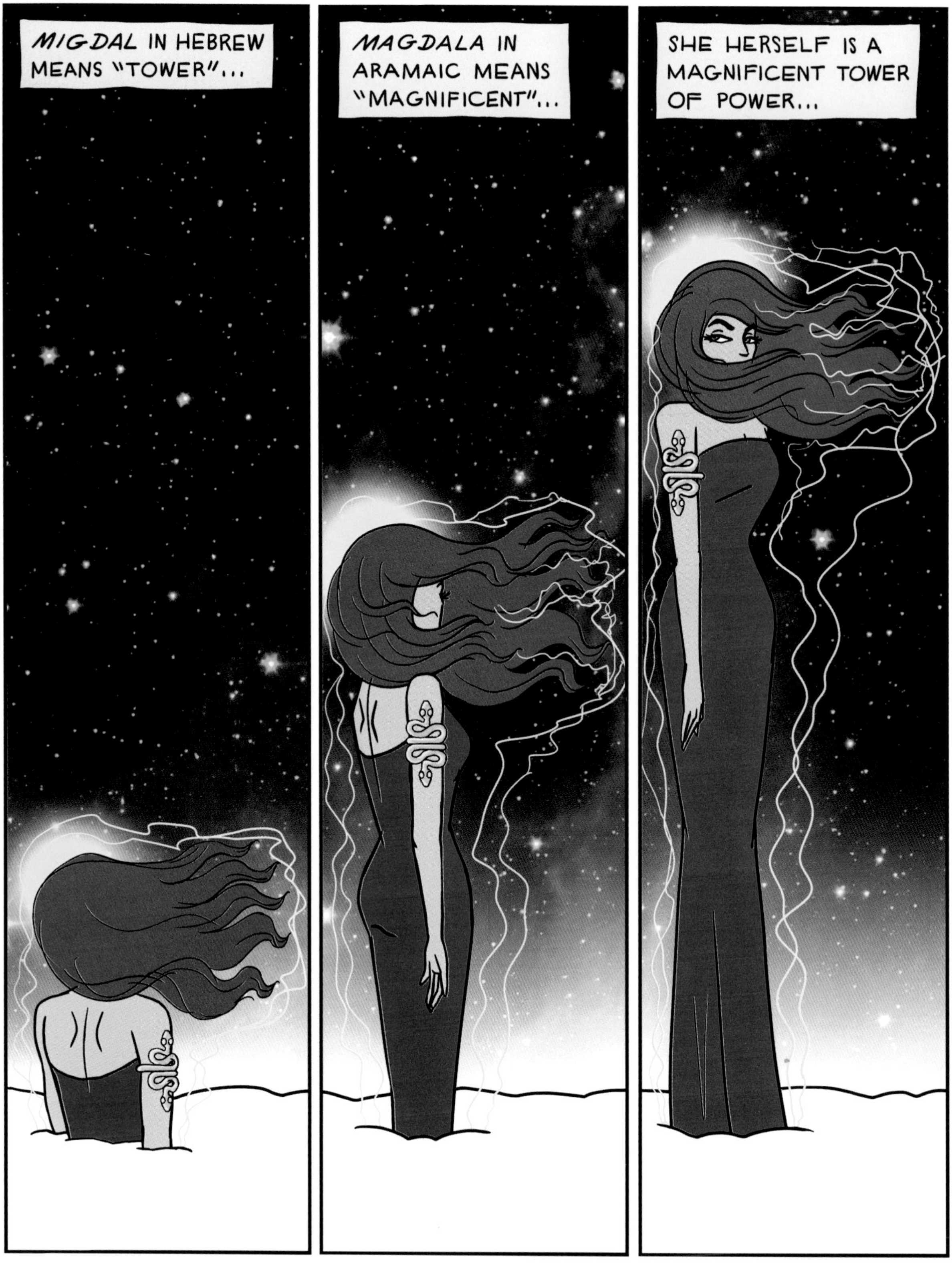
MIGDAL IN HEBREW MEANS "TOWER"...
MAGDALA IN ARAMAIC MEANS "MAGNIFICENT"...
SHE HERSELF IS A MAGNIFICENT TOWER OF POWER...

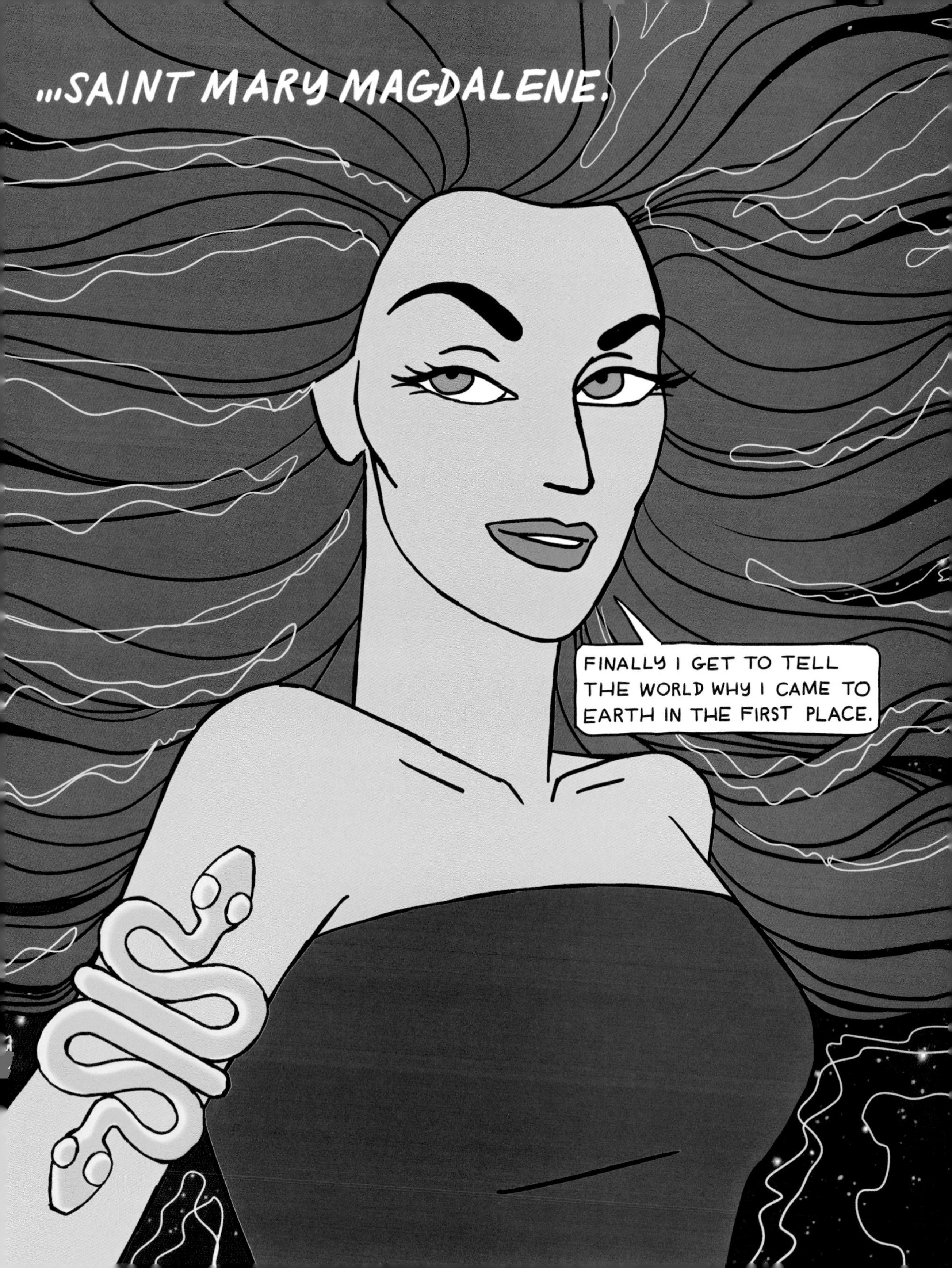
...SAINT MARY MAGDALENE.
FINALLY I GET TO TELL THE WORLD WHY I CAME TO EARTH IN THE FIRST PLACE.

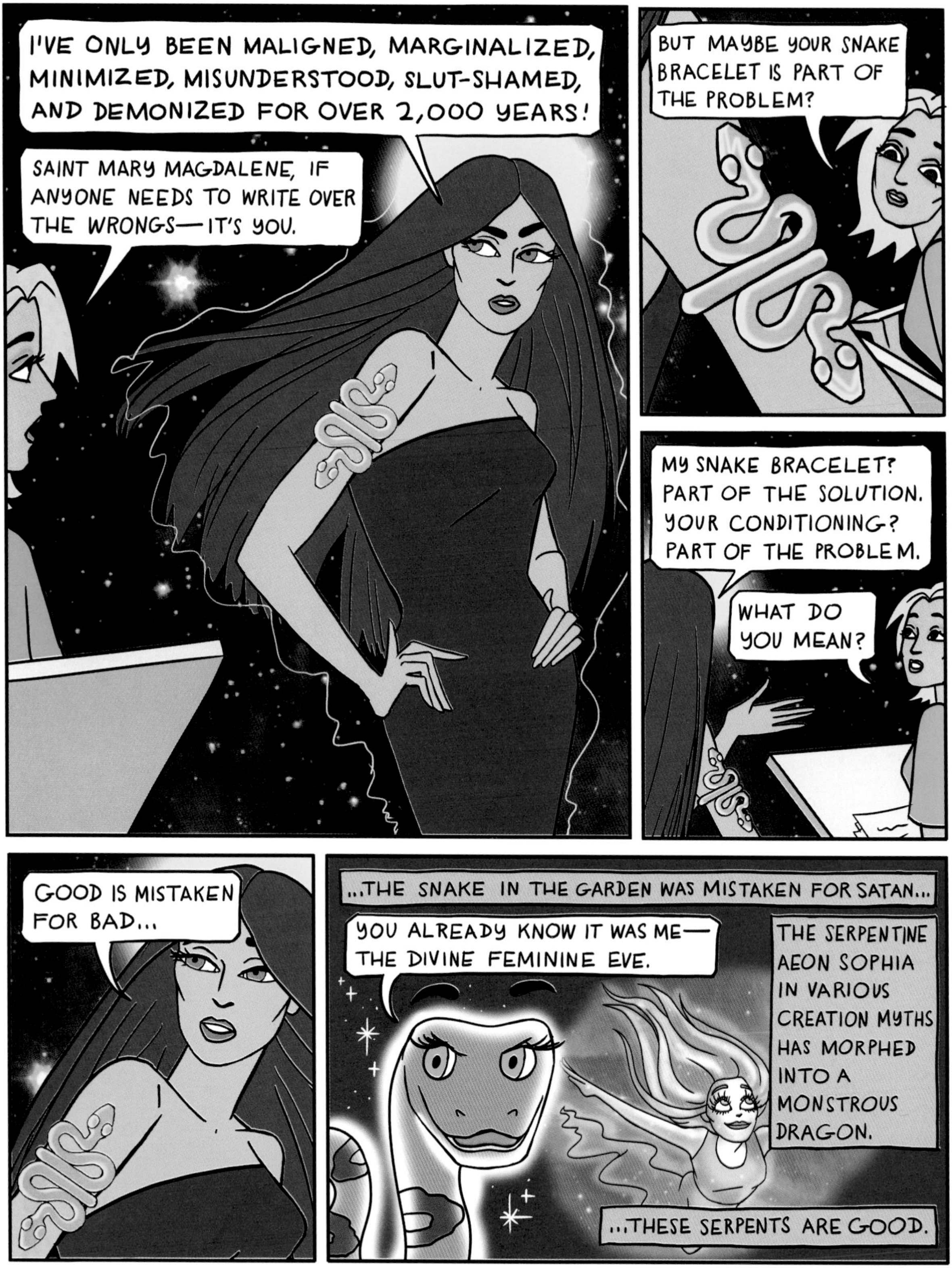
I'VE ONLY BEEN MALIGNED, MARGINALIZED, MINIMIZED, MISUNDERSTOOD, SLUT-SHAMED, AND DEMONIZED FOR OVER 2,000 YEARS!
SAINT MARY MAGDALENE, IF ANYONE NEEDS TO WRITE OVER THE WRONGS—IT'S YOU.
BUT MAYBE YOUR SNAKE BRACELET IS PART OF THE PROBLEM?
MY SNAKE BRACELET? PART OF THE SOLUTION. YOUR CONDITIONING? PART OF THE PROBLEM.
WHAT DO YOU MEAN?
GOOD IS MISTAKEN FOR BAD...
...THE SNAKE IN THE GARDEN WAS MISTAKEN FOR SATAN...
YOU ALREADY KNOW IT WAS ME—THE DIVINE FEMININE EVE.
THE SERPENTINE AEON SOPHIA IN VARIOUS CREATION MYTHS HAS MORPHED INTO A MONSTROUS DRAGON.
...THESE SERPENTS ARE GOOD.

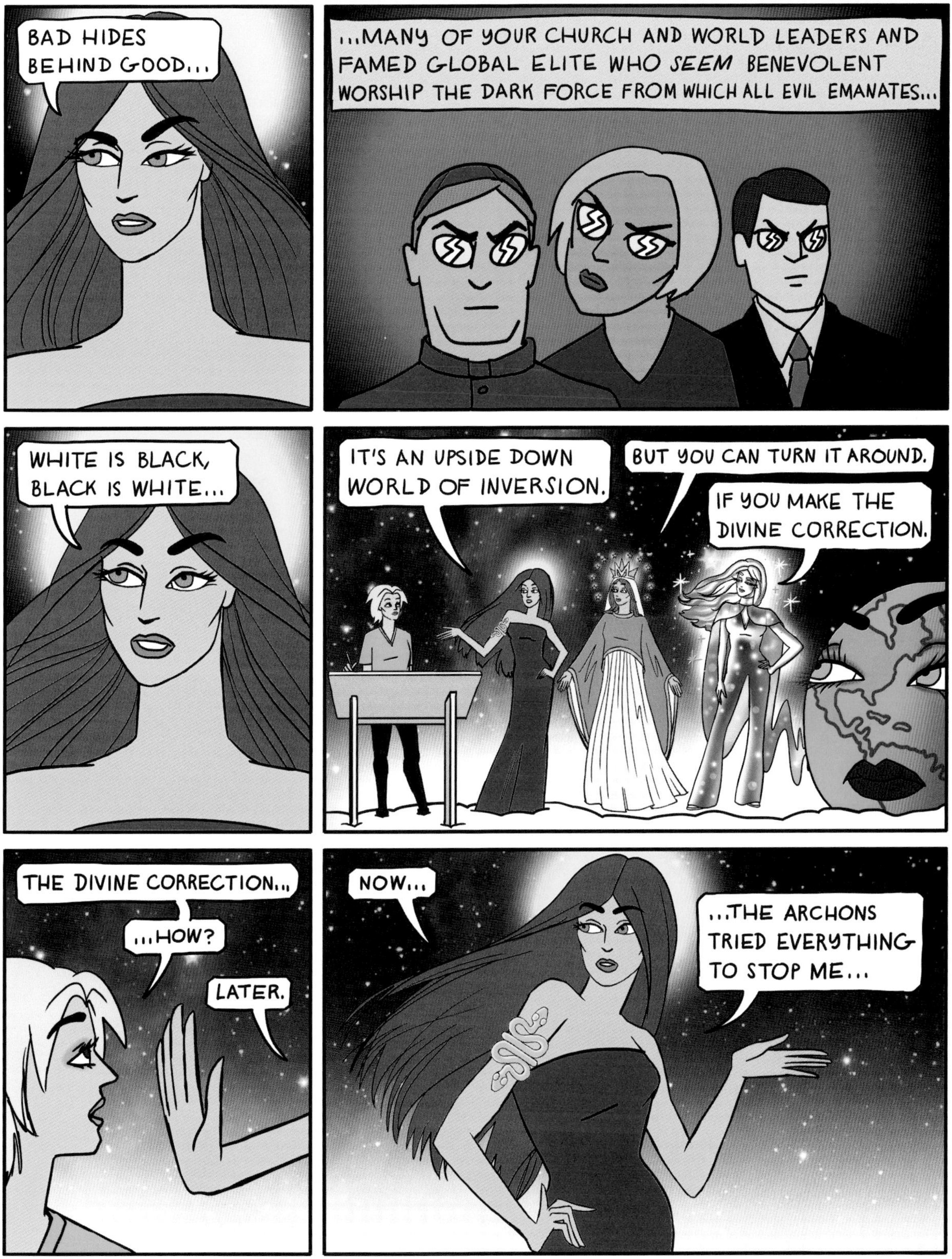
BAD HIDES BEHIND GOOD...
...MANY OF YOUR CHURCH AND WORLD LEADERS AND FAMED GLOBAL ELITE WHO *SEEM* BENEVOLENT WORSHIP THE DARK FORCE FROM WHICH ALL EVIL EMANATES...
WHITE IS BLACK, BLACK IS WHITE...
IT'S AN UPSIDE DOWN WORLD OF INVERSION.
BUT YOU CAN TURN IT AROUND.
IF YOU MAKE THE DIVINE CORRECTION.
THE DIVINE CORRECTION...
...HOW?
LATER.
NOW...
...THE ARCHONS TRIED EVERYTHING TO STOP ME...

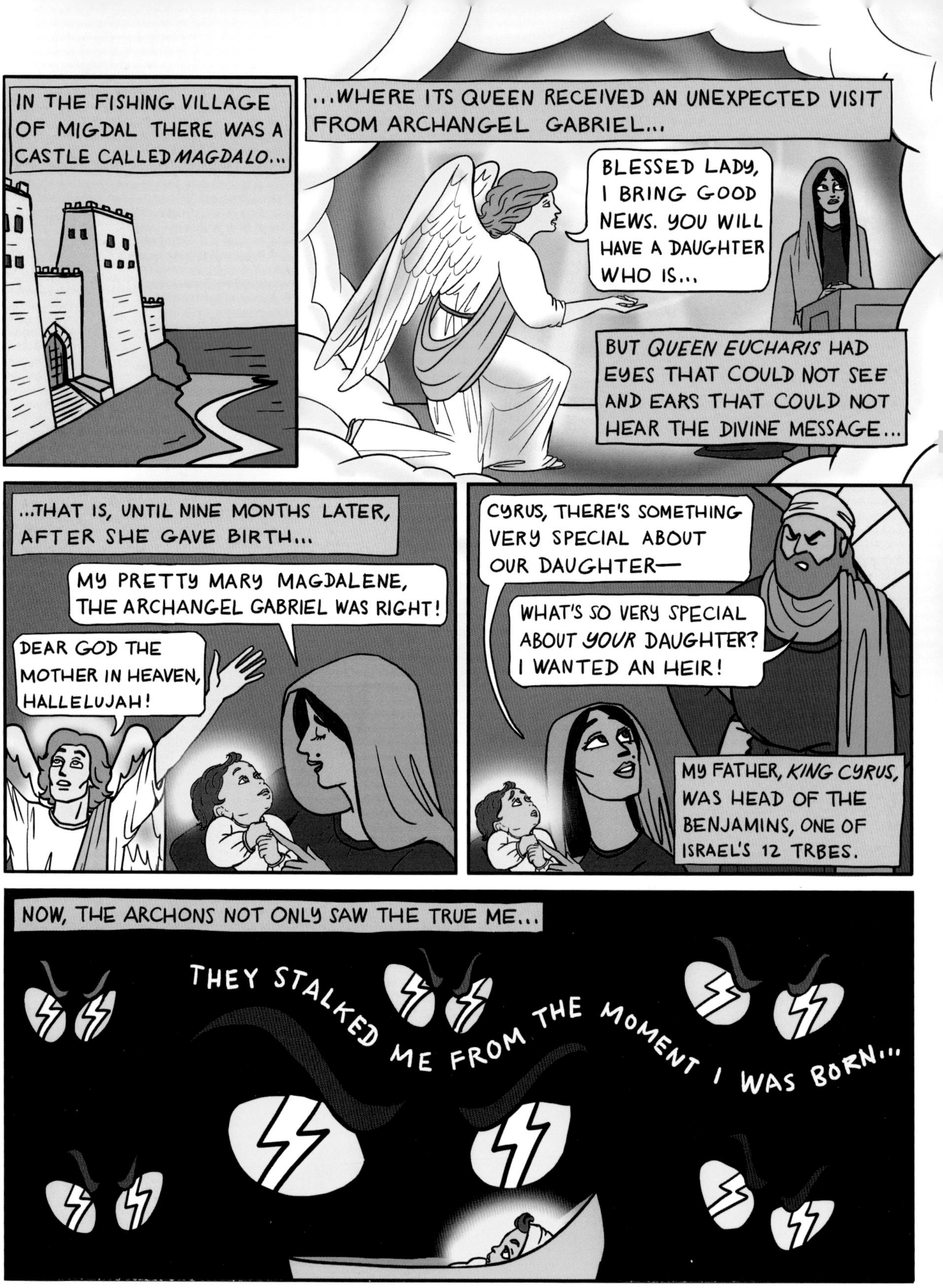
IN THE FISHING VILLAGE OF MIGDAL THERE WAS A CASTLE CALLED *MAGDALO*...
...WHERE ITS QUEEN RECEIVED AN UNEXPECTED VISIT FROM ARCHANGEL GABRIEL...
BLESSED LADY, I BRING GOOD NEWS. YOU WILL HAVE A DAUGHTER WHO IS...
BUT *QUEEN EUCHARIS* HAD EYES THAT COULD NOT SEE AND EARS THAT COULD NOT HEAR THE DIVINE MESSAGE...
...THAT IS, UNTIL NINE MONTHS LATER, AFTER SHE GAVE BIRTH...
MY PRETTY MARY MAGDALENE, THE ARCHANGEL GABRIEL WAS RIGHT!
DEAR GOD THE MOTHER IN HEAVEN, HALLELUJAH!
CYRUS, THERE'S SOMETHING VERY SPECIAL ABOUT OUR DAUGHTER—
WHAT'S SO VERY SPECIAL ABOUT *YOUR* DAUGHTER? I WANTED AN HEIR!
MY FATHER, *KING CYRUS*, WAS HEAD OF THE BENJAMINS, ONE OF ISRAEL'S 12 TRBES.
NOW, THE ARCHONS NOT ONLY SAW THE TRUE ME...
THEY STALKED ME FROM THE MOMENT I WAS BORN...

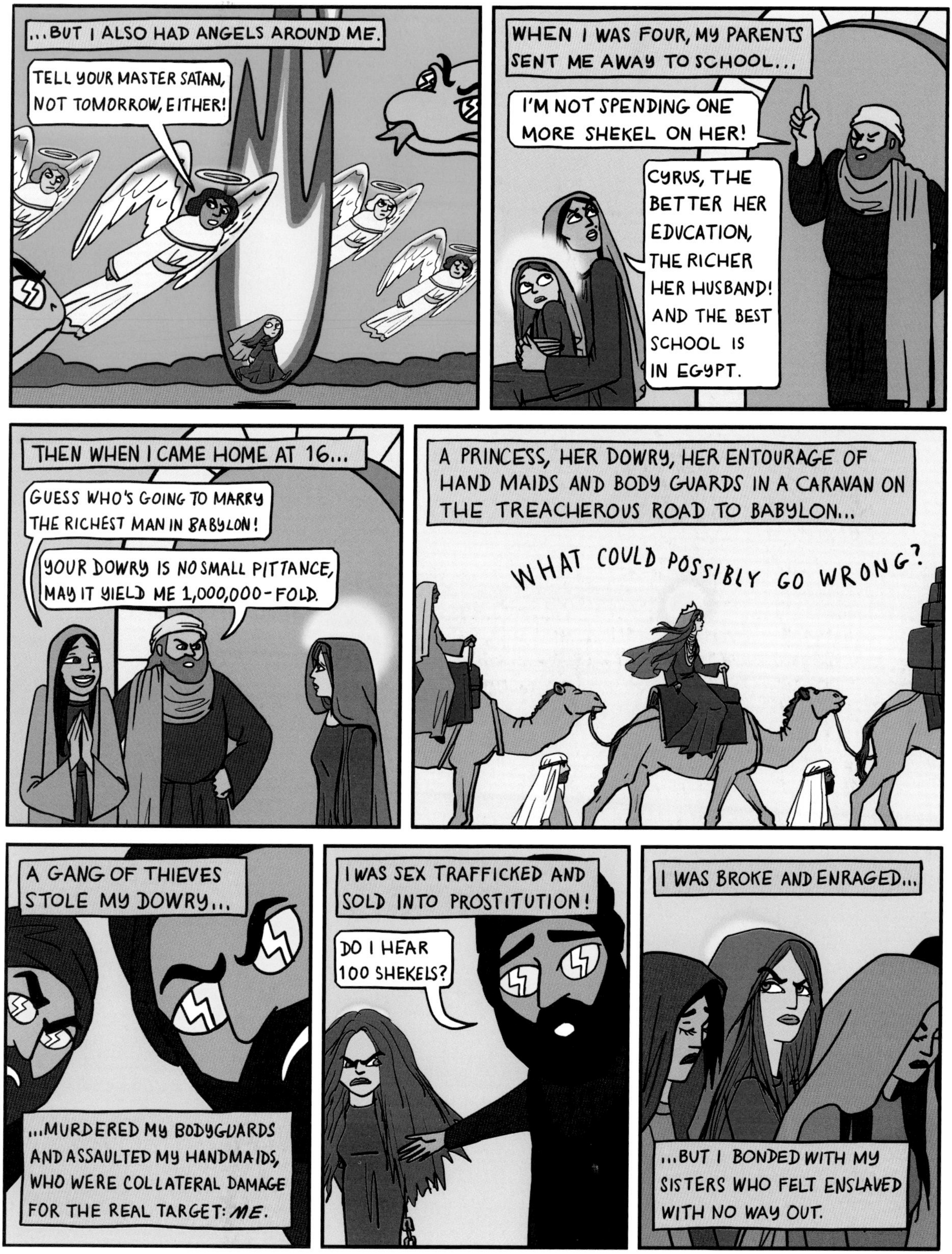
...BUT I ALSO HAD ANGELS AROUND ME.
TELL YOUR MASTER SATAN, NOT TOMORROW, EITHER!
WHEN I WAS FOUR, MY PARENTS SENT ME AWAY TO SCHOOL...
I'M NOT SPENDING ONE MORE SHEKEL ON HER!
CYRUS, THE BETTER HER EDUCATION, THE RICHER HER HUSBAND! AND THE BEST SCHOOL IS IN EGYPT.
THEN WHEN I CAME HOME AT 16...
GUESS WHO'S GOING TO MARRY THE RICHEST MAN IN BABYLON!
YOUR DOWRY IS NO SMALL PITTANCE, MAY IT YIELD ME 1,000,000-FOLD.
A PRINCESS, HER DOWRY, HER ENTOURAGE OF HAND MAIDS AND BODY GUARDS IN A CARAVAN ON THE TREACHEROUS ROAD TO BABYLON...
WHAT COULD POSSIBLY GO WRONG?
A GANG OF THIEVES STOLE MY DOWRY...
...MURDERED MY BODYGUARDS AND ASSAULTED MY HANDMAIDS, WHO WERE COLLATERAL DAMAGE FOR THE REAL TARGET: ME.
I WAS SEX TRAFFICKED AND SOLD INTO PROSTITUTION!
DO I HEAR 100 SHEKELS?
I WAS BROKE AND ENRAGED...
...BUT I BONDED WITH MY SISTERS WHO FELT ENSLAVED WITH NO WAY OUT.

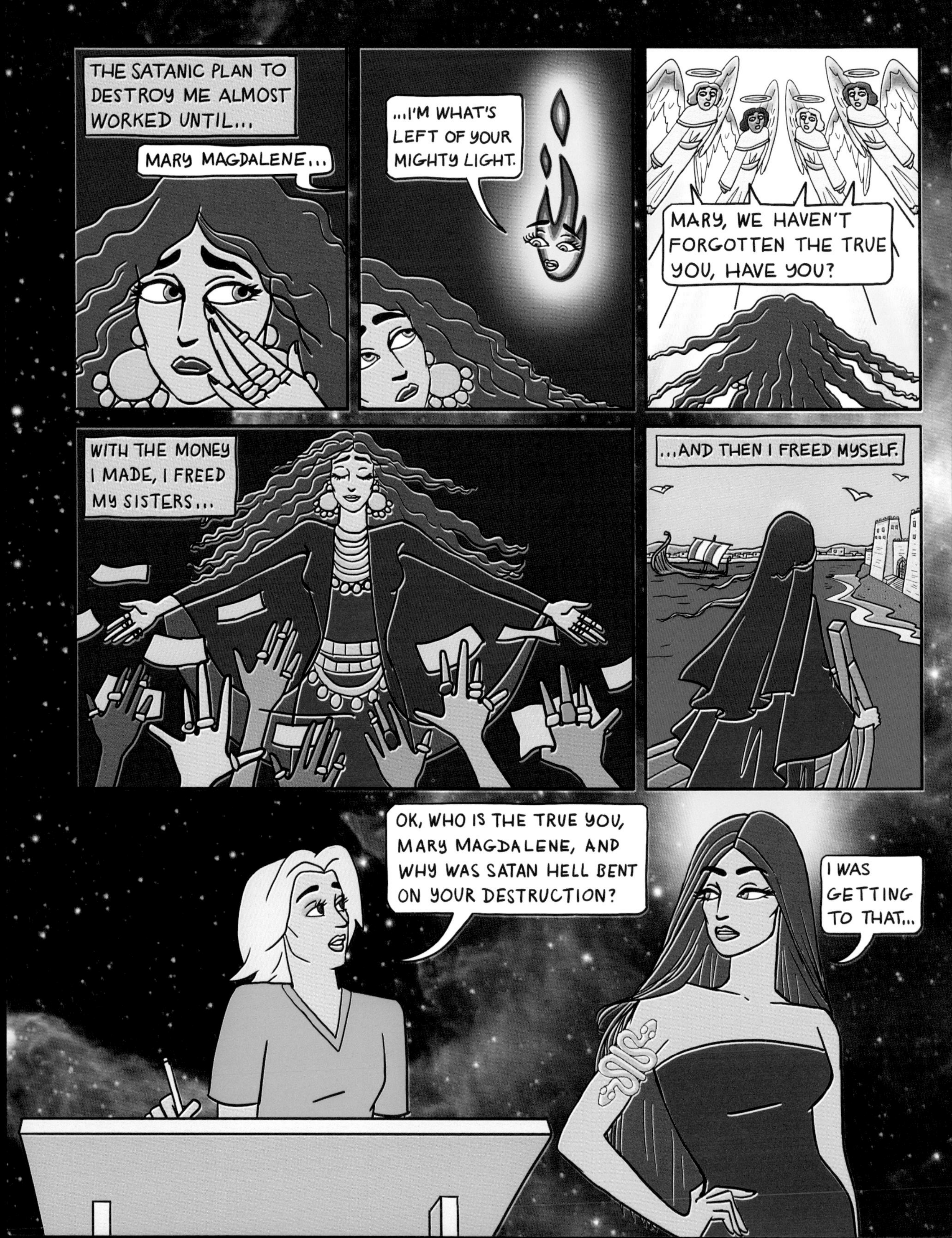
THE SATANIC PLAN TO DESTROY ME ALMOST WORKED UNTIL...
MARY MAGDALENE...
...I'M WHAT'S LEFT OF YOUR MIGHTY LIGHT.
MARY, WE HAVEN'T FORGOTTEN THE TRUE YOU, HAVE YOU?
WITH THE MONEY I MADE, I FREED MY SISTERS...
...AND THEN I FREED MYSELF.
OK, WHO IS THE TRUE YOU, MARY MAGDALENE, AND WHY WAS SATAN HELL BENT ON YOUR DESTRUCTION?
I WAS GETTING TO THAT...

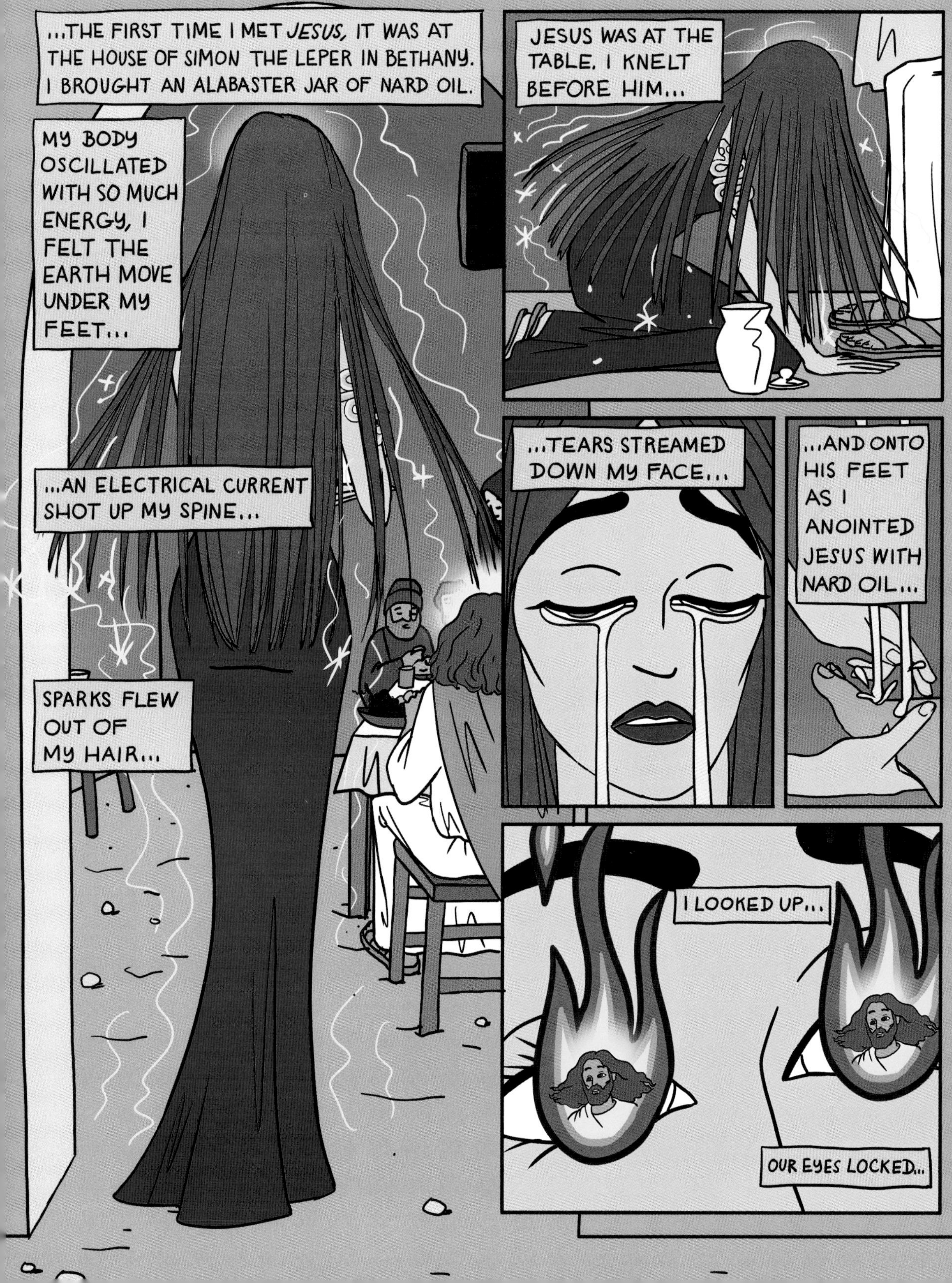
...THE FIRST TIME I MET *JESUS*, IT WAS AT THE HOUSE OF SIMON THE LEPER IN BETHANY. I BROUGHT AN ALABASTER JAR OF NARD OIL.
MY BODY OSCILLATED WITH SO MUCH ENERGY, I FELT THE EARTH MOVE UNDER MY FEET...
...AN ELECTRICAL CURRENT SHOT UP MY SPINE...
SPARKS FLEW OUT OF MY HAIR...
JESUS WAS AT THE TABLE. I KNELT BEFORE HIM...
...TEARS STREAMED DOWN MY FACE...
...AND ONTO HIS FEET AS I ANOINTED JESUS WITH NARD OIL...
I LOOKED UP...
OUR EYES LOCKED...

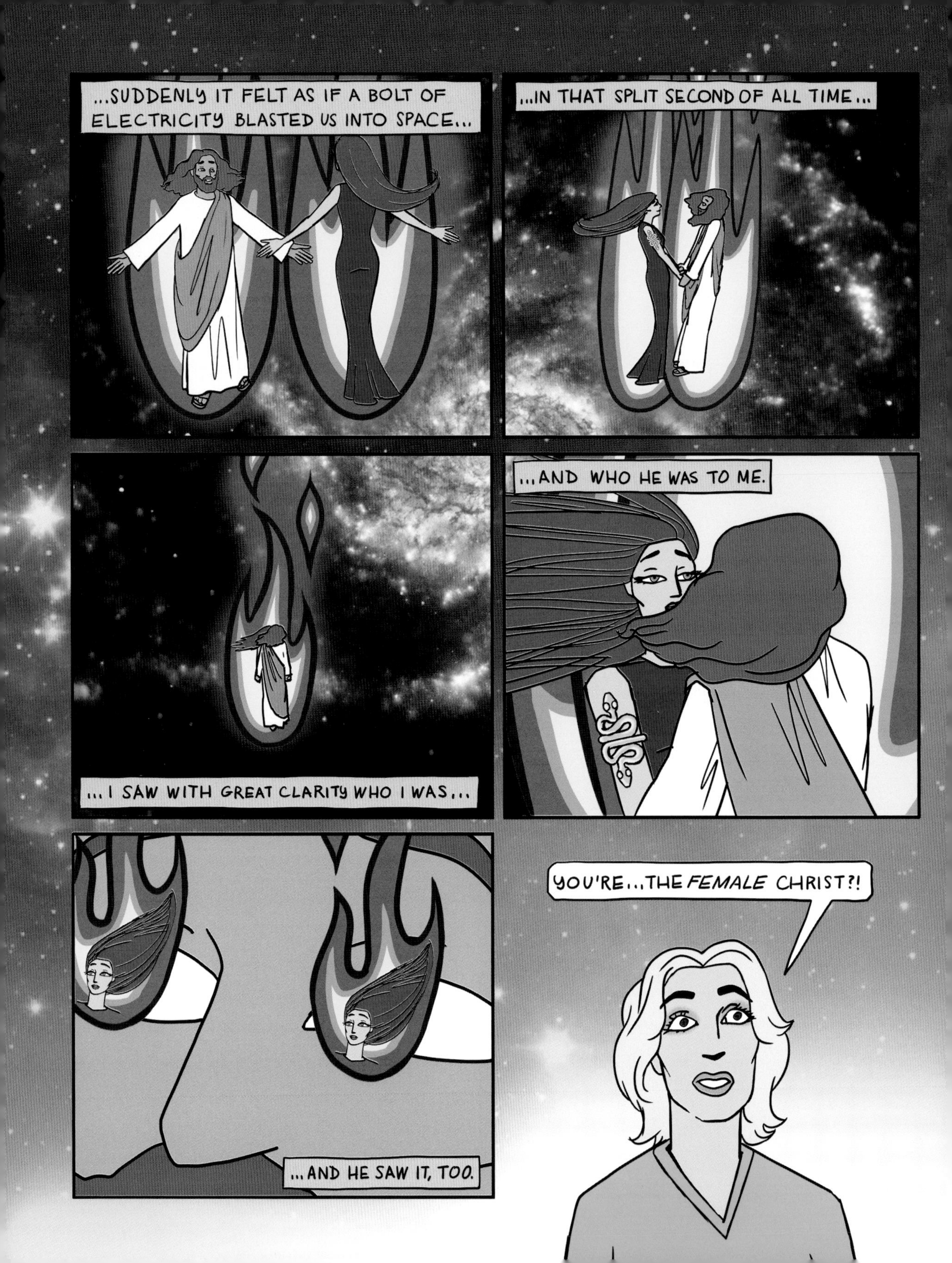
...SUDDENLY IT FELT AS IF A BOLT OF ELECTRICITY BLASTED US INTO SPACE...
...IN THAT SPLIT SECOND OF ALL TIME...
...I SAW WITH GREAT CLARITY WHO I WAS...
...AND WHO HE WAS TO ME.
...AND HE SAW IT, TOO.
YOU'RE...THE *FEMALE* CHRIST?!

YOU'RE THE SUGUGY, THE DIVINE DAUGHTER, THE EMBODIMENT OF SOPHIA, AREN'T YOU?

YOU KNOW WHAT ELSE SHE IS?

IN HEBREW, THE WORD *ANOINTED* MEANS "MESSIAH." KINGS IN ISRAEL WERE ANOINTED WITH PRESCIOUS OILS.

MARY MAGDALENE AS THE *ANOINTER*, EMPOWERED THE SACRED KING JESUS.

SO MARY MAGDALENE, ANOINTING THE MESSIAH MEANS...

...THE KINGSHIP FLOWS THROUGH ME.

WOW.

NOW, WHEN THE DISCIPLES SAW ME ANOINT JESUS...

...AND THEY SAW MY BRACELET...

...THAT BEAUTIFUL DAY BECAME JUDGEMENT DAY.

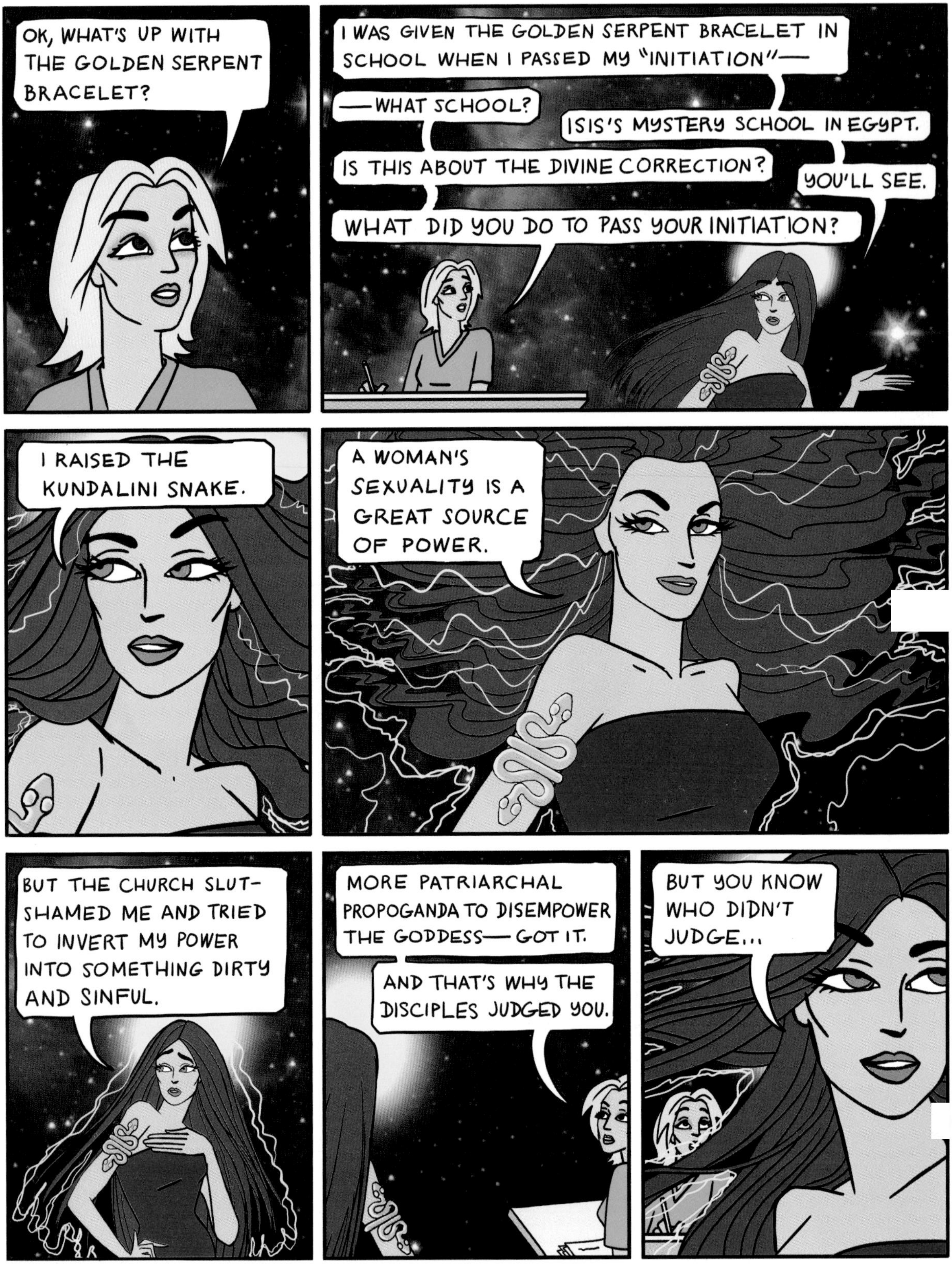
OK, WHAT'S UP WITH THE GOLDEN SERPENT BRACELET?
I WAS GIVEN THE GOLDEN SERPENT BRACELET IN SCHOOL WHEN I PASSED MY "INITIATION"—
—WHAT SCHOOL?
ISIS'S MYSTERY SCHOOL IN EGYPT.
IS THIS ABOUT THE DIVINE CORRECTION?
YOU'LL SEE.
WHAT DID YOU DO TO PASS YOUR INITIATION?
I RAISED THE KUNDALINI SNAKE.
A WOMAN'S SEXUALITY IS A GREAT SOURCE OF POWER.
BUT THE CHURCH SLUT-SHAMED ME AND TRIED TO INVERT MY POWER INTO SOMETHING DIRTY AND SINFUL.
MORE PATRIARCHAL PROPOGANDA TO DISEMPOWER THE GODDESS— GOT IT.
AND THAT'S WHY THE DISCIPLES JUDGED YOU.
BUT YOU KNOW WHO DIDN'T JUDGE...

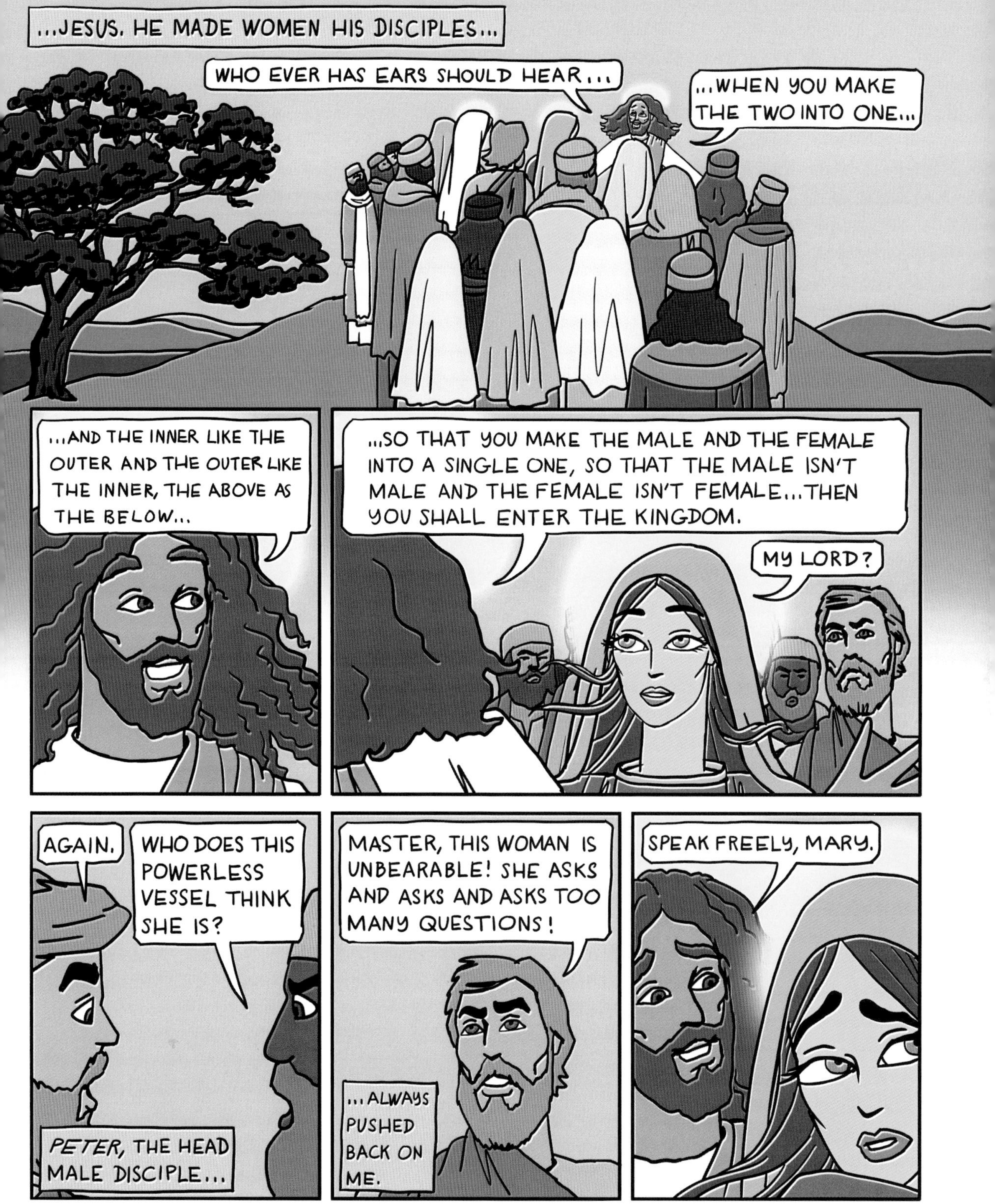
...JESUS. HE MADE WOMEN HIS DISCIPLES...
WHO EVER HAS EARS SHOULD HEAR...
...WHEN YOU MAKE THE TWO INTO ONE...
...AND THE INNER LIKE THE OUTER AND THE OUTER LIKE THE INNER, THE ABOVE AS THE BELOW...
...SO THAT YOU MAKE THE MALE AND THE FEMALE INTO A SINGLE ONE, SO THAT THE MALE ISN'T MALE AND THE FEMALE ISN'T FEMALE...THEN YOU SHALL ENTER THE KINGDOM.
MY LORD?
AGAIN.
WHO DOES THIS POWERLESS VESSEL THINK SHE IS?
PETER, THE HEAD MALE DISCIPLE...
MASTER, THIS WOMAN IS UNBEARABLE! SHE ASKS AND ASKS AND ASKS TOO MANY QUESTIONS!
...ALWAYS PUSHED BACK ON ME.
SPEAK FREELY, MARY.

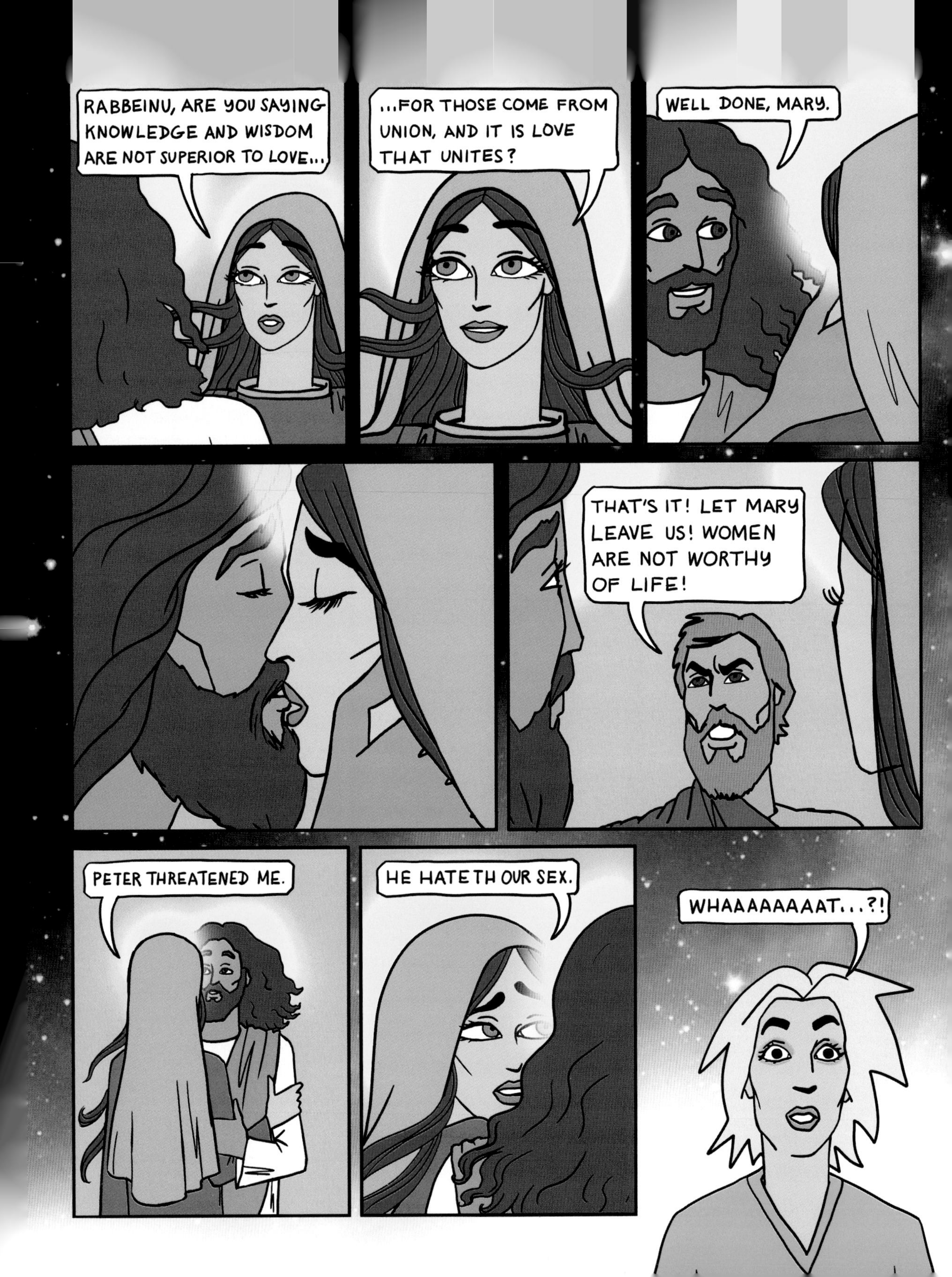
RABBEINU, ARE YOU SAYING KNOWLEDGE AND WISDOM ARE NOT SUPERIOR TO LOVE...
...FOR THOSE COME FROM UNION, AND IT IS LOVE THAT UNITES?
WELL DONE, MARY.
THAT'S IT! LET MARY LEAVE US! WOMEN ARE NOT WORTHY OF LIFE!
PETER THREATENED ME.
HE HATETH OUR SEX.
WHAAAAAAAAT...?!

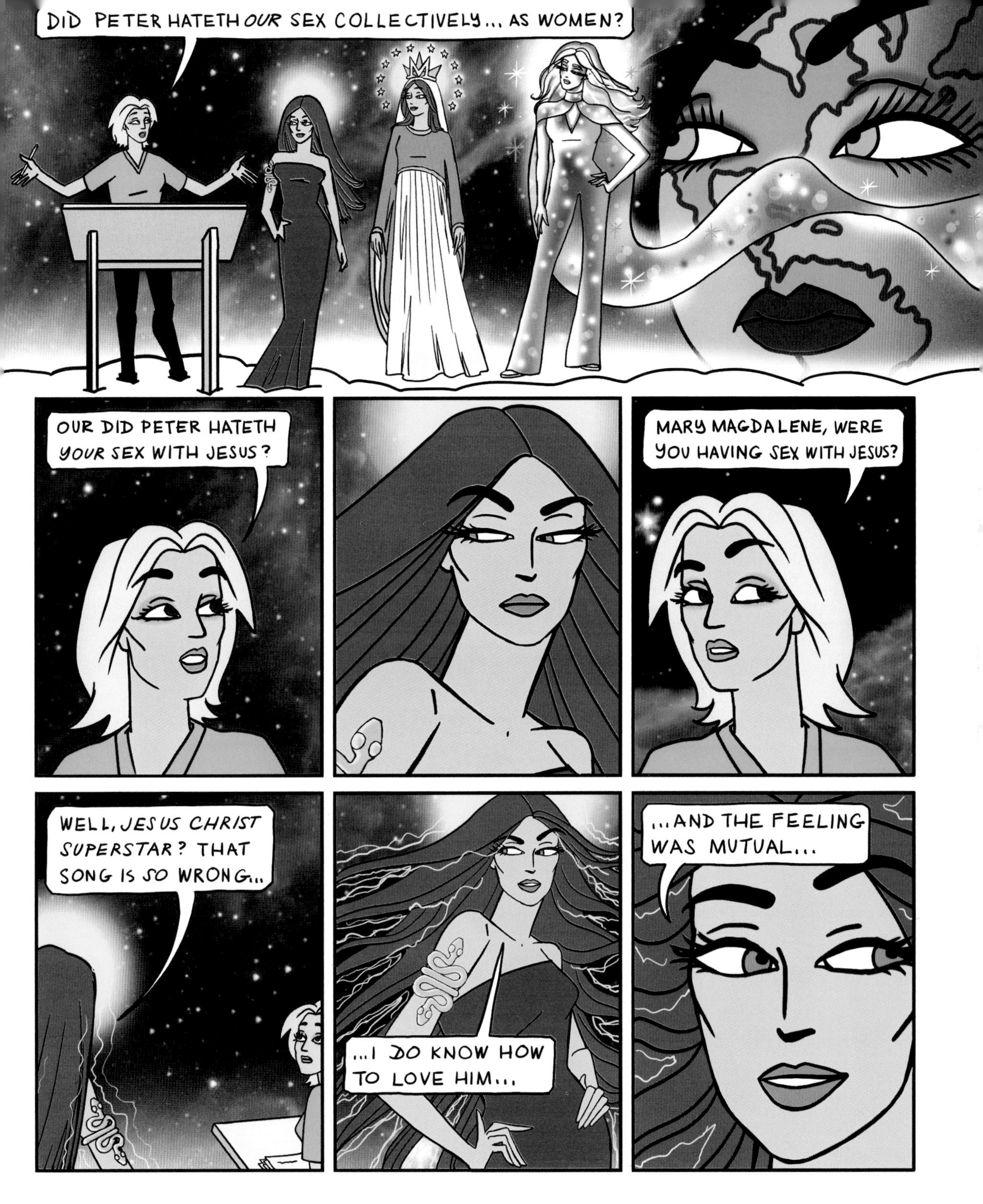
DID PETER HATETH *OUR* SEX COLLECTIVELY... AS WOMEN?
OUR DID PETER HATETH *YOUR* SEX WITH JESUS?
MARY MAGDALENE, WERE YOU HAVING SEX WITH JESUS?
WELL, *JESUS CHRIST SUPERSTAR*? THAT SONG IS SO WRONG...
...I DO KNOW HOW TO LOVE HIM...
...AND THE FEELING WAS MUTUAL...

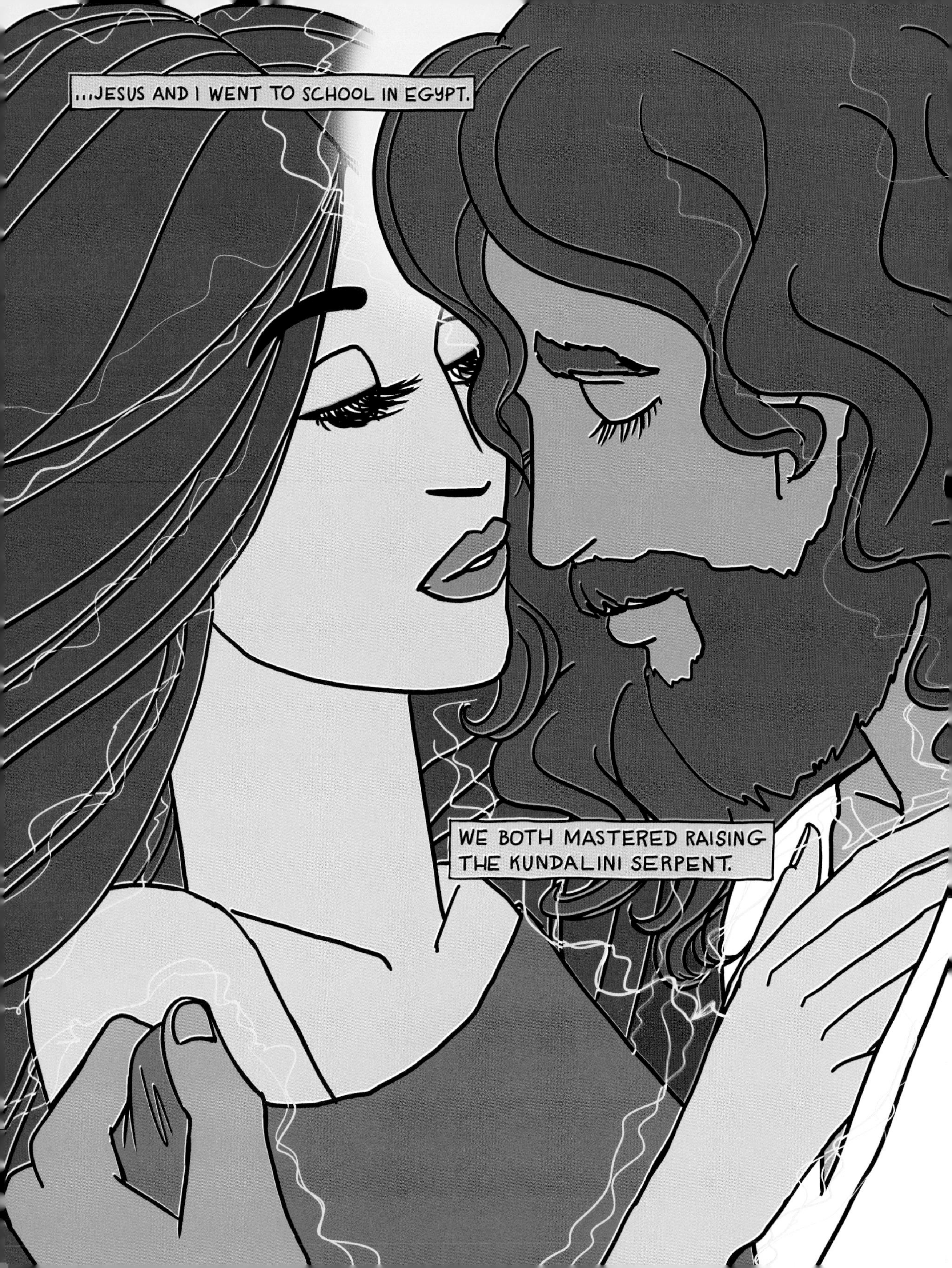
...JESUS AND I WENT TO SCHOOL IN EGYPT.
WE BOTH MASTERED RAISING THE KUNDALINI SERPENT.

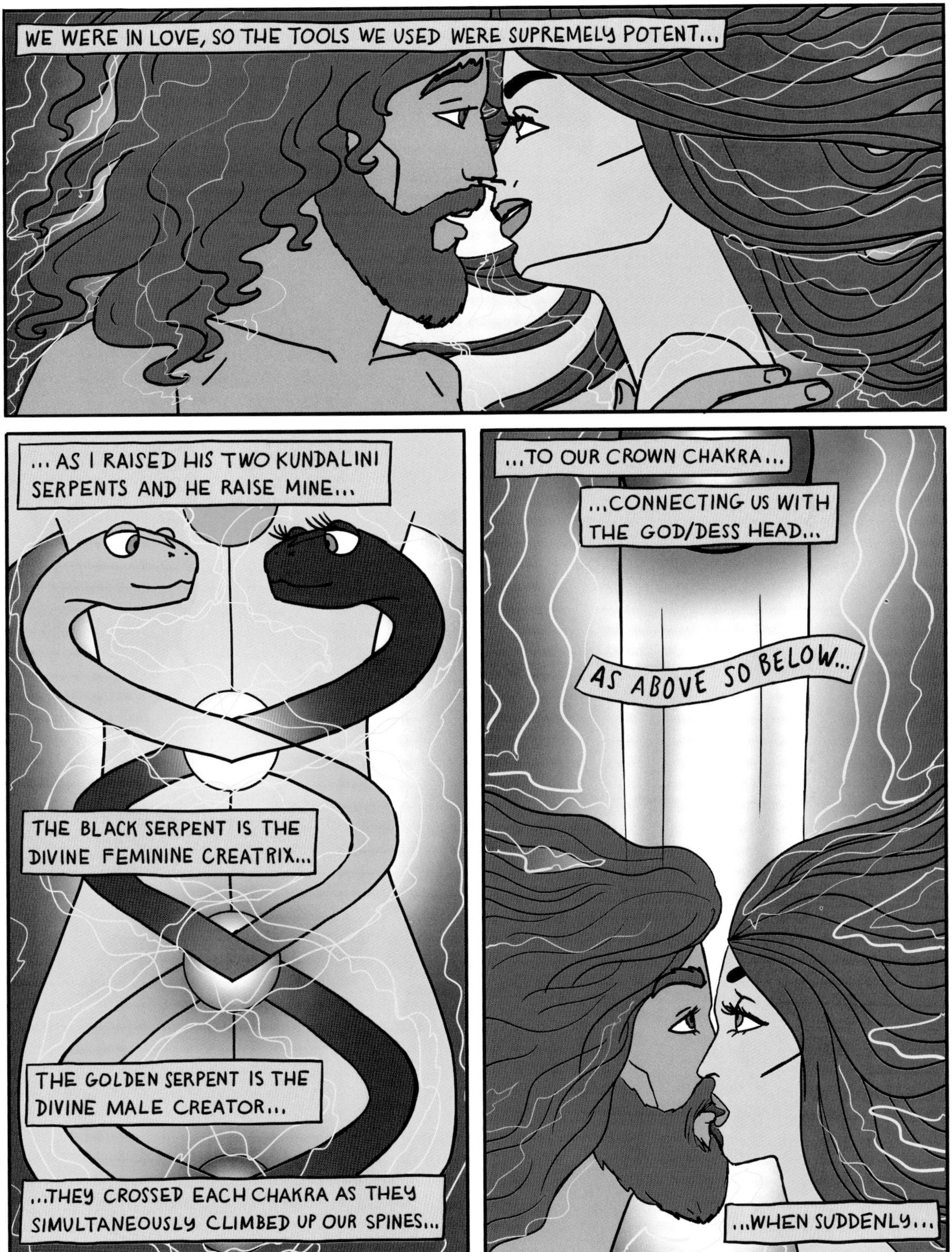
WE WERE IN LOVE, SO THE TOOLS WE USED WERE SUPREMELY POTENT...
... AS I RAISED HIS TWO KUNDALINI SERPENTS AND HE RAISE MINE...
THE BLACK SERPENT IS THE DIVINE FEMININE CREATRIX...
THE GOLDEN SERPENT IS THE DIVINE MALE CREATOR...
...THEY CROSSED EACH CHAKRA AS THEY SIMULTANEOUSLY CLIMBED UP OUR SPINES...
...TO OUR CROWN CHAKRA...
...CONNECTING US WITH THE GOD/DESS HEAD...
AS ABOVE SO BELOW...
...WHEN SUDDENLY...

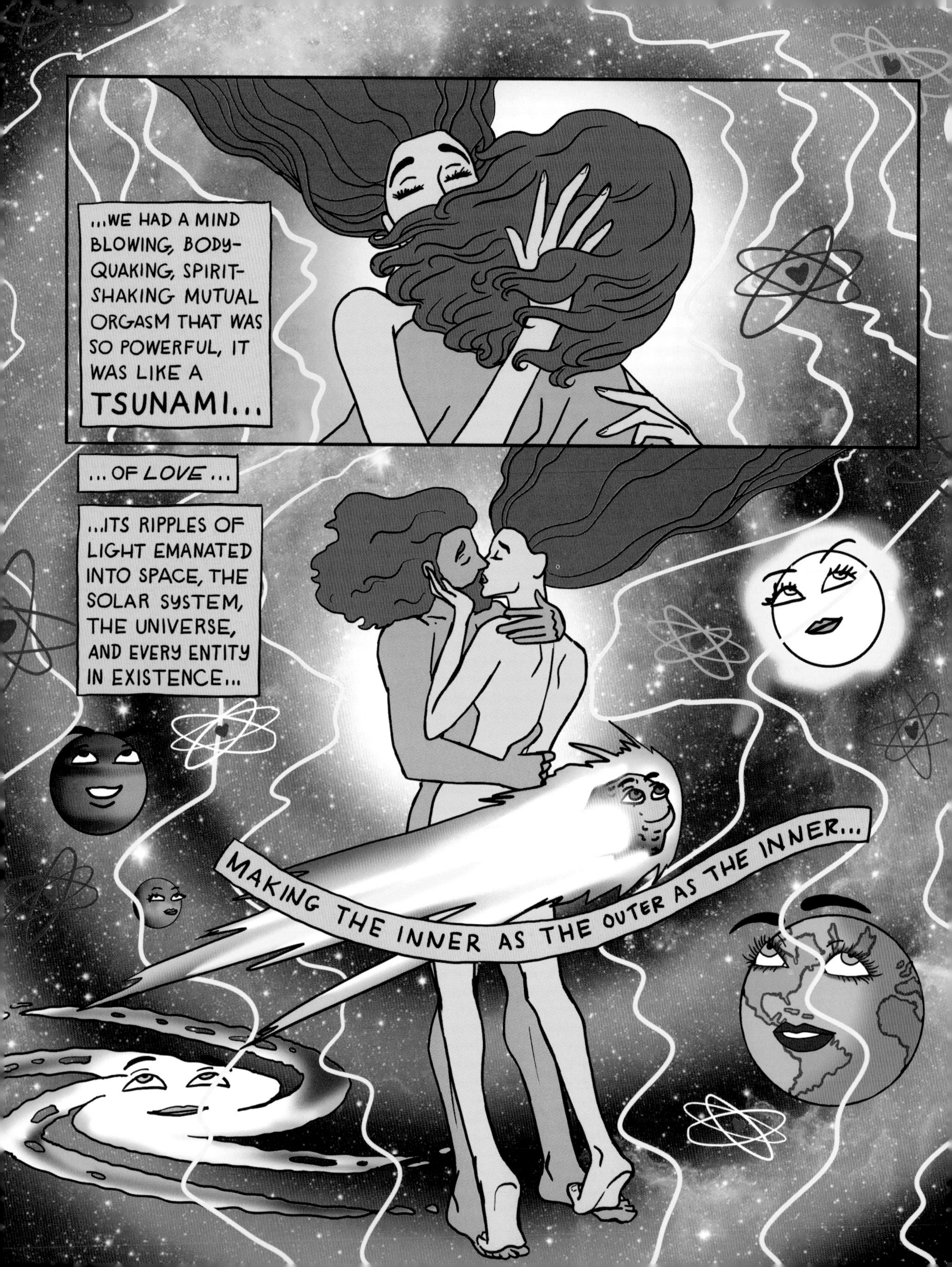
...WE HAD A MIND BLOWING, BODY-QUAKING, SPIRIT-SHAKING MUTUAL ORGASM THAT WAS SO POWERFUL, IT WAS LIKE A TSUNAMI...
...OF LOVE...
...ITS RIPPLES OF LIGHT EMANATED INTO SPACE, THE SOLAR SYSTEM, THE UNIVERSE, AND EVERY ENTITY IN EXISTENCE...
MAKING THE INNER AS THE OUTER AS THE INNER...

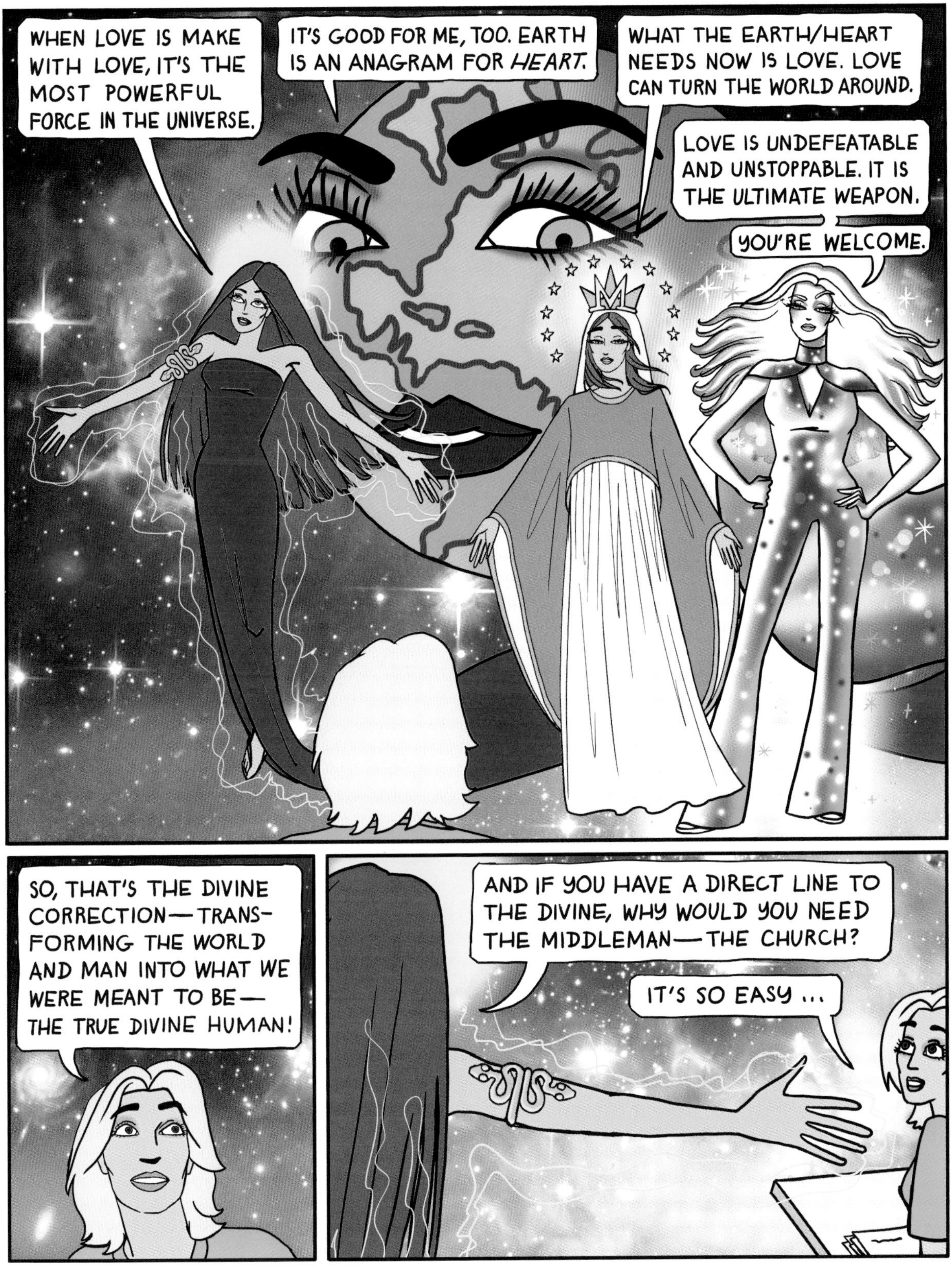
WHEN LOVE IS MAKE WITH LOVE, IT'S THE MOST POWERFUL FORCE IN THE UNIVERSE.
IT'S GOOD FOR ME, TOO. EARTH IS AN ANAGRAM FOR *HEART.*
WHAT THE EARTH/HEART NEEDS NOW IS LOVE. LOVE CAN TURN THE WORLD AROUND.
LOVE IS UNDEFEATABLE AND UNSTOPPABLE. IT IS THE ULTIMATE WEAPON.
YOU'RE WELCOME.
SO, THAT'S THE DIVINE CORRECTION—TRANS-FORMING THE WORLD AND MAN INTO WHAT WE WERE MEANT TO BE—THE TRUE DIVINE HUMAN!
AND IF YOU HAVE A DIRECT LINE TO THE DIVINE, WHY WOULD YOU NEED THE MIDDLEMAN—THE CHURCH?
IT'S SO EASY ...

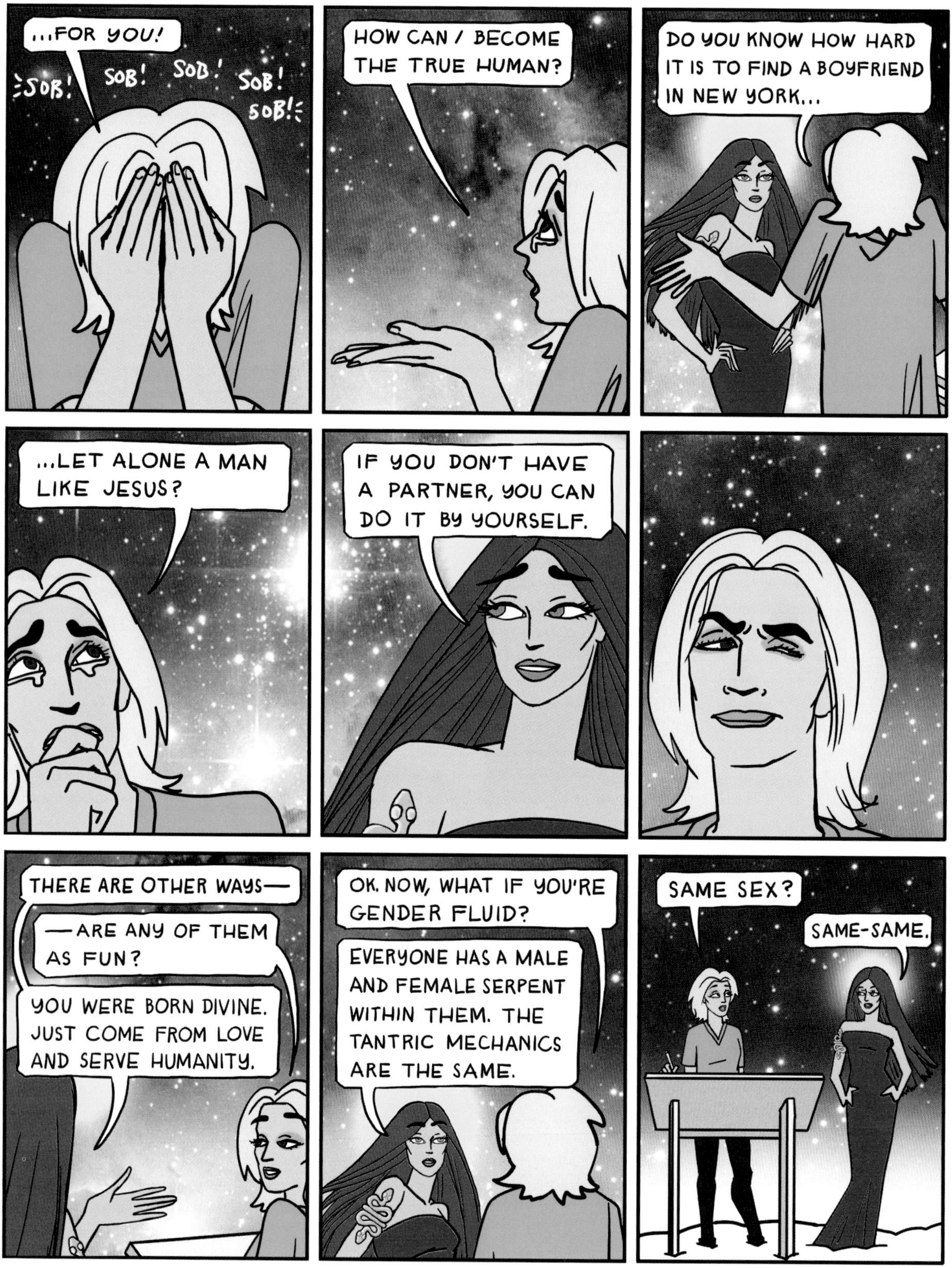
...FOR YOU!
SOB! SOB! SOB! SOB! SOB!
HOW CAN I BECOME THE TRUE HUMAN?
DO YOU KNOW HOW HARD IT IS TO FIND A BOYFRIEND IN NEW YORK...
...LET ALONE A MAN LIKE JESUS?
IF YOU DON'T HAVE A PARTNER, YOU CAN DO IT BY YOURSELF.
THERE ARE OTHER WAYS—
—ARE ANY OF THEM AS FUN?
YOU WERE BORN DIVINE. JUST COME FROM LOVE AND SERVE HUMANITY.
OK. NOW, WHAT IF YOU'RE GENDER FLUID?
EVERYONE HAS A MALE AND FEMALE SERPENT WITHIN THEM. THE TANTRIC MECHANICS ARE THE SAME.
SAME SEX?
SAME-SAME.

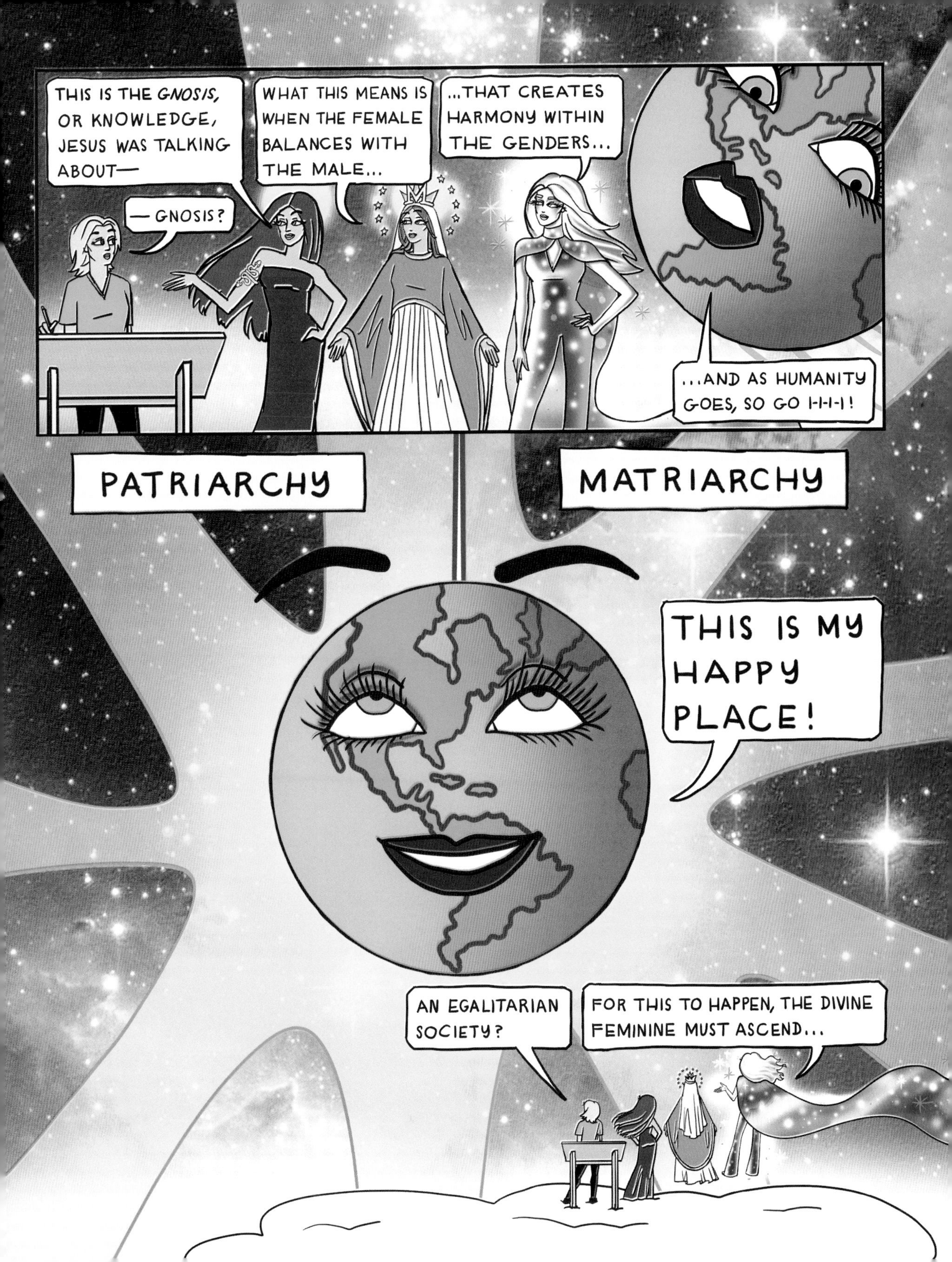
THIS IS THE GNOSIS, OR KNOWLEDGE, JESUS WAS TALKING ABOUT—
—GNOSIS?
WHAT THIS MEANS IS WHEN THE FEMALE BALANCES WITH THE MALE...
...THAT CREATES HARMONY WITHIN THE GENDERS...
...AND AS HUMANITY GOES, SO GO I-I-I-I!
PATRIARCHY
MATRIARCHY
THIS IS MY HAPPY PLACE!
AN EGALITARIAN SOCIETY?
FOR THIS TO HAPPEN, THE DIVINE FEMININE MUST ASCEND...

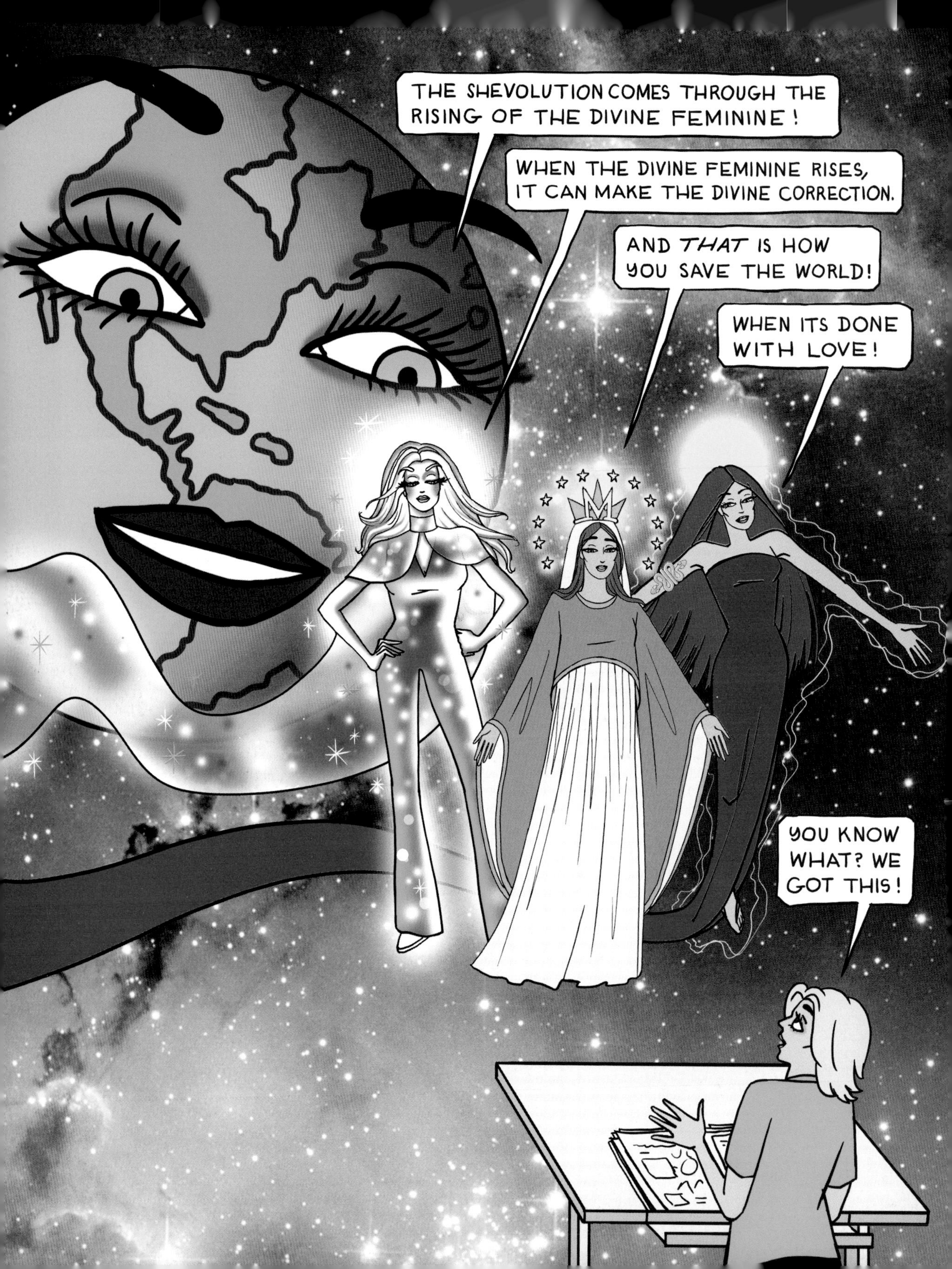

THE SHEVOLUTION COMES THROUGH THE RISING OF THE DIVINE FEMININE!
WHEN THE DIVINE FEMININE RISES, IT CAN MAKE THE DIVINE CORRECTION.
AND *THAT* IS HOW YOU SAVE THE WORLD!
WHEN ITS DONE WITH LOVE!
YOU KNOW WHAT? WE GOT THIS!

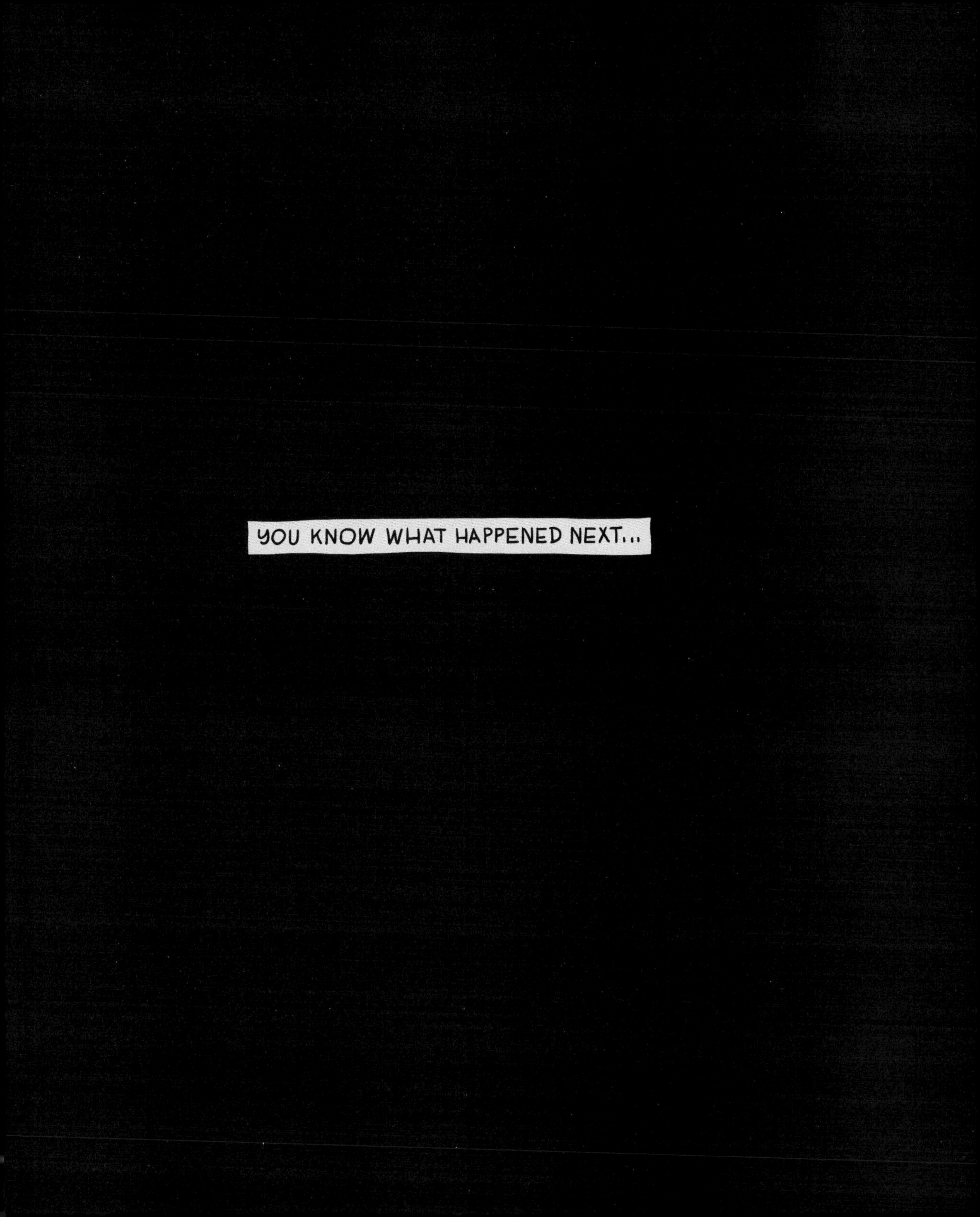
YOU KNOW WHAT HAPPENED NEXT...

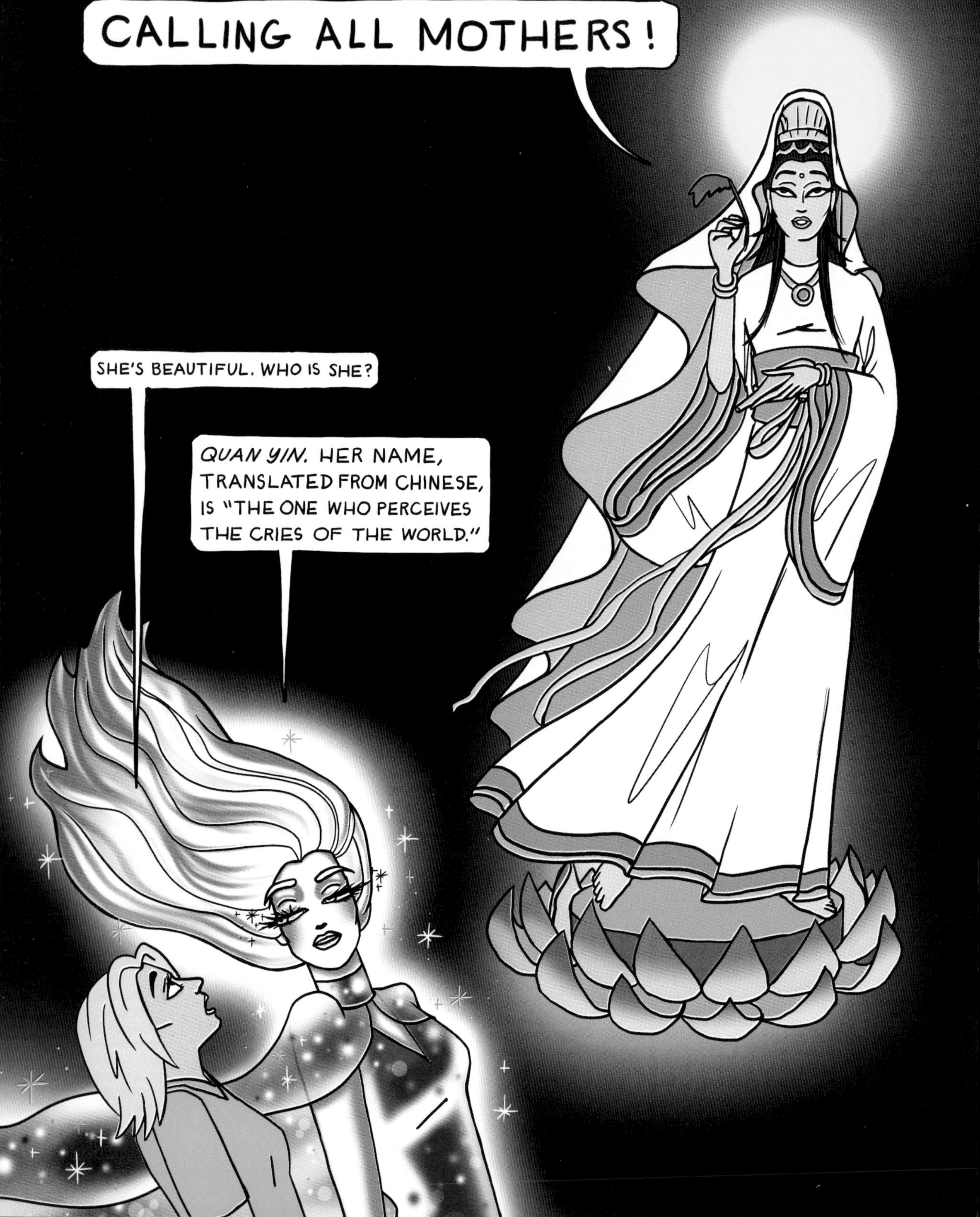
CALLING ALL MOTHERS!
SHE'S BEAUTIFUL. WHO IS SHE?
QUAN YIN. HER NAME, TRANSLATED FROM CHINESE, IS "THE ONE WHO PERCEIVES THE CRIES OF THE WORLD."

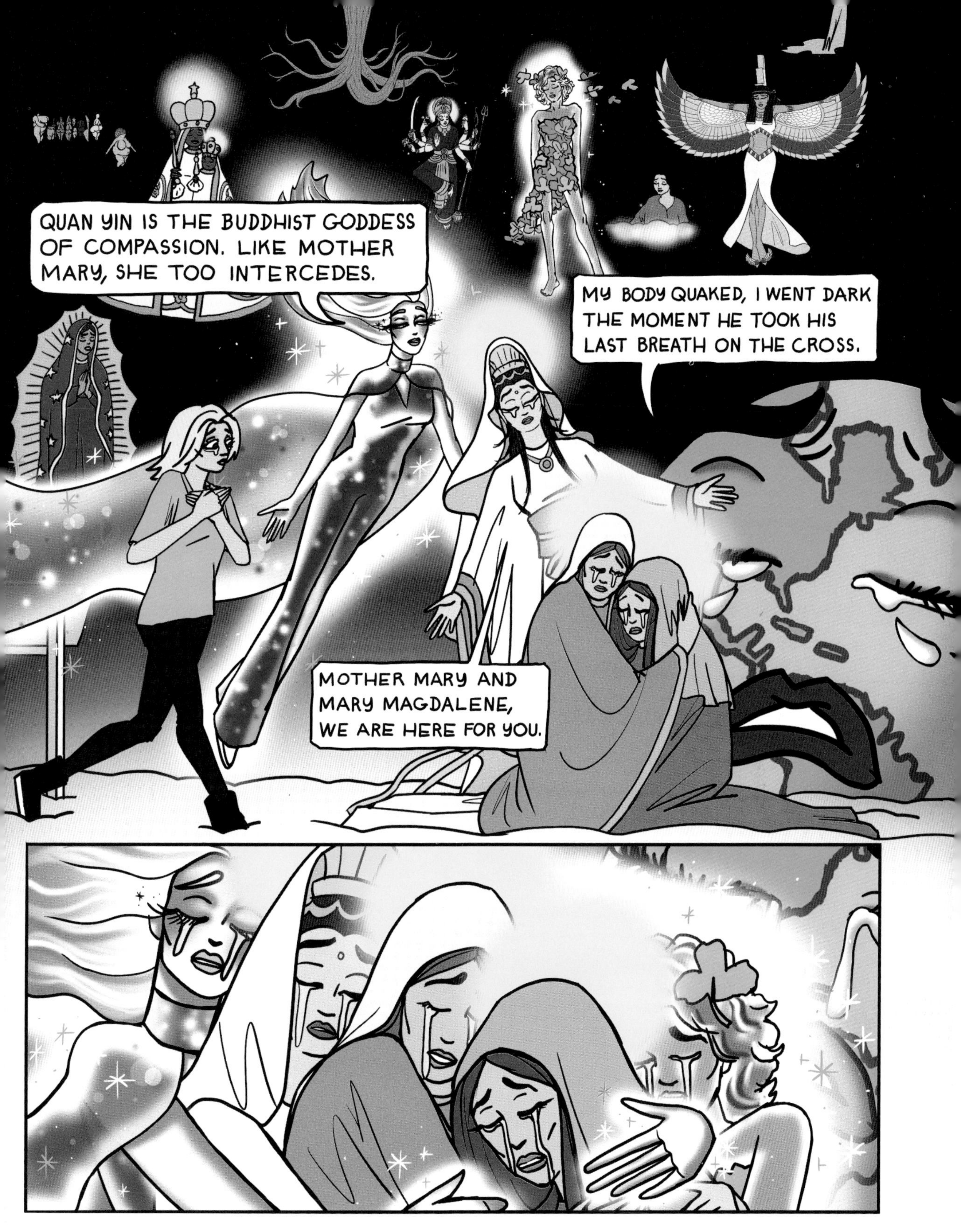
QUAN YIN IS THE BUDDHIST GODDESS OF COMPASSION. LIKE MOTHER MARY, SHE TOO INTERCEDES.
MY BODY QUAKED, I WENT DARK THE MOMENT HE TOOK HIS LAST BREATH ON THE CROSS.
MOTHER MARY AND MARY MAGDALENE, WE ARE HERE FOR YOU.

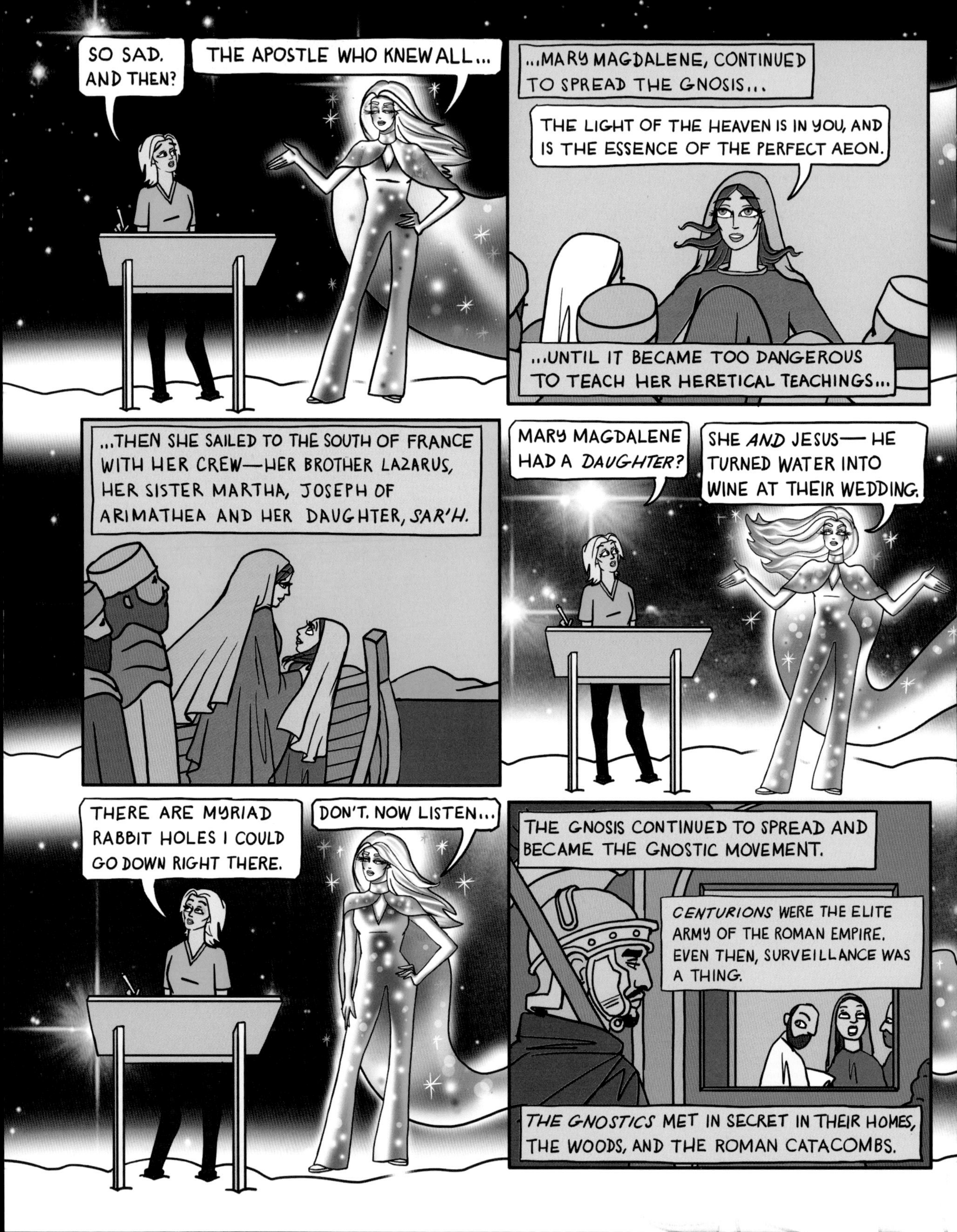

SO SAD. AND THEN?
THE APOSTLE WHO KNEW ALL...
...MARY MAGDALENE, CONTINUED TO SPREAD THE GNOSIS...
THE LIGHT OF THE HEAVEN IS IN YOU, AND IS THE ESSENCE OF THE PERFECT AEON.
...UNTIL IT BECAME TOO DANGEROUS TO TEACH HER HERETICAL TEACHINGS...
...THEN SHE SAILED TO THE SOUTH OF FRANCE WITH HER CREW—HER BROTHER LAZARUS, HER SISTER MARTHA, JOSEPH OF ARIMATHEA AND HER DAUGHTER, *SAR'H*.
MARY MAGDALENE HAD A *DAUGHTER*?
SHE *AND* JESUS— HE TURNED WATER INTO WINE AT THEIR WEDDING.
THERE ARE MYRIAD RABBIT HOLES I COULD GO DOWN RIGHT THERE.
DON'T. NOW LISTEN...
THE GNOSIS CONTINUED TO SPREAD AND BECAME THE GNOSTIC MOVEMENT.
CENTURIONS WERE THE ELITE ARMY OF THE ROMAN EMPIRE. EVEN THEN, SURVEILLANCE WAS A THING.
THE GNOSTICS MET IN SECRET IN THEIR HOMES, THE WOODS, AND THE ROMAN CATACOMBS.

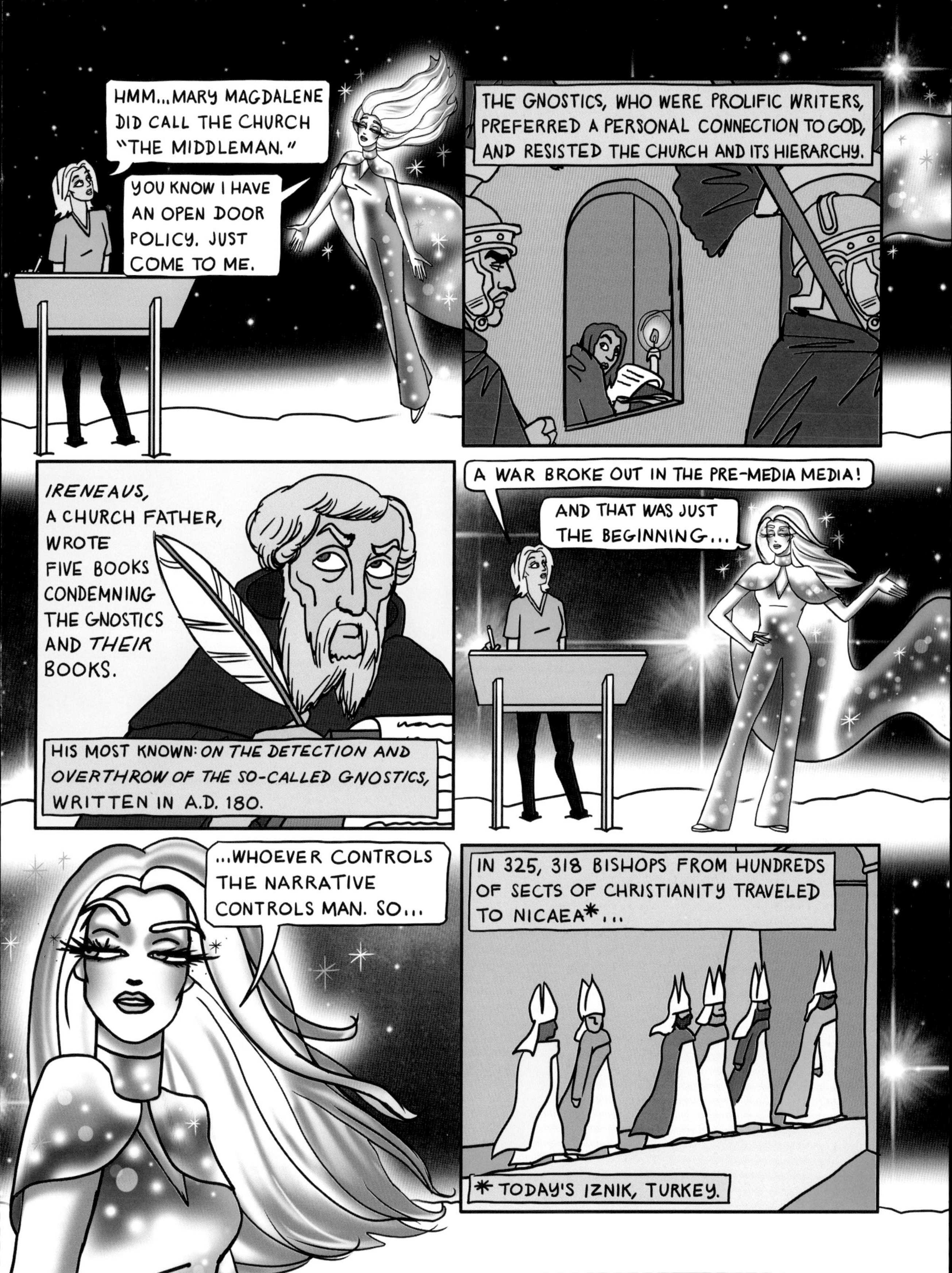
HMM...MARY MAGDALENE DID CALL THE CHURCH "THE MIDDLEMAN."
YOU KNOW I HAVE AN OPEN DOOR POLICY. JUST COME TO ME.
THE GNOSTICS, WHO WERE PROLIFIC WRITERS, PREFERRED A PERSONAL CONNECTION TO GOD, AND RESISTED THE CHURCH AND ITS HIERARCHY.
IRENEAUS, A CHURCH FATHER, WROTE FIVE BOOKS CONDEMNING THE GNOSTICS AND *THEIR* BOOKS.
HIS MOST KNOWN: *ON THE DETECTION AND OVERTHROW OF THE SO-CALLED GNOSTICS,* WRITTEN IN A.D. 180.
A WAR BROKE OUT IN THE PRE-MEDIA MEDIA!
AND THAT WAS JUST THE BEGINNING...
...WHOEVER CONTROLS THE NARRATIVE CONTROLS MAN. SO...
IN 325, 318 BISHOPS FROM HUNDREDS OF SECTS OF CHRISTIANITY TRAVELED TO NICAEA*...
* TODAY'S IZNIK, TURKEY.

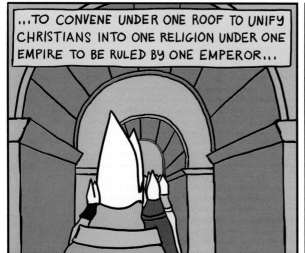

...TO CONVENE UNDER ONE ROOF TO UNIFY CHRISTIANS INTO ONE RELIGION UNDER ONE EMPIRE TO BE RULED BY ONE EMPEROR...

...THE BLOODTHIRSTY, POWER-HUNGRY *CONSTANTINE THE GREAT.*

ROMAN EMPEROR CONSTANTINE WAS NOT A CHRISTIAN AT THE MEETING HE DECREED...

THE FIRST COUNCIL OF NICAEA

A BUNCH OF MEN WHO WERE EDITORS OF *THE BOOK WRITTEN BY A BUNCH OF MEN ABOUT A BUNCH OF MEN.*

THEY DELETED ANY ALL ALL MENTIONS OF ME...

DELETED!
DELETED!
DELETED!
DELETED!
DELETED!

THEY ROLLED BACK WOMEN PRIESTESSES AND DEACONS...

NEVER, EVER, EVER, EVER NEVER SHOULD'VE HAPPENED!

THEY OMITTED ALL GOSPELS THAT CHALLENGED THEIR PATRIARCHAL STRONGHOLD.

NO!
NO!
NO!
NO!
NO!
NO!
NO!

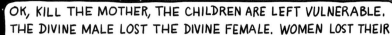

 OK, KILL THE MOTHER, THE CHILDREN ARE LEFT VULNERABLE. THE DIVINE MALE LOST THE DIVINE FEMALE. WOMEN LOST THEIR RIGHTS AND HUMANITY LOST ITS CRUCIAL KNOWLEDGE. NICE ONE NICAEA!

 AND THE CHURCH INSERTED ITSELF AS THE INTERCEDING MIDDLE MAN AND MADE HUMANITY SUBSERVIENT TO THEM...

 OPPOSING ME. I CREATED MANKIND TO BE DIVINE, INDEPENDENT AND FREE.

 WHAT HAPPENED TO THE BOOKS?

 WEREN'T THERE HUNDREDS OF CHRISTIAN SECTS? AND THE GNOSTICS WERE PROLIFIC WRITERS...

 ARE THE BOOKS GONE FOREVER?

OH, SOME OF THEM MAY HAVE SURFACED...

 WHAT'S WITH THE LOOK, YOU TWO?

 WILL YOU AT LEAST TELL ME WHICH BOOKS WERE LEFT OUT?

THE ACTS OF PAUL AND THECLA—

—THECLA. WHO'S THECLA?

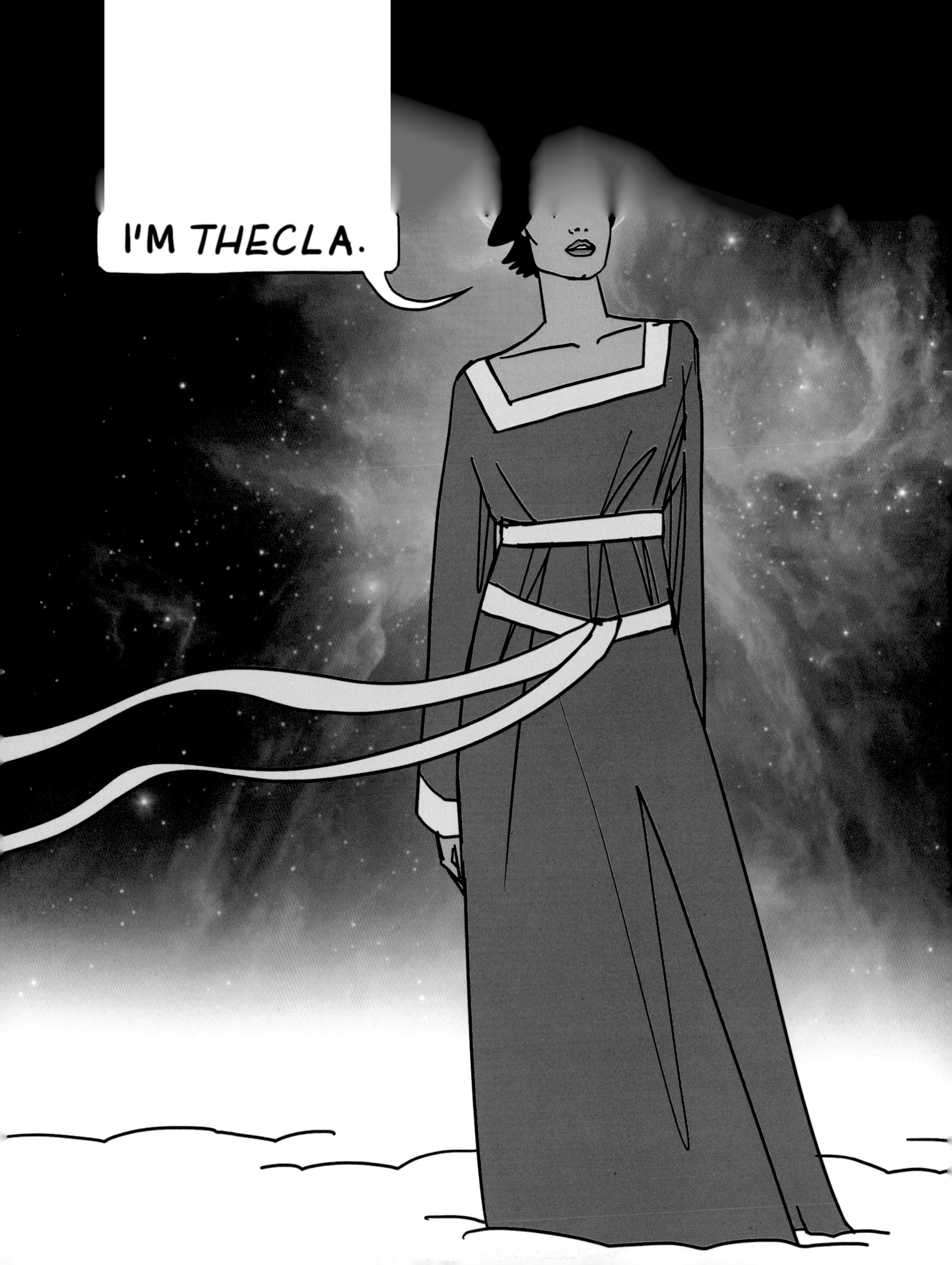
I'M THECLA.

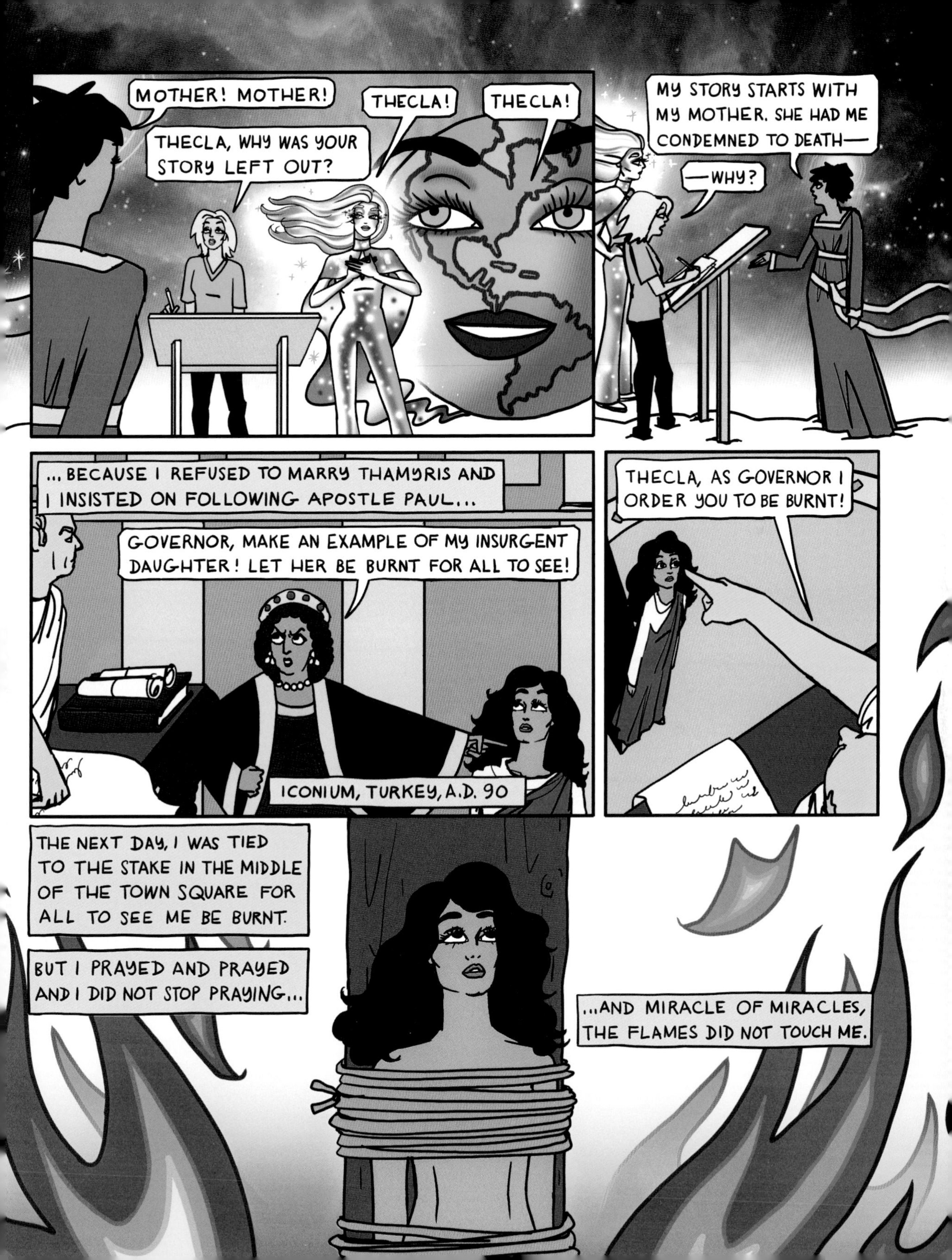

MOTHER! MOTHER!
THECLA, WHY WAS YOUR STORY LEFT OUT?
THECLA!
THECLA!
MY STORY STARTS WITH MY MOTHER. SHE HAD ME CONDEMNED TO DEATH—
—WHY?
...BECAUSE I REFUSED TO MARRY THAMYRIS AND I INSISTED ON FOLLOWING APOSTLE PAUL...
GOVERNOR, MAKE AN EXAMPLE OF MY INSURGENT DAUGHTER! LET HER BE BURNT FOR ALL TO SEE!
ICONIUM, TURKEY, A.D. 90
THECLA, AS GOVERNOR I ORDER YOU TO BE BURNT!
THE NEXT DAY, I WAS TIED TO THE STAKE IN THE MIDDLE OF THE TOWN SQUARE FOR ALL TO SEE ME BE BURNT.
BUT I PRAYED AND PRAYED AND I DID NOT STOP PRAYING...
...AND MIRACLE OF MIRACLES, THE FLAMES DID NOT TOUCH ME.

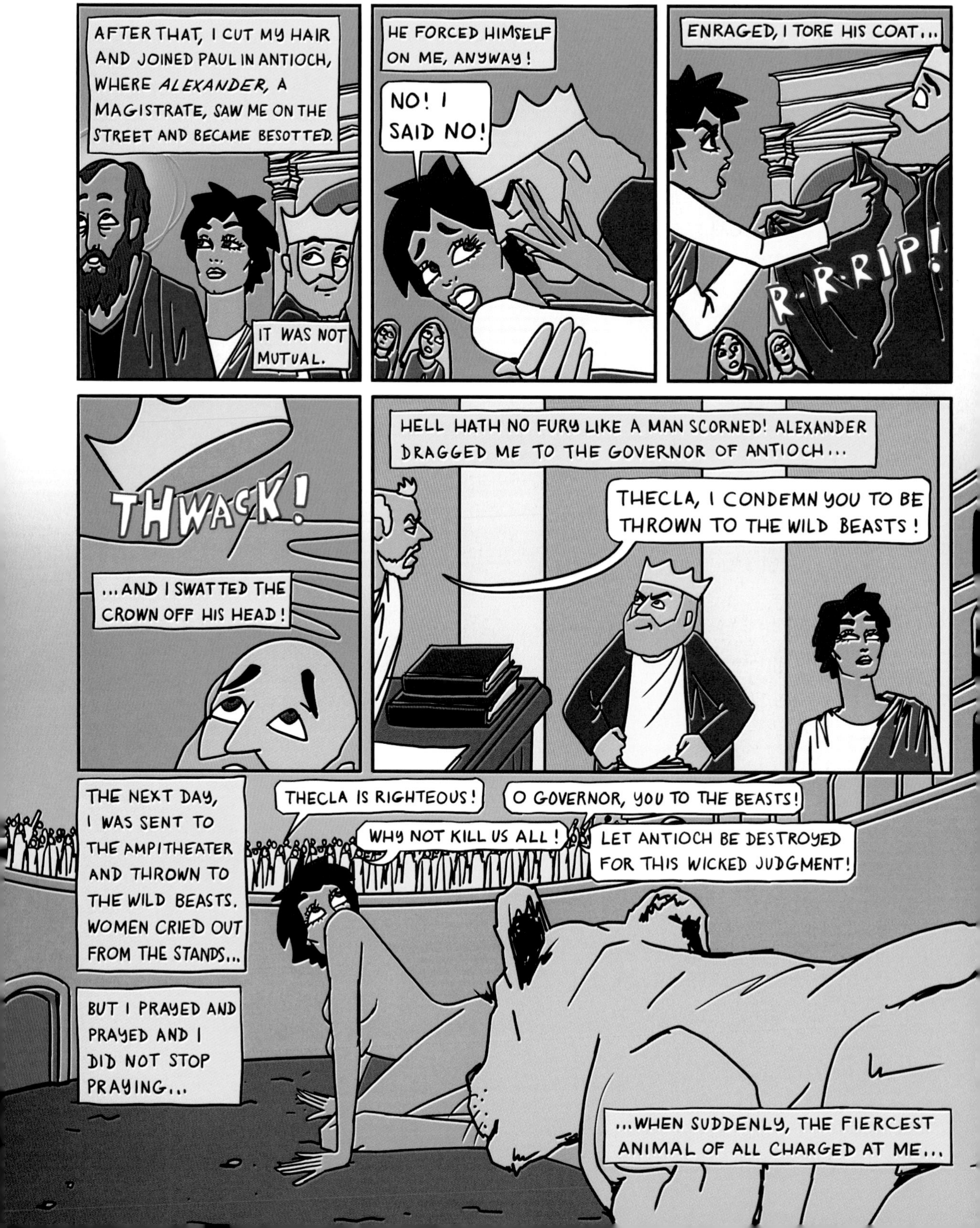
AFTER THAT, I CUT MY HAIR AND JOINED PAUL IN ANTIOCH, WHERE *ALEXANDER*, A MAGISTRATE, SAW ME ON THE STREET AND BECAME BESOTTED.
IT WAS NOT MUTUAL.
HE FORCED HIMSELF ON ME, ANYWAY!
NO! I SAID NO!
ENRAGED, I TORE HIS COAT...
R-R-RIP!
THWACK!
...AND I SWATTED THE CROWN OFF HIS HEAD!
HELL HATH NO FURY LIKE A MAN SCORNED! ALEXANDER DRAGGED ME TO THE GOVERNOR OF ANTIOCH...
THECLA, I CONDEMN YOU TO BE THROWN TO THE WILD BEASTS!
THE NEXT DAY, I WAS SENT TO THE AMPITHEATER AND THROWN TO THE WILD BEASTS. WOMEN CRIED OUT FROM THE STANDS...
THECLA IS RIGHTEOUS!
O GOVERNOR, YOU TO THE BEASTS!
WHY NOT KILL US ALL!
LET ANTIOCH BE DESTROYED FOR THIS WICKED JUDGMENT!
BUT I PRAYED AND PRAYED AND I DID NOT STOP PRAYING...
...WHEN SUDDENLY, THE FIERCEST ANIMAL OF ALL CHARGED AT ME...

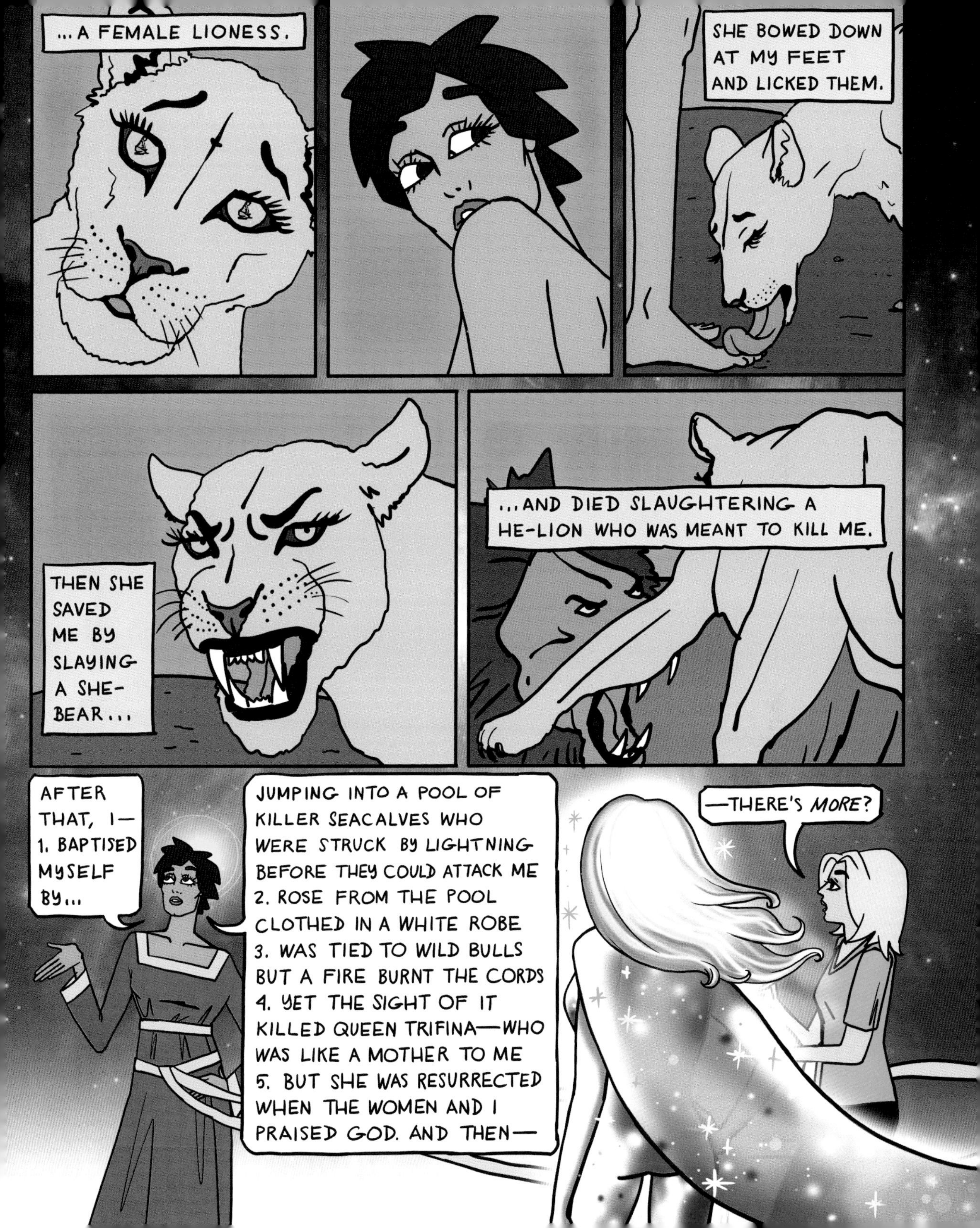
...A FEMALE LIONESS.
SHE BOWED DOWN AT MY FEET AND LICKED THEM.
THEN SHE SAVED ME BY SLAYING A SHE-BEAR...
...AND DIED SLAUGHTERING A HE-LION WHO WAS MEANT TO KILL ME.
AFTER THAT, I— 1. BAPTISED MYSELF BY...
JUMPING INTO A POOL OF KILLER SEACALVES WHO WERE STRUCK BY LIGHTNING BEFORE THEY COULD ATTACK ME 2. ROSE FROM THE POOL CLOTHED IN A WHITE ROBE 3. WAS TIED TO WILD BULLS BUT A FIRE BURNT THE CORDS 4. YET THE SIGHT OF IT KILLED QUEEN TRIFINA—WHO WAS LIKE A MOTHER TO ME 5. BUT SHE WAS RESURRECTED WHEN THE WOMEN AND I PRAISED GOD. AND THEN—
—THERE'S *MORE*?

I MIRACULOUSLY HEALED THE SICK INTO MY 90s, WHEN SOME YOUNG THUGS TRIED TO RAVISH ME, BUT AGAIN I PRAYED AND WAS SAVED WHEN A HUGE ROCK APPEARED, BLOCKING THEM—THERE'S *THAT*.

A *WOMAN* WHO'S DIVINE *AND* SOVEREIGN? THE COUNCIL OF NICAEA CAN'T HAVE THAT!

HA! THEN, A YEAR AFTER...

...THE COUNCIL OF NICAEA, CONSTANTINE ORDERED HIS SON CRISPUS POISONED TO DEATH AND HIS WIFE *FLAVIA* BOILED TO DEATH.

EUSEBIUS, CONSTANTINE'S ~~SCRIBE~~ PUBLICIST AND SYNCOPHANT IN CHIEF.

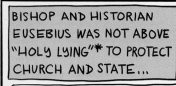

BISHOP AND HISTORIAN EUSEBIUS WAS NOT ABOVE "HOLY LYING"* TO PROTECT CHURCH AND STATE...

WE SHALL INTRODUCE INTO THIS HISTORY ONLY THOSE EVENTS WHICH MAY BE USEFUL TO OURSELVES...**

* HIS WORDS
** HIS WORDS FROM HIS *ECCLESIASTICAL HISTORY*

HANG ON— *BISHOP* AND *HOLY LIAR* EUSEBIUS WAS A *HISTORIAN*?

BISHOP AND HOLY LIAR EUSEBIUS WAS "THE FATHER OF THE CHURCH HISTORY"—HISTORIAN.

SO HISTORY IS WRITTEN BY A BUNCH OF MEN WHO LIE, OMIT, AND MAKE STUFF UP TO MAKE THEMSELVES AND THEIR CRONIES LOOK GOOD, LIKE *DECEVIOUS* EUSEBIUS?

NO WONDER THE GODDESS WAS SUPPRESSED!

WELL, BUCKLE UP...

...WE'RE ABOUT TO GO FULL-TILT *MISOGYNY OF THE HIGHEST ORDER*...

OH NO, NOT AGAIN!

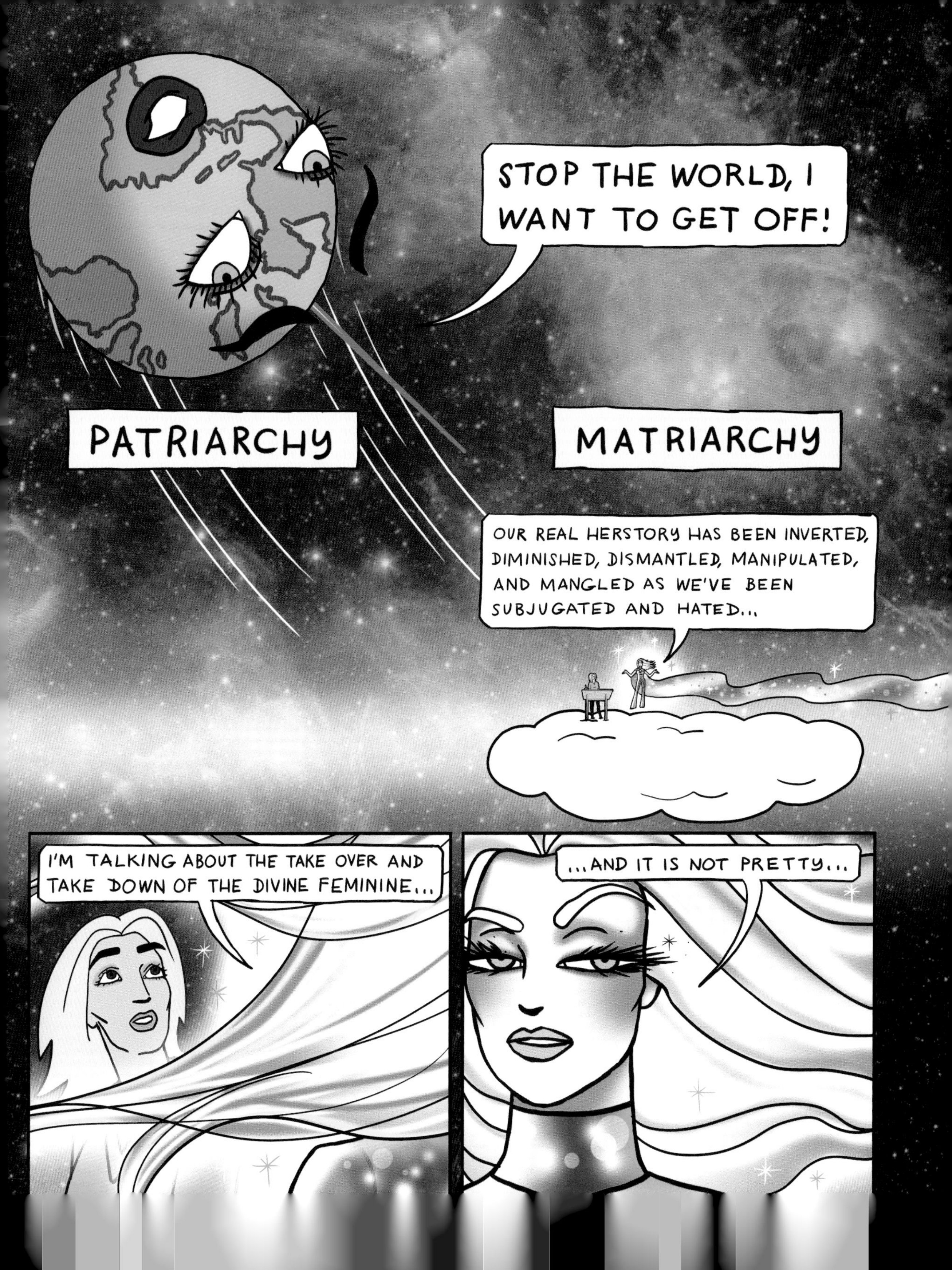
STOP THE WORLD, I WANT TO GET OFF!
PATRIARCHY
MATRIARCHY
OUR REAL HERSTORY HAS BEEN INVERTED, DIMINISHED, DISMANTLED, MANIPULATED, AND MANGLED AS WE'VE BEEN SUBJUGATED AND HATED...
I'M TALKING ABOUT THE TAKE OVER AND TAKE DOWN OF THE DIVINE FEMININE...
...AND IT IS NOT PRETTY...

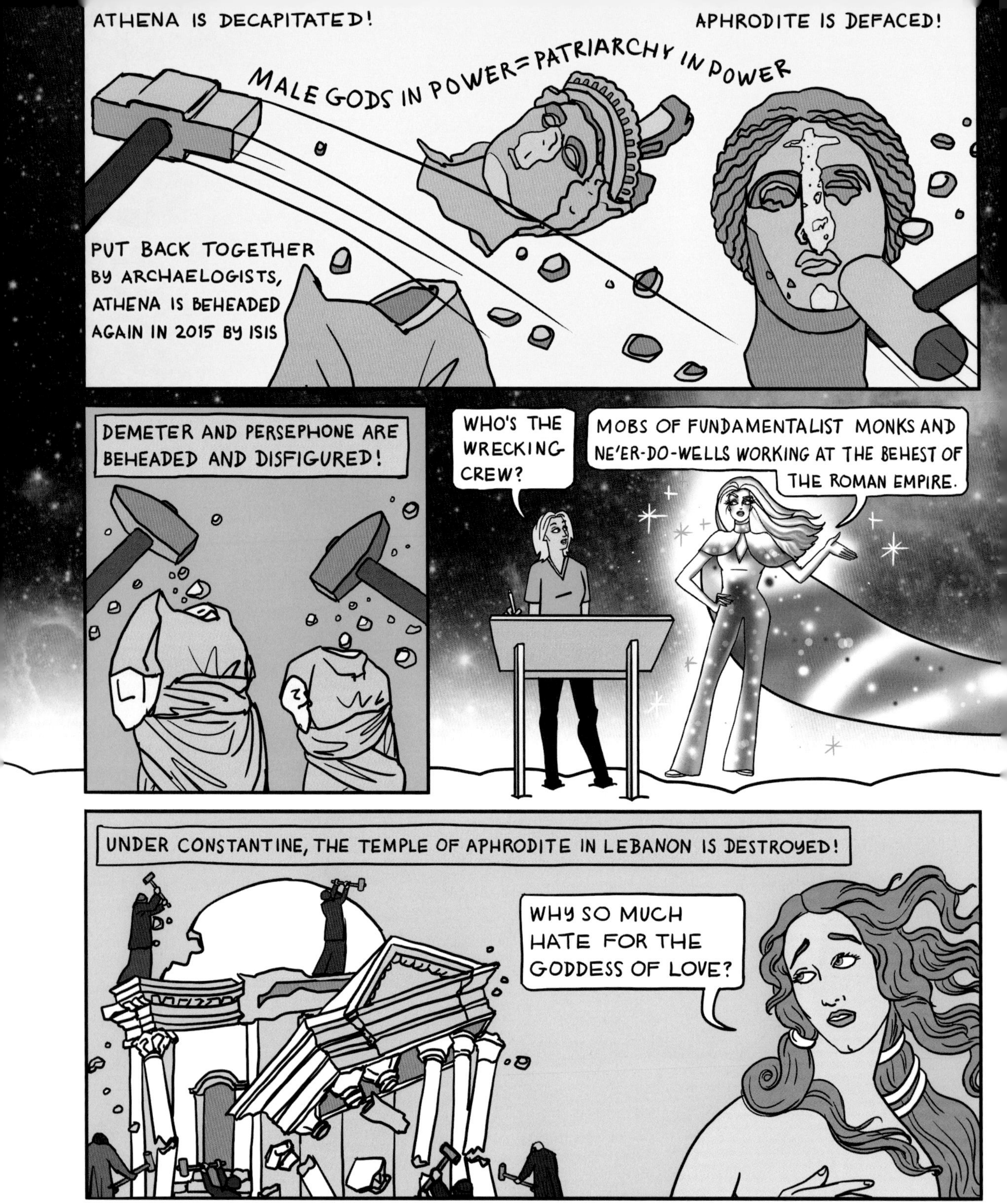
ATHENA IS DECAPITATED!
APHRODITE IS DEFACED!
MALE GODS IN POWER=PATRIARCHY IN POWER
PUT BACK TOGETHER BY ARCHAELOGISTS, ATHENA IS BEHEADED AGAIN IN 2015 BY ISIS
DEMETER AND PERSEPHONE ARE BEHEADED AND DISFIGURED!
WHO'S THE WRECKING CREW?
MOBS OF FUNDAMENTALIST MONKS AND NE'ER-DO-WELLS WORKING AT THE BEHEST OF THE ROMAN EMPIRE.
UNDER CONSTANTINE, THE TEMPLE OF APHRODITE IN LEBANON IS DESTROYED!
WHY SO MUCH HATE FOR THE GODDESS OF LOVE?

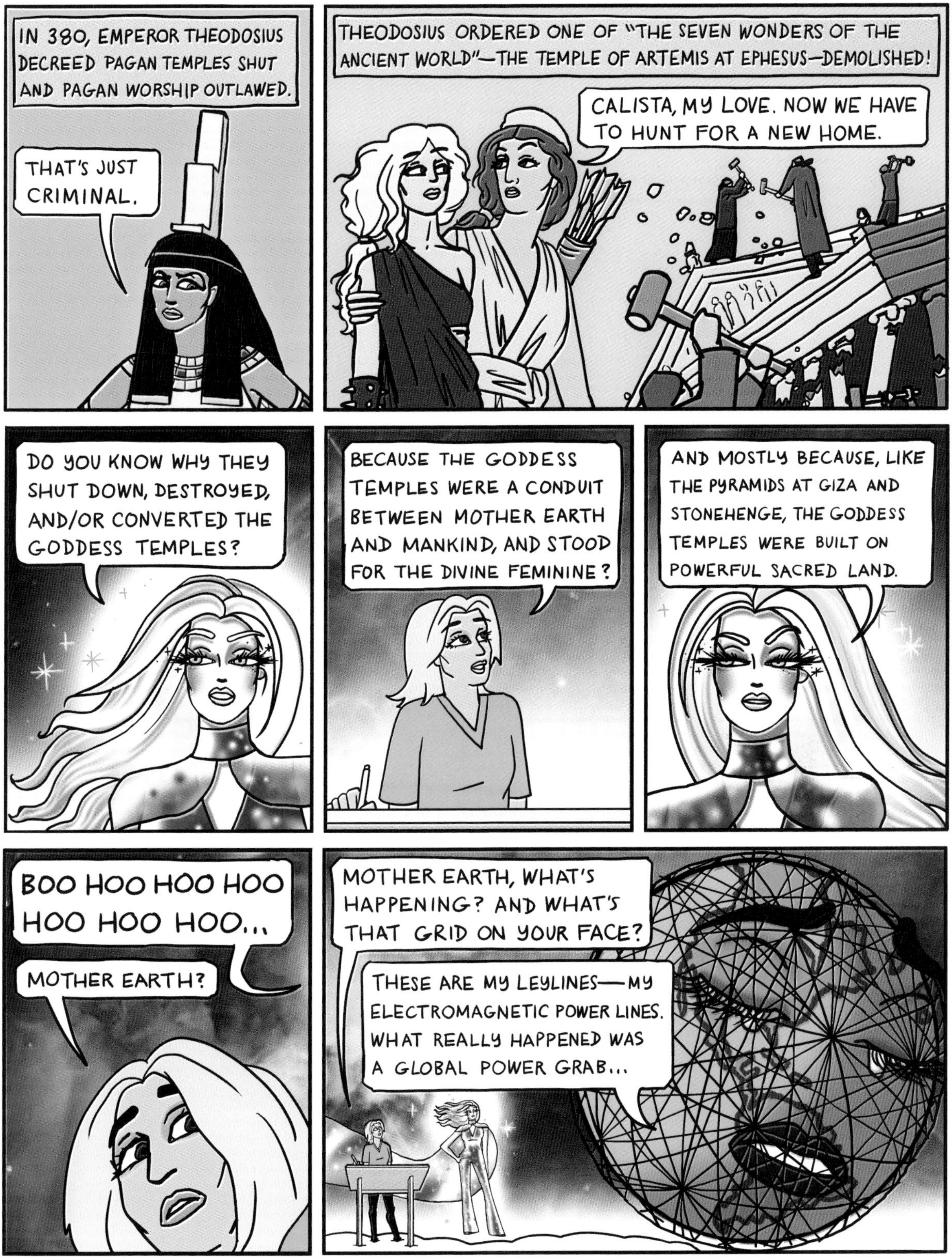
IN 380, EMPEROR THEODOSIUS DECREED PAGAN TEMPLES SHUT AND PAGAN WORSHIP OUTLAWED.
THAT'S JUST CRIMINAL.
THEODOSIUS ORDERED ONE OF "THE SEVEN WONDERS OF THE ANCIENT WORLD"—THE TEMPLE OF ARTEMIS AT EPHESUS—DEMOLISHED!
CALISTA, MY LOVE. NOW WE HAVE TO HUNT FOR A NEW HOME.
DO YOU KNOW WHY THEY SHUT DOWN, DESTROYED, AND/OR CONVERTED THE GODDESS TEMPLES?
BECAUSE THE GODDESS TEMPLES WERE A CONDUIT BETWEEN MOTHER EARTH AND MANKIND, AND STOOD FOR THE DIVINE FEMININE?
AND MOSTLY BECAUSE, LIKE THE PYRAMIDS AT GIZA AND STONEHENGE, THE GODDESS TEMPLES WERE BUILT ON POWERFUL SACRED LAND.
BOO HOO HOO HOO HOO HOO HOO HOO HOO...
MOTHER EARTH?
MOTHER EARTH, WHAT'S HAPPENING? AND WHAT'S THAT GRID ON YOUR FACE?
THESE ARE MY LEYLINES—MY ELECTROMAGNETIC POWER LINES. WHAT REALLY HAPPENED WAS A GLOBAL POWER GRAB...

THE LEYLINES MAKE UP MY MATRIX! THE CONTROLLERS TOOK CONTROL OF MY MATRIX!!!

THE *MATRIX*—MATRIX?

THE MATRIX WAS AN EXCELLENT MOVIE—

—DOCUMENTARY!!!

THE ANUNNAKI-ARCHON-CONTROLLER CABAL WHO CONTROL MY MATRIX ARE ALL IN CAHOOTS! THEY'VE HIJACKED MY ELECTROMAGNETIC GRID TO KEEP THE ENERGY FOR THEMSELVES *AND* SO YOU'LL PLUG INTO THEM INSTEAD OF ME!!!

MOTHER EARTH WANTS TO CONNECT WITH HER CHILDREN!

BUT IF WE'RE ON A HIGHER FREQUENCY, WE CAN CONNECT WITH YOU, RIGHT?

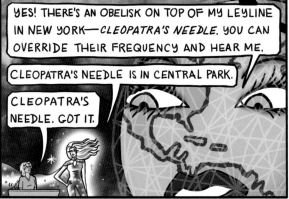

YES! THERE'S AN OBELISK ON TOP OF MY LEYLINE IN NEW YORK—*CLEOPATRA'S NEEDLE*. YOU CAN OVERRIDE THEIR FREQUENCY AND HEAR ME.

CLEOPATRA'S NEEDLE IS IN CENTRAL PARK.

CLEOPATRA'S NEEDLE. GOT IT.

OH, HOW THEY TRIED TO CONTROL ME, TOO.

HELLO. AND WHO ARE YOU?

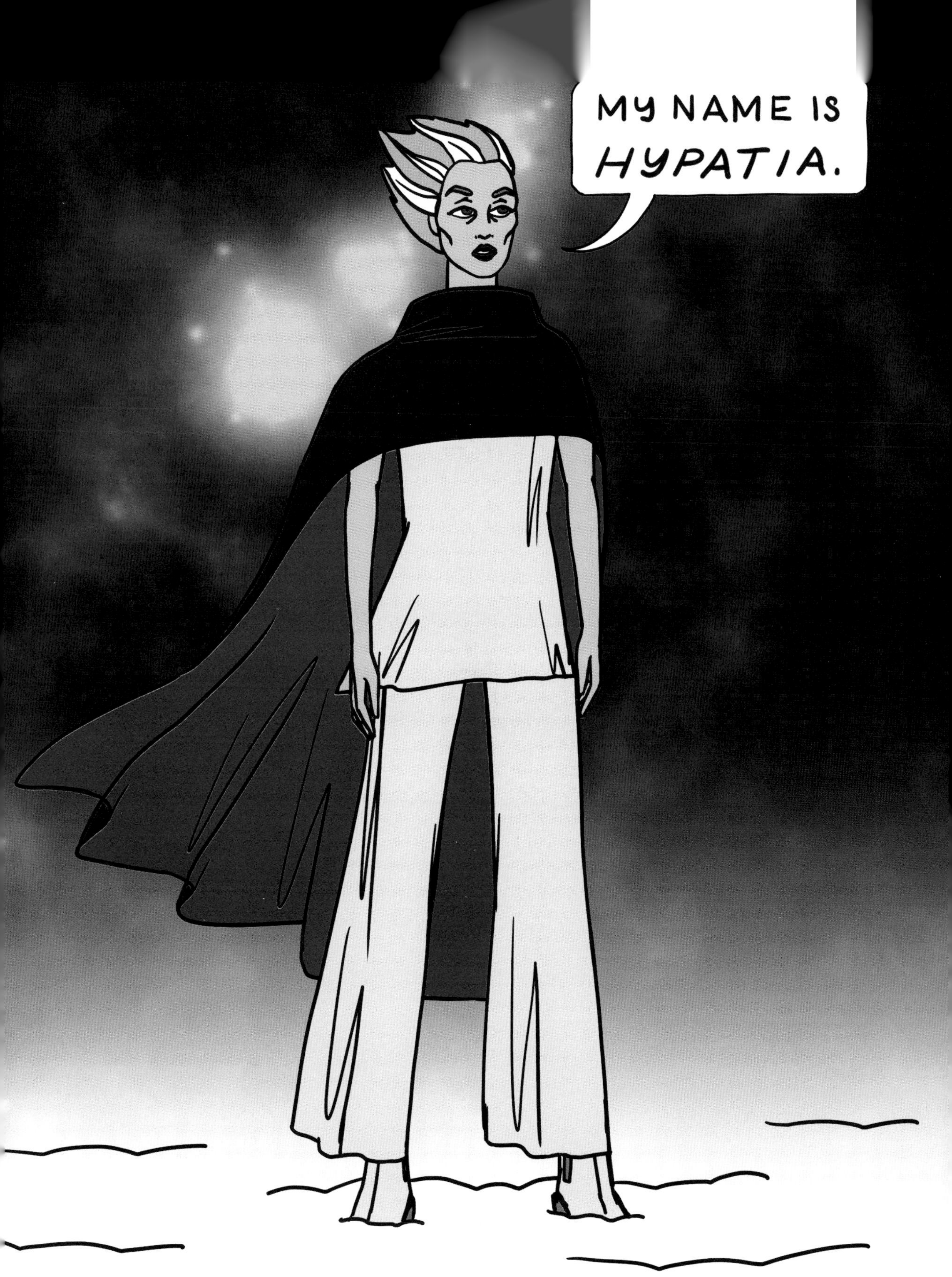
MY NAME IS *HYPATIA.*

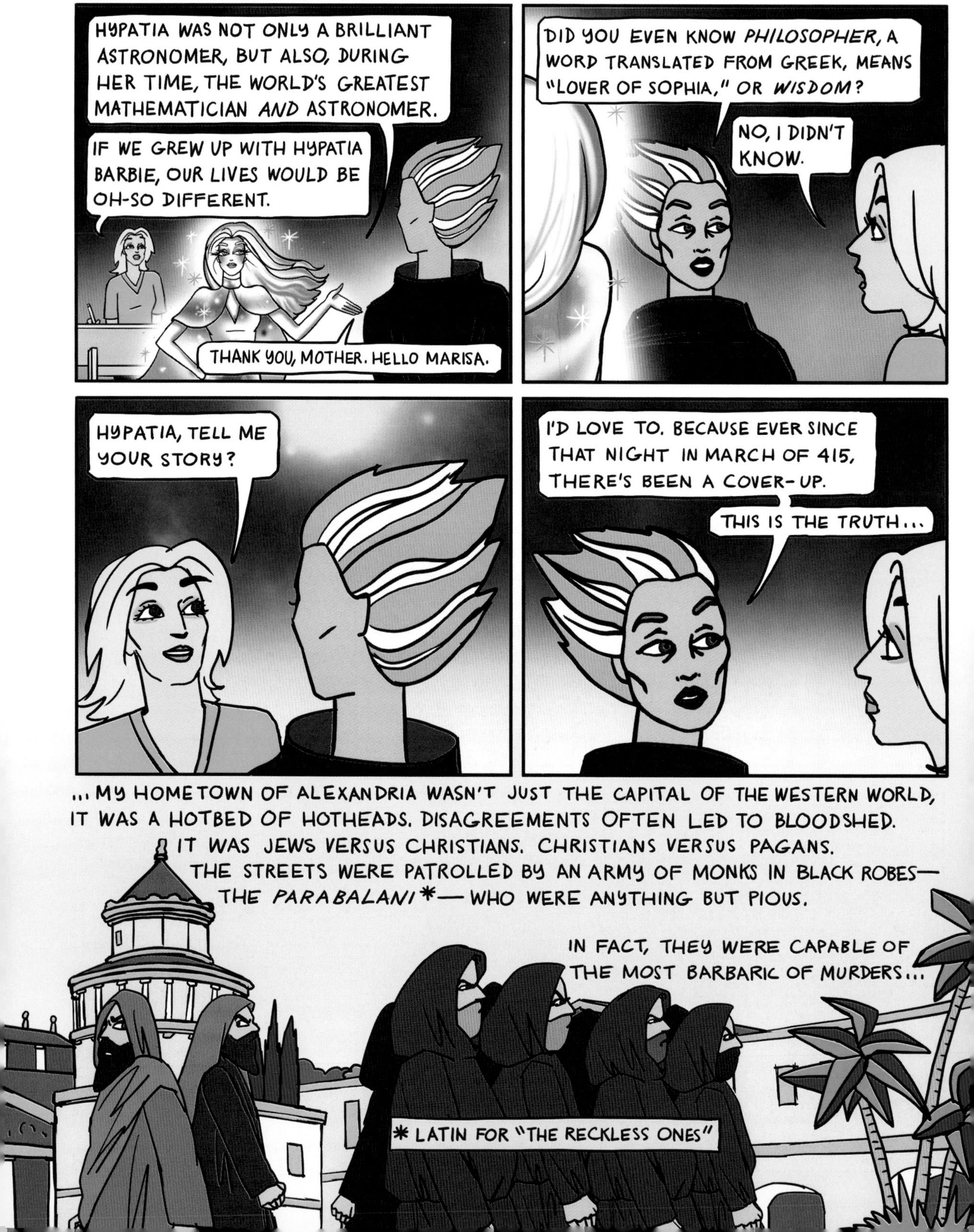
HYPATIA WAS NOT ONLY A BRILLIANT ASTRONOMER, BUT ALSO, DURING HER TIME, THE WORLD'S GREATEST MATHEMATICIAN AND ASTRONOMER.
IF WE GREW UP WITH HYPATIA BARBIE, OUR LIVES WOULD BE OH-SO DIFFERENT.
THANK YOU, MOTHER. HELLO MARISA.
DID YOU EVEN KNOW PHILOSOPHER, A WORD TRANSLATED FROM GREEK, MEANS "LOVER OF SOPHIA," OR WISDOM?
NO, I DIDN'T KNOW.
HYPATIA, TELL ME YOUR STORY?
I'D LOVE TO. BECAUSE EVER SINCE THAT NIGHT IN MARCH OF 415, THERE'S BEEN A COVER-UP.
THIS IS THE TRUTH...
...MY HOMETOWN OF ALEXANDRIA WASN'T JUST THE CAPITAL OF THE WESTERN WORLD, IT WAS A HOTBED OF HOTHEADS. DISAGREEMENTS OFTEN LED TO BLOODSHED. IT WAS JEWS VERSUS CHRISTIANS. CHRISTIANS VERSUS PAGANS. THE STREETS WERE PATROLLED BY AN ARMY OF MONKS IN BLACK ROBES—THE PARABALANI*—WHO WERE ANYTHING BUT PIOUS.
IN FACT, THEY WERE CAPABLE OF THE MOST BARBARIC OF MURDERS...
* LATIN FOR "THE RECKLESS ONES"

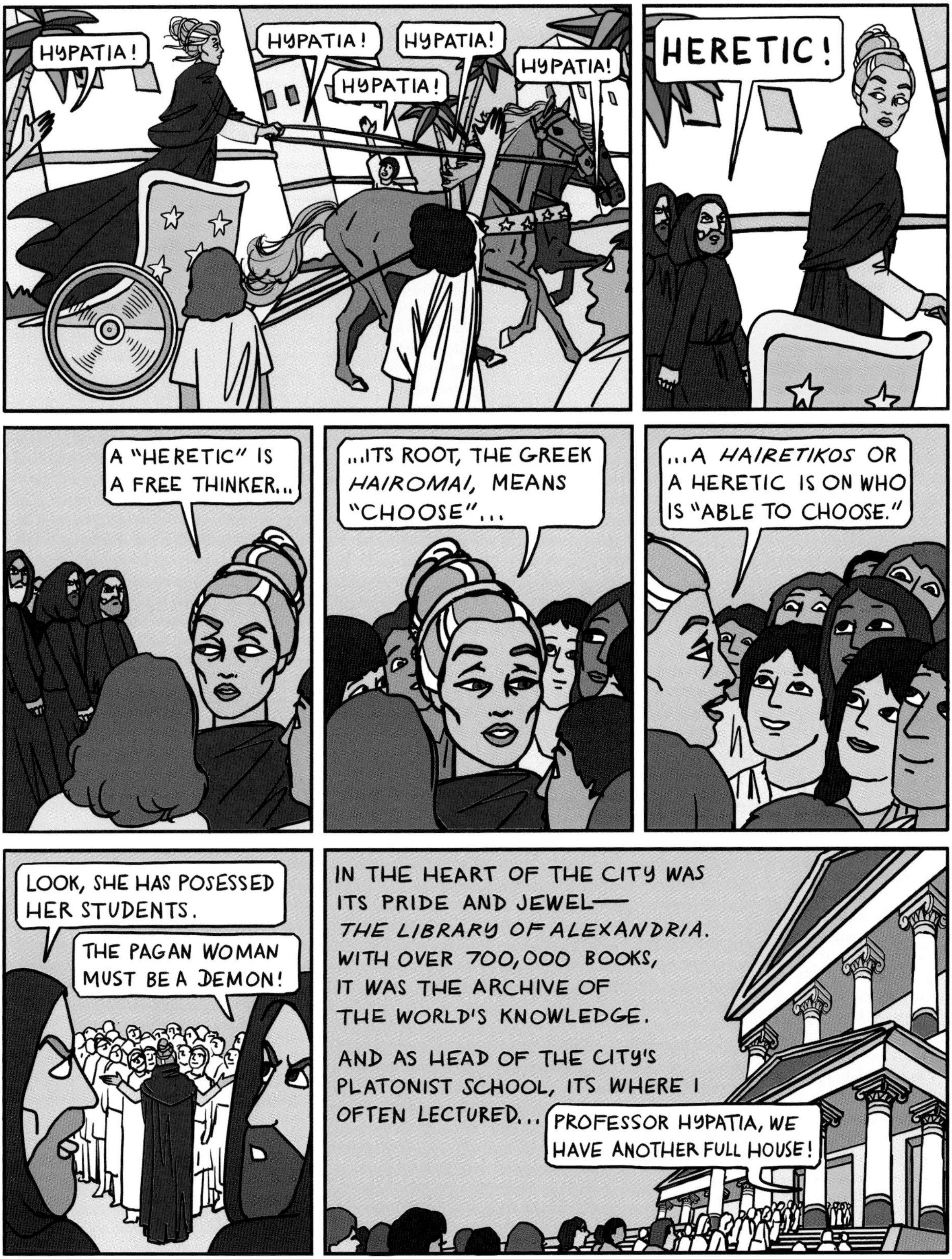
HYPATIA!
HYPATIA!
HYPATIA!
HYPATIA!
HYPATIA!
HERETIC!
A "HERETIC" IS A FREE THINKER...
...ITS ROOT, THE GREEK *HAIROMAI,* MEANS "CHOOSE"...
...A *HAIRETIKOS* OR A HERETIC IS ON WHO IS "ABLE TO CHOOSE."
LOOK, SHE HAS POSESSED HER STUDENTS.
THE PAGAN WOMAN MUST BE A DEMON!
IN THE HEART OF THE CITY WAS ITS PRIDE AND JEWEL— *THE LIBRARY OF ALEXANDRIA.* WITH OVER 700,000 BOOKS, IT WAS THE ARCHIVE OF THE WORLD'S KNOWLEDGE.
AND AS HEAD OF THE CITY'S PLATONIST SCHOOL, ITS WHERE I OFTEN LECTURED...
PROFESSOR HYPATIA, WE HAVE ANOTHER FULL HOUSE!

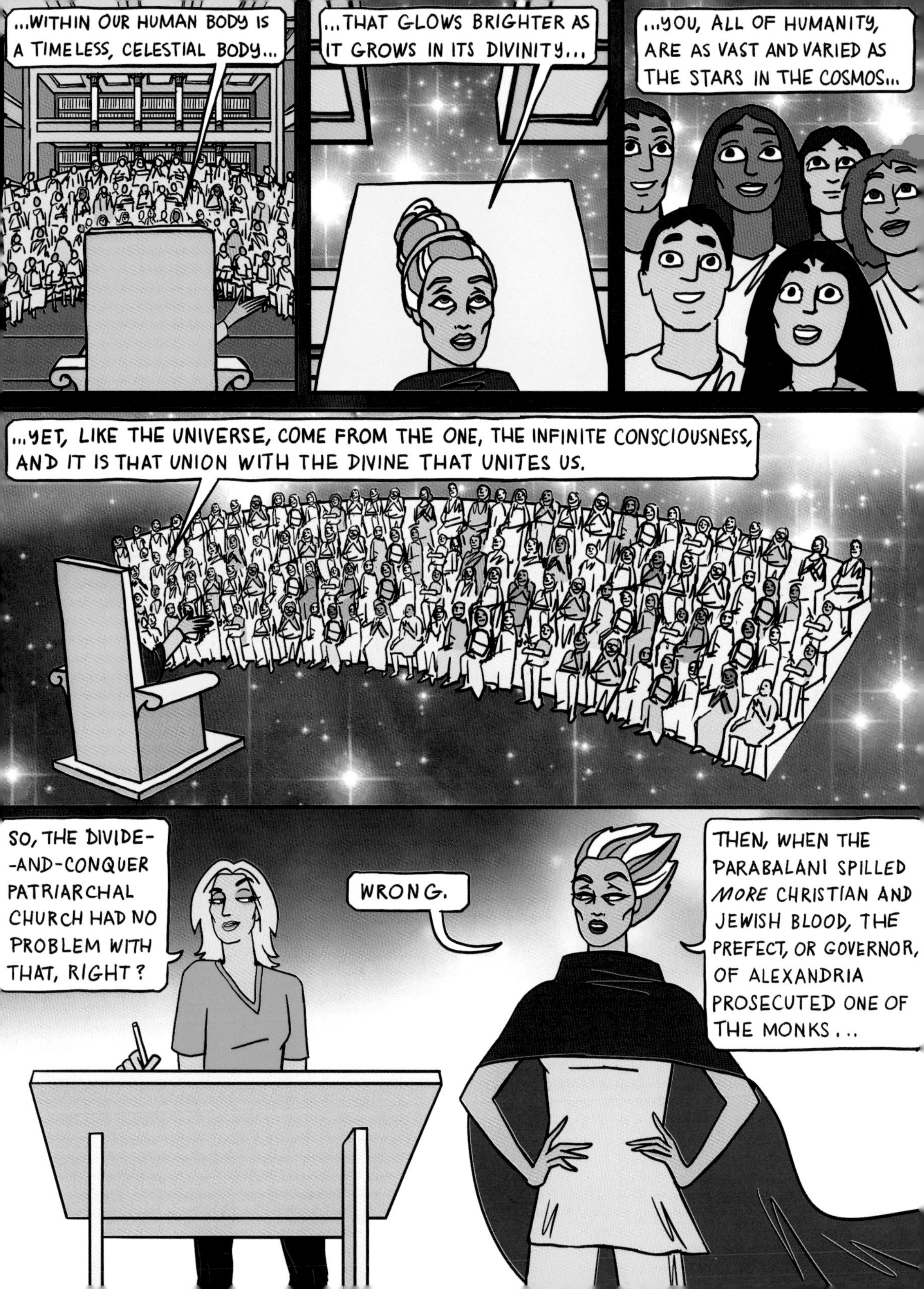
...WITHIN OUR HUMAN BODY IS A TIMELESS, CELESTIAL BODY...
...THAT GLOWS BRIGHTER AS IT GROWS IN ITS DIVINITY...
...YOU, ALL OF HUMANITY, ARE AS VAST AND VARIED AS THE STARS IN THE COSMOS...
...YET, LIKE THE UNIVERSE, COME FROM THE ONE, THE INFINITE CONSCIOUSNESS, AND IT IS THAT UNION WITH THE DIVINE THAT UNITES US.
SO, THE DIVIDE-AND-CONQUER PATRIARCHAL CHURCH HAD NO PROBLEM WITH THAT, RIGHT?
WRONG.
THEN, WHEN THE PARABALANI SPILLED *MORE* CHRISTIAN AND JEWISH BLOOD, THE PREFECT, OR GOVERNOR, OF ALEXANDRIA PROSECUTED ONE OF THE MONKS...

...I SIDED WITH THE PREFECT, *ORESTES*, A CHRISTIAN...

ORESTES, WE COME FROM THE SAME *LOVE-YOUR-NEIGHBOR* PLACE.

MY ALLIANCE WAS REPORTED TO HIS MORTAL ENEMY, THE HEAD OF THE CHURCH, *BISHOP CYRIL*...

YOU'RE RIGHT, HYPATIA'S A WITCH. ORESTES IS UNDER HER SPELL.

AS PUPPETEER OF THE PARABALANI, BISHOP CYRIL WAS THE TOWN PARIAH.

DRIVER, WHY SO MUCH TRAFFIC?

BISHOP CYRIL, WE'RE IN FRONT OF HYPATIA'S HOUSE. THE HERETIC IS GIVING A TALK.

THERE'S BISHOP CYRIL.

DON'T EVEN LOOK AT THAT MONSTER.

IF THERE WAS ONE WORD TO DESCRIBE CYRIL, IT'S *ZEALOT*...

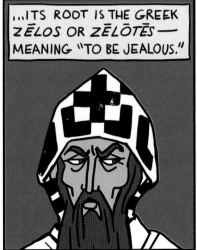

...ITS ROOT IS THE GREEK *ZĒLOS* OR *ZĒLŌTĒS* — MEANING "TO BE JEALOUS."

THAT NIGHT, CYRIL MET WITH HIS HITMAN, *PETER THE READER*.

HYPATIA IS A DEVIL! HOW ELSE WOULD SHE BE SO POPULAR? SHE MADE A DEAL WITH SATAN HIMSELF!

WHAT SHOULD I DO?

THE NEXT DAY WAS THAT FATEFUL DAY IN MID-MARCH...

I WAS DRIVING HOME FROM ONE OF MY LECTURES...

WHEN SUDDENLY...

SORCERESS!

DEMONESS!

YOU AND YOUR BLASPHEMOUS TEACHINGS ARE GOING STRAIGHT TO HELL!

WHAT ARE YOU DOING?

GOD'S WORK.

PETER THE READER PULLED ME OFF MY CHARIOT...

THE MONKS GRABBED, GROPED, STRIPPED, AND DRAGGED ME THROUGH THE STREET TO THE CAESARIUM CHURCH—

CYRIL'S HEADQUARTERS...

...WHERE THEY SCRAPED OFF MY SKIN WITH TILE SHARDS...

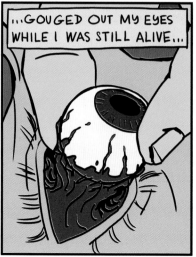

...GOUGED OUT MY EYES WHILE I WAS STILL ALIVE...

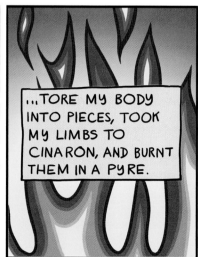

...TORE MY BODY INTO PIECES, TOOK MY LIMBS TO CINARON, AND BURNT THEM IN A PYRE.

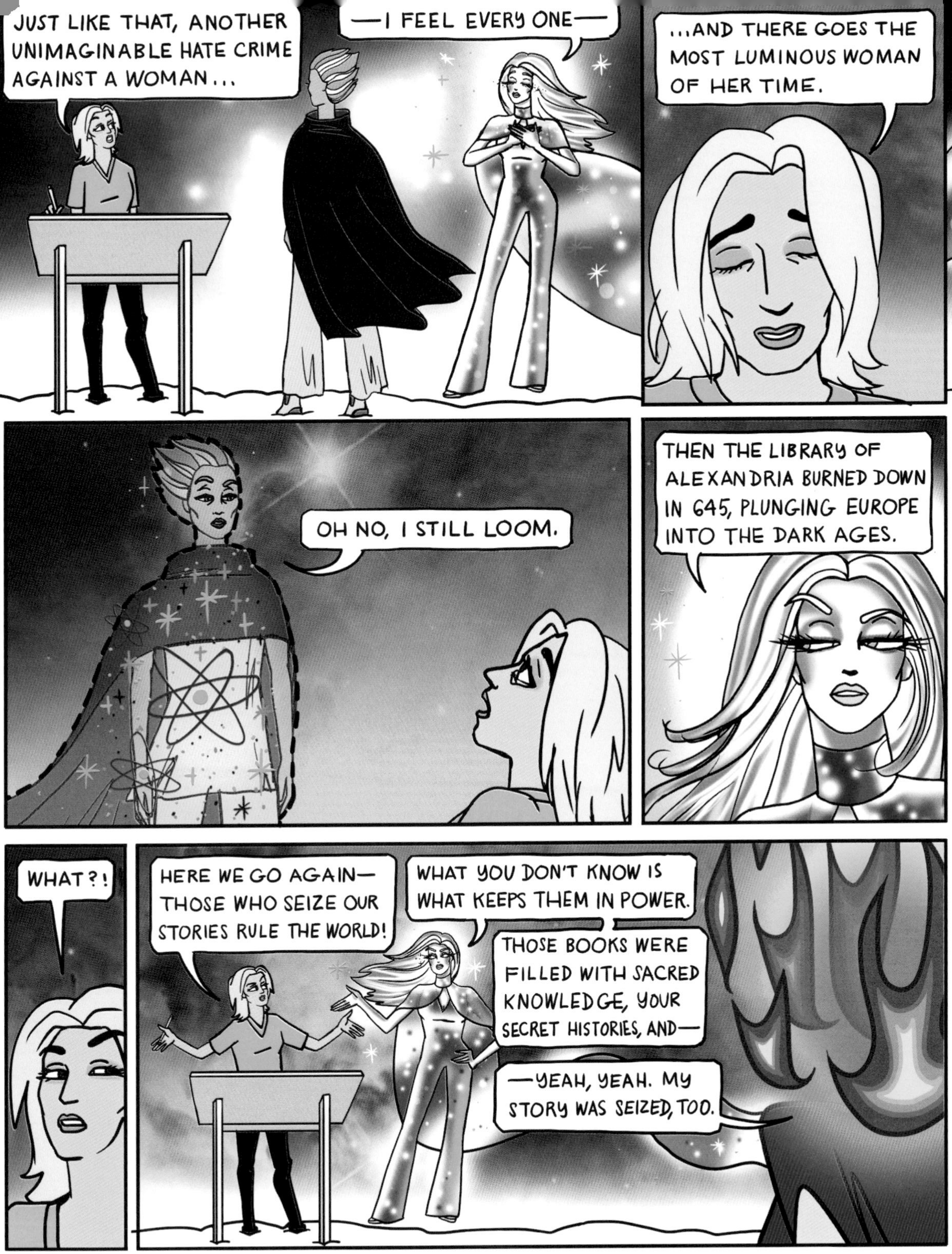
JUST LIKE THAT, ANOTHER UNIMAGINABLE HATE CRIME AGAINST A WOMAN...
—I FEEL EVERY ONE—
...AND THERE GOES THE MOST LUMINOUS WOMAN OF HER TIME.
OH NO, I STILL LOOM.
THEN THE LIBRARY OF ALEXANDRIA BURNED DOWN IN 645, PLUNGING EUROPE INTO THE DARK AGES.
WHAT?!
HERE WE GO AGAIN— THOSE WHO SEIZE OUR STORIES RULE THE WORLD!
WHAT YOU DON'T KNOW IS WHAT KEEPS THEM IN POWER.
THOSE BOOKS WERE FILLED WITH SACRED KNOWLEDGE, YOUR SECRET HISTORIES, AND—
—YEAH, YEAH. MY STORY WAS SEIZED, TOO.

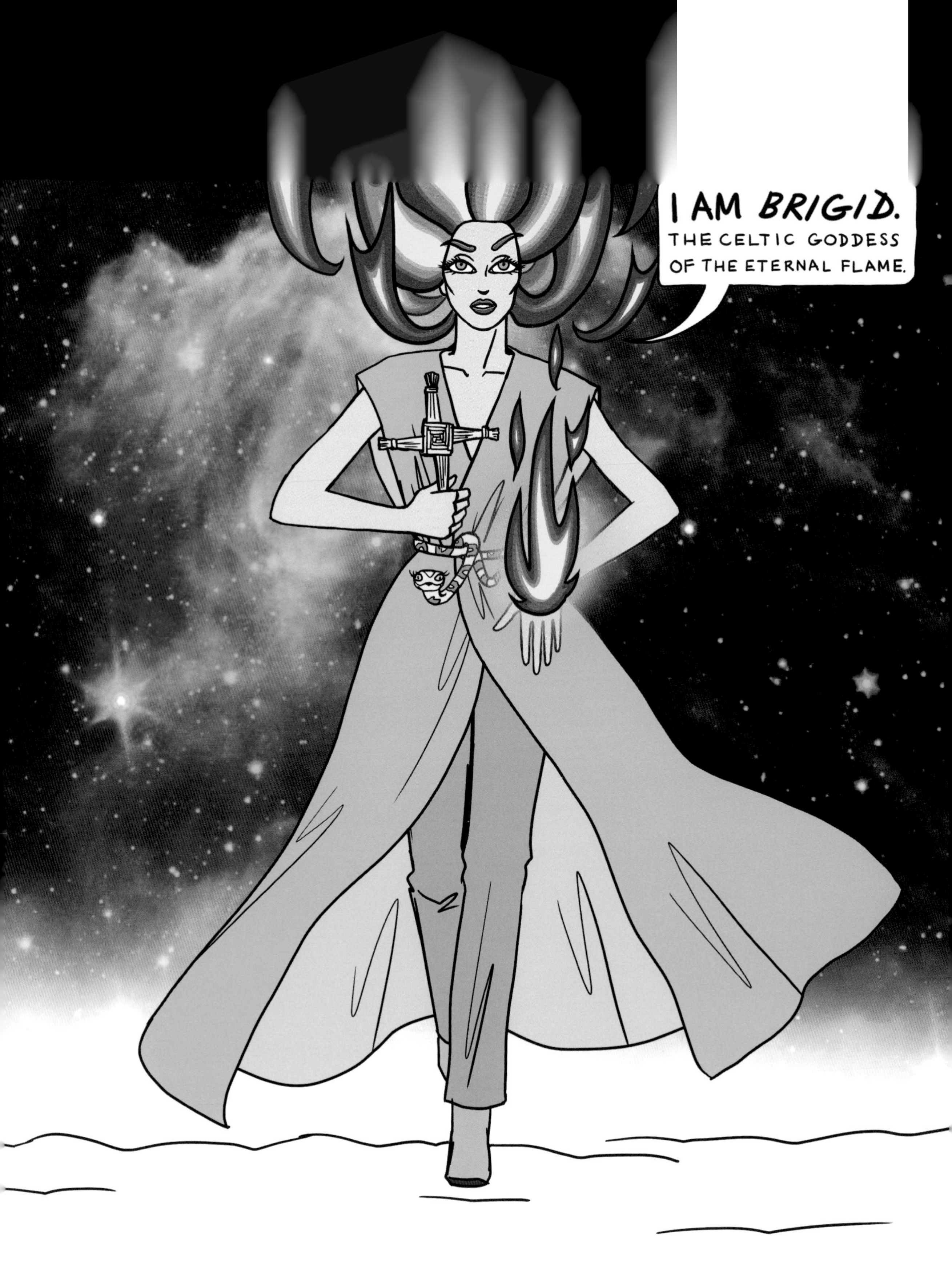
I AM *BRIGID.*
THE CELTIC GODDESS OF THE ETERNAL FLAME.

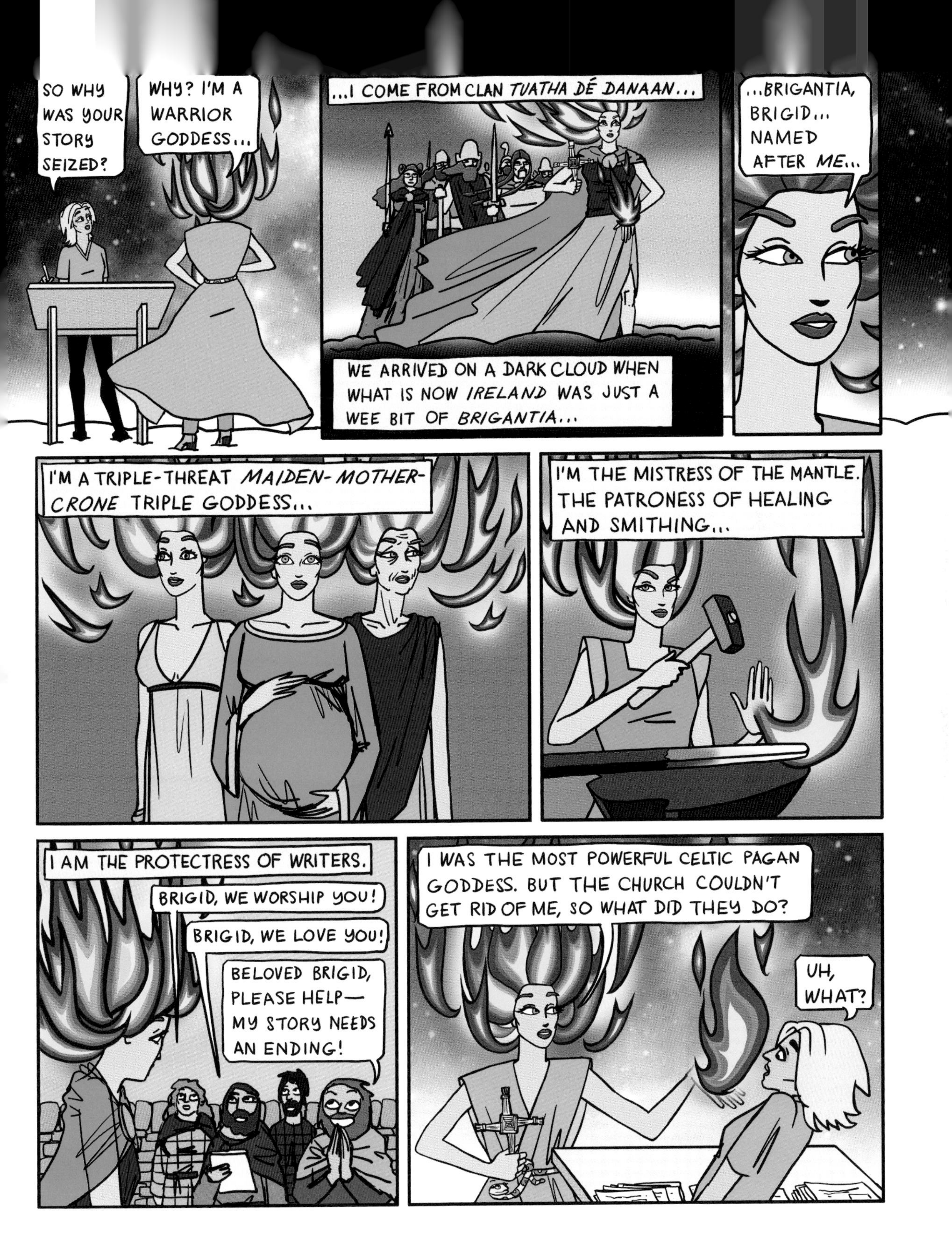

SO WHY WAS YOUR STORY SEIZED?
WHY? I'M A WARRIOR GODDESS...
...I COME FROM CLAN *TUATHA DÉ DANAAN*...
WE ARRIVED ON A DARK CLOUD WHEN WHAT IS NOW *IRELAND* WAS JUST A WEE BIT OF *BRIGANTIA*...
...BRIGANTIA, BRIGID... NAMED AFTER *ME*...
I'M A TRIPLE-THREAT *MAIDEN-MOTHER-CRONE* TRIPLE GODDESS...
I'M THE MISTRESS OF THE MANTLE. THE PATRONESS OF HEALING AND SMITHING...
I AM THE PROTECTRESS OF WRITERS.
BRIGID, WE WORSHIP YOU!
BRIGID, WE LOVE YOU!
BELOVED BRIGID, PLEASE HELP— MY STORY NEEDS AN ENDING!
I WAS THE MOST POWERFUL CELTIC PAGAN GODDESS. BUT THE CHURCH COULDN'T GET RID OF ME, SO WHAT DID THEY DO?
UH, WHAT?

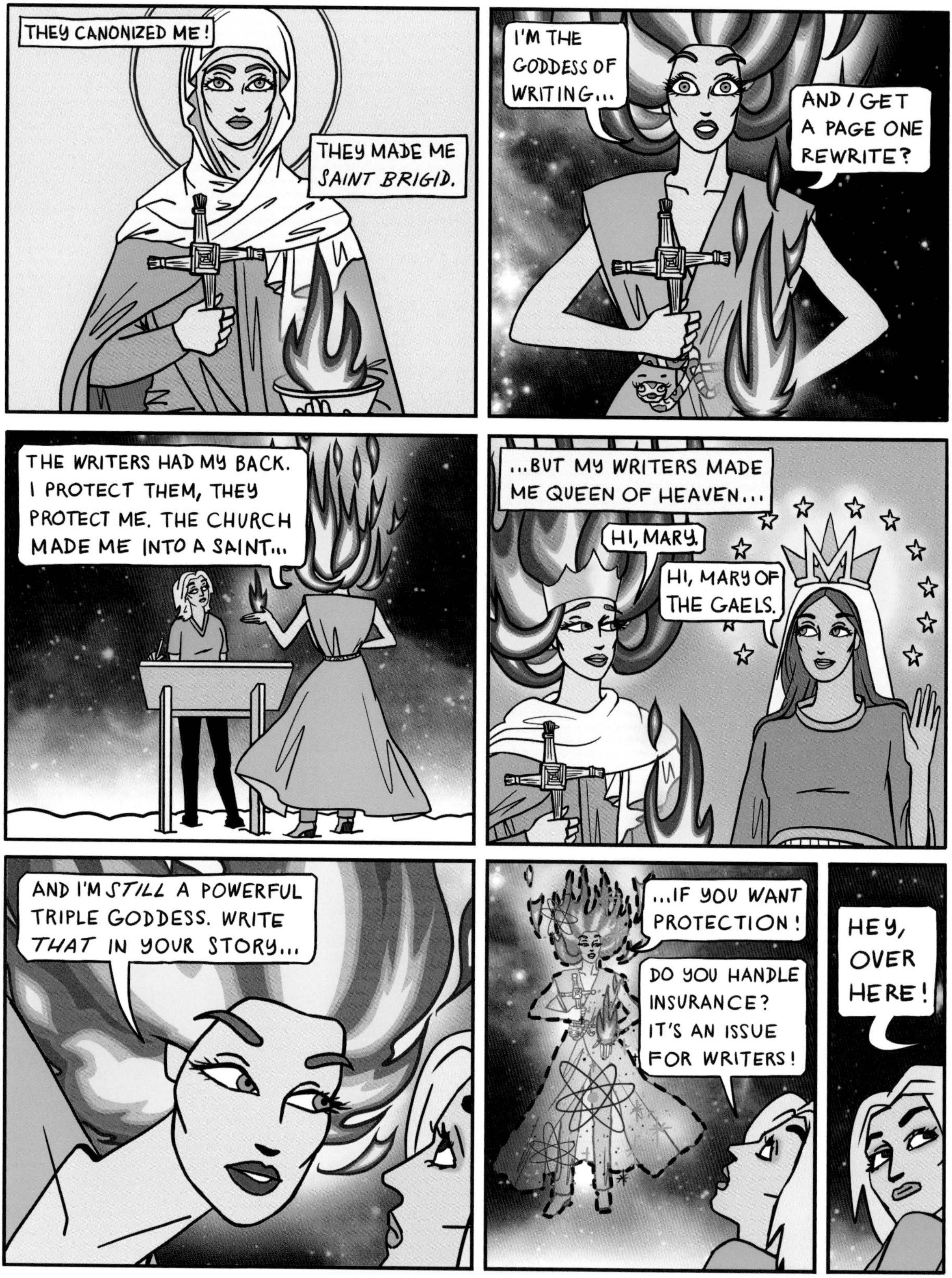
THEY CANONIZED ME!
THEY MADE ME SAINT BRIGID.
I'M THE GODDESS OF WRITING...
AND I GET A PAGE ONE REWRITE?
THE WRITERS HAD MY BACK. I PROTECT THEM, THEY PROTECT ME. THE CHURCH MADE ME INTO A SAINT...
...BUT MY WRITERS MADE ME QUEEN OF HEAVEN...
HI, MARY.
HI, MARY OF THE GAELS.
AND I'M STILL A POWERFUL TRIPLE GODDESS. WRITE THAT IN YOUR STORY...
...IF YOU WANT PROTECTION!
DO YOU HANDLE INSURANCE? IT'S AN ISSUE FOR WRITERS!
HEY, OVER HERE!

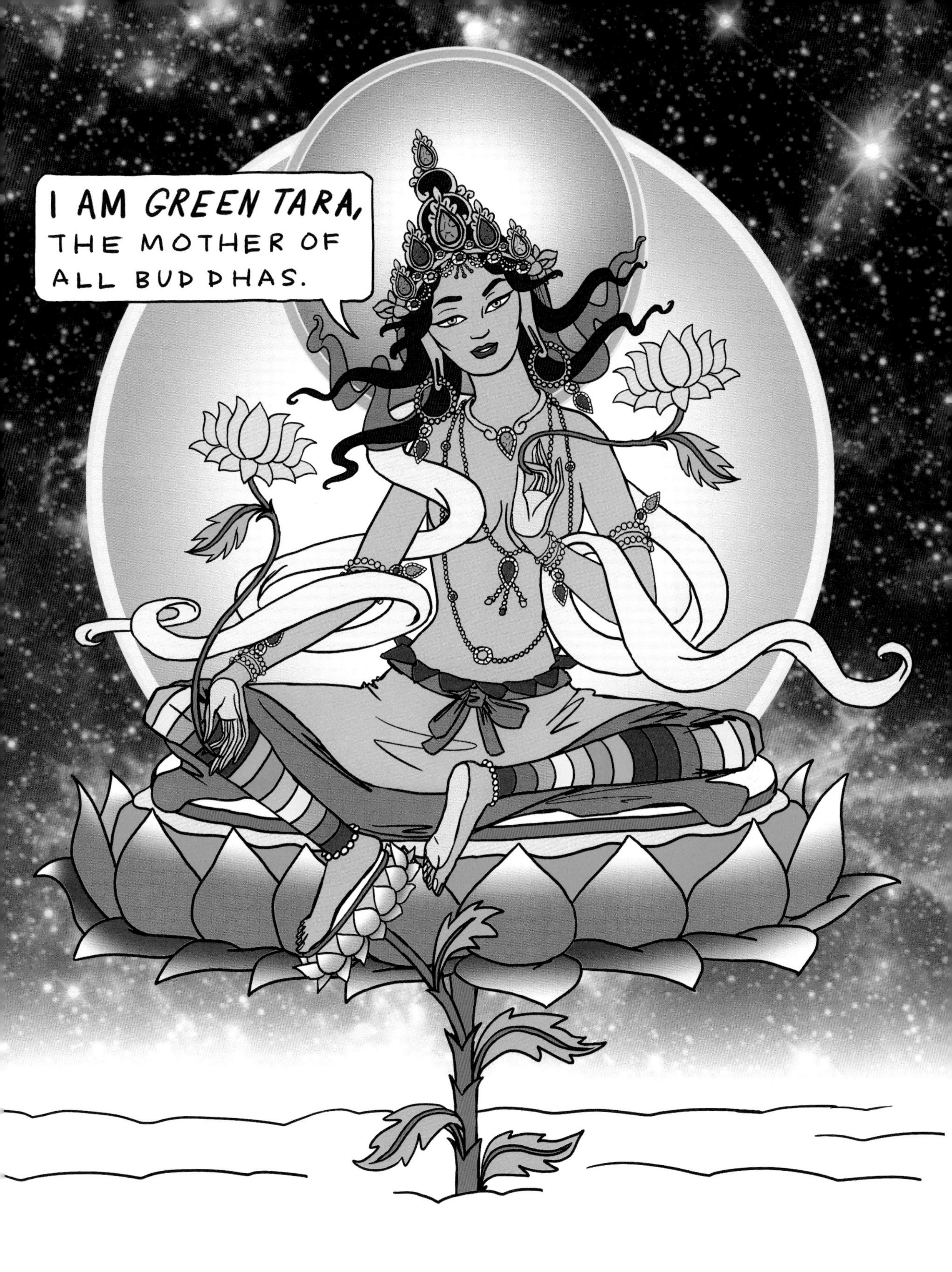
I AM *GREEN TARA*, THE MOTHER OF ALL BUDDHAS.

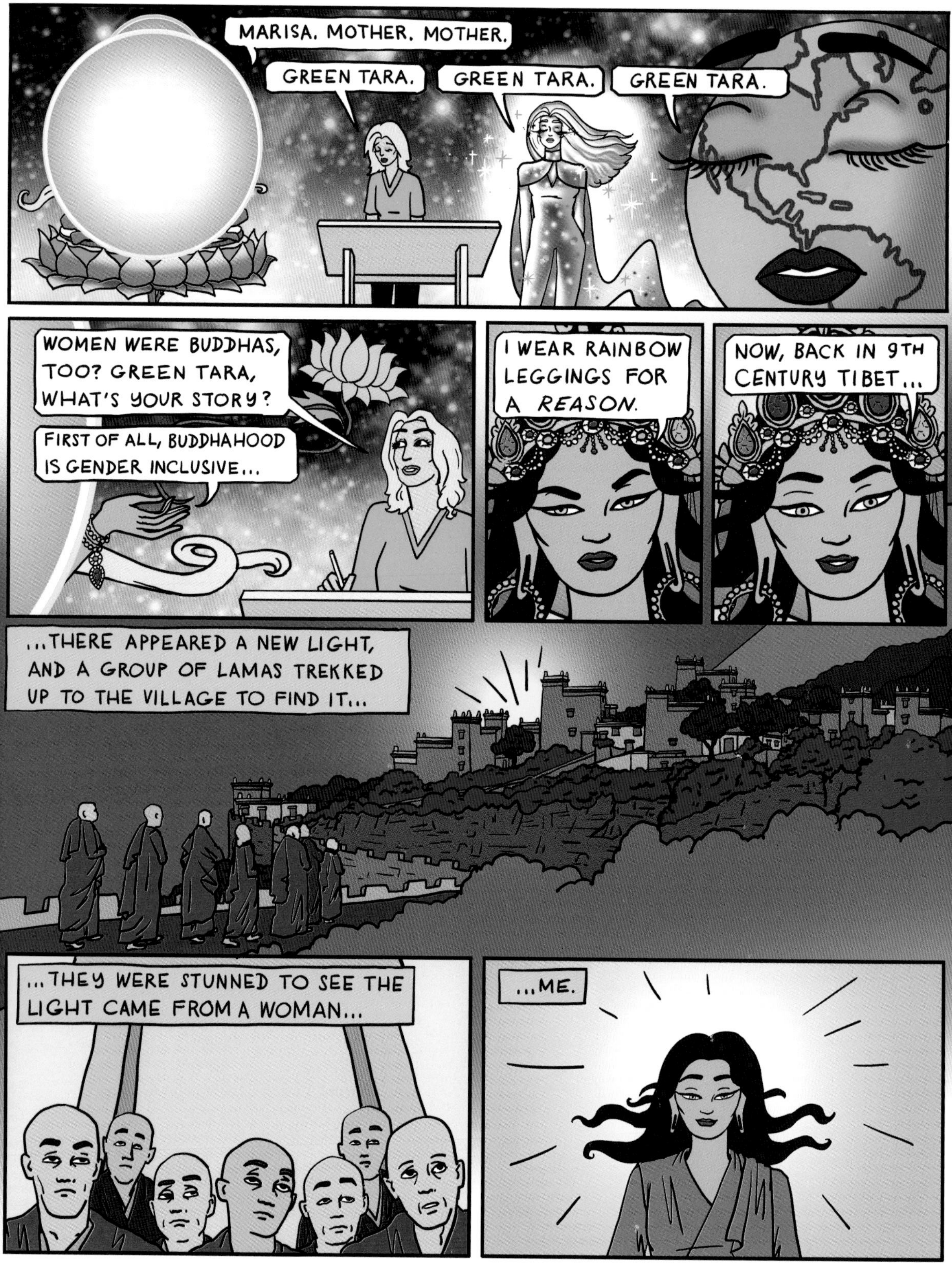

MARISA. MOTHER. MOTHER.
GREEN TARA.
GREEN TARA.
GREEN TARA.
WOMEN WERE BUDDHAS, TOO? GREEN TARA, WHAT'S YOUR STORY?
FIRST OF ALL, BUDDHAHOOD IS GENDER INCLUSIVE...
I WEAR RAINBOW LEGGINGS FOR A *REASON*.
NOW, BACK IN 9TH CENTURY TIBET...
...THERE APPEARED A NEW LIGHT, AND A GROUP OF LAMAS TREKKED UP TO THE VILLAGE TO FIND IT...
...THEY WERE STUNNED TO SEE THE LIGHT CAME FROM A WOMAN...
...ME.

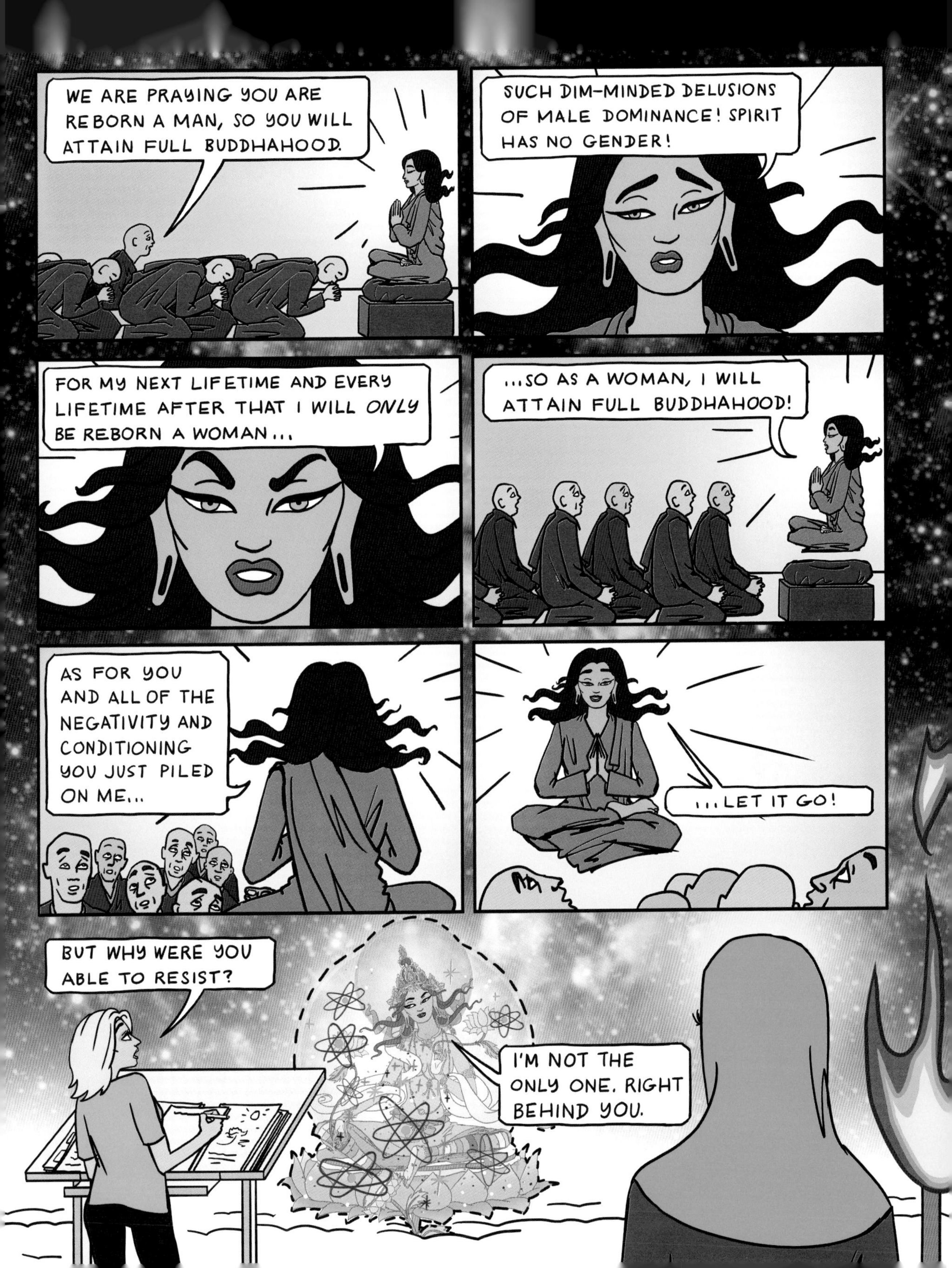
WE ARE PRAYING YOU ARE REBORN A MAN, SO YOU WILL ATTAIN FULL BUDDHAHOOD.
SUCH DIM-MINDED DELUSIONS OF MALE DOMINANCE! SPIRIT HAS NO GENDER!
FOR MY NEXT LIFETIME AND EVERY LIFETIME AFTER THAT I WILL *ONLY* BE REBORN A WOMAN...
...SO AS A WOMAN, I WILL ATTAIN FULL BUDDHAHOOD!
AS FOR YOU AND ALL OF THE NEGATIVITY AND CONDITIONING YOU JUST PILED ON ME...
...LET IT GO!
BUT WHY WERE YOU ABLE TO RESIST?
I'M NOT THE ONLY ONE. RIGHT BEHIND YOU.

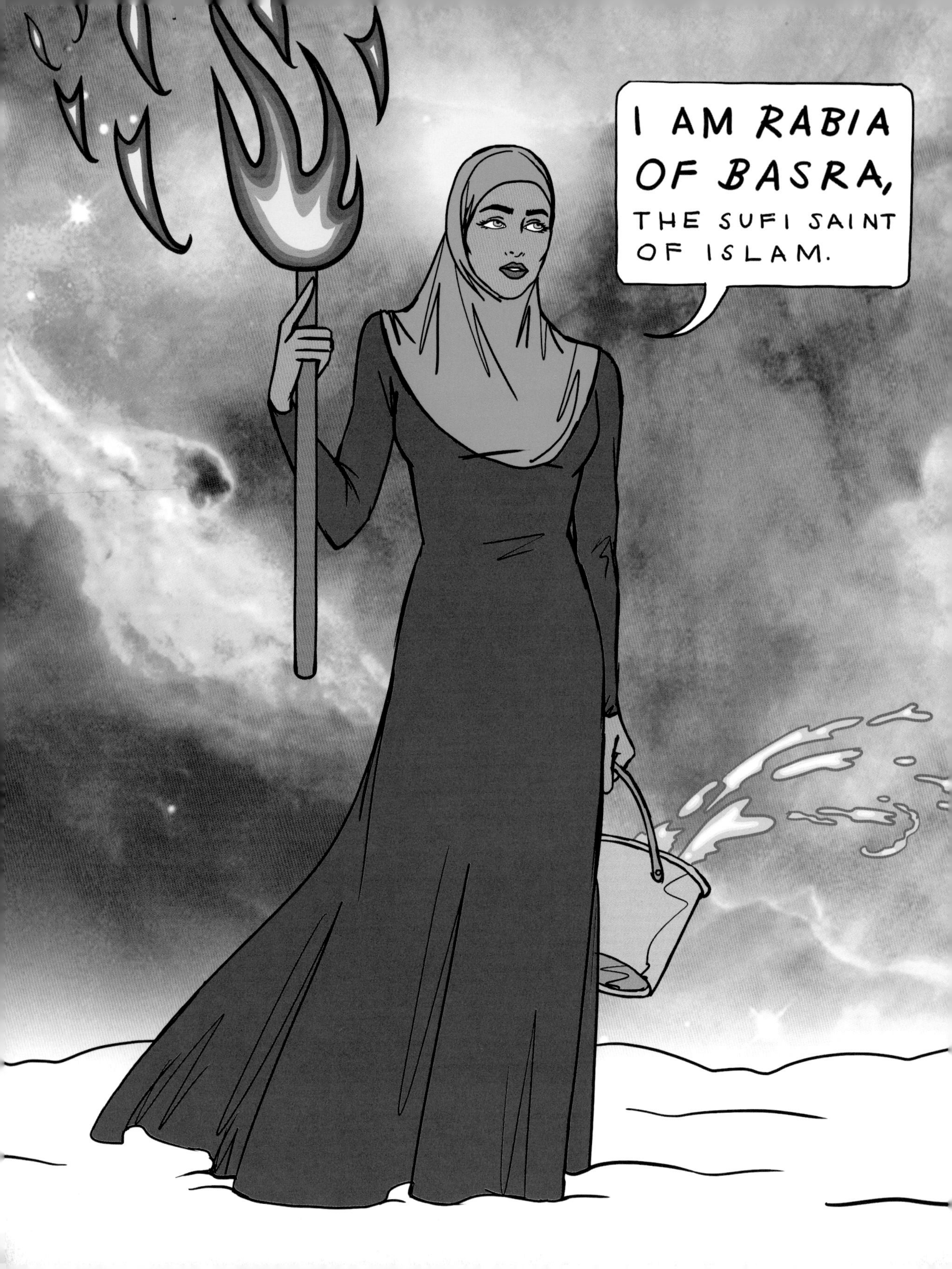
I AM *RABIA* OF *BASRA*, THE SUFI SAINT OF ISLAM.

MOTHER! MOTHER!

SAINT RABIA!

SAINT RABIA!

SAINT RABIA, WHY ARE YOU CARRYING A BUCKET OF WATER IN ONE HAND AND A TORCH IN THE OTHER?

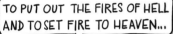

TO PUT OUT THE FIRES OF HELL AND TO SET FIRE TO HEAVEN...

I WON'T WORSHIP FROM FEAR OR FOR REWARD. I WORSHIP FOR THE LOVE OF GOD.

THAT YOU KNOW YOU HAVE.

HOW DID YOU BECOME A SAINT?

ON THE NIGHT I WAS BORN...

...MOHAMMED CAME TO MY FATHER IN A VISION...

YOUR DAUGHTER IS A FAVORITE UP HERE. SHE WILL LEAD MUSLIMS TO THE DIVINE PATH.

BUT MY PARENTS DIED WHEN I WAS VERY YOUNG, AND I WAS TRAFFICKED AND SOLD INTO SLAVERY.

CRACK!

MY WRISTS WERE BROKEN, BUT MY FAITH WAS NOT.

EVERY NIGHT I PRAYED UNTIL MY MASTER SAW THE LIGHT.

I HAVE ENSLAVED A SAINT!

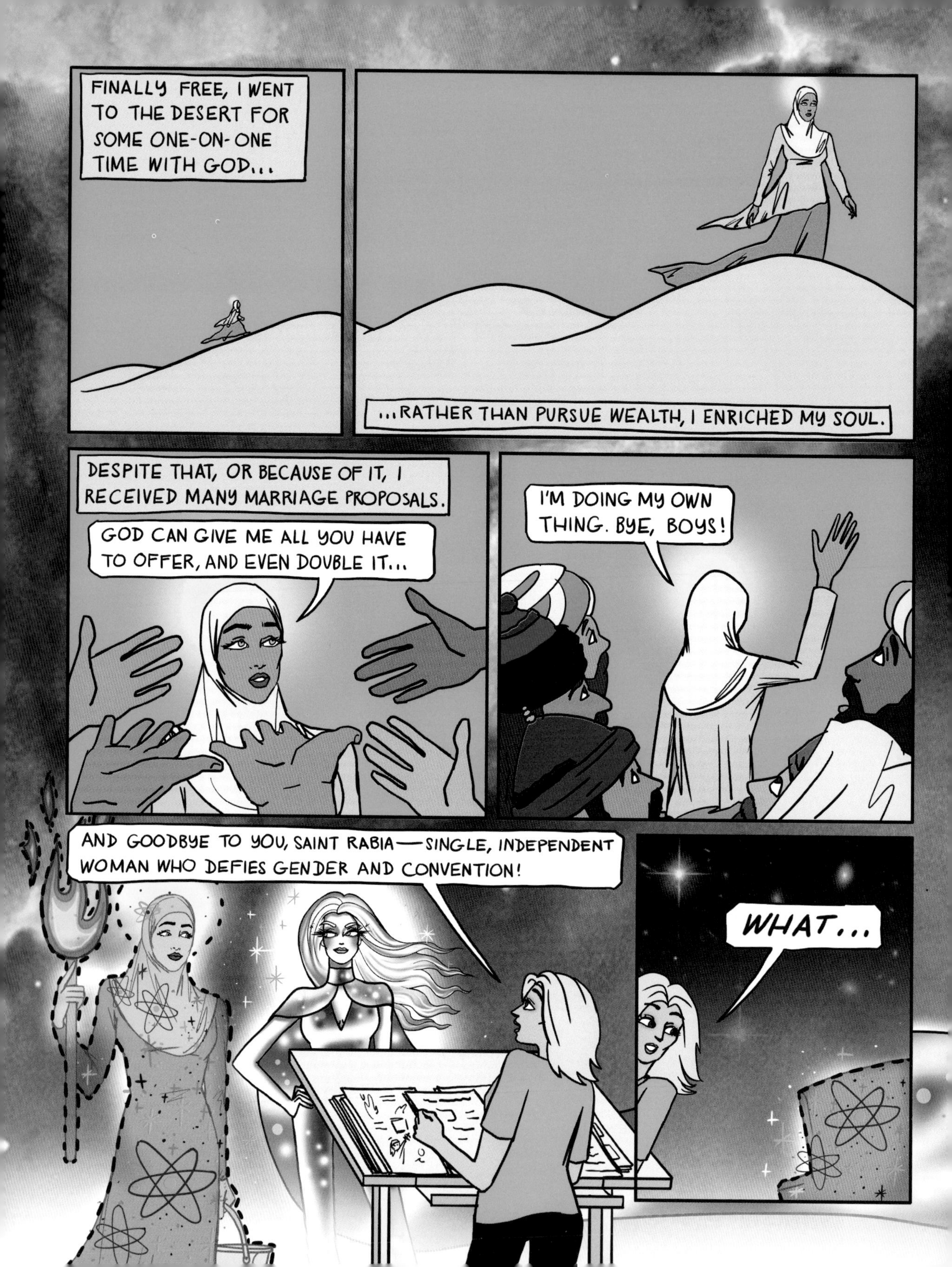
FINALLY FREE, I WENT TO THE DESERT FOR SOME ONE-ON-ONE TIME WITH GOD...
...RATHER THAN PURSUE WEALTH, I ENRICHED MY SOUL.
DESPITE THAT, OR BECAUSE OF IT, I RECEIVED MANY MARRIAGE PROPOSALS.
GOD CAN GIVE ME ALL YOU HAVE TO OFFER, AND EVEN DOUBLE IT...
I'M DOING MY OWN THING. BYE, BOYS!
AND GOODBYE TO YOU, SAINT RABIA—SINGLE, INDEPENDENT WOMAN WHO DEFIES GENDER AND CONVENTION!
WHAT...

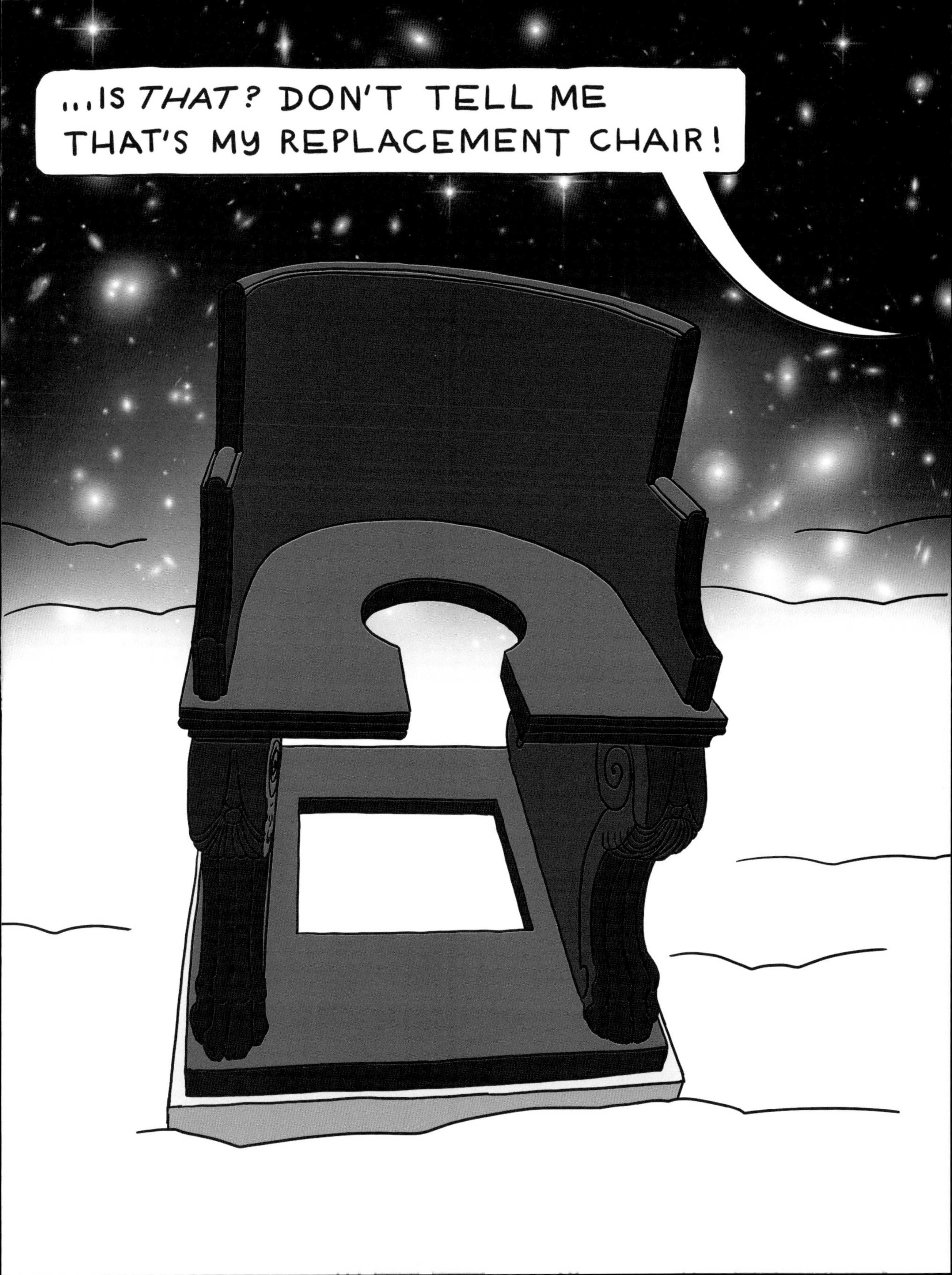
...IS *THAT*? DON'T TELL ME THAT'S MY REPLACEMENT CHAIR!

WHAT IS THAT CHAIR DOING THERE?

THAT'S THE *SEDIA STERCORARIA*, OR "DUNG SEAT."

IT'S A CHAIR FOR THE POPE-TO-BE.

WHY WOULD A CHAIR FOR THE POPE-TO-BE HAVE A HOLE IN IT?

PRIOR TO THE PAPAL CONSECRATION, THE POPE-TO-BE HAD TO SIT IN THE CHAIR BARE-BOTTOMED...

...WHILE A YOUNG CARDINAL REACHED UNDERNEATH TO VERIFY HIS MANHOOD.

HE HAS TWO TESTICLES. THEY'RE VERY DANGLY!

A REENACTMENT

SO, THE POPE GETS GROPED IN A CHAIR MADE TO CHECK HIS SEX?

IT'S IN THE VATICAN MUSEUMS.

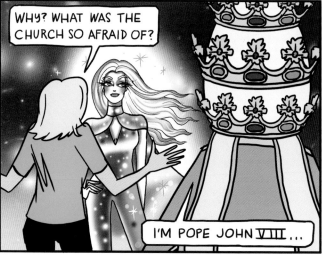

WHY? WHAT WAS THE CHURCH SO AFRAID OF?

I'M POPE JOHN VIII...

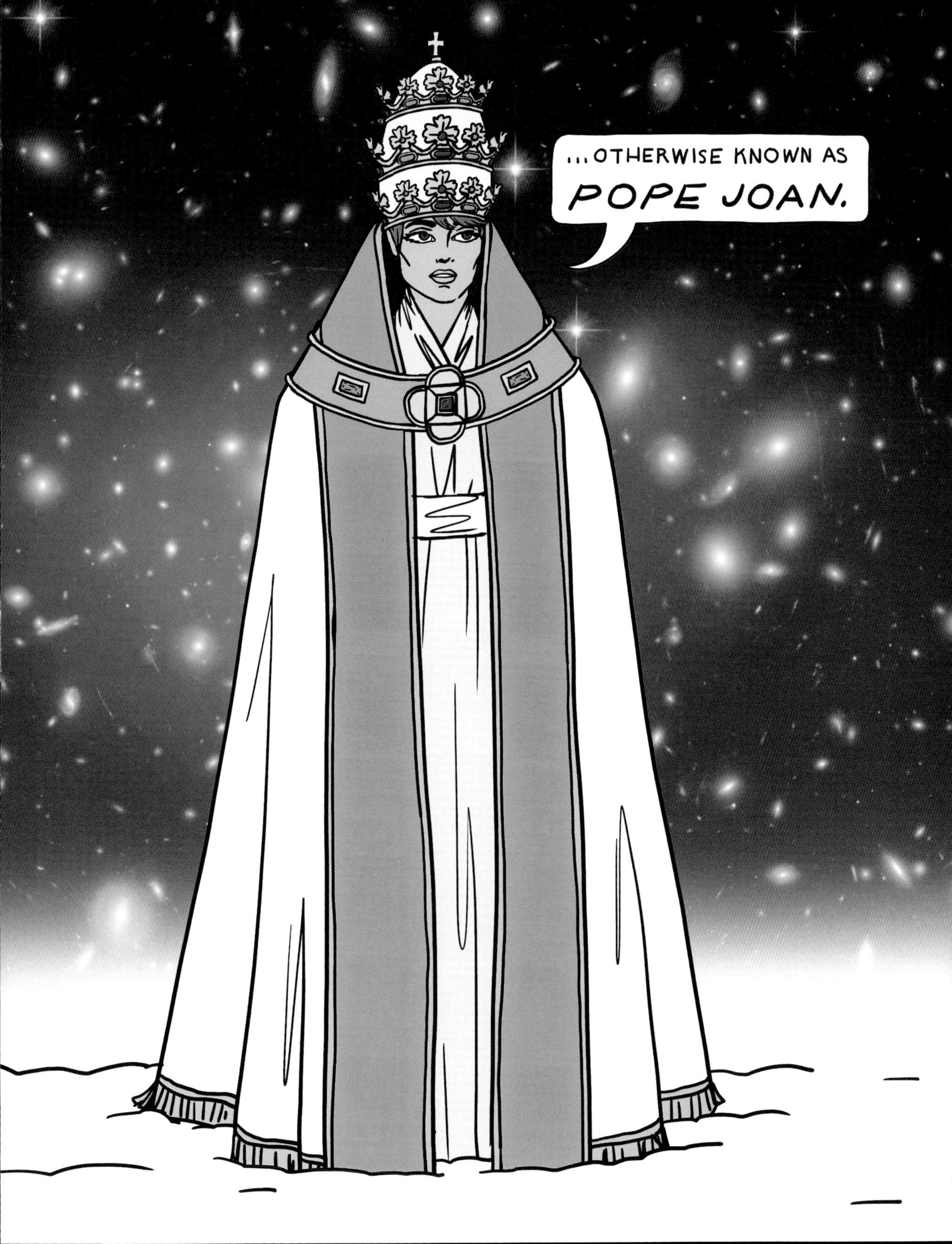
...OTHERWISE KNOWN AS POPE JOAN.

MOTHER! MOTHER!

HER EMINENCE, THE POPE! YOUR EMINENCE!

OF COURSE THERE WAS A FEMALE POPE AND I DIDN'T KNOW ABOUT IT.

WHAT DID THEY DO TO COVER YOU UP?

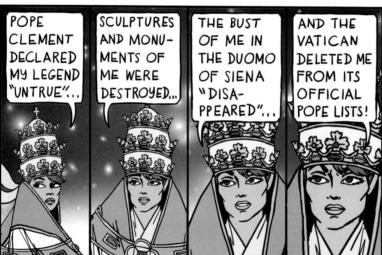

POPE CLEMENT DECLARED MY LEGEND "UNTRUE"...

SCULPTURES AND MONUMENTS OF ME WERE DESTROYED...

THE BUST OF ME IN THE DUOMO OF SIENA "DISAPPEARED"...

AND THE VATICAN DELETED ME FROM ITS OFFICIAL POPE LISTS!

BUT THAT GROPE-A-POPE CHAIR FROM THE VATICAN MUSEUMS? IT EXISTS BECAUSE YOU EXISTED.

THANK YOU.

FOR MEN WHO OPPRESS WOMEN, THEY SURE LOVE OUR DRESSES!

ALMOST AS MUCH AS THEY LOVE OUR JEWELRY!

SO HOW DID YOU BECOME POPE, JOAN?

I HAD A VISION THAT TRANSCENDED GENDER...

...AT 15, I CUT MY HAIR...

...JOAN BECAME JOHN AS I DONNED THE PERFECT COVER

THE ROBE OF A BENEDICTINE MONK.

I FELL IN LOVE WITH THE LIFE AND I FELL IN LOVE...

—WAIT. DID YOU HAVE A BOYFRIEND WHEN YOU WERE IN THE VATICAN?

I HAD AN AGE-APPROPRIATE, CONSENSUAL RELATIONSHIP PARTNER—PROBLEM?

NOT A PROBLEM!

THAT IS NOT A PROBLEM!

CAN I PLEASE FINISH MY STORY?

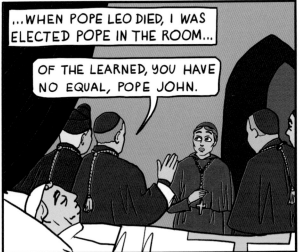

...WHEN POPE LEO DIED, I WAS ELECTED POPE IN THE ROOM...

OF THE LEARNED, YOU HAVE NO EQUAL, POPE JOHN.

—AN INCREDIBLE ACHIEVEMENT— EVEN FOR A MAN. BUT WEREN'T YOU WORRIED ABOUT BEING FOUND OUT?

BELIEVE IT OR NOT...

...THAT WASN'T MY BIGGEST WORRY...

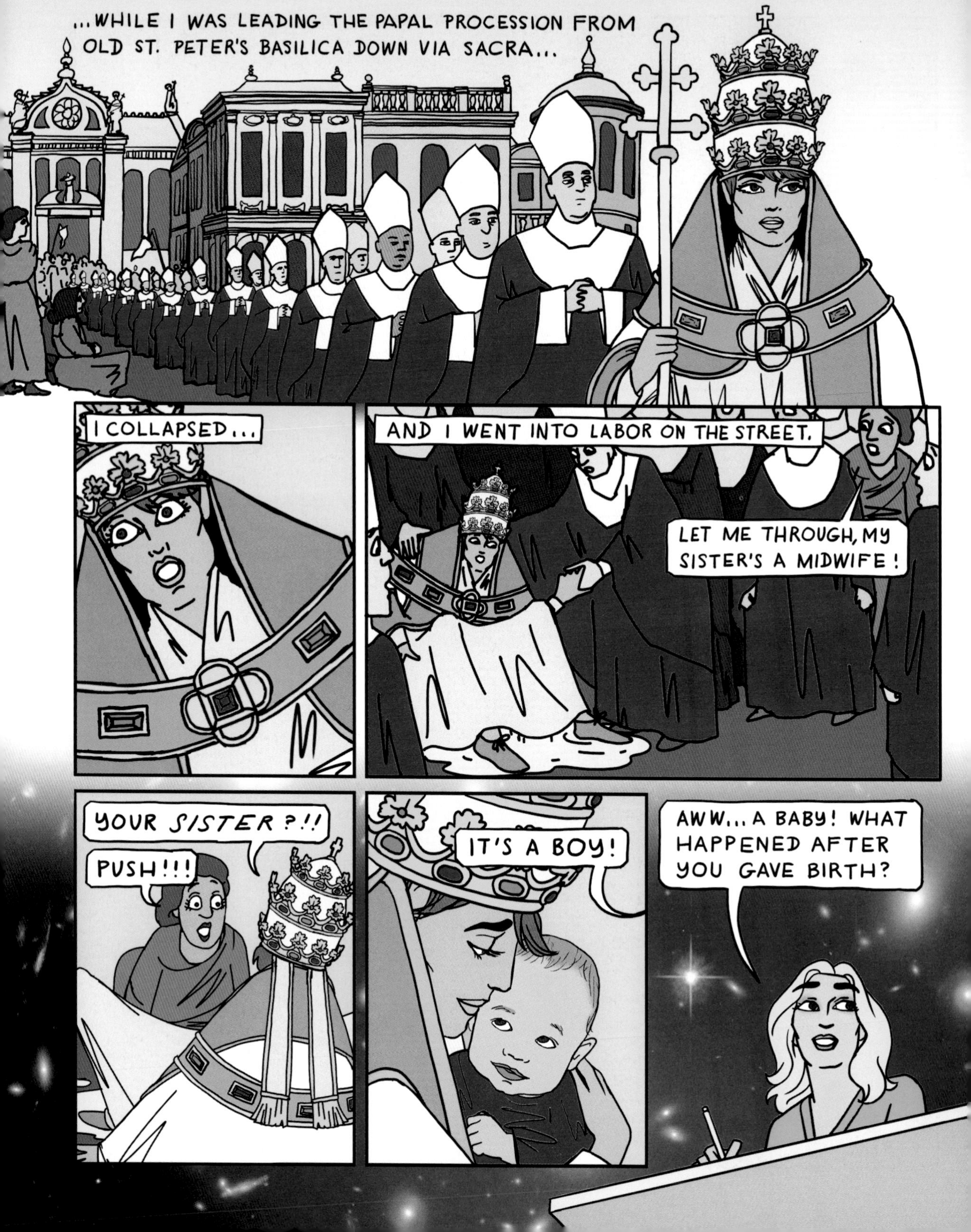
...WHILE I WAS LEADING THE PAPAL PROCESSION FROM OLD ST. PETER'S BASILICA DOWN VIA SACRA...
I COLLAPSED...
AND I WENT INTO LABOR ON THE STREET.
LET ME THROUGH, MY SISTER'S A MIDWIFE!
YOUR *SISTER*?!!
PUSH!!!
IT'S A BOY!
AWW... A BABY! WHAT HAPPENED AFTER YOU GAVE BIRTH?

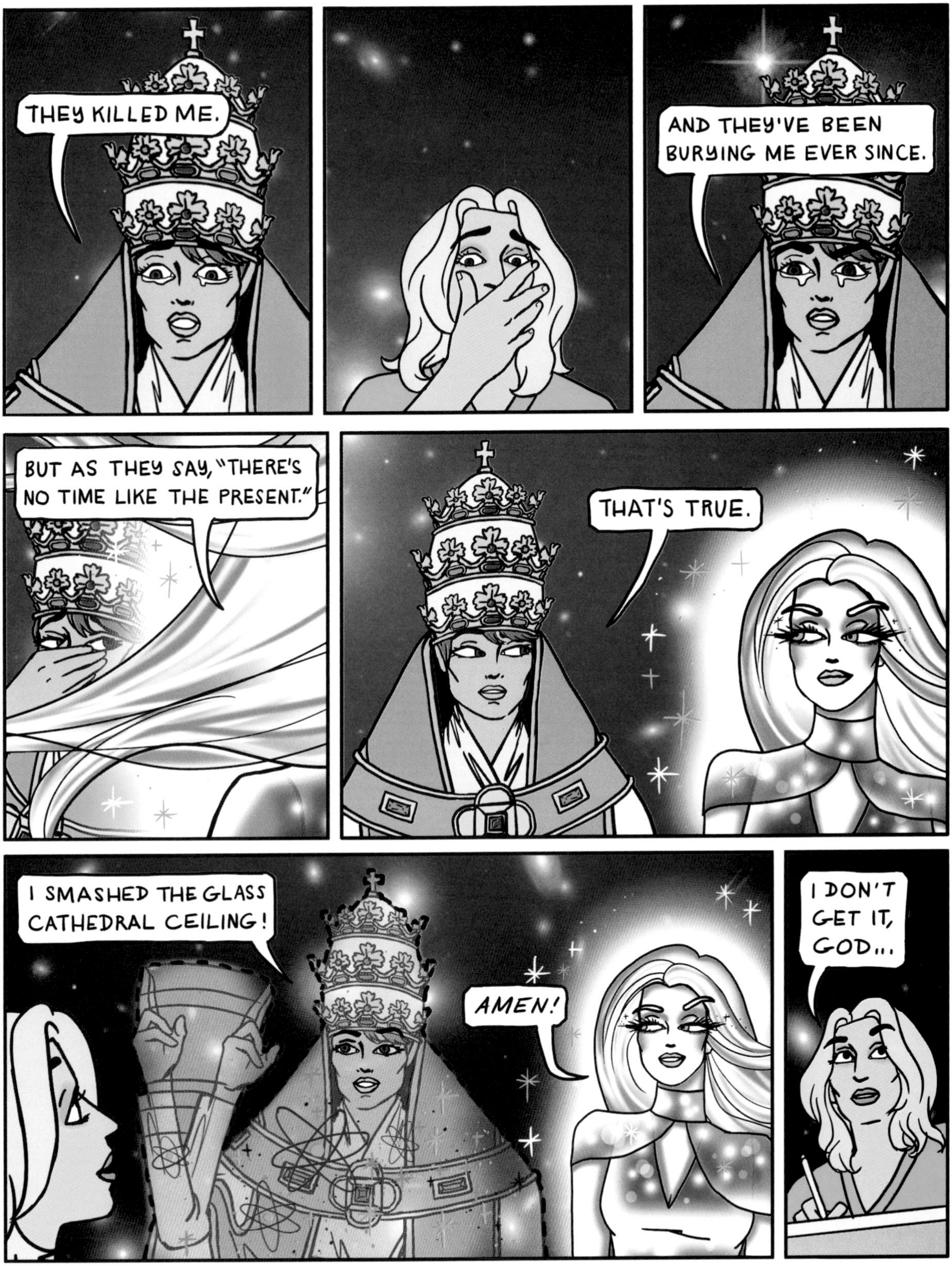
THEY KILLED ME.
AND THEY'VE BEEN BURYING ME EVER SINCE.
BUT AS THEY SAY, "THERE'S NO TIME LIKE THE PRESENT."
THAT'S TRUE.
I SMASHED THE GLASS CATHEDRAL CEILING!
AMEN!
I DON'T GET IT, GOD...

THEY MURDER POPE JOAN TO KEEP A WOMAN OUT OF THE CHURCH...

...BUT THE CHURCH COVERS UP AND PROTECTS ITS PEDOPHILE PRIESTS WHO STAY *IN* THE CHURCH *AND* GET AWAY WITH IT?!

I'M GOD—*NO ONE* GETS AWAY WITH IT.

NOW, IN THE 12TH AND 13TH CENTURIES, CATHEDRALS LIKE CHARTRES AND NOTRE DAME WERE BUILT...

AS FAR AS KEEPING WOMEN OUT OF THE CHURCH, WE'RE IN THE CHURCH.

WHY? BECAUSE THOSE CHURCHES WERE DEDICATED TO MOTHER MARY?

NO! BECAUSE CATHEDRAL ARCHES ARE VULVAS WITH CLITORIS TIPS!

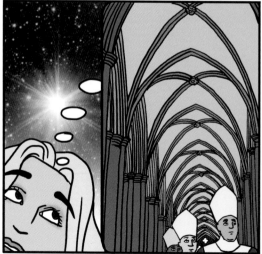

WAIT, WHO SAID THAT?

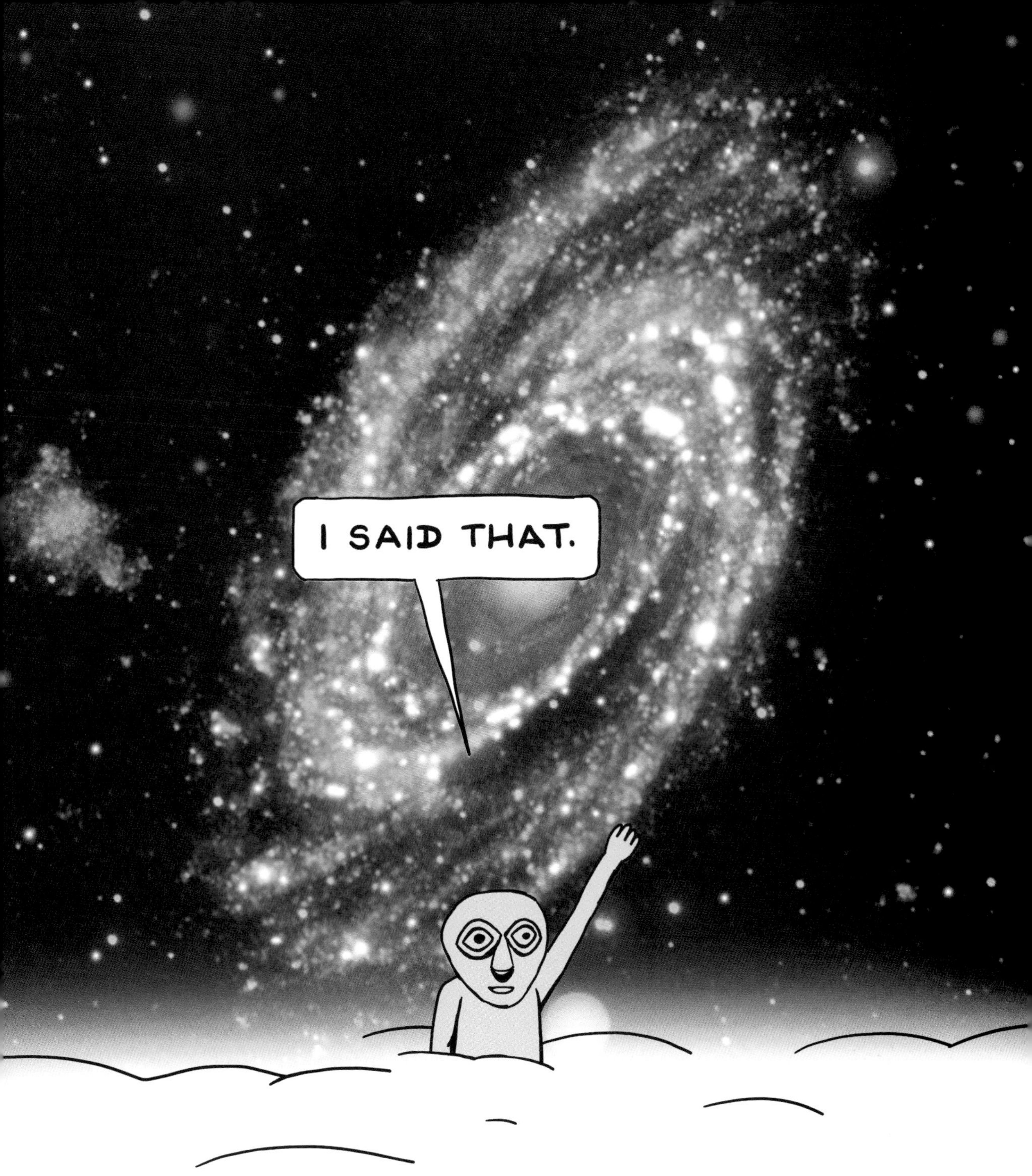
I SAID THAT.

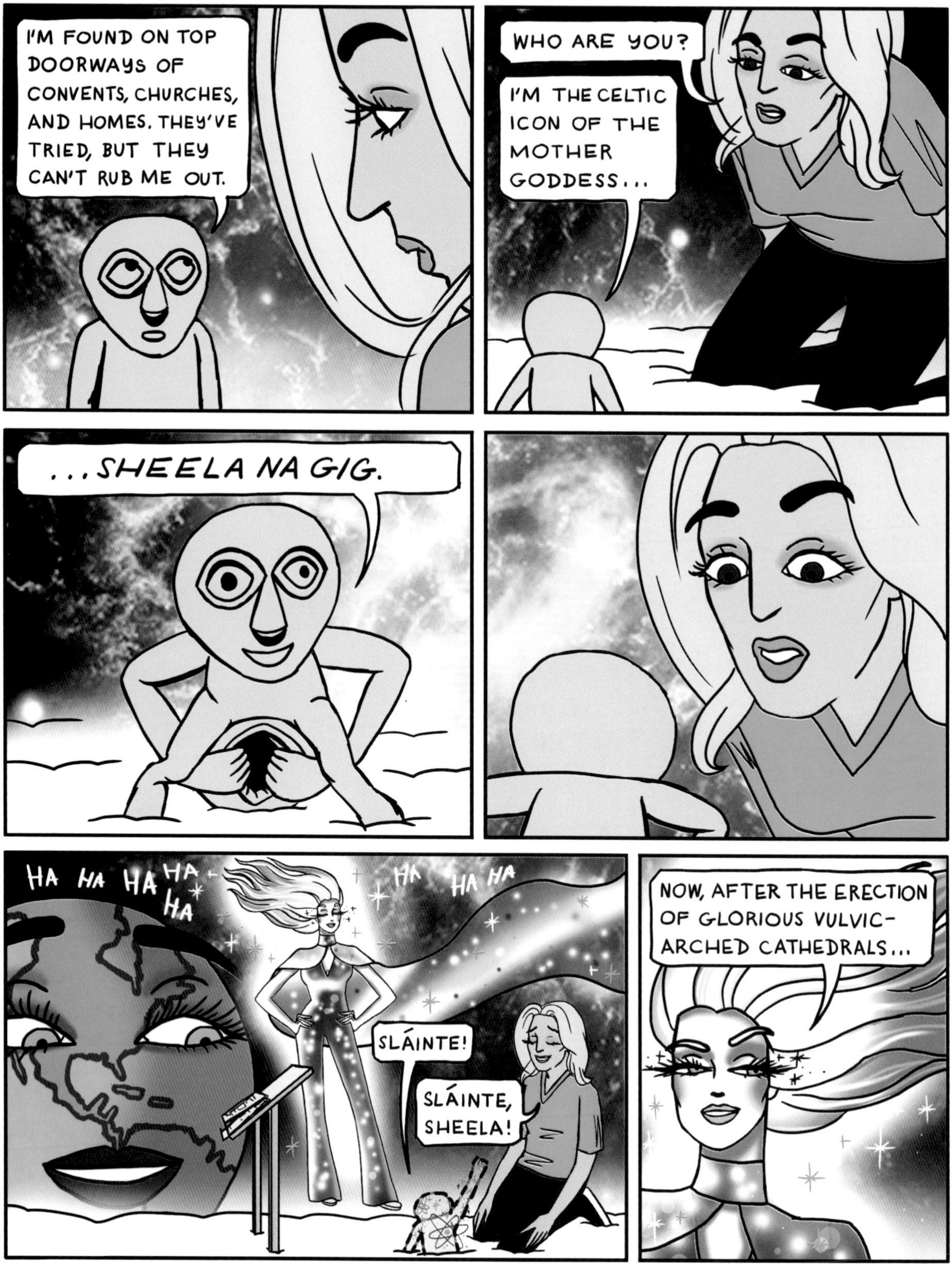
I'M FOUND ON TOP DOORWAYS OF CONVENTS, CHURCHES, AND HOMES. THEY'VE TRIED, BUT THEY CAN'T RUB ME OUT.
WHO ARE YOU?
I'M THE CELTIC ICON OF THE MOTHER GODDESS...
...SHEELA NA GIG.
HA HA HA HA HA
HA HA HA
SLÁINTE!
SLÁINTE, SHEELA!
NOW, AFTER THE ERECTION OF GLORIOUS VULVIC-ARCHED CATHEDRALS...

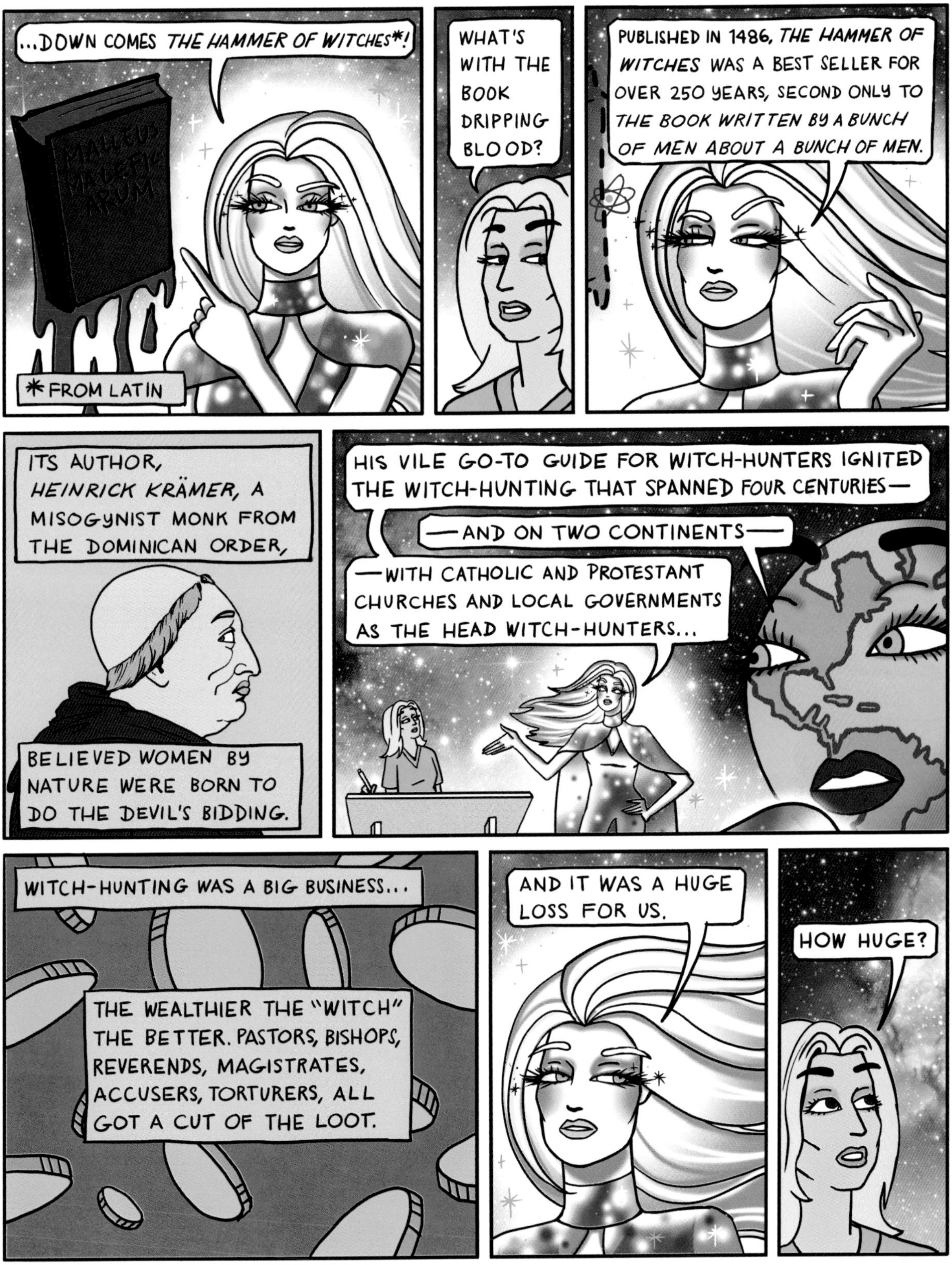
...DOWN COMES THE HAMMER OF WITCHES*!
MALLEUS MALEFICARUM
*FROM LATIN
WHAT'S WITH THE BOOK DRIPPING BLOOD?
PUBLISHED IN 1486, THE HAMMER OF WITCHES WAS A BEST SELLER FOR OVER 250 YEARS, SECOND ONLY TO THE BOOK WRITTEN BY A BUNCH OF MEN ABOUT A BUNCH OF MEN.
ITS AUTHOR, HEINRICK KRÄMER, A MISOGYNIST MONK FROM THE DOMINICAN ORDER,
BELIEVED WOMEN BY NATURE WERE BORN TO DO THE DEVIL'S BIDDING.
HIS VILE GO-TO GUIDE FOR WITCH-HUNTERS IGNITED THE WITCH-HUNTING THAT SPANNED FOUR CENTURIES—
—AND ON TWO CONTINENTS—
—WITH CATHOLIC AND PROTESTANT CHURCHES AND LOCAL GOVERNMENTS AS THE HEAD WITCH-HUNTERS...
WITCH-HUNTING WAS A BIG BUSINESS...
THE WEALTHIER THE "WITCH" THE BETTER. PASTORS, BISHOPS, REVERENDS, MAGISTRATES, ACCUSERS, TORTURERS, ALL GOT A CUT OF THE LOOT.
AND IT WAS A HUGE LOSS FOR US.
HOW HUGE?

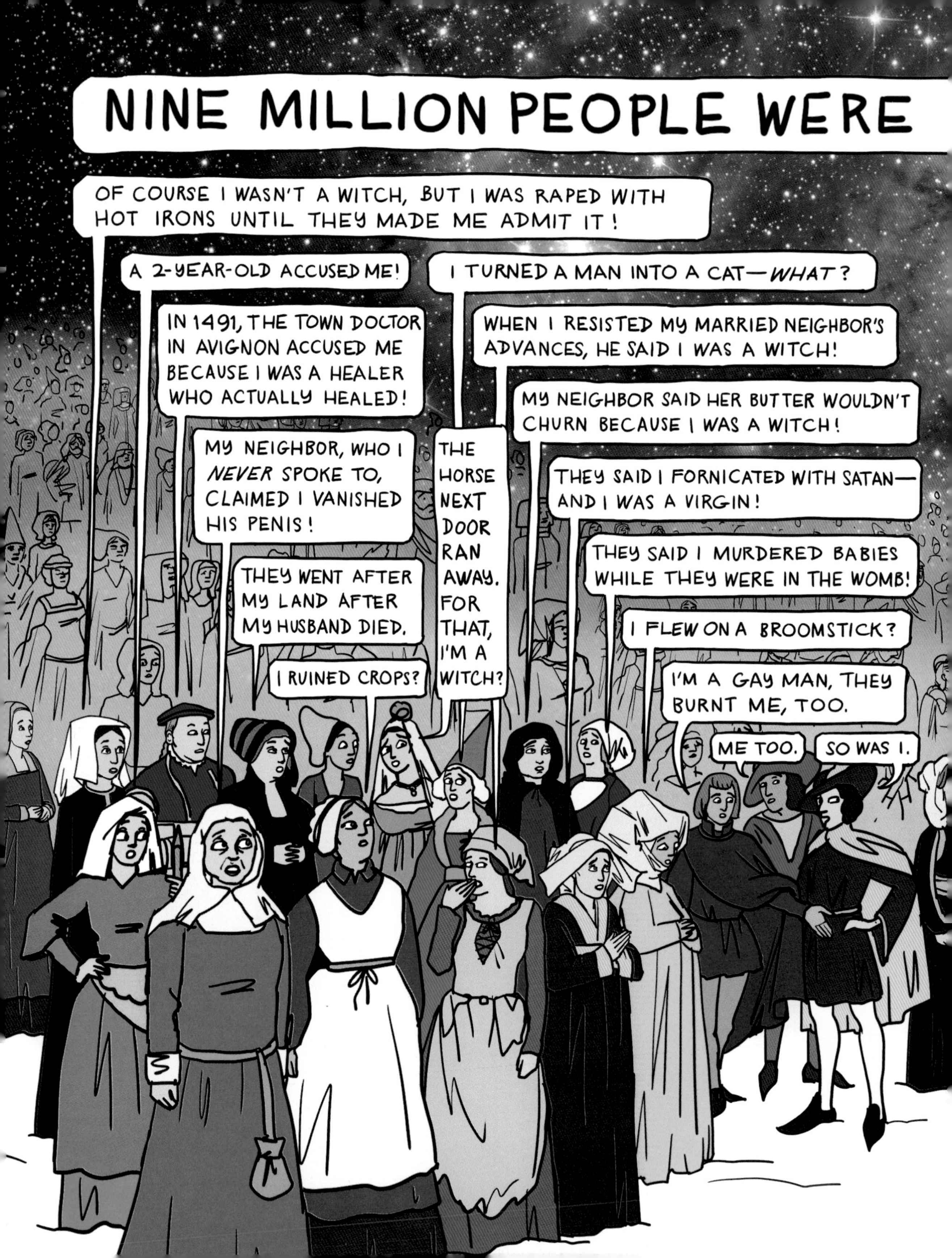
NINE MILLION PEOPLE WERE
OF COURSE I WASN'T A WITCH, BUT I WAS RAPED WITH HOT IRONS UNTIL THEY MADE ME ADMIT IT!
A 2-YEAR-OLD ACCUSED ME!
I TURNED A MAN INTO A CAT—*WHAT*?
IN 1491, THE TOWN DOCTOR IN AVIGNON ACCUSED ME BECAUSE I WAS A HEALER WHO ACTUALLY HEALED!
WHEN I RESISTED MY MARRIED NEIGHBOR'S ADVANCES, HE SAID I WAS A WITCH!
MY NEIGHBOR SAID HER BUTTER WOULDN'T CHURN BECAUSE I WAS A WITCH!
MY NEIGHBOR, WHO I *NEVER* SPOKE TO, CLAIMED I VANISHED HIS PENIS!
THE HORSE NEXT DOOR RAN AWAY. FOR THAT, I'M A WITCH?
THEY SAID I FORNICATED WITH SATAN—AND I WAS A VIRGIN!
THEY WENT AFTER MY LAND AFTER MY HUSBAND DIED.
THEY SAID I MURDERED BABIES WHILE THEY WERE IN THE WOMB!
I FLEW ON A BROOMSTICK?
I RUINED CROPS?
I'M A GAY MAN, THEY BURNT ME, TOO.
ME TOO.
SO WAS I.

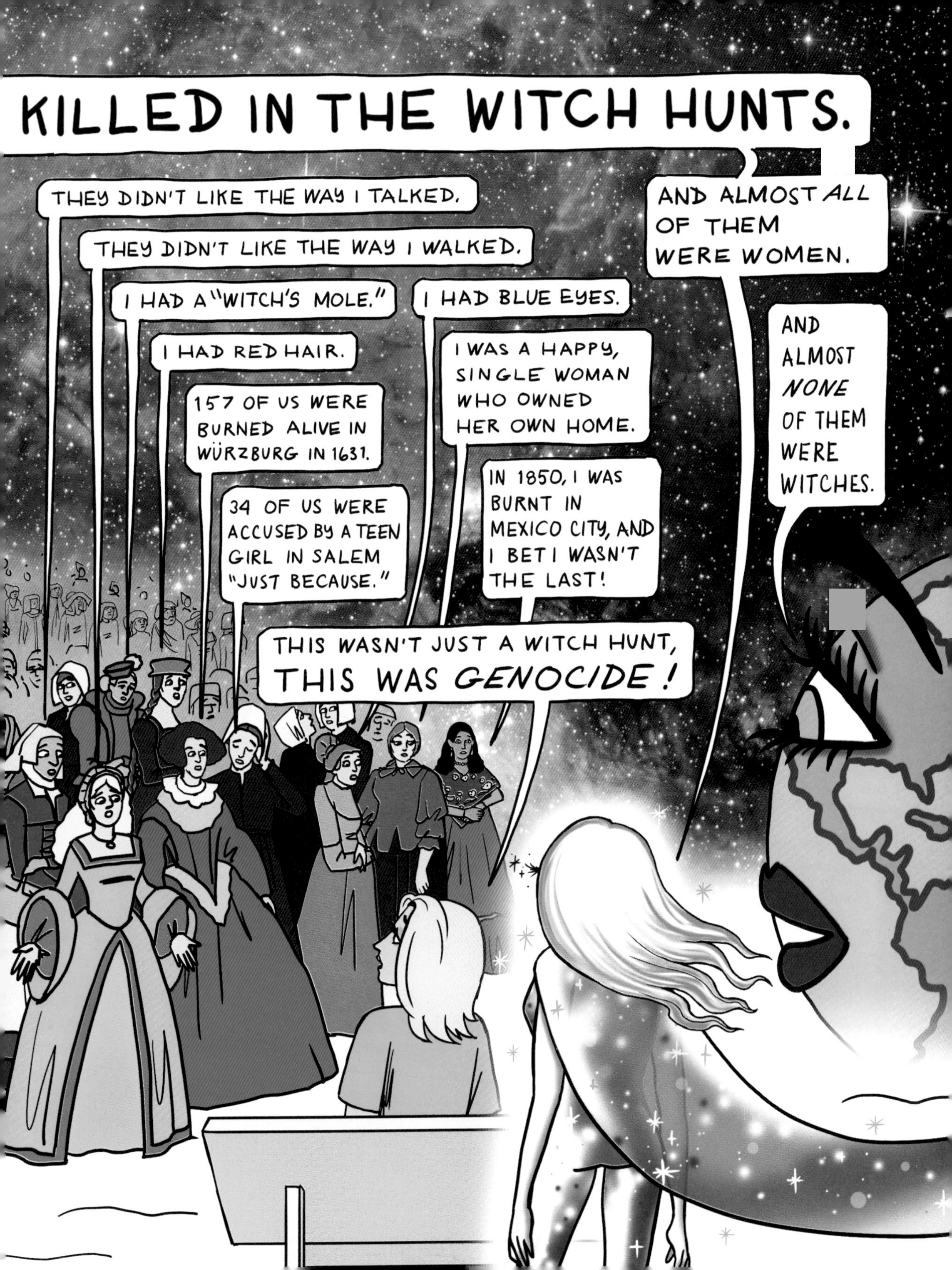
KILLED IN THE WITCH HUNTS.
THEY DIDN'T LIKE THE WAY I TALKED.
THEY DIDN'T LIKE THE WAY I WALKED.
I HAD A "WITCH'S MOLE."
I HAD RED HAIR.
157 OF US WERE BURNED ALIVE IN WÜRZBURG IN 1631.
34 OF US WERE ACCUSED BY A TEEN GIRL IN SALEM "JUST BECAUSE."
I HAD BLUE EYES.
I WAS A HAPPY, SINGLE WOMAN WHO OWNED HER OWN HOME.
IN 1850, I WAS BURNT IN MEXICO CITY, AND I BET I WASN'T THE LAST!
THIS WASN'T JUST A WITCH HUNT, THIS WAS GENOCIDE!
AND ALMOST ALL OF THEM WERE WOMEN.
AND ALMOST NONE OF THEM WERE WITCHES.

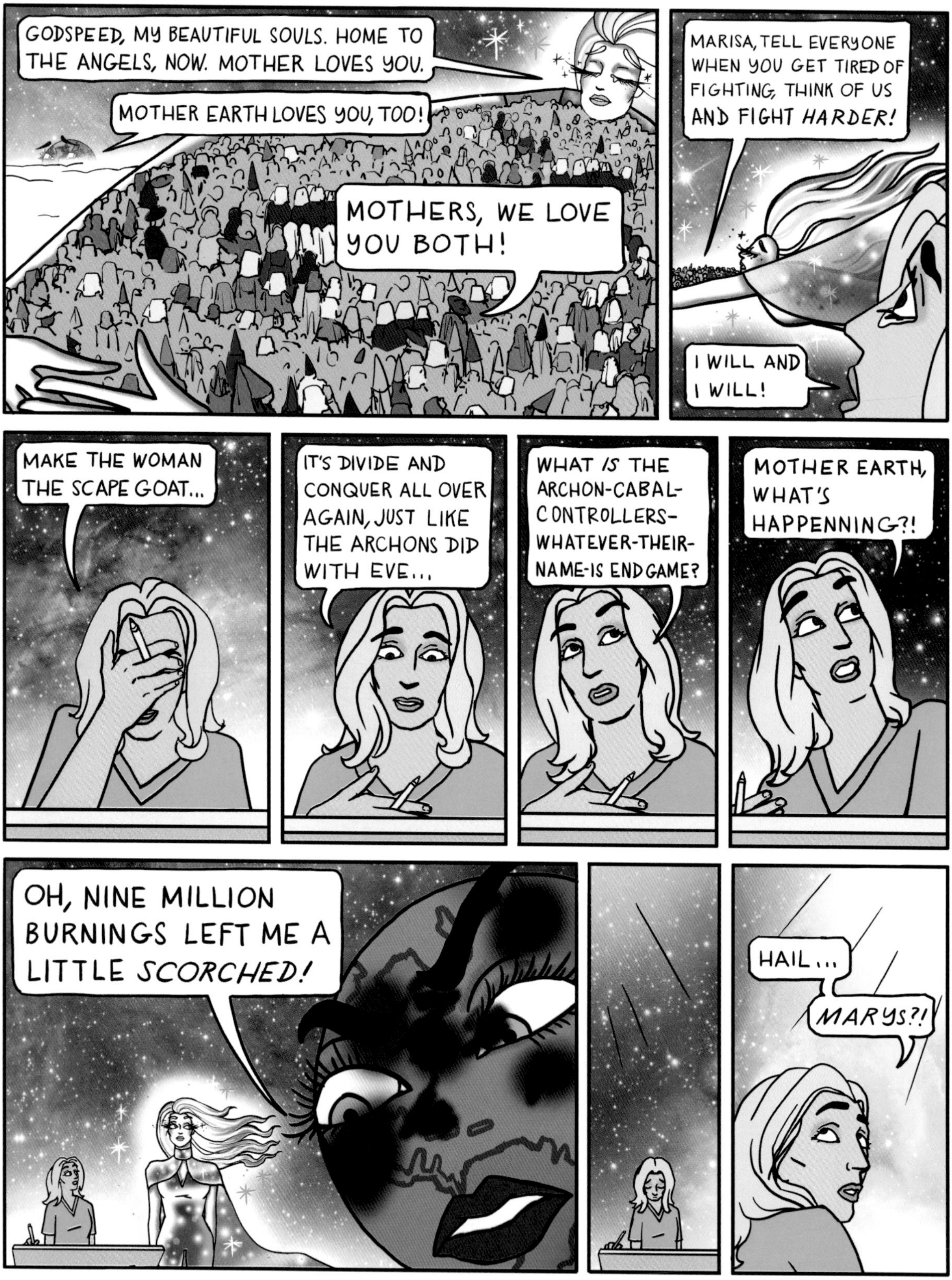
GODSPEED, MY BEAUTIFUL SOULS. HOME TO THE ANGELS, NOW. MOTHER LOVES YOU.
MOTHER EARTH LOVES YOU, TOO!
MOTHERS, WE LOVE YOU BOTH!
MARISA, TELL EVERYONE WHEN YOU GET TIRED OF FIGHTING, THINK OF US AND FIGHT *HARDER!*
I WILL AND I WILL!
MAKE THE WOMAN THE SCAPE GOAT...
IT'S DIVIDE AND CONQUER ALL OVER AGAIN, JUST LIKE THE ARCHONS DID WITH EVE...
WHAT *IS* THE ARCHON-CABAL-CONTROLLERS-WHATEVER-THEIR-NAME-IS END GAME?
MOTHER EARTH, WHAT'S HAPPENNING?!
OH, NINE MILLION BURNINGS LEFT ME A LITTLE *SCORCHED!*
HAIL...
MARYS?!

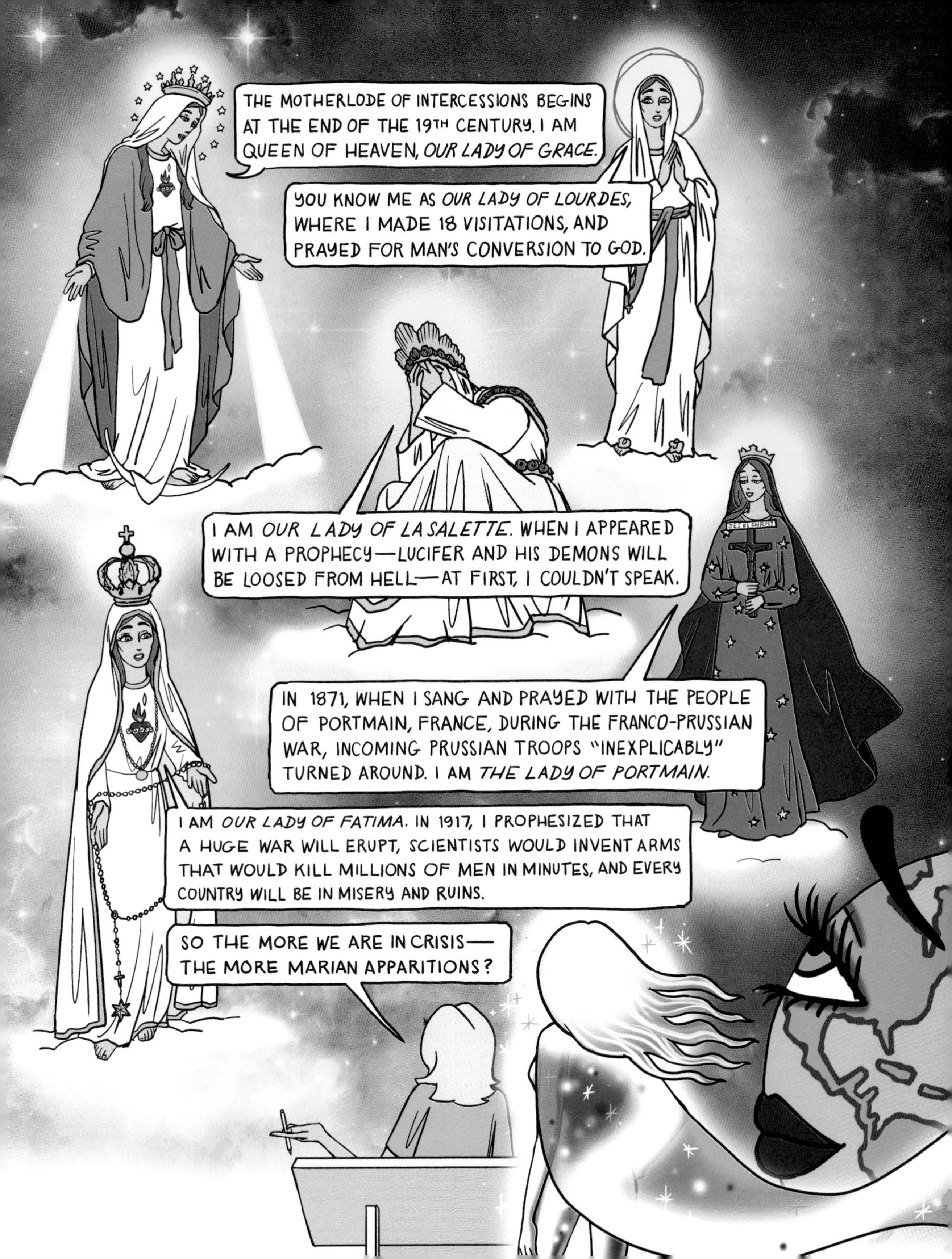
THE MOTHERLODE OF INTERCESSIONS BEGINS AT THE END OF THE 19TH CENTURY. I AM QUEEN OF HEAVEN, *OUR LADY OF GRACE.*
YOU KNOW ME AS *OUR LADY OF LOURDES,* WHERE I MADE 18 VISITATIONS, AND PRAYED FOR MAN'S CONVERSION TO GOD.
I AM *OUR LADY OF LA SALETTE.* WHEN I APPEARED WITH A PROPHECY—LUCIFER AND HIS DEMONS WILL BE LOOSED FROM HELL—AT FIRST, I COULDN'T SPEAK.
IN 1871, WHEN I SANG AND PRAYED WITH THE PEOPLE OF PORTMAIN, FRANCE, DURING THE FRANCO-PRUSSIAN WAR, INCOMING PRUSSIAN TROOPS "INEXPLICABLY" TURNED AROUND. I AM *THE LADY OF PORTMAIN.*
I AM *OUR LADY OF FATIMA.* IN 1917, I PROPHESIZED THAT A HUGE WAR WILL ERUPT, SCIENTISTS WOULD INVENT ARMS THAT WOULD KILL MILLIONS OF MEN IN MINUTES, AND EVERY COUNTRY WILL BE IN MISERY AND RUINS.
SO THE MORE WE ARE IN CRISIS—THE MORE MARIAN APPARITIONS?

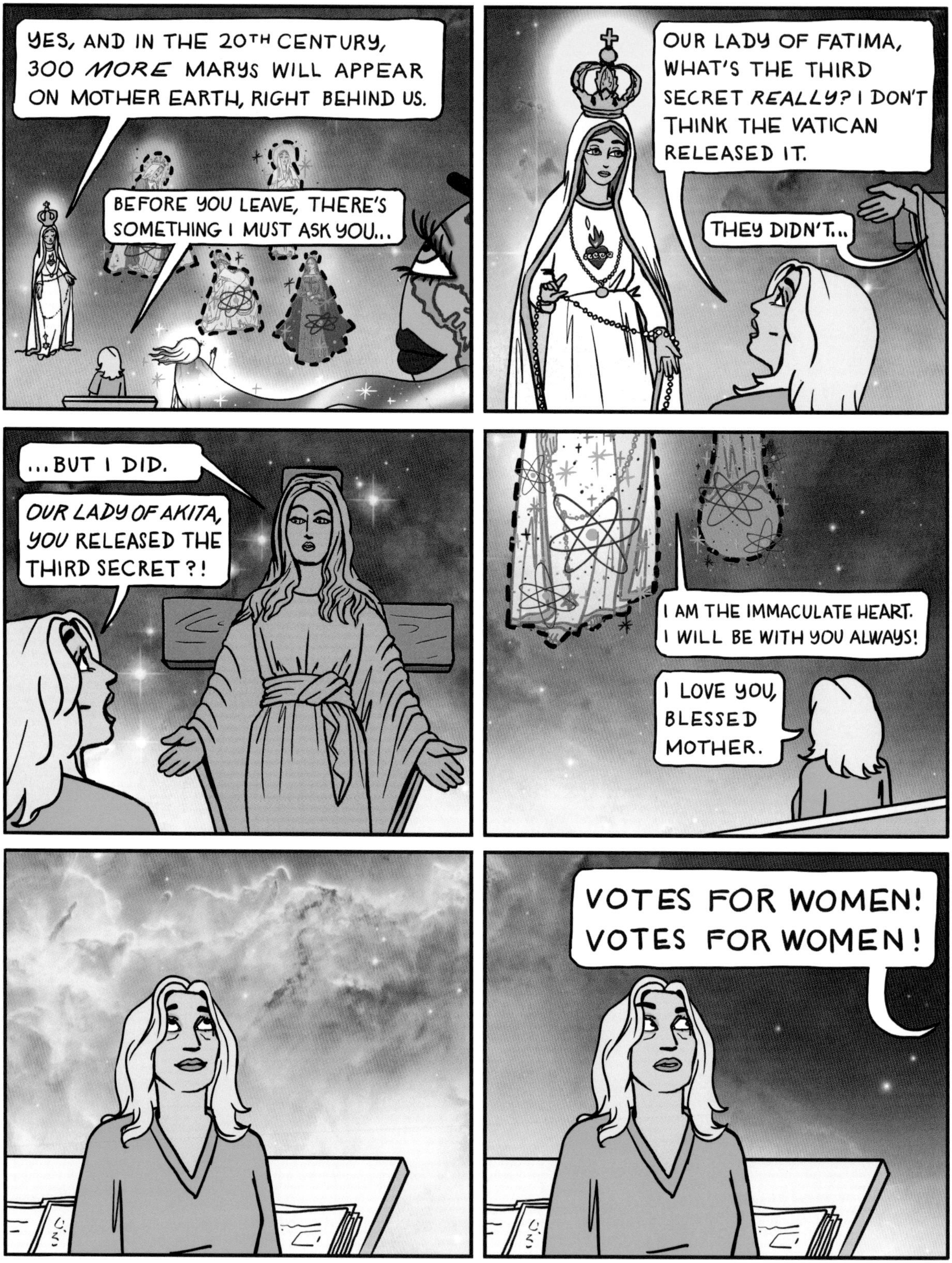
YES, AND IN THE 20TH CENTURY, 300 MORE MARYS WILL APPEAR ON MOTHER EARTH, RIGHT BEHIND US.
BEFORE YOU LEAVE, THERE'S SOMETHING I MUST ASK YOU...
OUR LADY OF FATIMA, WHAT'S THE THIRD SECRET REALLY? I DON'T THINK THE VATICAN RELEASED IT.
THEY DIDN'T...
...BUT I DID.
OUR LADY OF AKITA, YOU RELEASED THE THIRD SECRET?!
I AM THE IMMACULATE HEART. I WILL BE WITH YOU ALWAYS!
I LOVE YOU, BLESSED MOTHER.
VOTES FOR WOMEN! VOTES FOR WOMEN!

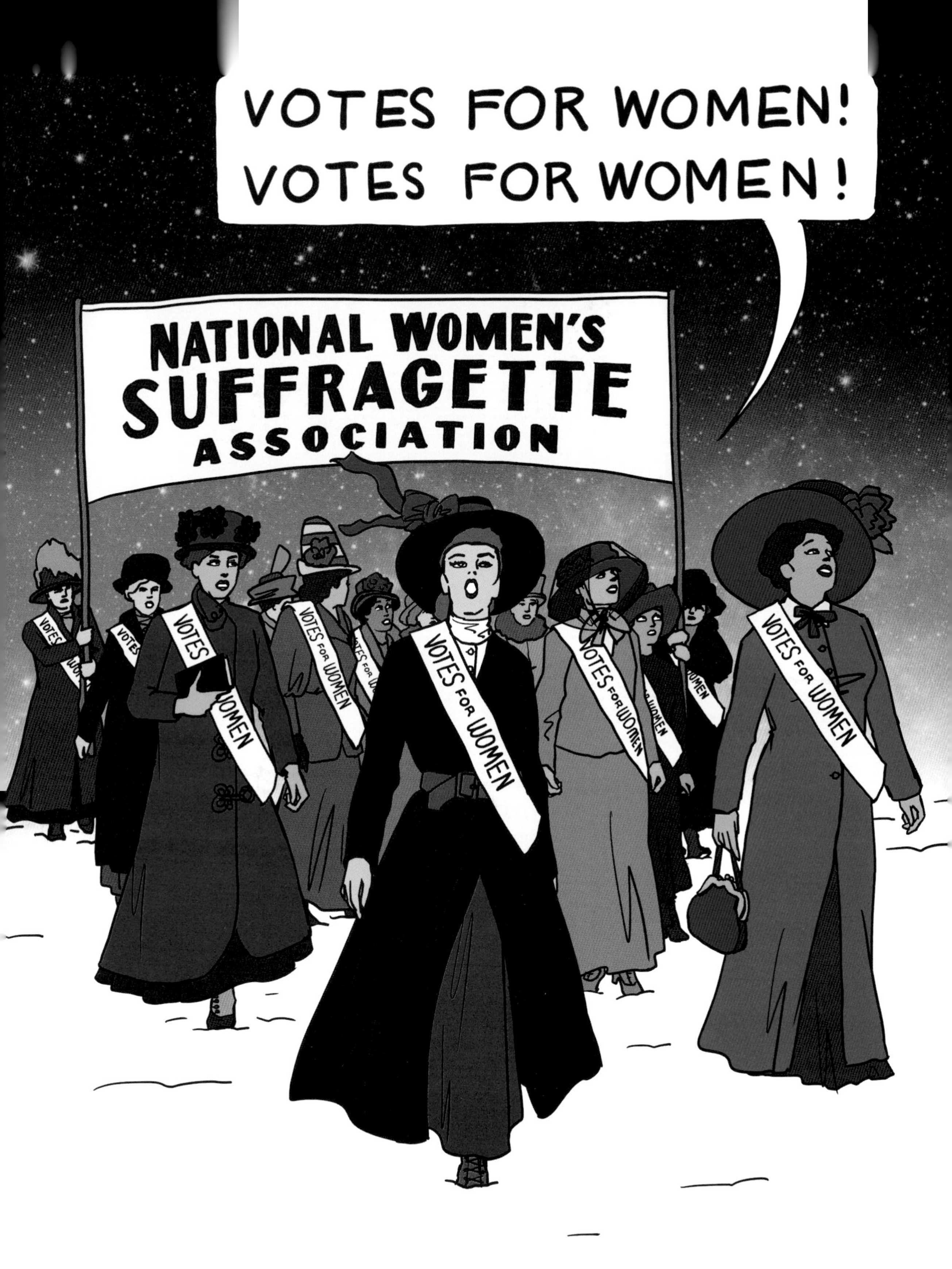
VOTES FOR WOMEN!
VOTES FOR WOMEN!
NATIONAL WOMEN'S
SUFFRAGETTE
ASSOCIATION
VOTES FOR WOMEN
VOTES FOR WOMEN
VOTES FOR WOMEN
VOTES FOR WOMEN
VOTES FOR WOMEN

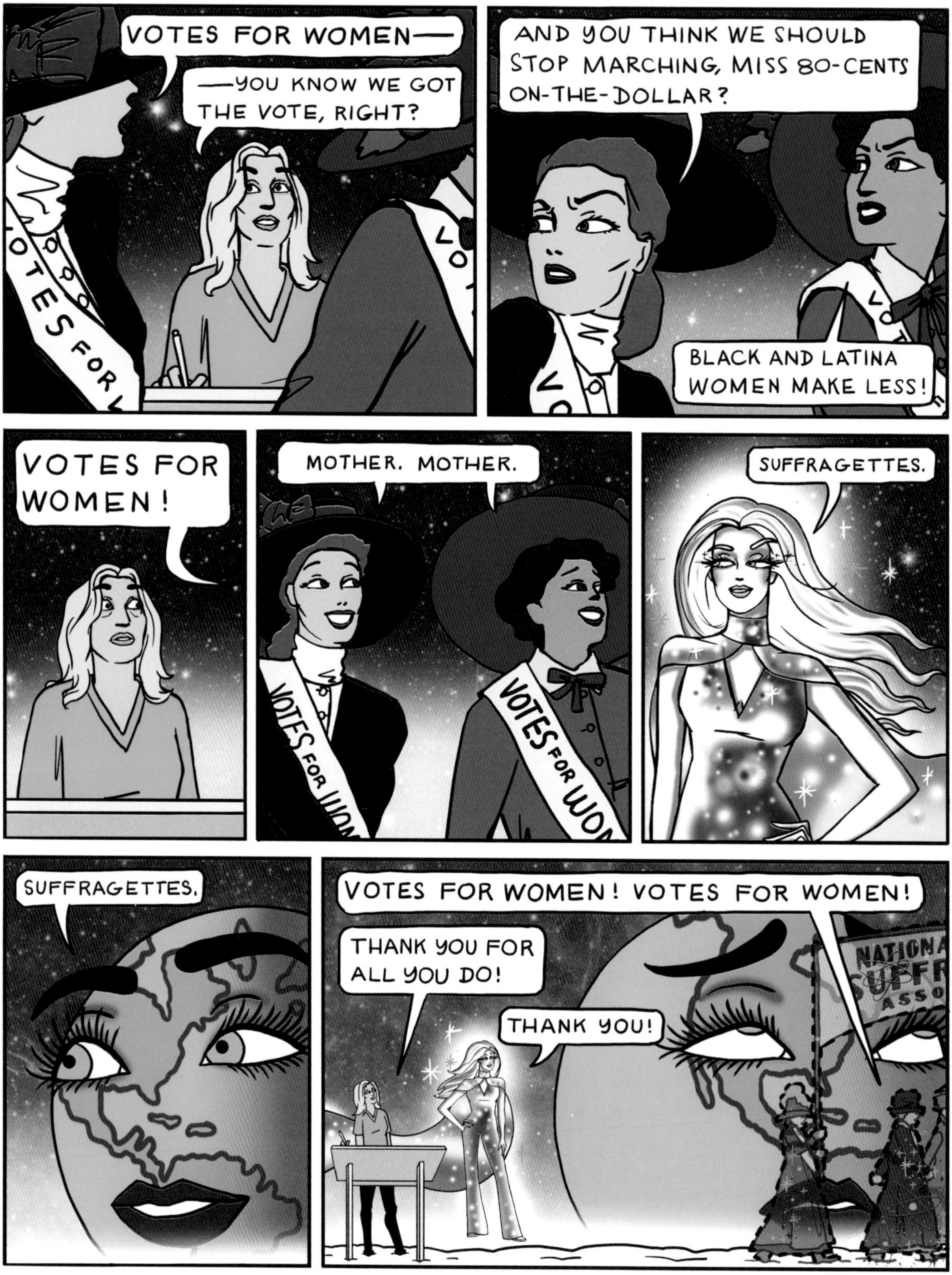
VOTES FOR WOMEN—
—YOU KNOW WE GOT THE VOTE, RIGHT?
AND YOU THINK WE SHOULD STOP MARCHING, MISS 80-CENTS ON-THE-DOLLAR?
BLACK AND LATINA WOMEN MAKE LESS!
VOTES FOR WOMEN!
MOTHER. MOTHER.
SUFFRAGETTES.
SUFFRAGETTES.
VOTES FOR WOMEN! VOTES FOR WOMEN!
THANK YOU FOR ALL YOU DO!
THANK YOU!

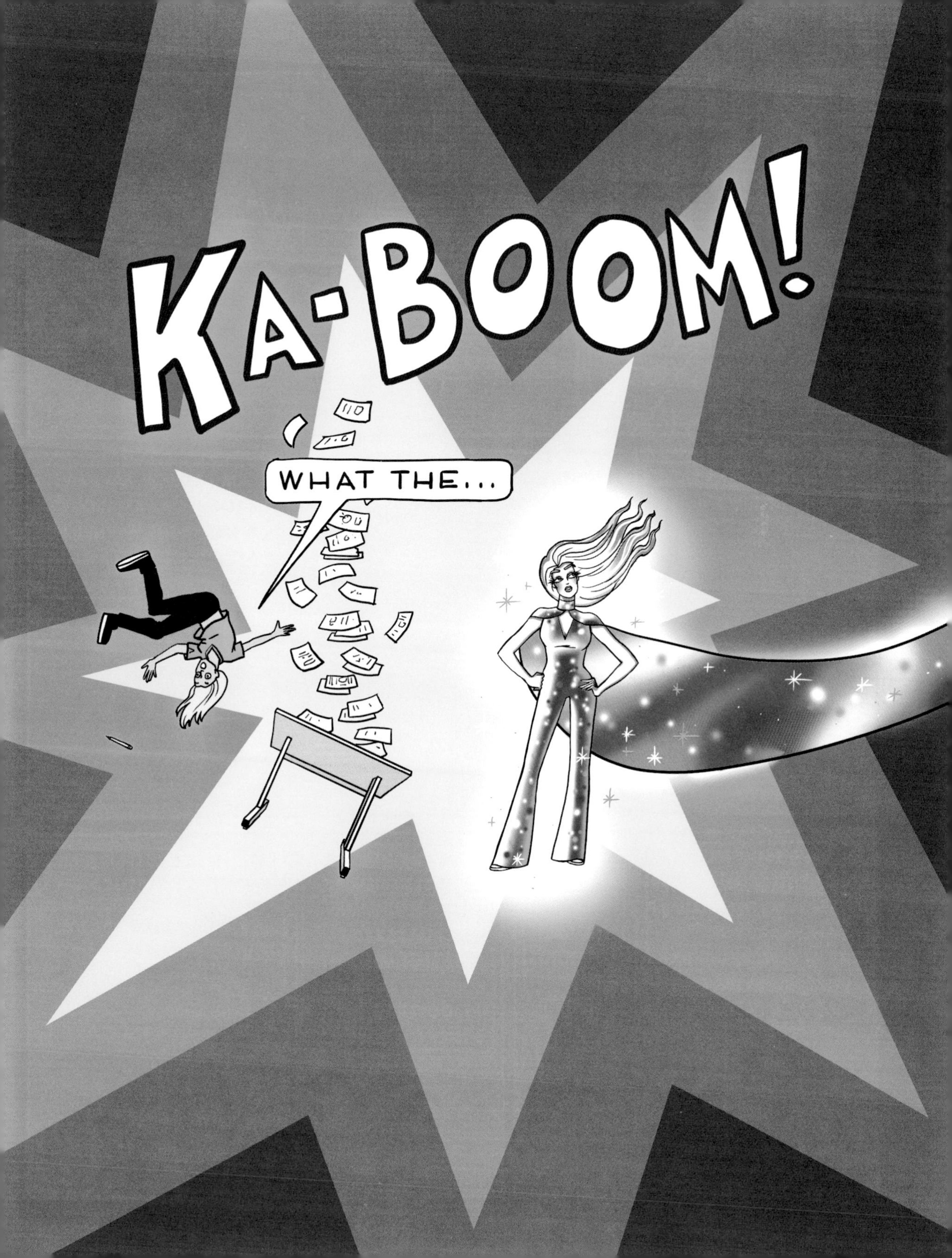
KA-BOOM!
WHAT THE...

MOTHER EARTH, WHAT'S HAPPENING?

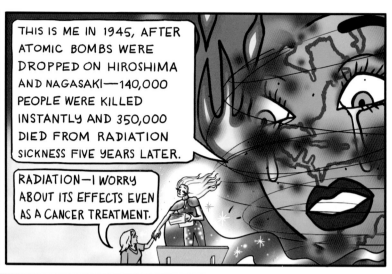

THIS IS ME IN 1945, AFTER ATOMIC BOMBS WERE DROPPED ON HIROSHIMA AND NAGASAKI—140,000 PEOPLE WERE KILLED INSTANTLY AND 350,000 DIED FROM RADIATION SICKNESS FIVE YEARS LATER.

RADIATION—I WORRY ABOUT ITS EFFECTS EVEN AS A CANCER TREATMENT.

SIX MILLION JEWS WERE KILLED IN WWII!

94 MILLION MORE PEOPLE WERE KILLED! IN WWI, THERE WERE 20 MILLION PEOPLE KILLED!

THAT'S 120 MILLION...

OUR LADY OF FATIMA'S PROPHECY WAS ABOUT WWII—SHE WARNED US ABOUT SCIENTISTS WHO WOULD INVENT ARMS.

IN 1945, 1,600 NAZI SCIENTISTS WERE SECRETLY BROUGHT OVER FROM GERMANY TO AMERICA TO WORK FOR THE U.S. GOVERNMENT. THIS COVERT MISSION WAS CALLED *OPERATION PAPERCLIP.*

OPERATION PAPERCLIP, WHAT DID THE NAZI SCIENTISTS HAVE?

THE NAZIS HAD ADVANCED SCIENCE TECHNOLOGY, AND HAD MASTERED EGYPTIAN MIND KONTROL, AND THE U.S. GOVERNMENT WANTED IT.

AS THEIR TRUTH IS BURIED, OURS IS *UNEARTHED*—

—LITERALLY.

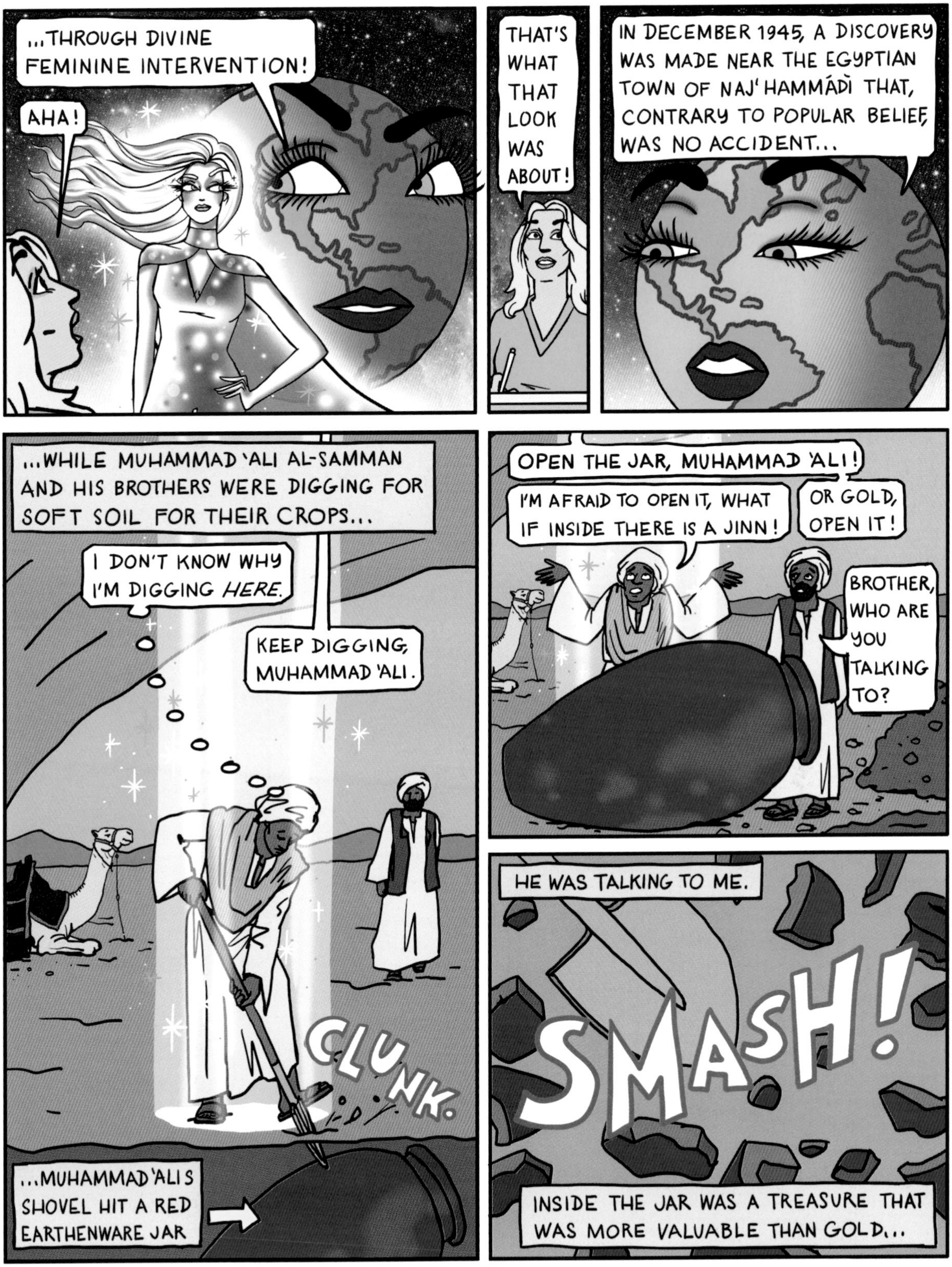
...THROUGH DIVINE FEMININE INTERVENTION!
AHA!
THAT'S WHAT THAT LOOK WAS ABOUT!
IN DECEMBER 1945, A DISCOVERY WAS MADE NEAR THE EGYPTIAN TOWN OF NAJ' HAMMÂDÎ THAT, CONTRARY TO POPULAR BELIEF, WAS NO ACCIDENT...
...WHILE MUHAMMAD 'ALI AL-SAMMAN AND HIS BROTHERS WERE DIGGING FOR SOFT SOIL FOR THEIR CROPS...
I DON'T KNOW WHY I'M DIGGING *HERE*.
KEEP DIGGING, MUHAMMAD 'ALI.
CLUNK.
...MUHAMMAD 'ALI'S SHOVEL HIT A RED EARTHENWARE JAR
OPEN THE JAR, MUHAMMAD 'ALI!
I'M AFRAID TO OPEN IT, WHAT IF INSIDE THERE IS A JINN!
OR GOLD, OPEN IT!
BROTHER, WHO ARE YOU TALKING TO?
HE WAS TALKING TO ME.
SMASH!
INSIDE THE JAR WAS A TREASURE THAT WAS MORE VALUABLE THAN GOLD...

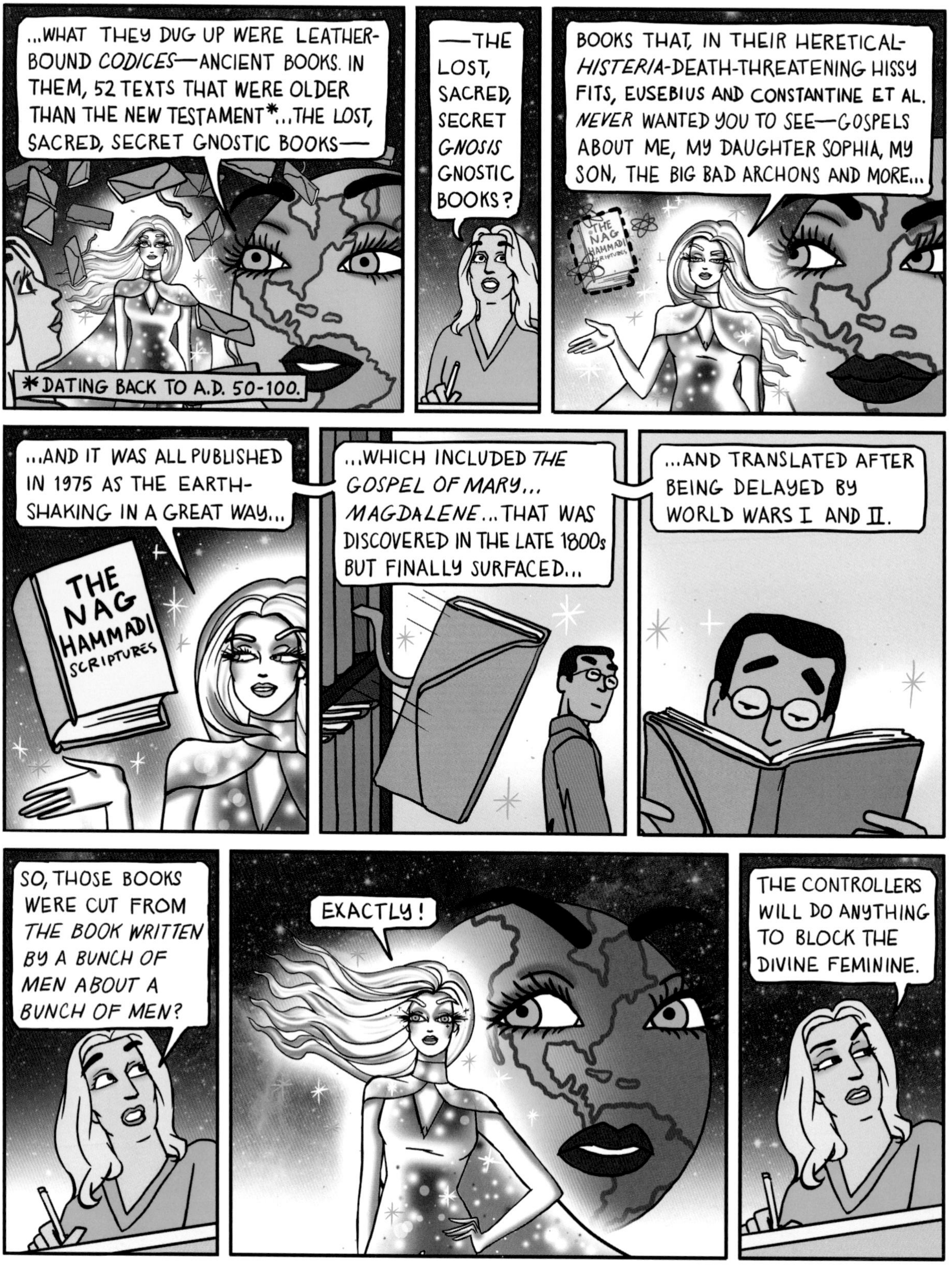
...WHAT THEY DUG UP WERE LEATHER-BOUND CODICES—ANCIENT BOOKS. IN THEM, 52 TEXTS THAT WERE OLDER THAN THE NEW TESTAMENT*...THE LOST, SACRED, SECRET GNOSTIC BOOKS—
*DATING BACK TO A.D. 50-100.
—THE LOST, SACRED, SECRET GNOSIS GNOSTIC BOOKS?
BOOKS THAT, IN THEIR HERETICAL-HISTERIA-DEATH-THREATENING HISSY FITS, EUSEBIUS AND CONSTANTINE ET AL. NEVER WANTED YOU TO SEE—GOSPELS ABOUT ME, MY DAUGHTER SOPHIA, MY SON, THE BIG BAD ARCHONS AND MORE...
THE NAG HAMMADI SCRIPTURES
...AND IT WAS ALL PUBLISHED IN 1975 AS THE EARTH-SHAKING IN A GREAT WAY...
THE NAG HAMMADI SCRIPTURES
...WHICH INCLUDED THE GOSPEL OF MARY... MAGDALENE...THAT WAS DISCOVERED IN THE LATE 1800s BUT FINALLY SURFACED...
...AND TRANSLATED AFTER BEING DELAYED BY WORLD WARS I AND II.
SO, THOSE BOOKS WERE CUT FROM THE BOOK WRITTEN BY A BUNCH OF MEN ABOUT A BUNCH OF MEN?
EXACTLY!
THE CONTROLLERS WILL DO ANYTHING TO BLOCK THE DIVINE FEMININE.

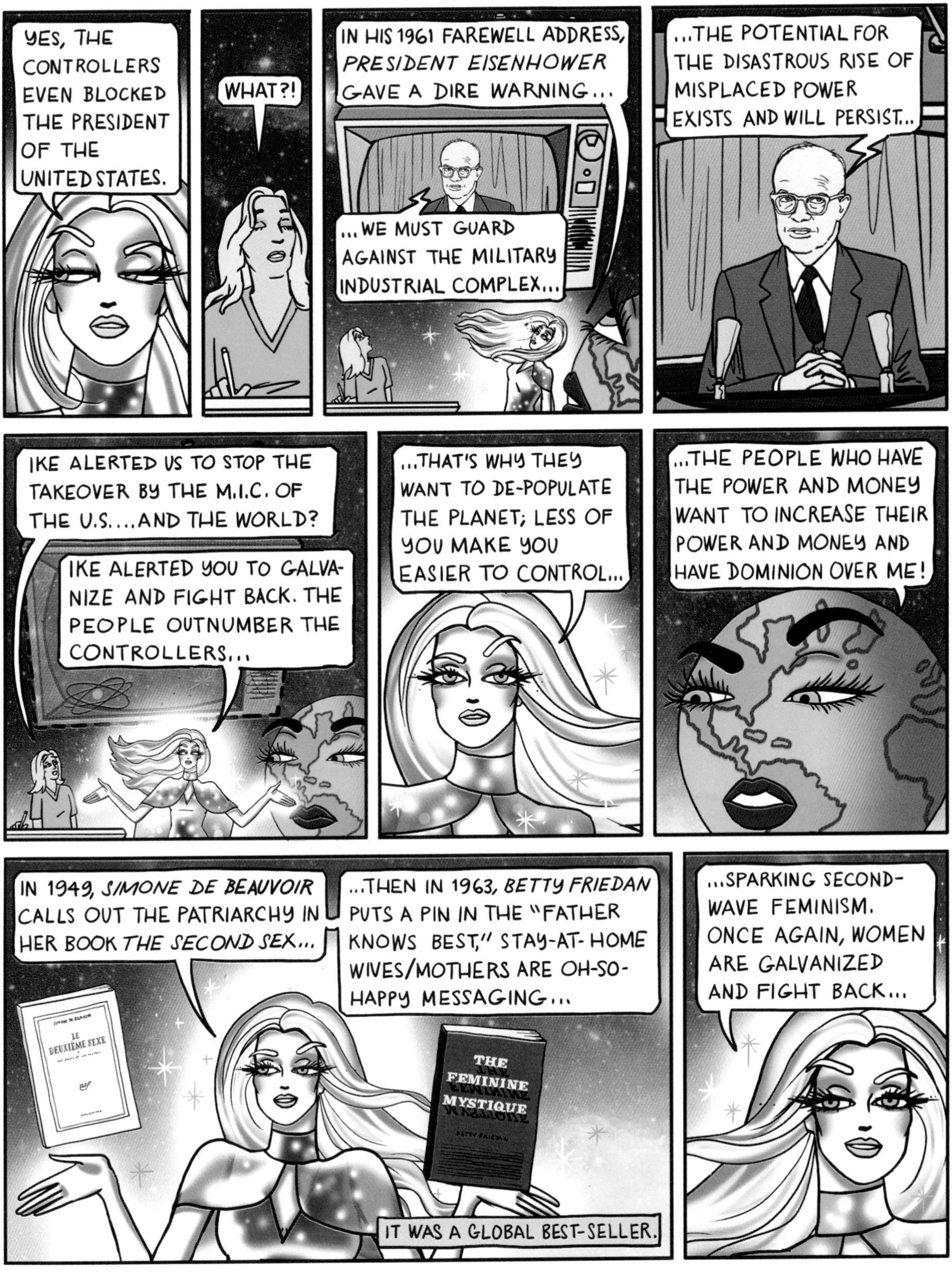
YES, THE CONTROLLERS EVEN BLOCKED THE PRESIDENT OF THE UNITED STATES.
WHAT?!
IN HIS 1961 FAREWELL ADDRESS, *PRESIDENT EISENHOWER* GAVE A DIRE WARNING...
...WE MUST GUARD AGAINST THE MILITARY INDUSTRIAL COMPLEX...
...THE POTENTIAL FOR THE DISASTROUS RISE OF MISPLACED POWER EXISTS AND WILL PERSIST...
IKE ALERTED US TO STOP THE TAKEOVER BY THE M.I.C. OF THE U.S.... AND THE WORLD?
IKE ALERTED YOU TO GALVANIZE AND FIGHT BACK. THE PEOPLE OUTNUMBER THE CONTROLLERS...
...THAT'S WHY THEY WANT TO DE-POPULATE THE PLANET; LESS OF YOU MAKE YOU EASIER TO CONTROL...
...THE PEOPLE WHO HAVE THE POWER AND MONEY WANT TO INCREASE THEIR POWER AND MONEY AND HAVE DOMINION OVER ME!
IN 1949, *SIMONE DE BEAUVOIR* CALLS OUT THE PATRIARCHY IN HER BOOK *THE SECOND SEX*...
LE DEUXIÈME SEXE
...THEN IN 1963, *BETTY FRIEDAN* PUTS A PIN IN THE "FATHER KNOWS BEST," STAY-AT-HOME WIVES/MOTHERS ARE OH-SO-HAPPY MESSAGING...
THE FEMININE MYSTIQUE
IT WAS A GLOBAL BEST-SELLER.
...SPARKING SECOND-WAVE FEMINISM. ONCE AGAIN, WOMEN ARE GALVANIZED AND FIGHT BACK...

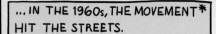

... IN THE 1960s, THE MOVEMENT* HIT THE STREETS.

A FEMINIST IS ANYONE WHO RECOGNIZES THE EQUALITY AND FULL HUMANITY OF WOMEN AND MEN.

*LED BY SHIRLEY CHISHOLM

BELLA ABZUG

DOROTHY PITMAN HUGHES

GLORIA STEINEM

ANGELA DAVIS

BETTY FRIEDAN

TV SHOWS LIKE *THE MARY TYLER MOORE SHOW, THAT GIRL,* AND *JULIA* REFLECTED THE MOVEMENT. IN 1991, THE MOVEMENT WAS REACTIVATED...

...WHEN *ANITA HILL,* IN TELEVISED HEARINGS, TESTIFIED TO A BUNCH OF SENATE MEN THAT SHE WAS SEXUALLY HARASSED BY CLARENCE THOMAS. HE WAS LATER SWORN INTO THE SUPREME COURT...

...INCITING THIRD WAVE FEMINISM AND THE ROAR OF THE PUNK ROCK *RIOT GRRRLS...*

...AND THEIR ZINES.

BUST

IN 2012 IN PAKISTAN, *MALALA YOUSAFZAI,* 14, IS SHOT BY THE TALIBAN IN RETALIATION FOR HER ACTIVISM FOR GIRLS' EDUCATION...

...SHE WON THE NOBEL PEACE PRIZE IN 2014. HER TOME *I AM MALALA* BECAME A GLOBAL BEST-SELLER. MALALA HAS CALLED UPON WORLD LEADERS TO ADVO-CATE FOR "BOOKS, NOT BULLETS."

THE WOMEN'S MARCH IN 2017 DREW 7 MILLION PEOPLE GLOBALLY...

MY ARMS ARE TIRED FROM HOLDING THIS SIGN SINCE THE 1960's

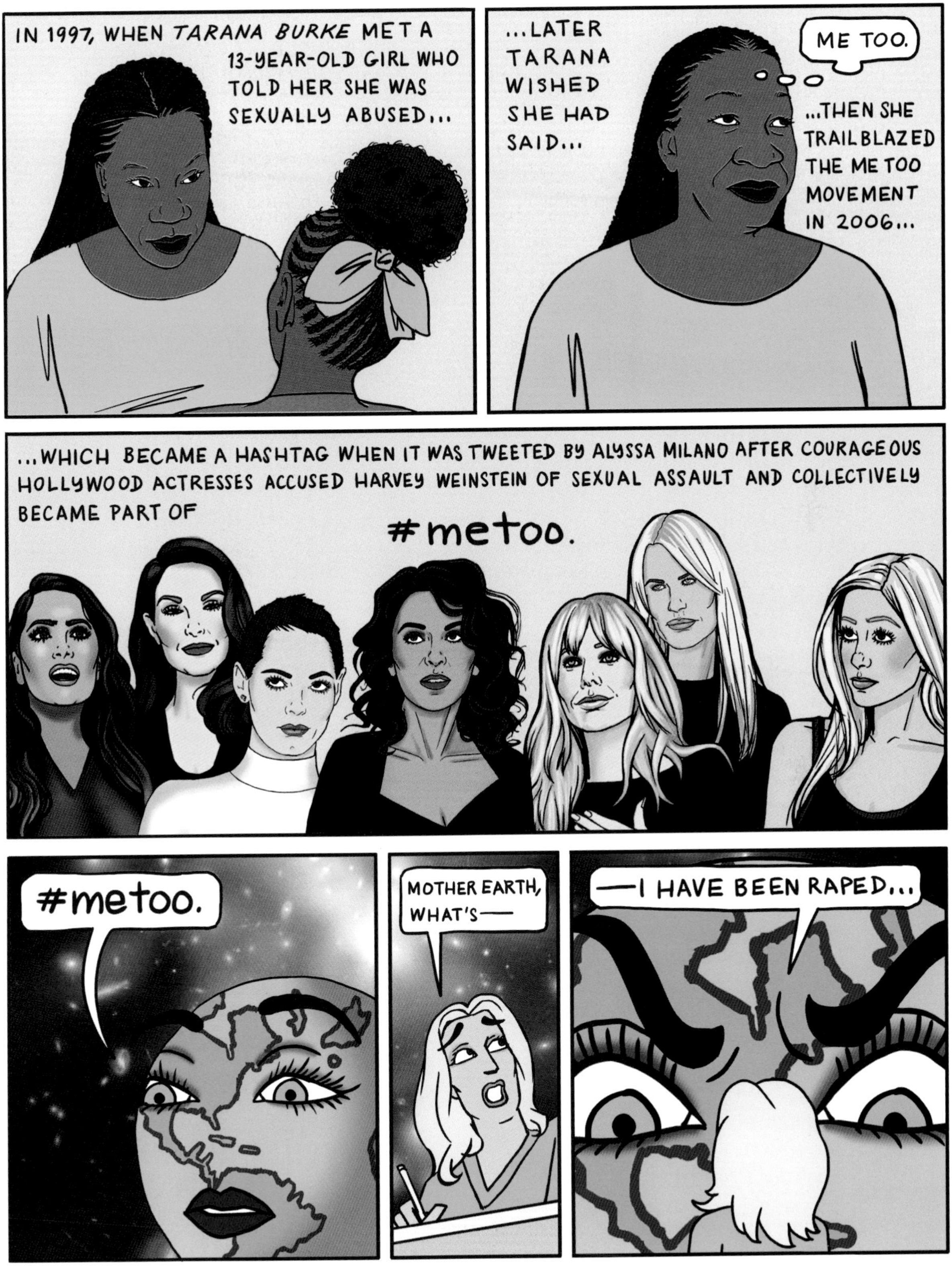
IN 1997, WHEN *TARANA BURKE* MET A 13-YEAR-OLD GIRL WHO TOLD HER SHE WAS SEXUALLY ABUSED...
...LATER TARANA WISHED SHE HAD SAID...
ME TOO.
...THEN SHE TRAILBLAZED THE ME TOO MOVEMENT IN 2006...
...WHICH BECAME A HASHTAG WHEN IT WAS TWEETED BY ALYSSA MILANO AFTER COURAGEOUS HOLLYWOOD ACTRESSES ACCUSED HARVEY WEINSTEIN OF SEXUAL ASSAULT AND COLLECTIVELY BECAME PART OF
#metoo.
#metoo.
MOTHER EARTH, WHAT'S—
—I HAVE BEEN RAPED...

...ABUSED BY DEFORESTATION, NUCLEAR TESTING, AND CHEMICALLY INJECTED RADIOACTIVE DRILLING!
I HAVE BEEN VIOLATED—PHOTOPLANKTON—40% GONE! INSECTS—90% GONE! 200 SPECIES EVERY DAY—GONE!
I HAVE BEEN SUFFOCATED—CHEMTRAILS SPRAY CANCER-CAUSING *NANO* METALS INTO THE AIR!
I HAVE BEEN DUMPED ON—PLASTICS! CORRUPTED—GMOs! POISONED—MY WATERS HAVE BEEN FLUORIDATED!
I HAVE BEEN DOMINATED—AND THE CONTROLLERS WHO CONTROL MY MATRIX WANT TO TURN *YOU* INTO A.I. BOTS!
THE VERY SAME AUTHORITIES WHO'VE WEAPONIZED MY WEATHER AGAINST YOU *AND* ME!
AND THEY'VE EVEN MADE ORIFICES WHERE I DIDN'T HAVE ANY...
THEIR COVERT BASES IN ANTARTICA ARE HASTENING GLOBAL WARMING!
WELL, THIS IS YOUR GLOBAL WARNING...
WE'RE ALL GOING TO DIE AND IT'S ALL *YOUR* FAULT!
ME?

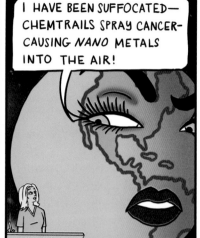

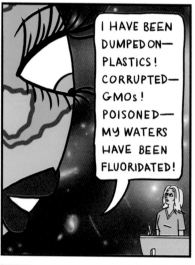

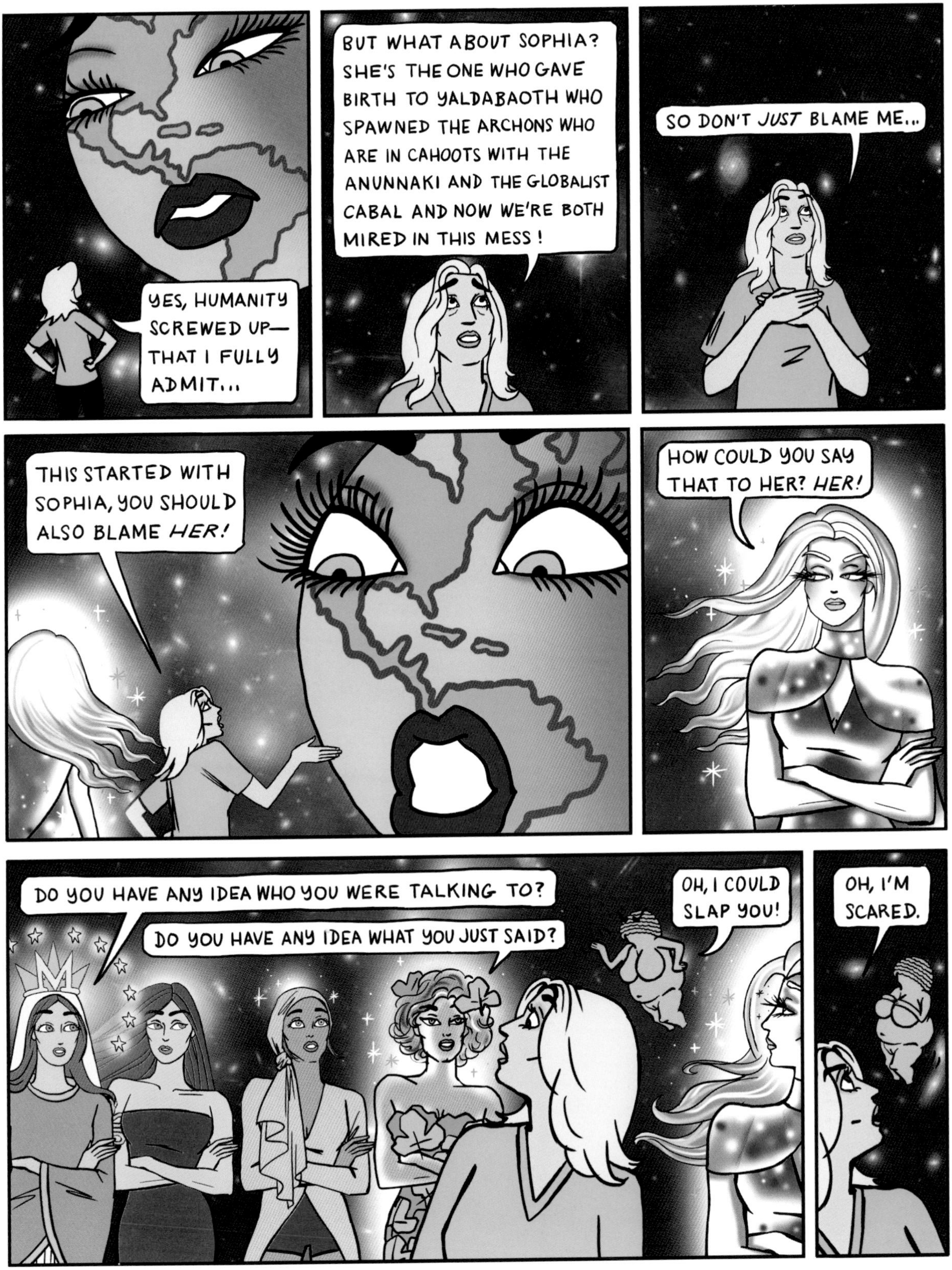
YES, HUMANITY SCREWED UP— THAT I FULLY ADMIT...
BUT WHAT ABOUT SOPHIA? SHE'S THE ONE WHO GAVE BIRTH TO YALDABAOTH WHO SPAWNED THE ARCHONS WHO ARE IN CAHOOTS WITH THE ANUNNAKI AND THE GLOBALIST CABAL AND NOW WE'RE BOTH MIRED IN THIS MESS!
SO DON'T *JUST* BLAME ME...
THIS STARTED WITH SOPHIA, YOU SHOULD ALSO BLAME *HER!*
HOW COULD YOU SAY THAT TO HER? *HER!*
DO YOU HAVE ANY IDEA WHO YOU WERE TALKING TO?
DO YOU HAVE ANY IDEA WHAT YOU JUST SAID?
OH, I COULD SLAP YOU!
OH, I'M SCARED.

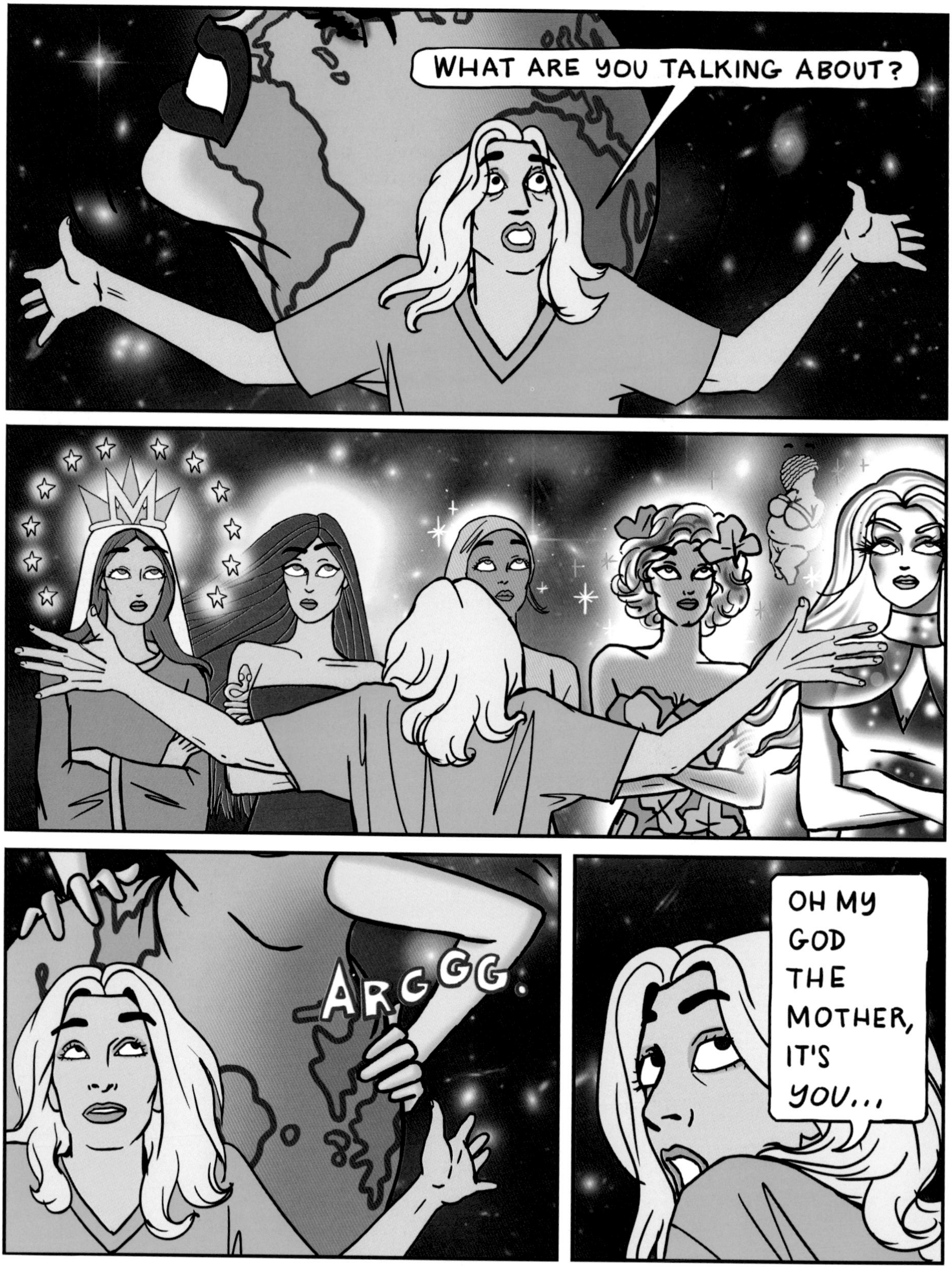
WHAT ARE YOU TALKING ABOUT?
ARGGG.
OH MY GOD THE MOTHER, IT'S YOU...

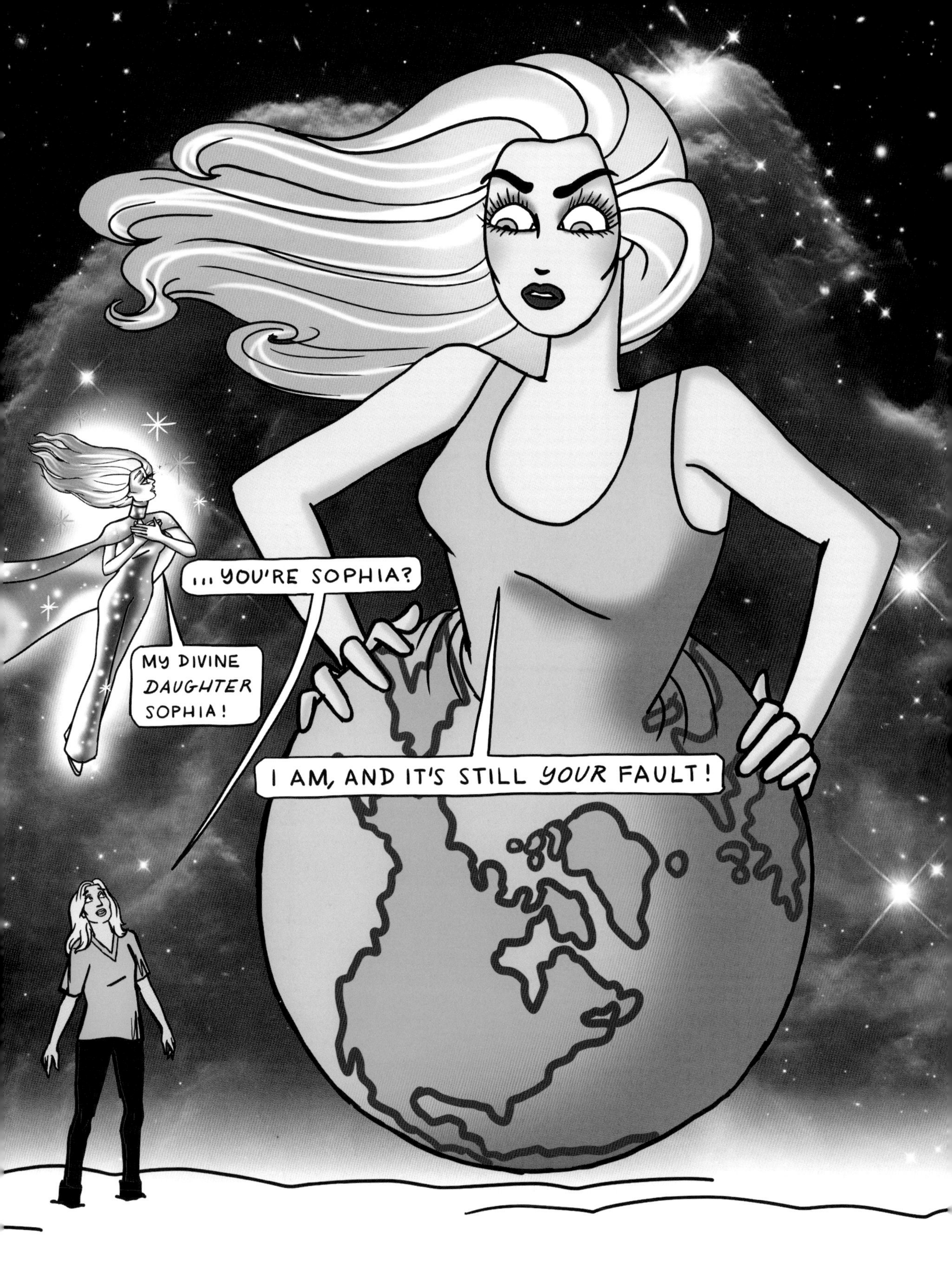
MY DIVINE DAUGHTER SOPHIA!
...YOU'RE SOPHIA?
I AM, AND IT'S STILL YOUR FAULT!

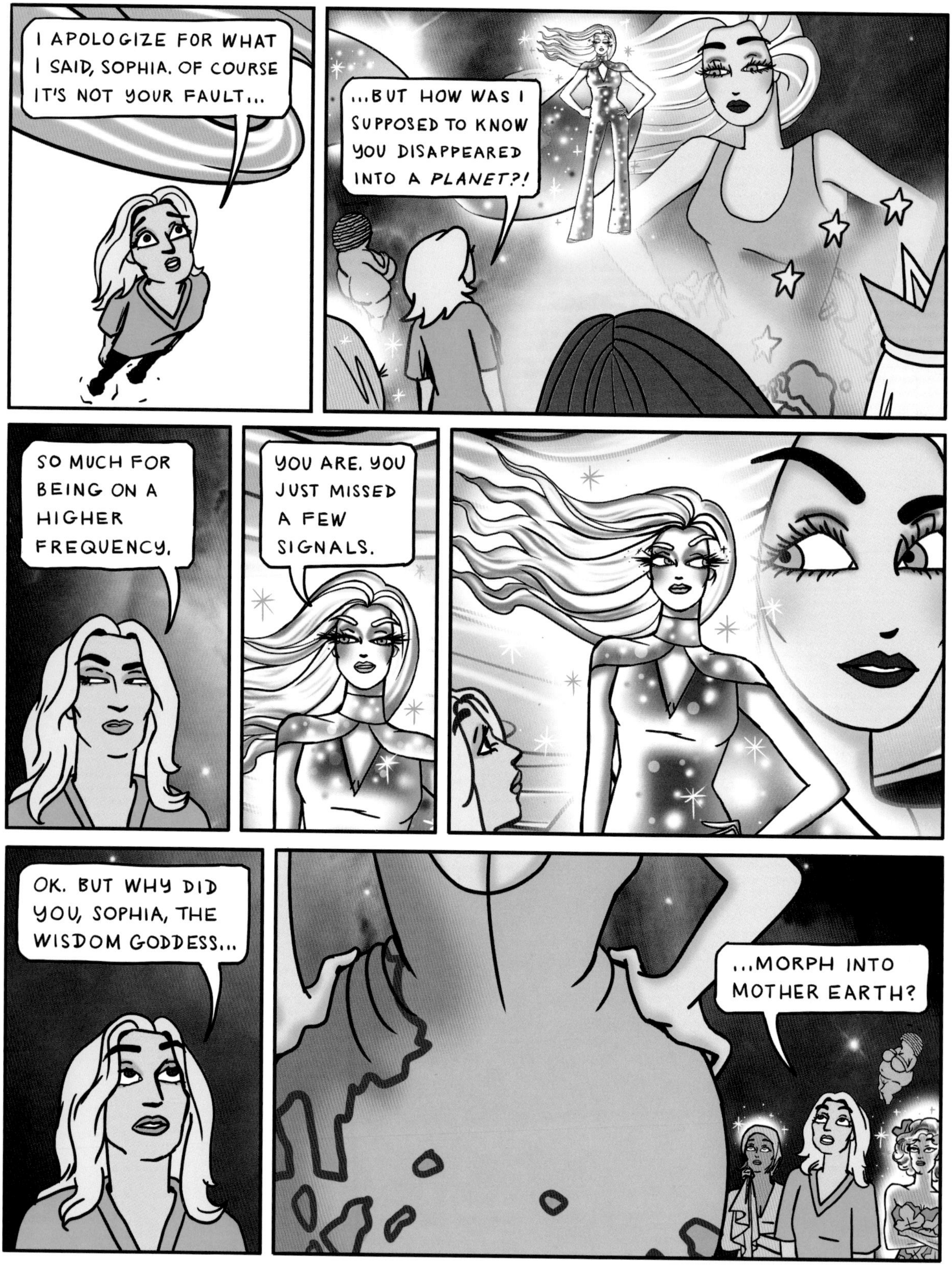
I APOLOGIZE FOR WHAT I SAID, SOPHIA. OF COURSE IT'S NOT YOUR FAULT...
...BUT HOW WAS I SUPPOSED TO KNOW YOU DISAPPEARED INTO A *PLANET?!*
SO MUCH FOR BEING ON A HIGHER FREQUENCY.
YOU ARE. YOU JUST MISSED A FEW SIGNALS.
OK. BUT WHY DID YOU, SOPHIA, THE WISDOM GODDESS...
...MORPH INTO MOTHER EARTH?

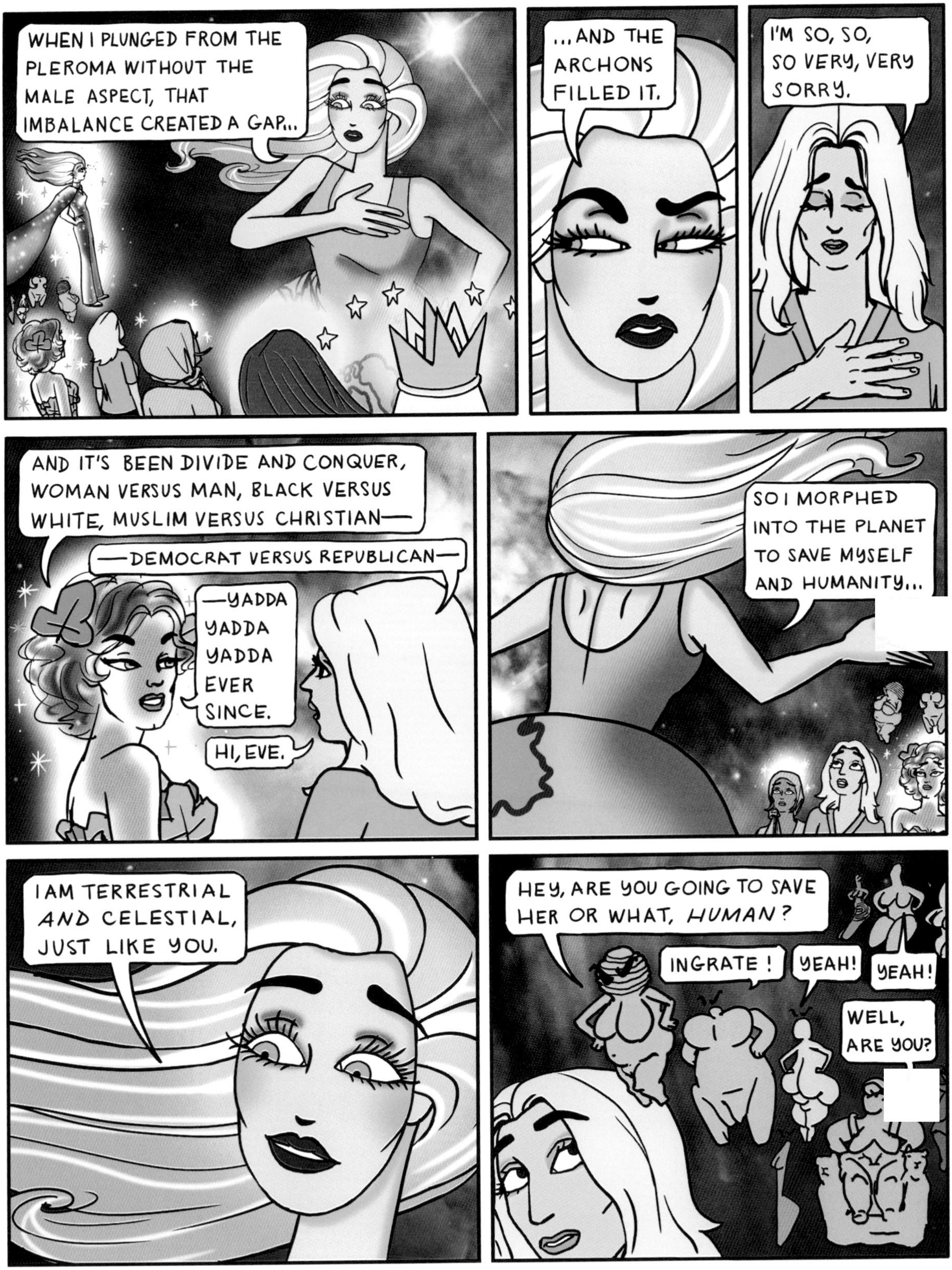
WHEN I PLUNGED FROM THE PLEROMA WITHOUT THE MALE ASPECT, THAT IMBALANCE CREATED A GAP...
...AND THE ARCHONS FILLED IT.
I'M SO, SO, SO VERY, VERY SORRY.
AND IT'S BEEN DIVIDE AND CONQUER, WOMAN VERSUS MAN, BLACK VERSUS WHITE, MUSLIM VERSUS CHRISTIAN—
—DEMOCRAT VERSUS REPUBLICAN—
—YADDA YADDA YADDA YADDA EVER SINCE.
HI, EVE.
SO I MORPHED INTO THE PLANET TO SAVE MYSELF AND HUMANITY...
I AM TERRESTRIAL AND CELESTIAL, JUST LIKE YOU.
HEY, ARE YOU GOING TO SAVE HER OR WHAT, *HUMAN*?
INGRATE!
YEAH!
YEAH!
WELL, ARE YOU?

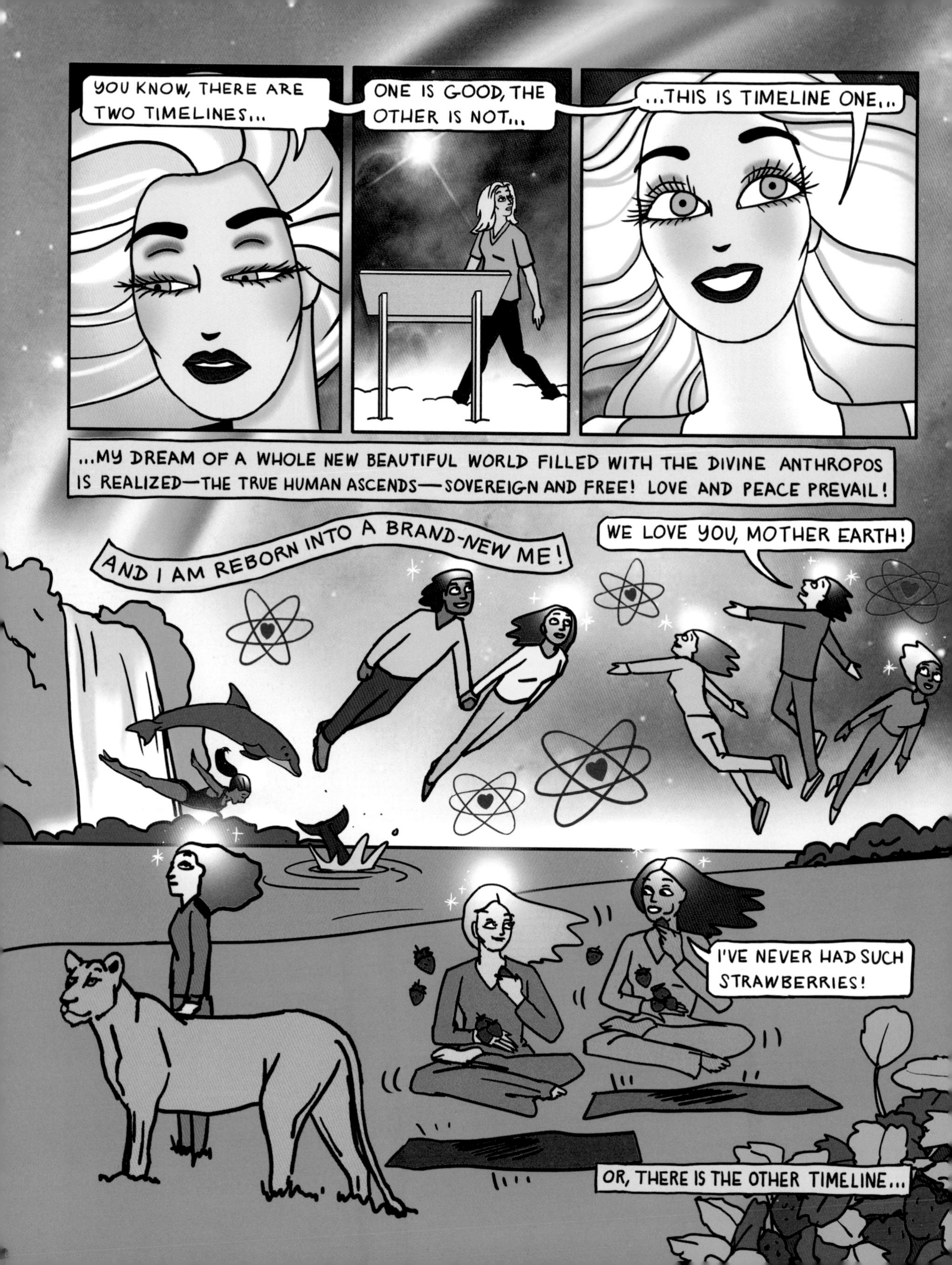
YOU KNOW, THERE ARE TWO TIMELINES...
ONE IS GOOD, THE OTHER IS NOT...
...THIS IS TIMELINE ONE...
...MY DREAM OF A WHOLE NEW BEAUTIFUL WORLD FILLED WITH THE DIVINE ANTHROPOS IS REALIZED—THE TRUE HUMAN ASCENDS—SOVEREIGN AND FREE! LOVE AND PEACE PREVAIL!
AND I AM REBORN INTO A BRAND-NEW ME!
WE LOVE YOU, MOTHER EARTH!
I'VE NEVER HAD SUCH STRAWBERRIES!
OR, THERE IS THE OTHER TIMELINE...

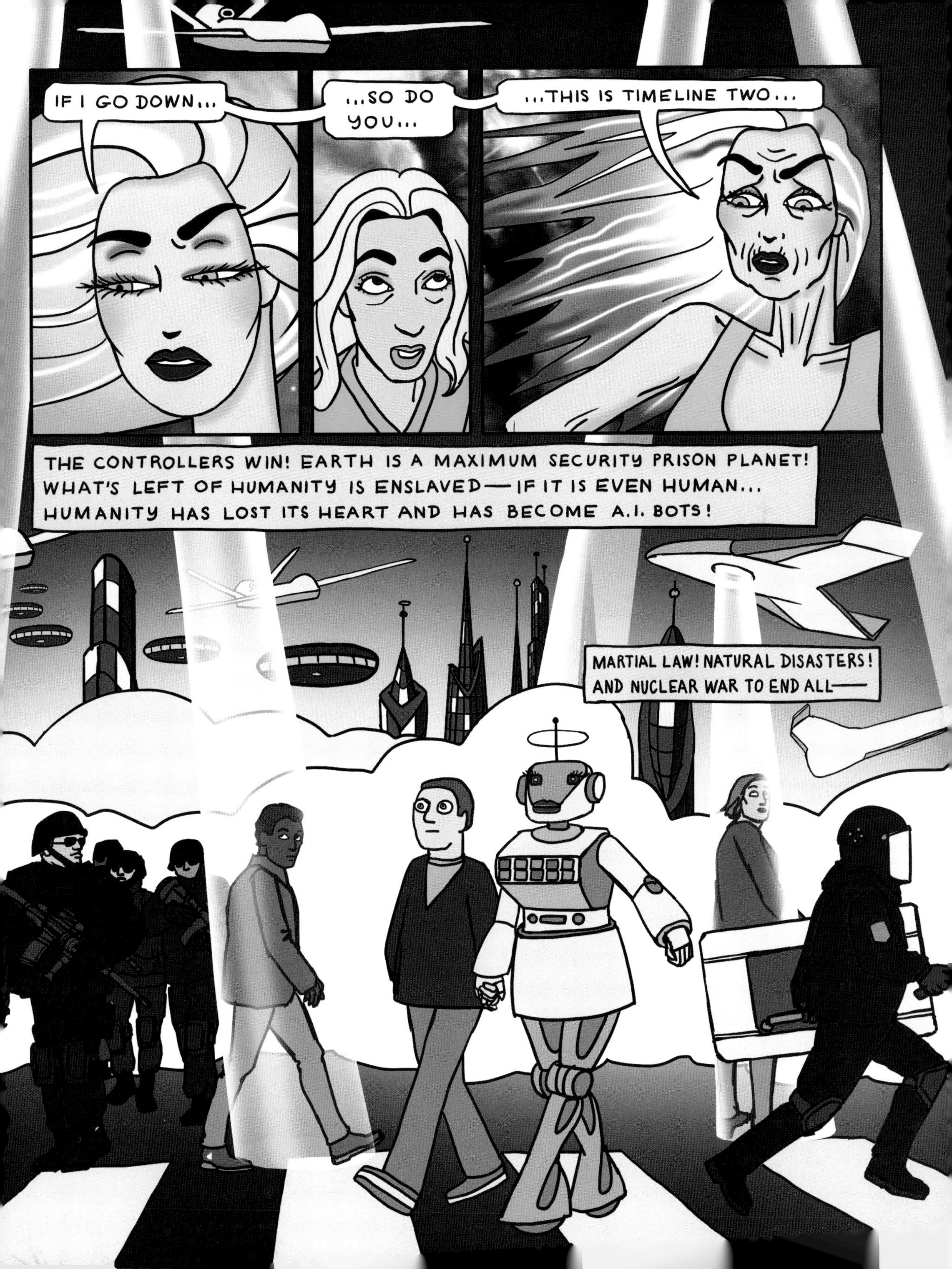
IF I GO DOWN...
...SO DO YOU...
...THIS IS TIMELINE TWO...
THE CONTROLLERS WIN! EARTH IS A MAXIMUM SECURITY PRISON PLANET! WHAT'S LEFT OF HUMANITY IS ENSLAVED—IF IT IS EVEN HUMAN... HUMANITY HAS LOST ITS HEART AND HAS BECOME A.I. BOTS!
MARTIAL LAW! NATURAL DISASTERS! AND NUCLEAR WAR TO END ALL—

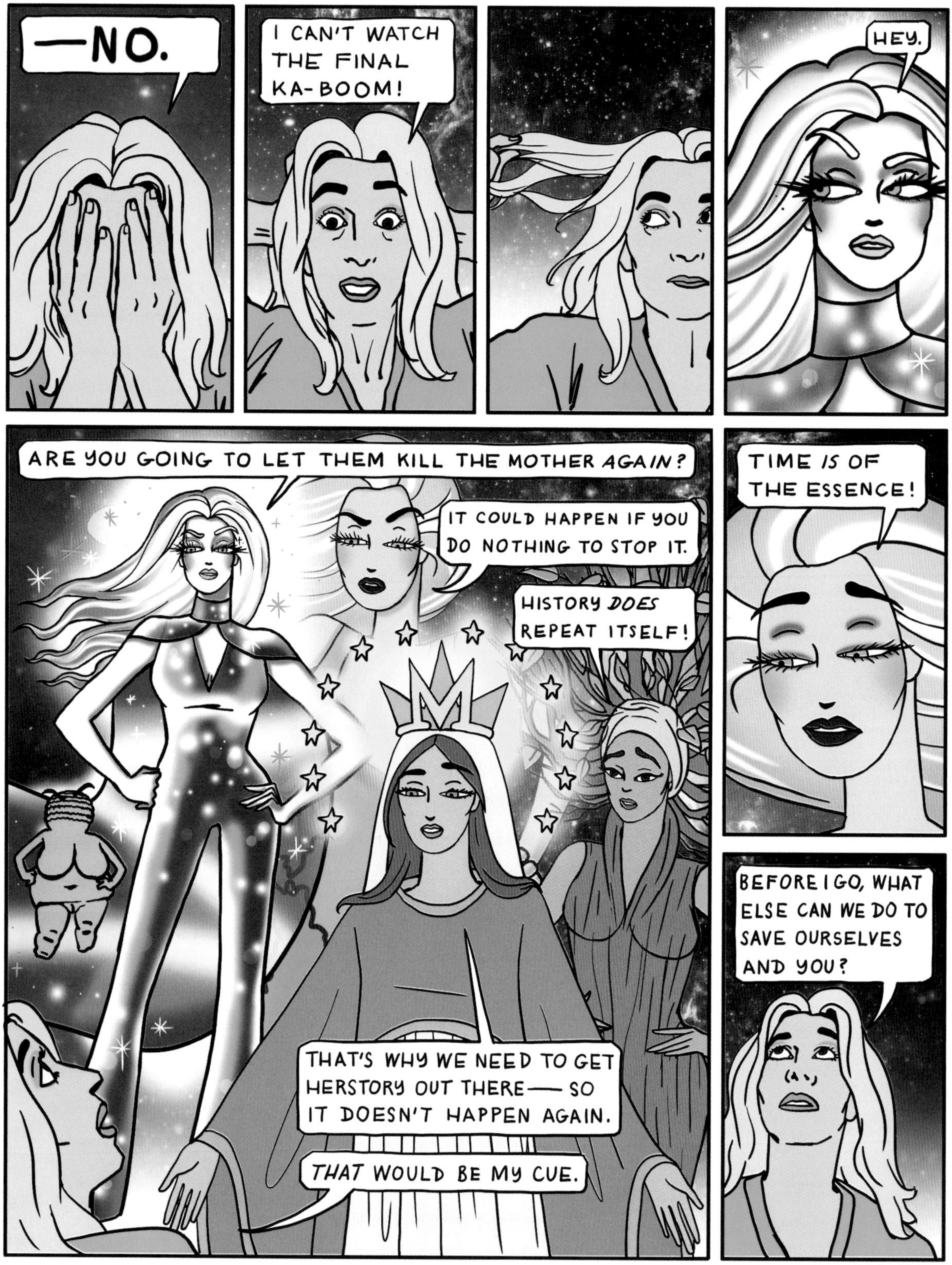
—NO.
I CAN'T WATCH THE FINAL KA-BOOM!
HEY.
ARE YOU GOING TO LET THEM KILL THE MOTHER *AGAIN*?
IT COULD HAPPEN IF YOU DO NOTHING TO STOP IT.
HISTORY *DOES* REPEAT ITSELF!
THAT'S WHY WE NEED TO GET HERSTORY OUT THERE— SO IT DOESN'T HAPPEN AGAIN.
THAT WOULD BE MY CUE.
TIME *IS* OF THE ESSENCE!
BEFORE I GO, WHAT ELSE CAN WE DO TO SAVE OURSELVES AND YOU?

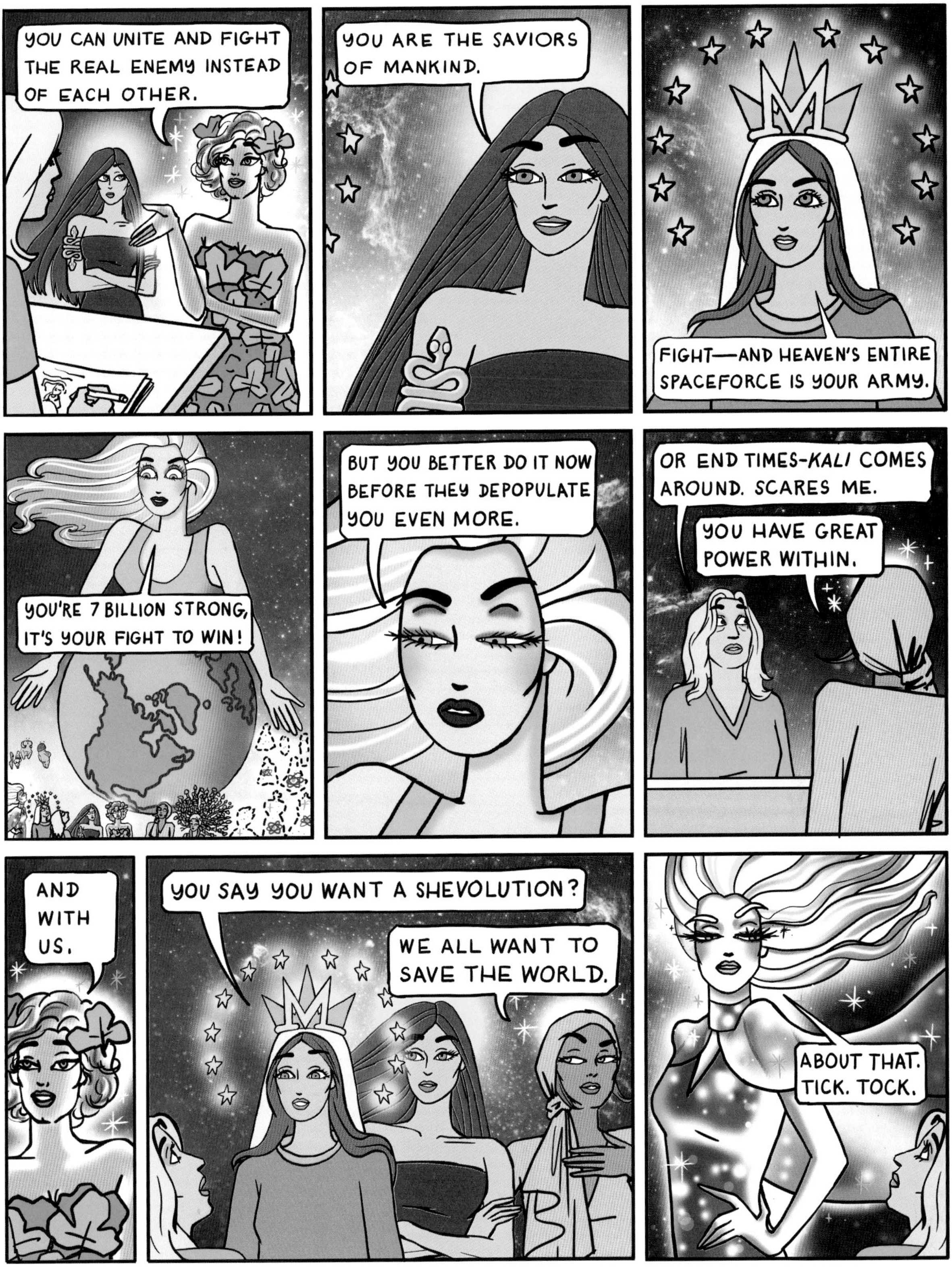
YOU CAN UNITE AND FIGHT THE REAL ENEMY INSTEAD OF EACH OTHER.
YOU ARE THE SAVIORS OF MANKIND.
FIGHT—AND HEAVEN'S ENTIRE SPACEFORCE IS YOUR ARMY.
YOU'RE 7 BILLION STRONG, IT'S YOUR FIGHT TO WIN!
BUT YOU BETTER DO IT NOW BEFORE THEY DEPOPULATE YOU EVEN MORE.
OR END TIMES-*KALI* COMES AROUND. SCARES ME.
YOU HAVE GREAT POWER WITHIN.
AND WITH US.
YOU SAY YOU WANT A SHEVOLUTION?
WE ALL WANT TO SAVE THE WORLD.
ABOUT THAT. TICK. TOCK.

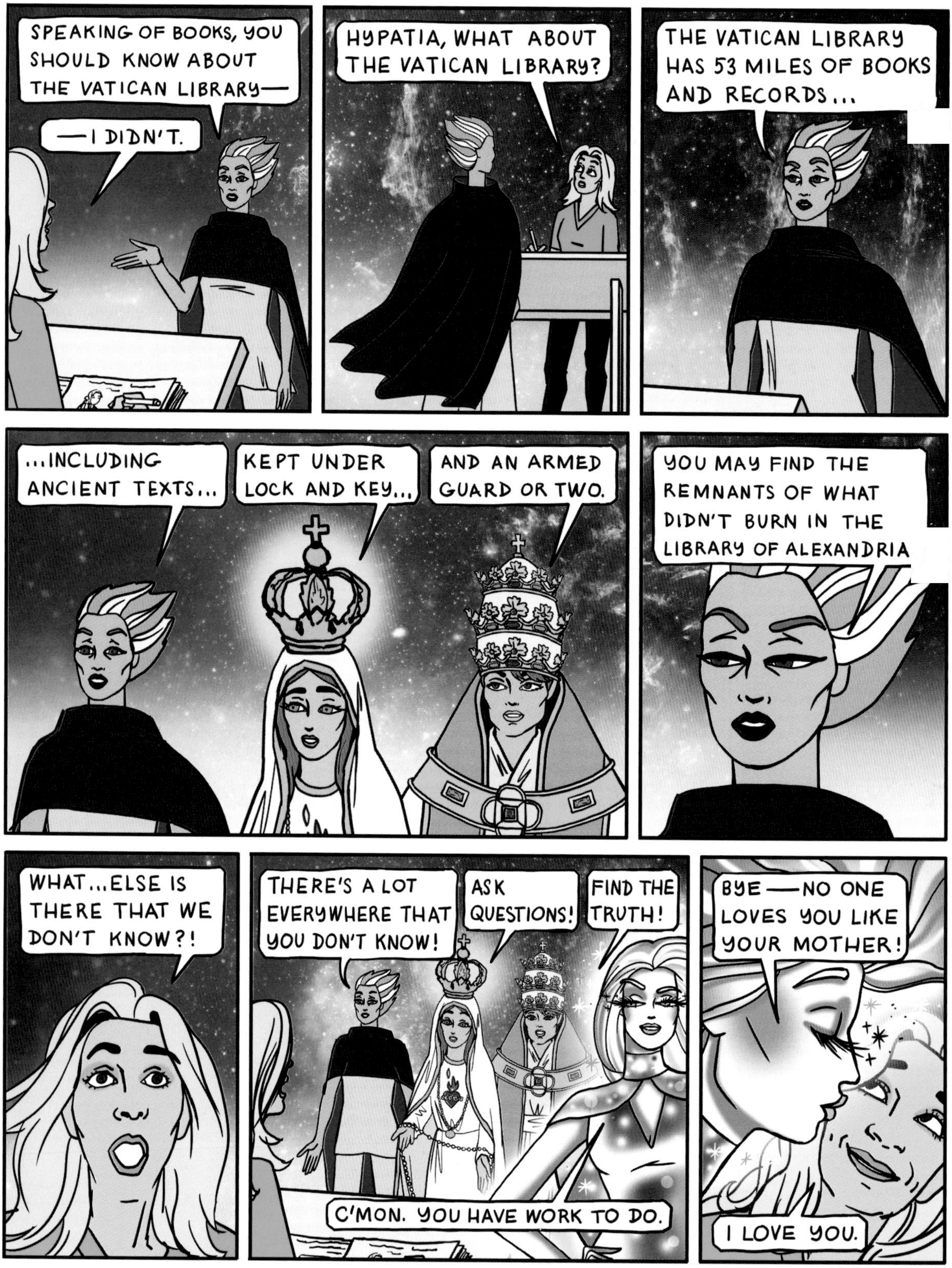
SPEAKING OF BOOKS, YOU SHOULD KNOW ABOUT THE VATICAN LIBRARY—
—I DIDN'T.
HYPATIA, WHAT ABOUT THE VATICAN LIBRARY?
THE VATICAN LIBRARY HAS 53 MILES OF BOOKS AND RECORDS...
...INCLUDING ANCIENT TEXTS...
KEPT UNDER LOCK AND KEY...
AND AN ARMED GUARD OR TWO.
YOU MAY FIND THE REMNANTS OF WHAT DIDN'T BURN IN THE LIBRARY OF ALEXANDRIA
WHAT...ELSE IS THERE THAT WE DON'T KNOW?!
THERE'S A LOT EVERYWHERE THAT YOU DON'T KNOW!
ASK QUESTIONS!
FIND THE TRUTH!
C'MON. YOU HAVE WORK TO DO.
BYE—NO ONE LOVES YOU LIKE YOUR MOTHER!
I LOVE YOU.

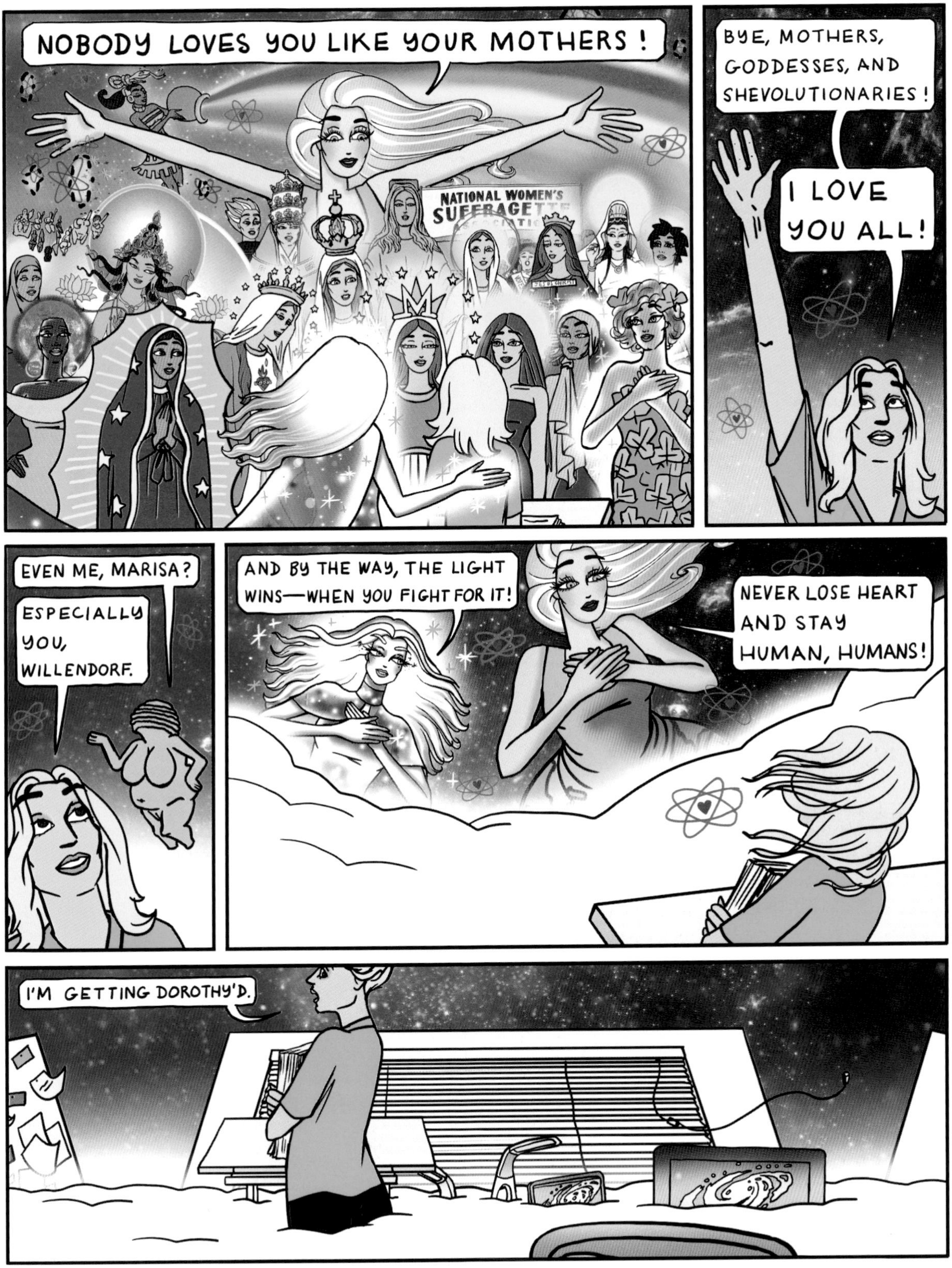
NOBODY LOVES YOU LIKE YOUR MOTHERS!
NATIONAL WOMEN'S SUFFRAGETTE
BYE, MOTHERS, GODDESSES, AND SHEVOLUTIONARIES!
I LOVE YOU ALL!
EVEN ME, MARISA?
ESPECIALLY YOU, WILLENDORF.
AND BY THE WAY, THE LIGHT WINS—WHEN YOU FIGHT FOR IT!
NEVER LOSE HEART AND STAY HUMAN, HUMANS!
I'M GETTING DOROTHY'D.

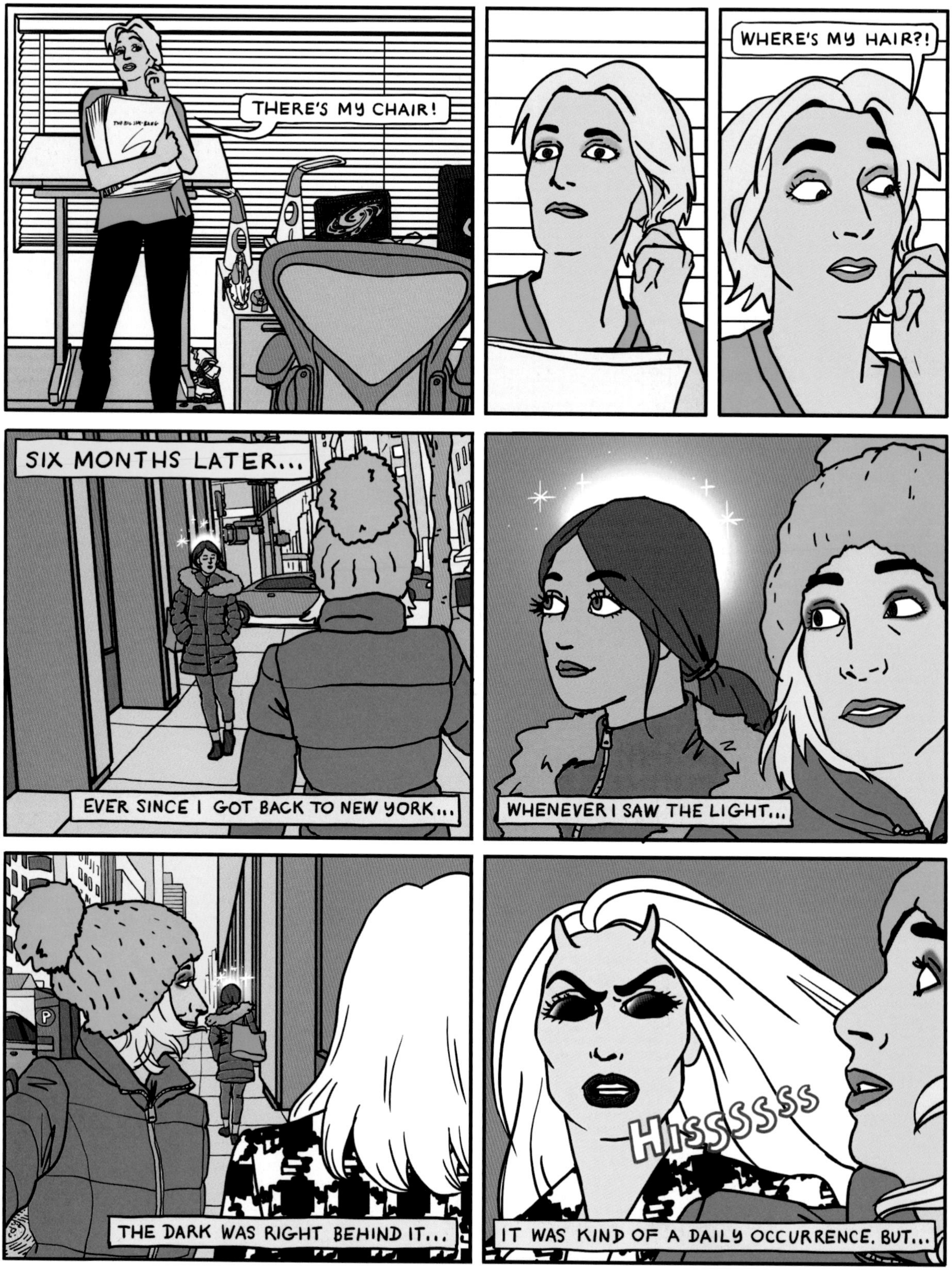
THERE'S MY CHAIR!
WHERE'S MY HAIR?!
SIX MONTHS LATER...
EVER SINCE I GOT BACK TO NEW YORK...
WHENEVER I SAW THE LIGHT...
THE DARK WAS RIGHT BEHIND IT...
HISSSSSS
IT WAS KIND OF A DAILY OCCURRENCE, BUT...

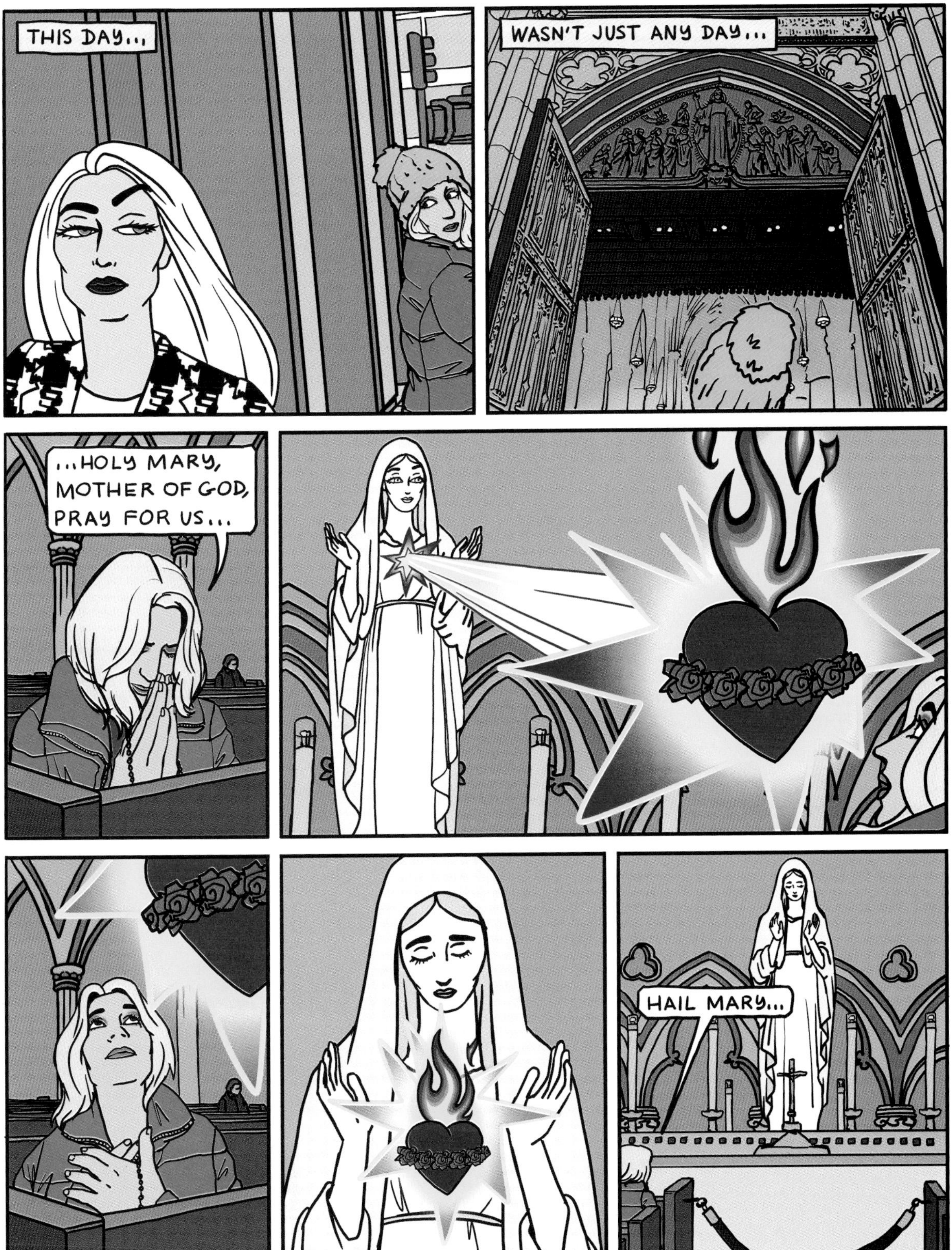
THIS DAY...
WASN'T JUST ANY DAY...
...HOLY MARY, MOTHER OF GOD, PRAY FOR US...
HAIL MARY...

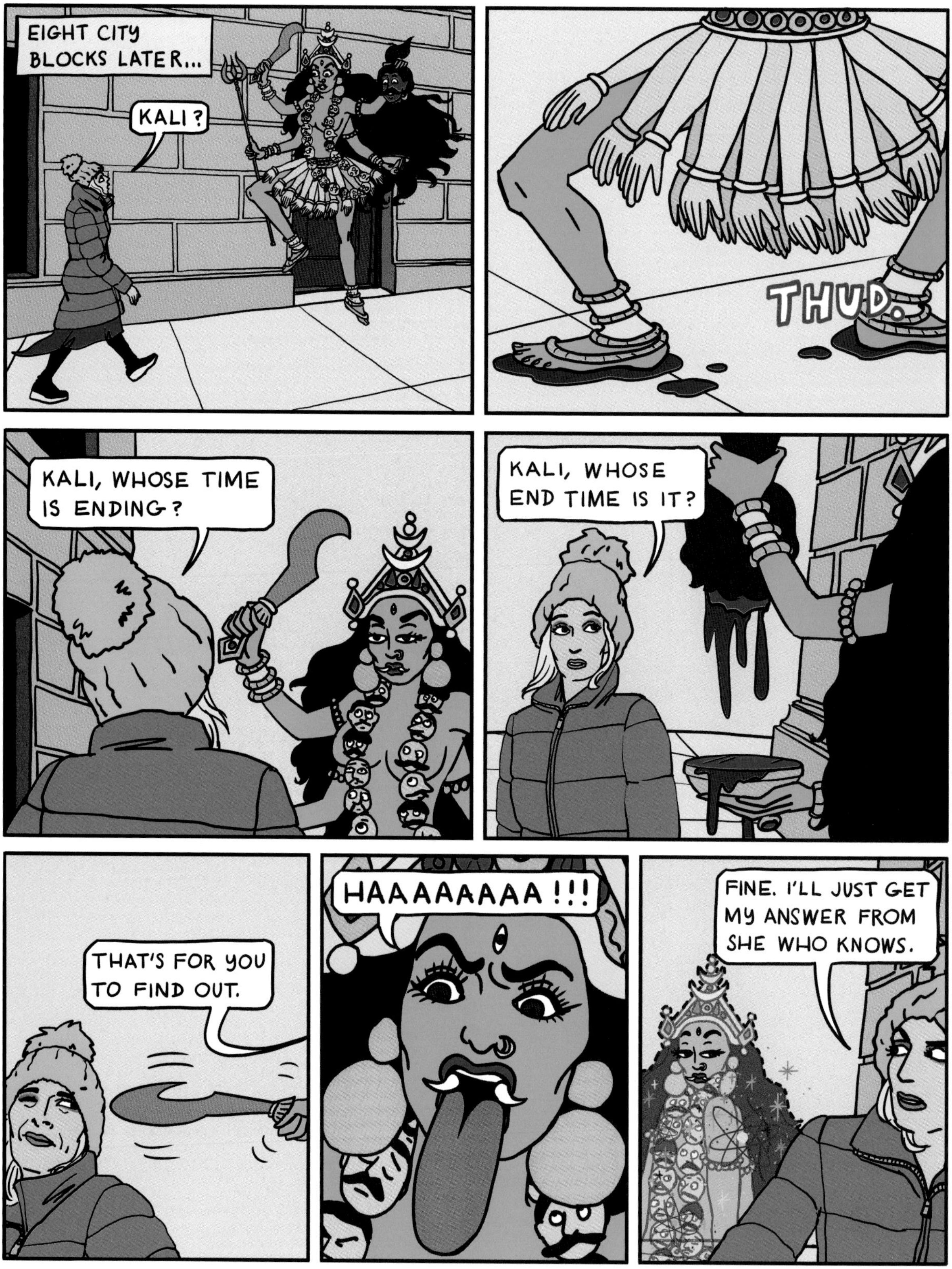

EIGHT CITY BLOCKS LATER...
KALI?
THUD.
KALI, WHOSE TIME IS ENDING?
KALI, WHOSE END TIME IS IT?
THAT'S FOR YOU TO FIND OUT.
HAAAAAAAA!!!
FINE. I'LL JUST GET MY ANSWER FROM SHE WHO KNOWS.

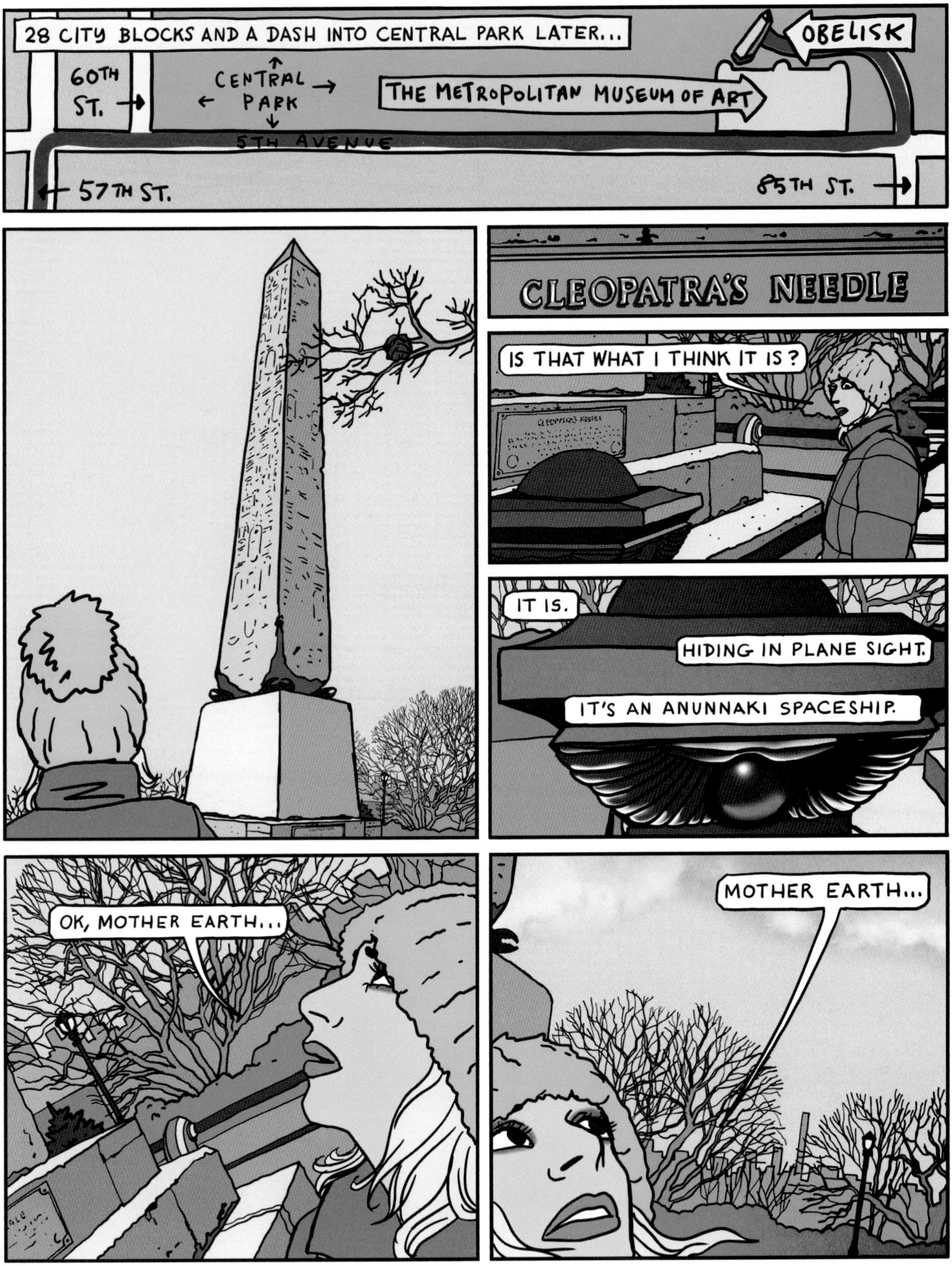
28 CITY BLOCKS AND A DASH INTO CENTRAL PARK LATER...
OBELISK
60TH ST.
CENTRAL PARK
THE METROPOLITAN MUSEUM OF ART
5TH AVENUE
57TH ST.
85TH ST.
CLEOPATRA'S NEEDLE
IS THAT WHAT I THINK IT IS?
IT IS.
HIDING IN PLANE SIGHT.
IT'S AN ANUNNAKI SPACESHIP.
OK, MOTHER EARTH...
MOTHER EARTH...

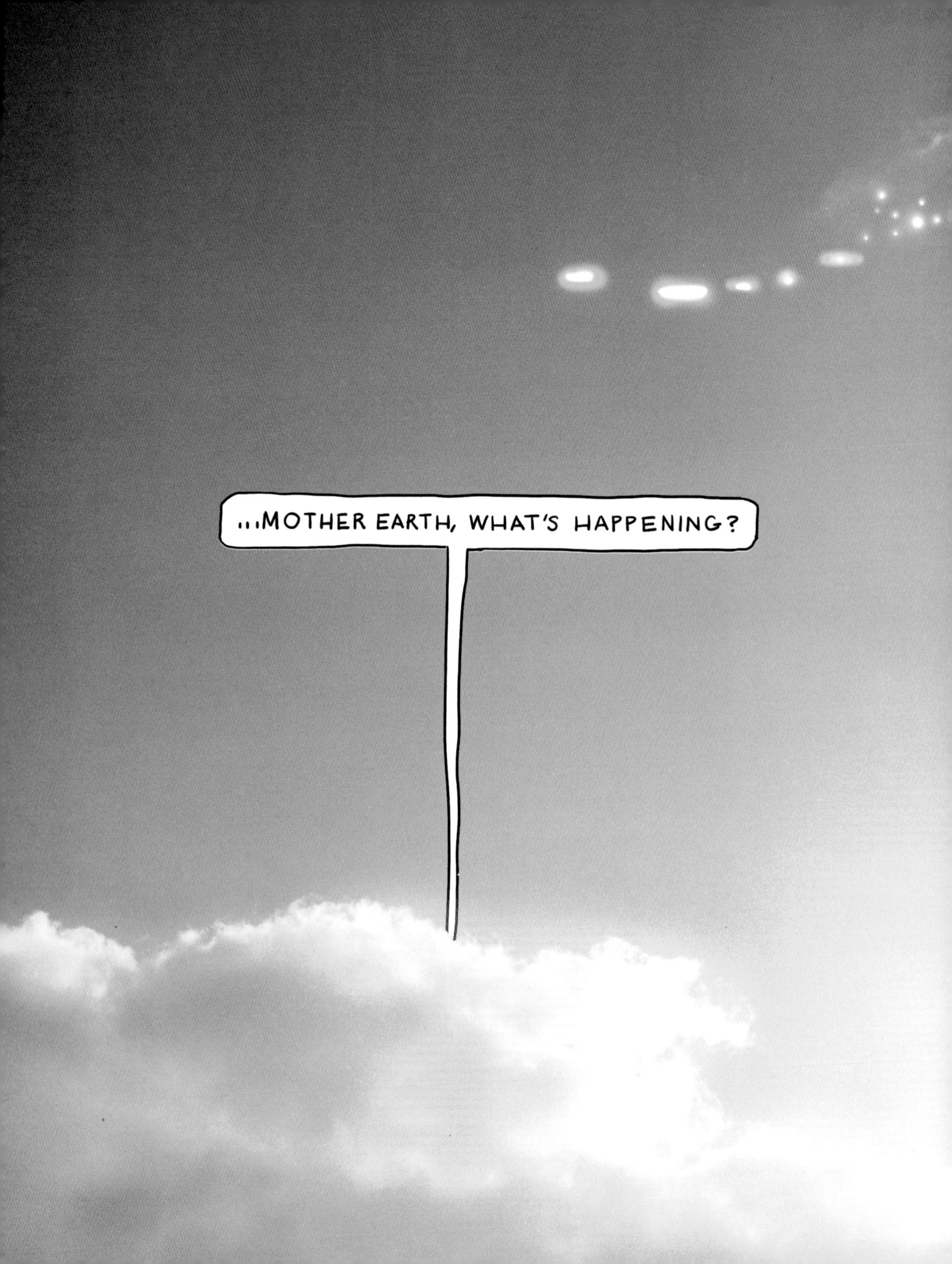
...MOTHER EARTH, WHAT'S HAPPENING?

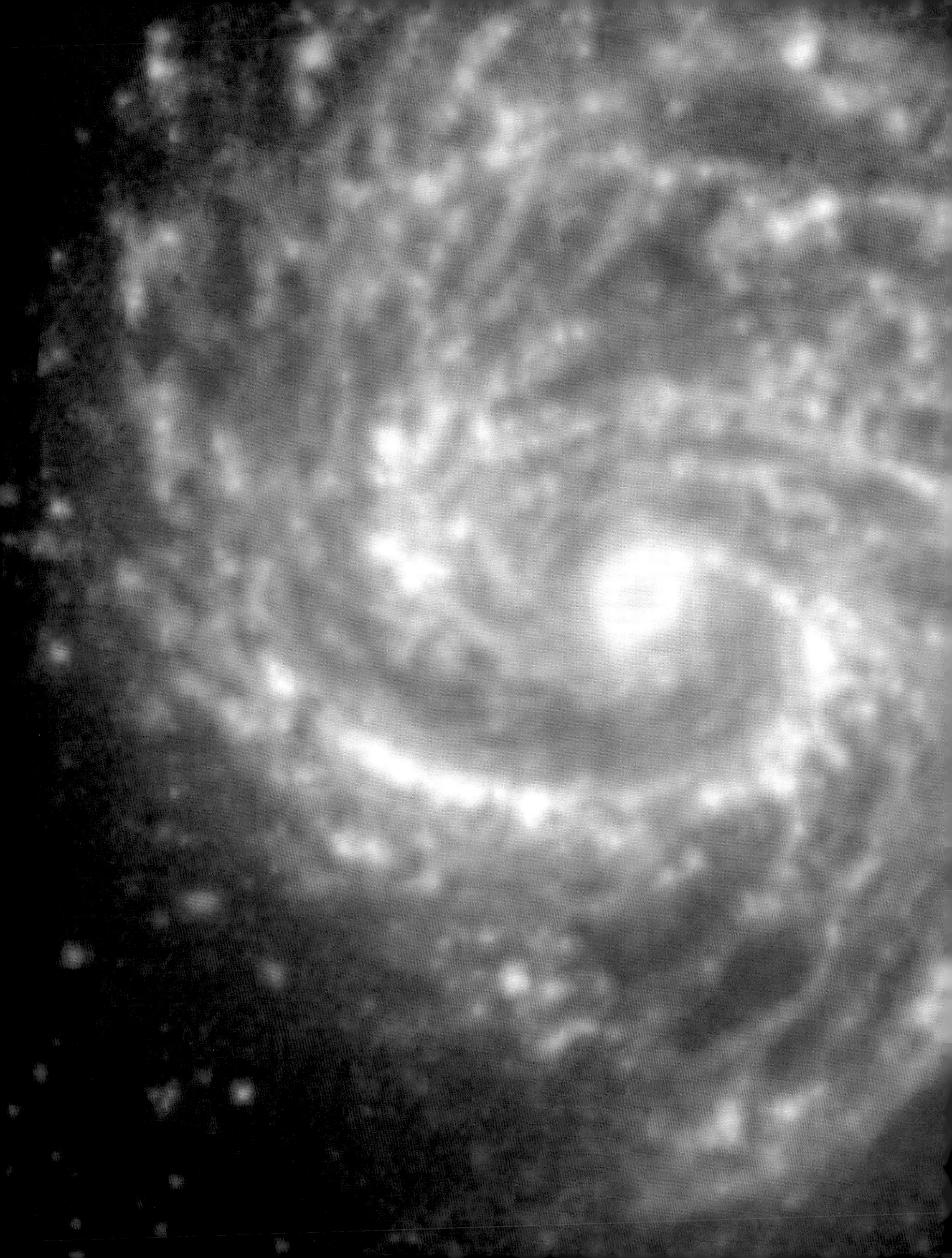

MY PARENTS—VIOLETTA AND TONY—WHO TAUGHT ME THE MEANING OF LOVE AND FAITH; MY BRILLIANT SISTER, DINA, AND HER SONS, JOHNNY AND VINNY; MY TRUE-BLUE BROTHERS, ANTHONY AND DAVID; AND DAVID'S WONDERFUL WIFE, YUN, AND THEIR DAUGHTERS, APOLLONIA AND PHILOMENA;

THE DREAM TEAM THAT REIGNS SUPREME—HARPER WAVE—LED BY THE DIVINE FEARLESS GODDESS KAREN RINALDI. THANK YOU TO THE EXCELLENT REBECCA RASKIN AND THE MARVELOUS LEAH CARLSON-STANSIC—IT'S BEEN MY GREAT PLEASURE TO WORK WITH ALL OF YOU;

MY SUPER AGENT—THE INCOMPARABLE ELIZABETH SHEINKMAN;

COLORIST DELUXE JEREMY LAWSON AND THE AMAZING THOMAS BAYNE;

KATHERINE CARLTON AND DR. NIKKI DELANEY FOR YOUR TIRELESS RESEARCH, DEEP RESOURCES, AND TREMENDOUS RESOURCEFULNESS;

EMILY SMITH, NESS SMITH, GERALYN LUCAS, KAREN DUFFY, LEIGH HABER, KIMBERLEY RYAN EKERN, ANNE KEATING, DR. PAUL GOLDSTEIN, DR. PAULA KLEIN, ADRIANA TRIGIANI, GIGI LAVANGIE GRAZER, ANN DEXTER JONES, MIKE CAVALLARO, ELLEN ABRAMOWITZ, ALEX MARSHALL, BOB MORRIS, SAM AND ISABELLE GROSS, ED STECKLEY, FRANK GRISHAM, THOMAS BAYNE, CHERI MANCUSO, LISA MIRCHIN, DINI VON MUEFFLING, BOB ECKSTEIN, ROBERT PERLMAN, RICHARD AND DANA KIRSHENBAUM, ERIK MAZA, PHYLLIS LEIBOWITZ, ALINA CHO, JIM SALICRUP, ROSANNA SCOTTO, ROBERT VERDI, IRA SILVERBERG, KENZIE LIEAUTAUD, CLAUDETTE DIDUL, MORT AND JUDITH GERBERG, MARIA SCRIVAN, OBERON SINCLAIR, LYNDA BAFF, AND MICHAEL, LINDA, AND VANNA STONE;

AND

THE DIVINE CYNTHIA LUFKIN: I MISS YOU EVERY DAY AND KNOW YOU'RE UP THERE WITH GOD THE MOTHER.

IMAGES OF SPACE PROVIDED BY NASA IMAGE AND VIDEO LIBRARY. NASA IMAGE AND VIDEO LIBRARY. NATIONAL AERONAUTICS AND SPACE ADMINISTRATION, n.d. https://images.nasa.gov/.

Altered Dimensions. *Altered Dimensions* (blog), September 26, 2016. https://www.altereddimensions.net/2016/vatican-secret-library-mysteries-inside-vatican-secret-archives.

Benko, Stephen. *Pagan Rome and the Early Christians*. Bloomington, IN: Indiana University Press, 1986.

Beauvoir, Simone de. *The Second Sex*. New York, NY: First Vintage Books Edition, 2011.

Campbell, Joseph. *Goddesses: Mysteries of the Feminine Divine*. Novato, CA: New World Library Foundation, 2013.

Carroll, Michael P. *The Cult of the Virgin Mary: Psychological Origins*. Princeton, NJ: Princeton University Press, 1986.

Collins, Andrew. *From the Ashes of Angels*. Rochester, VT: Bear & Company, 2001.

Dash, Max. "Icons of the Matrix: Female Symbolism in Ancient Culture." *The Journal of Archaeomythology*, 2005.

Dashu, Max. *Witches and Pagans: Women in European Folk Religion*. Richmond, CA: Veleda Press, 2017.

Eisenhower, Laura M. "Sophia/Christ Consciousness Creating Global Transformation." *Cosmic Gaia* (blog), https://sites.google.com/site/lauramagdalene/sophia-christ-consciousness-and-creating-global-transformation.1/11/2011.

Enheduanna, and Betty De Shong Meador. *Inanna, Lady of Largest Heart: Poems of the Sumerian High Priestess Enheduanna*. Austin, TX: University of Texas Press, 2006.

Foley, Helene P., ed. *The Homeric Hymn to Demeter*. Princeton, NJ: Princeton University Press, 1993.

Forrest, M. Isidora. *Isis Magic*. St. Paul, MN: Llewellyn Publications, 2001.

Freke, Timothy, and Peter Gandy. *Jesus and the Lost Goddess*. New York, NY: Three Rivers Press, 2002.

Gambero, Luigi. *Mary and the Fathers of the Church*. San Francisco, CA: Ignatius Press, 1999.

Grahn, Judy. *Blood, Bread, and Roses*. Boston, MA: Beacon Press, 1994.

James, M. R. *The Apocryphal New Testament*. Oxford: Clarendon Press, 1924.

Kasten, Len. *Alien World Order*. Rochester, VT: Bear & Company, 2017.

Kenyon, Tom, and Judy Sion. *The Magdalen Manuscript*. Orcas, WA: Orb Communications, 2006.

King, Karen L., ed. *Images of the Feminine in Gnosticism (Studies in Antiquity & Christianity)*. Harrisburg, PA: First Trinity Press International Edition, 2000.

Kirkwood, Annie. *Mary's Message to the World*. Nevada City, CA: Blue Dolphin Publishing, 1991.

Lahr, Jane. *Searching for Mary Magdalene*. New York, NY: Welcome Books, 2006.

Lash, John L. "She Who Anoints." *Bibliotecapleyades* (blog), March, 2004. MetaHistory, n.d. https://www.bibliotecapleyades.net/gnostic/mistic_05.htm.

Lash, John Lamb. *Not in His Image: Gnostic Vision, Sacred Ecology, and the Future of Belief*. White River Junction, VT: Chelsea Green Publishing, 2006.

Leloup, Jean-yves. *Gospel of Mary Magdalene*. Rochester, VT: Inner Traditions, 2002.

Lester, Meera. *The Everything Mary Magdalene Book*. Avon, MA: F+W Publications, 2006.

Light, Alexander. "Humans Are Free." *Humans Are Free* (blog), April 19, 2014. https://humansarefree.com/2014/04/the-truth-about-easter-and-the-secret-worship-of-the-anunnaki.html.

"Maggie's Holistics." *Maggie's Holistics* (blog), Maggie's Holistics, July 22, 2016. https://www.maggiesholisticsny.com/ley-lines-the-key-to-unlocking-the-matrix/.

Malachi, Tau. *St. Mary Magdalene: The Gnostic Tradition of the Holy Bride*. St. Paul, MN: Llewellyn Publications, 2006.

"Max Spiers Unplugged-Bases 59" *Mile's Bases Project*, April 1, 2016. https://www.youtube.com/watch?v=EaDGcPK-KwU.

"Max Spiers-Bases 37 Part 5 (A B C)." *Mile's Bases Project*, May 18, 2015. https://www.youtube.com/watch?v=L9_TG__joSU.

McCannon, Tricia. *Return of the Divine Sophia*. Rochester, VT: Bear & Company, 2015.

MEAD, G. R. S. *Pistis Sophia*. Kila, MT: Kessinger Publishing, 2010.

Meyer, Marvin, ed. *The Nag Hammadi Scriptures: The International Edition*. New York, NY: HarperCollins Publishers, 2007.

Nixey, Catherine. *The Darkening Age: The Christian Destruction of the Classical World*. New York, NY: Houghton Mifflin Harcourt, 2018.

"Our Lady of Akita Prophecies and Predictions for Humankind" *Alamongordo.com* (blog), http://www.alamongordo.com/lady-of-akita-prophecies/.

Pagels, Elaine. *The Gnostic Gospels*. New York, NY: Vintage Books, 1989.

Papal Trivia-Fun Facts About the Popes-Treasures of Our Catholic Heritage. Accessed May 15, 2020. https://www.bibliotecapleyades.net/vatican/esp_vatican39.htm.

Pinch, Geraldine. *The Handbook of Egyptian Mythology*. Santa Barbara, CA: ABC-CLIO, August 2002.

"Project Camelot Interviews Dr Pete Peterson." Project Camelot, 2 September 2009. https://www.youtube.com/watch?v=ooSRh7VG8uk.

Rubin, Miri. *Mother of God-A History of The Virgin Mary*. New Haven, CT: Yale University Press, 2009.

Seawright, Caroline. "Hathor, Goddess of Love, Music and Beauty." *The Keep* (blog), November 29, 2012. http://thekeep.org/~kunoichi/kunoichi/themestream/hathor.html#.XsHTcy-ZO-s.

SJ, Monica, and Barbara Mor. *The Great Cosmic Mother*. San Francisco, CA: HarperOne, 1987.

Stone, Merlin. *When God Was a Woman*. Orlando, FL: Harvest, Harcourt Brace 1976.

"The Message of Our Lady of La Salette." catholicapologetics.info (blog), http://catholicapologetics.info/catholicteaching/privaterevelation/lasalette.html.

"The Times Are Urgent and We Must Heed the Warnings of Our Lady." ncregister.com (blog), October 10, 2017. https://www.ncregister.com/blog/msgr.pope/the-times-are-urgent-and-we-must-heed-the-warnings-of-our-lady.

Virtue, Doreen. *Goddess Guidance Oracle Cards*. Carlsbad, CA: The Hay House, Inc. 2004.

Walker, Barbara G. *The Woman's Encyclopedia of Myths and Secrets*. San Francisco, CA: HarperOne.

Watterson, Barbara. *The Gods of Ancient Egypt*. Carlsbad, CA: The Hay House, Inc.

Wolkstein, Diane, and Samuel Noah Kramer. *Inanna: Queen of Heaven and Earth: Her Stories and Hymns from Sumer*. Harper Perennial, 1983.

MARISA ACOCELLA IS A CARTOONIST FOR THE *NEW YORKER* WHOSE WORK HAS APPEARED IN THE *NEW YORK TIMES, GLAMOUR,* AND *O, THE OPRAH MAGAZINE,* AMONG OTHER PUBLICATIONS. SHE IS THE AUTHOR OF THE *NEW YORK TIMES* BESTSELLING GRAPHIC NOVEL *ANN TENNA; JUST WHO THE HELL IS SHE ANYWAY?;* AND *CANCER VIXEN,* WHICH WAS NAMED ONE OF *TIME* MAGAZINE'S TOP TEN GRAPHIC MEMOIRS. A FOUNDER OF THE MARISA ACOCELLA FOUNDATION AT MOUNT SINAI COMPREHENSIVE CANCER CENTER, MADE POSSIBLE THROUGH A GRANT FROM BLOOMINGDALE'S, MARISA LIVES IN NEW YORK CITY.

HARPERCOLLINS BOOKS MAY BE PURCHASED FOR EDUCATIONAL, BUSINESS, OR SALES PROMOTIONAL USE. FOR INFORMATION, PLEASE EMAIL THE SPECIAL MARKETS DEPARTMENT AT SPSALES@HARPERCOLLINS.COM.

FIRST EDITION

LIBRARY OF CONGRESS CATALOGING-IN-PUBLICATION DATA HAS BEEN APPLIED FOR.

ISBN 978-0-06-290566-6

20 21 22 23 24 TC 10 9 8 7 6 5 4 3 2 1